THE COMPLETE WORKS OF JAMES SHIRLEY

THE COMPLETE WORKS OF
James Shirley

VOLUME 7

The Constant Maid, *The Doubtful Heir*,
The Gentleman of Venice, and *The Politician*

GENERAL EDITORS
EUGENE GIDDENS
TERESA GRANT

ASSOCIATE EDITOR
EMIL RYBCZAK

EDITORIAL BOARD

NIGEL BAWCUTT   DAVID BEVINGTON
MARTIN BUTLER   BRETT GREATLEY-HIRSCH
ANDREW HADFIELD   PETER HOLLAND
ANTHONY W. JOHNSON   LUCY MUNRO
ALISON SEARLE

Great Clarendon Street, Oxford, OX2 6DP,
United Kingdom

Oxford University Press is a department of the University of Oxford.
It furthers the University's objective of excellence in research, scholarship,
and education by publishing worldwide. Oxford is a registered trade mark of
Oxford University Press in the UK and in certain other countries

© the several editors, 2022

The moral rights of the authors have been asserted

First Edition published in 2022

Impression: 1

All rights reserved. No part of this publication may be reproduced, stored in
a retrieval system, or transmitted, in any form or by any means, without the
prior permission in writing of Oxford University Press, or as expressly permitted
by law, by licence or under terms agreed with the appropriate reprographics
rights organization. Enquiries concerning reproduction outside the scope of the
above should be sent to the Rights Department, Oxford University Press, at the
address above

You must not circulate this work in any other form
and you must impose this same condition on any acquirer

Published in the United States of America by Oxford University Press
198 Madison Avenue, New York, NY 10016, United States of America

British Library Cataloguing in Publication Data

Data available

Library of Congress Control Number: 2020945956

ISBN 978–0–19–886892–7

Printed and bound in the UK by
TJ Books Limited

Links to third party websites are provided by Oxford in good faith and
for information only. Oxford disclaims any responsibility for the materials
contained in any third party website referenced in this work.

In memory of David Bevington (1931–2019)

Only the actions of the just
Smell sweet and blossom in their dust.

CONTENTS

List of Illustrations	ix
Acknowledgements	xi
A Note on Modernization and Spelling	xiii
The Constant Maid *edited by Teresa Grant*	1
The Doubtful Heir *edited by Rebecca Yearling*	141
The Gentleman of Venice *edited by Lucy Munro*	257
The Politician *edited by Duncan Fraser and Andrew Hadfield*	393
Bibliography	533

LIST OF ILLUSTRATIONS

1. *The Constant Maid*, quarto title-page (1640), Library of St Catharine's College, Cambridge, Z.42. — 3

2. *The Doubtful Heir*, quarto title-page (1652), Cambridge University Library, Y.10.57. — 143

3. *The Gentleman of Venice*, octavo title-page (1655), Library of St Catharine's College, Cambridge, Z.50. — 259

4. *The Politician*, quarto title-page (1655), Library of St Catharine's College, Cambridge, Z.49. — 395

ACKNOWLEDGEMENTS

The general editors would like to thank the following, without whose help the edition would have been impossible to produce:

Our institutions, Anglia Ruskin University and the University of Warwick, for support both logistical and financial, including funding from the Warwick Humanities Research Fund and a series of Warwick University and Anglia Ruskin Undergraduate Research Studentships to work on the Shirley project. We would also like to thank the staff in our research offices, particularly Liese Perrin, Katie Klaassen, and David Duncan at Warwick for help beyond the call of duty.

Funding bodies. The project has received generous funding for various stages in the form of a major research grant from the Arts and Humanities Research Council; two research grants from the British Academy; a Modern Humanities Research Association research associateship; a public engagement grant from the Society for Renaissance Studies; and a minor research grant from the Bibliographical Society. We are grateful to the following for providing library fellowships which facilitated textual work: UCLA and the Huntington Library for a Clark-Huntington Joint Bibliography Fellowship; the Harry Ransom Center, University of Texas, Austin, for a Pforzheimer Fellowship; and The Daiwa Anglo-Japanese Foundation for work in Meisei University collections.

The editorial board, whose input has been crucial throughout. Also Jonathan Bate and Julie Sanders, former members of the editorial board, and the anonymous reviewers at various stages of the process, all of whom have spotted errors and encouraged improvements. We thank our eagle-eyed proofreaders John Harding, Emil Rybczak, and Nicola Sangster.

Our project research associates and PhD students: Emil Rybczak (MHRA); Alison Searle, Jennifer Young, and Eva Griffith (AHRC); Emily Hargreaves (British Academy); Justine Williams and Stefania Crowther (AHRC-funded PhDs).

The rare books librarians at every institution that holds a copy of Shirley, but particularly Colin Higgins (St Catharine's College, Cambridge); Noriko Sumimoto (Meisei University); and Wayne G. Hammond (Chapin Librarian, Williams College). Considerable early help was also provided to the project by Jill Whitelock (Cambridge University Library) and Suzan Griffiths (St Catharine's College, Cambridge).

Ari Friedlander and Paul Schaffner for providing the project with electronic text, and David Gants for early advice on it. Brian Vickers and Marcus Dahl for guidance on authorship. Martin Wiggins for putting on the tremendous Shirley Marathon in 2015.

All the team at Oxford University Press, especially Andrew McNeillie (for commissioning Shirley in the first place), Matthew Humphrys, and our editor Eleanor Collins, whose patience seems to know no bounds.

A NOTE ON MODERNIZATION AND SPELLING

By and large, the spelling of Shirley (or his compositors) is already quite modern. Shirley likes contracted forms; an elliptic mode of expression is often visible, both in terms of syntax and morphology.

In the edition, spelling variants give way to modernized forms, unless there is compelling evidence of dialectal use, wordplay, or typical Shirleian colloquialisms. Editors have been encouraged to preserve the spelling of Shirley's colloquialisms even when their usage seems unfamiliar now. This applies in particular to auxiliaries or auxiliary microphrases (see table below).

In general, spaces and apostrophes have been adopted as set out in this list of elisions:

auxiliary phrases

	original spelling	*modernized*
do	dee, d'ee, de'e, d'yee, dee see, how d'ee, etc. (*as in* Madam, what dee meane?)	d'ye
have	th'ast	th'ast
	(*as in* thast deserv'd my blessing)	
	ha yee (*as in* ha yee done?)	ha'ye
	y'ave	y'have
shall	shannot, shan'ot, shanot, etc. (*as in* you shannot trouble friends)	sha'not
	shall's	shall's
	(*as in* what shall's do this evening?)	
	sha't	shalt
	(*as in* thou sha't have another gowne)	
will	weele	we'll
	(*as in* weele place you where you shannot be so merry)	
won't	woonnot, wonot, wo'not, wo-not, etc. (*as in* you wonot understand me yet)	wo'not
	twonot, 'twonot, 'twon'ot, etc. (*as in* 't wonot come to that)	't wo'not (*but* 'twill not)
would	wod, woo'd, wood, wo'd, wot, etc. (*as in* wod I could stay)	would
	woot, wot, wo't, etc.	wo't
	(*as in* thou wot not be a murderer)	(*if the meaning is* thou wilt)
	wod ha	would ha'
	(*as in* we did expect this wod ha' made you merry)	

A NOTE ON MODERNIZATION AND SPELLING

prepositions, articles and pronouns

	original spelling	*modernized*
in	ith (*as in* ith meane time)	i'th'*noun*
other	tother, t'other, to'ther, etc. (*as in* belch out My Lord, and tother cosin in a baudihouse *or* he told me to'ther day)	t'other
	the tother (*as in* whats the tother rat thats with him?)	the tother
to	t'ee	t'ye
	toot, toote, too't, etc.	to't
	toth' court, toth' cave, etc.	to th'*noun*
with	wo'me, wo me, wo'yee, wo't (*as in* be plaine wo'me)	wi'me, wi'ye, wi't, etc.
	we'e, w'ee (*as in* I ha done we'e sir)	wi'ye

xiv

The Constant Maid

EDITED BY

Teresa Grant

THE
CONSTANT
MAID.

A Comedy.

Written by *James Shirley.*

LONDON,
Printed by *J. Raworth*, for *R. Whitaker.* 1640.

1. *The Constant Maid*, quarto title-page (1640), Library of St Catharine's College, Cambridge, Z.42.

General Introduction

THE PLAY

The Constant Maid is not a staple of the undergraduate canon but it has much to recommend it.[1] It is a mainstream Caroline comedy very like Shirley's other 1630s plays including the much more famous *Lady of Pleasure* and *Hyde Park*. Its design is recognizable from other plays of the era: the usury plot owes much to Massinger's *A New Way to Pay Old Debts* (*c.* 1626) and Shirley's country-bumpkin 'new gentleman', Startup, is a version of Jonson's Cokes in *Bartholomew Fair* (1614), and perhaps even the Ward in Middleton's *Women Beware Women* (1623/4?). Refractions of this character appear in many other Shirley plays too: for instance Nicholas Treedle in *The Witty Faire One* (perf. 1628; pb. 1633) and Captain Underwit in *The Country Captain* (pb. 1649, evidently—in part, at least—a collaboration between Shirley and William Cavendish, Earl of Newcastle).

The plot is as follows: Hartwell, a young gentleman of an established family that now has little income, has been forced to turn away his servants and rent out his ancestral home. Hartwell's father 'had an office which brought in / A fair revenue' (1.1.8–9), but he himself has inherited only the family estate with no way to maintain it. Yet there is hope, because Hartwell and Mistress Frances, the daughter of a rich widow, are in love with each other, and so her prudent mother devises an intricate plan to test Hartwell's faith. Widow Bellamy pretends to Hartwell that she has herself fallen in love with him. She withdraws her permission, already given, to the marriage of her daughter and Hartwell, supposedly in the hope that he will marry her instead. The widow has another suitor, the usurer Giles Hornet, who bears a strong resemblance to the infamous Jacobean projector Sir Giles Mompesson, and his avatar Sir Giles Overreach in *A New Way to Pay Old Debts*. The most inventive parts of *The Constant Maid* involve metatheatrical attempts by Hartwell's friend, Playfair, to rescue Hornet's niece from his malevolent guardianship, so that he can marry her himself. This ruse has Playfair's cousin impersonating the King and some of Hartwell's former servants playing various court functionaries as they gull Hornet into thinking he has been specially selected for a knighthood, on account of his 'ability' (3.2.75). In fact, the point of all this dressing up is rather simple—to give Playfair a chance to divest Hornet of his keys in order to rescue the niece who is locked in Hornet's house. A disguise-related misunderstanding prompts some lover-like hysteria on Hartwell's part, but the play ends happily, with the

---

[1] I would like to thank Emil Rybczak (including extensive help with collation) and Eugene Giddens for their painstaking editorial work along the way. My thanks are due also to Anthony W. Johnson and Alison Searle, who read the completed edition. The final version has been much improved by incorporating their corrections and suggestions. All errors that remain, naturally, are my own.

DATING AND PERFORMANCE

As A. P. Riemer noted in 1966, 'the dating of *The Constant Maid* has proved one of the most difficult tasks in the establishment of the canon of James Shirley's plays' (141). This is partly because of the dearth of information we have on its performance history. Another problem is that the play does not appear in any of the usual places that supply supplementary information, such as Abraham Wright's Caroline commonplace book (see Kirsch 1969). Our only solid information is that it was entered into the Stationers' Register on 28 April 1640 and printed that year by J. Raworth for R. Whitaker (see Textual Introduction). An altered version of the play, entitled *Love Will Find Out the Way*, was printed in 1661 and reissued in 1667 with a new title page. This new edition is of Q1 (1640). Because the intricacies of the relationship between it and Q2/3 need more space than a *Complete Works* can provide, the later quarto will be edited for the Shirley electronic edition in due course. Riemer was flummoxed probably because most of the rest of Shirley's work has left strong documentary traces at least as far as dating, publication, and performance are concerned. Recent work (e.g. Williams 2010; Ravelhofer 2017; Crowther 2017) has reconstructed and reconsidered earlier scholarly work so that we now have a clearer idea of the chronology of the plays. *The Constant Maid*, however, remains a problem. Riemer dealt with this uncertainty by constructing an elaborate revision scenario in which Q1 and Q2 were both reliant on an Ur-text of the play, and in which sections found both in Q2 and in *The Lady of Pleasure* (lic. 1635; pb. 1637) originated in this Ur-text, from the early 1630s. Esche (2006) has described this as 'absurd logic' and it is hard not to agree. There is no particular reason to think that the borrowing was this way round; indeed, it is more likely that the extra sections in Q2 (1661) were borrowed from a play already in print, i.e. *The Lady of Pleasure*. As Jeremy Lopez (2017) has argued, *The Constant Maid* is not the finest of Shirley's plays, and the amplifications of 1661 suggest that someone, maybe even Shirley, felt that more work needed to be done on it. Perhaps Riemer wanted to date it early in Shirley's stage career because of this clunkiness, but even Shirley's novice work generally made it to both stage and print relatively speedily: *The School of Compliment* (lic. 1625) was printed in 1631 and *The Wedding* (probably written 1626, though the licence is missing) was printed twice, in 1629 and 1633 (Bentley 1941–68, 5.1163). So, a ten-year gap between playing and printing was not normal at this stage in Shirley's career, even if the play was early and relatively unpolished.

A much more likely date for the composition of *The Constant Maid* would be 1636–7, making it the next play after *The Lady of Pleasure* (1635) and *The Duke's Mistress* (lic. 18 Jan 1636). Bentley notes that 'there is some evidence that [Shirley] aimed at an autumn play and a spring play each year' (5.1068), which might suggest that *The Constant Maid* was intended as the play for autumn 1636. This would make it what Shirley was working on when the plague closed the London theatres for seventeen months on

THE CONSTANT MAID: GENERAL INTRODUCTION

12 May 1636; they did not reopen until long after Shirley had left for Dublin, which was probably on 23 November 1636 (Williams 2010, 44). Williams argues that local references to particular parts of London in *The Constant Maid* indicate that it was not written for the Dublin stage, though Fleay reads these as nostalgia (Williams 2010, 280). These references chime with Richard Brome's use of London locales in, for instance, *The Asparagus Garden* (1635) and with Shirley's own mid-period comedies such as *The Lady of Pleasure* (1635). Shirley's very early plays make little or no use of location-as-meaning, and in his use of such a technique in *The Constant Maid*, he would seem to be participating in a current trend. Most persuasive of a date after 1636 is the fact that the manuscript was handed to the printer with *St Patrick for Ireland* (see Textual Essay), which very strongly implies that Shirley had it with him in Ireland. It also might suggest that Shirley felt that these two plays were unsuitable for the London stage, since neither was performed there but were instead batch-published in 1640. Shirley made brief visits home to London in 1637 and in 1638, on the latter occasion delivering *The Royal Master* to the printer, while perhaps also seeking the Poet Laureateship (Williams 2010, 117ff). The other 'Dublin' plays were not printed until the 1650s but both *The Gentleman of Venice* and *The Doubtful Heir* were licensed for London performance, in 1639 and 1640 respectively. *The Politician* was not licensed for performance, nor was it printed with the other unlicensed Dublin plays in 1640, having to wait until 1655 to reach the public via the press. The manuscript of *The Gentleman of Venice* must have been in London for the licensing on 30 October 1639, even though Shirley was still in Ireland, but Herbert's office-book does not record it as licensed to a particular company (Bawcutt 1996, 206; Bentley 1941–68, 5.1112). *The Doubtful Heir*, on the other hand, was licensed after Shirley returned from Ireland (probably with Wentworth in April 1640) on 1 June 1640 but to the King's Company (Bawcutt 1996, 208), unlike his previous London plays bar one (*The Changes* (1632)), which had all been performed by Queen Henrietta's players at the Cockpit. One possible conclusion might be that *The Constant Maid* was, like *St Patrick*, performed in Dublin but not considered suitable by Shirley for a London transfer.

The Constant Maid is unusual among Shirley's plays because there is no documented performance licence for it (Bentley 1941-68, 5.1095), and we are left to speculate on scanty evidence what the writing and early performance conditions of the play might have been.[2] As Bentley notes, scholars think that the play may have been given a first performance at the Werburgh Street Theatre in Dublin (see Williams 2010, 280) and was not, contrary to the claim on the 1661 title page, 'Acted with great Applause, by Her Majesties Servants, at the Phoenix in Drury Lane', or at least not in the 1630s (see King 1965a). Because at least three of the Dublin plays—*The Royal Master* (lic. 1638), *Rosania* (lic. 1640) and *The Gentleman of Venice* (lic. 1639)—do appear in Herbert's office-book with approval for playing on the London stage, it is likely that *The Constant Maid* was never licensed. Barring any illegal interregnum performance, it seems not to have been played in London until the rewritten version, *Love Will Find Out the Way* (1661), apparently hit the Restoration stage sometime between 1661 and 1667, as the 1667 title page

---

[2] We are missing performance licences for only five of his other plays: *The Wedding* (written *c.* 1626; perf. Cockpit before pb. 1629); *St Patrick* (pb. 1640; perf. Dublin); *The Politician* (pb. 1655; perf. Dublin); *The Arcadia* (pb. 1640; perf. unclear); *The Court Secret* (pb. 1653; not acted until 1664).

7

claims: 'at the new playhouse called the Nursery, in Hatton-Garden' (see Crowther 2017, 125). Unfortunately there is no corroborating evidence that George Jolly's Nursery troupe did act *The Constant Maid* but we do know that neither Davenant nor Killigrew had rights to the play, and that neither of them seems to have staged it (Crowther 2017, 128). Though none of the plays we can trace to the Nursery company can be identified as any version of *The Constant Maid* (see Hume 1985 and Astington 2004), Jolly did use the Cockpit on and off between 1660 and 1662 (Crowther 2017, 129) and, without a valid licence, in 1664–7 (Hotson 1928, 186). On balance, the evidence points to three possible windows when performances of either *The Constant Maid* or *Love Will Find Out the Way* might have taken place: for the former, in Dublin during Shirley's trip between 1636 and 1640; for the latter, first at the Cockpit by Jolly's troupe between his licensing on 24 December 1660 and the temporary hold placed on that licence on 1 November 1661 and, second, between April 1667 and the end of that year, the dates generally agreed for the founding of the Nursery in Hatton Garden (Hotson 1923, 442).

In terms of performance, then, one has to ask for which theatre did Shirley write *The Constant Maid*, rather than where was it eventually performed. Whichever date in the 1630s one accepts as correct, the overwhelming likelihood is that the company and theatre for which it was written were Queen Henrietta's Men at the Cockpit/Phoenix in Drury Lane. As Andrew Gurr has explained, the three main Hall playhouses—the Blackfriars, the Cockpit, and Salisbury Court—were roughly similar in design and size (Gurr 2009, 201–2). Their stages were about half the size of those of the open-air amphitheatres, making the playing conditions very intimate especially with the fad for audience members paying extra to sit on the stage (Gurr 2009, 195). If Gurr is right that the refitting of the Drury Lane cockpit as a theatre in 1616 is reflected in the John Webb copy (*c.* 1660) of an Inigo Jones design, then we know quite a lot about the physical resources of the stage for which *The Constant Maid* was written (2009, 197–8). It had three doors in the back wall of the stage, two smaller on either side of a larger, in front of which hangings could be hung to create a discovery space; there was a musicians' gallery above; there seems not to have been a railing at the front of the stage as there is in the de Witt Swan drawing (Gurr 2009, 201–2). *The Constant Maid* specifically requires hangings for Frances and Startup to hide behind, as Startup suggests they do at 2.4.56 to catch Hartwell and Mistress Bellamy in the act of courting.[3] These hangings were probably also used to shield Hornet from the audience's eyes in 3.2 as he changes his whole set of clothes while the conspirators steal his keys (see 3.2.118–45 and note to 122–3). In 4.3 Hornet is called upon to man an outside door and restrict entry to the masque, which results in comic knocking 'within' and the need for more than one door at the back of the stage.[4] Finally, the action of 5.3 requires at least two doors—one to the 'next room' and one from outside—as the whole cast assembles on the stage for the denouement. Gurr argues that the Webb drawing indicates there was no trap at the Cockpit, a conclusion corroborated by T. J. King in his earlier article on the staging requirements for the Cockpit plays (Gurr 2009, 202; King, 1965b *passim*);

---

[3] For the extensive use Shirley makes of hangings in his other plays, see Stevens 1977, 499–503.
[4] Shirley does the same trick with 'rude' pressing crowds in *The Humorous Courtier* 5.3 and there is 'saucy' knocking in *The Example* 1.1 (see Stevens 1977, 496–7).

THE CONSTANT MAID: GENERAL INTRODUCTION

certainly *The Constant Maid* has no requirement for one. Even the one time when it might have been used—to stage the ditch in 4.1—the stage directions indicate Startup's 'Exit' at l. 34 and it is clear from the action of the scene that he is not within earshot of the conversation between Hartwell and Close from ll. 49–84.[5]

Critics have noticed that *The Constant Maid* has similarities with *The Wedding* (see Forsythe 1914, 382), and it was partly on these grounds that Riemer wanted to assign an earlier date to the play. This is not just pertinent to the plot but also suggests some casting possibilities for two of the key roles—those of Hornet and Startup—as well as giving some hints as to how Shirley conceived those characters. *The Wedding*'s three suitors are stock types of the Jacobean and Caroline stage: Beauford 'a passionate louer', Rawbone 'a thin Citizen', and Lodam 'a fat Gentle-man' (Shirley 1629, A2v). These stock characters also appear in *The Constant Maid* in the persons of Hartwell, Hornet, and Startup. If Shirley were writing for the same actors in these similar roles, then they were intended for the talents of Michael Bowyer as Hartwell, William Robins as Hornet, and William Sherlock as Startup—each of whom are assigned to parts in the *Wedding* cast list. All three actors were still available to Shirley in the Cockpit company until the plague struck in May 1636, although William Sherlock was transferred to the company working out of Salisbury Court in late 1637. It is possible that Bowyer and Robins were part of the troupe that Shirley took to Dublin with him (Stevenson 1942, 149–50) and, though Bowyer's name at least seems to be associated with the King's Men somewhere between 1635 and 1641, the vagueness of the dates in the complaint which provides this information would also allow Bowyer to play in Ireland (see Hotson 1928, 31–5). In the case of Robins particularly, the plays given on the Dublin stage provided roles which seem to play to his strengths as 'a famous funnyman': 'Bombo in *The royall master*, Rodamant in *St. Patrick for Ireland*, Pickadill in *No wit no help like a womans*, and perhaps the Captain in *Rosania*' (Stevenson 1942, 153). So, if one thinks about roles—and specifically the paired comic parts of Rawbone and Lodam being translated into Hornet and Startup—several suggestions can be made for *The Constant Maid*. The first of these is that Startup is supposed to be portly like Lodam, which explains why the 'running scene' in 2.2 is especially funny. The metre in Startup's speeches in this section (from ll. 66–80) runs almost consistently one foot short as if he were out of breath (though Close and Bellamy still have regular length lines) and his comment at l. 71, 'If I live', seems strange unless he is gasping for breath. The second thing is that the main way in which Rawbone and Hornet differ is in terms of age—Rawbone is young but Hornet old—which argues that when Shirley was writing *The Constant Maid* he was writing for an actor considerably more advanced in years, and at a date in the late rather than early 1630s.[6] The third thing is that the break-up of the Cockpit company in 1636/7 and the splitting of its personnel must have affected Shirley's ability to stage a play that was reliant on the double-act of a thin and fat clown. This might be an added reason for the critical assessment of the play as being

---

[5] Stevens (1977, 496) suggests that Shirley only uses a trap in *The Arcadia* but this is a problematic conclusion given the very uncertain performance history of this play, and the suspicions of some critics that it may not even be by Shirley (Bentley 1941–68, 5.1073–6).

[6] Popular tradition has it that Robins, while fighting for the king, was shot in the head in 1645 *after* having laid down his arms (quoted in Hotson 1928, 13). He can probably be traced to Queen Anne's Men in 1617 but with no further information to tell us his date of birth (Tucker Murray 1910, i.188).

underwritten, perhaps because what we have in Q1 is an unacted version which Shirley left unrefined when he lost William Sherlock, one of his major character actors, during the move to Dublin.

THE GEOGRAPHY OF THE PLAY

Julie Sanders has shown how cultural geography enhances our understanding of Caroline drama, and *The Constant Maid* certainly repays such attention (Sanders 2011). Though they are not as identifiable as in *Hyde Park* (perf. 1632) or Brome's *The Weeding of Covent Garden* (after 1632), we see in Shirley's choice of locations a sense of character development which depends upon the complex political relations between court, city, and country so typical of plays of this era. Martin Butler has written that *The Constant Maid* is 'the completest example' of Caroline comedy's distinguishing feature: 'the Town is not the only centre of attention, but the other localities of the realm are invoked besides and the behaviour of the metropolis is measured against them' (1984, 164). The play stages several locations—Hornet's house in the City; Mistress Bellamy's London house, nearby but not precisely located; the fields on the way to Islington; Sir Clement's London residence—and it uses another to locate the character of Startup, the Northamptonshire 'gentleman' (see note to 4.2.24). References to London landmarks—the Fleet, the Bear-garden, Bedlam, the New Prison, St Paul's—and allusions to London characters such as Dick Whittington serve to anchor the play firmly in the lived experience of the London audience-member. But because *The Constant Maid* knowingly uses spaces which, as well as being real, are staples of earlier plays (particularly in Jonsonian drama, on which see Johnson 2018, *passim*), the locating is at once a geographical and cultural act. Shirley could be said to use his sources geographically.

In fact, most of the play does not take place within the city walls—we do presume that Hornet the usurer's house (2.3) is located in the City but its exact location is not speci-fied. We know that he keeps moving house to avoid 'subsidies' (i.e. to the Crown, see note to 2.3.101–3) and he says he 'always live[s] obscurely to avoid / Taxations' (104–5) but we do expect a usurer to operate from the financial centre rather than the suburbs. Jonson's 1626 play, *The Staple of News* (3.Int.2) offers, perhaps jokingly, Silver Street in Cheapside as the fit location for usury. It is also possible that a hint in Middleton's much earlier *A Trick to Catch the Old One* (1607) might fix the action in the Fleet Street/ Holborn area: the usurer Dampit's recollection of fleecing people out of their money is 'motions of Fleet Street, and visions of Holborn' (1.4.55), and his maid Audrey echoes this in her song at 4.5.3. Dampit clearly started life as a lawyer but Middleton makes strong associations between law and usury which were carried forward through Massinger's *A New Way to Pay Old Debts* (c. 1626) into *The Constant Maid*. The Holborn area has the benefit of being near the locations that are more definitely indicated in the text and is west of the city walls—so it is much nearer to the Cockpit than other possible locales.[7] Another speculation might be the more-than-coincidence of Seacoal Lane,

---

[7] e.g. Crutched Friars (off Old Jewry in the far east of the city), where Pisaro the Portuguese usurer resides in Haughton's *An Englishman for My Money* (1616).

THE CONSTANT MAID: GENERAL INTRODUCTION

which ran between Fleet Street and Holborn Bridge, literally round the corner from St Andrew's Holborn at which three of Shirley's children were baptised between 1628 and 1633. Hornet is associated throughout the play with sea-coal both because it is a money-saving measure and because of its connections with the fires of Hell: at 2.1.85–6 'He smothers a poor gentlewoman / At home with sea-coal', and the niece fantasizes that he and the devil will 'stink the poor souls so' when they try to save money by using it to heat Hell (2.3.47). There is a final alluring possibility which connects the location of Hornet's house to the niece's allusion to Dick Whittington (2.3.55): Seacoal Lane is next to a dead end called Turnagain Lane, so-called 'for that it goeth downe West to Fleete dike, from whence men must turne againe the same way that they came, for there it is stopped' (Stow 1598, 316). But surely it is also resonant with the words the bells played: 'Turn again, Whittington, Lord Mayor of London' (see note to 2.3.55–7)?

The night-walk in 4.1 is easier to evidence. Since Close says that 'such things [spirits] use to walk the fields' (4.1.18), he must have led Startup out into a less built-up area. Close tells the Watch that he has been 'about business' in Islington (4.1.109), so the most likely area for their night-time ramble might be the fields between Clerkenwell and Islington, bounded to the west by St John Street and to the east by Goswell Road. Shirley's London residences were in the parishes of, first, St Giles Cripplegate, and subsequently St Andrew Holborn, between which two churches lie these roads north. This area is also close to the New Prison, Clerkenwell, to which the Watch say they are going to take Close at 4.1.117. There are other possibilities further east—Moorfields, Mallow Field, or Finsbury Field (depending how far north towards Islington they have got). Stow's description of this area might encourage that idea: 'Thomas Fawconer Mayor ... builded the Posterne called Mooregate, for the ease of the Citizens, to walke that way upon Causwayes into the fieldes towards Iseldon and Hoxton. Moreouer, he caused the Ditche of the Citie, and other Ditches thereabout, to be new cast and clensed, by meane whereof, the said Fen or Moore was greatly dreyned and dried' (Stow 1908, 351). Not only is this the way to Iseldon (i.e. Islington) but there are plenty of ditches for Startup to hide in, as he does at 4.1.37–8, though the same would presumably be true of the fields further west too. Stow also gives us evidence that when they bump into Hartwell—a young member of the gentry—he is wandering in fields he already knows from more pleasant visits to 'speciall wels, in the Suburbes: sweete, wholesome, and cleare, amongst which Holywel, Clarkes wel, & Clementes wel, [which] are most famous and frequented by Schollers, and youths of the City in sommer euenings, when they walke foorth to take the aire' (Stow 1598, 14).

The geographical centrality of Clerkenwell is evident in the play—so close to the New Prison and on the way to Islington—and may give us a hint as to the intended location of Mistress Bellamy's and Justice Clement's houses. We know Sir Clement is the 'next Justice' (5.1.19) when Hartwell is apprehended wandering the fields, which implies his house is fairly near to the site of arrest. We also know that it must have been relatively easy for Hartwell, and Close and Startup, to leave Mistress Bellamy's house for the fields at the end of Act 3, so this rules out a city residence and an exit through one of the gates of the city wall. Martin Butler notes that the diarist Sir Humphrey Mildmay's London residence was a house rented from his brother-in-law 'in unfashionable Clerkenwell' (1984, 110), and the Earl of Newcastle's London house was also located there, in Clerkenwell Close, built on the ruins of the nunnery (Thornbury

11

THE COMPLETE WORKS OF JAMES SHIRLEY, VOLUME 7

1878, 329–30). Other residents included the antiquary John Weever (author of *Ancient Funeral Monuments*, 1631); the fourth Earl of Clanricarde (the third husband of Frances Sidney); Izaak Walton in the 1650s, and allegedly even Oliver Cromwell (Thornbury 1878, 329). This list of residents demonstrates the country-party tone of the area, making it fit for the minor gentry figures we find in the play, with their Jonsonian views of hospitality and good order. What is notable throughout the play is the strong social connectedness of the different parties involved, so that in the last scene Sir Clement's 'You'll meet with friends in the next room' (5.3.133) comes as no surprise. Sir Clement is uncle to both Playfair and his cousin; Hartwell and Playfair are friends and, therefore, Playfair is able to make free with the house of Mistress Bellamy (2.1): and she, in her turn, has been putting Hartwell up since he 'broke up house' (1.1.3). But the offer of hospitality does not stop with kith and kin: even Startup is accommodated when he visits and when the unknown Countryman shows up at night out of the blue, Mistress Bellamy offers him lodging and the aid of her servants. In strong contrast to Hornet's miserly household, the Clerkenwell milieu observes the rules of hospitality and are rewarded for it—there is poetic justice for adhering to traditional social mores in Shirley's plays.

No matter which date of composition we accept, the play was certainly written during Charles I's Personal Rule, when (according to country peers, at least) middle-class men of ability were preferred to those aristocrats who had previously held sinecures of government offices. Shirley had strong patronage relationships with both Sir Thomas Wentworth (later the Earl of Strafford), who was regularly locked in battles for the King's favour in the 1620s and 1630s, and with William Cavendish, Earl of Newcastle, who wrote slightingly of 'meane People' who lived off the King (Butler 1984, 195). Depending on your mind-set and allegiances, Wentworth was arguably either just the sort of new man by whom Hartwell has been replaced, or a version of Hartwell himself (though Wentworth was never in such financial distress that he was forced to break up house). Shirley's play responds directly to the country party's assessment of the evils of the city and the new-fangled. As Martin Butler suggests, it engages specifically with the broad context of the 'estates of the realm' and places its support firmly behind the values of the country gentry (Butler 1984, 164–5). As Butler relates, Cavendish's attitude to modishness, unsurprisingly, chimes with Close's and Hartwell's grief over the passing of the old ways (Butler 1984, 195). Cavendish would have agreed with Close that 'hospitality / Went out of fashion with crop-doublets' (1.1.3–4) and lamented that Hartwell's 'annual profits' could not 'encourage [him] to live at the same height [as his father]' (1.1.10–11). Equally, Hornet's tight-fisted advice about how to run a house describes as undesirable the old traditions of hospitality for which the Sidney/Jonson tradition was famous (see Celovsky 2009). Mistress Bellamy shows her allegiance to the traditional party when she tells Hornet roundly: 'I sha'not practise these in haste, and must / Declare these precepts make not for your welcome' (1.2.98–9).

USURY AND HOSPITALITY

There are real connections, then, linking the gentry-set love affair between Hartwell and Frances, Startup's status as a new man with money but no class, and Hornet's

THE CONSTANT MAID: GENERAL INTRODUCTION

dodgy business doings. Shirley's treatment of usury is broad-brush, based very much on the theatrical tradition of plays-gone-by: *The Jew of Malta* (1589), *The Merchant of Venice* (*c.* 1598), *A Trick to Catch the Old One* (1607), and *A New Way to Pay Old Debts* (*c.* 1625, pb. 1633) as well as other less well-known usury plays (of which there are many). *The Jew of Malta* and *A New Way* were both revived by Queen Henrietta's Men in *c.* 1632 and *c.* 1633 respectively (Gurr 2009, 292; 294), which seems to suggest a resurgence of interest in usury plays in the mid-1630s. *The Constant Maid* clearly draws on *A New Way* not just in terms of the usury plot but also on the complex socio-political questions surrounding impoverished gentlemen (though Hartwell, unlike Wellborn, is not to blame for his pecuniary difficulties), and the ways in which the servant-master bond is explored. Shirley had already drawn a sketch of a usurer in Rawbone (*The Wedding*) but Hornet draws deeply on Shylock, even to the extent of verbal parody in 5.2.1–2: 'She's gone! She's gone! I shall run mad! My niece! / Robbed of three thousand pound in her escape!' (cf. *Merchant* 2.8.15).[8] As Lloyd Kermode points out, the debate on usury went on throughout the whole of the sixteenth and seventeenth centuries and was a popular topic in pamphlets, plays, and essays (2009, 1–78). Because England had particularly high interest rates—though capped at 10 per cent, these were much higher than, for instance, in the Netherlands where they lent at 6 per cent—it made more sense for lenders to borrow abroad and do their moneylend-ing in England (Kermode 2009, 7). This is how foreigners, and particularly Jews, became the scapegoat usurers on the early modern stage, lumped together as 'anti-Christian' and 'un-English' (Kermode 2009, 16). The confusion over whether Hornet is Jewish or not is rooted in this tradition of conflating Jews and usurers, but it is important to understand that all English Jews—who, after having been expelled by Edward I in 1290, had slowly returned from *c.* 1540 onwards—were officially converts anyhow. The play ends with Playfair's intertheatrical joke, aimed at Shylock and at Barabas, who had been recently treading the same boards as Hornet: 'I'm glad of your conversion: ye are the first / Jew that in my remembrance has turned Christian' (5.3.220–1). Shylock's forced 'conversion', it seems from this, was as problematic for Caroline theatre-goers as it is today, though perhaps in different ways. The only other direct mention of Jewishness in the play is Hornet's own elaborate joke in 4.3 address-ing his scrivener, 'Jew's ears I know they are' (153). The usurer was often accompanied by two side-kicks, a broker and a scrivener, whose entanglement in usury might prop-erly qualify them as 'Jews' also (Kermode 2009, 23). However, there are also jokes about the devil (e.g. 1.2.112–14 and 2.3.42–8) and damnation (e.g. 1.2.91–4; 2.1.99; 5.2.17) as was traditional in usury tracts on account of the fact that it was held that both usurers and Jews were denied salvation (Kermode 2009, 13–14). In Sir *Giles* Hornet, Shirley uses a refraction through Massinger's Sir Giles Overreach of Giles Mompesson, the Jacobean monopolist and projector, whose sharp schemes came tumbling down spectacularly in 1621. Monopolies, used by Charles to make money during his per-sonal rule, were a contentious issue in the 1630s. Hornet is a kinder version of Overreach—where the latter has to be dragged raving off the stage, the former accepts his fate (along with his new nephew) fairly gracefully and is most worried about being

---

[8] It is no accident that the niece's portion is three thousand pounds, to match the three thousand ducats that Antonio owes Shylock.

ridiculed: 'charm thy friends they do not laugh at me', he begs a victorious Playfair (5.3.205).

Usury plots are often intimately tied to the theme of hospitality and this would have been a connection the audience would readily have seen in *The Constant Maid*. Shirley makes it clear several times that Hornet's way to salvation is to renounce the arguments against hospitality he voiced early in the play, because by embracing this vision of Christian charity he will align himself with the gentry and with traditional notions of hospitality. More serious than Hornet's advice to Mistress Bellamy that 'Your table / Is a devourer, and they shut up doors / First that keep open house and entertainments' (1.2.71–3) is his refusal of charitable giving in general, as is indicated by his niece in her 'mad' speeches in 2.3. Her exhortation that he imagine he had 'undone a widow, / Or turned an orphan begging' (50–1), coupled with her advice of how to avoid spending charitably until he dies (69–74), demonstrates how tenuous his hope of salvation is at this stage of the play. In direct contrast to the way he was depicted in Act 2, Hornet's conversion in 5.3 is signalled by his willingness to embrace charitable giving:

> I'll be a knight too, if I live, and build
> An hospital for twenty more o'th'order,
> Which I'll reduce myself out of the suburbs.
>
> (206–8)

For Hornet, the reformed usurer, 'It is a shame such men should lose their spurs . . . For want of fit provision' (209; 212).

Hospitality, as practised by most of the characters in the play, is a question of sensible money management. Unlike Wellborn (in *A New Way*), Hartwell's behaviour is not profligate and his fortune, though reduced, has not disappeared—as Frances puts it, 'Nor are the means of Hartwell so contemptible' (1.2.173). She makes the point to her mother that they do not need to marry money—'Your estate / Is above needy providence' (1.2.169–70). Mistress Bellamy might argue that Startup's 'wealth [is] / Able to guild deformity' (1.2.147–8), but even she runs out of arguments and resorts to telling Frances 'No more' in the hope that she will 'shape / Another answer' when she has 'considered well' (1.2.174–5). As Celeste Turner Wright has pointed out of usurers, 'one who feeds neither himself nor his neighbor is a hard master for servants' (Wright 1934, 187) and Hartwell's relationship with Close is a continuation of the lesson about generous hospitality. Hartwell's *largesse* with the servants he is forced to turn off with 'somewhat more, / Not worth the name of bounty' (1.1.41–2), is part of Shirley's characterization of him in that it indicates that even pecuniary distress does not stop him from more than meeting his obligations. Close's refusal to leave him, both in 1.1 and in the fields in 4.1, demonstrates the importance of a bond more emotional than contractual, even for such a canny operator as Close. In contrast, Startup's inability to know the value of money, even though he has lots of it, is demonstrated in the absurd sum he gives Close to buy tobacco at 2.2.27 and results in Close treating him with contempt in their dealings.

Mistress Bellamy's character and behaviour are harder to read. She has already agreed to the marriage of Frances and Hartwell by the beginning of the action, an agreement which seems to be threatened by Hornet revealing that Hartwell's estate is less secure and profitable than she had thought, 'he's a beggar, or must be very shortly'

THE CONSTANT MAID: GENERAL INTRODUCTION

(1.2.42). Given that she soon bates and ridicules Hornet, it is surprising that she takes what he says seriously. In response to his counsel that Frances 'throw [Hartwell] off betime' (48–9), her 'You direct well' could either mean 'That's good advice' or 'You're very bossy'. The appearance of Startup's letter at 1.2.105 is either an indication that Mistress Bellamy is already having doubts about Hartwell (and therefore is in marriage negotiations with Startup), or a fortuitous coincidence which she seizes upon in order to test Hartwell's fortune-hunting propensities. But her moral position is muddied when she demands that her daughter give him up and then tries to seduce him herself—and what is more, uses her money to do so:

> Add unto this my wealth, no narrow fortune
> And without competition—my daughter
> Depending on my love, whose portion must
> Flow from my bounty or be nothing.
>
> (1.2.231–4)

Reading Mistress Bellamy's tone is difficult: she is a very convincing tyrannical mother and seductive widow. We are only informed that she is actually neither of these things by the nurse—who lets the trick slip, 'your mother did but counterfeit / The love-sick widow all this while, to try him' (3.4.2–3)—or by Mistress Bellamy herself who admits this to Frances the second time she tries to bully her into giving him up:

> I had no other thought
> At first but wisely to distinguish whether
> His heart was fixed on thee or my estate.
>
> (4.2.66–8)

But alas, Hartwell's sterling qualities mean that 'Love / Hath changed both scene and title in our comedy... And made me his indeed, his perfect lover' (4.2.71–2; 77). Frances finally gets her way by dint of *not* being the dutiful daughter, by admitting that she thinks her mother is tyrannical and—most convincing of all—proving to her mother that she trusts Hartwell beyond all reason: 'I know he loves me' (4.2.154).

Jeremy Lopez has commented of Frances' passionate main speech in this scene that its 'rhetorical form might best be described as *unrepressed*: it glosses, without warning, the most volatile conflicts of late Caroline society' (Lopez 2017, 23). Lopez offers a political reading of the play where the 'half-covert language of religious freedom and aristocratic resistance to tyranny come easily precisely because Shirley is writing in a pre-revolutionary moment' (24). It is certainly true, as shown by Butler, that fundamental to Caroline drama was a displaced commentary on the themes and problems of the political state. But Mistress Bellamy's 'repressed-feeling capitulation' (Lopez, 24) is not quite as surprising as Lopez thinks it is; rather than the characters displaying 'infuriating theatrical fickleness' (22), the nurse has prepared us for this 'love test' (24), and Frances' easy acceptance of the explanation that her mother is counterfeiting (at 3.4.11) prepares an audience for the capitulation which provides the happy ending in 4.2. In the long exchange between Frances and Bellamy in 4.2, Shirley plays with the audience who have been seduced into expecting a speedy end to the love test now that the nurse has revealed it to Frances. The further twists that the Widow has *actually* fallen in love with Hartwell, and then actually *has not*, are part and parcel of a strategy which Lopez identifies as 'searching for unimagined ground' (23). We might compare to this the denouement of *The Cardinal*, the finest example in Shirley's works of 'the dramatist's compulsive need to demonstrate...mastery of...conventions' (Lopez, 23). The rapid twists in 4.2 are surely a variation of this action of employing convention after convention in order to keep the audience on its toes. But Lopez's argument that the play 'shifts radically between discordant registers' could be said of others of Shirley's comedies, where the heightened tragicomic register often appears (e.g. *The Wedding, The School of Compliment*). All of the 1630s tragicomedies also use the passionate register of Frances' speech at some point. Hartwell's speeches (and behaviour) at both 4.1.41–58 and 5.3.47–79 are, likewise, in this heightened register and it might be that we are better thinking of *The Constant Maid* as an attempt at tragicomedy, especially in respect to the Frances and Hartwell plot. This is additionally true of *Much Ado About Nothing*, which obviously influenced *The Constant Maid*.

SOURCES AND INFLUENCES

Lopez notes that he wants to 'imagin[e] Shirley's artistic energies directed not toward the future but the past—that he briefly seized upon an opportunity to create something really new on the stage' (23). Indeed, *The Constant Maid* is very striking in the huge debt it owes to Shakespeare, specifically to two of Shakespeare's Elizabethan comedies, *The Merchant of Venice* and *The Taming of the Shrew*. We saw earlier how Shirley recalled Barabas and Shylock, especially in the way his ending to *The Constant Maid* plays with the unlikelihood of conversion and nods so deliberately at the one Jew-turning-Christian that everyone in the audience would remember. But the Hornet subplot takes as much from *The Taming of the Shrew* as it does from *The Merchant of Venice*. The whole premise—persuading a delusional protagonist that he is something he is not, dressing him in better clothes than he deserves, enacting a 'court' scene—reuses the Christopher Sly plot. And it is not just in the Hornet subplot that the influence of this play can be detected. For much of Act 4, Startup hides in ditches divested of his clothes and wrapped in a blanket, surely an idea suggested by the treatment of Sly in *The Taming of the Shrew*. The culmination of this plot, though, is not Hornet's meeting the Player King but Hornet being appointed 'Controller of the ['King's'] masque' (4.3.47), a masque which represents the story of the Judgement of Paris. Shirley delights in layering one metatheatrical device upon another. We have several concurrent games of 'musical clothes': Hartwell steals and wears Startup's to gain access to Frances' bedroom; Playfair's cousin dons two different disguises as the Player King and as a doctor treating Hornet's 'mad' niece; the servants dress up as courtiers and pursuivants; Hornet himself is divested of his clothes and dressed as his betters; finally, in the masque, Playfair impersonates Paris and Hornet's niece pretends to be Helen of Troy. These multiple disguises would seem excessive even in Shakespearean comedy, but Shirley redoubles them wherever possible to stress metatheatrical effect. For instance, the masque which is, after all, given in front of a Player King contains the stage direction 'To Juno enter one like a King' and ends with Hornet recognizing and then doubting his recognition of his own disguised niece

(4.3.178–83). This last point is crucial, and indicative of the way Shirley's suggestive metatheatre works: the internal logic Hornet uses 'Nay, if she be my niece I am sure she was not / Married this morning' (4.3.182–3) is correct for the real world but not for the world of the play. As he comments, 'I do dream still' (4.3.186) and this has been his conviction—that this is somehow a dream—since the start of Playfair's scheme. Shirley's destabilization of the reality of the play is deliberate, and a more profound debt to Shakespeare, especially to *The Taming of the Shrew*, than the lifting of plot. Shirley's primary aim is not to steal the plot and characters. Instead, he is negotiating with Shakespearean metatheatre by replaying it, just as we see Shakespearean devices in *The Constant Maid*—the Player King, the 'musical clothes'—iterated for an audience so as to reinforce their power. We might think of this now as a postmodern impulse, but I would argue that it is esemplastic—a moulding into unity—rather than parodic, aiming not to reject but to create, as Lopez suggests.

Shirley does not just reuse the works of other playwrights, of course; his work is constantly in conversation with itself (see earlier under The Play). Katherine Heavey has noted that Shirley reuses the Judgement of Paris story in his later masque *The Triumph of Beauty* (pb. 1646) (Heavey 2014, 439). In this masque Shirley reframes the myth, though, by making it the 'real' action rather than the inset play, which is to be Jason and the Golden Fleece presented by bumbling amateurs (this anticipated play-within-the-play never materializes). Almost without exception the plays contain 'set-piece' metatheatrical devices: from schoolroom training in the aping of Petrarchan poetry (*The School of Compliment*), to the murders-within-a-masque in *The Cardinal*—a scene which itself offers a metatheatrical reading of the metatheatrical devices in revenge tragedies. One might argue that a consciousness of their theatricality is fundamental to the plays' method and certainly it is something that Shirley does self-consciously and pointedly. *The Constant Maid* makes this explicit as early as its first scene: Playfair's entrance is greeted stichomythically by Hartwell's three manumitted servants with three quotations from *The Spanish Tragedy*, one from *Mucedorus* and one (substantially altered) from Beaumont's *Swetnam, The Woman-Hater* (see note to 1.1.53–7). Playfair wishes to stage what he variously terms a 'device', a 'project', a 'trick' and he recruits the servants as actors in the drama. Their performance, Hornet's gulling, is also repeatedly interpreted as a 'dream' by Hornet whose new 'clothes already have / Made him forget himself' (4.3.21–2). As Heavey notes, 'the main joke is on Hornet, who is unable to read Playfair's retelling of Helen's myth for what it really is' (2014, 439), and this lack of right sight is a theme elsewhere too: for Hornet, who cannot read the apocryphal story found in the hangings (4.3.40–1), and for Hartwell, who misreads first Mistress Bellamy and then Frances.

Elsewhere, Heavey uses Shirley's choice of masque subject in *The Constant Maid* to argue that the niece is merely a player in a 'plot concocted by men', 'aligned . . . with the silenced and objectified Helen of the medieval Troy-narratives, whose speech is rarely recorded' (Heavey 2009, 8). This is truer than she meant it: the Judgement of Paris trope has little to do with women, chaste or otherwise, and is all about how (young) men should exercise their judgement. The earliest moralizing readings of the tale, such as that of Fulgentius, stress the stupidity of Paris for choosing the worst of the three ways of life represented by the goddesses' gifts: 'the contemplative, that is, the search for knowledge and truth, represented by Athena; the active, accumulating worldly riches and possessions, signified by Hera; and the voluptuous, seeking after lust, personified by Aphrodite' (Stróbl 2018, 210). By the fifteenth century, Marsilio Ficino used the story to explain that there are three kinds of life: the contemplative, the active, and the pleasurable. His praise of Lorenzo de Medici stresses that the ideal nobleman neglects none of the goddesses, choosing to combine the best of all their attributes in his virtuous way of life (Stróbl 2018, 210–11). It is not fanciful, therefore, to think of the masque in *The Constant Maid* as urging all three of the goddesses' gifts as constitutive of the combined virtues of gentility, of the 'complete man' (4.3.177). Of course, the masque does celebrate the power of love but the fact that it is used primarily as a trick to confuse and humiliate Hornet surely undercuts this as the moral lesson. Hornet identifies Venus as the eventual victor—'No, no: that fairy must / Win the ball' (177–8)—but thinks this is the wrong choice, commenting 'more fool he!' when Paris refuses Juno's 'state and kingdoms' (173–4).

Any moral intended by the play as a whole is less clear-cut than that of the inset masque. Although Hartwell begins the play with Pallas Athene's virtues of wisdom and strength, he cannot attain the status of a 'complete man' until he has also acquired the worldly success bestowed by Juno and love by Venus; his lesson turns out to be to trust the power of love since it brings him fortune also. Hornet's conversion shows him embracing love too, partly in his acceptance of Playfair and his niece's love match but more specifically in the loving-kindness he displays in his charitable plans (5.3.206–12). The play's last words demonstrate a Christian piety which is not explicit elsewhere in the text, but is fundamental to the salvific old-fashioned kindness of *The Constant Maid*:

> 'Twixt Love and Fortune now the accounts are even—
> A chain of hearts and the first link in heaven.
>
> (5.3.223–4)

Textual Introduction

The Constant Maid was entered in the Stationers' Register on 28 April 1640, together with *St Patrick for Ireland*, as follows: 'Master Whitaker. / Entred for his Copies vnder the hands of doctor Wykes and Master Fetherston Warden / two Playes . . . / Saint Patrick for Ireland. And / The Constant Maide. by James Shirley' (Bergel and Gadd, SRO10348). Both plays were printed by J. Raworth, for R. Whitaker and the rows of ornaments above HT on A2r of *Constant Maid* are from the same setting as A3r of *St Patrick*, as is (probably) the imprint (Greg 1939–59, 729 and 731). The title page reads:

THE / CONSTANT / MAID. // A Comedy. //Written by *James Shirley*. // [ornament, similar to McKerrow 379] // LONDON, / Printed by *J. Raworth*, for *R. Whitaker*. 1640. [STC 2nd ed. S22438]

In 1657, these plays were re-issued with a new title page as part of a nonce collection of two plays, of which there is only one copy known to be still extant (in the Chapin Library of Williams College):

TWO / PLAYES // THE / Constant Maid. / A / COMEDY / AND / St *PATRICK* / FOR / IRELAND. // Written by / *James Shirley* Gent. // *LONDON*: / Printed for *Joshua Kirton*, at his shop in S. *Pauls* Church- / yard, at the sign of the Kings-Arms 1657.

The bottom of the title page of *Constant Maid* has been cut off to remove the original imprint and the *St Patrick* title page has been cancelled, and that play starts with the prologue (A2r).[1] There is one more extant copy of *St Patrick* in the Folger Shakespeare Library which was most probably detached from this issue (STC 22455 copy 2): the copy note in the library catalogue has 'Lacking t.p.; bound in its place is lower half of t.p. from his "Two playes" (Wing S3490)'. This Folger *St Patrick*, then, is probably a copy which had previously been bound as part of the 1657 nonce collection but has subsequently lost its *The Constant Maid* and the upper part of the 1657 t.p. has been cut to remove any reference to it. *The Constant Maid* was very substantially revised and augmented in 1661 as *Love Will Find Out the Way* (pb. 1661, reissued 1667). This later play is bibliographically unconnected to *The Constant Maid* and will be edited separately for the electronic edition of *The Complete Works of James Shirley*.

This edition is based on a full collation of twenty copies of Q (see collation record).[2] Across all sheets, there is only one substantive variant which cannot be accounted for by poor printing, which is a change at E4r, 24 from a colon to a question mark. There

---

[1] I am indebted and very grateful to Wayne G. Hammond, the Chapin Librarian at Williams College, for substantial help relating to this exemplar.

[2] The collations were carried out by Emil Rybczak and Teresa Grant.

THE COMPLETE WORKS OF JAMES SHIRLEY, VOLUME 7

is a similar instance at A3r, 24 of a colon apparently corrected to a stop, but in some copies (e.g. C11.2) there is a faint imprint of what looks like the upper point of a colon but which is probably caused by poor inking or damaged or worn type during printing; this could account for the apparent colon in half the copies. There are also instances of under-inking at C1r, 3 (where 'selfe' gives way to 'self~') and at D4r, 5 (HN1 and L.1 have 'wont' rather than 'went', where damaged type has picked up too much ink). Poor inking may also account for a missing catchword on F3v of O.3. The one substantive correction at E4r, 24 is a puzzle: there are three uncorrected errors on this sheet— E1v, 5] Sinbe (Since), E1v, 25 you (your), and E3v, 32] side, (side)—yet the compositor chose to amend only the relatively minor punctuation error. In his edition of *St Patrick for Ireland*, John P. Turner Jr. notes that there are no substantive variants in the thirty copies of that play that he collated (Turner 1979, 7). As the shared setting of some of their quires A demonstrates, *The Constant Maid* clearly went through the press at roughly the same time as *St Patrick*, possibly set by the same compositors with the same habits, so the lack of stop-press correction is not a surprise. In the case of *St Patrick* too, Turner finds 'poor inking or damaged type to account for each instance [of variant]', and surmises that Raworth did not proofread the text, 'a circumstance that could account for Shirley's ceasing to do business with Whitaker' (1979, 13; 15).

The collation of the play is: Quarto, A to I (nine full sheets).

[A1] Title page

[A1v] *The names of the Persons*

A2 Row of ornaments / THE / CONSTANT MAID // Act. I. and beginning of text.

[A2v] through [I3v] Text of play (five acts in verse)

[I4] Blank

[I4v] Blank

The Constant Maid contains thirty-six unnumbered leaves. The gatherings are regularly signed throughout like B (B, B2, and B3), except A which is unsigned on A1. A running title '*The Constant Maid.*' appears throughout the text [A2v] to [I3v]. There are catchwords at the foot of each page which correspond correctly in all cases to the first word of the next page.

Broken type and other distinctive markers in the running titles make it relatively easy to determine that the play was set on two skeleton formes in which the running titles are largely consistent, possibly by two compositors—one of whom seems to have been more prone to errors than the other. There are two basic settings: one consistent with B(i) and one with C(o), which may make it possible to determine an approximate order of printing.

Q	Inner	Outer
A	Skeleton forme 1a	Skeleton forme 2a
B	Skeleton forme 1b	Skeleton forme 1b
C	Skeleton forme 1b	Skeleton forme 2b
D	Skeleton forme 1b	Skeleton forme 2b
E	Skeleton forme 1b	Skeleton forme 1b

THE CONSTANT MAID: TEXTUAL INTRODUCTION

F	Skeleton forme 1b	Skeleton forme 2b
G	Skeleton forme 2b	Skeleton forme 1e
H	Skeleton forme 1d	Skeleton forme 2b
I	Skeleton forme 1c	Skeleton forme 2c

The second skeleton forme (2) comes in fewer states than forme 1, and we will start there because it is easier to surmise a possible printing order. There are three states of forme 2, accounting for the title page (a), the text (b), and the last (blank) page (c).

A outer (2a)		C outer (2b)		I outer (2c)	
t. p.	vii	vi	v	viii	blank
v	vi	vii	viii	v	vi

It is likely that state 2a was printed first because a correction in running title v (a turned 'n' in *Constant* on A2v) was made between the printing of A(o) and C(o) but that running title is not otherwise altered. For C(o), A(o) was turned, and another running title (viii) was added, with a swash C in *Constant* with a distinctive broken top, apparent throughout the rest of the printing. Running title vii is also distinctive, by virtue of *Constant*'s odd st ligature with a tail pointing slightly forwards and the only non-swash C on the running titles of this forme. Running title vi has a particularly straight tail on its st ligature which can be used to track its progress throughout the play. C(o), D(o), F(o), G(i), and H(o) are printed from skeleton forme 2b, in the same orientation. I(o), state 2c, has the same orientation as A but is blank on a different page (4v).

Skeleton forme 1 is more complicated, with five separate arrangements of its running titles. 1b is the most common state of this setting and first appears on B(i), which is consistent also with B(o), C(i), D(i), E(i), E(o), and F(i). It pairs two titles (i and iv) with swash C in *Constant* on the near pages (i.e. 1v and 4r or 2v and 3r), the right of which (title iv) also has a broken e in *The*, which contracts the hole of the e. On the far pages are titles (ii and iii) with non-swash C, the right of which (iii) has a distinctive dropped 'a' in '*Constant*'. All the running titles are retained without resetting and these are used in the various arrangements of formes 1a, 1c, 1d, and 1e, which are each unique but based on this skeleton. The arrangement of running titles on the sequence of formes is as follows:

A inner (1a)		B inner (1b)		I inner(1c)		H inner (1d)		G outer (1e)	
start of text	Ii	iii	ii	blank	ii	Iv	Iii	Iv	i
d.p.	Iv	i	iv	i	iv	Ii	I	iii	ii

Given that we have evidence that skeleton forme 2 was printed A>C>I and the printing shop would have an interest in perfecting sheets (otherwise it would have a jumble of half-sheets), we might surmise that forme 1 also started with A. It is

21

possible that A(i) might have been printed between I(i) and H(i) but this evidence from the sequence of skeleton forme 2 suggests that A was probably printed first. The most likely printing order for the sheets with versions of skeleton forme 1 might therefore be A(i), B(i), B(o), C(i), D(i), E(i), E(o), F(i), I(i), H(i), G(o). A(i) (state 1a) was set with running titles ii and iv, then running titles iii and i were added for the run from B(i) to F(i) (state 1b), and then running title iii was removed to print I(i) (state 1c). This is consistent with the practice on forme 2 as far as we can determine it. For H(i) (state 1d) the compositor seems to have turned the forme and reinstated running title iii but swapped its position with i; however, importantly, retaining iv and ii in their previous positions suggests a continuity with 1a–c. Something then caused G(o) (1e) to be completely rearranged since no turning or swapping of existing arrangements of skeleton forme 1 can account for its unique placement of running titles. It is notable that H(i) and G(o) have disproportionate numbers of uncorrected errors, one explanation for which might perhaps be haste to finish the job with a possible implication that these sheets were last to be printed. G(o), with its disordered running titles, (arguably) has seven uncorrected errors, the largest number on any sheet.[3]

It may be reasonable to investigate if these data support a theory that the play was printed in formes by two compositors, one of whom—responsible for skeleton forme 1—was less accurate than the other. This is already problematic since compositors did not always stick to their own formes and it is possible that a novice might be responsible for the maintaining of formes, redistributing type, etc., but it is worth an attempt to distinguish characteristic composition styles of skeleton formes 1 and 2. Skeleton forme 1 has twenty-three uncorrected errors over eleven impressions (average 2.1); skeleton forme 2, nine mistakes over seven impressions (average 1.3). D(i), G(o), and H(i) are particularly error-filled, with four, six, and four respectively. However, there are only two error-free formes, B(o) and F(i), both of which were set by the usually less accurate compositor if we are to insist on one compositor per forme. There is also another complication to this conclusion, which is that ten formes of the eighteen use a distinctive over-large capital U, especially in the words Uncle, Usurer, and Upon. It appears once in B(i), C(o), D(i), D(o), E(o), I(i), and I(o) and twice in F(o), G(o), and H(i). Unfortunately, though, this arrangement does not correspond to a scenario where skeleton 1 was set from one case of type and skeleton 2 from another, since formes set from both skeleton 1 and skeleton 2 include examples with and without this oversized U. Some, but not all, of the formes reproduce what has come to be known as Shirley's extended dash: these, used most commonly to indicate the silence of a loss for words (sometimes because of interruption), appear only on D(i), D(o), F(o), G(i), G(o), and H(o) but cross-comparing them with instances of the over-size U or with the basic skeleton forme does not yield any clear conclusions about how many compositors were involved because the dashes appear on sheets with and without the U and on both skeleton forme 1 and 2. It is curious that the dash is not used at all on the remaining formes, which might seem to imply that the same person set both sides

---

[3] For the sake of argument here I have counted all possible uncorrected errors (some might have plausible but unprovable explanations, e.g. to adjust for metre).

THE CONSTANT MAID: TEXTUAL INTRODUCTION

of quire D and G (and adjacent F(o) and H(o)) and none of the rest of the play. There is a rough correlation, however, between the incidence of use of dashes and uncorrected errors (D(i) and G(o) particularly), and it is nearly certain that the compositor for H(i) (also with a high number or errors) also set G(o) since it is only on these two formes that an over-size J is used in addition to the over-size U. Turner notes of *St Patrick* that, though 'the evidence makes it possible that two compositors set the type...each working from a different type case, the evidence does not bear out this assumption' (1979, 11). This is true, too, of *The Constant Maid*: though two or more compositors are possible, if this were the situation they must have worked from a single case of type and were not both setting separate formes at the same time. Recurring type evidence is suggestive that the formes were not consistently set or redistributed, although they were distinctively given a skeleton of headlines (in one case) and a rough skeleton in another (see earlier). There is evidence of redistribution of headlines and there are two discernibly different patterns of dealing with skeletons, but not of composition: that might be indicative of two compositors but that is probably as far as we can go.

The relationship of *The Constant Maid* to its stablemate publication, *St Patrick for Ireland*, will be discussed fully in the general Textual Introduction to *The Complete Works* but it is clear from existing evidence that they were printed together. A preliminary investigation of the imprints of both plays suggests that *St Patrick* was printed first, since in all copies of *The Constant Maid* that I have inspected 'Printed' has clearly shifted during the loosening of the forme from the *St Patrick* imprint, so that the 'P' is raised and the 'i' has dropped. Turner's description (1979, 12) of the features of *St Patrick* are all consistent with *The Constant Maid*: there are no 'troublesome' errors and the printing never obscures the meaning of the play; the plays are set in Roman type but italics are consistently used for speech headings, proper names, and stage directions including those that describe the masque in 4.3. The play proved shorter than the printer expected, as evidenced by the two blank sides at the end (I4r-v) and the very generous spacing given to the masque on H1r-v. There are thirty-six printed lines on a standard page (and fewer on those with such things as act divisions) but only twenty-nine and twenty-five on H1r-v; additionally, the compositor(s) have introduced instances of spaces before and after stage directions on B(i), C(i), C(o), D(o), E(i), E(o), F(o), H(i), and H(o), though these last two are as part of the masque. There are spaces before (but not after) stage directions on E(i), H(i), and I(o). In fact, only B(o), F(i), G(i), G(o), and I(o) show the usual measures employed for not wasting space that one would expect in a play of this era, though on all pages the line length is consistent and there is no turnover. I think G(o)—the one with the disordered running titles—was probably the last to be printed, so this explains the economy there, but there is no obvious pattern with the other instances. In fact, the play is short; at 1,948 lines, it is shorter than every Shakespeare play except *The Comedy of Errors*, and about half the length of *Hamlet*. *The Constant Maid* is short even for Shirley, with, for example, *Bird in a Cage* totalling 2,344 lines and *The Lady of Pleasure* 2,554. In this context, the augmentation of the text to create *Love Will Find Out a Way* (1661) makes sense, since readers might have felt cheated by a playbook weighing in at less than 2,000

23

THE COMPLETE WORKS OF JAMES SHIRLEY, VOLUME 7

lines.[4] John Raworth (active 1638–45) was not a particularly experienced printer of playbooks by the time he printed Shirley's two in 1640—he had reprinted Massinger's *The Bondman* and *The Duke of Milan* in 1638, both for Edward Blackmore; reprinted *If You Know Not Me You Know Nobody* for Nathaniel Butter in 1639; reprinted *The Duchess of Malfi* for John Waterson and John Benson in 1640, but it is not possible to determine whether this last came before or after the Shirleys. His *Duchess* looks very different from *The Constant Maid*, with a marked tendency to print speeches continuously in an effort to save space, just as the first edition 1623 *Duchess* (Okes for Waterson) had done. *The Constant Maid* presented the opposite problem, demanding extra spacing to fill the allotted sheets. The publisher and printer collaborated only once after Shirley, on *The foure cardinall-vertues of a Carmelite-fryar observed by Sir Edward Dering* (1641; Wing / D1109), though Whitaker did send work to the print shop between 1646 and 1648, when it was run by Raworth's widow Ruth, after John's death. Shirley's two plays were the only first edition playbooks Raworth ever printed, so we are forced to conclude with Turner and Stevenson that his failure to make stop-press corrections was an issue and that Shirley must have known he was sending these second-string plays (in the sense that he did not intend them for the London stage in 1640) to a second-string printer.

Like *St Patrick*, its companion through the press, it is most probable that *The Constant Maid* was printed from an author's manuscript rather than a prompt book (Turner 1979, 16ff). For a start, there is no record of performance of the play which could have given rise to such a prompt book. Furthermore, the stage directions concerning servants, particularly in the last scene of the play, demonstrate that the entrances and exits required had not been accurately plotted in the manuscript as would have been necessary for a production. As Turner says of *St Patrick*, the stage directions generally show the playwright's conception of the scene, clearly evident in the directions for the masque in 4.3 of *The Constant Maid*. The same might be said of the speech prefixes in 3.2 where there is a shift from *Cous.* (up to l. 53) to *War.* (l. 73ff) to mark the speeches of the Cousin when disguised as the King. This shift takes place only on Hornet's entrance, so is clearly a continuation of the learned joke at 3.2.57 where Playfair calls his player-king cousin 'Excellent Warbeck', rather than a practical measure suitable for a prompt book.

An unpublished 1958 M.Litt. dissertation by J. L. Hall contained editions of *The Constant Maid* and *The Grateful Servant* in original spelling (so of limited help to this modern spelling edition). The only published post-seventeenth-century edition of *The Constant Maid* is in *The Dramatic Works and Poems of James Shirley* (1833), eds. Gifford and Dyce. Spelling and punctuation were modernized, scene divisions and corrected stage directions were added, and Shirley's characteristic contractions like 'wo'not' and 'shannot' were regularized to 'will not' and 'shall not' and 'ha" becomes 'have'. Gifford's main intervention—a temptation for any editor—was the regularization of Shirley's metre, not an easy task. I have adopted some of Gifford's suggestions and recorded these in the collation.

---

[4] *St Patrick* is also short, extending only to quire I (most Shirley plays fill I and K), and one might speculate that this accounts for the texts being printed together by Whitaker and Raworth who were not Shirley's normal publishers. See Stevenson (1944a) for an account of Shirley's change of publisher.

24

THE CONSTANT MAID: TEXTUAL INTRODUCTION

THE CONSTANT MAID—STOP-PRESS COLLATION OF 1640 QUARTO

Copies collated:

BRISTOL	Central Library, Bristol, SR 74
C	University Library, Cambridge, Syn.7.63.381
C11.1	St Catharine's College, Cambridge, Z.59
C11.2	St Catharine's College, Cambridge, Z.42
CH	Chapin Library, Williams College, MA, Wing S3490
E	National Library of Scotland, Edinburgh, Bute.555
ETON	Eton College, S.170.Plays 30(04)
HN1	Huntington Library, 69451
L.1	British Library, C.12.f.18. (2.)
L.2	British Library, 644.c.59
L6	National Art Library (V&A), Dyce 25.C.93
LEEDS	Leeds University Library, Brotherton Lt SHI
MEISEI.1	Meisei University Library, Tokyo, MR 1319
MEISEI.2	Meisei University Library, Tokyo, MR 1320
O.1	Bodleian Library, 4mo P 2(1) Art.BS.
O.2	Bodleian Library, Mal. 255 (6)
O.3	Bodleian Library, Harding D 2027
O6	Worcester College, Oxford (no classmark)
O7	Wadham College, Oxford, Stack A70000002850 (A35.23)
O9	All Souls College, Oxford, p.14.15(20)

Variants by forme:

	State 1	*State 2*
E(i)		
E4r		
24	love:	love?

Distribution of variants:

	State 1	*State 2*
E(i)	C11.1; MEISEI.2	BRISTOL; C; C11.2; CH; E; ETON; HN1; L.1; L.2; L6; LEEDS; MEISEI.1; O.1; O.2; O.3; O6; O7; O9.

Uncorrected errors

A2v, headline]	*Coustant*
A4r, 23]	kinred [kindred]
B4r, 12]	manage [first a turned]

THE COMPLETE WORKS OF JAMES SHIRLEY, VOLUME 7

C2r, 35]	wo'mee [?wi'me]
C2v, 36]	you [your]
C4r, 4]	Faith [a turned]
D1v, 33]	*Ztart* [Start]
D3v, 8]	lik [like]
D3v, 15]	him. [stop turned]
D4r, 24]	Pageans [?Pageants]
D4v, 3]	he [possibly she?]
E1v, 5]	Sinbe [Since]
E1v, 25]	you [your]
E3r, 2]	Be [By]
E3, r28]	ſttragling [ſtragling]
E3v, 32]	side, [side]
F4v, 14]	but [u turned]
F4v, 27]	childen [children]
G2v, 26]	chang' [?chang'd]
G2v, 29]	excused [excuses]
G3r, 24]	somewhat a [somewhat]
G3v, 29]	I [It]
G3v, 35]	banque t [banquet]
G4v, 20]	missing SH
G4v, 33]	*La*. [Lo.]
G4v, 34]	subject [u turned]
H1v, 18]	*Clos* [*Cous*]
H2r, 10]	*Horn* [*Hart*]
H3r, 35]	yet [get]
H3v, 4]	guilt [guilt' or guilty]
H4r, 19]	*Cotntrey-man* [*Countrey-man*]
I1v, 3]	joyes [joy]
I1v, 29]	Gentlewoman [Gentlewomen[
I2v, 34]	*Hart*. [no speech heading needed]
I3r, 10]	belongs [Belongs]

The Constant Maid

A Comedy

THE NAMES OF THE PERSONS

HORNET, *a rich usurer*

HARTWELL, *a young gentleman, lover of Mistress Frances*

PLAYFAIR, *a gallant*

A gentleman, COUSIN *to Playfair* [*sometimes disguised as the king*]

Sir CLEMENT, *a justice* 5

STARTUP, *a foolish* [*country*] *gentleman*

COUNTRYMAN

PERSONS Dramatic characters.

1 HORNET 'insect of the wasp family...much larger and stronger than other wasps, and inflicting a more serious sting'. As such, it is a fitting name for a usurer, especially as its figurative connotations are of an 'enemy that attacks persistently and with virulence' (*OED, n. 2*).

1 *usurer* 'money-lender, esp. in later use one who charges an excessive rate of interest' (*OED, n.*). Usurers were roundly condemned by early modern commentators, who focused on the excessive interest usurers charged and considered it an unchristian profession, with usury being particularly associated with Jews (see Kermode 2009, Introduction, *passim*).

2 HARTWELL Both lover-like (i.e. pursuing the Petrarchan hart) and good-hearted.

3 PLAYFAIR The name encompasses the idea of being a good sport as well as reinforcing the idea that the pursuit of love is a game.

3 *gallant* fashionable gentleman.

4 COUSIN He remains unnamed throughout, like the niece and the nurse.

5 CLEMENT A name which means 'merciful, lenient, kindly' (*OED, n. 1*), suitable for his personality and his role as justice. The justice in Jonson's *Every Man In His Humour* (1598) is also Clement.

5 **justice** justice of the peace, i.e. magistrate.

6 STARTUP 'Person recently or suddenly sprung into prominence, existence, or importance,...upstart or parvenu' (*OED, n. 1*). Appropriate for the character's low birth and his recently acquired wealth and gentlemanly status.

7 COUNTRYMAN In performance this could be demonstrated by his appearance or manner, though his is not a comic simpleton role unlike, e.g., Shepherd and Clown in *Winter's Tale* or William in *As You Like It*. He is obviously a yeoman farmer, not a country bumpkin.

Master and Sir have been silently expanded from their various early modern contractions, but not collated. Changes in punctuation have only been collated when they make a potential difference to the sense, so are confined to !, ? and –.

4 *sometimes... king*] *this edn; not in* Q   6 *country*] *this edn; not in* Q

THE COMPLETE WORKS OF JAMES SHIRLEY, VOLUME 7

CLOSE, *servant to Hartwell*

THREE SERVANTS, [*formerly in Hartwell's employ,*] *disguised sometimes as lords,*
[and] *one of them once disguised as a pursuivant*   10

A CONSTABLE

THREE WATCHMEN

MASQUERS

OFFICERS

SERVANTS and ATTENDANTS   15

[MISTRESS] BELLAMY, *a widow*

FRANCES, *her daughter*

NURSE, *their servant*

NIECE *to Hornet*

8 CLOSE So-called both because he is Hornet's intimate servant (*OED, adj.* 17) and because he is capable of secrecy (*OED, adj.* 7), as he tells Startup at 3.1.43.

10 *pursuivant* 'royal or state messenger, esp. one with the power to execute warrants' (*OED, n.* 2a).

11 CONSTABLE 'officer of a parish or township appointed to act as conservator of the peace' (*OED, n.* 5a & c); perhaps in this case specifically 'constable of the watch' (see *OED*, Watchman, *n.* 4).

12 WATCHMEN 'men formerly appointed to keep watch and ward in all towns from sunset to sunrise' (*OED*, Watchman, *n.* 4).

13 MASQUERS The masquers can be doubled by actors in other minor roles.

14 OFFICERS In 5.1 Hartwell is seen having been apprehended by the officers who escort him to Clement in 5.3.17 SD. They are clearly not supposed to be the same dramatic characters as the watchmen. The constable enters with another set of officers at 5.3.102 SD2, and they all leave together, probably at l. 118.

15 SERVANTS...ATTENDANTS Mistress Bellamy has lent a servant to the Countryman in 5.1 and at least one servant is needed in 5.3 to open the door as all the characters assemble on the stage for the finale.

16 MISTRESS Female head of household, what today would be 'Mrs.'

16 *widow* In early modern drama the widow is simultaneously attractive because she generally has wealth, and threatening because she has sexual experience, which is supposed to make her insatiable. Mistress Bellamy's seduction of Hartwell plays with this convention.

18 NURSE Like the nurse in *Romeo and Juliet*, Shirley's is rather silly.

19 NIECE Unnamed throughout in the play. Niece can just mean kinswoman and her exact relationship to Hornet is never revealed.

9 *formerly...employ,*] *this edn; not in* Q   16 MISTRESS] *this edn; not in* Q

THE CONSTANT MAID

THE SCENE: LONDON.

1[.1]

Enter HARTWELL, CLOSE, [*and three*] SERVANTS.

HARTWELL Nay, let's not part so heavily.

CLOSE   For mine own part
It does not trouble me so much that you
Have broke up house – for hospitality
Went out of fashion with crop-doublets
And cod-pieces – but I, that have worn out   5
So many liveries under the worshipful
Old gentleman, your father –

HARTWELL My father had an office which brought in
A fair revenue; I inherit but
His little land, whose annual profits won't   10
Encourage me to live at the same height.
Ye may meet better fortunes: there's enough
Preferment in the world, my love and best
Assistance promise to yourselves.

CLOSE   I do not
Stand upon wages, sir. I will not leave you.   15

HARTWELL How wo't thou live?

---

0 The scene is set in a London street.

1 **heavily** with sorrow, grief, displeasure, or anger; grievously (*OED, adv.* 3). Hartwell may also mean 'let's not drag this out', an implication present in *OED, adv.* 2. Close is making a fuss and, as we see, refusing to be discharged.

3–5 **hospitality…cod-pieces** Close draws attention through clothing to Caroline nostalgia for the Elizabethan period, an idea Shirley partly borrowed from Dekker and Middleton's *The Roaring Girl* (1611), 'in the time of the great-crop doublet, your huge bombasted plays, quilted with mighty words to lean purpose, was only then in fashion' ('The Epistle', ll. 2–5 in Bevington *et al.* 2002, 1377).

4 **crop-doublets** close-fitting padded short jackets, called 'doublet' from the garment being made of double stuff padded between (Fairholt 1896, 149). By this date, the short length was very unfashionable.

5 **cod-pieces** A cod-piece was 'a bagged appendage to the front of the close-fitting hose or breeches worn by men from the fifteenth to the seventeenth century: often conspicuous and ornamented' (*OED, n.* a). By 1600, men's fashionable breeches and coats had become fuller and longer and the cod-piece was no longer generally visible (Vicary 1989, 10).

6 **liveries** characteristic uniforms or insignia worn by a household's retainers or servants, typically distinguished by colour and design (*OED, n.* 6b). This comment is self-reflexive since acting companies wore livery (Cerasano 1999, 328–9).

12–14 **there's…yourselves** i.e. Hartwell means that he still prizes them ('my love') and he'll do his best to help them find another place. This is a characteristic example of Shirley's often contracted and inverted verse syntax – in prose it might read 'My care and best assistance will make sure that there is ample preferment available to you in the outside world'.

14–15 **I…wages** i.e. Wages are not necessary for me. (See *OED*, Stand *n.* 18.)

16 **wo't** i.e. wilt (a characteristic abbreviated form in Shirley).

1[.1]] *Gifford subst.* (ACT I. SCENE I.*)*; Act. I. Q
0 SD *and three*] *this edn; and three other Gifford; not in* Q   7 father -] *Gifford;* father. Q
10 won't] *this edn;* wo'not Q

29

I.I THE COMPLETE WORKS OF JAMES SHIRLEY, VOLUME 7

CLOSE As other mortals do. Yet I'll not play
　　The thief; that is a course by which a man
　　May soon ascend the ladder of preferment,
　　But I ne'er loved these climbing trees. I cannot　　　　　　　　20
　　Cheat – though I have heard there is an art,
　　A devilish deal of knowledge in the dice –
　　And if men wo'not part with money, some
　　Will fetch it out o'th'bones. But the best casting
　　Is in a tavern, when the wine and reckoning　　　　　　　　25
　　Come up together: some do spin a living by't.
　　And there are many secret ways for serving-men
　　To live: it is not wages does maintain
　　All of our tribe, sir – and especially
　　Those that have mistresses.
HARTWELL　　　　　　　　　　But I am a bachelor.　　　　　　　30
CLOSE I pray let me be one of your buttons still then:
　　I am not half worn-out. You know what mould
　　I'm made of: I did ever honest service,
　　And though my fellow vermin can forsake
　　Your falling house, I do not fear the rafters.　　　　　　　35
　　By this hand, sir, I'll wait upon you, though
　　Like great men's servants I do live on nothing
　　But looks and the air of commendations.
HARTWELL Well, since you are so resolute, attend me.

---

19 **ladder…preferment** i.e. punning on the steps up the scaffold as a thief's punishment. Shirley frequently associates theft with hanging—see *Gentleman of Venice*: 'Canst though not steal and so deserve a hanging?' (1.1.113).
　20 **climbing trees** i.e. trees you can climb (the ladders of preferment one can ascend in l. 19).
　21–6 **Cheat…by't** Close taps into the early modern fascination with 'cony-catching' (swindling or cheating)
by describing various tricks used by unscrupulous gamblers to cheat the unsuspecting of their money. (For a
selection of cony-catching texts see Salgado 1972 and Judges 2002).
　24 **fetch…bones** In card games of the period the 'bone-ace' was a prize of half the stake (*OED*, Bone ace *n.*
and Bone *n.* 2), so this is a way of cheating to win the stake. Bones also means simply dice. As the many references
in his plays and poems attest, Shirley was interested in dice games. In 'A Catch', he uses printed images of dice
throws within the poem (*Poems etc.* (1646), 51. See Stern 2011, 312).
　24 **casting** punning on 1) counting (the tab); 2) throwing (the dice); and 3) vomiting (the wine).
　29–30 **especially…mistresses** Close implies sexual 'services' are part of pleasing your employer.
　31 **buttons** Close means something unimportant attached to Hartwell's person (*OED*, Button *n.* 1a and b).
Early modern buttons were often silk-covered so could 'wear out', especially when transferred (as they typically
were) from suit to suit. In this context of liveries and service, Close may also bring to mind the button as identifying 'badge' (Fairholt 1896, 105–6) and of the 'button boy' (*OED, n.*), a manservant (usually in livery), from
which we get Buttons the pantomime character.
　34–5 **vermin…house** variant of Tilley M1243 'Mice (Rats) quit a falling house (sinking ship)'.
　37–8 **Like…commendations** '[G]reat men' were typically considered to be bad payers of their servants,
both those in their service and their political clients. It was common, however, for great men's servants to receive
gifts/bribes from their clients in order to facilitate access to them.

---

33 of] *this edn;* off Q

30

THE CONSTANT MAID

I.I

The rest I here discharge: [*giving them money*] there's somewhat more, 40
Not worth the name of bounty. I wish all
A happier entertainment.

SECOND SERVANT   An there be
No remedy, heaven bless you, sir.

CLOSE Pray give me leave to wet my lips with these
My fellows. Sorrow has made but a dry proverb; 45
I must to th'tavern and condole a quart.

HARTWELL Meet me at Mistress Bellamy's then.   *Exit.*

CLOSE I shall, sir.

    Enter PLAYFAIR.

PLAYFAIR   How now, masters.

CLOSE   You speak not
To me, sir: I am a servant still indeed.
With them the case is altered: they are masters, 50
For they want services.

FIRST SERVANT   Oh, Master Playfair!

SECOND SERVANT It is not now as when Andrea lived.

THIRD SERVANT This place was made for pleasure, not for death.

FIRST SERVANT There was a time when mortals whetted knives.

SECOND SERVANT In time of yore, when men killed brutish beasts. 55

THIRD SERVANT Oh, cruel butcher, whosoe'er thou wert!

CLOSE Do not you know what all this signifies?

PLAYFAIR Not I.

CLOSE My master has given over house-keeping.

FIRST SERVANT He has committed burglary, broke up the cellar, 60
And thrown the kitchen out at the hall window.

---

42 **An** If.

45 **Sorrow...proverb** That sorrow is dry *is* actually a proverb (Tilley S656), derived from Proverbs, 7.22: 'A merry heart doeth good like a medicine: but a broken spirit drieth the bones' (*AV*). Tilley's examples demonstrate that sorrow is often, as here, an excuse for a drink.

50–51 **masters...services** Close's joke is complicated: his fellow servants are now masters because they are masterless men, but we are supposed to hear in it the fact that players were potentially subject to the Act against Vagabonds of 1574, made doubly ironic by Playfair engaging the three servants as players in his device to fool Hornet.

52–6 **It...wert!** Like much of Shirley's dramatic writing, this section nods to past plays. From *The Spanish Tragedy* (in Bevington *et al.* 2002), Forsythe identifies, 'It...lived' (3.14.11); 'This...death' (2.5.12) and 'Oh...wert!' (2.5.30). 'In...beasts' is modified from *Mucedorus* (1598, E2v), 3.4, 'In time of yore when men like brutish beasts / Did live their lives in loathsom celles and woodes'. 'There...knives' is substantially altered from Beaumont's *Swetnam, The Woman-Hater* (1606, D1r) 'About the time that mortals whet their knives'—i.e. dinner time. This last alteration at once undercuts the quotations, over-dramatic for the situation, from *The Spanish Tragedy* and suggests that the visit to the tavern may involve the partaking of food as well as drink.

60–1 **He...window** i.e. By removing the contents which make a house a home—such as food and drink (and the servants required to serve them)—it is as if Hartwell has burgled his own house.

---

40 SD] *Gifford subst. (after 'bounty.' l. 41); not in* Q
42 SH] *this edn;* 2 Serv. Q; *1, 2. and 3. Serv. are normalized as* FIRST, SECOND *and* THIRD SERVANT *throughout this scene*
42 An] *Gifford;* And Q   51 Playfair!] *this edn; Playfare.* Q   56 wert!] *Gifford;* wert. Q

31

I.I   THE COMPLETE WORKS OF JAMES SHIRLEY, VOLUME 7

CLOSE His house, sir, has a superscription,
    And is directed to his loving friend
    Will pay the rent. You'll hardly know me now
    I have no fellow.
PLAYFAIR   You are very merry, sir.   65
SECOND SERVANT He has some cause; we are discharged.
CLOSE For certain, my master only
    Belongs to me. If you would speak with him,
    He's gone to Mistress Bellamy's, sir.
    In the meantime, please you to understand: 70
    I, Close, follow my master and shall feed still,
    Although my fellows here are become blanks,
    And do want filling.
PLAYFAIR   Lads, I have known you long:
    Although you be at loss, in confidence
    Of all your future honesties I'll employ ye   75
    In a device which, if it hit, may
    Reward your pains.
CLOSE   All?
PLAYFAIR Your master only, sir, belongs to you.
    Follow him still and, if there be occasion,
    I shall enquire for you. [*To the others*] You will be faithful?   80
ALL SERVANTS Doubt not, Master Playfair.
PLAYFAIR   I have a project:
    Follow me for instructions. Farewell Close –
    Commend me to your master.
SECOND SERVANT Buoy, Close! Buoy, honest Close! We are blanks, blanks.
CLOSE Roll up yourselves in paper liveries, and   85
    Be drawn at the next lottery. I wo'not

---

62 **superscription** i.e. Hartwell has put a 'To Rent' sign up.
63 **friend** friend (who).
67–8 **my...me** i.e. he's only my master now.
72–3 **blanks...filling** Close means that the other servants are contractless (their names are not in the blank spaces on any contract of employment and they will go hungry) but it is also an insult—they are nothing.
76 **device** piece of entertainment, interlude, play; also a trick.
78 **Your...you** Playfair parrots Close's slightly smug words at ll. 67–8 back at him.
84 **Buoy...blanks** By enthusiastically (and hypocritically) cheering him up (Buoy, *OED, v.* 3b.) the servants get back at Close for his smugness, reminding him by repeating his 'blanks'.
85–6 **Roll...lottery** Close suggests that they could disguise themselves as lottery tickets if they wrapped themselves in paper. Lotteries were not uncommon in Elizabethan and early Stuart England and were often state-sponsored: for instance, Elizabeth issued a proclamation for one in 1566–9 to improve the Cinque Ports and there were two under James to benefit the settlement of Virginia (Richards 1934, 58).
86 **wo'not** 'would not' here, though Shirley sometimes also uses it to mean 'won't'.

---

71 I, Close,] *Gifford;* I *Close* Q   80 SD] *this edn;* – *Gifford; not in* Q   80 faithful?] *Gifford;* faithfull. Q
81 SH] *this edn; Ser. omnes.* Q   84 Close!...Close!] *this edn; Close,...Close,* Q

32

THE CONSTANT MAID   1.2

Forsake my certainty for all your projects.
If it should fail I shall find some of you
Sneaking in Paul's behind a pillar, with
A zealous prayer some gentleman would read   90
The bed-roll of your commendation
And pity a very serviceable fellow
That would fain wait on him but wants a cloak.

Go, prosper with your project.   *Exeunt.*

[1.2]

    Enter HORNET [*and*] MISTRESS BELLAMY.

HORNET Widow, be ruled by me. I know the world,
  And I have studied it these fifty years:
  There's no man to be trusted.
BELLAMY   Without good
  Security, you mean?
HORNET   No young man, widow,
  That talks, and says he loves you, writes you verses,   5
  And swears he shall go hang himself unless
  You pity him. Take me an old man –
BELLAMY – So, take you an old man. –
HORNET Seasoned with care and thrift, not led away
  By vicious conversation, nor corrupted   10
  With pride and surfeit, one that knows the use
  Of money. Do ye mark the use?

88–93 **I...cloak** Close conjures up a vision of the servants having to seek work in St Paul's Cathedral, a popular place to transact business in the early modern period. He plays on the ecclesiastical setting with 'zealous prayer' and the conflation of bed-roll with 'commendation' (i.e. employer's reference) implies, without actually stating it, that the servants are sleeping rough in the Churchyard. Several early modern plays used the middle aisle of St Paul's as a setting for this kind of business, e.g. *Every Man Out of His Humour* 3.1, and *Englishmen for My Money* 2.2 in which Frisco is seeking a French tutor for his master's daughters (ed. Kermode 2009).

  0 The scene is set in Mistress Bellamy's house.

  4 Security Property, *etc.*, deposited or pledged by or on behalf of a person as a guarantee of the payment of a debt, and liable to forfeit in the event of default (*OED*, *n.* 5). The usurer in *Eastward Ho!* is named Security. Bellamy's comment is supposed to alert the audience to Hornet's character early.

  6 hang himself stock claim made by a despairing, rejected lover, and often used parodically.

  7–8 Take...man Hornet's use of the ethic dative, i.e. 'if one were to take', here creates the possibility of his deliberate double meaning: 'Take *me*, an old man'. Bellamy's response retains that double sense, and delivery in performance will determine which meaning is primary. It might be said, aside in interruption, with Bellamy indicating to the audience in her 'so' that she understands Hornet's ethic dative to be hiding his real motive. (See Abbot 1869, 147 for the ethic dative as used in Shakespeare.)

[1.2]] *Gifford subst.* (SCENE II.*); not in* Q   **0 SD** *and*] *Gifford; not in* Q   **4** mean?] *this edn;* meane. Q
7 man –] *this edn;* man. Q

33

I.2   THE COMPLETE WORKS OF JAMES SHIRLEY, VOLUME 7

BELLAMY   Yes, sir.
  – Use upon use, you mean. –
HORNET And dares not spend it prodigally, knowing
  The principal end it was ordained to was   15
  To relieve our necessity and lay up
  What is above.
BELLAMY   To help the poor.
HORNET   You may,
  If you be so disposed, but 'tis as commendable
  To give it in your will, to build an hospital,
  And so our charity comes altogether.   20
  I would not have your state be eaten up
  By caterpillars, but preserved and made
  Greater by marrying some discreet old man.
BELLAMY And such an one you show yourself?
HORNET   You happily
  Interpret me.
BELLAMY   I would not tell you, sir,   25
  Till our next meeting, how much you have won,
  By your good counsel, on me.
HORNET [*Aside*]   She inclines.
  [*Aloud*] 'Tis your good nature. I am plain and have
  No tricks. I'll tell you all my fault: I am
  Addicted very much to gather wealth;   30
  I have no children to devour my state,
  Nor kindred – only a niece left to my trust,
  One that is never like to marry.
BELLAMY Why?
HORNET   She never thrived since she came to me.
BELLAMY [*Aside*] I easily believe it.
HORNET   Melancholy   35

---

13 Use…use Compound interest; (more generally) excessive interest (*OED*, *n.* P17), i.e. usury. This is
another comment probably not intended to be heard by Hornet and it interrupts the otherwise regular meter.
14–17 And…above Hornet adopts religious language here in an effort to legitimize his usury.
16 lay up i.e. save (for). To deposit or put away in a place for safety; to store up (*OED*, lay up PV3 in Lay *v.*).
21–2 eaten…caterpillars a common early modern metaphor derived from its regular biblical use for something that consumes the crops.
24 show present (as).
35 Melancholy In early modern medicine, a pathological condition thought to result from an excess of black
bile in the body, characterized in early references by sullenness, ill temper, brooding, causeless anger, and
unsociability, and later by despondency and sadness (*OED*, *n.*[1] 2b). Hornet's resort to the doctor shows he takes
it as a medical condition. It is very common on the early modern stage, especially in humours plays—see
Dowsecer in Chapman's *An Humorous Day's Mirth* (1597).

---

27 SD] *Gifford subst.; not in* Q   **28 SD**] *this edn; not in* Q   **35 SD**] *this edn; not in* Q

THE CONSTANT MAID   I.2

Will kill her, and yet I pursue all ways
That promise her delight. I spare no cost
Of physic: what her doctor says, is done.

BELLAMY 'Tis lovingly performed.

Enter HARTWELL *and* FRANCES.

HORNET   What's he?
BELLAMY A gentleman that bears my daughter much   40
    Affection.
HORNET   Sure I have seen him?
BELLAMY   Master Hartwell.
HORNET Oh, he's a beggar, or must be very shortly.
BELLAMY Have you his lands in mortgage?
HORNET   Not yet, not yet;
    But he'll want money, widow.
BELLAMY   He has had
    Good breeding.
HORNET   Hang breeding, 'tis unlucky: 45
    They never keep their state that have too much on't.
    Counsel your daughter, Mistress Bellamy,
    To throw him off betime.
BELLAMY   You direct well.
HORNET When we are married, I'll provide a match for her.
BELLAMY You have care on's.
HORNET   It will become me. [*They walk aside.*]   50
HARTWELL Is he suitor to your mother, lady?
FRANCES He would be such a thing. Were not I blessed
    In such a jolly father-in-law?

---

39 performed both in the sense of 'done' and of 'pretended'. Bellamy expects Hornet to hear the former but shows herself aware of his motives in the double meaning.

41 Sure...him? Surely I recognize him?

42–4 Oh...money Though he has not met him, Hornet has already heard what is to him the most important thing about Hartwell—that he is in financial trouble. Bellamy suspects Hornet of being more nearly involved by being about to foreclose on Hartwell's mortgage but Hornet indicates merely that acquiring the mortgage (presumably for this purpose) is a future aim. Sir Giles Overreach in *A New Way to Pay Old Debts* (with whom, by design, Shirley's Hornet shares much, including a first name) exemplifies business practices where usurers prey on those in financial difficulty to ruin them at law (e.g. at 2.1.1–10). His whole plot against Wellborn including Overreach's original purchase of Wellborn's mortgage is recounted at 5.1.160ff (in Bevington *et al.* 2002).

46 on't of it

48 betime quickly.

48 You...well You give good advice (but also a sense of 'you are bossy').

50 on's of us; very common in Shirley's drama.

50 become me be fitting for me (because he intends to marry Bellamy; the 'become' also quibbles on that future).

52 Were...I Would I not be.

53 jolly father-in-law jolly step-father. Frances is being sarcastic.

---

39 SD FRANCES] *this edn;* Mistresse Frances Q   **41** him?] *this edn;* him. Q
43–5] *lineation this edn;* morgage? / Not...widdow. / He...breeding. / Hang Q   **50 SD]** *this edn; not in* Q

35

THE COMPLETE WORKS OF JAMES SHIRLEY, VOLUME 7

HARTWELL He looks like some cast money-bag, that had given up
 The stuffing and for want of use grown mouldy.   55
 He dares not keep much fire in's kitchen, lest
 Warming his hands – which rather look like gloves,
 So tanned and thin – he let 'em scorch, and gather
 Into a heap. I do not think he ever
 Put off his clothes: he would run mad to see   60
 His own anatomy. That such a wretch
 Should have so vast a wealth!
FRANCES   I would not be his
 Niece for all his fortune.
HARTWELL   I presume
 Your mother is more noble than to encourage him
 In his pretence; and her estate would mix   65
 But ill with his ill-gotten wealth, extorted
 From widows and from orphans, nor will all
 His plenty keep his soul one day from famine.
 'Tis time ill-spent to mention him; let's talk
 Of something else.
FRANCES   Of what?
HARTWELL   Of love again,   70
 Whose flame we equally divide. [*They walk aside.*]
HORNET   Your table
 Is a devourer, and they shut up doors
 First that keep open house and entertainments.
 This lord is feasted, and that young lady's
 Sweet tooth must have a banquet; t'other old   75
 Madam with ne'er a tooth must have some marchpane
 Coral to rub her gums withal. These are
 Ridiculous expenses.

54–61 He...anatomy Hartwell's description of Hornet relies upon entrenched conventions about the usurer in early modern drama: his body is lean and dried up ('cast' = empty) and he never changes his already second-hand clothes because of fear of seeing himself naked ('anatomy') (Stonex 1916; Wright 1934).

66–7 extorted...orphans Another convention is that usurers prey upon these vulnerable groups (see also 2.3.50–1 where Hornet's niece encourages him to laugh by imagining 'you'd undone a widow, / Or turned an orphan begging').

67–8 nor...famine i.e. since avarice is one of the deadly sins, usurers' money cannot buy them into heaven (with 'famine' poking fun again at Hornet's skinniness).

71 divide share.

76–7 marchpane coral marzipan which either serves as a teething aid (for babies normally, but in this case for an old lady who has lost her teeth) or covers one made of another material such as glass or bone (*OED*, Coral *n.*[1] 3).

---

62 wealth!] *Gifford;* wealth. Q   **71 SD**] *this edn; not in* Q

36

THE CONSTANT MAID   I.2

BELLAMY   Far from thrift.
HORNET This room has too rich furniture and worse
   Hangings would serve the turn. If I may be   80
   Worthy to counsel, costly pictures are
   Superfluous, though of this or t'other master's
   Doing: hang Michelangelo and his oils!
   If they be given, you're the more excused
   To let 'em show, but have a care you let not   85
   Appear, either in arras or in picture,
   The story of the prodigal. 'Twill fright
   Young gentlemen that come to visit you
   From spending o'their portions, whose riot
   May enrich you with their forfeited estates.   90
   I have a thousand precepts more.
BELLAMY   But do not
   Think all this while of heaven?
HORNET   Tis in my chest,
   And multiplied in every bag.
BELLAMY   Or hell?
HORNET A fable to fright fools or children. But
   I cannot stay, my scrivener doth expect me;   95
   I'll visit you another time, sweet widow,
   And give you more instructions.
BELLAMY   Spare your travel.
   I sha'not practise these in haste, and must
   Declare these precepts make not for your welcome:
   My patience was a virtue all this while.   100
   If you but think you have a soul, repent!

---

78 Far…thrift Bellamy's comment is again deliberately ambiguous. While seeming to agree with Hornet—it is not thrifty to keep open house—she also manages to make the point that thrift is not a good thing. Hospitality should *not* be thrifty, but liberal.

81–3 costly…oils Having criticized the liberality of Bellamy's board in the last speech, Hornet moves on to a subject close to Charles I's heart. The king was a connoisseur of Italian masters who amassed a fine collection of art, larger than that of any other British monarch (*ODNB*, Kishlansky and Morrill).

87 story…prodigal The very well-known parable of the prodigal son (Luke 15.11–32) was a common motif in plays of the period (see Horbury 2019). Prodigals were often paired against usurers and it is no surprise that Hornet does not wish to put young men off being profligate with their money. Like Overreach did Wellborn, he hopes to cheat Hartwell out of his estate and, as we hear later in the play, he has already lent Playfair money on unfavourable terms.

89 portions inheritances.

92 chest pun on money-chest and heart.

95 scrivener notary or clerk acting as financial agent or broker; (more generally) a person engaged in the business of moneylending, investing money at interest on behalf of clients, *etc.* (*OED*, *n*. 1c). In early modern drama the usurer was often accompanied by two side-kicks, a broker and a scrivener (Kermode 2009, 23).

---

83 Michelangelo] *this edn; Michael Angelo* Q   **83** oils!] *Gifford;* oyles. Q
92 heaven?] *this edn;* heaven. Q   **93** hell?] *his edn;* hell. Q   **101** repent!] *this edn;* repent; Q

1.2   THE COMPLETE WORKS OF JAMES SHIRLEY, VOLUME 7

Your rules I am not covetous to follow,
Good Master Hornet.
HORNET   Live and be undone then:
You'll tell me another tale hereafter, widow.   *Exit* [*Hornet*].
    Enter NURSE *and* CLOSE.
NURSE [*To Bellamy*] Letters from Master Startup, the country gentleman.   105
HARTWELL What's he?
FRANCES A suitor of my nurse's commendations.
CLOSE Now heaven deliver me, what have I seen?
This monster once was shown i'th'fair, or such
Another furred baboon for all the world.   110
[*To Nurse*] Dost know him? Why do I ask such a question?
He's such a thing the devil would not own's
Acquaintance.
NURSE   Master Hornet, the great usurer.
CLOSE Hornet? Nay then, my wonder's over and the
Devil be but such another. They   115
May be sworn brothers, yes, and divide hell
Betwixt 'em.
HARTWELL   Who is that you talk on, sir?
CLOSE The beast that, heaven be thanked, has left you –
Hornet; but I ha' news for you.
BELLAMY   Frances!
HARTWELL I'll hear it in the garden.   *Exeunt Hart*[*well and*] *Close*.
BELLAMY   Do you love   120
That Master Hartwell? Do not blush, but answer.
FRANCES I hope you move not this as if you doubted;
I took him first, upon your character,
Into my good opinion.
BELLAMY   But things alter:
What then I thought, I delivered ye,   125
Nor since hath he deserved a less esteem

105–6 Shirley's flexible metre sometimes makes it difficult to decide whether he intended verse or prose. This is such an instance: the nurse and Hartwell seem to be speaking prose but Frances' line is verse.
109–10 **This…world** Close pretends that Hornet's appearance is so outlandish that he mistakes him for a performing ape. Usurers traditionally wore fur (typically fox, with its connotations of trickiness), rather in contradiction to their otherwise parsimonious clothing (Wright 1934, 189). Fur was also a sign of social climbing which fitted another common stereotype of the usurer (Kermode 2009, 27).
112–13 **He's…acquaintance** This is the first of many occasions in the play where characters associate Hornet with the devil (e.g. 1.2.115 and 2.3.42–8), as was traditional in usury tracts (Kermode 2009, 13–14).
123 **character** description, delineation, or detailed report of a person's qualities (*OED, n.* 12a).

---

104 SD1 *Hornet*] *this edn; not in* Q   **105 SD**] *this edn; not in* Q   **111 SD**] *this edn; not in* Q
118 you –] *this edn;* you; *Gifford;* you, Q   **119** Frances!] *this edn; Frances.* Q
120 SD] *this edn; Exeunt Hart. and Close. Gifford; Exit Hart. Close.* Q

38

THE CONSTANT MAID

I.2

In his own person. But the circumstance
Is not the same: his fortune I have examined,
Which rises not to such a value I
Did apprehend; and it becomes my care,   130
Being at one gift to depart with thee
And my estate, to look for one whose purse
May carry a proportion.
FRANCES   Make me not
Imagine you would wed me to a heap
Of shining dust, a golden bondage –
BELLAMY   Nor   135
To penury. His birth and education
Are not unworthy; he's a handsome man too,
But be not governed by your eye too much.
Children and age pursue and many storms
Hover about our frail conditions.   140
All these must be provided for; they are not
Kisses will arm you against winter. Therefore,
Confident of your obedience, I propound
Another to your best thoughts.
FRANCES   – Oh, my unhappiness! –
BELLAMY A country gentleman of spreading fortunes,   145
Young too, and not uncomely. For his breeding,
It was not spun the finest, but his wealth
Able to guild deformity and make
Even want of wit a virtue when your life
Renders itself more sweet by your command.   150
His name is Master Startup, whom I expect
Our guest tomorrow. That's his letter: read it.

---

128 his...examined Bellamy seems to imply that her previous examination of Hartwell's means overplayed his fortune, but it must appear to an audience that she is basing her revised opinion on Hornet's gossip. Given we have just seen her reject his suit on the good grounds that he has all the wrong priorities, we might think Bellamy unwise to base any of her actions on his advice.

132–3 one...proportion i.e. someone whose fortune is more equal to hers (*OED*, Proportion *n*. 1).

135 shining dust dust here implies the bodily form (as in *OED*, *n*. 3b) and encapsulates Frances' sensible depiction of the worthlessness of such a marriage, shining/moneyed though it may be.

135 golden bondage i.e. marrying for money. The notion of *aurea compedes* (fetters of gold) could refer to this, as to other situations where mental freedom had to be sacrificed in order to gain riches (see Whitney 1586, 202).

139 children...pursue i.e. children and age follow marriage, but pursue also has a predatory overtone.

141–2 they...winter stocked up kisses are not food in the winter, i.e. no practical use in any kind of crisis.

144 Oh...unhappiness! This is a kind of aside—it interrupts the regularity (such as it is) of Bellamy's verse and it is unclear whether Frances intends her mother to hear it or not. Certainly it does not disturb the trajectory of Bellamy's speech.

148–50 make...command i.e. Startup being stupid is a good thing because Frances will have his considerable fortune at *her* command because of her superior intelligence, so can order her life to suit herself.

---

135 bondage –] *this edn;* bondage. Q   **144** unhappiness!] *Gifford;* unhappinesse. Q

39

I.2 THE COMPLETE WORKS OF JAMES SHIRLEY, VOLUME 7

This may seem strange at the first coming toward you,
But when discretion comes to examine what
A fruitful consequence attends it, you 155
Will thank me for't.
FRANCES   But with your pardon, mother,
Although I could dispense with my own thoughts
And frame them to obedience, will this change
Be for my honour or my fame when such
A noble gentleman shall boast he had, 160
With your consent, my love? Or, pray, admit
That which we gain by riches of the second
Seem to authorize and may justify
The act with some, how can it cure the wound
Which the poor heart, which loves, shall find too soon 165
When 'tis neglected, and so cruelly
Where it did hope for cherishing? Oh, think
How you did love my father first and be
More gentle to your daughter. Your estate
Is above needy providence or grafting 170
Into a new stock; it doth grow already
Fair from his own root, and doth want no piecing:
Nor are the means of Hartwell so contemptible.
BELLAMY No more. Y' have considered well, you'll shape
Another answer; i'th'meantime dispose 175
Your countenance to entertain this new
And able lover. Leave the satisfaction
Of Hartwell to my care. He's here – to your chamber.   [*Exit Frances.*]

161–7 admit...cherishing 'even if the gain in riches we'd get from the change (from Hartwell to Startup)
would be understood and explained by some people, how could these explanations cure the wound which the
loving heart would suffer when it noticed (only too soon) that it was neglected by the one person it expected to
love it, which is especially cruel.' Frances may be referring to either Hartwell's or her own heart—if the latter,
she may also mean that she will no longer be able to feed/cherish her feelings for Hartwell because her mother
has told her to stop loving him.

170–2 grafting...piecing Frances uses a metaphor from gardening. Grafting is used to replace the root-
stock of a plant, usually to make it more resistant to disease. 'Piece-root grafting' uses each piece of a cut seedling
root as a stock, so piecing (also a term in dress-making) is to join together in this way (*McGraw-Hill Dictionary
of Technical and Scientific Terms* 2003). Frances' point is that the House of Bellamy does not need new roots or
finance from another source.

174 Y'...well (When) you have thought it over carefully.

177 able suitable (*OED*, *n.* 2a), and also in the specific financial sense of the word, 'having material resources;
rich, influential, powerful' (*OED*, *n.* 6). There is irony here, since there is almost no other way in which Startup
has ability.

178] *lineation Gifford;* care: / He's Q   178 SD1] *Gifford; not in* Q

THE CONSTANT MAID   1.2

 Enter HARTWELL [*and*] CLOSE.

CLOSE I know not what's the trick on't, nor themselves yet,
 But he has a project to employ 'em all.   180
HARTWELL I wish it well. But do you work yourself
 Into the opinion of her nurse: she is
 The major-domo and has all the intelligence.
CLOSE Let me alone, I'll work her, sir, like wax,
 To print what form you please upon her. 'Tis   185
 A loving crone already to me: I
 Will speak her fair and in my drink may marry her.
BELLAMY Master Hartwell.
HARTWELL [*To Close*] About your business.   *Exit Close.*
BELLAMY There is a matter, sir, which I must open,
 And you perhaps will wonder at.
HARTWELL   You prepare   190
 My attention.
BELLAMY   You do love my daughter;
 At least I think so.
HARTWELL   If you knew my heart,
 You might be confident in her I sum
 All my desires on earth.
BELLAMY   Be not so fixed.
HARTWELL How, lady?
BELLAMY   When you have heard me out, you'll find 195
 Your consent easy to call back a promise
 Made to your disadvantage.
HARTWELL   I acknowledge
 This makes me wonder; pray interpret, lady,
 And speak the dialect I understand:
 I love your daughter.
BELLAMY   But must never glory   200

 179–80 At the end of the conversation they have been having in the garden, Close has been filling Hartwell in on Playfair's employment of his former servants on his 'project'.

 182 opinion i.e. good opinion (*OED, n.* 6b).

 183 major-domo chief official of an Italian or Spanish princely household. Subsequently also the head servant of a wealthy household in a foreign country; a house-steward, a butler (*OED, n.* 1). Hartwell's point is that the nurse is very powerful.

 183 intelligence knowledge concerning events communicated by or obtained from another; information, news (*OED, n.* 6a).

 184–5 I'll...her Close imagines the nurse as sealing wax they can stamp with their own impression (form) and, therefore, with their intentions. (See *Midsummer Night's Dream* 1.1.49–50.)

 195–7 you'll...disadvantage 'you'll consent easily to go back on your promise (to marry Frances) which will then seem disadvantageous'.

---

178 SD2 *and*] *Gifford; not in* Q **188 SD1**] *this edn; not in* Q
190–1] *lineation this edn;* You [do] / Prepare...attention. *Gifford;* You...attention. Q

41

I.2   THE COMPLETE WORKS OF JAMES SHIRLEY, VOLUME 7

In the reward which you expect should be –
Her marriage.
HARTWELL   In the number of my actions
There is not one that's guilty of so much
Offence to you that I should be so soon
Lost to your favour.
BELLAMY   Have no thought so poor   205
You can deserve less; my opinion
Is richer laden with your merit.
HARTWELL Now I fear again – this violent turn of praise
Makes me suspect my state. If I be fallen,
Teach me to know my trespass.
BELLAMY   I ne'er looked   210
With such clear eyes into your worth, and 'twere
A sin to general goodness to delay
The free resign of that your worth may challenge.
HARTWELL If this be meant, pray pardon my mistake
Of something went before. Love made me fear: 215
You said I never should enjoy your daughter
In marriage, which yourself so late inclined to.
BELLAMY And must again repeat, you cannot call
Her bride.
HARTWELL   Can you forbid this happiness
And love me?
BELLAMY   Yes, so dearly, Hartwell, I   220
Present myself to thy affection.
HARTWELL You fright my understanding.
BELLAMY   Does the name
Of widow sound displeasing? I have learned
Already to obey; my years are not
So many, with the thought to freeze your blood;   225
I wear no print of time deep in my brow.
Have my hairs the innocence of age

213 **that** i.e. her own body and estate.
213 **challenge** assert one's title to, lay claim to, demand as a right (*OED, v.* 5a).
225 **freeze…blood** horrify you, make your blood run cold (*OED*, Freeze *v.* 5c). There may also be a sexual
overtone here—Bellamy suggests that she can still stir his passion (*OED*, Blood *n.* 12 & 13).
226 **print…time** i.e. wrinkles.
227–8 **my…child** her hair is not white, i.e. innocent (like a child again). Old age is often so described (*OED*,
Second childhood *n.* 2).

201 be –] *this edn;* be, Q   208 again –] *this edn;* agen, Q   223 displeasing?] *Gifford;* displeasing, Q

42

THE CONSTANT MAID   I.2

To speak me twice a child? Gentlemen active,
And of great birth, have courted my affection
And, if they flatter not, commend my person.   230
Add unto this my wealth, no narrow fortune
And without competition – my daughter
Depending on my love, whose portion must
Flow from my bounty or be nothing. Make
A sober apprehension of this tender   235
And think I was not able to suppress
My silent flame, increased still by your virtues.
This minute give all hopes up for my daughter:
I can admit no rival. 'Tis within
Your election to be happy, sir: 240
My love accepted comes with fair attendance;
Denied, you hasten your own exile. Think on't;
I will expect your answer.   *Exit.*
HARTWELL   I am destroyed.
Was it her mother that spake all this while?
As pilgrims, by mistake of some small path,   245
Having told many weary steps, at night
When their hopes flatter 'em they are not far
From some kind entertainment, find themselves
Lost in a wilderness, so am I miserable.
Thus Love delights to wound and see us bleed;   250
He were a gentle god to kill indeed.   *Exit.*

---

228 active She means both young enough to be energetic and also the financial sense of being in credit rather than in debt (*OED*, Active, *adj.* 5a). She has been courted by men in the prime of life and with means.
230 person appearance.
232–4 without…nothing Bellamy lays out her financial circumstances: she legally controls all the Bellamy money and Frances will have no share in this fortune except what dowry and inheritance she gives her out of love.
235 sober well considered.
235 tender offer (though with an implication of the French *tendre*, affection).
239 admit permit.
240 election choice (but gesturing towards religious election in the sense of being 'chosen').
245–9 As…miserable 'Just as pilgrims, having narrowly missed the way and walked far, imagine hopefully they are within reach of shelter as night draws in, but find they are lost in a wilderness.' Hartwell means he had assumed he was on the verge of marrying Frances and suddenly finds that he has taken a wrong turn and now is deeply confused in an unfriendly place.
251 gentle kinder.
251 indeed in real life, instead of metaphorically (with his arrows).

232 competition –] *this edn;* competition, Q

43

THE COMPLETE WORKS OF JAMES SHIRLEY, VOLUME 7

2[.1]

     Enter CLOSE *and* NURSE.

CLOSE A word of thy mouth does it – I am weary
    Of these indentures. Like a fool, I was
    In hope he should have married Mistress Frances.
NURSE A beggar? She his wife? No, Master Startup,
    Whom I preferred, must carry her. He's a man   5
    Of lands and money; I must tell you by
    The way, he is little better than a fool.
CLOSE The fitter for her husband, and my master.
NURSE You're in the right: he's innocent to your hands.
    You may soon come to manage his estate.   10
CLOSE Which if I do, thou shalt have all.
NURSE   All what?
CLOSE Why, all that I can beg, borrow, or steal
    From him. What should he do with so much riches?
    I'll prompt my mistress, after the first year,
    To put him to his pension; he should pay   15
    For's very diet, and after a month or two,
    For every time he comes aloft.
NURSE Nay, I would wish her to begin betimes
    If she do mean to rule the roast – I can

---

  0 The scene is set in Mistress Bellamy's house.

  1–22 A...way The verse is quite rough here, but Close speaks in verse throughout the play. His blank verse is regular when in conversation with 'high' characters like Hartwell, but here, in conversation with the nurse whose metre and line length is always more approximate, it relaxes a bit.

  1 A...it Shirley often starts a scene (or a new entrance) like this, with the audience expected to surmise what one character has just said to another. In this case, the nurse has just told Close that Bellamy has reversed her decision to allow Frances to marry Hartwell. (See also e.g. 1.2.178–9 where Close has just told Hartwell about Playfair employing his former servants in his 'project'.)

  1–2 weary...indentures Close is now chafing in his service (indentures) to Hartwell. As he tells us in the next line, he was counting on Hartwell reviving his fortunes by marrying Frances.

  5 preferred The nurse means both that she recommended him to her mistress and that she likes him best (*OED*, prefer, *v.* 2 and 4. There is also a specific sense referring to marriage (1d) which may be in play).

  8 Close points out that a foolish husband's complaisance would be an advantage for Frances—who would be able to control him—and for Hartwell, presumably either because Frances would not love a fool or because she and Hartwell can continue their love affair behind his back.

  9 innocent...hands The nurse probably means both innocent when 'in your hands' (i.e. that Close can manipulate him), and unaware of Close's machinations (analogous to the 'hands' used when playing cards).

  14–17 As part of his husband-management scheme, Close's advice to his mistress (i.e. Frances) will be that after the first year she should make Startup live as if he were a boarder in lodgings (*OED*, pension *n.* 7b) and make him pay her for food ('diet') and sex ('com[ing] aloft').

  19 rule...roast have full sway or authority (*OED*, roast *n.*, P2a).

2[.1]] *Gifford subst. (*ACT II. SCENE I.*); *ACT. II. Q
4 beggar?... wife?] *this edn;* beggar!... wife! *Gifford;* beggar,... wife; Q   19 roast –] *this edn;* rost, Q

44

THE CONSTANT MAID   2.1

Give her some documents. And be you sure   20
To stick close to your mistress: there is something
To be got that way.
          Enter HARTWELL [*and*] PLAYFAIR.
CLOSE   My most exquisite Verges,
How I do love thy documents – but he's here.
I'll not be seen with thee: farewell, we'll talk
The rest at night over a sack-posset.   *Exit Close.*   25
NURSE I will use this advantage to o'erhear 'em.   [*Withdraws.*]
PLAYFAIR You tell me strange things. Is it possible
The widow herself loves you?
HARTWELL   Would I had
But reason to suspect.
PLAYFAIR   Possible!
Turn'd colt again? This love will kill us all!   30
And can she make no choice but where her daughter
Has the same longing? Not her dancing days
Done yet? Why, there's no remedy: you must love her.
HARTWELL And violate my faith made to her daughter?
PLAYFAIR Thou would not be so much an infidel   35
To think I mean thou shouldst forsake the wench.
Tell me the mother a fine tale of love,
Print kisses on her paper-lip and hug

---

20 documents instructions, lessons (*OED*, 'document' *n.* 2).

22 Verges Close calls her this because of 'verge' (*OED*, *n.* 4a), the rod or wand carried as an emblem of authority or symbol of office, just as Hartwell described her as 'major-domo' at 1.2.82. It may also be that Shirley recalls Verges in *Much Ado*, and that this is double-edged, a joke about her (limited) competence, especially since that play has a character called George Seacoal (3.3.10), a commodity which is mentioned twice in this act of *Constant Maid* (2.1.86 and 2.3.47).

25 sack-posset beverage popular in the seventeenth century especially at weddings and christenings. Properly a type of liquid syllabub, it was made with eggs, sugar, sack (white wine from Spain and the Canaries), and seasonings such as nutmeg. It was also apparently a treat for (foolish) old women—see *Cynthia's Revels* 2.4.22 where Madam Moria mixes a good sack-posset.

30 Turned...again Gone back to her youth (*OED*, Colt *n.* 2), including a figurative overtone of lasciviousness (sense 2b).

32 dancing days i.e. youth. Early modern drama often draws an analogy between dancing and courtship and/or sex.

37 Tell me The 'me' is the ethic dative, signifying that the person denoted has an interest in or is indirectly affected by the event (*OED*, Ethic dative, in Ethic *adj.*). (See also note to 1.2.7–8.)

38 paper-lip i.e. her lip is dried up, as frail as paper; thin, flimsy, fragile (*OED*, Paper *n.* 3), like wood with the sap removed (youth v. age).

---

22 SD *and*] *Gifford; not in* Q   **22** Verges] *this edn;* Varges Q   **26 SD**] *this edn; Retires. Gifford; not in* Q
30 all!] *this edn;* all: Q   **34** daughter?] *Gifford;* daughter. Q

2.1 THE COMPLETE WORKS OF JAMES SHIRLEY, VOLUME 7

Her reverend body; anything but lie with her.
Write sonnets on the ivory tooth afore, 40
Swear she does cough distinctly, get a rhyme
To bless her when she sneezes, and cry up
The method of her nose, which sweats and falls
So perpendicular upon her face;
Admire the wart upon her chin and motion 45
Of her blue eyes that look three ways at once;
Praise her above thy reason, or her daughter,
And then she will believe thou mayst be mad for her.

HARTWELL Is this the way to do me good? She comes
Too fast on me already.

PLAYFAIR   Let her fly to thee, 50
Thou mayst clip her wings the sooner. This secures thee.
Should you hold off and play the modest creature –
Nay, but deny as maids do when they love it,
And bending of your hams, cry, 'No, forsooth',
Profess with coxcomb-like civility 55
You are not worthy of her carnal favours –
She may believe it and in very spite
Marry her daughter to a citizen.
Or should you be so mad to think to win her
To your first choice with howling out your passion 60
For Mistress Frances, plaining how Don Cupid
Hath scarified your heart, you may go hang yourself.
Go to the barbers, let him firk your hair up,

---

39 reverend worthy of the respect due to age (*OED*, *adj.* 2).

40–6 Playfair offers Hartwell advice based on lovers' conventional praise of their mistresses' beauty, adapted parodically for Bellamy's advanced age.

50 Too fast Both 'too quickly' and 'too firmly-attached' (adverbial here; see *OED*, Fast *adj.* I and II).

50–1 Let...sooner Playfair means 'if you let her fly to you, you may clip her wings the sooner'. To cut (a bird's) wings was to disable it from flight; hence, to check aspirations or ambition, cripple strength, resources, or action (*OED*, Clip *v.*² 1d).

54 bending...hams kneeling (i.e. supplicant) or bowing (i.e. being very polite, see 'making a leg' in *OED*, Leg *n.* 4).

55 cockscomb-like foolish, with a sense of foppish and deceitful (because he would be pretending he did not consider himself worthy of her).

56 carnal favours gift of sexual access.

57 Marry...citizen i.e. Beneath her.

61 Don Cupid As 'Don' is a contraction of *dominus* (master, sir), Cupid here is seen as schooling lovers. It is a formulation which is not uncommon in early modern drama, such as in *Love's Labour's Lost* 3.1.166, and dates back at least to Chaucer.

62 scarified wounded, especially by making incisions or scratches.

63 firk...up do your hair (*OED*, Firk *v.* 2c).

THE CONSTANT MAID   2.1

Or get a periwig, wash your sullen face,
And starch your infant upper lip, to look   65
Like one that would run desperate on a widow.
NURSE [*Aside*] Precious conspiracy!
PLAYFAIR   This is the way.
At leisure you may tell your maiden mistress,
Like Jove you have put another shape on
To cheat the beldam Juno.
NURSE [*Aside*]   Foul-mouthed rascal!   70
HARTWELL I apprehend: th'ast given me good counsel.
I'll watch the first occasion to assure
I have preferred her in my heart already.
NURSE [*Aside*] I'll conjure up a cross-plot – and that quickly –
Shall mar your mirth and pay your fine dissembling   75
As it deserves, my confident love-gamester.   *Exit Nurse.*
PLAYFAIR I'll take my leave then. You've no other service
To use my stay? I have a project, Hartwell,
That must not be neglected.
HARTWELL   May not I
Communicate?
PLAYFAIR   Thou art engaged to wait   80

64 periwig Playfair may be suggesting that Hartwell Frenchify himself, wigs being at this stage more common in France owing to their adoption by Louis XIII to hide his premature baldness. This accords with his
advice to Hartwell to make himself presentable to Bellamy rather than mooching around looking heart-broken
for Frances.

64 sullen serious and gloomy.

65 starch...lip By suggesting that he starch his undergrown moustache in order to be taken seriously as a
suitor, Playfair draws attention to Hartwell's youth in comparison to Bellamy.

67 Precious Used here as an intensifier, meaning complete, utter, out-and-out (*OED*, *adj.* 4a). There may also
be an overtone of the nurse using it as oath (sense 1b), which could be intended to characterize her as rather
old-fashioned and simple.

69–70 Like...Juno Jove/Jupiter often adopted other forms (e.g. swan, golden shower) in order to get away
with marital infidelity to Juno who watched his every move; 'beldam' = grandmother (or older female) (*OED*, *n.*
1 & 2) but the nurse understands it in the depreciative sense of a loathsome old woman, a hag (sense 3), as her
response in the same line indicates.

74 cross-plot counter, or opposing plot.

76 love-gamester one playing the game of love (*OED*, Gamester, *n.* 2a), perhaps with other connotations
implied, such as risk-taking or play-acting (senses 1a and 4).

78 stay attendance.

79–80 That...wait Q typesets this on three lines but Hartwell's question is between quite regular verse and
completes the two half lines spoken by Playfair.

79–80 May...communicate? Hartwell asks if he can take part in the project (*OED*, Communicate, *v.* 6a: to
share (in), partake of), but he also means 'tell me what you are doing'.

67 SD] *this edn; not in* Q   **67** conspiracy!] *Gifford;* conspiracie. Q   **70 SD**] *this edn; not in* Q
70 rascal!] *Gifford;* Rascall. Q   **74 SD**] *this edn; not in* Q
79–80] *lineation Gifford;* May...communicate? Q

47

2.1   THE COMPLETE WORKS OF JAMES SHIRLEY, VOLUME 7

Upon thine own affairs, or I should trouble thee
To be an actor in't. Thou knowest old Hornet?
HARTWELL He is a suitor to the widow,
And, after the rate we cast the plot, my rival.
PLAYFAIR I'll rival him! He smothers a poor gentlewoman   85
At home with sea-coal and allows her no
More light than serves to read in painted cloth
The exposition of the harlot's story.
Hartwell, I love her, and before her father
Died we interchanged our hearts. 'Tis here   90
To free her from that slavery she lives in
Under the iron-hearted jailer, else
I shall repent my aim. He broods upon
Her portion still but I have a trick may spoil
His hatching of young bags: thou shalt know all   95

---

84 after...rate roughly means 'at this rate' (where 'this' corresponds to 'the plot'). *OED* has 'after the rate' (Rate, *n.* P1a) with a stronger sense of value proportion than Shirley's use here, where 'after the rate we cast the plot' simply means 'if I follow through on your suggestions on how to woo Bellamy'.

85 rival contend or vie with (*OED*, *v.* 1). Playfair will challenge Hornet not as a love rival (which he will be to Hartwell), but in order to outwit him to rescue the niece.

85–6 smothers...sea-coal Sea-coal, as distinct from coke, is coal in the modern sense. The rising price of timber in the late sixteenth century meant coal was increasingly burnt instead. It was energy efficient, but 'smothers' because it is very polluting (Cavert 2016, *passim*). This, and the subsequent line's description of the niece's lack of light (wax candles were expensive), are typical of Hornet's meanness.

87 painted cloth Wall-hangings with pictures, either tapestry or painted, were popular both domestically and in the theatre. They provided decoration and also, in a domestic situation, insulation.

88 harlot's story Good, not bad, ends are made by the biblical harlots who might be depicted in the cloth: Rahab (from Joshua 2) rescues the Israelite spies and is redeemed to become an ancestor of Christ; the female disciple Mary Magdalene witnesses Christ's resurrection. So this might be a misapplication of example by Hornet since, presumably, the painted cloth is there to warn the niece against being a 'harlot'. Gifford glosses this section thus 'i.e. what Hornet calls just before, the story of the prodigal' (Gifford 464). At 1.2.85–90, Hornet tells Bellamy not to have such a thing on display because it discourages prodigality, on which he depends for his fortune. However, a distinction must be made between the two things, since the niece cannot be prodigal with a fortune she does not even have access to and, since Hornet's main concern is to prevent her marriage so he retains control of her fortune, a minatory hanging which depicts a fallen harlot is more appropriate. Versions of the harlot's progress (made famous by Hogarth's painting and engravings in the eighteenth century) were available in Italian in the sixteenth century and may have made it into London-printed broadside ballads by the early seventeenth century (Kurz 1952, *passim*). This seems the likeliest story to make Hornet's point, unfair as it is to his blameless niece.

90 'Tis here i.e. Here is the project, possibly gesturing to himself. It is his responsibility to free her.

92 iron-hearted hard-hearted, perhaps (fittingly for Hornet) especially in a context of lack of charity (see *OED*, *adj.* quotation from Sylvester, 1618). The iron is surely meant also to remind us of the jail's bars.

93 repent...aim i.e. be sorry because I have failed.

94 portion dowry. The niece has inherited money (her portion) which will go to her husband as a dowry unless she does not marry, in which case it remains with her guardian (Hornet).

93–5 He...bags Playfair imagines Hornet as a mother bird who sits on eggs (broods) until they hatch, though Hornet is trying to hatch money from bags. The sexualizing of money in this way—where it 'breeds'—is a common feature of early modern writings against usury (Kermode 2009, 3–4).

---

85 him!] *Gifford;* him; Q

48

THE CONSTANT MAID   2.2

Hereafter. To the widow, Hartwell! I am
For state affairs: be faithful and pray for me!
We must be bold. Farewell. If something hit
We'll laugh in spite of Dives and the devil.   *Exeunt.*

[2.2]

> *Enter* [*together*] STARTUP, MISTRESS BELLAMY, [*and*] FRANCES, [*and*
> *separately*] CLOSE, NURSE, [*and*] HARTWELL.

CLOSE [*Aside to Hartwell*] This is the thing, sir, that must carry away
The garland. They have given him a cup
Or two of sack, and has the prettiest humour –
He does so whistle out his compliment.
He wears his feather like the captain of   5
A country team and would become a horse-collar

97 state affairs literally matters relating to the State or national government—an excellent excuse for leaving—but Playfair really means the mock court he is planning to create to cozen Hornet. This is the first inkling we have of the form that his 'project' is going to take.

99 Dives...devil Dives is the Latin word for 'rich (man)', and is used generically with this meaning (*OED*, Dives, *n.* 1). Dives and the devil are commonly yoked together in usury writing, perhaps because Dives was taken as the proper name of the rich man in Luke 16 who dies and is damned for his lack of charity to a beggar at his gate (see also Kermode 2009, 22–4).

0 The scene is set in Mistress Bellamy's house.

1 thing being without life or consciousness (*OED*, Thing *n.* 15). Close is suggesting Startup is unworthy to be called a person (cf. *OED*, sense 10) because he is such a dunce.

3 has i.e. he has

3 humour particular disposition, inclination, or liking, esp. one having no apparent ground or reason; a fancy, a whim (*OED*, Humour *n.* 6a), such as is particularly displayed by the characters in seventeenth-century humours comedies (by Ben Jonson and others). See Edelman (in Chapman 2010) for a discussion of humours in early modern drama.

4 whistle...compliment Startup's humour is an exaggerated courtesy which does not differentiate correctly between its objects (e.g. he mistakes Close for a gentlemen) and is repetitive and ungainly. He 'whistles out' his compliments for several reasons: it is a shrill, unpleasant sound; he is like a horse with broken wind (see notes to ll. 5–6) (*OED*, Whistle *v.* 2b); it is idle and to no purpose (sense 9a).

5 feather in this case, the badge of a fool (*OED*, Feather *n.* 8b, see especially quotation: 'He has a Feather in his Cap, a Periphrasis for a Fool' (1699), and Shakespeare, e.g. *Love's Labours Lost* 4.1.92). This is also a pun which glosses the 'country team' of l. 6: all horses have a 'feather' (according to Gervase Markham in 1607), which is the name for the 'centrical division, and different directions, of the surrounding hair in a horse's forehead' (see quotations in *OED*, Feather *n.* 11b).

5–6 captain...horse-collar Close imagines the animal-like Startup happily jogging along yoked in a horse collar as part of a rural team (pair or more) of horses. By the nineteenth century, being yoked in a horse-collar in a grinning competition was a sign of low humour (*OED*, Horse-collar *n.* quotations 1801 and 1878), so it is possible this was understood earlier. Startup certainly fits the bill as a low grinning fool.

---

96 Hartwell!] *this edn;* Hartwell.– *Gifford;* Hartwell, Q
97 me!] *this edn;* me. *Gifford;* me; Q   **99 SD**] *this edn;* Exit. Q   [2.2]] *this edn; not in* Q
0 SD] *this edn; Enter Startup, Mistresse Bellamy, Mistresse Frances, Close, Nurse, Hartwell.* Q
1 SD] *this edn; not in* Q   **3** h'as] *this edn;* has Q   **3** humour –] *this edn;* humour! *Gifford;* humour, Q
4 compliment.] *this edn;* complement: Q

49

2.2   THE COMPLETE WORKS OF JAMES SHIRLEY, VOLUME 7

Rarely; I do not think but, were he put to't,
With little switching he would draw the cart well.

STARTUP Sweet lady, I'm your humble servant. 'Tis
Well-known what I am, where I live; my father   10
Died since I was of age and left me, thank him,
A younger brother's portion.

BELLAMY   A younger brother?

STARTUP I know, sweet lady, what you'd say. My father
Had no more children, but I must speak modestly
Of my estate. I have land, I know, enough   15
For two or three wives. I have a horse in town –
Your daughter, if we please, shall ride behind me.
Sweet lady, did you ever see the country?

FRANCES What country, sir?

STARTUP   Why, any country living.
Sweet lady – [*bowing*] I am your humble servant – if   20
You affect hawking, hunting, or drinking,
There be good fellows will bear you company, but you have

---

8 **switching** hitting with a riding whip.

8 **cart** i.e. the cart that Startup the horse is drawing in Close's fantasy. Cuckolds were sometimes punished in this way.

9 **Sweet...servant** Startup's catchphrase, as noted by Forsythe (384–5), is not untypical of the early modern stage where rustic or conventional characters often have wholesome mottoes, such as Touchstone's 'Work upon that then!' in *Eastward Ho!* Startup's is absurd, though, because it is acquired rather than natural and he has clearly bought it, as he intends to buy the 'wit' he mentions at l. 49. Shirley deals with these kinds of money-for-comportment exchange in *School*.

12 **younger...brother** younger brothers often inherited little or nothing and were in constant financial difficulty. Bellamy seems dismayed by this turn of events, having been told he is wealthy, and this reminds us that she is strongly motivated by financial concerns despite the short shrift she gave Hornet in Act 1.

16 **two...wives** basically comic in that it reveals his lack of sense, but also an adumbration of the plot as it turns out.

16–17 **I...me** Startup is rich enough to keep a horse in town (stabling was expensive). A gentleman would have a coach of some sort in town in which to convey his wife in style, but Startup is too ungentrified to realize that only a yeoman would take a woman up behind him, and that riding like this would imply sexual impropriety unless she were his wife (Agnes Beaumont suffered from such accusations when Bunyan took her up behind him (see Beaumont 1998, 197–8)). Following the last comment about two or three wives, Startup reveals an (accidental?) tendency to suggest sexually inappropriate behaviour which continues throughout this scene. Echoing l. 8, it may also allude to skimmington rides.

18–19 **country...living** As in Hamlet 3.2.104, 'country' is an obscene pun, though certainly unintentional on Startup's part. This conversation is at cross-purposes, with Startup thinking of the countryside and Frances of other countries—though this may be mischievous on her part. It underlines their lack of compatibility, as Frances may mean it to do.

21 **hawking...drinking** These activities are those of uncouth country youths and not ones which are likely to interest Frances.

---

12 brother?] *this edn;* brother! *Gifford;* brother. Q   20 SD] *this edn; not in* Q

THE CONSTANT MAID   2.2

better sack, sweet lady. Is there good tobacco in London?
CLOSE Virginia tobacco grows here, sir.
STARTUP Sweet sir – [*bowing*] I am your humble servant – you   25
   Seem to be a gentleman, will you fetch me a pipe?
   There's half a piece, an I be not troublesome.
   Perhaps, sweet lady, 'twill offend you – then
   Let it alone.
CLOSE   A very precious widgeon.
   Gramercy sack!
STARTUP [*Singing and dancing*] Ta la la la lero, etc.
FRANCES   You dance well, sir.   30
NURSE [*Aside to Close and Hartwell*] He has a strong back, I warrant him.
STARTUP Sweet lady, is this your daughter?
CLOSE [*Aside*] Ask that now?
BELLAMY   I was her mother, sir.
STARTUP That may be too. [*Indicating Hartwell*] What gentleman is that?
   Sweet sir – [*bowing*] I am your humble servant likewise.   35

23 **good tobacco** unadulterated tobacco. Startup's obsession with tobacco is indicative of his *nouveau riche* status—young men learned to 'drink tobacco' in order to be gentlemen (see Jonson, *Every Man Out of His Humour* 3.3, for Fastidious Brisk's smoking display). Shirley's *Lady of Pleasure* uses the taking of tobacco to signify something similar at 3.2 and 5.1.

24 **Virginia...here** This is partly a joke in that Virginia tobacco cannot grow in London, but underlying it is a reference to the Caroline monopoly system. Charles issued a series of edicts from 1627 onwards particularly trying to restrict the domestic cultivation of tobacco which might threaten Crown receipts (see Butler 2009, *passim*).

26 **gentleman** Close is not a gentleman but a servant. Startup's comportment lessons clearly did not extend to how to be ceremonious to those who are not his social equals.

27 **half...piece** a piece was one of various English gold coins—in this case the 'unite' of James I (*OED*, Piece *n*. 16c and Unite *n*. 1). In 1611 its value was raised from 20 to 22 shillings, so Startup seems to be handing Close 11 shillings to buy him tobacco (Jonson 1994, 72). This was about a week's wages for a skilled tradesman so would have bought a great deal of tobacco: Startup is both rich and does not know the value of money.

29 **precious widgeon** foolish or stupid person (*OED*, *n*. 2), alluding to the stupidity of the bird of the same name. For precious see note to 2.1.67.

30 **Gramercy** Thanks to. They have the alcohol in the sack to thank for revealing the foolishness of Startup, who cannot hold his drink.

30 SD *Singing...dancing* The sack has clearly given Startup energy—he dances here and races around the stage from l. 66. Startup must have been played by an actor with a developed capacity for physical comedy.

30 *Ta...etc.* Startup sings an unidentified song. Plays typically gave only the first line with the '*etc.*' but Startup would have sung more than just this snatch. It is possible that he sings the tune (no longer extant) called *Falero lero lo* connected with *Walking in a Country Town*, itself associated in Continental sources with English-style comedy. Startup might be singing something like STC 22555.5, 'A country new Iigge betweene Simon and Susan, to be sung in merry pastime by bachelors and maydes. To the tune of I can, nor will no longer lye alone: or, Falero lero lo' (Duffin 2018, 656–7).

31 **has...back** i.e. is fit for physical labour, possibly with a sexual undertone.

---

25 SD] *this edn; not in* Q   27 an] *Gifford;* and Q   29–30] *lineation this edn;* A...Sack Q
30 sack!] *Gifford;* Sack. Q   30 SD] *this edn;* dances. *Gifford; not in* Q   30 etc.] *this edn;* &c. Q
31 SD] *this edn; not in* Q   33 SD] *this edn; not in* Q   34 SD] *this edn; not in* Q
35 SD] *this edn; not in* Q

2.2   THE COMPLETE WORKS OF JAMES SHIRLEY, VOLUME 7

HARTWELL   You are too humble, sir; to stoop so low,
　　[*bowing*] It would become my duty.
STARTUP   Sweet sir, 'tis all one:
　　A leg or an arm is not cast away
　　Among friends. I am a country gentleman;
　　All the world knows, sweet sir, I ha' no business   40
　　In town.
BELLAMY   I thought you came to see my daughter?
STARTUP   That may be too, sweet lady. Pray, uncase me:
　　I honour your fair daughter, for I know
　　As well as another what belongs to a gentlewoman.
　　She's not the first, sweet lady, I have loved   45
　　I'th'way of matrimony.
HARTWELL   Were you ever married?
STARTUP   Sweet sir, no: all men are not alike.
HARTWELL   For some are fools.
STARTUP   Sweet sir, I do confess it,
　　But wit is never good till it be bought.
　　They say there are good wits in town – I ha'   50
　　Brought money a purpose with me for it.
　　If any will sell me a penny-worth,
　　I'll give him a hundred pieces 'cause I would
　　Carry a little down into the country.

37–40 It…business The metre of these lines is regular if one discounts Startup's 'sweet sir's, so one suspects this is deliberate on Shirley's part.

40 no business Startup seems to mean being in town is a thing which he does not have the right to meddle
with or involve himself in, following *OED*, *n*. 16b, though the first quotation for this colloquial sense is not until
1692. In the next line Bellamy understands him literally, though this is probably a joke at his expense.

42 uncase Uncover, lay bare, expose to view or observation (*OED*, *v.* 2a) is the primary meaning but it also
humorously introduces the idea of undressing him, realised in 3.3.

45–6 She's…matrimony Startup incidentally confesses what turns out to be the truth, though his audience
does not recognize it at this stage. Hartwell's subsequent question and Startup's response seem like pointless
joking, but turn out to have considerable retrospective irony.

47–8 all…fools This exchange quibbles on two proverbs—Tilley A167, 'All that is alike is not the same' and
Tilley A111, 'All are fools'.

49 wit…bought Tilley W545, 'Bought wit is best', but also alluding to the kinds of transaction, such as
being able to buy a poem in order to feign wit, that Shirley dramatizes in *School* Act 3.

52–3 If…pieces Startup's willingness to exchange vast sums of money (220 shillings) for a penny-worth of
wit demonstrates his stupidity (see l. 60 for a similarly unfavourable financial bargain). See note to 2.2.27.

---

37 SD] *this edn; not in* Q   **41** daughter?] *this edn;* daughter. Q
50–7] *lineation this edn;* They…towne, / I…it; / If…I'll / Give…carrie / A…Countrey. / Is there /
A…Countrey? / Sweet…no; / There's plentie. / Of…much / To…still. Q
51 with me] *Gifford;* wo'mee Q

52

THE CONSTANT MAID   2.2

HARTWELL Is there a dearth, sir, in your country?   55
STARTUP Sweet sir, no. There's plenty.
CLOSE [*Aside*]   Of wild oats.
    [*To Startup*] I heard you had much to sow still.
STARTUP My servants have, sweet sir, but 'tis all one:
    This lady shall be lord o'the soil. I won't
    Give any man sixpence for a bushel o'money.   60
    I am a gentleman; my father was
    A yeoman; but, sweet lady, howsoe'er,
    I'm yours and every limb is at your service:
    My hands shall walk; my feet shall run.
FRANCES Away, away.   65
STARTUP By this gold they shall. [*Running about the stage*]
CLOSE   He keeps his oath.
STARTUP   Not run?
    My grandfather was a nobleman footman,
    And indeed he ran his country;
    My father did outrun the constable.

  55–6 Is…oats Q chops these lines up into shorter lines in a rather odd fashion. The verse is discernible
(if very rough) with Startup's lines being particularly irregular.
  56 wild oats youthful excesses or follies, with a sense of sowing the wrong kind of grain (*OED*, Wild oat
n. P). Close's intervention, both aside and then to Startup, extends the 'dearth of wit' joke that Hartwell makes
at l. 55, by introducing a bawdy suggestion and, specifically, an allusion to semen.
  59 lord…soil owner of an estate or domain, so-called because typically the lord of the manor was owner of
the soil under common land (*OED*, Soil *n.* 5a; Tomlins 1820, 1: 212, 'common II').
  60 A bushel is a measure of capacity used for corn, fruit, *etc.*, containing four pecks or eight gallons. A 'bushel
of money' means a large quantity or number (*OED*, Bushel *n.* 1d). Startup's ridiculous statement seems to operate around the notion that he would not give even sixpence to swap his land (which makes him a gentleman) for
lots of ready money.
  62 howsoe'er in what manner soever; anyhow.
  65 My…run Deliberately ridiculous.
  65 Away, away Frances means 'don't be silly' (as in *OED*, Get *v.* PV1, 'to get away', 1b (b)). Startup thinks
she means 'run', so he does.
  66 By…shall Startup seems to be putting money on a wager without anyone offering him one (see *Hyde
Park* Act 3 for Shirley making similar fun of pointless betting).
  68 ran…country (of a hunting dog) ran directly forward (rather following a scent), ran away (*OED*, Run his
country P2, in Run, *v.*).
  69 outrun…constable run away from the constable (i.e. his father was wanted by the law), though perhaps
Startup's intended sense is that his father could beat the constable in a running race.

  56 SD] *this edn; not in* Q   **57 SD]** *this edn; not in* Q   **59** won't] *this edn;* wo'not Q
  60 sixpence] *Gifford;* six pence Q   **62** howsoe'er] *this edn;* howsoever Q
  66–87] *lineation this edn; set as prose* Q   **66 SD]** *this edn; not in* Q   **68** ran] *Gifford;* run Q

                                        53

2.2 THE COMPLETE WORKS OF JAMES SHIRLEY, VOLUME 7

CLOSE And he, sweet lady, being his father's issue,   70
Must run naturally.

STARTUP   If I live.

CLOSE   He'll run
Himself out of all.

STARTUP   Not run, sweet lady? [*Still running*]
If you have occasion to use me,
I won't stand upon my feet.

FRANCES   No, sir.

STARTUP Nay, I won't stand upon my head,   75
Sweet lady, to do you courtesy.

FRANCES That were the clean contrary way.

BELLAMY Please you, a sorry dinner stays for you.

STARTUP [*Stops running*] Sweet lady, I am your servant.
Will this gentleman dine with us?   80

BELLAMY I'll prevail with Master Hartwell.

CLOSE [*Aside to Startup*] Do ye know what you ha' done? He's your rival!
Invite him?

STARTUP   Sweet sir, I invite nobody,
[*To Hartwell*] If you love anybody here?

HARTWELL   What then?

---

71 run naturally After we discover that Startup's grandfather was a footman who ran his country and his father outran the constable, it makes genetic sense that he run *naturally*. There is also a quibble on 'natural' meaning foolish (*OED*, *n.* 7).

71–2 He'll…all i.e. He'll lose Frances by being idiotic and, Close suggests, eventually spend every penny he has. (See *OED*, Run *v.* PV2, 'to run out of', 2 *trans.*)

72–80 Not…us The metre of this section is consistently short in Startup's lines, exploiting the comic potential afforded by him running around the stage and getting out of breath. There is a hint in l. 90 ('valiant…at meals') that the actor playing Startup likes his food and is overweight which might make his puffing more likely. It may be related to his being habitually short of breath, described as 'whistling out his compliments' at 2.2.4. This would be consistent with the casting of William Sherlock (who we know also played Lodam in *Wedding*) in this part. See Stevenson (1942) for the actors who went to Ireland with Shirley and the Introduction to this edition for a discussion of casting.

73–4 If…feet Startup appears to mean that if Frances has any use for him he is at her disposal, the 'stand upon' meaning something like 'I'll jump to it' (related to the sense of *OED*, Stand *v.* PV2, to stand upon, 4). More nonsense, allowing a quibble on l. 75 (see next note).

75 stand…head a quibble related to l. 74, connected to the expression 'not to know whether one is standing on one's head or one's heels', meaning to be in a state of utter bewilderment (*OED*, Stand *v.* 8), a good fit for Startup throughout the play.

77 clean contrary exact opposite (as well as being true also of being on one's head or one's heels, in ll. 74 and 75).

78 sorry…stays Bellamy's comment is slightly barbed—she means it may only be an inferior (sorry) dinner but you are still letting it get cold.

---

72 SD] *this edn; not in* Q   **74 won't**] *this edn;* wo'not Q   **75 won't**] *this edn;* wo'not Q
79 SD] *this edn; not in* Q   **82 SD**] *this edn; not in* Q   **82 your**] *Gifford;* you Q
82 rival!] *this edn;* rivall, Q   **84 SD**] *this edn; not in* Q

54

THE CONSTANT MAID   2.3

STARTUP Sweet sir, I sha'not take it kindly;   85
    I do not use to quarrel.
CLOSE [*Aside*]   But when you're beaten.
    [*To Startup*] Lay him o'er the face, he sha'not wrong you.
STARTUP Sweet sir, 'tis dinner time. Fair lady.

                                        Exeunt [all but Close].

CLOSE I had a great mind to have him beaten,
    But he's not valiant but at meals. Would I   90
    Were hired to beat him handsomely after dinner,
    And make him thank me for't. I'll have a plot
    Upon your precious body, my sweet sir.   *Exit.*

[2.3]

        Enter HORNET [*and*] *Playfair's* COUSIN, *like a doctor.*
HORNET You tell me wonders, sir.
COUSIN   I tell you truth.
    Alas, you know I have no ends of profit;
    I practise not for wealth.
HORNET   You're virtuous;
    For that you were commended, sir, to me.
    You have a conscience and wo'not take   5
    Fees for a compliment, nor make poor your friends
    To enrich apothecaries.
COUSIN   I have
    Cured her melancholy; but she's a't'other side
    Now: extreme merry, dance and sing, all air.

86 I…quarrel I do not make a habit of quarrelling (*OED*, Use *v.* 21). Quarrel meaning here 'a dispute or argument' (*OED, n.*² 3), though Close affects to misunderstand it (see next note).
86 But…beaten Close understands 'quarrel' in the sense of 'to lay a complaint against someone' (*OED, n.*² 1), which he imagines Startup doing when someone has beaten him (presumably for being stupid and annoying).
87 Lay…you Close is trying to get Startup to start a quarrel with Hartwell by slapping him (*OED*, Lay *v.* 34).
90 not…meals Close means that Startup eats a lot.
o The scene is set in Hornet's house.
o SD *like* disguised as.
5 wo'not would not.
7 apothecaries those who prepared and sold drugs for medicinal purposes.
7–9 I…air In humours theory the opposite of melancholy (earth-like, cold and dry) was sanguine (air-like, warm and moist). It makes medical sense, therefore, for the doctor to have purged the melancholy but produced a patient who is now too sanguine, as he describes in ll. 12–15. It also allows the niece and Playfair's cousin to have some fun at Hornet's expense.

86 SD] *this edn; not in* Q   **87 SD**] *this edn; not in* Q   **88 SD**] *Gifford subst.; Exeunt* Q
[2.3]] *Gifford subst.* (SCENE II.*); not in* Q   **o SD** *and*] *Gifford; not in* Q
7–8] *lineation this edn;* I…cur'd / Her *Gifford;* I…side Q

55

2.3   THE COMPLETE WORKS OF JAMES SHIRLEY, VOLUME 7

HORNET 'Tis strange, methinks: nothing but extremities.   10
     Good Master Doctor, could you not ha' pared
     Her t'other leaden humour?
COUSIN   Sir, I could not
     Kill the malignity of her melancholy
     Another way: extremities must be cured
     With extreme applications. My next work   15
     Shall be to abate this levity of her brain,
     And qualify her spleen, sir, by degrees,
     So state her body in that modest temper
     She was possessed of.
HORNET   I complained before
     Of quietness; now she's all noise and madness,   20
     By your description.
COUSIN   You must have patience
     A month or so: she is not mad, but merry,
     Some few vagaries. You must understand
     I have opened, sir, her fancy – wherein lay
     All her imaginations confused,   25
     And on a heap, smothered for want of vent –
     And now the spirits that were imprisoned
     Rush out, which causes all her faculties,
     Before oppressed, to exercise so strangely
     As the agitation of her tongue will manifest.   30
     She's here.

          Enter NIECE.

NIECE Uncle, how does your body? You appear
     As lean as Lent; I've a great mind to dance
     About a maypole. Shall we?

---

10 **extremities** extremes.

12 **leaden** heavy, as in heavy-hearted or sad. This is a traditional symptom of melancholy.

17 **qualify...spleen** The spleen was thought to produce black bile, and laughter (Schulten 2001, 71), so the doctor is going to moderate or mitigate the action of the spleen so as to reduce its effects to a more satisfactory or normal condition (*OED*, Qualify *v.* 9).

18 **state** put into or cause to be in a specified state, condition, or set of circumstances (*OED*, State *v.* 4a. This use from *Constant Maid* is given as one of the examples.)

23 **vagaries** departures or strayings from the ordered, regular, or usual course of conduct, decorum, or propriety (*OED*, Vagary *n.* 3a).

33 **as...Lent** On account of it being a period of penitence and fasting Lent was traditionally personified as an emaciated character, such as in Breughel's *The Fight between Carnival and Lent* (1559) (see https://www.bl.uk/collection-items/the-fight-between-carnival-and-lent).

33–4 **dance...maypole** The niece suggests this because such a festive, pagan ritual is in straight opposition to Lent. Maypole dancing was one of the things William Prynne's anti-theatrical polemic *Histriomastix* (1632/3) particularly abhorred, as the index entry to 'May-games, and may-poles' demonstrates (Prynne 1633, Pppppp4r).

---

12 humour?] *Gifford;* humor. Q

56

THE CONSTANT MAID   2.3

HORNET   She is mad.
NIECE This doctor has so tickled me,   35
  I cannot choose but laugh: ha, ha!
  Uncle, if you'll procure a dispensation
  To marry me yourself, deduct the charge
  Out of my portion. I could love an old man
  Rarely: *an old man with a bed full of bones* etc.   *Singing.*   40
  Uncle, when did you put on a clean shirt?
  D'ye hear, I dreamed o'th'devil last night.
  They say 'tis good luck. Do you know him, uncle?
HORNET I know the devil?
NIECE   He's a fine old gentleman,
  And something like you. No such bugbear as   45
  The world imagines; you and he'll keep house
  Together one day, but you'll burn sea-coal
  To save charges, and stink the poor souls so.

35 **tickled me** The niece uses a medical term, meaning to be affected or excited by a pleasantly tingling or thrilling sensation; to be stirred or moved with a thrill of pleasure: said of the heart, lungs, blood, 'spirits', *etc.*, also of the person (*OED*, Tickle *v.* 1a—though the niece uses it transitively here). But doctors were also seen as sexual predators in the seventeenth century, so there is a bawdy pun too where tickle equals sexual activity (Williams 1994, 308).

37 **procure...dispensation** in order to marry his niece, Hornet would have to get a dispensation from ecclesiastical authorities. We do not know the exact relationship which this uncle/niece pairing determines: she might be his actual niece or she may be less nearly related to him. Her suggestion that it might be possible indicates that it is a more distant relationship—it was not until the late seventeenth century that first cousins were legally allowed to marry, and you could not marry your sibling's child (only royal petitioners had a chance of a dispensation in this situation) (see Trumbach 2013, 18ff). The niece's suggestion might simply be calculated to tease Hornet, and to underscore the 'extreme merr[iment]' of her new disposition.

40 *an...etc.* The title 'An Old Man is a Bed Full of Bones' comes from a song, four lines of which are quoted in Rowley's *A Match at Midnight* (1.1): 'An old man is a bedful of bones, / And who can it deny? / By whom a young wench lies and groans / For better company' (B3v). These words could be sung to the tune 'Cock Laurel', itself a song found in Jonson's *Gypsies Metamorphosed*, or there is a tune called 'Old Man...Bones' extant by 1651 at least, when it appears in the first edition of John Playford's *English Dancing Master* (76). This song gives the boy actor playing the niece a chance to showcase his singing voice.

42–3 **dreamed...luck** In *Astrologaster, or, The figure-caster* (1620), number 19 in 'A Catalogue of many superstitious ceremonies...[which] to this day are held for certain and true observations' is 'That to dreame of the deuill is good lucke' (46).

43–7 **Do...day** See notes to 1.2.112–13 and 2.1.99.

45 **bugbear** imaginary evil spirit or creature said to devour naughty children; bogeyman (*OED*, *n.* 2).

46–7 **keep...together** presumably in Hell, or perhaps Purgatory (see note to l. 48 'poor souls').

47–8 **burn...charges** Sea-coal had a high sulphur content, but was cheaper than wood.

48 **poor souls** used sometimes loosely to describe the damned, but more particularly those who end up in Purgatory (see More's *Supplication of Souls* 1990, 27).

36 laugh: ha, ha!] *this edn;* laugh; ha! ha! *Gifford;* laugh, ha, ha. Q
40 *an...bones* etc.] *this edn; – An...bones. – Gifford;* An...bones, &c. Q
40 SD] *this edn; Sings.* Q   42 dreamed] *this edn;* dreamt Q   43 uncle?] *Gifford;* Vnckle. Q
46 and] *Gifford;* an Q

57

2.3   THE COMPLETE WORKS OF JAMES SHIRLEY, VOLUME 7

Uncle, you are not merry! I pray laugh
A little: imagine you'd undone a widow,   50
Or turned an orphan begging. Ha, ha, etc.
Faith, how many churches do you mean to build
Before you die? Six bells in every steeple,
And let'em all go to the city tune,
'Turn again, Whittington', who, they say,   55
Grew rich, and let his land out for nine lives,
'Cause all came in by a cat. But let me counsel you
To die at all adventures: great men do't in policy.
HORNET   Why does she talk of dying? She's stark mad.
Could you not put into the next receipt   60
Something to make her sleep well? Opium
In a good quantity, they say, will do't.
COUSIN   I'll so proportion it, she shall never wake.
I did it for a merchant's wife last week,
Which loved a knight; a great man, not long since   65
Was weary of his countess, and I cured him
So artificially of his disease.

---

51 Ha...etc. The niece has a laughing fit here, in keeping with her airy sanguine 'madness' (see commentary 2.3.7–9).

53 six bells The introduction of 'scientific changing' bell ringing (also known as 'method' ringing, where each bell plays a pattern memorized by its ringer) in the early seventeenth century made it fashionable to increase the number of church bells from five to six (Clouston 1947–8, 146). It is possible that Shirley is thinking of a specific church, perhaps St Mary-Le-Bow which, by 1635, had six bells and was supposedly the peal which had turned Dick Whittington back to London (see l. 55). There is a bell change called 'Whittingtons', rung 531246—see next two notes.

55 Turn...Whittington Here Q does not indicate (as it often does) whether this is sung. But it is possible that the niece sings this snatch rather than just using the title of the song.

55–7 Turn...cat The legend of Dick Whittington (c. 1350–1423), Lord Mayor of London, tells us that the sale of his cat brought his fortune. He was prevented from leaving London in penurious despair, by hearing the bells pealing to the words 'Turn again, Whittington, Lord Mayor of London'. He was a notable philanthropist—leaving all his money to the poor—so is a particularly apposite example to offer Hornet (*ODNB*).

56 nine lives a joke depending on the tradition that cats (l. 57) have nine lives.

58 at...adventures as chance directs, at random; (hence) whatever the consequences may be, recklessly (*OED*, Adventure *n.* P1b).

58 in policy as a matter of policy, as a stratagem.

60 receipt recipe, i.e. prescription. Common alternative use in the seventeenth century.

61 Something...well This is intentionally sinister. Hornet may be suggesting the big sleep—death —as he subsequently mentions 'Opium in good quantity' (ll. 61–2). If the niece dies, he gets her fortune.

63–7 I'll...disease Playfair's cousin, as the 'doctor', understands Hornet's sinister intention and cheerfully assures him he has killed at least two people already in this manner.

---

55 'Turn...Whittington'] *this edn; Turn...Whittington Gifford;* Turneagen *Whittington* Q

58

THE CONSTANT MAID

2.3

HORNET   She hears.

COUSIN   But collects nothing; all her senses are scattered.

NIECE   Stay, you shall give towards the building of a church –
   Nothing. See the money first laid out   70
   That's given already – it were sin and pity
   To abuse the dead. But 'tis no matter, uncle:
   You'll be as famous for pulling down the parish,
   The church will fall of itself. With *ding dong bell.*   *Singing*
   Why did they put the poor fellow in prison?   75

HORNET   Whom? What fellow?

NIECE   Why, the corn-cutter.
   Poor gentleman, he meant no hurt to the city,
   His feet were very weary, and that made him
   In every street cry out, 'ha' ye any corns
   In your head or toes?' That head spoiled all.   80

          Enter PURSUIVANT.

PURSUIVANT   Which is Master Hornet?

HORNET   Ha, with me?

PURSUIVANT   A word, sir. [*They walk aside.*]

NIECE   [*To Cousin*]   Prithee, what's he? He comes to borrow money
   On his wife's wedding-ring or his child's whistle.
   You may see by his nose he has no land; he looks   85
   As a hawk. What do you dream on?

70–2 See...dead i.e. before Hornet spends anything he should ensure that any legacy money from others is 'laid out' (spent). The niece is sarcastically encouraging his avarice by pretending that religious piety demands he do this to respect the wishes of the donors.

73 pulling...parish weakening the parish, in a financial sense but also in physically and morally destructive ways (*OED*, to pull down, PV 1 & 2 in Pull *v.*).

74 ding...bell a traditional catch sung in response to death in many songs of the period, as in *The Tempest* (1.2). See e.g. Hilton 1652.

75 Why...prison? See note to ll. 79–80.

76 corn-cutter chiropodist. Part of the itinerant class of London low-life, the corn-cutter was regarded as particularly contemptible (quot. in *OED*, Corn-cutter, *n.*²). See *Bartholomew Fair* 2.4.

79–80 'ha'...toes?' The niece has substituted the word 'head' in place of the traditional 'feet'. As she points out in the same line, offering to cut someone's head is dangerous and might explain his imprisoning (l. 75).

84 wife's...whistle The last things anyone would pawn, indicating extreme desperation.

85–6 You...hawk His hooked or aquiline nose makes him look hungry and predatory.

---

69 church -] *this edn;* Church Q
74 With *ding...bell.*] *this edn;* With...*bell. – Gifford;* With...bell. Q   **74 SD**] *this edn; Sings.* Q
80 SD] Q *subst. (Enter Pursevant.);* Enter 4 Servant, *disguised as a Pursuivant. Gifford*
82 SD] *this edn; not in* Q   **83 SD**] *this edn; not in* Q

2.3   THE COMPLETE WORKS OF JAMES SHIRLEY, VOLUME 7

What lady's tympany is your next cure?
Or whose stale body must be rectified
Next with a clyster?
PURSUIVANT [*Aloud*] There is no disputing; I must attend you.   90
HORNET I am sent for by a pursuivant to his highness.
   Alas, I am undone. I never saw him –
   How should he know me, a poor wretch?
COUSIN   Is't not
   Some complaint, think you?
HORNET   That's my fear. There be
   Too many knaves i'th'world, and a man cannot   95
   Grow rich but one state-surgeon or other
   Must practise on his purse – before this judge
   A vein is opened in the other court,
   So many ounces he must bleed again.
   Let me see: all the treason I committed   100
   Is that I shifted houses, for I took
   Delight to cozen him of his subsidies.
   I always live obscurely to avoid
   Taxations; I never pay the church

---

87 **tympany** distension of the abdomen by gas or air in the intestine, the peritoneal cavity, or the uterus (*OED*, *n.* 1a), thus sometimes confused with or referring to pregnancy (sense 1b). Also used more vaguely to mean a swelling or tumour.

87 **cure** 'care', not necessarily indicating success (*OED*, Cure *n.*[1] 1 & 5).

88 **stale** past the prime of life (*OED*, *adj.* 4a).

88 **rectified** restored to a normal or healthy condition (said of an organ or part of the body, *OED* Rectify *v.* 1a).

89 **clyster** 'medicine injected into the rectum, to empty or cleanse the bowels [or] to afford nutrition'. (*OED*, *n.*). Shirley uses the form 'glister' but both were seventeenth-century usages.

92 **undone** brought to decay or ruin, esp. financially (see ll. 101–5).

93 **poor wretch** Hornet means he is not worthy (and is also hiding his wealth), but, ironically, the phrase has religious overtones similar to those of l. 48.

96 **state-surgeon** Hornet sees tax collectors as doctors who bleed him of money in order to 'cure' him of excess wealth (in ll. 98–9).

100–4 **all…Taxations** As a man of property Hornet would expect to appear on Exchequer lists as a 'subsidy-man'. This would make him eligible for paying not only 'subsidies' (l. 103), but also other direct taxes which were assessed on them. These included Privy Seal loans, benevolences, and distraint of knighthood (levied on all non-knighted subsidy-men) and, in collusion with the authorities, evasion and avoidance were widespread (Braddick 1996, 15, 163ff). Hornet's strategy seems to be to move house frequently enough to prevent his name from being returned to the Exchequer. He has been operating under the radar of the Caroline state by living 'obscurely' (l. 104).

---

89 clyster] *Gifford;* glister Q   90 SD] *this edn; not in* Q
93–4] *lineation this edn;* Is't … you Q

THE CONSTANT MAID   2.3

Her superstitious tithes, nor come to trouble   105
Sermons for fear of homilies before
That beg for burning.
NIECE   Why how now, uncle,
  Is your scrivener broke, you talk such lamentation?
HORNET   I am sent for the king, niece, and shall be made a beggar
  As I was born. I see my chattel ceased,   110
  This chest is ransacked, and that bag deflowered,
  My door sealed up, and with this hungry messenger,
  I am already marching to the Fleet.
NIECE Nay, an you be at that ward, I must leave you.
  Farewell. Pray, do not lift my uncle too hard;   115
  And so I leave you both to the mercy of the bear-garden.   [*Exit.*]
COUSIN Best make fast her chamber.
HORNET   [*Pursuivant makes signs to hurry.*] Aye, aye, cursed dog!

---

105 superstitious tithes It was early modern practice to pay a tenth of household income as a tax (originally
in kind) for the support of the church and clergy (*OED*, Tithe *n.*² 1a). Hornet deems such religious observance
superstition.

105–7 nor…burning Hornet avoids church in case he has to sit through a homily which judges his way of
life to be sending him to Hell (beg for burning). The traditional distinction between sermons and homilies is that
the latter were pre-written and read out by less educated priests, whereas sermons were written by the orator.
However, Hornet's greater fear of the homily may be that it commonly offered practical advice for living, whereas
sermons offered grander theological musings (see Wabuda 1994, *passim*).

108 Is…lamentation Are you passionately expressing grief because your scrivener (see note to 1.2.95) has
lost all his money? The niece is mocking Hornet's use of 'sermons' and 'homilies' by continuing in this vein (the
Lamentation was part of the service of *Tenebrae*), but 'sing the lamentation' is also a common formulation in
ballads which fits with the niece's extensive knowledge of popular song.

110 chattel ceased capital lost (*OED, n.* 2).

111 deflowered In keeping with Playfair's earlier joke about money breeding (2.1.95), Hornet imagines his
virgin money-bags being violated.

112 hungry avaricious.

113 Fleet Fleet Prison, used for offences heard by Chancery Court and Star Chamber, north of Ludgate Hill
(Chalfant 1978, 81). It is unclear whether Hornet thinks his imprisonment will be for debt (the Fleet was the
debtors' prison) or for transgression against the Crown which would be a Star Chamber affair. His tax evasion
could presumably fall under either jurisdiction.

114 ward A pun on the senses of having a guardian (*OED*, Ward *n.*² 6a) and prison (sense 17a).

115 lift…hard The niece means both physically and in the sense of levy (contributions, fines, *etc.*) (*OED*,
Lift *v.* 7).

116 bear-garden arena for animal baiting on Bankside. The niece may mean that Hornet is in for rough
treatment in the Fleet, or the comment may be intended to indicate her madness.

117 Best…chamber As we discover later, Playfair's project to extract the niece from Hornet's house relies
on him stealing Hornet's keys so that he can spirit her away. Hornet needs to think she is safely confined during
the period of his visit to 'court', so the cousin reminds him to lock her in.

107–8] *lineation this edn;* Why…broke, / You Q   **109** and] *Gifford;* & Q   **114** an] *Gifford;* and Q
115 Farewell] *Gifford;* Fare well Q   **116 SD**] *this edn; not in* Q   **117 SD**] *this edn; not in* Q
117 Aye, aye] *Gifford subst. (*Ay, ay*);* I, I Q   **117** dog!] *Gifford;* dog Q

2.4   THE COMPLETE WORKS OF JAMES SHIRLEY, VOLUME 7

COUSIN Won't some money qualify your haste?
PURSUIVANT [*To Cousin*] Deal in your own affairs. [*To Hornet*] Will you go, sir?
HORNET Go! I must go.
COUSIN   I'll take my leave.   120
   Have comfort, sir; this cloud may soon blow over.   *Exit.*
HORNET Yes, when I am blown up.
   I read imprisonment in his very looks
   And all my gold confiscate.   *Exeunt [Hornet and Pursuivant].*

[2.4]

    Enter NURSE *and* STARTUP.

NURSE I heard her say she would walk up to her chamber;
   The trick was but to teach him whither he
   Should follow (who as nimbly apprehended)
   To acquaint her with his new affections.
   I do this for your good, that Mistress Frances,   5
   Whom I'll send to you presently, may be
   Convinced in Hartwell's falsehood and transplant
   Her love on you.
STARTUP   This will be excellent.
   So we shall strangle him in his own noose,
   And he ne'er know who hurt him.
NURSE   I'll lose no time.   10
   You know my instructions.
STARTUP   I had almost

---

122 **blown up** ruined (*OED*, Blow up *v.* 25a).
0 The scene is set in Mistress Bellamy's house.
1 **her** i.e. Bellamy.
2 **him** i.e. Hartwell.
3 **nimbly apprehended** quickly understood.
8–18 **Her…worship** Q sets this as prose, but the verse cadence is apparent.

---

118 **Won't]** *this edn;* Wo'not Q
119 **SD1]** *this edn; not in* Q   119 **SD2]** *this edn; – Gifford; not in* Q   120 **Go!]** *Gifford;* Go, Q
121 **SD** *Cousin] this edn; not in* Q   124 **SD** *Hornet and Pursuivant] this edn; not in* Q
[2.4]] *Gifford subst. (*SCENE III.*); not in* Q
10–17] *lineation this edn;* I'll…instructions. / I…more. / They…away. / If…thee / Lighter…weight. /
If…about you, / Your…departed. / There. Q

62

THE CONSTANT MAID   2.4

Forgot: there is a cast of angels more.
NURSE They are not cast away.
STARTUP   If thou dost fear
   They'll drown, nurse, I can give thee lighter.
   I have some want weight.
NURSE   If you have an evil   15
   Angel about you, your business will
   Thrive better when 'tis departed.
STARTUP   There.
NURSE Now all the good ones wait upon your worship.   *Exit.*
STARTUP These things that go to and again, must have
   Their fees; they'll never speak in cause else.   20

      Enter FRANCES.

   Save you, sweet lady.
FRANCES   Kind Master Startup.
STARTUP Yes, I am kind if you knew all, but you are
   Deceived in somebody. Love, and love your heart out,
   The party does not care a button for you.
FRANCES What party?   25
STARTUP No, I am a fool, a country clod, sweet lady,

---

12 cast...angels in the senses of: 1. a 'throw' (Startup has passed her money, as if throwing dice); 2. 'moulded metal' (of the coins); and 3. 'two at a time' (analogically with hawks, maybe pointing here to angels) (*OED*, Cast *n*. 3a, 29, 14). The nurse and Startup exchange an extended quibble on the various meanings of 'cast', 'angel', and the weight of coins.

12 angels gold coins first coined in 1465 by Edward IV and last issued as currency during the reign of Charles I, it was worth 10*s* from 1619. Pertinently for the subsequent jokes about ship-wreck, Jacobean and Caroline angels bore on them a galleon at full sail (Baker 1959, 89).

13 cast away both 'squandered', and 'lost', particularly at sea (see l. 14) (*OED*, to cast away in Cast *v*. PV 4 & 5).

14 drown quibble depends on 'cast away' meaning 'ship-wrecked'.

14–15 I...weight Startup jokes that he can give the nurse some coins which have been clipped and are lighter than they should be (and therefore less valuable). Being lighter, they will not sink as quickly and may not 'drown'.

15–16 evil angel The nurse quibbles on evil angel meaning one of Satan's followers and a coin not at full weight.

16–17 your...departed both if you give me more money I will facilitate your business better, and your business will do better without diabolical intervention.

18 good ones the money he has given her (which ensures she 'waits upon' him) and a version of a conventional good wish that angels keep someone.

19 These...again i.e. messengers, go-betweens.

20 in cause in support.

21 Kind Frances means Startup to understand 'benevolent, agreeable' but the many meanings of 'kind' allow her some personal satisfaction that it could also be insulting: e.g. '(typically in depreciative contexts) fully warranting a particular description or label by one's very nature' (*OED*, Kind *adj*. 4c); or possibly 'malleable' (9a); or by using it ironically in the sense 'noble' (6b).

24 does...you cares very little about you. See note to 1.1.31.

25 What party? Both here, and at l. 29 ('How sir?'), Frances interpolates exclamations which do not interrupt the metre of Startup's relaxed verse.

26 clod blockhead, but playing on clod meaning made of earth (suitable for someone from the country, such as Clod in *Honour and Riches*).

---

20 SD] Q *subst. (after 'Lady.' l. 21)*

63

THE COMPLETE WORKS OF JAMES SHIRLEY, VOLUME 7

Not worth one of your shoe-ties; no, not I.
I do not know who makes an ass of you.

FRANCES How sir?

STARTUP A gull, a coxcomb, I am ashamed you have 30
So little wit. Tell me, and tell me truly,
Who loves this face of yours besides myself?

FRANCES Although it were immodest to commend it,
I must thus far, in gratitude to nature,
Acknowledge it no monster. I have seen 35
One more deformed.

STARTUP   Sweet lady, I know that.
A worse face would become the country; nay,
There are but fifteen women in the parish
I live in, of which twelve are counted witches
And wear beards. But it troubles me, sweet lady, 40
You should be such an owl –

FRANCES   This is coarse language.

STARTUP Not to see who abuses you. Oh, I could
Now find in my heart to baste you, baste you soundly:
You think Master Hartwell loves you.

FRANCES   I –
Believe he hates me not.

STARTUP   You lie.

FRANCES   Good words. 45

STARTUP You lie most basely; he affects your mother.

38–40 There...beards The tiny community from which Startup comes seems only to have three women of marriageable age. The twelve with beards are presumably old women, in keeping with early modern understandings of what 'witches' were like.

41 owl Like an owl in daylight, Frances cannot see things in plain sight (see *OED*, owl-eyed and owl-sighted, in Owl *n.*).

41 coarse rough or rude, but allowing a pun on 'course' (Shirley's spelling) meaning a passage at arms (*OED*, *n.* 5) and to pursue an animal in chase (*OED*, *v.*). Frances seems to mean 'this is fighting talk'.

43 baste beat soundly, thrash, cudgel (*OED*, *v.*³). A surprising threat which seems to imply a tongue lashing until Startup expresses the wish that women wore swords at l. 48. This confusion of what is proper treatment of women accords with his inappropriate suggestions for pastimes for Frances at 2.2.20–2.

44–5 I...not In Q the lines are set 'I / Believe he hates me not'. There is clearly a pause intended between 'I' and 'believe', as Frances thinks of a politic but true way to answer Startup's question, given her mother's wishes that she encourage him as a suitor.

46 affects is in love with.

---

32 myself?] *Gifford;* my selfe. Q   **41** owl –] *this edn;* owle. Q
41 coarse] *Gifford;* course Q   **44** I –] *this edn;* I Q

64

THE CONSTANT MAID   2.4

FRANCES My mother? This fool's mad!
STARTUP   I would it were
  The fashion for women to wear swords.
FRANCES   What then?
STARTUP I'd breath you into a little understanding:
  I say again – and she is the son of darkness   50
  Denies it – Master Hartwell loves your mother.
FRANCES I hope he does.
STARTUP   Oh, I could kick your ignorance!
  He does love her in the way of matrimony,
  And makes a property of you. I'll justify it.
FRANCES It is impossible.
STARTUP   D'ye know that couple?   55

        Enter HARTWELL [*and* MISTRESS] BELLAMY.

  Step behind the hangings, and you may
  Both hear and see. I say no more, sweet lady –
  I am a rustic puppy and know nothing.

        [*Frances and Startup hide behind the hangings.*]

HARTWELL I have considered perfectly and, if
  You will vouchsafe me hearing, dare pour forth   60
  My heart which, full of love, tenders itself
  To your acceptance. I acknowledge, lady,

47–55 My…couple Q sets as prose but it is probably verse. As we saw when Startup's running messed up his breathing in 2.2, Shirley does pay attention to the way stage business can affect verse. In this case it seems possible that Startup's irregular long lines demonstrate his having reached his wits' end with Frances, and that this is demonstrated linguistically. See next note.

47–8 I…swords Having come to his argumentative limit, in bluster supposed to be typical of underbred young blades, Startup now wishes he could fight her. As Close surmised at the end of 2.2, he is not much good at that either.

50–1 she…it a phrase one might imagine to be typical of fictional 'quarrels', the grammar of which is described by Touchstone in *AYLI* 5.4. Startup has to change 'he' to 'she' which makes a nonsense of the phrase and turns the whole thing comic.

54 property means to an end.

54 justify prove.

56 Step…hangings Shirley makes reference to the 'hangings' in fourteen of his twenty-two plays for Beeston at the Cockpit, often to assist with stage business (Stevens 1977 and King 1965b). In *Bird* Mardona and Fidelia use the 'arras' to conceal themselves in preparation for their entry during the ladies' amateur performance of their *Danae* play, and there are several allusions to the figures depicted on the arras being their 'audience' (4.2). The hangings are used for eavesdropping in several other plays, including *Ball, Traitor,* and *Opportunity.*

58 rustic puppy unrefined and foolish young man (*OED*, Puppy *n.* 2a).

---

47 SH2] *Gifford subst. (Start.); Ztart* Q   **55 SD** MISTRESS] *Gifford subst.; not in* Q
58 SD] *this edn; Fran. and Start. retire. Gifford; not in* Q

65

2.4　THE COMPLETE WORKS OF JAMES SHIRLEY, VOLUME 7

My passions are but young, for could I hope
You should with so much favour look upon me?
BELLAMY　But may I credit this?
HARTWELL   But to suspect   65
Were an injustice to my faith, which looks
Upon your virtue with as much religion
As love is able to receive. Your age
Hath struck a reverence into my eye,
And what you want of youth and spring upon you,   70
Your wisdom richly satisfies. Those characters
Which time hath writ upon your careful forehead
Are but his virtue and your ornament,
When it shall come to pass by your example
That youth shall be esteemed an infancy,   75
And women never ripe for love or marriage
Without your age upon 'em. 'Tis a fault
That men, not guided by the tract of reason
But heat and wantonness of blood, run giddy
To seal such weighty covenants; better 'twere   80
The world should end in our virginities
Than spin itself more length by inconsiderate
And hasty marriages.
BELLAMY   Have you already
Retrieved the affection that pursued my daughter?
Shall I believe no seed of love remains,   85
Which may grow up and ripen with repentance
For this exchange? I do allow you, sir,
The consideration of my fortune, which
Might of itself incline you to accept me.
HARTWELL　That is but an attendant; as you use it,   90

---

65 to Both Gifford and 1661 supply 'to' in order to correct this line in meaning and metre.
65–71 But...satisfies Hartwell's version of wooing an older woman is elegant, rather than comical like the suggestions Playfair made. His use of religious language ('faith'; 'virtue'; 'religion'; 'reverence'; 'wisdom') is nicely calculated in that it is plausible, flattering, and seemingly sincere.
71–3 Those...ornament In disagreeing with Bellamy's earlier assertion (1.2.225) that she has no wrinkles on her face, Hartwell seems to underline his sincerity—he loves her *because* of them—and proves he is not just flattering her.
80 weighty covenants serious contracts (i.e. marriage).
90 as...it i.e. the way in which Bellamy manages her money (liberally but sensibly).

65–6] *lineation Gifford;* this? / But...lookes Q　**65 to]** *Gifford; not in* Q
84 Retrieved] *Gifford subst.* (Retriev'd); Retriv'd Q　**87 exchange?]** *Gifford;* exchange; Q

66

THE CONSTANT MAID

2.4

I must confess a welcome one. Although
The mind is the first beauty which true love
Aspires to, when 'tis waited on with person
And estate, it comes with greater privilege
To win upon's. I do not wish you, lady,   95
Rashly believe what I profess, but measure
My service by the trial: I'll expect
And write your smiles a competent reward,
Till time and your command demonstrate me,
Although not equal to your full deservings,   100
Yet one that has ambition to be thought
Not too unworthy.
BELLAMY   And I guess ere long,
Such an occasion will present itself.
HARTWELL Till then, have Hartwell in your loving memory,
Who wishes no more happiness of life   105
Than to be called yours.   *Exeunt [Hartwell and Mistress Bellamy]*.
          [*Frances and Startup step out from behind the hangings.*]
FRANCES   What have I understood?
STARTUP Will you believe me another time, sweet lady?
If I loved you not, what would become on you?
FRANCES It is not he. Some devil does but cozen us
And mock our sense with these fantastic bodies.   110
Hartwell?
STARTUP Nay, 'tis the man. I hope you'll be converted
And think a country gentleman worth favour,
That brought you to this knowledge. I deserve –
FRANCES My curses for this black discovery.   115
When as before 'twas not impossible,
In time I might be brought to pity thee,

---

93 person living body or physical appearance of a human being (*OED*, *n.* 4a), but Hartwell's use has an overtone of 'personable', i.e. pleasing in appearance.

108 become on become of. A Shirley-ism, perhaps indicating the speech of the country, found throughout the plays, and also in Cavendish's *The Country Captain* (1649) in which Shirley had some sort of hand.

110 fantastic Modernized spelling loses the sense of 'phantasm' – Frances means that they must be apparitions, not just that it is unbelievable.

111–12 Hartwell…man Frances' one-word orphaned question comes in the middle of verse, perhaps signifying a lengthy pause on one or both sides of the word. Startup's impatience, which may be as a result of Frances' dumbfounded pause, is evident in his response.

---

102 guess] *Gifford;* ghesse Q
106 SD] *this edn; Exeunt Hart. and Bell. – Start. and Fran. come forward. Gifford; Exit.* Q
110 fantastic] *Gifford;* phantastick Q   **111** Hartwell?] *this edn;* Hartwell! *Gifford;* Hartwell. Q

67

3.1 THE COMPLETE WORKS OF JAMES SHIRLEY, VOLUME 7

Henceforth I'll look upon thee as my sins,
And beg as much forgiveness that I knew thee.
STARTUP Nay, d'ye but hear?
FRANCES   Die quickly, and be forgotten.   120
STARTUP This is very fine i'faith, sweet lady!
FRANCES My mother? Oh, my fate! [*To Startup*] See me no more,
And I'll forgive thee.   [*Exit.*]
STARTUP   Thank you, most sweet lady!
Is my discovery come to this? I'd better
Ha' been tongue-tied. Curse me and call me her sins,   125
And see her no more? Why, this is worse and worse!
I must suck better counsel from the nurse.   *Exit.*

3[.1]

Enter NURSE *and* STARTUP.

NURSE   Fie, fie!
I am ashamed of you – a gentleman
Of your high promising, and be put off
So slightly?
STARTUP Why nurse, what would you ha' me do?
NURSE Do? I would have you do something. A man   5
Of your ability, and cannot turn
And wind a woman?

---

127 suck...nurse a rustic joke which depends on the physical purpose of wet-nurses, and which is reflected in *OED*, *v.* 5, 'to derive or extract (information...etc) from'.

0 The scene is set in Mistress Bellamy's house.

1 Fie, fie! The nurse is in the middle of speaking as they enter. In order for the verse to work in the next 20 lines, this exclamation should be taken as the second part of a line shared with Startup which he delivered out of earshot.

4 slightly lightly (*OED*, *adv.* 2a).

6 ability See note to 1.2.177 for the financial sense of 'able'. The nurse may also have faith, which is obviously misplaced, in his other abilities.

6–7 turn...wind turn this way and that, as a rider his horse; *fig.* to manage according to one's pleasure, to do what one will with (*OED*, Turn, *v.* 64b).

---

120 Nay...hear?] *this edn;* Nay, do you but hear. *Gifford;* Nay d'ee but hear. Q
121 lady!] *this edn;* Lady. Q
122 mother?...fate!] *this edn;* mother!...fate! *Gifford;* mother,...fate, Q
122 SD] *this edn;* – *Gifford; not in* Q   **123 SD**] *Gifford; not in* Q
123 lady!] *this edn;* lady. *Gifford;* Lady, Q   **126** worse!] *this edn;* worse; Q
3[.1]] *Gifford subst.* (ACT III. SCENE I.); ACT. III. Q
1 Fie, fie! *Gifford;* Fye, fye, Q   **1–2**] *lineation this edn;* Fye...Gentleman Q

68

THE CONSTANT MAID   3.1

STARTUP   You would not ha' wished me
  To ha' put her to't behind the hangings?
NURSE You should ha' been round with her.
STARTUP   I was round
  With her. I called her ass and coxcomb,   10
  And twenty more names; unless I should
  Ha' called her whore, I could not be more round with her.
NURSE I do not mean that way.
STARTUP   And she called me –
  I thank her.
NURSE   What?
STARTUP   Why, no worse than her sins,
  Heaven forgive her. She has the more to answer: 15
  Nay, she did not stick to bid me die too,
  In that desperate estate.
NURSE   Come, you shall take
  Another course –
        Enter CLOSE.

CLOSE [*Aside*] What ails my master's sweetheart? She frighted?
  I met and asked her for my master, and   20
  She turned tail like a hound had lost the scent.
  There's something in the wind. My three-piled worship,
  Are you there with my lady o'th'larder?

---

  8 put...to't forced her (to have sex) (*OED*, Put, *v.* P2).
  9 round The nurse's primary meaning is 'straightforward', though she may mean that if he *had* put her to it behind the hangings, she might be pregnant (round). Startup takes the meaning to be 'rude' rather than 'straightforward' (compare *OED*, Round *adj.* senses 19 and 21a).
  13 And...me Startup is so upset by the recollection that Frances said he was as bad as her sins that he cannot get the words out until l. 14, after the nurse prompts him.
  17 desperate despairing of salvation, i.e. unshriven of sin and therefore going to Hell.
  17 estate state.
  20 I...master Close has just met Frances off-stage and enquired of her for Hartwell.
  22 three-piled thick-piled, like velvet (*OED*, Three-piled, *adj.*[1]); also both of the highest quality and excessive (*OED*, *adj.*[1] 2). Startup is mocked throughout the play for his fine clothes. It may also be mocking his humble origins by gesturing towards heraldic piles (upside-down triangles) on coats of arms, which 'new men' like Startup (and Sogliardo in *Every Man Out*) had to buy.
  23 lady o'th'larder i.e. a servant responsible for providing food, in this case the nurse.

  9–10] *lineation this edn;* I was...coxcombe, Q   **13** me –] *Gifford subst.;* me, Q
  14–18] *lineation this edn;* Why...forgive her, / She...did / Not...desparate / Estate. / Come...course. Q
  18 course –] *this edn;* course. Q   **19 SD]** *this edn; not in* Q
  22 worship,] *Gifford;* worship Q   **23** larder?] *Gifford;* larder, Q

3.1   THE COMPLETE WORKS OF JAMES SHIRLEY, VOLUME 7

Now, in that posture, do not they two look like
A fine brick house and a thatched barn in the country,   25
Laying their heads together? They ha' spied me.
NURSE Come hither, Close. [*To Startup*] Nay, he's faithful, and one that
    Has a desire to serve you: you may trust him.
CLOSE Your worship may trust me abed with ye. I
    Have had an itch this great while, sir, a kind   30
    Of longing to be one of your appurtenances.
    I have some faults, and I'll confess 'em. I have
    A humour now and then, when I am asked
    A question, to tell true, though I be chid for't;
    And I do not love blows: you may sooner beat   35
    My brains out, than a word of flattery.
    I cannot batten upon commendation,
    Without my wages, nor be valiant
    Upon small beer; I am not overmuch
    Given to be drunk, but I've a trick o'th'Dutchman,   40
    To do your business as well drunk as sober.
    I have not impudence enough to pimp
    For you, but I have a gift I can say nothing.

24–6 do...together Close compares Startup to the 'fine brick house', probably because of his smart clothes;
the nurse, the 'thatched barn', leaning towards him, is low-lying and—one might extrapolate—less smartly
dressed and messily coiffed.
  29 with ye Q has 'with —', whereas 1661 supplies ''ye'. Close means that he can be trusted a great deal, as
kings did their gentlemen of the bedchamber, necessary as one is most vulnerable when asleep. It is possible that
the — indicates that a bawdy meaning was being hidden, an *entendre* which might easily be missed but for the
attempt to cover it up.
  31 appurtenances appendages, servants, hangers-on.
  32–49 I...wit Close's set-piece 'humorous servant' speech, 'admitting' his many faults, is intended to draw
attention to his honesty so that he can gull Startup and maintain Hartwell's interests.
  33 humour 'temporary state of mind or feeling' in this case, but Close intends to ridicule the Jonsonian idea
of humour meaning 'particular disposition, inclination, or liking, esp. one having no apparent ground or reason'
(compare *OED*, Humour *n*. senses 5a, 6 and 7). This is also humour ('capacity to elicit laughter or amusement',
sense 9b) on Close's part.
  35–6 you...flattery if you beat me, my brains will come out before flattering words (i.e. I will die before I
flatter you).
  37–9 I...beer Unlike his claim to Hartwell 1.1.37–8 that he can live on 'looks and the air of commendation',
Close tells his prospective new employer that he cannot live on praise without money and cannot be brave if he
is not given strong rather than weak (small) beer.
  37 batten thrive, feed.
  40 Dutchman The Dutch were reputed to be hard-drinking and are used often in early modern drama to
connote drunkenness (see Verbeke 2010).
  43 I...nothing i.e. my talent is keeping quiet.

27 Close.] *Gifford;* Close, Q   27 SD] *this edn; – Gifford; not in* Q   29 ye.] *this edn; –* Q
30 an] *Gifford;* a Q

70

THE CONSTANT MAID 3.1

I was born upon Shrove Tuesday, and shall be
Now and then given to rebellion. 45
My flesh will once a year rise at a chamber-maid;
If none such take me down, I shall in malice
And deep revenge, fling out upon May Day,
Among the prentices, without fear or wit.

STARTUP I like this humour.

NURSE   Nay he has a sense, 50
And shall be of our counsel. Look you, Close,
There is a plot to help this gentleman
At night when they're abed. [*To Startup*] And if you went
To bed betimes, to avoid suspicion,
'Twere ne'er the worse – I'll say you are not well. 55
D'ye mark? [*To Close*] This honest, honest gentleman shall be
Let into Mistress Frances' bedchamber.

CLOSE Without her knowledge?

NURSE   You shall only attend
To give him notice from me when to come,
And watch about the house – he may get off 60
Without discovery. This is all.

CLOSE So, so, I sha'not keep the door.

NURSE   I can do that.

CLOSE Let me alone to give you notice who
Stirs about house.

---

44 Shrove Tuesday The last day of carnival before the penitential religious period of Lent, traditionally an excuse for gorging on food banned in Lent (such as eggs and fat).

45 rebellion Close claims his being born on Shrove Tuesday means he is likely to exercise the licence to rebel traditionally associated with this day.

46 My...rise i.e. I will get an erection. This is also an irreligious pun on 'flesh shall rise' in the sense of the resurrection of the body and, as an allusion to Easter (Christ's physical resurrection) 'flesh shall rise' is placed, with calendrical correctness, in Close's speech between Shrove Tuesday and May Day.

46–9 My...prentices Close will require sexual congress with a convenient chambermaid once a year, and if he does not get it he will take revenge on the world by rioting on May Day, another festival (this time civic) noted for offering an excuse for civil unrest, especially for apprentices who were given the day off. In 1517, for instance, the 'Evil May Day' unrest resulted in Henry VIII sending the Duke of Norfolk to put down a xenophobic riot with over 1,000 troops.

50 sense that which is wise, reasonable, or sensible (*OED*, Sense *n.* 5a), i.e. good sense.

54 betimes in good time, early.

56 honest, honest The repetition draws attention to the fact that neither Startup nor the nurse are honest.

60 he (in order that) he.

---

53 abed.] *this edn;* a bed Q   **53 SD]** *this edn; – Gifford; not in* Q   **56 SD]** *this edn; not in* Q
57 Frances'] *Gifford; Francis* Q   **60** house –] *this edn;* house, Q

3.1   THE COMPLETE WORKS OF JAMES SHIRLEY, VOLUME 7

Enter HARTWELL.

NURSE   Away, 'tis Mr Hartwell.
We'll not be seen together.   [*Exeunt Nurse and Startup.*]
CLOSE   Go your ways!   65
A foolish knave and bawd, that do want nothing
But carting. I would sooner see that triumph,
Than all the pageants, a day after Simon
And Jude, when the fine city goes a-feasting.
Oh sir, I have news – yes, they are gone – brave news.   70
Your gentlewoman can hold out no longer.
This night there will be a stratagem:
Old Madam Humpy-Pumpy, the nurse, has promised
To admit the country gentleman, when all
Are abed, into her chamber. Yes, your mistress!   75
I'm o'th'plot, to lie perdu, and give
The word if any firelock approach
The rest. Imagine if he have not art to
Persuade her to the feat with him, yet there
Be tricks and he may be surprised in the chamber,   80
And she may be compelled to marry him in
Her own defence. There have been such devices.

65 **Go…ways** i.e. Be off with you!
66 **foolish knave** Knave means 'villain', and according to *OED* (Knave *n.* 3a) is often contrasted with 'fool'. Close means that Startup is not only foolish but also unprincipled.
66 **bawd** Close correctly identifies the nurse as a procuress, a common assumption in early modern drama.
  67 **carting** the act of carrying someone in a cart through the streets, by way of punishment or public exposure (esp. as the punishment of a bawd) (*OED*, Cart *v.* 2).
  67 **triumph** public festivity or joyful celebration; a spectacle or pageant (*OED*, *n.* 4).
  68–9 **all…feasting** In the seventeenth century the Lord Mayor's pageants took place on 29 October, the day after the feast day of St Simon and St Jude. In this festival, the twelve livery companies marched in great pomp up Cheapside, with a procession of their members dressed in various outlandish costumes (depending on the theme). This was known as the 'pageant' (see Leinwand 1982).
  73 **Humpy-Pumpy** Q has 'Humpe a Pompe'. This modernized version reflects the still current 'rumpy-pumpy' (*OED*, *n.*), meaning sexual intercourse.
  76 **lie perdu** to be hidden and on watch, to be lying in ambush (a military term, also in extended uses, *OED*, Perdu *adj.* 2a & b).
  77 **firelock** i.e. soldier armed with a firelock gun (*OED*, *n.* 3). Close continues the military metaphor from l. 76.
  80–2 **he…defence** If Startup is discovered in Frances' bedroom her chaste reputation would be compromised and she might have to marry him to rectify it. As Close points out in l. 80, the nurse might employ 'tricks' in order to have Startup discovered so as to force the marriage.

65 SD] *Gifford subst. (Exeunt Nurse and Start.); not in* Q   65 ways!] *this edn;* wayes, Q
68 pageants] *Gifford;* Pageans Q   73 Humpy-Pumpy] *this edn;* hump-a-pump *Gifford;* Humpe a pompe Q
75 mistress!] *this edn;* mistress['s.] *Gifford;* Mistris: Q   76 perdu] *Gifford;* Perdue Q
82 devices] *Gifford;* devises Q

72

THE CONSTANT MAID   3.1

HARTWELL Does she consent?
CLOSE   She is betrayed to't, sir.
HARTWELL Then thou wo't be so base?
CLOSE   An I had meant it,
  I never had told you this. Can you make use   85
  Of this intelligence?
HARTWELL   Thou art my honest servant.
CLOSE I promised to be his.
HARTWELL   I have it! Canst
  By any means procure me but his clothes?
CLOSE With ease. He'll go to bed betimes, to avoid
  Suspicion – that's a part of our design.   90
HARTWELL I could not wish a happy opportunity
  To try how she affects this gaudy fool
  And clear my faith to her, which her mother's watch
  Will not permit. She has, I fear, perceived
  My new familiarity with her mother,   95
  Which I am compelled to, and must clear this way.
  Fail me not, Close, and propound thy own reward.
CLOSE   Tell me your purpose, and let my wit
  Dispose of him.
HARTWELL   Prosper me, Love, in this!
CLOSE An you fall to prayers   100

83 she Q has 'he', amended to 'she' in 1661. 'She' makes more sense, given Close's response that 'She is
betrayed to't'.
84 wo't wilt.
86 intelligence information (*OED*, *n*. 6a).
88 but just, only.
91 a happy i.e. such a happy.
92 try test.
92 gaudy fool highly ornate or showy jester. The word gaudy has overtones of trickery and is often associated
with fools (see e.g. *OED*, Gaudy *adj*. 2, quot.).
96 clear...way i.e. make it plain to Frances that this is a ruse.
97–104 In Q, the compositor has clearly struggled to find the rhythm when setting this irregular verse, making
some odd decisions, such as the orphaned 'Reward' of l. 97 which I have reunited with its line. Line 100 is very
short (three feet if 'prayers' is two syllables) but it is Shirley's practice to end a scene on a full not a half line, so
there seems to be no other rational way to set Close's last speech. 'Ceremony' (l. 103) must be tri-syllabic here,
but even so the line is still a foot too long.
97 propound propose.

83 she] *Gifford;* he Q   84 An] *Gifford;* And Q   85 never] *this edn;* nere Q
87 it!] *this edn;* it. *Gifford;* it; Q   97] *lineation Gifford;* owne / Reward. Q
99 me,...this!] *Gifford;* me love in this. Q   100 An] *Gifford;* And Q

73

3.2   THE COMPLETE WORKS OF JAMES SHIRLEY, VOLUME 7

With good Love, look about us! I shall suspect
You wo'not thrive. You should go to a wench,
As gentlemen to oysters, without ceremony
Or saying grace. Devotion will spoil all.   *Exeunt.*

[3.2]

    Enter PLAYFAIR *and his* COUSIN.

COUSIN Right as an arrow, coz.

PLAYFAIR   Witty engineer!
But was she taken with the plot?

COUSIN   I was
Compelled to frame the outside of a reason,
Lest our own mirth should play the traitor with us.
Her spleen was so dilated, he believed   5
I have made her mad, which change makes for us.

PLAYFAIR Excellent.

COUSIN   And he that we employed,

---

101 look…us watch out; we had better look sharp.

102 wo'not would not, i.e. don't want to.

103–4 As…grace Oysters were popular in the seventeenth century, in life as well as art. Because oysters have to be eaten immediately they are shucked, they became a by-word for quick and unceremonious snacking. George Peele invites a visitor to 'stand to and eat an oyster' (Peele 1627, 6); a song of the period exhorts that we 'loose no time with such good meat' (Ravenscroft 1614, 9). The Protestant communion table (rather than high altar) was commonly compared to an oyster board on account of a supposed lack of ceremony (*OED*, 'oyster board' in Oyster *n.*). Furthermore as 'the oyster is a symbol with multiple meanings of pleasure, sins and their consequences' (see Cheney 1987, 158), Close's *carpe diem* advice in matters of love makes it a fitting comparison.

104 Devotion Refers to saying grace (with the reminder of the proper ceremony of l. 103) and treating a mistress too reverently.

0 The scene is set in Sir Clement's house.

1–23 Compositor confusion continues here, where the verse is set more or less as if it were prose. However, there are some lines which are clearly verse (e.g. ll. 5–6) and only a little reordering makes relative sense of the half lines.

1 Right…arrow This is another scene which starts in the middle of a conversation – Playfair has obviously asked his cousin if the plan worked.

1 coz cousin.

1 engineer author or designer of something; a plotter, a schemer (*OED*, Engineer *n.* 5).

2–4 I…us I was forced to make up a barely plausible explanation (that in 'curing' the niece, the doctor has made her mirthful), in case we were given away by our laughing.

5 Her…dilated i.e. she was laughing so hard. Compare *Twelfth Night*, 3.2.59–60.

6 change…us has changed things for us.

7 he…employed Here we learn, from the logical conclusion of the pursuivant being in their employ, that Hornet's summons to meet the 'King' is a stratagem.

---

101 Love…us!] *this edn;* love,–look about us,– *Gifford;* love, look about us, Q

[3.2]] *Gifford subst.* (SCENE II.*); not in* Q   **1** engineer!] *Gifford;* enginere; Q

2–3] *lineation Gifford;* I…reason, Q

7–20] *lineation this edn;* And…Pursevant, / Shewed…Usurer / Trembled…lash. / He…then? / With… hanging: / He…Church / In…sheet. / That…him. / Nay…fine / For…it, / For…apprehend / Nothing… earth-quakes. / How…rampant / With…musick / Be…flourishes; / But…part, / My Q

74

THE CONSTANT MAID   3.2

The pursuivant, showed such a fiery rascal,
The poor usurer trembled, as bawds
Beneath the lash.
PLAYFAIR   He comes then?
COUSIN   With as much joy,   10
    As to receive a hanging. He would be whipped,
    And say his prayers i'th'church in a white sheet.
PLAYFAIR That were no penance to him.
COUSIN   Nay, he would pay
    As much as he should fine for alderman –
    Though half his soul went with it – for his quietness.   15
    He doth apprehend nothing but earthquakes.

        Enter [SERVANTS *disguised as*] *three lords.*

PLAYFAIR How am I rampant with the imagination!
    [*To Cousin*] Bid the music be ready; they know all
    Their flourishes. But shift you quickly for
    Your other part.   [*Exit Cousin.*]
    [*To Servants*]   My honourable lords!   20
    How they do look like statesmen! Where's your toothpick?
    Excellent. Bear your staff handsomely, contract
    The brow, and look more superciliously.

8 **fiery** hot tempered. The pursuivant was indeed forcefully insistent and would not take no for an answer.
9–10 **bawds…lash** Whipping was a traditional punishment for bawds.
11 **would** would (rather).
12 **in…sheet** i.e. as a penitent. Offenders for such crimes as adultery had to stand in front of the congregation wearing a white sheet and bearing placards (Edelman 2014, 50).
14 **fine…alderman** Also known as distraint of knighthood (see note to 2.3.100–4 and Leonard 1978).
17 Q makes this a question, but Playfair is celebrating his stratagem here.
18 **Bid…ready** This might be a cue for the cousin to tell the musicians to get into place since, by l. 64 when the lutes play softly, they are presumably in the musicians' gallery. If the audience witnesses them making their way to the gallery the metatheatricality of the 'device' is neatly foregrounded.
19 **flourishes** fanfares (of horns, trumpets, *etc.*), *esp.* to announce the approach of a person of distinction (*OED*, *n.* 7a).
19–20 **shift…part** go and change your clothes quickly for your other role (as the king). Presumably the cousin is still dressed as a doctor.
21 **toothpick** an affectation of courtiers (see Jonson, *Cynthia's Revels* 1.1.54).
22 **staff** As part of the ceremonial retinue of the 'King', one of the servants is carrying a staff of office.
22–3 **contract…brow** frown.
23 **look…superciliously** Playfair directs the servants to look haughtily as befits the retainers of the king.

8 pursuivant] Q *subst.* (Pursevant*)*
16 **SD**] *this edn; Enter three* Servants, *disguised as Lords. Gifford; Enter three Lords.* Q
17 imagination!] *Gifford;* imagination? Q   18 **SD**] *this edn;* – *Gifford; not in* Q
20 **SD**1] *Gifford; not in* Q   20 **SD**2] *this edn; not in* Q   20 Lords!] *Gifford subst.;* Lords; Q
21 statesmen!] *Gifford;* States-man, Q

75

3.2   THE COMPLETE WORKS OF JAMES SHIRLEY, VOLUME 7

FIRST SERVANT I warrant you for my part.

SECOND SERVANT   We came now
  From practice.

PLAYFAIR   Can ye do't with confidence?   25

THIRD SERVANT These very clothes have made me proud already:
  It was some lord's cast suit, I'll lay my life.

          Enter one with perfume.

FIRST SERVANT And mine: it smells of honour.

PLAYFAIR [*Directing the perfuming*]   So, so.
  [*To First Servant*] How now, man?

SECOND SERVANT   He looks pale! My lord, how d'ye?

FIRST SERVANT Well, well, I hope; 'tis but conceit!

THIRD SERVANT   Of what?   30

FIRST SERVANT Will the pox lie in clothes? I cannot tell.
  I find some alteration in my body
  Since I shifted.

PLAYFAIR   'Tis a mere conceit.
  They were an honest man's, upon my knowledge:
  A captain of the trainband in the country.   35

24 **I…part** I assure you that I know my part.

26–7 **These…suit** The Third Servant says that his posh new clothes make him feel superior. Theatrical costumes were often cast-offs from deceased courtiers, sold on by their servants (see Gurr 2009, 238–9).

26 **very** specific, particular.

27 **SD** Not an uncommon SD in the period, appearing in several plays, including *The Malcontent* and *Ball* (Dessen and Thomson 1999, 161). In *Malcontent* 1.1 the perfume is supposed by Prepasso to protect him from the stench of a brothel (Dugan 2011, 119ff); in *Ball* 5.1 Monsieur Le Frisque wants to make the musty house smell sweet for the ladies. *Cynthia's Revels* also associates this with courtiers: 'Pray Jove the perfumed courtiers keep their casting-bottles, pick-tooths, and shuttlecocks from you' (2.3.54–5; see note to l. 21 above).

28 **smells…honour** A joke to coincide with the splashing of perfume.

28 **So, so** A direction to do something in a particular manner (*OED*, So *adv.* and *conj.* 5d), in this case presumably controlling the amount and direction of the perfuming.

29 **How…man** How are you, man? (Playfair notices something is wrong, probably because the First Servant 'looks pale' (l. 29).

30 **conceit** fanciful notion.

31 **Will…clothes** The First Servant, having realized that the clothes might have belonged to a courtier (implying an unsavoury lifestyle), is worried that he will catch a sexually transmitted disease from them.

32–3 **I…shifted** The First Servant already feels physically different since he donned the finery; it could be a feeling of superiority like the Third Servant (l. 26), or the pox.

33 **'Tis…conceit** you are just imagining it.

34–5 **They…country** Playfair is clearly being economical with the truth here, but it does reassure the First Servant.

35 **trainband** trained company of citizen soldiery, organized in London and other parts of Britain in this period.

24 SH1] *this edn;* 1. Q; *1., 2. and 3. are normalized as* FIRST, SECOND *and* THIRD SERVANT *throughout this scene*
27 SD] Q*subst. (in margins of ll. 26–7)*   28 SD] *this edn; not in* Q
28 So, so.] *this edn;* So, so! *Gifford;* So, so, Q   28–9] *lineation this edn;* So…man? Q
29 SD] *this edn;* – *Gifford; not in* Q   29 pale!] *this edn;* pale: Q
30 conceit!] *this edn;* conceit. Q   33 Since] *Gifford;* Sinbe Q
35 trainband] *this edn;* train-band *Gifford;* traine Band Q

THE CONSTANT MAID   3.2

They were brought against the general muster last;
He wore 'em that day, and to church the
Sunday following, and most carefully
Sent 'em up, to taste our London lavender.

FIRST SERVANT Sir, you have satisfied me.

PLAYFAIR   Be sprightly!   40
Where's this prince? See, and attend him in fit state.

SECOND SERVANT He's here.

    Flourish [sounds]. Enter COUSIN *[disguised as] the King,* LORDS, *[and]*
    SIR CLEMENT.

PLAYFAIR   Now by that sprig, a pretty majesty!
But wo't thou not be out of thy king's part
And when the wine is wanting at the banquet,
Call upon drawers, quarrel with your nobles;   45
Or when we shall present our man of mortgages,
Take him aside, and borrow half a crown,
To give your whore benevolence, which trusted
For your last tilting; or be drunk too soon
And leave our project in the dirt?

36 general muster training day for citizen soldiery when all are expected to perform training manoeuvres and where a census of the militia is taken.

39 Sent...up No matter from which part of the country they come, things always go 'up' to London.

39 London lavender Lavender was supposed to repel the plague, so presumably might also be efficacious against the pox. Lavender sellers were a common sight in London, perhaps because infection was a serious threat.

40 sprightly energetic, alert.

41 this prince i.e. Playfair's cousin in disguise as the 'King'.

41 in...state as befits his state.

42 SD LORDS i.e. Servants as Lords. They are already on the stage but 'enter' their disguises at this point and subsequent speech headings reflect this.

42 by...sprig Though not an exact sense in *OED* Playfair means that his cousin's costume (in which he is 'sprigged out' or decorated) is fine enough for a king.

43–4 But...banquet 'But won't you forget to keep in character as the player king when the wine is running low at the banquet?' A drunken Cousin might forget he is not in a tavern, un-regally demand more wine from a drawer, and pick a fight with the actors playing his nobles.

45–9 Call...tilting All behaviour more appropriate for the ordinary than the court.

45 drawers those drawing and serving wine for guests.

48–9 give...tilting In this conceit, the cousin owes his doxy money from the last time they had sex ('tilting', metaphorically appropriate both as tipping something over (*OED*, Tilt *v.* 1) and thrusting with a lance (sense 6)), so he pays her a (borrowed) 'benevolence', a gift or grant of money (*OED*, *n.* 3) with an overtone of it being a forced payment (as in *OED*, sense 4).

50 in...dirt i.e. unsuccessful, on the rubbish heap.

37–41] *lineation this edn;* He...Sunday / Following,...up, / To...Lavender. / Sir,...me. / Be...Prince? / See Q

40 sprightly] *this edn;* sprightly; Q

41 SD] *this edn;* Flourish.–*Re-enter* Cousin, *disguised as the King, three* Servants *as Lords, followed by sir* CLEMENT. *Gifford; Enter Cousen for the King, and Lords, Sir Clement. Flourish.* Q

42 majesty!] *Gifford;* Majesty; Q **43** part] *Gifford subst.* (part,); part? Q

49 your] *Gifford;* you Q **50** dirt?] *Gifford;* dirt. Q

77

3.2   THE COMPLETE WORKS OF JAMES SHIRLEY, VOLUME 7

COUSIN   My lords,   50
This fellow's insolence must be corrected;
Dispose him in what prison you think fit.
FIRST LORD He's mad, I think.
COUSIN   To Bedlam with him then.
Is this a place for fools or madmen?
Who admitted him? Take him – see you he be   55
Well whipped, and let him thank our mercy, bandog.
PLAYFAIR I quake already, excellent Warbeck.
Cool, cool thy lungs, and whisper with some lord;
Thou wo't be a key too high else. Good Sir Clement,
Master of the house, at whose cost we are entertained.   60
SIR CLEMENT My part is rotten in my head, doubt not!

        Enter PURSUIVANT.

PLAYFAIR Is he come?
PURSUIVANT   He waits in the first chamber.
PLAYFAIR Let the lutes begin, and their best voice,
And then admit him.
                        Soft music [plays].

        Enter HORNET.

50–2 **My...fit** The cousin is already in role, pretending that Playfair is behaving inappropriately in the presence of majesty.
53 **Bedlam** Bethlehem Hospital, famous institution for 'lunaticke people' (Stow 1908, 2.144), situated outside the city, just north of Bishopsgate and east of Moorfields.
54 **Is...madmen** The rhetorical question is deliberately ironical: is the court a place for fools or madmen?
56 **bandog** dog tied or chained up, either to guard a house, or on account of its ferocity, and in the associated phrase 'to speak bandog and Bedlam', i.e. furiously and madly (*OED*, Bandog *n.* b), appropriate to ll. 53–4, and to the idea that Playfair speaks inappropriately to the 'King' at ll. 43–50.
57 **Warbeck** Playfair's cousin plays at being king, like Perkin Warbeck [Pierrechon de Werbecque; *alias* Richard Plantagenet, duke of York] (*c.* 1474–99), impostor and claimant to the English throne (*ODNB*). John Ford's play *The Chronicle History of Perkin Warbeck* (*c.* 1632–34) was presumably in Shirley's mind.
58 **Cool...lungs** stop speaking so heatedly. But there is also a medical overtone since, in early modern medicine, the purpose of the lungs was to use fresh air to cool the heart (Meli 2008, 679).
59 **too high** too loud, over the top (*OED*, High *adj.* 17a).
59–60 **Good...entertained** Strictly speaking in prose not verse, this utterance is for information only but is rather clumsy (almost as if Shirley had forgotten about him). Q sets it as verse.
61 **rotten...head** thoroughly prepared and rehearsed (*OED*, Rotten *adj.* P3; this quotation used as the example).
61 SD The Pursuivant is of course one of the servants in disguise.
62 **first chamber** next room.

54 madmen?] *Gifford;* madmen, Q
54–6] *lineation this edn;* Is...who / Admitted...you / He...mercy, / Bandog. Q
59 Sir] *Gifford subst.;* Sʳ. Q   61] *lineation Gifford;* rotten / In Q
61 SD *Enter* PURSUIVANT.] Q *subst.* (Enter Pursevant.); Enter 4 Servant, *disguised as a Pursuivant. Gifford*
63–6] *lineation this edn;* Let...Lutes / Begin,...him. / Here's...for't: / That's...they are Q
64 SD1] *this edn; Soft music, and a song. Gifford; Soft Musicke.* Q

78

THE CONSTANT MAID   3.2

HORNET [*Aside*]   Here's revelling –
My purse must be squeezed for't. That's the king;   65
The rest are bare. How supple they are
I'th'hams – that courtier has oiled his joints.
He looks this way; they point at me – a rot
O'that knave's finger.
FIRST LORD [*Indicating Hornet*] What fellow's this? Who waits?
PURSUIVANT It was His Grace's pleasure he was sent for,   70
My good lord.
FIRST LORD   Master Hornet?
Let me have the honour to present him.
COUSIN Is this the man whom all so much commend
For his ability?
HORNET   [*Aside*] I smell no good from that word, ability.   75
COUSIN   Discreet and read
I'th'commonwealth, a man fit for
Employment in the state?
SECOND LORD   The very same.
COUSIN His countenance is promising.

65 My...for't Hornet imagines his purse as a sponge which will let out money rather than water when squeezed. *OED* has a similar compound phrase, 'purse-milking' meaning swindling (*OED*, Purse *n*. C2).

66 bare i.e. have taken their hats off as is fitting in the presence of royalty. Hornet can identify the king because his head is still covered.

66–7 How...joints Hornet is observing them bow low and elegantly, drawing their right legs back almost as if dancing.

68–9 a...finger Hornet is trying to escape notice and does not want to be pointed out.

71 A short line, in more uneven verse.

73 SH Q has *War.* for Warbeck here (the first time the cousin speaks after Playfair calls him this) and in all the SHs until his exit at l. 99.

74–6 For...read Hornet's line (75) is interpolated into the cousin's longer speech, which is metrically discrete. 'Discreet' is on the same line as 'ability?', but a modern edition must number them separately.

75 ability Hornet initially understands this to mean 'pecuniary power' (*OED*, *n*. 5), and so worries for his fortune, but the 'King' demonstrates in ll. 76–8 that he means personal talent or mental capacity (senses 3 & 6). Gifford points out that it is also 'bitter', presumably meaning that by this time in the 1630s men of 'ability' had got a bad name (though, as he notes, it did not have nearly so bad a 'scent' as 'a few years afterwards' (4: 485).

76 Discreet Having sound judgement.

76–7 read...I'th'commonwealth experienced, versed, or well-informed by reading (*OED*, *adj*. 1a) in the matters of the nation or state or the body politic (*OED*, *n*. 2), i.e. knowledgeable, a man of the world.

78 state government (*OED*, *n*. 26a).

79 His...promising His face and expression suggest we can expect good things from him.

---

64 SD] *Gifford* (at end of l. 69); *not in* Q
69 SD] *this edn; not in* Q
73 SH] *Gifford subst.* (*Co.*); *War.* Q; *War. is used throughout the remainder of this scene in Q, but is here normalized as* COUSIN   **74** ability?] *Gifford;* ability. Q   **75 SD**] *Gifford subst.; not in* Q
76–8] *lineation this edn;* Discreet...man / Fit...State. Q   **78** state?] *Gifford;* State. Q

79

3.2 THE COMPLETE WORKS OF JAMES SHIRLEY, VOLUME 7

SIR CLEMENT   If the
King of Spain had but his head, that politic head,   80
I know who might go fish for the Low Countries.
COUSIN   His garments are but coarse.
SIR CLEMENT   His mind is rich.
HORNET [*Aside*] They praise me – I am a thousand pound the worse for't.
THIRD LORD Wilt please your majesty?
COUSIN   Kneel down. Thy name?
HORNET [*Kneeling*] Giles Hornet, your poor creature.
COUSIN   Rise up,   85
Sir Giles Hornet.
HORNET   But am I knighted?
LORDS We congratulate your honour.
HORNET   What must I pay for it?
I'll sell it any friend of yours again
For half the money.
COUSIN   Some have care to give
His body more becoming ornaments.   90

79–81 **If…Countries** The Thirty Years' War (1618–48), a Europe-wide conflict was initially religious but became imperial when the Catholic French entered on the 'Protestant' side in 1635 (though they had been offering support since 1631 to counter the Habsburgs). The Low Countries had been a major site of conflict since 1581, which had seen the secession of the Seven United Provinces as the Dutch Republic; the ten provinces of the Spanish Netherlands continued to be occupied by Habsburg armies as they attempted intermittently to re-take the Protestant states. France declared war on Spain in 1635 and on the Holy Roman Empire the following year, opening theatres of war in the Low Countries. See following two notes.
80 **King of Spain** Philip IV, the Great, reigned 1621–65.
80 **politic** judicious, but perhaps also with an overtone of crafty.
81 **I…who** A coy way of saying Cardinal Richelieu, King Louis XIII of France's chief minister from 1624 to 1642, who was a major player in the Thirty Years' War, funding the anti-Habsburg faction since *c.* 1625 and committing France militarily from 1635.
81 **go fish** try to get something, with the implication of being unsuccessful.
82 **coarse** of inferior quality or value; in comparison to 'rich' in the same line.
84–9 The verse here is irregular, with the Lords' congratulations interposing between Hornet's half lines at ll. 86 and 87. Relineating it like this allows the cousin a dramatic pause after 'Rise up' (l. 85).
85 **creature** person who owes his or her fortune and position, and remains subservient to a patron (*OED*, *n.* 4). Tri-syllabic here.
87–9 **What…money** Because of his own obsession with money, and because distraint of knighthood was a common way for the Crown to raise funds, Hornet thinks he is being made to buy his knighthood. He plans to re-coup some of the money by selling it on for half what he spent.
89–90 These lines are directed generally at the servants who subsequently help Hornet into his new clothes.
90 **more…ornaments** attire which suits him, and his new status, better.

79–80] *lineation this edn;* If…*Spaine* / Had…head, Q
83 SD] *Gifford subst.; not in* Q
84–7] *lineation this edn;* Wilt…Majesty? / Kneel…name? / Giles…creature. / Rise…*Hornet.* / But… Knighted? / We…honour. / What…it? / Q
85 SD] *this edn; not in* Q

THE CONSTANT MAID   3.2

He shall be like himself and then we will confer
More honours on him.   *Exit Pursuivant.*

FIRST LORD [*To Hornet*] Do you make haste. His Grace
    Will have you new-thatched; you must have clothes
    Fitting your state and honourable title.
HORNET These will be good enough for me;   95
    'Las I am not able.
FIRST LORD   Nay, you must have 'em
    From his wardrobe, sir. They'll cost you nothing.
    You'll not look in those like a poor knight of Windsor.
COUSIN When he is ready, give us knowledge.
FIRST LORD   Yes, sir.

     Exeunt [all but Hornet and First Lord]. Flourish [sounds].

HORNET What will become of me?
FIRST LORD   You were best prepare: 100
    Your clothes will be here presently; the king
    Will send for you before you be ready. Cast
    Your old skin off. Do you not to save sheets
    And trouble, wrap yourself a' nights i'th'blankets?
    Or are they ashamed to show the linings?   105
HORNET Hmm? If this be but preparative to a whipping,

---

91 **like himself** i.e. the way he should be.

93 **new-thatched** i.e. given a general make-over, but there is an association between thatch and hair so it also anticipates the visit of the barber which comes later in the scene.

94 **state…title** i.e. both his new position as royal counsellor and as *Sir* Giles.

95–8 **These…Windsor** more uneven verse set as prose by the compositor.

96 **I…able** i.e. I can't afford (new clothes).

97 **wardrobe** the 'office or department of the royal household responsible for supplying and maintaining clothing, armour, furnishings, and other valuable goods and objects belonging to the monarch' (*OED, n.* 3). In Playfair's device the theatrical sense (5b) of the word is also present, especially as deliberate attention has been drawn earlier to the servants getting dressed up in their borrowed clothes.

98 **poor…Windsor** poverty-stricken military officers (Military Knights of Windsor) who have royal pensions and apartments in Windsor Castle (*OED,* Knight *n.* P2a). In the seventeenth century, in order to qualify the holder must have less than £20 p.a. The First Lord's point is that Hornet's existing clothes would only be appropriate to one of these knights, and not to a knight of the court.

102–3 **Cast…off** Take your old clothes off. Like a snake, Hornet will renew himself and emerge with a glorious new casing.

103–5 **Do…linings?** 'They' (l. 105) are the old clothes which Hornet has to remove, but the First Lord suspects that Hornet is too mean to wear underclothes. In this metaphor, the blankets are the outer clothes and Hornet saves 'sheets' (underwear) by putting them on without anything beneath them.

106 **preparative** tri-syllabic.

---

92 SD1 *Pursuivant*] Q *subst. (Pursevant)*   92 SD2] *this edn; not in* Q
95–8] *lineation this edn;* These…able. / Nay,…sir, / They'll…those, / Like…Windsor.
99 SD] *this edn; Flourish.–Exeunt all but Hor. and* 1 *Serv. Gifford; Exeunt. Flourish.* Q
104 yourself] *this edn;* your selves Q

81

3.2   THE COMPLETE WORKS OF JAMES SHIRLEY, VOLUME 7

What case am I in?

    Enter SERVANTS *with clothes.*

FIRST LORD   Well said! Now they are come.
[*To Servants*] Be nimble now and help to fit Sir Giles.
HORNET Alas, must I wear this doublet? It would yield
Heaven knows how much to burn.
FIRST LORD   You may be desperate   110
When 'tis on and burn your body with it, sir.
HORNET I sha'not know myself.
FIRST LORD   By that time we ha' done wi'ye.
FIRST SERVANT [*Dressing Hornet*] Fit as they were made, sir.

    Enter PLAYFAIR.

PLAYFAIR   Which is Sir Giles?
HORNET I am the man you please to call Sir Giles.
PLAYFAIR Then I congratulate your happy fortune.   115
You're like to be exalted. His Grace talks
Much on you: I'll be proud to be your servant.
[*To First Lord*] My lord, a word. [*They walk aside.*]
HORNET   What Gentleman is that?
FIRST SERVANT The bridegroom, sir. In great favour, I can tell you,
And new created by his highness, Baron   120
Of Landscape – his living is far off.

---

107 case pun on outfit and situation.

107 Well said! A meaning in the period is 'well done', so the First Lord might be congratulating the servants on bringing Hornet's new clothes, or agreeing with what he takes to be Hornet's lamenting the state of his clothes. It also draws ironic attention to the project to defraud Hornet, as does the pun on 'fit' in l. 108. It could also be drawing ironic attention to the project to defraud Hornet, even as it congratulates him for noticing that something is not as it seems.

108 fit both (a) dress/supply with the necessaries and (b) visit (a person) with a fit penalty, punish (*OED*, Fit *v.* 11 &12).

109 doublet close-fitting body-garment, with or without sleeves.

109–10 It...burn Hornet instantly assesses the worth of the rich doublet and translates its sale value into the payment of heating bills (presumably for sea-coal, his fuel of choice—see note to 2.1.85–6).

110–11 You...it The doublet may also be comically thick and therefore hot; perhaps the fear expressed by the First Servant at 3.2.31 that you could catch 'the pox' from borrowed clothes is also in ironic play.

113 Fit...made A perfect fit, as if they were made for you.

114 Hornet still refuses to accept that he has been knighted.

116 like...exalted likely to be promoted.

120–1 Baron...Landscape Like the Duke of Drowned-lands in Jonson's *The Devil is an Ass* (2.4.20), this is a made-up title. 'Landskip', as it appears in Q, was a new term borrowed from Dutch painting (see Trevisan 2013).

121 his...off His estates are far from London (a joke about the background nature of all landscapes).

---

107 said!] *Gifford;* said, Q   **108 SD**] *this edn; – Gifford (at end of l. 107); not in* Q
108 Sir] *Gifford subst.;* Sʳ. Q   **112** By] *Gifford;* Be Q   **113 SD1**] *this edn; not in* Q
118 SD1] *this edn; – Gifford (at end of l. 117); not in* Q   **118 SD2**] *this edn; not in* Q
121 Landscape] Q *subst.* (Landskip)

82

THE CONSTANT MAID   3.2

HORNET My very good lord, my breeches are
    Almost on.
FIRST SERVANT [*Aside to Playfair, pointing*] There be the keys.
HORNET His Grace has pleased to shine upon
    A piece of barren earth.
PLAYFAIR   You are too modest.   125
    The king has been informed, Sir Giles, you are
    One of the ablest men in his dominion.
    Should virtue still be clothed in rags? Advance it
    To honour and regard you waste your brain
    At home in cheap and low engagements, sweat   130
    Your soul out for a poor and paltry living.
    Old houses, let 'em fall to the dull lord
    O'th'manor; switch me up a town together,
    Or meddle not. This or that straggling acre's

122–3 my...on We might imagine in ll. 118–45 that Hornet is in the Cockpit's discovery space passing his clothes out and, as here, poking his head out comically to deliver his lines. Certainly, Playfair's long speech (ll. 125–42) might be designed to allow Hornet time to change his clothes.

123–4 Almost...upon The First Servant's 'There be the keys' is an interruption of Hornet's metrically (almost) correct 'Almost on. His Grace has pleased to shine upon.' This is common in Shirley, who writes as if he hears his metre carried over such interpolations. Other, similar, examples occur at 1.2.13 and 2.4.25 and 29.

123 There...keys In all the joking about over Hornet's new clothes, the audience may have forgotten that the whole point is to extract his keys when he is not looking so that Playfair can elope with his niece. The First Servant spots them as Hornet divests himself of his old breeches—keys were often kept on the belt—and a performance could make much comic business out of the conspirators' attempts to steal them by the time Playfair leaves at l. 157. They have to end up in Playfair's possession (since he leaves first) but he provides the grandiose speech designed to distract Hornet, presumably while the First Lord and First Servant try to edge towards the keys without Hornet seeing. Gifford ignores the action implied later in the scene and has another servant give the keys to the First Servant at l. 123, and he conflates the First Lord with the First Servant so that a further exchange is not necessary at l. 145, but this does not account for the whispered conversation in ll. 144–5.

128 it i.e. virtue.

129–30 regard...engagements think that by staying at home thinking about matters of no consequence you are wasting your talents.

130–1 sweat...living There is an implication here that by being a courtier one can get great riches for less work, a point reinforced by Playfair's mention of monopolies in l. 135 (see note). An 'and' is implied before 'sweat'.

132–40 Old...pension Playfair argues in this speech that the old ways are obsolete. In place of old houses and land-based wealth, he advocates the money markets (in their various forms) as the way forward.

133 manor Q's 'manner' quibbles on the two spellings.

133–4 switch...not Drive a whole town as if with a switch or don't bother (i.e. you would need a lot more than one 'old house' to make investing in property worth it).

134 straggling acre dispersed land (i.e. not part of a single large estate).

122–3] *lineation this edn;* My...on. Q
123 SD] *this edn; not in* Q

83

3.2　　THE COMPLETE WORKS OF JAMES SHIRLEY, VOLUME 7

Not worth your care: study some monopoly　　　　　　　135
May sweep the kingdom at a stake; despise
A project wo'not bring in half the city;
Find out a way to forfeit all the charters;
Have an exchequer of your own and keep
The princes round about in pension.　　　　　　　140
These are becoming businesses and speak
An active statesman.

HORNET　　　　　　　　You do talk strange things,
My lord.

PLAYFAIR　[*Aside to First Lord*]　His keys are things very material
To our business.

FIRST LORD　[*Aside, discreetly showing keys to Playfair*]　And I have 'em.

PLAYFAIR　　　　　　　　　　　　　　　So, so.　　145

[*First Lord hands keys to Playfair who pockets them.*]

135 **study** consider.

135 **monopoly** exclusive privilege conferred by a monarch, state, *etc.*, of selling a particular commodity or of trading with a particular region (*OED*, *n.* 2). Since an organized monopolies system had been instituted under Elizabeth I, abuses had crept in and Parliament acted several times to right these by annulling all monopolies in 1601, 1607, and 1624. (See Johnson 1905, lviiiff.) However, during Charles's personal rule Parliament had no way of exercising control, and the King's need for funds meant that farming of monopolies was extensive and unregulated. Monopolies were very much associated with Sir Giles Mompesson, the infamous Jacobean projector, who was the satiric source of several stage characters after his fall including Sir Giles Overreach in Massinger's *A New Way to Pay Old Debts* (*c.* 1625) and indeed, here, in the choice of name for Giles Hornet. Holding a monopoly was often a way to get rich quick, though some—such as the project to drain the Fens in 1605 by Sir John Popham and Sir Thomas Fleming—were a complete failure.

136 **sweep...stake** Playfair represents the seeking of monopolies as a kind of race with the sums of money subscribed by the bidders who enter the contest as the stake. This was one way that the Crown made money out of monopolies.

138 **Find...charters** According to Hobbes 'Charters are Donations of the soveraign; and not Lawes, but exemptions from Law' (*Leviathan* 26:45). If this is the case, finding a way to revoke all of these documents which granted privileges or rights to certain people could make different people very rich at a stroke.

139 **exchequer** office or department of the public service, which is charged with the receipt and custody of the moneys collected by the several departments of revenue (*OED*, *n.* 4a). Playfair is, in effect, advising Hornet to start his own bank.

140 **in pension** See note to 2.1.14–17. The Princes would borrow money and then pay a monthly sum to Hornet for the privilege.

141 **becoming** befitting, suitable (perhaps also with a sense of up and coming).

141–2 **speak...statesman** reveal one to be a mover and shaker.

142 **strange things** Even Hornet is nonplussed by Playfair's financial schemes.

143 **My lord** This seemingly orphaned phrase is actually the first half of l. 146. See note to ll. 123–4.

144 **very material** crucial (but also drawing attention to the difference between the unfamiliar 'strange things' (l. 42) and the solidity implied by materiality).

145 **So, so** i.e. Give the keys to me quickly (see note to 3.2.28).

144 **SD**] *this edn; not in* Q　144–5] *lineation this edn;* His...verie / Materiall...businesse. Q
145 **SD1**] *this edn; not in* Q　145 **SD2**] *this edn; not in* Q

84

THE CONSTANT MAID

3.2

[*To Hornet*] I will account it one of my felicities
　To be a witness of your honour, sir.

HORNET Oh, my good Lord of Landscape.

FIRST SERVANT [*Aside to First Lord, showing clothes*] How shall we dispose these?

FIRST LORD [*Aside*] The hangman will not have them, and I fear　　　　150
　They will corrupt a well. 'Faith, give them stable-room.　　[*Exeunt Servants.*]
　　　　Enter THIRD LORD.

THIRD LORD [*To Playfair*] My lord, the king asks for you. [*To Hornet*] Good Sir Giles,
　Write me i'th'number of your faithful friends.

PLAYFAIR We must attend.

FIRST LORD　　　　　　　Do not yet say he's ready!
　The barber has a duty to dispatch –　　　　　　　　　　　155
　He will be hours a-rubbing, washing, powdering –
　Then I'll attend him to his presence.

PLAYFAIR We shall excuse him so long; still your servant.　　　　[*Exit.*]

FIRST LORD The barber, sir, attends in the next room.

HORNET I wo'not shave.　　　　　　　　　　　　　　　　160

---

146 I...my This is the second half of the line that begins with Hornet's 'My lord' (l. 143), and is interrupted by the byplay over the keys.

148–9 The verse has deteriorated here; perhaps Shirley imagines l. 148 as a line of verse interrupted by the First Servant's aside.

150–1 The...stable-room Hornet's old clothes will not even be acceptable to the hangman (who sold off the clothes he took from the bodies) and the First Lord thinks they are so disgusting that they might poison a well, so the only option is to send them to be used in the dirty stables, e.g. for mucking out.

151 corrupt...well An interesting choice of words, perhaps coming from the association in the early modern mind of usurers and Jews who were purported to poison wells (see *The Jew of Malta* 2.3.180 in Bevington 2002). It was not normal practice to dispose of old clothes into wells.

153 Write...of Put me down as one of.

154 Do...ready An expression of feigned disbelief, to which this edition adds an exclamation mark.

155 barber The conspirators have to find an excuse to keep Hornet busy without missing his keys for as long as it takes them to rescue his niece. The barber's ministrations, as we are told in l. 156, will take hours.

157 his presence the king's ceremonial audience.

158 still (I am) still.

158 SD It is possible that the Third Lord exits with Playfair here, but more likely that he stays to be the recipient of the First Lord's aside at l. 161 and to constitute the 'we' of the last line of the scene.

160 wo'not would not (i.e. rather not).

160–3 These lines are set as prose here but it is likely that Shirley thought of l. 160 and l. 162 as corresponding half lines and of l. 163 as a continuation of l. 161. See note to ll. 123–4.

---

146 SD] *this edn;* – *Gifford (at end of l. 145); not in* Q　**148** Landscape] Q *subst. (*Landskip*)*

149 SD] *this edn; not in* Q　**150 SD**] *this edn; not in* Q

151 SD1] *this edn; Exeunt Servants with Hornet's clothes. Gifford; not in* Q

151 SD2 THIRD] Q *subst.* (3.)　**152 SD1**] *this edn; not in* Q　**152 SD2**] *this edn;* – *Gifford; not in* Q

154 ready!] *this edn;* ready. *Gifford;* ready, Q　**158 SD**] *this edn; not in* Q

85

3.3   THE COMPLETE WORKS OF JAMES SHIRLEY, VOLUME 7

FIRST LORD [*Aside*] He fears his throat.

HORNET I never give above three-pence.

FIRST LORD Talk not you of charge.

> You have but yet your welcome: do not you
>
> Think, good Sir Giles, but we can shave you too?   *Exeunt.*   165

[3.3]

> *Enter* CLOSE [*and*] STARTUP *in his shirt.*

STARTUP Where is he, Close?

CLOSE   I told him, sir,

> You lay in a chamber o'th'tother side
>
> The house, whither he is gone with his sword drawn
>
> And curses of themselves able to kill you.
>
> You did affront him once and now his mistress   5
>
> Has quite neglected him for your love, he thinks –
>
> He'll make you an example to all rivals.
>
> I'll bring your clothes hereafter, yet your fear –
>
> And running, sir – will keep you warm enough.

---

161 fears…throat fears the barber will cut his throat. Seventeenth-century barbers used straight 'cut throat' razors which gave a very close shave but were potentially quite dangerous.

164 You…welcome i.e. we have only just started.

165 shave you remove your beard; but, also, strip you clean of money or possessions, fleece you (*OED*, Shave *v.* 4 & 7a).

0 Gifford suggests that scene is set in the street near Mistress Bellamy's house, but it could equally be set inside it, or in the entrance doorway. Startup is being bundled out of the house without his clothes but it is not clear from the short scene how far out of the house Close has got him yet.

0 SD in…shirt 'widely used like the nightgown to indicate that a male figure is unready, surprised, or vulnerable' (Dessen and Thomson 1999, 195). Given that Startup has undressed already (he went to bed early on a pretext) and Close has manoeuvred him out of his bedroom so that Hartwell can steal his clothes, it is possible he is actually in his nightshirt. But at the very least he is without his outside clothes which explains why he is so desperately cold in the fields later in the play.

1 Where…Close This is yet another scene that starts mid-conversation, with the 'he' being the violently angry Hartwell that Close has described to Startup.

2 o'th'tother Q has 'o'th t'other'. This is a common Shirley-ism which makes no sense as 'on the the other' but is a distinct way of expressing the sentiment verbally. Similar examples can be found across Shirley's works irrespective of who printed them, implying that the construction is an authorial choice. 'Tother' is common in Shirley and in Beaumont and Fletcher, who also regularly precede it by a definite article.

4 curses…you Hartwell's (supposed) words are so violent that they alone could kill Startup.

7 i.e. by killing him.

8 clothes The whole point of hurrying Startup out of his chamber by telling him he is being pursued by an angry Hartwell is to steal his clothes so that Hartwell can impersonate him in Frances' chamber. Of course, 'honest' Close (see l. 10) has no intention of fetching him his clothes.

---

161 SD] *this edn; not in* Q   **165 too?**] *this edn;* too. Q

[3.3]] *Gifford subst.* (SCENE III.); *not in* Q

0 SD and] *Gifford; not in* Q   **2** o'th'tother] *this edn;* o' the t'other *Gifford;* o'th t'other Q

THE CONSTANT MAID   3.4

STARTUP Honest Close, thou hast saved my life.   10

CLOSE [*Starting as if at a noise*] Death, is he not behind you? This way, good sir.

Exeunt.

[3.4]

Enter NURSE *and* FRANCES.

NURSE Ha'you not made a fine choice? I did ever
  Think he was false – your mother did but counterfeit
  The love-sick widow all this while to try him –
FRANCES Try him, nurse?
NURSE   She told me so herself –
  Assuring him the state was hers and you   5
  At her devotion, put him to his choice
  To take her with the wealth or you with nothing.
  What followed you have heard. Come be wise yet
  And love the country gentleman that dotes on you –
  He's rich and half a fool. I'll fetch him to you.   [*Exit.*]   10
FRANCES My mother counterfeit? Why, may not Hartwell
  Pretend as well as she, fearing her anger
  And policy if he refused her love?
  I have observed some sorrow in his gestures
  As he were willing to deliver something   15
  If opportunity would give him leave.

---

 11 **SD1** Close pretends to hear Hartwell coming from behind them.
 11 **Death** i.e. 'Sdeath (*OED*, *int.*, euphemistically shortened from God's death). Close chooses this oath because it reminds Startup that Hartwell is supposedly chasing him with murderous intent.

 0 The scene is set at night in Frances' bedchamber.
 1–3 The nurse's verse is, as so often, metrically approximate.
 1 **fine choice** i.e. in choosing Hartwell as her lover.
 2–3 **your...him** This is the first we hear that this has been a ruse; up until this moment an audience has had little reason not to take Mistress Bellamy's romantic approaches to Hartwell at face value.
 4–6 **She...devotion** This is probably true since we did not observe the nurse eavesdropping on Bellamy and Hartwell's conversation and, though she did overhear the one between Playfair and Hartwell, Hartwell did not tell Playfair that Bellamy said this to him.
 5 **state** estate i.e. money and property.
 6 **devotion** command, disposal (*OED*, *n.* 6a).
 13 **policy** course of action.
 15–16 **willing...leave** would like to say something (to me) if he got a chance.

---

 11 **SD1**] *this edn; not in* Q
 [**3.4**]] *Gifford subst.* (SCENE IV.*); not in* Q
 0 SD FRANCES] Q *subst.* (*Mistresse Frances*)   3 him –] *this edn*; him. Q
 4 nurse?] *this edn*; nurse! *Gifford*; Nurse. Q   4 herself –] *this ed*; herself, *Gifford*; her selfe, Q
 10 SD] *Gifford; not in* Q

3.4   THE COMPLETE WORKS OF JAMES SHIRLEY, VOLUME 7

He cannot be so false. Now I suspect
He does obey some dire necessity:
'Twould puzzle a wise lover to be so
Severely put to't.

> NURSE *brings in* HARTWELL *in Startup's clothes.*

NURSE   On like a bold captain!   20
Give her a broadside – she's within your shot.
I'll leave you.   [*Exit.*]
FRANCES   'Tis the fool! Why, nurse?
HARTWELL   Nay, fly not
Before you hear!
FRANCES [*Aside*] 'Tis Hartwell.
HARTWELL [*Aside*]   If my voice
Betray me not –
FRANCES [*Aside*]   Why in this shape? Some trick in't.
He hides his face. I'll put him to't, however.   25
[*Aloud, as if to Startup*] Although the hour be unseasonable, any time
We may express our joy. My nurse once told me
You were not well and gone to bed; your health

---

18 dire necessity terrible need. Frances means financial difficulties as well as the awkwardness of his potential mother-in-law having declared her love for him.

20 put to't forced to do his utmost, driven to extremities (*OED*, Put *v.* P2b).

20–1 On…shot The military images here (captain, broadside, shot), as well as being typical in early modern descriptions of wooing, carry on from those used by Close at 3.1.76–82.

21 broadside simultaneous discharge of the artillery on one side of a ship of war (*OED*, *n.* 2).

21 within…shot within range.

22–4 'Tis…in't The sharing of the lines and the rapidity implied in this exchange magnify the confusion in the dark of Frances' room.

22 Why, nurse? Both 'why have you brought him' and 'why, really, nurse – this is unacceptable'.

23–4 If…not If she does not recognize my voice. Hartwell may be trying to disguise his voice in order to sound like Startup, but in 'Nay, fly not/Before you hear!' (ll. 22–3) he does not succeed, either because Frances recognizes his voice even disguised or because in his haste to stop her leaving he does it badly. There would have been great comic potential in Hartwell pretending to sound like Startup the country fool.

24 Why…shape Why is he dressed like this?

25 hides his face Hartwell is carrying a dark lantern which makes it hard to see him (see note to l. 48) but he may also be turning his head into the shadow or possibly making comic play with a hat to try to avoid discovery.

25 put…to't challenge him (*OED*, Put *v.* P2a); also, possibly, embarrass him (sense P2b). Frances means she will use this opportunity to tease or test him by pretending she thinks he is Startup.

---

20 captain!] *Gifford;* Captaine, Q   **22 SD**] *Gifford; not in* Q   **22** fool!] *Gifford;* foole, Q
22–3] *lineation this edn;* Nay,…heare. Q   **23** hear!] *this edn;* heare. Q
23 SD1] *Gifford subst.; not in* Q   **23 SD2**] *this edn; not in* Q   **24** not –] *this edn;* not. Q
24 SD] *Gifford subst. (at end of l. 25)*   **26 SD**] *this edn; not in* Q

88

THE CONSTANT MAID 3.4

Is welcome as my own. I dare not, sir,
In modesty presume to bid you stay 30
And to requite your pains. Kind Master Startup –
HARTWELL [*Aside*] She knows me not!
FRANCES   Forgive me if I blush:
I have no other way but to declare
My eyes that late frowned on your love shall smile.
HARTWELL On me?
FRANCES   On none but you. I have been too 35
Unkindly dealt withal by Hartwell, whom
How dearly I affected good heaven knows.
But I have read discretion to my fancy
And, were he here, he should be witness of
My vows to you. If you accept my heart 40
And can with equal truth embrace it, I
Will choose my husband here: you, only you.
This faith, be registered in heaven, shall challenge
From me a wife's obedience.
HARTWELL   Planet-struck!

     Enter NURSE.

NURSE Away, your mother's up! I would not for 45
A thousand pound she find you in this chamber.

38 **read…fancy** taught my amorous inclination sound judgement (See *OED*, Read *v.* 18a for this use which is common in Jonson). Frances means it is more sensible to favour Startup—for financial reasons, but also because Hartwell has 'unkindly dealt' with her (l. 36). She is probably also alluding jokingly to the 'sound judgement' in worldly terms that Hartwell's defection to her mother might show in him.

39 **were…here** pointedly ironic, since he is.

41 **equal truth** More irony, since she is speaking in earnest to Hartwell though pretending that she is committing herself to Startup.

42 **you…you.** i.e. Hartwell, though it seems as though she means Startup.

43–4 **This…obedience** This agreement – heaven witness it – will, when called upon, mean I marry you.

44 **Planet-struck** Stricken or afflicted, as by paralysis or other sudden physical disorder, as a result of the supposed malign influence of a planet (*OED*, *adj.*).

46 **you** i.e. Startup. The nurse does not yet know that it is Hartwell, and her reluctance that Startup be discovered speaks better of her than Close's suspicions (at 3.1.79–82) that trapping Frances into marriage was part of the plan.

32 **SD**] *Gifford subst.; not in* Q   32 not!] *this edn;* not. Q
44 Planet-struck!] *Gifford;* Planet-struck. Q   45 up!] *Gifford;* up; Q

89

4.1   THE COMPLETE WORKS OF JAMES SHIRLEY, VOLUME 7

FRANCES I have undone myself.   *Exit Frances.*

NURSE   Sweet Master Startup,
   To your own lodging! Take that close lantern
   With you! Passion of me, what makes her rise?

HARTWELL I will discover yet.

NURSE   Discover what?   50
   [*Hartwell reveals his face.*] Ha, Master Hartwell!

HARTWELL   You ha' midnight plots.

NURSE Oh, we are wretched, miserable! What have I done?

HARTWELL Oh, who shall lead me to a world where are
   No women? Farewell all: I'll be above
   Your charms and find out death, a cure for love.   *Exeunt [separately].*   55

4[.1]

             Enter STARTUP [*and*] CLOSE.

STARTUP Where are we now? 'Tis very cold – why dost not
   Lead me to some house?

CLOSE   What, at this time a' night?
   All people are abed; the very owls
   Are in their dead sleep. Or, if we could
   Be admitted, would you venture a' this fashion   5

---

   47 I...myself Because she has no time to tell Hartwell that she knew him all along and was just teasing him.
   48 close lantern i.e. a dark lantern, with a sliding panel to dim the light. The stage has apparently been very faintly lit throughout by a dark lantern which explains why no-one can see Hartwell properly.
   51 SD Hartwell probably slides the panel on the dark lantern so that the nurse can see it is him but there might be other ways of managing this.
   51 midnight plots plots which take place at night (but also with overtones of last-minute, and, from the extreme darkness of that hour, secret and nefarious).

   0 The scene is set in the fields in the northern suburbs of London (see Introduction).
   1 Where...now? This is a good point—see discussion in Introduction.
   1 This line, with its focus on the cold, recalls (probably deliberately) *Hamlet* 1.4.1–2.
   3–4 very...sleep It is so late that even the owls—night birds—have gone to sleep.
   4 dead sleep very deep sleep (as in 'sleep like the dead').
   5 a'...fashion i.e. in this fashion, dressed like this (i.e. in his nightgown; see l. 62).

47–9] *lineation this edn;* Sweet...Startup, / To...you.– / Passion *Gifford;* Sweet...lodging, / Take...you: / Passion Q
48 lodging!] *this edn;* lodging, Q   **48** lantern] Q *subst.* (lanthorne)
49 you!] *this edn;* you: Q   **51 SD**] *this edn; not in* Q   **51** Hartwell!] *Gifford;* Hartwell. Q
52 miserable!] *Gifford;* miserable, Q   **55 SD**] *this edn; Exit.* Q
4[.1]]] *Gifford subst.* (ACT IV. SCENE I.*);* ACT. IV. Q   **1** dost] *Gifford;* do'st Q
2 a'] *this edn;* o' *Gifford;* a Q   **5** a'] *this edn;* o' *Gifford;* a Q

90

THE CONSTANT MAID   4.1

And publish your disgrace, proclaim yourself
Coward, and lay some imputation
Upon the place you came from – where your hopes
May yet be fair for marriage, this brunt over?
To meet some drunkard now were comfortable,   10
Whose eyes inflamed might serve for torches,
Or he might spit flap-dragons from his fire
Of sack and light us. But no sober man,
Considering what case you are in, sir,
By my consent should see you.
STARTUP   Ha, what's that?   15
CLOSE Where? Where? A firedrake.
STARTUP   Now, 'tis gone – 'tis bright
Again. Is't not a spirit? Oh, deliver me!
CLOSE I have heard some such things use to walk the fields.
STARTUP What shall I do?
CLOSE   Pray! Pray with as much strength
As if you had no land or were confined   20
To my annuity. Now I fear no spirits:
This riches makes us cowards. Hide yourself;

6–9 publish…marriage Close makes the point that seeking shelter in a nearby house would reveal that
Startup is wandering about the fields half-dressed because: a) he was too cowardly to face Hartwell and b) the
(by implication inadequate) hospitality of Mistress Bellamy allowed this to happen. The latter point is that
exposing Mistress Bellamy to such public shame would scupper Startup's chances of marrying Frances, which
might still be on the cards.

9 this brunt Close means 'this present crisis' (attack or onslaught, *OED*, Brunt *n.* 2).

10–13 To…us Close's fantasy depends on the common biblical trope 'inflamed with wine' (Isaiah 5.11 *inter
alia*), punning on the idea that the light by which they need to navigate might emanate from this inner 'flame'.

12 flap-dragons raisins caught out of burning brandy and eaten to extinguish the flame (from the drinking
game of that name (*OED*, Flap-dragon *n.*)).

14 case meaning both clothes and situation.

16 firedrake light seen hovering or floating at night, esp. over marshy ground, that appears to move away
when approached; a will-o'-the-wisp (*OED*, *n.* 2b).

17 Is't…me! Startup is predictably superstitious about will-o'-the-wisps, thinking that they are spirits
rather than natural physical phenomena. The *OED* quotation from Chapman demonstrates why Startup might
be terrified: 'So haue I seene a fire drake glide at midnight / Before a dying man to point his graue' (*OED*,
Firedrake *n.* 2b quot.).

18 use to are accustomed or wont to. This is an example of the present tense use of this grammatical construction, now rare (*OED*, Use *v.* 21).

19–21 Pray…annuity i.e. pray as if you were desperate.

22 This…cowards Close seems to be saying he is braver, because he is so poor that he has nothing to lose,
unlike Startup whose riches make him fearful of losing them.

---

9 marriage,…over?] *Gifford;* marriage?…over. Q   11 inflamed] *Gifford;* enflamed Q
16 Where? Where?] *this edn;* Where. where? Q   17 me!] *Gifford;* me. Q
19 Pray!] *this edn;* Pray; *Gifford;* Pray, Q
21 annuity.…spirits:] *this edn;* annuity.–Now, I fear no spirits; *Gifford;* annuity: Now I feare no spirits; Q

4.1   THE COMPLETE WORKS OF JAMES SHIRLEY, VOLUME 7

I will go nearer.
STARTUP Dost know the devil if thou see'st him, Close?
A pox on love if this be the reward on't!   25
Some call it fire but I find no such matter.
I am frozen to the blanket and my teeth
Strike one another and keep time like hammers
That beat a psalm upon the virtuous anvil.
I do believe if they were beaten out   30
They would make false dice: there's quicksilver in 'em –
I know already by their dancing.
CLOSE   Sir, where are you?
STARTUP   Here I am still.
CLOSE   You're a dead man.
STARTUP More terror? What's the matter?
CLOSE   'Tis my Master
With a dark lantern that pursues us. By   35
This darkness, 'tis his voice. Wrap yourself up
And roll into some ditch – flight will betray us.
STARTUP I had as good be killed, but yet I'll venture.   *Exit.*

24 Dost...Close? This is the second time someone in the play has been asked this question; Hornet's niece asks him the same thing at 2.3.24, though her implication is that he is friends with the Devil.
26 it i.e. love.
27 to...blanket i.e. to the bone.
27–9 my...anvil i.e. his teeth are audibly chattering. This is a curious layered metaphor which depends on 'virtuous' being paired with 'psalm' and 'hammer' with 'anvil'. In this case the anvil makes virtue rather than being virtuous: 'in figurative contexts, esp. with reference to the use of an anvil as a block on which something is forged or shaped' (*OED*, Anvil *n*. 2a). Metrical psalms have a strong beat which might sound like hammering.
31–2 false...dancing Dice could be weighted to fall one way or another in order to cheat a competitor of his money. *The Compleat Gamester* (1674) detailed at length methods for making such false dice, including 'the old ways...by drilling them and loading them with Quicksilver' (Cotton 1674, 13). This meant that they were unbalanced and when you held them gently between your fingers they 'danced' or pulled towards the weighted side because the liquid mercury kept them moving.
33 where...you? Having returned from going 'nearer' at l. 23, Close cannot find Startup in the dark.
35 dark lantern see note to 3.4.48. Although we might have thought Close was only pretending to see a firedrake and Startup hallucinating in his terror, a light is now visible—which Close pretends to identify as Hartwell in pursuit. The fact that we last saw Hartwell with a darkened lantern is not something that Close knows.
37 roll...ditch The fields to the north of London were criss-crossed with a series of drainage ditches and causeways which allowed travellers to make their ways across previously muddy terrain.
38 I...killed I might as well be killed (see *OED*, Good *adj*. P4b).
38 venture take the risk, make the effort.

25 on love] *this edn;* of love, Q   25 on't!] *Gifford;* on't; Q
31 dice:...'em –] *this edn;* dice; there's quicksilver in them, *Gifford;* Dyce, there's quicksilver in 'em, Q
34–5] *lineation Gifford;* 'Tis...darke / Lanthorne Q   35 lantern] *this edn;* Lanthorne, Q
38 SD *Startup*] *this edn; not in* Q

92

THE CONSTANT MAID   4.1

CLOSE 'Tis he indeed and more than I expected!
    The matters do not fadge well with his mistress.   40

       Enter HARTWELL.

HARTWELL What a sweet thing is night! How calm and harmless!
    No whispering but of leaves, on which the breath
    Of heaven plays music to the birds that slumber.
    Here are no objects to betray our sense
    To repentance, nor can women, thus   45
    Advantaged by the tapers of the night,
    Spread their temptations to undo poor man.
    What a fine book is heaven which we may read
    Best now – when every star is a fair letter.
    How much they wrong thee, Night, which call thee guilty   50
    Of rapes and murders! 'Tis the day that, like
    A glorious whore, engages men to act 'em
    And, taking then the darkness to obscure 'em,

---

39 'Tis…expected! i.e. It *is* Hartwell, which I was not expecting. (Close admits he pretended to Startup that he had spotted Hartwell pursuing them and is actually surprised to see him.)

40 fadge succeed, thrive.

41–58 What…home Hartwell's long speech is typical in its representation of the ambiguous feelings that early modern people had about night. On the one hand it was threatening and potentially violent; on the other Shirley was not alone in speaking of it as a time of calm (see Koslofsky 2011, 5, 6, 9, and *passim*). This whole scene is a deliberate dramatization of the various facets of 'night', from Hartwell's set speech, following hard on the heels of Close and Startup getting lost in the dark, to the appearance of the more-or-less comic Watch, a force which only operated during hours of darkness and for which there was no day-time equivalent (Koslofsky 2011, 9).

44–5 Here…repentance Shirley's characteristically concise syntax occludes the meaning, which must be something along the lines of 'There is nothing visible here to tempt our senses (or good sense) into doing something which will make us repent'.

46 Advantaged…night i.e. The half-light given by candles makes women look better or hides their wiles.

48–9 It had long been customary in both biblical and classical tradition to read *liber naturae* (the Book of Nature) in order to contemplate and try to understand the works of God. Hartwell's speech suggests that the stars resemble letters which give clarity to the message, and divination from the stars was as ancient as man.

50 Night *Nyx*, in Greek mythology, personification of Night, called in Latin *Nox*. She was mother to unsavoury children, including *Keres* (Destruction, Death), *Thanatos* (Death), *Momus* (Blame), *Oizys* (Pain, Distress), *Eris* (Strife), *Nemesis* (Retribution), and the *Moirai* (Fates). However, in keeping with the ambivalence noted at ll. 41–58, she also gave birth to *Hypnos* (Sleep), *Oneiroi* (Dreams), *Philotes* (Friendship), and the *Hesperides* (the guardians of the golden apples).

51–4 'Tis…brows Hartwell argues that men conceive and plan their crimes during the day and then choose to enact them at night to avoid detection, which makes us mistakenly blame Night for the crimes.

51–2 like…'em By being beautiful, a 'glorious whore' compels men to 'act' in the same way as the light of day tempts them to crimes. There may be a suggestion that the actual 'act' takes place, like the crimes, under cover of darkness.

52 'em The antecedents are 'rapes and murders' (l. 51), as well as 'whore' (l. 52).

---

39 expected!] *this edn;* expected: Q   **41** night!…harmless!] *Gifford;* night?…harmlesse? Q
48 heaven] *this edn;* heaven! *Gifford;* heaven? Q   **50** Night] *Gifford;* night Q
51 murders!] *Gifford;* murders: Q

4.1 THE COMPLETE WORKS OF JAMES SHIRLEY, VOLUME 7

We unjustly lay the shame upon thy brows,
That art so innocent: thou never saw'st them 55
Befriended with this silence. I begin
To wander – there's no wilderness abroad
To him that's lost at home.

CLOSE   Sir!

HARTWELL   Who's that?

CLOSE One that has taken pains for you tonight.
I am Close.

HARTWELL   What mak'st thou here?

CLOSE   I wait upon 60
My charge: I led your rival a procession
In's shirt, persuading him you had resolved
To cut his throat else. He's hard by at's prayers
And thinks you ha' pursued him.

HARTWELL   Ha, I'll do't!
Show me the fool – by all my hopes I'll kill him 65
And send his base heart as a present to her.
Fate has preserved me with this revenge
And I will not delay his death a minute.

CLOSE You wo'not kill him basely?

HARTWELL   No.

CLOSE   Why then
There is no fear, but he'll live long enough. 70
I'll undertake he ne'er shall go provided
To fight wi'ye, and for other satisfaction,
Name it and take it. So, I'll fetch him to ye.

55–6 That…silence i.e. That Night is so innocent that she does not afford the criminals the friendly silence under which to hide their crimes; or that she does not notice their crimes. Q's punctuation favours the former reading. 'Saws't them befriended' means 'ensured that they were befriended' (*OED*, See *v.* 20b).

60–1 I…charge Close could mean either 'I'm looking after Startup' or 'I'm waiting for instructions from you'.

64 do't i.e. cut Startup's throat, as Close suggests at l. 63.

67 Fate…revenge Fate giving me this opportunity to revenge has saved my life.

69 basely unfairly or by stealth, by not respecting the rules of combat.

69–72 Why…wi'ye In that case I am convinced that he'll survive for a good while yet. I am sure that he'll never accept your challenge, i.e. because Hartwell will respect the rules of combat Startup will not meet an untimely end. At the moment, in his nightshirt, Startup is certainly not 'provided' (wearing a sword) and Close's judgement is that he'll never don said sword in order to fight Hartwell.

72 other satisfaction Satisfaction is a word strongly associated with duelling (*OED*, Satisfaction *n.* 4), so some sort of humiliation of Startup will be necessary in place of the duel, such as a good beating, which his pusillanimous nature will force him to accept.

---

58 Sir!] *Gifford;* Sir. Q   **64** do't!] *this edn;* do't. *Gifford;* do't; Q
65 fool –] *this edn;* fool; *Gifford;* foole, Q

94

THE CONSTANT MAID   4.1

HARTWELL Stay! I have been too passionate: let him live
    To be her punishment – that's revenge enough,   75
    While I pursue my own ways.
CLOSE   Whither now?
HARTWELL Whither thou must not follow. By thy honesty,
    I charge thee come not after me.
CLOSE   That binds
    My attendance, sir.
HARTWELL   But not when I command
    The contrary. If thou dost move this way   80
    Thou draw'st my anger. Mind the preservation
    Of the tame thing you undertook. Farewell!
    If thou dost love me, follow not, nor question
    'Tis in my power to lose thee or myself.   *Exit.*
CLOSE I cannot see i'th'dark with spectacles   85
    And mine own eyes ha' lost him o'th'sudden.
    Well, I must hope the best. What shall I do
    With my hen-hearted lover, that would give
    Half his estate his cold fit were well over?
    I shall make work for the physicians: 90
    Caudles and cullises will ne'er restore him.

75 **punishment** For any sensible woman, being married to someone as stupid and crass as Startup is bound
to be a punishment, one Hartwell thinks Frances deserves for her perfidy. His focus seems much more on
revenging himself on her than on Startup, who is beneath contempt.

77 **Whither…follow** Hartwell the disappointed lover rejects the services of his faithful retainer, with the
melodramatic implication that he is off to do something desperate.

78–9 **I…attendance** Close correctly realizes that the proper reaction to such melodramatic orders to leave
is to stay, because it is part of true service to work in the interests of your master even against his commands.

82 **tame thing** Startup, in comparison to Hartwell's new-found disappointed-love wildness. Hartwell
comments upon Startup's lack of courage and poor-spiritedness (*OED*, Tame *adj.* 4 and 5).

83–4 **nor…myself** Because Hartwell has a lantern he can lose Close by disappearing into the night; he can
also dispense with Close's services. He can lose himself both by wandering away over the fields (*OED*, Lose *v.*
10a) and by taking his own life (*OED*, Lose *v.* 2a), which is what Close fears.

85 **I…spectacles** Close means he cannot see in the dark *even* with spectacles.

88 **hen-hearted** timorous or cowardly (i.e. Startup).

91 **caudles** warm drinks consisting of thin gruel, mixed with wine or ale, sweetened and spiced, given chiefly
to sick people (*OED*, Caudle *n.*).

91 **cullises** strong broths, made of meat, fowl, *etc.*, boiled and strained; used especially as a nourishing food
for sick persons (*OED*, Cullis *n.* 1a). This may be a pun too, since by *c.* 1627 the word had acquired the transferred and figurative use 'a sound beating' (*OED*, 1b), which harks back to a possible 'other satisfaction' for
Hartwell's anger at l. 72 and is presumably what Close would most like to do to Startup.

74 Stay!…passionate:] *this edn;* Stay;…passionate; *Gifford;* Stay,…passionate, Q
78–9] *lineation Gifford;* That…sir Q   82 Farewell!] *this edn;* Farewell; *Gifford;* Farewell, Q
84 lose] *Gifford;* loose Q   86 o'th'] *this edn;* o'the Q   89 over?] *Gifford;* over: Q

95

4.1 THE COMPLETE WORKS OF JAMES SHIRLEY, VOLUME 7

If he but 'scape with life I am not sorry:
He may be a soldier and endure the trenches –
I put him first to the becoming sufferance.
But what are these? An army of horns and halberds?   95
Upon my conscience: the watch. I thought
The fields had not been haunted with these goblins.
I cannot run; if I should squat and they find me
There were no mercy but Bridewell
Or some such lovely place. I am resolved   100
To cast away a few good words upon 'em:
A leg, and worshipping the constable

---

93 trenches punning on the ditch in which Startup is hiding and the military sense.

94 I...sufferance Close views Startup as a raw army recruit to whom Close delivers the initial training test which he may pass with a patient endurance befitting his manhood i.e. it may be the making of him.

95 But...these? Close either hears or sees people approaching. It is hard to know if the implied SD is aural or visual. Certainly by the end of the line, he can see them enough to discern their accoutrements.

95 horns synecdoche for lanterns, which in the early modern period often used thin horn as 'glass' to cover the flame. 'The form *lanthorn* is probably due to popular etymology, lanterns having formerly been almost always made of horn' (*OED*, Lantern *n.* etymology). Glass was expensive and easily broken. Horn was very tough and long lasting, and while yellow and not clear like glass, it allowed enough light through by which to see.

95 halberds weapons 'consisting of a spear and battleaxe combined...and having a spearhead or spike above an axe blade with a hooked back, on a pole typically around 1.8 metres long' (*OED*, *n.* 1) By the seventeenth century they had become more ceremonial than fighting weapons. The frontispiece to Thomas Dekker's *The Belman of London* (1608) depicts a watchman bearing a halberd, a lantern, and a bell.

96 the watch 'those who watch, for purposes of guarding and protecting life and property, and the like;...[a] body of watchmen, who patrolled and guarded the streets of a town, proclaimed the hour, *etc.*' (*OED*, Watch *n.* 11). See *Much Ado* (esp. 3.3) for the most famous dramatization of them as comic characters.

97 these goblins Close calls them this figuratively—in the sense that they are likely to try to cause him harm—and because it was possibly their lights that he and Startup saw earlier, attributed then to will-o'-the-wisps, themselves goblin-like in that they are imaginary beings which frighten the gullible (*OED*, Goblin *n.*).

98–9 if...mercy Close risks being taken up for vagrancy or some other crime if he hides and is caught, so he is hoping to brazen it out (ll. 100–5). Koslofsky mentions as specific night crimes 'walking without a light, keeping a public house open too late, disturbing the peace, lantern-smashing, dueling (at dusk or dawn), and grave-robbing' (2011, 9).

98 squat hide by crouching, referring specifically to hares: 'to sit close to the ground in a crouching attitude; to crouch or cower down, esp. in order to avoid observation or capture' (*OED*, Squat *v.* 5a).

99 Bridewell Prison for 'idle persons and women of ill repute located on the west side of the Fleet ditch near where it discharged into the Thames' (Chalfant 1978, 47). It may be the threat of being taken up for vagrancy which suggests Bridewell to Close: John Taylor the Water Poet says that Bridewell houses 'Vagabonds and Runnagates...Whores, and idle knaues' (Taylor 1630, sig. Mm2r), and in *Every Man In* (1616) Cob thinks he is 'a vagabond, and fitter for Bridewell' (Jonson 2014, 3.6.35).

100 lovely sarcastic.

100–4 I...often Close decides that the most likely way of getting out of being arrested is to speak politely to the watch, bow, and be excessively respectful to the constable, a strategy which has proved effective for him in the past.

102 leg gesture of deferential respect, esp. a bow or curtsy (*OED*, Leg *n.* 4).

102 worshipping calling someone 'your worship' (as Close does at l. 107), but also habitually treating with honour or respect (as in *OED*, Worship *v.* 2a).

92–4 life...sufferance.] *this edn*; life, I am not sorry, / He may be a souldier, and indure the trenches; / I put him first to the becomming sufferance: Q

96

THE CONSTANT MAID   4.1

That leads the rusty regiment will quit me –
I pass the gates wi't often and so may
The devil if he pay the porter.

> *Enter* CONSTABLE *and* WATCHMEN.

                       Bless you,   105
My masters! What o'clock is't?
FIRST WATCH   Who's there?
CONSTABLE I charge you, stand!
CLOSE   Your worship may do much.
CONSTABLE Where have you been?
CLOSE At Islington, an't please you, about business.
CONSTABLE Some thief, I warrant him; no honest man.   110
I know by his basket hilt – some rogue that watches.
The fields are pestered with such sturdy robbers.
CLOSE He is a rogue that watches, for my part.
CONSTABLE He calls my watchmen rogues.
FIRST WATCH   How, Master Constable?

---

103 rusty regiment the watch. Such men were volunteers and resembled (according to Graham–Dixon 2019) the Home Guard in WW2, often not fit for active military service.

104 wi't i.e. with such politeness.

104–5 so...porter This recalls 2.3 of *Macbeth* and draws on the same theatrical tradition, the knocking of Christ on the doors of Hell in the 'Harrowing of Hell' pageants of the mystery cycles (see, *inter alia*, Schreyer 2010). Close, though, misremembers who is doing the knocking and imagines the Devil paying to get through the gates—presumably not those of Hell. The consistent connection between the Devil and money continues from Hornet's association with him earlier in the play.

107 stand stand still, i.e. stop

107 may...much has a lot of authority; i.e. I'll do what you tell me (reminiscent of Olivia saying 'You might do much' to Viola in *Twelfth Night* 1.5.258).

108–9 See note to 4.1.1. 'In the early seventeenth century "Islington" usually denoted the small settlement half a mile beyond Moorfields...[and] was the most popular of London's recreational locales' (Chalfant 1978, 107). It may be, therefore, that the idea of being at 'business' in Islington is oxymoronic and this makes the Constable more suspicious of Close's story, prompting especially his notion that Close's 'business' may be as a thief.

109 an't if it

111 basket hilt woven-style metal hand guard indicative of an out-dated civilian sword.

111 rogue...watches i.e. someone up to no good who is either set as the look-out for a crime or lying in wait to perpetrate one.

113 rogue...watches Though he thought he would avoid it by seeming to agree with the Constable, Close gets caught playing with words to suggest the watch are rogues. His need to make this joke does away with his plan of 'cast[ing] away a few good words' (l. 101) in order to 'quit' himself (l. 103).

---

104 wi't] *Gifford subst. (*with it*); wo't Q   **105 SD**] *this edn; after 'you:'* Q

105–6 you,...masters!] *Gifford;* you:...masters Q

106–8 *lineation this edn*; theere? / I...stand. / Your...much. / Where...beene? Q

106 o'clock] *Gifford;* a clocke Q

106 SH] *this edn;* 1. Q; *1. and* 2. *are normalized as* FIRST *and* SECOND WATCH *throughout this scene*

107 stand!] *Gifford;* stand. Q   **109** an't] *Gifford;* and Q

97

4.1   THE COMPLETE WORKS OF JAMES SHIRLEY, VOLUME 7

You are one yourself.

CONSTABLE   Away with him!   115

CLOSE Good sir!

SECOND WATCH   We will provide you a lodging.

CLOSE Where?

CONSTABLE   New Prison.

CLOSE   But are you in earnest,
Gentlemen? If there be no remedy.

SECOND WATCH We'll humble you.

CLOSE   I have a companion
Hereabouts. [*Calling*] Where are you, sir?

STARTUP   Here – in the ditch.   120

CONSTABLE They seldom go alone. We'll find him out.   [*Exeunt Watchmen.*]

     [*Re-*]enter WATCHMEN *and* STARTUP.

Ha, sirrah!

STARTUP I thank you, honest men. Where art thou, Close?

CLOSE Here. These good men will help us to a lodging.

STARTUP Blessing on their hearts! I am almost starved.   125

---

115 **You...yourself** The First Watch points out to the Constable that he himself is a watchman and therefore Close is also calling him a rogue. It may be this insult which prompts the Constable's summary 'Away with
him' in the next line.

117 **New Prison** One of the four minor prisons, it was situated in Clerkenwell and was used to house prisoners awaiting examination of trial (see Taylor 1630, sig. Mm2r and Drouillard 2018).

118 **If...remedy** i.e. If there is nothing I can do about it (I will come with you). Close gives in rather easily
here, making one suspect that he has now changed his plan to trying to get them taken to prison for the night
where at least it might be warm and dry. With Hartwell's pursuit of Frances now off, Close has no reason for
keeping Startup out of the Bellamy house.

119 **humble you** i.e. bring you low, chastise you.

120 **in...ditch** In keeping with their supposed location in the fields of north London, Startup has hidden
himself in a ditch as instructed by Close at l. 37 (see note to l. 1). This can provide comic stage business as the
members of the watch search for him off-stage.

121 **They** i.e. The 'sturdy robbers' of l. 112.

122 **sirrah** 'term of address used to men or boys, expressing contempt, reprimand, or assumption of authority
on the part of the speaker' (*OED*). The Constable asserts his authority over Startup.

123 **honest** Startup probably means 'honourable' (*OED*, Honest *adj.* 2a) but there is a patronizing overtone
(cf. sense 2b).

124 **These...lodging** Close encourages Startup's delusion that he is not in the hands of the Law.

125 **almost starved** nearly dead. 'To starve' (*OED, v.* 1) means to cause to die, but can be used specifically
to mean 'to die of cold', or hyperbolically 'to be extremely cold' (sense 2c).

114–15] *lineation Gifford; How...selfe.* Q   115 him!] *Gifford;* him. Q   116 sir!] *this edn;* Sir. Q
117–18] *lineation this edn;* But...Gentlemen? / If Q   119–20] *lineation this edn;* I...Sir? Q
120 SD] *this edn; – Gifford; not in* Q   120 Here –] *this edn;* Here! *Gifford;* Here Q
121–2] *lineation this edn;* alone. / We'll...sirra. Q
121–2 out....sirrah!] *Gifford subst. (*out.– Hah, sirrah!*); out; ha sirra. Q
121 SD1] *this edn; after l. 120 Gifford; not in* Q   121 SD2 Re-enter] *Gifford subst.; Enter* Q
125 hearts!] *Gifford;* hearts, Q

THE CONSTANT MAID   4.2

CONSTABLE Yes, we'll do you that favour. Come away, sir!

STARTUP Whither shall we go now?

CLOSE   To prison.

STARTUP   How, Close?

FIRST WATCH You shall be close enough.

STARTUP D'ye hear, sweet gentleman?

CLOSE   I follow, sir!
    I cannot leave you in adversity.   130
    All this is for your health: clean straw is warm, sir.
    You have the benefit of being naked;
    I shall have work tomorrow in the woollen.

CONSTABLE Away, away; bring them away.   *Exeunt.*

[4.2]

    [*Enter*] MISTRESS BELLAMY *and* NURSE.

BELLAMY I heard some noise. Look! Call up the servants!
    See if the gentlemen be abed!   [*Exit Nurse.*]
    I'm troubled.

    [*Re-enter* NURSE.]

---

127 How, Close? How come (i.e. why), Close? but understood by the Second Watch as How close?

128 close enough i.e. in tight prison quarters.

129 gentleman Q has 'gentlemen'. but 'I follow, sir!' seems to be a response to Startup calling out (still in the dark) for Close.

132–3 benefit...woollen Close, as usual, tries to persuade Startup of something counterintuitive, in this case that his lacking his clothes is a good thing because Close will be picking the prison straw out of his clothes tomorrow whereas Startup will not have that problem.

0 The scene is set in Mistress Bellamy's house.

1 noise This explains why she has woken and called the nurse. It may be that the scene is supposed to take place immediately after 3.4 and the noise she has heard is Hartwell leaving the house. In this case, the scene takes place simultaneously with 4.1 but in a different location.

1 servants The invisible but oft-mentioned manservants who must help run Mistress Bellamy's establishment (see also 4.2.46).

2–3 See...troubled Mistress Bellamy seems to be starting to worry that her plan to test Hartwell has backfired.

---

126 sir!] *this edn;* sir. Q   **127** Whither] *Gifford;* Whether Q

127 How, Close?] Q *subst.;* How, Close! *Gifford*   **129** gentleman] *this edn;* Gentlemen Q

129 sir!] *this edn;* sir; *Gifford;* Sir, Q   **129–30** *lineation Gifford;* I...adversity; Q

131 health:...sir.] *this edn;* health;...sir. *Gifford;* health,...sir; Q

[4.2]] *Gifford subst. (*SCENE II.*); not in* Q

0 SD *Enter*] *Gifford; not in* Q

1 Look!] *this edn;* looke, Q   **1** servants!] *this edn;* servants. *Gifford;* servants, Q

2–3] *lineation this edn;* See...troubled. Q   **2** abed!] *this edn;* abed. *Gifford;* a bed; Q

2 SD] *Gifford subst.; not in* Q   **3 SD**] *Gifford subst. (*Re-enter Nurse, *with Hartwell's clothes.); not in* Q

4.2   THE COMPLETE WORKS OF JAMES SHIRLEY, VOLUME 7

NURSE   Oh, mistress!
BELLAMY   What's the matter?
NURSE Master Startup is not abed, and here [*Showing Hartwell's clothes*]
    Is all is left of Master Hartwell.   5
BELLAMY This is very strange.
NURSE [*Aside*] I dare not tell her of his shift. [*Aloud*] They're gone:
    The doors I found left open and no sign
    Which way they are bestowed.
BELLAMY   This puzzles me.
    Pray heaven there be no mischief in this absence.   10
    Is Frank abed?
NURSE   Yes.
BELLAMY   What should move 'em
    To leave my house so late and Master Hartwell
    Without his clothes? Some knock there!   [*Exit Nurse.*]
    Beshrew me but I trembled!

    [*Re-enter* NURSE.]

NURSE   'Tis a stranger
    And says he would speak with you.
BELLAMY   At this late hour?   15
    What accidents are these? From whence?
NURSE   I know not.

---

6 Hartwell and Close's anti-Startup machinations create a mystery for Mistress Bellamy because it seems very strange that Startup, whose suit was in favour as they retired for the night, would have fled the house and even stranger that Hartwell appears to have left without his clothes on.

7 I...shift The nurse cannot tell Mistress Bellamy that Hartwell has changed into Startup's clothes because then she will have to confess that she had plotted to conduct Startup into Frances' bed chamber. 'Shift' in this context may mean either Hartwell's change of clothes, or his scheme in general.

8 left open probably not wide open but certainly without the internal locking bar in place which could only be operated from the inside.

9 bestowed located (*OED*, Bestow *v.* 1) or lodged/quartered (sense 3).

10 mischief ill fortune or trouble (according to *OED* literally 'ill' (mis) 'end' (chief)).

11 Frank (spelled Franck in Q), i.e. Frances. Mistress Bellamy is checking that she has not eloped with either suitor.

14 Beshrew...trembled Plague on it but I got a shock (i.e. the knock made her jump out of her skin).

16 accidents happenings, perhaps here with a sense of being unforeseen (*OED*, Accident *n.* 5).

16 From whence? From what place?

---

3 mistress!] *Gifford;* Mistris? Q
4–5] *lineation this edn;* Mᵣ.... left / Of Q   4 SD] *this edn; not in* Q
7 SD1] *Gifford subst. (after 'shift.'); not in* Q   7 SD2] *this edn;* – *Gifford; not in* Q
13 there!] *this edn;* there: Q   13 SD] *this edn; Nurse goes to the door, and returns. Gifford; not in* Q
14 trembled!] *this edn;* trembled. Q   14 SD] *this edn; not in* Q

THE CONSTANT MAID 4.2

BELLAMY Has he no name? What should this mean?
NURSE   He says
    He is a countryman of Master Startup's.
BELLAMY Admit him: he perhaps does bring some news.

        Enter COUNTRYMAN.

COUNTRYMAN By your leave, mistress. Pardon my importunity   20
    At so unfit an hour.
BELLAMY   You're welcome, sir.
COUNTRYMAN I met with fortunate directions,
    Though I came late. I understand you have
    A guest, one Startup of Northamptonshire,
    That comes a-wooing to your daughter.   25
BELLAMY Such an one there was that supped with us and went
    To bed. But since, as I have faith, I know not
    Which way he has conveyed himself. Another
    Gentleman too is missing – and his rival.
COUNTRYMAN Pray do not mock me, lady, I ha' rid   30
    A great way, and the business much concerns him.
BELLAMY You may believe me he is no such treasure
    I should conceal him.

        Enter FRANCES.

COUNTRYMAN   Then I see you dally

---

18 countryman This has a double sense of 'from the same part of the country' as Startup, and of being a rural type, possibly even a 'dependent upon' him.

20–1 Pardon...hour Forgive me for being a nuisance so late at night.

21 welcome Mistress Bellamy's response recalls the importance of good hospitality alluded to at 1.1.3 and 1.2.78.

22–3 I...late I was lucky enough to meet someone who gave me good directions despite it being night-time.

24 Northamptonshire The significance of Startup being from Northamptonshire seems to be that it was known to be a particularly wealthy county, in Camden's words 'The soile very fertile both for tillage and for pasture...in every place, as else where also in England, it is ouer-spread and as it were beset with sheepe' (Camden 1610, 505). This idea is reiterated in *The Northamptonshire Lover* (1625)—a ballad sung (perhaps not coincidentally) to the same tune that Startup sings at 2.2.30. In this ballad Northamptonshire is 'that country rich and faire' and the lover owns, besides 'Three hundred goodly Akers', 'full three thousand sheepe' (Anon. 1625, Part 1).

28 conveyed himself stolen or slipped away.

29 and...rival who is also his rival (i.e. Hartwell).

30 do...me Mistress Bellamy's story is so outlandish that the Countryman thinks she is teasing him.

31 the...him my business is very much about him. 'Business' has two syllables here.

32–3 You...him Mistress Bellamy admits jokingly and ruefully (and for the first time) that Startup would not be worth concealing in order to keep hold of him.

33 dally delay (with a sense of trifling or mocking engendered by Mistress Bellamy's joke in the previous line (*OED*, v. 4 & 5)).

17–18] *lineation Gifford;* He sayes *... Startups.* Q

4.2   THE COMPLETE WORKS OF JAMES SHIRLEY, VOLUME 7

Know, mistress, you may slack your preparations.
Your daughter must look out another husband –   35
He is contracted.
BELLAMY   How?
COUNTRYMAN   And something more –
Gotten with child one that, without blushing,
I cannot call my daughter. He shall make
Her credit straight again; although my fortunes
Have no equality with his, I shall   40
Find law to force him.
FRANCES [*To Bellamy*]   You preferred this suitor?
[*Aside*] This news returns my blood.
BELLAMY   Sir, you shall find
All truth I have delivered. I am not sorry
To hear this news. This is no time to seek him:
Please you accept the lodging that was his;   45
My servant shall attend you in the morning
To help your search.
COUNTRYMAN   You seem a noble
Gentlewoman; I take your courtesy.
BELLAMY Nurse, a light! Pray walk, sir.   *Exeunt Countryman* [*and Nurse*].

34 **slack...preparations** i.e. for the wedding of Startup and Frances.
36 **contracted** betrothed, affianced (*OED*, Contracted *adj.* †2).
37–8 **one...daughter** i.e. he is embarrassed to call her his daughter because she has got pregnant out of wedlock.
38–9 **make...again** make a decent woman of her by marrying her. Hair (1970) presents evidence that in seventeenth-century England as many as one fifth of brides were pregnant on marriage, so marriage after the fact was common and also, according to Hair (1966, 239), not shameful. There was a small risk of being summoned by a Church Court and made to do penance, but Hair (1970, 68) argues that this was a relatively small price to pay in comparison to bearing a child out of wedlock. To all intents and purposes Startup marrying the Countryman's daughter will right the wrong he has done her.
38–41 **He...him** The punctuation of Q is a comma after again (l. 39) and another after his (l. 40), allowing 'although my fortunes / Have no equality with his' to pertain to the clauses either side of it. It is not possible to do this with modernized punctuation, but there are two implications here: even though the daughter is not a financial catch, Startup will have to marry her; even though he has not got as much monetary clout as Startup, the Countryman has the Law on his side.
42 **returns...blood** restores my life-blood and/or courage (*OED*, Blood *n.* 4 and 12). The prospect of escaping marriage to Startup cheers Frances up immensely.
43 **All...delivered** i.e. I have spoken nothing but truth.
46 **servant** one of Mistress Bellamy's invisible servants (see also 4.2.1).
48 **courtesy** i.e. putting him up for the night and helping him search in the morning.

---

41 **SD**] *this edn; not in* Q   41 suitor?] *this edn;* suitor! *Gifford;* sutor, Q
42 **SD**] *this edn; not in* Q   47–8] *lineation this edn;* You...Gentlewoman, / I Q
49 light!] *this edn;* light.– *Gifford;* light; Q
49 **SD**] *this edn; Exeunt Coun. and Nurse. after* 'nothing.' *l. 51 Gifford;* Exit Countrey-man. *after* 'nothing.' *l. 51* Q

102

THE CONSTANT MAID   4.2

FRANCES [*Aside*] I was unkind to Hartwell; he not wise.   50
    But love still apprehends too much – or nothing.
BELLAMY Frances, a word. Do not you know what is
    Become o' these gentlemen.
FRANCES   Not I. Their absence
    Is strange to me.
BELLAMY   Oh, Frank, I am undone!
FRANCES Good heaven forbid!
BELLAMY   This gentleman, Master Hartwell,   55
    Whom we shall never see again, I fear –
FRANCES How, mother? Are you acquainted with any
    Cause to fear thus?
BELLAMY   'Tis in vain to tell thee
    How I loved him –
FRANCES   Bless my senses! You love him?
BELLAMY 'Bove all the world, affectionately placed him   60
    Too near my heart.
FRANCES   I heard you made pretence
    Of love to try him for my sake, and
    Pardon me if yet I dare not believe more.
BELLAMY Oh, Frank –
FRANCES [*Aside*]   My heart doth thrill – I feel a
    Coldness run through all my veins already.   65
BELLAMY I had no other thought

---

50 Frances very sensibly recognizes that there has been fault on both sides: she was ungenerous, and Hartwell was silly.

51 A lover always fears/understands everything, or nothing. Frances probably means 'apprehend' in the sense of 'fear' but might mean 'understand'; the point is that lovers tend to extremes.

54 undone brought to ruin.

57 How i.e. How come, why?

61–2 I...sake see 3.4.1–8.

64 thrill affect or move with a sudden wave of emotion, but not necessarily, as is common now, one of joy (*OED*, Thrill *v*. 5). Frances is horrified.

64–5 I...veins her blood is freezing with horror, a deliberate comparison to l. 42.

66 This is metrically the second half of Bellamy's 'Oh, Frank –' (l. 64).

66–77 I...lover Shirley likes manipulating the audience by allowing the frisson of possibility throughout that Mistress Bellamy is serious in her intentions towards Hartwell.

---

50 SD] *this edn; not in* Q   **51** much –] *this edn;* much, Q   **54** undone!] *Gifford;* undone. Q
55 forbid!] *Gifford;* forbid. Q   **56** fear –] *Gifford;* feare. Q
57–9] *lineation this edn;* acquainted / With...thus. / 'Tis...vaine / To...him. Q
58 thus?] *Gifford;* thus. Q   **59** him –] *this edn;* him. Q
62–5] *lineation this edn;* Of...me, / If...more. / Oh Franck– / My...run / Through Q
64 SD] *this edn; not in* Q   **64** thrill –] *this edn;* thrill, Q

4.2 THE COMPLETE WORKS OF JAMES SHIRLEY, VOLUME 7

At first but wisely to distinguish whether
His heart was fixed on thee or my estate,
With resolution if I found him more
A courtier of thy fortune than thy person   70
To punish him with loss of both. But Love
Hath changed both scene and title in our comedy
And what I meant should shipwreck all his hopes
Hath ruined us. His modest and calm answer
To accept my tender with such force and reason   75
Directed to my fancy, turned my purpose
And made me his indeed, his perfect lover.
But now we ha' both lost him.
FRANCES [*Aside*]   All the piety
That ever taught children to love their mother
Will but suffice to keep my heart obedient.   80
Was ever maid so miserable? Was there
No other in my fate to rival me?
I live too long! Oh, break, break my poor heart
For she that gave me life, hath took it from me.
BELLAMY Why do you weep?
FRANCES   I do not weep; or if   85
I do, I know not why.
BELLAMY   Now I perceive
Thy duty was but counterfeit: you love him!
Upon my life, you love him still! Have my
Commands no more respect? My care and love

74–6 **His…fancy** i.e. In accepting what I offered, his modest and calm response was both cordial and respectful to my wishes.

77 **perfect lover** someone who loves him totally.

80 **Will…suffice** Will only just be enough.

81–2 **Was…me?** i.e. no-one has suffered the same fate so piteously as I do.

85 **Why…weep?** Mistress Bellamy's question reinforces the supposition that Frances' last speech should be delivered as an aside. Shirley uses Frances' asides very effectively in this scene to stage her conflict between love and duty.

87–8 **Thy…still** In fact, we have not witnessed Frances agreeing to love Startup rather than Hartwell. At 1.2.174–5, Mistress Bellamy optimistically instructed her daughter that when she had 'considered well' she would be able to promise to stop loving Hartwell but this was clearly as unrealistic in the early modern period as it would be now.

69 resolution] *this edn;* resolution, Q   78 SD] *this edn; not in* Q
83 long!] *this edn;* long. *Gifford;* long; Q   87 him!] *this edn;* him, Q
88 still!] *this edn;* still. *Gifford;* still; Q

104

THE CONSTANT MAID   4.2

So ill-rewarded that my heart desiring   90
One comfort in the world and shall my child
Rise up to take it from me?
FRANCES   Alas I knew not
You loved him too; indeed I had rather die
Than you should call me rebel.
BELLAMY   Now I see
The cause of his departure in this fashion!   95
Pray heaven he have not made away himself.
Did ever child deceive a mother so?
I have a sad presage. You may to bed
And rise without my blessing; yet
You may stay. Wherefore should I despair   100
Of his return? You say you could not tell
That I affected him.
FRANCES   Indeed not I
And do believe it now against my will.
But I am your daughter –
BELLAMY   Show it in conforming
Yourself to my desires, and what is past   105
I can forgive you. If he come again,
Will you be ruled and show no favour to him?
For 'tis in you, I see, to make me happy.
I will not tie you to affect the other –
Choose any for your husband but this man,   110

91 **One...world** i.e. Marrying Hartwell.
91–2 **shall...me?** The audience must perceive that this is grossly unfair because the opposite has happened—Mistress Bellamy has taken Hartwell away from Frances.
95 **in...fashion** i.e. secretly at night.
96 **made...himself** killed himself, presumably because he is desperate at being torn between the two women.
98 **sad presage** foreboding of seriousness or sadness.
98–9 **You...blessing** A sign that Mistress Bellamy is very cross with her daughter is that she dismisses her to bed, and will refuse the next morning to give her the customary parental blessing.
99–100 **yet...stay** Frances may make to leave at this point, but this contradictory command demonstrates the supposedly disordered state of Mistress Bellamy's mind.
100–1 **Wherefore...return?** Mistress Bellamy apparently realizes that if her 'sad presage' is not fulfilled she will need a promise from her daughter about the future.
104 **conforming** Bellamy means 'showing compliance' in modern terms, though Q has 'confirming'. *OED* notes that there was considerable confusion between conform and confirm (Conform, *v.* etymology).
107 **be ruled** 'submit to counsel, guidance, or authority; ... listen to reason' (*OED*, Rule *v.* 1b).
109 i.e. I won't insist that you love Startup.

95 fashion!] *this edn;* fashion. *Gifford;* fashion, Q   104 daughter –] *this edn;* daughter. Q
104 conforming] *Gifford;* confirming Q

4.2 THE COMPLETE WORKS OF JAMES SHIRLEY, VOLUME 7

My love and prayers shall go along with you.
Answer!
FRANCES   Indeed I dare not, yet could I
    Put off the knowledge that you are a mother –
BELLAMY What then?
FRANCES Though in imagination I allow you   115
    The greatest woman in the earth whose frown
    Could kill and eyes at pleasure make alive
    Again, I could say –
BELLAMY   Pray, let's hear!
FRANCES   I durst tell you,
    In confidence of my cause, that you betray
    Two innocents to sorrow and – though heaven   120
    Look on and seem to smile upon your cruelty –
    Yet there is punishment for divorcing those
    Whose hearts that hath conjoined. I durst tell you –
    Though all your terrors were prepared to punish
    My bold defence – you were a tyrant.
BELLAMY   How?   125
FRANCES A most unjust, a sacrilegious tyrant.
BELLAMY You would not be so violent.
FRANCES   That thus,
    Not only ruin and deface the altar
    But steal away the very sacrifice.
    And I durst add (and smile upon your anger   130
    Though, as you frowned, death stood in every wrinkle):
    My soul's above your tyranny and would
    From torturing flame receive new fire of love
    And make your eye faint to behold the brightness

113 put off forget
118 durst past tense of dare. In Frances' imagination, she dared to tell her mother how cruel she was being.
121 seem...cruelty i.e. the heavens seem to approve Mistress Bellamy's cause because it looks like she has
the upper hand and is going to get her way.
123 that i.e. heaven (l. 120).
127–38 That...suffered Frances' speech recalls metaphysical poetry which uses the language of violent love
for religious martyrdom, as well as e.g. John Ford's *Tis Pity She's A Whore* (*c.* 1633) where the disembodied heart
is a material manifestation of love.
128 altar i.e. the institution of marriage.
129 steal...sacrifice Frances probably means herself, withheld from Hartwell, but she could mean him
being stolen from her by her mother's machinations.
131 as...wrinkle As a tyrant (l. 126), Mistress Bellamy's displeasure holds the power to condemn her
daughter to death with a frown.
132–3 would...love A typically metaphysical idea that extreme violence only encourages love—cf. Donne's
'Batter My Heart'.

112 Answer!] *this edn;* Answer. Q   118 hear!] *this edn;* heare. Q   126 tyrant –] *Gifford subst.;* tyrant. Q

106

THE CONSTANT MAID   4.2

Of my poor body's martyrdom; and, if ever   135
Love showed a miracle, my heart should bear
The characters of him you have torn from it
With beams about it like a saint that suffered.
But as you are my mother, thus I kneel
And beg a pardon for my innocence   140
If that offend you. Live you happy still
And be the mistress of your vows! Live to
Enjoy whom you affect! May every hour
Return new blessings on you both, renew
Your spring and let him think you young again.   145
And let me beg but this, for all my duty:
Against that day you marry him to provide
My coffin, for I fear I sha'not have
Breath many minutes after to pray for you.
The herbs that shall adorn your bridal chamber   150
Will serve my funeral and deck my hearse,
Beneath which you should say – there lies your daughter
That dies to show obedience.
BELLAMY   Why shouldst thou
    Continue thus to him?
FRANCES   I know he loves me,
    Yet hereafter your affections may not.   155
BELLAMY But never procure thee one sad thought!
    Now I have tried you both. Assure, my child,
    I loved him but for thee. Dispose thyself
    To be his bride – this news, at his return,
    Will make all well to rest.

135 my...martyrdom Here this seems part of the exaggerated language of violent love, but we realize
further on (l. 147ff) that Frances is threatening her literal death as a result of her mother's cruelty.
136–7 my...him Hartwell's name should be found inscribed on her heart.
138 with...suffered Frances imagines an emblem of her heart surrounded by the beams of sainthood. Early
modern emblem books associate halo-like beams with God's love, and Shirley amalgamates the sacred and
profane in Frances' image.
147 Against In preparation for (*OED*, Against *conj.* 1).
150–1 recalling *Hamlet* 1.2.180-1, 'the funeral baked meats / Did coldly furnish forth the marriage tables'.
155 hereafter...not Frances thinks her lack of duty risks losing her mother's love.
156 never...thought never let all this cause you to have one sad thought.
157 tried tested.
157 Assure Be assured
158 Dispose thyself Get yourself ready.
160 make...rest make everything right.

142 vows!] *Gifford;* vowes, Q   143 affect!] *Gifford;* affect, Q
145 again.] *this edn;* again! *Gifford;* againe, Q   154–5] *lineation this edn;* I...affections / May Q
156 thought!] *this edn;* thought; Q

107

4.3   THE COMPLETE WORKS OF JAMES SHIRLEY, VOLUME 7

FRANCES   Can this be true?   160
BELLAMY 'Twere sin to mock thee any more. To bed!
FRANCES I'll spend all night in prayers for you, mother!
    Oh, my Hartwell!   *Exeunt.*

[4.3]

        Enter PLAYFAIR *and his* COUSIN.
PLAYFAIR I am bound ever to thee.
COUSIN   Does she not become
    Her rich clothes, too?
PLAYFAIR   The morning never looked
    So fresh nor Venus with more charms upon her!
    Adon would melt before her eye and woo her
    Her kisses at expense of his last breath;   5
    Cupid himself, could he but see, would fall
    In love with her and, throwing away his shafts,
    Offer the empty quiver to her eyes,
    Ambitious to fill it with her beams –
    The least of which would wound more hearts than all   10
    His stock of golden arrows!
COUSIN   No more raptures.

161 **'Twere...more** It would be a sin to continue to deceive you.

0 The scene is set in Sir Clement's house.

1 **bound...thee** i.e. forever in your debt (for the favour of his help in the charade to trick Hornet).

1–2 **Does...clothes** We must assume from this comment that the niece has been kept in mean clothes by Hornet's parsimony, so that her appearance later in this scene in 'rich clothes' is markedly different from when we last saw her in 2.3.

3 **Venus** Roman goddess of Love who surpassed all the other goddesses in beauty, as the interlude later in the scene suggests.

4–5 Adonis, in classical legend, was the extremely handsome young man for whom Venus conceived an unrequited passion. Playfair thinks the niece is so beautiful that even Adonis (famously unsusceptible to love) would succumb to her charms and woo her for (implied) her kisses, at the risk of his very life.

6–7 **Cupid...her** If Cupid, the blind god of Love, could see the niece he would fall in love with her. This is especially significant because Cupid generally treats Love as a game, shooting arrows blindly which causes people to fall in love inappropriately.

7 **shafts** arrows.

8 **quiver** portable case or bag for holding arrows.

9 **beams** radiance emitted from her eyes associated with her beauty.

10–11 **The...arrows** Even the smallest beam from the niece's eyes would have the power to make more people fall in love than all of Cupid's golden arrows.

11 **raptures** expressions of intense delight or enthusiasm.

---

161 bed!] *this edn;* bed. Q
162 mother!] *this edn;* mother.– *Gifford;* Mother: Q   162–3] *lineation this edn;* night / In...*Hartwell* Q
163 Hartwell!] *Gifford;* Hartwell Q

[4.3]] *Gifford subst.* (SCENE III.*); not in* Q
1–2] *lineation Gifford;* Does...too? Q   3 her!] *this edn;* her. *Gifford;* her: Q
11 arrows!] *this edn;* Arrowes. Q

108

THE CONSTANT MAID

4.3

PLAYFAIR Didst thou not know before that love is able,
  Without the help of sack, to make a poet,
  My nimble Mercury, Jove's herald in
  Reversion?
COUSIN   I must confess I had   15
  A trick of Mercury when I picked his
  Pocket for the keys.
PLAYFAIR   He never missed 'em?
COUSIN His eyes were drenched in suds and I returned 'em
  'Ere they recovered light.
PLAYFAIR   'Twas excellent.
  He walks in darkness still.
COUSIN   D'ye think he'll know her?   20
PLAYFAIR His clothes already have made him forget
  Himself, or, if he have but the remembrance
  Of such a woman, the more he sees her now
  The more he'll think the change impossible.
COUSIN Where ha' you left him?   25
PLAYFAIR I'th'gallery, where, with much patience,
  He does expect his highness will send for him.
COUSIN Then all runs smooth: his wonder still continues.
PLAYFAIR I fed that humour artificially.
  He is half persuaded all's but a dream,   30
  To which imagination his clothes

12–13 love...poet Behind this idea is probably the concept from Plato's *Phaedrus* that divine madness can be split into four subcategories: love, Dionysian frenzy, oracular prophecy, and poetic composition. Three of these—love, drink, and poetry—make it into these lines directly, and prophecy is glanced at in the sense that Playfair is speaking an unknown truth to his cousin.
14 **Mercury** Messenger of the gods, fitting for Playfair's cousin who has acted as a go-between for him with the niece.
14 **Jove's herald** Jove was the king of the gods and sent the others to do his bidding.
14–15 **herald...Reversion** Playfair is suggesting that should Mercury give up his post, the cousin will be next in line to succeed him. 'Reversion' means the 'action or fact of succession to an office or post after the death or retirement of the holder' (*OED, n.* 3b and Pb).
16–17 **trick...keys** Mercury was also the god of financial gain, patron of tricksters and thieves.
18 **drenched...suds** The barber mentioned at 3.2.155ff has clearly done his best to keep Hornet busy and incapacitated for as long as he could.
19 **'Ere...light** i.e. Before he could see again.
20 **walks...still** i.e. has not yet discovered their schemes.
20 **know** recognize.
29 **that humour** i.e. his wonder.
29 **artificially** with deliberate design.
30–2 **He...'em** The free clothes reinforce Hornet's feeling that he is dreaming, presumably because he cannot believe he has been so lucky.
31 **imagination** All six syllables are pronounced here.

15–17] *lineation this edn;* confesse / I...pick'd / His...keyes. Q
21–4] *lineation this edn;* have / Made...have / But...woman; / The...thinke / The Q

109

4.3   THE COMPLETE WORKS OF JAMES SHIRLEY, VOLUME 7

Are a great help because he paid not for 'em.
Sometimes he is very merry; then again
He struts about with such a scurvy pride,
As some new-crept into nobility   35
When men of their first livery come to see 'em.
His honour has so changed him that he now
Knows not of what religion he is –
Or, if he chance to think of his first faith,
He spits o'th'hangings and excuses with   40
'I do not like the story; 'tis apocryphal'.
Sometimes he'll offer at a jest and talk
Nonsense with him that has been seven years lorded –
Frown upon any man that will presume
To have more knowledge, in worse clothes. I told him   45
It was his grace's pleasure he should be
Controller of the masque, and he did sweat
As he were studying for some mighty oaths
To clear the presence. He is here! Away!   *Exeunt.*

      [*Enter*] HORNET *and Sir* CLEMENT.

HORNET   And you are master of the house, Sir Clement? –   50

---

34 scurvy contemptible (but perhaps with an overtone of 'quasi' as in *OED, adj.* 2†b).

34–6 Hornet is preening about like a newly ennobled citizen, exceptionally proud when he encounters his own liveried servants for the first time.

38 religion Money-lenders were traditionally Jewish, so it is possible that this is an allusion to this, but it could merely be that Hornet is supposed to have been converted from his miserliness by the grandeur of the 'Court'.

39 first faith either Judaism or miserliness.

40–1 The tapestry hangings obviously relate some sort of improving story of which Hornet might have approved before his conversion to courtly behaviour. See also 2.1.87–8. The use of the word 'apocryphal' does associate Hornet with Judaism because the Apocrypha refers properly to those books of the Old Testament not written in Hebrew and therefore not counted genuine by the Jews. At the Reformation, Protestant theologians also excluded them from the biblical canon, so this implies that the subject of the hangings in question was contained in one of the deuterocanonical books of the Old Testament.

42–3 Hornet laughs and makes small talk with someone who has been a lord for a seven years already. He probably congratulates himself on moving in such exalted circles, but Shirley's implication is that this milieu is still 'new money' not traditional landed gentry.

44–5 Frown…clothes Hornet has become snobbish about appearances and is looking down his nose at people who are not as well-dressed as he is, even if they seem better informed.

47 Controller…masque This is probably the managerial role, a 'court official charged…with conveying decisions', discussed by Daye (1996, 16). Daye thinks that this might often have been the dancing master, 'amongst the highest servants in rank' (16), so being given this office is extremely flattering to Hornet.

47–9 he…presence Hornet is taking his new role very seriously, and in Playfair's description we recognize Hornet's later peremptory attitude to the task. The 'mighty oaths' are indicative of the manner in which he will exercise his power.

---

37 changed] *Gifford;* chang' Q   **40** excuses] *this edn;* excuses 't *Gifford;* excused Q
49 here! Away!] *this edn;* here; away! *Gifford;* here; away. Q   **49 SD1**] *this edn; Exit.* Q
49 SD2] *Gifford subst; Hornet and* Sʳ. *Clement.* Q   **50** Clement? –] *Gifford subst.* (Clement?*);* Clement. Q

110

THE CONSTANT MAID   4.3

For so I heard you called.
CLEMENT   It is my name,
    Sir Giles, unworthy of this grace his highness
    Is deigned to show in honouring of my daughter.
HORNET And was she married this morning, say you?
CLEMENT This morn she lost her virgin name.   55
HORNET I have not seen her yet, nor any of the ladies.
    You have but little noise, methinks, in the house.
CLEMENT It would offend his grace.
HORNET   Who, as you say,
    Came hither privately, with a small train
    Of lords. Would I might see his face again.   60
    I am not sent for yet – I have been ready,
    Sir Clement, these three hours and I do wonder
    His grace forgets himself so much. *Flourish.*
CLEMENT That music speaks him on entrance.

        Enter COUSIN *and* LORDS.

COUSIN   Aye, that garb becomes him.   65
    How was his person lost within that shape
    He was first presented to me.
HORNET Indeed, the case is somewhat
    Altered by Your Highness' bounty
    To your poor subject, Hornet.

53 **Is...show** i.e. condescends to show.
57 **but...noise** Hornet has noticed that it is much quieter than one might expect a court to be. There may also be an association with the missing 'ladies' of the previous line, following the popular opinion that women were particularly noisy, reinforced by the whole plot of Jonson's *Epicoene*.
58–60 **Who...lords** Sir Clement has already offered a plausible explanation by reinforcing the private nature of the royal visit.
63 **forgets himself** loses remembrance of his station, position, or character; loses sight of the requirements of dignity, propriety, or decorum; behaves unbecomingly (*OED*, Forget *v.* 5b), but also 'gets lost' (sense 5c) and 'overlooks' (sense 4).
64 That music announces his entrance.
65 **garb** dress (especially when elegant and fashionable); outward bearing or behaviour.
66 **his person** both his outward appearance and his personality. The 'King' means that the true personality of Hornet is now visible.
67–9 Gifford relineates these lines but fails to regularise the meter.
68–9 **the...altered** Literally, the outward appearance has been somewhat changed but also figuratively, the boot is on the other foot or the situation has changed. This may also be also a nod to Jonson's *The Case is Altered* (pub. 1609).
69 **bounty** generosity.

52 Sir] *Gifford;* Sᵣ. Q
58–9] *lineation Gifford;* Who,...train Q   61 yet –] *this edn;* yet; *Gifford;* yet, Q
62 Sir] *Gifford;* Sᵣ. Q   63 SD] *Gifford; after entry SD l.* 64 Q   67 me.] *this edn;* me! *Gifford;* me? Q
68 somewhat] *Gifford;* somewhat a Q   69 Altered] *this edn;* Altered, Q

4.3   THE COMPLETE WORKS OF JAMES SHIRLEY, VOLUME 7

PLAYFAIR [*Aside*]   Now he looks   70
    As he did scorn the quorum and were hungry
    To eat a statesman. 'Las an office in
    The household is too little for a breakfast,
    A baron but a morning's draught – he'll gulp it
    Like a round egg in muscadine. Methinks   75
    At every wiping of his mouth should drop
    A golden saying of Pythagoras;
    A piece of Machiavel I see already
    Hang on his beard (which wants but stroking out);
    The Statutes and the Magna Carta have   80
    Taken a lease at his tongue's end.
COUSIN   I will think on't;
    He shall be – but to th'banquet.
    Then, let the masque be ready! There we shall

70–2 he...statesman Hornet has developed such taste for court life that he looks like he would reject an appointment to the quorum, the select body of (usually eminent) justices of the peace, as he is instead ambitious to become a statesman. The following speech comically details Hornet's burgeoning and overweening pride by imagining him eating the offices in question.

72–3 office...household position as a royal servant, such as the one discussed in the note to l. 47.

74 baron i.e. baronetcy, the lowest rank of nobility, invented by James I to raise revenue and therefore derided as a worthless 'rank'.

74 morning's draught alcoholic drink taken in the morning, from post-classical Latin *haustus matutinus*. But in *Historia vitae et mortis* (1623, 308), Bacon uses this phrase to mean a medicinal tonic rather than an alcoholic pick-me-up—the examples he gives are '*succorum*' (juices), '*decoctionum*' (decoctions), '*seri lactis*' (whey), and '*hordeatorum*' (barley-water).

75 round...muscadine A traditional way of judging when the right amount of sugar had been added during the making of wine from muscadine grapes was to place a fresh egg in it and wait for it to float—this happened when the liquid was sufficiently saturated with sugar as to make it heavier than the egg (see Verstille 1866, 201). Eggs, particularly in muscadine, had acquired a reputation as an aphrodisiac by this period (see Williams 1994, 433 for examples from early modern drama).

75–9 Methinks...beard Playfair thinks Hornet fancies himself transformed and will start dropping statesmanlike *bons mots* from the Greek philosopher Pythagorus and the Italian Renaissance diplomat and politician Machiavelli.

79 which...out The piece of Machiavelli stuck in his beard just needs to be stroked out, but there is a secondary image of the wise old statesmen stroking his beard thoughtfully.

80 Statutes In England, Scotland, and Ireland, 'statute' is generally synonymous with 'Act of Parliament', though the term also denotes enactments made by the king and his council before the rise of regular parliaments (*OED*, Statute *n*. 2a). The 'statutes at large' is (the title of) the published collection of legislative acts understood to commence with Magna Carta (see *OED*, P2, quot. 1745).

80 Magna Carta Charter of English personal and political liberty, obtained from King John in 1215, repeatedly confirmed, and appealed to in all disputes between the sovereign and his or her subjects.

81 Taken...end Hired his tongue (i.e. Hornet has internalized the law and the bill of rights and he keeps quoting them).

81 I...on't The 'King' will consider what to do about Hornet. During Playfair's imaginative aside, discussion has clearly been continuing about Hornet's status and reward, the 'it' in question.

82 He...banquet Q1 and Q2 (1661) mark the long 'thinking' pause in this line with a double-length and triple-length dash respectively. Q1 sets this as rough verse, and clearly expects the dash to stand for one metrical foot, though this section of the play is metrically uneven. One can imagine an actor having great fun with the pregnant pause—which never delivers a suggestion of which office might be offered to Hornet.

---

70 SD] *this edn; not in* Q   **78** Machiavel] *Gifford; Machiævell*; Q   **80** Carta] Q *subst. (Charta)*
83 ready!] *this edn;* ready; *Gifford;* ready, Q

112

THE CONSTANT MAID 4.3

Employ your worthy diligence.
HORNET Heaven bless your mighty grace!   85
COUSIN You'll follow.   *Exeunt [all but* HORNET].
HORNET   I attend you presently.
I know not what to think of these things yet:
'Tis very strange I should be thus exalted
Without desert, best known unto myself.
Princes, I see, are mortal and may be   90
Deceived in placing of their honours. I
Am little better than a favourite
If this be true. If? 'Tis a question
Let me consider wisely: it may be
I am not I. No, no: I am a knight.   95
Are these my clothes? I did not use to wear such.
A pocket in my sleeve and velvet hose
Six times translated since they were a midwife's
Fore-part were things I wore on holidays.
The price of these would break a camel's back   100

---

84 **worthy diligence** meritorious assiduity in service (see *OED*, Worthy *adj*. 1c).
86 **You'll follow** This is an order.
86 **I...presently** I'll wait on you promptly. *OED* says 'presently' could mean both 'immediately' and 'in a little while' in the seventeenth century but what Hornet clearly means here is that he will come at the apposite moment, which from a theatrical perspective is after he has delivered his speech in ll. 87–108 and, from the perspective of the 'Court', when the 'King' is ready for him.
88 **exalted** praised and promoted.
89 **Without desert** Undeserving. There is certainly a joke here about courtiers not deserving their favour, which carries on at ll. 90–3.
89 **best...myself** The antecedent is 'desert'; Hornet means only he knows how deserving or undeserving he is.
90–3 **Princes...true** Shirley manages to criticize favourites at court but, since this is not a real court, side-steps implicating the Caroline regime.
93 **this** the whole situation.
93–4 **'Tis...wisely** Let me consider this question sensibly.
94–9 **it...holidays** This metatheatrical speech relies upon the audience understanding that Hornet is at once the character and an actor, and that as the actor playing Hornet he is dressed up in second-hand finery. Hornet the character is in properly fine clothes, in comparison to his former parsimonious practice of wearing sixth-hand finery *but only on a holiday*; the joke is that the actual costume the actor is wearing is certainly more than sixth-hand (see note to 3.2.26–7).
97 **hose** article of male clothing for the leg, like leggings or tights.
98 **Six...translated** The material has been refashioned six times into different garments.
98–9 **midwife's fore-part** A 'forepart' was an ornamental covering for the breast worn by women; a stom-acher. There is comic effect from it belonging originally to a midwife: dirt, cross-dressing, and class are all at stake and so it is particularly undignifying for Hornet.
100 **these** i.e. the rich clothes he has been changed into.
100 **break...back** Proverbially, the straw that breaks the camel's back is the little thing added to extreme weight, but Hornet clearly means that the expense is so great that merely the huge cost of the clothes would be too much, in that even a camel could not carry the weight of money required to buy these clothes.

---

85 grace!] *this edn;* Grace. Q
86 SD] *Gifford subst.;* Exit. Q

113

4.3　　THE COMPLETE WORKS OF JAMES SHIRLEY, VOLUME 7

And yet some men walk under 'em like elephants,
And have variety, as the devil were
Their tailor, who best knows where all their land lies.
Then why this cost on me? It is a dream,
And I am very glad on't; 'tis impossible　　　　　　　　　105
I should be true – it does not hang together.
It will have patience till I wake again,
And care not what becomes on't.

　　　　Enter Sir CLEMENT.

CLEMENT　　　　　　　　　　　　'Tis His Highness'
Pleasure, now the banquet's done.
HORNET　How, the banquet done? I was coming to't.　　　　110
You could hardly say grace by this time!
CLEMENT　That's a ceremony grown out of use:
It was a running banquet.
HORNET　　　　　　　　　A running?
So it seems – it made great haste. I do dream,
Certainly: there's no sense nor reason　　　　　　　　115
In any thing they say.
CLEMENT　　　　　　　　You know your place.
The masque will straight begin and his grace wo'not
Have any one admitted. He resolves,
If the conceit affect him, it shall be
Performed i'th'court hereafter. I'th'meantime　　　　120

---

101 **some…elephants** some men wear such clothes just as elephants carry castles. Elephants in medieval and early modern art were very often shown bearing a castle on their back: the point is that the clothes are very weighty, both literally and in richness.

102 **variety** i.e. more than one set of rich clothes.

102–3 **as…lies** If the tailor-devil knows the full extent of the purchaser's land he can presumably encourage him to overspend on finery knowing full well he can go after the land in the event of being unpaid.

106 **hang together** make sense.

107 **wake again** Hornet imagines himself to be in a dream. As in *A Midsummer Night's Dream*, the playful connection of dreams, reality, truth, and playacting was common on the early modern stage.

110 **How…done?** How can the banquet be over (already)?

112 i.e. Saying grace has gone out of fashion. See also note to 3.1.103–4.

113 **running banquet** buffet.

113–14 **running…haste** Hornet takes it to mean that the banquet itself ran, which accounts for it taking so little time.

116 **You…place** This has a primary meaning of 'you know where to stand/sit', but it also works well both as a response to Hornet's dissatisfaction at missing the banquet by reminding him of his inferior status (*OED*, Know *v.* 15b) and as a confirmatory response to his comment in the previous lines that it is all a dream.

118–20 **He…hereafter** The 'King' has decided that if he likes the subject and execution of the masque he will subsequently have it performed at court.

---

106 true –…together.] *this edn;* true,…together, Q　　106 It] *Gifford,* 1661; I Q
108 SD SIR] *Gifford subst.;* Sʳ. Q　　111 time!] *this edn;* time. Q
113–15] *lineation this edn;* A…haste: / I…reason Q

114

THE CONSTANT MAID
4.3

He does command all privacy: there are
Some set to guard the door, but your care must
Provide His Highness be not interrupted. *Knock*[*ing within*]
[*Calling out*] Back! [*To Hornet*] They are rude already.

HORNET   Let me alone.

                                         Exit [*Sir Clement*].

What turbulent knave is that?   125
WITHIN I am a country gentleman, Sir Giles,
    And if I may presume upon good clothes,
    You may before his grace call me your cousin
    And not be ashamed. Here is a lady, too.
HORNET A lady too? Is she with child? What makes   130
    She here, an she be with child already?
    'Tell thee none shall be admitted while
    I am in place. [*More knocking*] More rapping? Keep the doors!
    If I do fall a-swearing once, look to't.
WITHIN I beseech you for my wife's sake.
HORNET   Thy wife's?   135
    What's he that pleads *in forma pauperis*?
WITHIN A citizen, an't like you.
HORNET Like me? Thou lie'st – I am more like a lord.
    Thou shalt fare ne'er the better for that word.

---

124 Back Sir Clement presumably directs this to those knocking.
124 rude unmannerly. The 'crowd' outside is pressing for entry in boisterous and uncivilized fashion.
124 Let…alone Leave me alone (to manage it).
125 Hornet presumably shouts this through the barred 'door', which is one of the two at the back of the Cockpit's stage (see King 1965b).
125 turbulent knave unruly rogue.
127 presume…clothes rely on (my) respectable attire.
128 cousin The 'country gentleman' means that he is related to Hornet both because he is the 'country' cousin version of Hornet's city gentleman and by virtue of the 'good clothes' they have in common.
130–1 A…already Hornet wilfully misunderstands l. 129's 'too' as 'two' which allows him to pretend he thinks she is pregnant as a strategy for excluding those knocking.
134 If I start to swear you had better look out.
136 in…pauperis in a humble or abject manner (*OED*, In *prep.²*, 9).
137 an't…you if it please you. Q has 'and like you', a deliberate homophonic quibble meaning that Hornet is a citizen like the speaker.
138 Hornet pretends to understand that he is being called a citizen which he denies because he is more like a Lord in his finery. Hornet's fight-picking is again a strategy to refuse the crowd entry to the house.
139 You won't get special treatment by using the word citizen.

---

123 SD] *this edn; Knocks. in margin of l. 123* Q   **124 SD1**] *this edn; not in* Q
124 Back!] *Gifford;* Back, Q   **124 SD2**] *this edn; not in* Q   **124 SD3**] *this edn; Exit. in margin of l. 123* Q
126 Sir] *Gifford subst.;* Sʳ. Q   **130–1**] *lineation this edn;* A…makes she / Here,…already? Q
131 an] *Gifford;* and Q   **133 SD** *Gifford subst. (knocking within.); not in* Q
133 doors!] *Gifford;* doores, Q   **137** an't] *Gifford;* and Q

4.3   THE COMPLETE WORKS OF JAMES SHIRLEY, VOLUME 7

Knock down the women, an there be a hundred,   140
And make their husbands drunk. The guard are lazy.
These women's insolence will force a statute:
I will petition to the king myself
They may have liberty but once a year
To see the galley-foist, then be confined   145
To their chamber and one prentice – [*knocking*] yet again.
WITHIN Sir Giles! Sir Giles! You know me well enough.
HORNET But while I am in office I'll know nobody.
SCRIVENER I am your scrivener!
HORNET   Draw thy purse wherein
Thou keepest thy ears, and leave 'em at the door.   150
The guard trust none without a pawn: they'll serve,
If they be ne'er redeemed, to seethe in milk
For a sore throat – Jew's ears I know they are.
SCRIVENER Sir Giles, here's your niece.

---

142 statute type of statutory law specified as regulating a person or thing (*OED*, Statute *n.* 3), here as a joke recalling Hornet's quoting the Statutes in Playfair's flight of fancy (ll. 80–1).

145 galley-foist metonymic for Lord Mayor's parade, from a state barge, esp. that of the Lord Mayor of London (*OED*, Galley-foist *n.*).

145–6 then...prentice Hornet wants insolent women put under house arrest and limited to one apprentice. There is a sexual overtone to this last prescription since women were rumoured to take sexual advantage of their apprentices.

148 in office performing his official role as controller of the masque (which seems to consist largely of being doorkeeper).

149 your scrivener see note to 1.2.95. The point is that Hornet should let him in because, as a usurer's side-kick, his scrivener is the closest companion Hornet has. They are teasing Hornet, who knows perfectly well that it is not actually his scrivener; the point is to confuse him to the extent that he won't believe that the 'niece' who speaks at l. 155 is his real niece (even though she is).

149–50 Draw...door Hornet seems to mean that he can only come in if he promises to keep the proceedings completely private by leaving his ears (i.e. his ability to hear) at the door with his purse, presumably as a bribe for Hornet. The implication of the scrivener keeping his ears in his purse is that he is paid not to hear certain things.

151 pawn pledge, something left as surety.

152 ne'er redeemed This points forward to l. 153 and quibbles on the idea that the Jews will never be converted and therefore never redeemed.

152 seethe...milk stew in milk. Shirley probably chose this method of cooking ears because it is linguistically reminiscent of a scriptural prohibition given to the Jews not to 'seethe a kid in its mother's milk' (see Exodus 23:19; Exodus 34:26; Deuteronomy 14:21).

153 Jew's ears This can be read both literally and as enabling a joke based on the edible cup-shaped fungus growing on the roots and trunks of trees, chiefly the elder, formerly in repute as a medicine (*OED*, Jew's-ear *n.* 1), which might have included a recipe where it was seethed in milk.

153 Jew's...are The scrivener, according to Hornet, is either actually or figuratively Jewish (cf. 4.3.38 and see Introduction).

---

140 an] *Gifford;* and Q   **143 myself**] *Gifford;* my selfe, Q
146 SD] *Gifford subst. (knocking within.); not in* Q   **149 scrivener!**] *Gifford;* scrivenor. Q

116

THE CONSTANT MAID 4.3

HORNET   My niece? The devil she is.

NIECE (*Within*) Pray, uncle, let me in!

HORNET   Her very voice!   155

  Ha? Open the doors there. Where is she?

WITHIN Whom?

HORNET   My niece that called to me.

WITHIN None called, nor was there any woman here.

HORNET No, nor my scrivener bawling out 'Sir Giles'?

WITHIN Not at any hand, your worship.

HORNET   Then I dream   160

  And I am a fool to make a question on't.

WITHIN Ha, ha, ha.

HORNET   The knaves laugh at me, but let 'em! I

  Shall be as merry with this tale tomorrow.

  What fancies men have in their sleep sometimes!

  His Highness –

      Enter COUSIN, LORDS, [*and Sir* CLEMENT].

  [*To Sir Clement*] Where be the ladies?

CLEMENT   They are all i'th'masque.   165

HORNET Nay, 'tis no matter. Why do I ask the question?

CLEMENT You'll see 'em, sir, anon.

FIRST LORD (*Giv[ing] papers to* [*Cousin*] *and* [*Hornet*]) Wil't please your grace?

  And you, Sir Giles – the subject of the masque.

---

155 very voice actual or true voice.

156 Open...there In performance Hornet may open the doors and look 'within' or there may be no response to this demand.

160 at...hand on any side (with a quibble on 'hand' since scriveners write for a living).

162 Ha, ha, ha This edition retains Q's reading which prints the sound of laughter rather than adding a SD, such as (*Laughter within*).

162–3 I...tomorrow Tomorrow I will find this just as funny as they do now (or possibly 'tell it to raise laughs').

167 Nay...question? Hornet muses that where the women are is not important, but he can't shake the feeling that something is wrong.

169 subject...masque This may be a programme with the plot outline on it, or possibly something slightly more substantial, similar to the *livrets* (printed programmes) for entertainments developed in France under Louis XIII (see Nevile 2018, 65).

---

155 SD] Q *subst. (set as part of SH)*   **155** in!] *this edn;* in. Q   **155** voice!] *Gifford;* voice: Q

155–6] *lineation this edn;* Her...there; / Where Q   **159** Gyles'?] *this edn; Giles! Gifford; Gyles,* Q

160 SH1] *Gifford subst.; not in* Q   **162** 'em!] *this edn;* them; *Gifford;* 'em, Q

164 sometimes!] *Gifford;* sometimes? Q   **165** Highness –] *this edn;* Highnesse. Q

165 SD1 *and* SIR CLEMENT] *this edn; Re-enter sir* CLEMENT *Gifford; not in* Q   **165 SD2**] *this edn; not in* Q

168 SH] *this edn;* 1 *Serv. Gifford;* 1 *La.* Q

168 SD] *Gifford subst. (after l. 169); Gives papers to the King and S^r. Gyles in margins of ll. 168–9* Q

4.3 THE COMPLETE WORKS OF JAMES SHIRLEY, VOLUME 7

HORNET What's here? 'The Three Goddesses' Contention   170
For the Golden Ball'?

Enter PLAYFAIR, *dancing, with a golden ball in his hand.*

This is Paris. So –

Enter [THREE PLAYERS as] *Juno, Pallas,* [*and*] *Venus.*

These are the three goddesses: Juno, Pallas, Venus.

The goddesses dance and court Paris for his ball.

Enter [*to Juno*] *one like a king.* [*She*] *takes his crown and sceptre* [*and*] *offers it to Paris,* [*who*] *refuses.*

FIRST LORD Juno doth woo him with her state and kingdoms.

HORNET But he refuses – more fool he!

Enter [*to Pallas*] *one like a soldier, armed, with a book in his hand.*
She presents [*the arms and book*] *to Paris,* [*who*] *neglects* [*them*].

CLEMENT He is not for her service, though she offer   175
To make him a scholar and a soldier:

170–1 The...ball This story from classical mythology explains the cause of the Trojan War. Paris, son of Priam, was asked to award one of the golden apples from the Garden of the Hesperides to the most beautiful of three goddesses, Juno, Pallas Minerva, and Venus. Each goddess tried to bribe him with a present which comes under her sway—Juno (as Queen of the Gods) with worldly power, Pallas with knowledge/wisdom and military might and Venus with love, in the person of the most beautiful woman in the world (Helen, wife of Menelaus, king of Sparta). Paris chose Venus, ran off with Helen, and the Trojan War resulted when the Greeks sailed to reclaim Menelaus' wife. For uses of the myth in entertainments see Introduction.

171 SD1 *dancing* The correct early modern term for acting in a masque was to 'dance'. Playfair is clearly moving elegantly while engaged in the action of the masque but this need not mean he is dancing formally, as we would understand it.

171 SD1 *golden ball* golden apple from the tree in the Garden of the Hesperides.

172 SD2 *crown...sceptre* attributes of worldly power, and the costume of a king.

174 SD *arms...book* attributes of military might and wisdom.

174 SD *neglects* ignores.

176 a scholar Q omits the 'a', probably an uncorrected error. Not only does the missing 'a' complete the metre, but without it the line seems ungainly.

---

170 here?] *Gifford;* here, Q   **170–1**] *lineation this edn;* Goddesses / Contention...ball? Q

170–1 'The...Ball'? *this edn; Gifford italics;* the three Goddesses / Contention for the golden ball? Q

171 So –] *this edn;* So. Q   **171 SD2**] *this edn; Enter Juno, Pallas, Venus.* Q

172] *lineation Gifford;* Goddesses; / Juno, Q

172 SD2] *this edn; To Juno enters one like a King; Takes his Crowne and Scepter, offers it to Paris, he refuses.* Q

174 he!] *this edn;* he. Q

174 SD] *this edn; To Pallas, enter one like a Souldier arm'd, with a Booke in his hand; She presents them to Paris, he neglects.* Q

176 a] *this edn;* both a *Gifford; not in* Q

THE CONSTANT MAID   4.3

A complete man.
HORNET   No, no: that fairy must
Win the ball.
[*Enter*], *to Venus*, CUPID, *leading in Hornet's* NIECE [*who is*] *richly dressed.*
                Ha? That's my niece!
CLEMENT   Which, Sir Giles?
HORNET That whom Dame Venus and her dandiprat
Are busy withal.
FIRST LORD   Why, that's the bride!
HORNET   Bride, quotha?   180
CLEMENT Married this morning: 'tis my daughter, sir!
HORNET Nay, if she be my niece I am sure she was not
Married this morning.
                Paris receives the niece, and gives Venus the ball.
                        Exeunt Juno [*and*] *Pallas, with their masquers.*
                She's safe enough at home
And has but half her wits, as I remember.
The devil cannot juggle her from my   185
Custody. Ha, ha! I do dream still.
        Cupid joins [*Paris' and the niece's*] *hands and sings, which done, exeunt masquers.*
COUSIN 'Tis time to break off revels. How like you
This, Sir Giles?
HORNET   A very fine dream, i'faith.
COUSIN   I see you'd be abed; you are not used

    177 **complete** fully equipped or endowed; perfect, accomplished, consummate.
    177 **that fairy** Venus, towards whom Hornet is presumably pointing. Appropriate when referring to a god-
dess, Hornet uses 'fairy' to mean 'likened to a fairy in possessing extraordinary or supernatural power; an
enchantress' and more generally 'a woman, esp. an attractive or seductive young woman' (*OED*, Fairy *n.* 4a).
Shirley uses the word in a similar sense in *WFO* 4.4.
    179 **Dame** Prefixed as a title to the name of a lady or woman of rank (*OED*, Dame *n.* 6a).
    179 **dandiprat** young lad, little boy, urchin (in this case Cupid).
    180 **quotha?** he said?; used with contemptuous, ironic, or sarcastic force after repeating words said by some-
one else, thus 'indeed!' (*OED*).
    184 **has...wits** is mad.
    185–6 **juggle...Custody** steal her away from me by magic or conjuring, or by trickery or deceit.
    187 **break...revels** end the performance; bring the whole evening's entertainment to an end.

177–8] *lineation this edn;* fairy / Must *Gifford;* No, no,...ball. Q
178 SD *Enter...*CUPID] *this edn; To Venus comes Cupid* Q
178 niece!] *this edn;* Neece. Q   178 Sir] *Gifford subst.;* Sr. Q   180 bride!] *this edn;* Bride. Q
181 sir!] *this edn;* sir. Q   183 SD2] *this edn: Juno, Pallas, with their Masquers, Exeunt.* Q
185–6] *lineation this edn;* The...custody. / Ha, Q   186 Ha, ha!] *Gifford;* Ha, ha, Q
186 SD *Paris'...niece's*] *this edn;* their Q   187–8] *lineation this edn;* 'Tis...this, / Sr. Q
188 Sir] *Gifford subst.;* Sr. Q

119

5.1   THE COMPLETE WORKS OF JAMES SHIRLEY, VOLUME 7

To these late hours.

CLEMENT [*Calling*]   Lights for His Highness!   190

HORNET I humbly beg your licence I may return
    To my own lodging.

COUSIN   Well, sir, 'tis easily granted.   *Exit.*

FIRST LORD [*Calling*] Lights for Sir Giles!
               [*To Hornet*] One shall attend you home.

HORNET Ha, ha, ha.

CLEMENT   Why do you laugh?

HORNET   At a conceit; at a conceit.
    What did I eat last night to make me dream thus?   *Exeunt.* 195

5[.1]

    Enter HARTWELL, *apprehended,* COUNTRYMAN, OFFICERS, [*and*] SERVANT.

HARTWELL You have done well!

COUNTRYMAN   Would you had done no worse.
    These are his clothes, and you must give account
    How you came by 'em and produce him safe
    Ere you acquit yourself. We may suspect
    You ha' killed him.

---

190 late hours Court revels went on much later than working citizens would be used to (see Koslofsky 2011, chapter 4, *passim*).

194 conceit fanciful notion; a fancy, a whim.

195 The *somnium naturale* (in medieval dream theory) was a dream which had a bodily cause, such as partaking of certain foods, just as today cheese still has a popular reputation for causing vivid dreams.

0 The scene is set in the street or the fields near Mistress Bellamy's house.

0 SD The list of characters matches the search party which Mistress Bellamy promised to furnish in 4.2, so the scene must be set the following morning. The Countryman and Mistress Bellamy's servant are joined by officers and they have apprehended Hartwell rather than having found Startup, as was their original intention.

1 done well i.e. in catching him.

1 Would...worse If only you hadn't done something worse (i.e. killed Startup, as they suspect).

2 his clothes Hornet is still in Startup's clothes from the previous evening as (we assume) he has been wandering about all night.

3 him i.e. Startup.

4 Ere...yourself Before you can prove you did not commit this crime.

---

190 SD] *this edn; not in* Q   **190** Highness!] *Gifford;* Highnesse. Q

191–2] *lineation this edn;* license / I...lodging. Q   **192 SH**] *Gifford subst.; Clos.* Q

193 SD1] *this edn; not in* Q   **193** Giles!] *Gifford; Gyles:* Q   **193 SD2**] *this edn; not in* Q

5[.1]] *Gifford subst. (*ACT V. SCENE I.*);* ACT. V. Q

0 SD and] *Gifford subst.; not in* Q   **1** well!] *this edn;* well. *Gifford;* well? Q

THE CONSTANT MAID   5.1

HARTWELL   Then I obey my destiny: 5
    Justice, I see, pursues the guilty person.
    Dispose me where you please.
OFFICER   He does confess.
HARTWELL Whate'er you be, you can but have my life
    For his – all your revenge can reach no higher –
    And to the law I yield myself.
COUNTRYMAN   My hopes are cold   10
    As his blood whom thou hast slain. Thou hast
    Been cruel in this act to me and mine,
    Whose fames in him are miserably wounded.
    But look for the reward!
HARTWELL   I must expect it.
    In the meantime I do not beg your mercy: 15
    Life is a burden – I would fain be rid on't.
    Does He weary me to carry it?
SERVANT I'll acquaint my mistress.
COUNTRYMAN Do so.   [*Exit Servant.*]
                    To the next Justice! Come away!   *Exeunt.*

---

5 obey...destiny Hartwell is still in the fatalistic mood of the disappointed lover, so his 'destiny' is
to die.

6 Hartwell is innocent but his desperate strategy is to try to get himself convicted of murder because fickle
women make life not worth living. Even so, he does not actually confess to having killed Startup.

7 dispose me put me into the proper or suitable place (i.e. prison) (*OED*, Dispose *v.* 1b).

8 Whate'er...be Whoever you are (Hartwell has not met the Countryman yet).

8–9 you...higher The basic law of revenge was reciprocity (an eye for an eye), although early modern drama
took great pleasure in exploring 'revenges' which theatrically surpassed the crimes they avenged (see, e.g., *The
Revenger's Tragedy*).

10 hopes i.e. his hope of getting Startup to marry his daughter and thus restore her (and the Countryman's)
credit.

12 me...mine me and my daughter (and. more generally, family, because Startup's death without marrying
the daughter brings shame on all of her relations).

13 fames reputations.

14 reward i.e. the death penalty.

17 Does God still weary me by making me live?

18 my mistress i.e. Mistress Bellamy.

19 next nearest.

---

14 reward!] *this edn;* reward. Q   **17** He] *this edn;* he Q   **19 SD1**] *this edn; not in* Q
19 Justice!...away!] *this edn;* justice!...away. *Gifford;* Justice;...away Q

121

[5.2]

Enter HORNET.

HORNET She's gone! She's gone! I shall run mad! My niece!
Robbed of three thousand pound in her escape!
I find too late I am awake and gulled,
Nor know I whom to accuse for my tormentors.
Devils or men? But sure they were not men   5
But very fiends I revelled with last night!
That I could meet the prince of devils that knighted me –
The poets call him Pluto, god of riches –
I and my learned counsel would undo him
In law, in very law, which he should find   10
Hotter ere I had done than hell itself,
And call his place of torment in three terms
But a refreshing to't. Yet let me see:
I have the portion still though she be vanished –
That's better than my niece. But if she marry,   15
I lose it all there. There's the vexation.

---

0 The scene is set in Hornet's house.

1–2 Shirley consciously draws on *The Merchant of Venice* here, from the (possibly exaggerated) description given by Solanio of Shylock's reaction to finding Jessica missing: 'My daughter, O my ducats, O my daughter!' (2.8.15ff).

1 run mad Possibly this draws on Solanio's reports of Shylock, 'I never heard a passion so confused, / So strange, outrageous, and so variable' (*MV*, 2.8.12–13).

2 If the niece marries, her huge fortune of £3000 will pass to her husband and we know from 2.1.93–4 that Hornet 'broods upon her portion'. Although he still has the money, Hornet will be forced to give it up by law if he cannot reclaim his niece unmarried.

3 awake...gulled not dreaming (as he suspected he was last night) and tricked.

4 Because they were all in disguise Hornet cannot take out a writ or complaint against any known individual.

6 very fiends 'true-born' devils.

7 prince...devils Satan is the Prince of Devils, but Hornet quibbles on the cousin being a 'king'.

8 Pluto...riches Hornet conflates Pluto, god of the underworld, with Plutus, god of riches, which suits his extended metaphor about the devil and pertains to the loss of the niece's money. Plutus appears as a character in Ben Jonson's *Love Restored* (1612) and in George Chapman's *The Memorable Masque* (1613).

10 very true and to its full extent (as at l. 6, another intensifier which may be supposed to demonstrate Hornet's passion or madness).

10–13 he...to't The devil will find being taken to court by Hornet much more painful (hotter) than hell and, after he has had to endure the case throughout three legal terms, will say that hell is a refreshment in comparison.

14–16 I...there See note to l. 2. Shirley lays out the situation for the audience in preparation for the cousin's impending visit.

16 vexation annoyance.

[5.2]] *Gifford subst. (SCENE II.); not in* Q   **1** gone!...gone!] *Gifford subst.;* gone,...gone, Q
1 mad!...niece!] *this edn;* mad....niece! *Gifford;* mad;...Neece, Q   **2** escape!] *this edn;* escape, Q
5 men?] *this edn;* men; *Gifford;* men, Q   **6** night!] *this edn;* night. Q
14 vanished –] *this edn;* vanished; *Gifford;* vanish'd Q

THE CONSTANT MAID   5.2

Enter COUSIN [*as himself*].

COUSIN Save Master Hornet!

HORNET   'Tis too late! Away –
  I do not love unnecessary compliment.

COUSIN This he?

HORNET Yes, I am he. Am I not very fine?   20
  What do you think this trim will cost me, ha?
  Three thousand pounds? No more?

COUSIN   The broker wo'not
  Lend half the money.

HORNET   Will you, sir, be gone?
  I ha' no money to lend now; it is not,
  You know, in fashion with rich clothes.   25

COUSIN I came for other purpose and with news
  Perhaps you would be willing to receive.
  You have a niece?

HORNET   No. Such a creature was
  In my possession. Do you know where she is?

COUSIN Faith, I imagine.

HORNET   Ha, good sir? Pray, forwards!   30

17 **Save…late** In response to the cousin's customary greeting of '(God) save', Hornet responds that it's too late to save him because the disaster (his niece's disappearance) has already happened, but Shirley also intends a pun about salvation—Hornet's behaviour, or his being Jewish, will prevent him from going to heaven.

18 **compliment** either 'politeness' or 'company' (Q has complement).

19 **This he** The cousin affects not to recognize Hornet in his finery.

20 **fine** showily dressed.

21 **trim** outfit (*OED*, Trim *n.* 4a).

22 **Three thousand pounds** Hornet is balancing the loss ('cost') of his niece and her fortune against the suit of finery.

22–3 **The…money** The cousin pretends to take the demand to gauge the worth of the garment seriously and thinks that Hornet could not pawn it for £1,500.

22 **broker** pawnbroker (and see note to 1.2.95).

24–5 **it…clothes** Hornet's barbed comment suggests that those who have spent their money on rich clothes have little left to lend out, or that courtly types think money-lending is beneath them.

29 **In…possession** Hornet thinks of the niece as a chattel rather than a person.

30 **Faith…imagine** In truth, I think I might know. In performance, this could be said very teasingly.

30 **good sir** Hornet changes his tune and becomes very polite as soon as he thinks the cousin may know where his niece is.

30 **forwards** out with it! tell me!

16 SD *as himself*] *this edn; not in* Q   17 Hornet!] *Gifford;* Hornet. Q
17 late! Away –] *this edn;* late; away! *Gifford;* late, away, Q
18 compliment] Q *subst.* (complement*)   22 pounds?] *this edn;* pounds, Q   23 gone?] *Gifford;* gone, Q
26–9] *lineation this edn;* I…perhaps, / You…have / A *Neece?* / No;…possession: / Do Q
30 forwards!] *this edn;* forwards: Q

123

5.2   THE COMPLETE WORKS OF JAMES SHIRLEY, VOLUME 7

You shall have money upon good security.
COUSIN I thank you, sir, for nothing. I do owe you
    Too much already on these terms.
HORNET   My niece,
    As you were saying –
COUSIN   Were you knighted lately?
HORNET Is that talked abroad?   35
COUSIN No general rumour. By a chance I came
    Where such a thing was whispered – only whispered.
    [*As if to himself*] Just as he was described.
    [*To Hornet*] In my opinion you're very handsome
    And do look as like a reverend –
HORNET   Ass.   40
COUSIN Why, you shall have it, sir.
HORNET   But touching my niece,
    Good sir – that most ungracious giglet
    That's run or stolen away, juggled last night
    Out a' my doors –
COUSIN   Did not she leap the casement?
HORNET Do not increase my agony; you came –   45
COUSIN With civil meaning to discover how
    You may be abused.

---

31 I will lend you money if you have something to secure the loan (a change from his claim of poverty at l. 24).
32–3 I…terms I have already taken too many secured loans from you. (This is the first time we learn that the cousin has a reason other than his kinship with Playfair for conspiring against Hornet.)
34 knighted lately The cousin pretends this was not a charade and, interestingly, in the next few lines Hornet seems to half forget his earlier realization that he has been tricked.
35 abroad openly, publicly.
36 general widespread.
38 The cousin pretends he has already heard a description of Hornet in his finery being knighted.
40 Ass Idiot. Hornet has recalled that he has been tricked.
41 you…it if you say so.
42 ungracious giglet wicked strumpet.
43 juggled stolen by trickery or magic (see 4.3.185n).
44 leap…casement jump out of the window.
46 civil courteous and neighbourly.
46–7 discover…abused reveal how you have been abused or work out a way to abuse you further.

---

33 terms] Q *subst.* (tearmes)   33–4] *lineation Gifford;* My…saying. Q   34 saying–] *this edn;* saying. Q
38 SD] *this edn;* – *Gifford; not in* Q   39 SD] *this edn;* – *Gifford; not in* Q
38–42] *lineation this edn;* Just…opinion / Y'are…reverend– / Asse. / Why,…sir. / But…sir, / That Q
44 doors –] *this edn;* doores. Q

THE CONSTANT MAID   5.2

HORNET   What money do you want, sir?
  Your own bond shall suffice.
COUSIN   I ha' sworn never
  To write my name or mark. But I can tell –
HORNET Where I may find this girl?
COUSIN   More I can do,   50
  If need require: 'tis in my power to give
  Her back to your possession, and I am willing –
HORNET An honest man –
COUSIN On reasonable conditions, and such
  As shall not trench on borrowing money –   55
HORNET Honester yet.
COUSIN For you shall give it freely and get by't.
  For you must understand if I do this
  I shall betray a friend of mine that has
  Put me in trust, one that intends to marry her   60
  (For truth to tell they are not yet contracted) –
  To marry her, d'ye mark? – and get ere morning
  Three thousand pounds upon her. Is't not so much?
  One that has lent me sums too without parchment
  Or foolish circumstance to be repaid,   65
  Which you were never yet so much a Christian

48 **Your…suffice** Your signed contract without security will be enough.
48–9 **I…mark** I have sworn that I will not sign anything. A rather bizarre excuse to get out of borrowing more money.
53 **honest** fair, free from deceit.
55 **trench on** i.e. cause me to (borrow money).
56 **Honester yet** Even fairer.
57 **give…by't** i.e. buy a service, a transaction rather than usury.
60 **Put…trust** Trusted me.
61 Actually they are not yet legally married.
62 **d'ye mark** are you taking note? are you paying attention?
62–3 **get…her** Instead of getting her pregnant (the normal sense of *get upon her ere morning*), he will get his hands on her £3,000.
63 **Is't…much** Isn't that how much it is?
64 **One** i.e. the friend (Playfair) of l. 59.
64 **without parchment** without a written contract.
65 **foolish circumstance** silly conditions.
66–7 **you…of** i.e. you were never sufficiently Christian to lend without contract or conditions. It was popular lore in early modern England that usurious rates of interest were only charged by Jewish lenders, but as Kermode demonstrates, this is not borne out by the facts (2009, 7).

50 girl?] *Gifford;* girle. Q   50–1] *lineation Gifford;* More…require; / Tis Q
52 willing –] *this edn;* willing. Q   53 man –] *this edn;* man! *Gifford;* man. Q
55 money –] *this edn;* money. Q   62 get] *Gifford;* yet Q

125

5.2   THE COMPLETE WORKS OF JAMES SHIRLEY, VOLUME 7

As to be guilt' of, in your usurer's gallon
Of conscience-melting sack. This deserves something,
But 'cause some expedition is required –
You have a bond of mine.

HORNET   For fifty pound.   70

COUSIN I had but forty and your scrivener paid,
With whom, perhaps, your worship too divided.
If you remember, there were precious dinners
Ere I could count my chickens altogether,
Which was your thrift and my expense. You shall   75
First cancel that bond – nay, this wo'not do't –
And give – d'ye mark? – give me a hundred pieces.
Perhaps I'll drink your health. This shall retrieve
Your niece and give her into your hands,
Though for my treachery I be sung in ballads   80
And have the town curse if ever I marry.

HORNET 'Tis too much for no more labour, sir.

---

67 guilt' Q2 (1661) has 'guilty', and guilt is not found adjectivally in the *OED*. Q 'guilt' may therefore be an attempt to compress a metrically long line or simply an uncorrected error.

67 usurer's gallon 'An Usurers Gallon, that's just halfe a pint' (Davenport's *A New Trick to Cheat the Devil* (1639), C4v), i.e. a measure that cheats the drinker out of all but one sixteenth of his gallon.

68 conscience-melting sack Usurers plied their victims with alcohol in order to cloud their judgement (conscience).

69 expedition speed, prompt execution.

70 bond...mine contract between us detailing a loan you have given me.

71–5 I...expense Although the contract is for £50, in fact the cousin only got £40 in cash because he had to pay the scrivener out of the money he was borrowing; he suspects moreover that Hornet split that with his scrivener. The cousin also had to pay for expensive dinners for Hornet before he could be sure he had secured the money.

74 count...chickens To count your chickens before they are hatched is to rely on something happening before it can be guaranteed (Tilley C292). It is also a joke about the dinners of l. 73.

76 cancel...bond void the contract of my debt (i.e. not require repayment).

76 nay...do't Hornet obviously starts to agree, but the cousin has not finished laying out his terms.

77 give...give The cousin stresses the idea of giving because it is alien to Hornet who only lends money.

77 hundred pieces One hundred 'unite' pieces was a lot of money (c. £11 in 1630 and worth over £1,300 today), enough to buy two cows (or a horse and a half) or pay a skilled labourer for 157 days; see note to 2.2.27.

80 for...ballads Ballads were popular (usually narrative) songs, often printed without the music in the seventeenth century. Their subjects were commonly the betrayal of friends or lovers, as well as grisly murders.

81 Marriage should garner the town's blessing but his infamy will be so great that they will curse him instead.

82 'Tis...labour i.e. it is too much money considering you don't have to do anything else to get it (because the cousin already knows where the niece is). Hornet tries to negotiate terms.

---

67 guilt'] *this edn;* guilty *Gifford;* guilt Q   **69** 'cause] *Gifford;* cause Q
69 required –] *Gifford subst.* (required,–); required; Q   **77** mark?] *Gifford subst.;* marke, Q

THE CONSTANT MAID 5.3

COUSIN If I consider –
  Three hundred will not bring me to't again.
  Thus fair I'll deal with you: I'll not touch your money 85
  Till I ha' done't, but then I will be sure –
  Fetch, fetch the business.
HORNET   The bond is ready. [*Showing bond*]
COUSIN I will have ready money too. You have
  Bags of all sizes and denominations? [*Hornet shows him money bags.*]
  Aye, these things promise well. Now I'll attend you. 90
HORNET Do this feat for me and 'tis all thine own.   *Exeunt.*

[5.3]

    Enter [Sir CLEMENT *the*] *Justice,* PLAYFAIR, *and* NIECE.

CLEMENT Now we may wish you joy! The priest has tied
  That knot no subtlety nor malice can
  Dissolve, and I repent not I have been
  An actor in your comedy, though I should not
  Be tempted easily to such another 5
  Engagement. For your sake I have dispensed with
  My person and my place.

83–4 If I think about it, I won't do it for three hundred. In performance, the cousin probably pauses between 'consider' and 'Three' to tease Hornet with the idea that he is really willing to negotiate.
85–6 **I'll...sure** i.e. I won't take a penny now, but I have to be sure that everything is set up for payment after I have found your niece.
87 **business** things necessary to do business.
87 **SD** Hornet may rummage in a box in order to produce it.
89 **denominations** units of money.
90 **attend** listen to; accompany you.

0 The scene is set in Sir Clement's house.
0 **SD Justice** In this scene, Q has '*Justice*' in SD and *Just.* in SH but it is clear that the 'next Justice' of 5.1.19 is in fact Sir Clement.
2 **subtlety** cunning, trickery.
4 **your comedy** i.e. the events ending with their wedding, as comedy should.
4–6 **I...Engagement** I would not be easily persuaded to be involved in another undertaking like this (perhaps, following 'actor in your comedy', with a sense of 'theatrical engagement' meaning contract to perform, although this is only documented in later use).
6–7 **dispensed...place** i.e. disguised himself and acted in such a way as to disregard the office of magistrate.

83 consider –] *this edn;* consider, *Gifford;* consider, Q   84 again.] *Gifford;* agen; Q
86 done't] Q *subst.* (don't*)*   87 SD] *this edn; not in* Q   89 denominations?] *this edn;* denominations. Q
89 SD] *this edn; Hor. opens a cabinet. Gifford;* not in Q

[5.3]] *Gifford subst.* (SCENE III.*); not in* Q
0 SD SIR CLEMENT] *Gifford subst.; not in* Q
1 SH] *Gifford subst.* (Clem.*);* Just. Q; *Just. is amended to* CLEMENT *throughout this scene*
1 joy!] *this edn;* joy; Q

127

5.3   THE COMPLETE WORKS OF JAMES SHIRLEY, VOLUME 7

PLAYFAIR   You always were
    My loving uncle.
NIECE   Sir, you have, in this,
    Deserved our lives and fortunes.
PLAYFAIR   It was good mirth
    To hear him confident all our device   10
    Was but a dream.
CLEMENT   He is awake by this time.
    Should your cousin fail, we'll have another way
    To invite him and, if honesty prevail not,
    Force him till he consent.

            Enter SERVANT.

SERVANT Some offenders are brought to be examined.   15
CLEMENT Nephew, withdraw! And you, fair bride. These troubles
    Are incident to my place; I'll soon dispatch 'em.

                [Exeunt Playfair and Niece, with Servant.]
        Enter COUNTRYMAN, HARTWELL, *and* OFFICERS.

    How now, my masters? Master Hartwell? Ha!
HARTWELL Look on me, sir, as a delinquent. These
    Are able to accuse me.
CLEMENT   What offence?   20
OFFICER Nothing, but for killing of a man.
CLEMENT What proof?

    8 uncle Sir Clement turns out to be uncle to both Playfair and the cousin, to whom he refers as 'my kinsman'
at 5.3.101.
    13 honesty It is hard to see what has been honest about the conspirators' behaviour towards Hornet, but the
point is that usury is dishonest, so outwitting a usurer is honest by default (*OED*, Honest *adj*. 4b, 'done with
truthfulness, fairness, or integrity').
    14 Urge him until he is compelled to consent [to hand over his niece's dowry]. There may be an overtone of
physical coercion (see *OED*, Force *v.*), but the threat of exposing Hornet's foolishness will be the primary means
of persuasion.
    15 As a magistrate, Sir Clement is appointed to give the first hearing to a wide range of criminal offences,
committing defendants to trial before a judge and jury in more serious cases and dealing with minor cases
himself.
    16–17 These...place These disturbances are part of being a magistrate.
    18 Master Hartwell Sir Clement is surprised to see Hartwell, whom he recognizes and probably mixes with
socially, as they are from a similar class.
    19 delinquent one guilty of an offence against the law, an offender (*OED*, *adj*. and *n*. B1).
    21 Nothing Hartwell is still using double-speak (ll. 19–20), in order to implicate himself without saying any-
thing untrue. One could take the officer's 'Nothing' to mean a sarcastic 'Not much', or that Hartwell has
offended no-one because no-one values Startup anyway, or that he has not committed an offence at all (although
only Hartwell can take it this way, since no-one else knows the truth of the matter).

    16 withdraw!] *this edn;* withdraw, Q   **17 SD1**] *this edn; Exeunt Play. and Niece. Gifford; not in* Q
    17 SD2 COUNTRYMAN] Q *subst. (Cotntrey-man)*

128

THE CONSTANT MAID

5.3

COUNTRYMAN   He has confessed it, sir.

Enter MISTRESS BELLAMY *and* FRANCES.

CLEMENT Mistress Bellamy –
    You are come in a sad time: here's Master Hartwell
    Accused for killing.
BELLAMY   'Tis not possible!   25
    Good sir, believe it not!
CLEMENT   He does confess.
HARTWELL I am not worth your pity, gentle lady.
    In vain I should extenuate my fact
    To have the troubles of examinations.
    Here I confess again: my hand is guilty   30
    Of killing him whose feeble arm durst not
    Lift up a weapon to defend himself.
CLEMENT That was not manly.
HARTWELL   I but slew a coward,
    Startup, and – could I call his life again –
    As soon I should destroy it. You perhaps   35
    Know not my provocation: he was
    My rival, sir. Pardon me, Mistress Bellamy –
    To whom I only seemed a proselyte
    In love – I had no heart to give from her,
    And in my study to decline your anger   40
    I fell upon her scorn, which in few minutes
    Engaged me to this fate. Nor am I troubled

24 **sad** serious (as well as the modern sense of unhappy).

28–9 The fact of his action will not be extenuated by the exertions of investigations (i.e. investigation won't exculpate him).

31–2 **him…himself** Contrary to what he told Close at 4.1.69, Hartwell now claims he killed Startup 'basely' because Startup was too cowardly to defend himself. Because Hartwell is *only* guilty of killing a man who did not defend himself, he is effectively confessing to having killed no-one. He did not even encounter Startup, let alone challenge him to a fight. At ll. 33–5, he comes closer to claiming Startup's death was at his hands, though there is still some ambiguity.

33 **manly** showing qualities befitting a man, i.e. courageous, honourable. An early modern classicist such as Shirley would no doubt have had the Latin *virtus* 'manly excellence' in the back of his mind.

38 **proselyte** convert.

39 **her** i.e. Frances.

40 **study** thought or attention directed to the accomplishment of a purpose (*OED*, *n*. 13).

40 **decline** avoid, turn away.

23 Bellamy–] *this edn; Bellamy*, Q   25 possible!] *this edn;* possible: Q   26 not!] *this edn;* not. Q
37 Bellamy –] *this edn; Bellamy*, Q   39 her,] *this edn;* her; [*Pointing to Frances. Gifford;* her: Q

129

5.3　THE COMPLETE WORKS OF JAMES SHIRLEY, VOLUME 7

That I must die when she, upon whose faith
I durst have laid the hopes of my eternity,
Hath violated all the trust of woman. 45
COUNTRYMAN Will't please you, sir –
CLEMENT　　　　　　　　　　Forbear a little.
HARTWELL [*To Frances*] Tell me, most unkind, if thou didst love
At all? How couldst thou think I should be such
A desperate atheist that thou so soon,
And with a strange apostasy, shouldst revenge it? 50
These swelling drops which in thy innocence
Might ha' prevailed to ha' restored the dead,
Heaven now doth look on and despise. And though
Thou shed moist tribute on this tomb, 't shall slide
Neglected o'er the marble and be lost, 55
As if the stone had sense to punish thy
Disdain of me. I can behold that weeping
And not be moved to wish I were not guilty
Of killing him whose love had been thy triumph.
And I dare boldly – still in the contempt 60
Of what I am to suffer and the justice
Of my own truth – challenge thy soul to answer
In what I was beneath that gaudy fool,
Excepting that he had more earth than I

43–4 **upon…eternity** i.e. I would have wagered my salvation on her faithfulness.
45 **hath…woman** i.e. by failing to keep faith, Frances the paragon has demonstrated that all women are untrustworthy.
49 **atheist** someone who fails to keep faith; apostate (see note to l. 50). Hartwell is here inverting the traditional religious metaphors of love to rebuke Frances.
50 **strange** unfamiliar; distant; unfriendly (see *OED*, Strange *adj*. esp. 10a and 11b).
50 **apostasy** renunciation of their vows (of love); properly, abandonment or renunciation of one's religious faith or moral allegiance.
51 **swelling drops** tears. Frances is crying.
51 **in…innocence** i.e. before she was unfaithful.
54 **moist tribute** i.e. tears as an offering or gift.
54 **this tomb** Hartwell probably means his heart.
57–9 **I…triumph** i.e. I can watch you weep without getting upset and wishing that I had not killed Startup. This denial gives a big clue to how Hartwell is really feeling.
60 **in…contempt** with scorn, disregard.
62–3 **challenge…fool** i.e. ask yourself if there were any ways I was less worthy (of your affections) than Startup.
63 **gaudy fool** see note to 3.1.92.
64 **earth** land (and, thus, wealth).

47 **SD**] *this edn; not in* Q

130

THE CONSTANT MAID   5.3

To help his scale which yet he may be in debt for   65
To his father's sins. Alive, he could not merit
One cold disdain from thee; and dead, how comes it
He should be worth thy tears? But let thy eyes
Chide this unruly sorrow: dress thy cheeks
With their fresh blood again, and let thy face   70
Open a book of smiles in the assurance
I have not long to live. When I have numbered
A few sad minutes, thou shalt be revenged
And I shall never trouble thee. If this
Be not enough, extend thy malice further,   75
And, if thou find'st one man that loved me living
Will honour this cold body with a grave,
Be cruel and corrupt his charity.
So fare ye well.
FRANCES   Yet you must stay and hear me!
He sha'not suffer if my friends or state   80
Can purchase him a pardon. Where's the body
Of him that's slain?
COUNTRYMAN   We know not, but you hear
His free confession of the fact.
CLEMENT   This may
Proceed from discontents. Life to some men

65 **help…scale** tip the balance in his favour.

65–6 he…sins Hartwell imagines that the wealth that Startup's father passed down to him might be tainted with sins he committed in amassing it. Hartwell's image is based on the idea that God weighs good deeds against bad in a balance before making a determination about whether or not to save a soul.

67 **One…disdain** even one cold look of scorn or disregard.

67 **and dead** and when he is dead.

67–8 and…tears Hartwell thinks Frances is weeping over Startup's death; actually, she is weeping because of Hartwell's predicament and her consequent loss of him.

69–70 dress…again i.e. stop looking so pale and get some colour back in your cheeks.

70–1 let…smiles i.e. change your mood and start smiling.

71–2 When…minutes An elaborate way of saying in a few minutes; 'sad' because Hartwell is heading off to his execution.

72 **thou…revenged** i.e. Frances will get her revenge on Hartwell for taking Startup's life.

75 **extend…further** further your desire to do me harm.

78 **corrupt…charity** dissuade him from being charitable.

79 **Yet…me** This is primarily to Hartwell, but she addresses also the rest of the company as she does at ll. 80–2 too.

80 **friends…state** relations/supporters or estate (so both a personal and financial intervention as necessary).

83–4 This…discontents i.e. his confession may be prompted by despair or unhappiness. Only Sir Clement is sensible enough to realize this may be Hartwell's motivation.

65 in debt] *Gifford;* indebt Q   79 me!] *this edn;* me.– *Gifford;* me: Q

131

5.3 THE COMPLETE WORKS OF JAMES SHIRLEY, VOLUME 7

Is but their torment in whose pain they will, 85
As on the rack, confess what never
Was in their thought.

HARTWELL [*To Frances*] Speak it again, and I
Dare promise thee to live!

FRANCES   My heart was ever
Constant. My mother's love was but thy trial,
As mine a seeming change, in thy disguise, 90
Which was not able to secure thee from me:
The words were 'I would choose my husband here'.
But what will this avail us?

HARTWELL   Master Justice –
I here discharge you.

CLEMENT   How?

HARTWELL   My joy obeys
No limits! I accused myself unjustly: 95
The fool's alive.

COUNTRYMAN   Startup? Where?

HARTWELL   I know not that.
My servant's with him – but if he ha' played
The hangman, starved or smothered him in a ditch,
I ha' made fair work.

ALL   This were a welcome truth.

     Enter SERVANT.

SERVANT   Sir, the constable. 100

CLEMENT   I had rather it had been my kinsman and the usurer,

---

87 Speak…again i.e. Repeat what you said in ll. 80–1.

90 seeming change apparent (rather than real) alteration.

90–1 in…me i.e. while you were disguised but not well enough for me not to see through it.

92 I…here This is repetition of what Frances said at 3.4.42 and may be accompanied by a gesture towards Hartwell.

93 But…us But what use is this (rapprochement) to us? A rhetorical question because she still thinks Hartwell is guilty and so lost to her.

94 I…you I relieve you now of your duty as magistrate. (This is not something that Hartwell can actually do in a legal sense.)

95 unjustly inaccurately, contrary to the principles of justice.

98 starved killed (see note to 4.1.125).

99 made…work done a good job.

101 my kinsman i.e. the cousin.

---

87 SD] *this edn; not in* Q   **88 live!]** *this edn;* live. Q   **93** Justice –] *this edn;* Justice, Q
93–4] *lineation Gifford;* Mʳ…. you. Q   **94** joy obeys] *this edn;* joys obey *Gifford;* joyes obeyes Q
95 limits!] *this edn;* limits. *Gifford;* limits; Q   **96** Startup?] *Gifford; Startup,* Q
97 him –] *this edn;* him; *Gifford;* him, Q   **99 SH]** *this edn; Omnes.* Q

132

THE CONSTANT MAID   5.3

But wait and give me knowledge when they come.   [*Exit Servant.*]

  Enter CONSTABLE, STARTUP [*in ragged clothes*], CLOSE, [*and*] OFFICERS.

CONSTABLE Where's Master Justice?

HARTWELL   It is he and Close –

 Then I am secure. [*To Bellamy*] Your pardon, [*to Frances*] and thy love?

BELLAMY You have it freely and a mother's prayers   105

 For both your happiness.

CONSTABLE   Please your worship, these

 We took last night i'th'fields suspiciously

 And by my own authority I condemned 'em.

STARTUP Shall we be hanged, Close? We are condemned already!

CLEMENT This is the gentleman was killed?

STARTUP   Sweet sir, no,   110

 Not killed outright – but I was almost starved

 With cold. These gentlewomen know me,

 And I should know that hose and doublet too.

 Those garments which you wear I have oft seen, sweet sir.

CLOSE [*Aside*] Well said, Hieronimo!

STARTUP   I was fain to borrow   115

 These of a prisoner that lies in, upon

 My diamond ring.

CLEMENT [*To Hartwell*] You are discharged.

---

104 **secure** i.e. certain to remain safe from conviction.

107 **suspiciously** i.e. behaving suspiciously by wandering around in the dark.

108 **condemned** The Constable cannot condemn them (despite Startup's fears in the next line). Shirley may be glancing at *Much Ado* 4.2, a scene full of Dogberry's malapropisms, one of which is 'thou wilt be condemned into everlasting redemption' (ll. 49–50).

111–12 **almost...cold** See note to 4.1.125.

113 **that...too** i.e. the ones that Hartwell is wearing and that belong to Startup.

113 **hose** article of male clothing for the leg (see note to 4.3.97).

113 **doublet** close-fitting padded jacket (see note to 1.1.4).

114 **Those...seen** A quotation from Kyd's *The Spanish Tragedy* 2.5.13.

115 **Well...Hieronimo** Hieronimo is the protagonist of *The Spanish Tragedy* to whom the King of Spain does indeed say 'Well said' at 4.4.68.

115 **fain** glad.

116 **These** i.e. The ragged clothes Startup is wearing.

116 **lies in** is incarcerated.

116–17 **upon...ring** using my diamond ring as a pledge.

117 **discharged** freed without charge.

---

102 **SD1**] *Gifford subst.; not in* Q 102 **SD2**] *this edn; Enter Constable, Startup, Close, Officers.* Q
103 Close –] *this edn; Close;* Q 104 **SD1**] *this edn; – Gifford; not in* Q 104 **SD2**] *this edn; not in* Q
104 love?] *this edn;* love. Q 109 Close?] *Gifford; Close,* Q 109 already!] *this edn;* already. Q
110 killed?] *this edn;* kill'd Q 115 **SD**] *this edn; not in* Q
115 Hieronimo!] *this edn;* Jeronimo! *Gifford; Ieronimo.* Q 117 **SD**] *this edn; not in* Q

133

5·3   THE COMPLETE WORKS OF JAMES SHIRLEY, VOLUME 7

STARTUP   And we too?
CLEMENT Yes; and joy in every bosom.   [*Exeunt Constable and Officers.*]
STARTUP Close, you must know this your mistress. [*To Frances*] Sweet lady.
FRANCES How?
CLOSE   'Tis enough for you to know her, sir,   120
    And me to acknowledge.
COUNTRYMAN   Do you know me, sir?
STARTUP Hmm! Yes. Who brought you to town? And your
    Daughter too, sweet sir?
COUNTRYMAN   And you shall right her.
STARTUP Is she grown crooked? I knew her too well.
    [*Aside to Countryman*] Peace; not a word more – I know your meaning.   125
    Do not discredit me, sweet sir, and we'll steal down
    And marry her ere any be aware on't.
    I wo'not stay to shift me, take no leave.
    The jest will be when I am in the country
    How like an ass he'll look in my apparel.   *Exeunt Startup [and] Countryman.*   130
        Enter SERVANT.

SERVANT Sir, Master Playfair's cousin and the t'other gallant.

119 **Close...mistress** Because he has missed the rapprochement between Hartwell and Frances, Startup
still thinks he is going to marry Frances. He also seems to assume that Close will remain in place as his regular
servant.
120 **How** What's going on? This word is used repeatedly as the denouement plays out, and its repetition demonstrates how confused things seem.
120–1 **'Tis...acknowledge** Close quibbles on the biblical sense of 'know' (l. 119), be sexually intimate with
(*OED*, Know *v.* 13), and points out that it is not his place to do more than acknowledge (i.e. recognize) Frances.
121 **Do...sir** The Countryman uses 'know' to mean recognize but maybe also with overtones of 'admit the
claims of' and 'confess' (*OED*, senses 3 & 4). In performance the 'me' would be stressed.
122 **Hmm** Either Startup is genuinely trying to think who he is or this is an expression of surprise, perhaps
with an overtone of 'oops'. At 3.2.106, Hornet's use suggests the former, but it is a decision for performance
here.
122–3 **And...sir** In 'knowing' the Countryman, Startup naturally thinks of his daughter whom he has previously 'known' (back to sense 13).
123 **you...her** you shall redress or rectify (the wrong you have done) her.
124 **crooked** Startup understands 'right' to mean 'straighten (a crooked object)' (*OED*, Right *v.* 1b).
124 **I...well** Startup admits that he got rather closer to her than he should have done (i.e. sexually).
125 **I...meaning** I understand what you mean (another sense of 'know', *OED*, 10b).
126 **discredit me** harm my reputation; bring me into disrepute (by telling the truth in public).
126 **steal down** travel secretly.
128 **I...leave** I will not stay to change my clothes or say goodbye.
129–30 Startup clearly looks more ridiculous in his rags than Hartwell does in the gaudy finery, but Startup is
a master at making the best of a bad job and appears to leave the play as buoyantly as he entered it.
131 **t'other gallant** i.e. Hornet who is still in his finery.

118 SD] *this edn; Exeunt Const. Watchmen, and Officers. after 'discharg'd.' l. 117 Gifford; not in* Q
119 SD] *this edn; – Gifford; not in* Q   122 Hmm!] *this edn;* Hum; Q
122–3] *lineation this edn;* Hum; ...Daugh- / ter *(set as prose)* Q   125 SD] *this edn; not in* Q
130 SD *and*] *Gifford; not in* Q

134

THE CONSTANT MAID   5.3

CLEMENT I must entreat your patience a little.
　　You'll meet with friends in the next room.　　　　[*Exeunt all but Sir Clement.*]
　　　　Enter COUSIN [*and*] HORNET.
COUSIN Excuse my boldness, sir: [*presenting Hornet*] this gentleman –
CLEMENT Master Hornet, you are very welcome.   135
HORNET Good sir, no ceremony. We are come
　　'Bout business. I have lost my niece and would
　　Know where she is.
CLEMENT　　　　　　　　D'ye take me for a wizard?
COUSIN Sir, our desires are modest: that you would
　　Be witness to a bargain and receive   140
　　Some trifles, sir, in trust, to be delivered
　　To me if I restore his kinswoman.
HORNET Not else. On that condition I deposit
　　These hundred pieces and a bond. [*Handing money and bond to Sir Clement*] If he
　　Deliver me my niece, they are his fraught;   145
　　If not, they call me owner.
COUSIN　　　　　　　　Pardon, sir,
　　That I presume to bring this trouble to you.
CLEMENT 'Tis none at all.
COUSIN [*To Hornet*]　　You sha'not long expect,
　　So rest you merry.　　　　　　　　　　　　　　[*Exit.*]
CLEMENT [*To Hornet*] How fare you, sir?
HORNET As you see, fallen away an inch since morning,   150

133 Playfair and his bride, who retired into the next room at l. 17, are known to the rest of the company.
134 **Excuse...boldness** Forgive my barging in. The cousin deliberately adopts a formal tone, presumably to hide the fact that he and Sir Clement are related so as to persuade Hornet that their deal is above board.
134 **gentleman** Hornet is not a gentleman but the cousin is being excessively polite and slyly reminding Hornet of his 'knighting' at the same time.
136 **no ceremony** Hornet is impatient to get on with business, so he is trying to forestall lengthy courtesies.
138 **D'ye...wizard** Do you expect me to find her by magic? Sir Clement is having fun at Hornet's expense.
141 **Some trifles** In fact, the bond and the money are rather more than trifles, but the cousin is playing it cool.
145 **fraught** cargo (now obsolete for freight).
146–7 **Pardon...you** The cousin maintains his formality with Sir Clement to keep their connection hidden.
148 **'Tis...all** i.e. It is no trouble at all.
148–9 **You...merry** You won't have to wait long, so be cheerfully confident.
150 **fallen...inch** deteriorated or diminished (*OED*, Fall *v.* PV Fall away, 5a) and lost weight (5b) but also perhaps become less cheerful or hopeful (*OED*, Fall *v.* 20b).
150 **morning** Hornet and Sir Clement last met during the late night 'revels'.

133 SD1] *this edn; Exeunt Hart. Bell. Fran. and Close. Gifford; not in* Q　　133 SD2 *and*] *Gifford; not in* Q
134 SD] *this edn; not in* Q　　134 gentleman –] *Gifford;* Gentleman. Q　　144 SD] *this edn; not in* Q
148 SD] *this edn; not in* Q　　148–9] *lineation Gifford;* You...merry. Q
149 SD1] *Gifford; not in* Q　　149 SD2] *this edn; not in* Q

5.3 THE COMPLETE WORKS OF JAMES SHIRLEY, VOLUME 7

But this will physic me. If I possess
This harlotry again, I'll make her sure.
Trust not a woman: they have found the herb
To open locks. Not brazen towers can hold 'em
Or, if they get not loose, they have the virtue   155
Of loadstones: shut up in a box, they'll draw
Customers to them. Nay, being dead and buried
There is a suspicion they will break the grave,
Which puts so many husbands to the charge
Of heavy stones to keep their bad wives under.   160

CLEMENT You are moved?

HORNET   Oh, Master Justice, you are honest:
I ha' been abused, so miserably cheated
I am ashamed to think on't. [*Music plays.*] Stay, what? Music?

    Enter COUSIN, *leading the* NIECE.

Ha! 'Tis my niece – the very same.

COUSIN There, sir, you have her; and I must ha' these. [*Taking money and bond*]   165
HORNET Take 'em. [*To Niece*] But you shall go with me. Have I found you?
NIECE How, uncle? A reveller? You'll lead me
    A coranto.
HORNET   You shall dance homewards.

    Enter PLAYFAIR.

PLAYFAIR What make you so familiar with my wife?
HORNET How wife? Is she married?

---

151 **physic me** act as medicine on me (as one who had lost weight might require).
152 **harlotry** harlot; a term of opprobrium for a woman (i.e. his niece). At 2.1.88 (see note) Playfair tells Hartwell that Hornet displays the harlot's story as an example for his niece so this is consistent with her uncle's view of her.
152 **sure** safe in one's possession or keeping; not liable to be lost or to escape (*OED*, Sure *adj.* †4).
153 **herb** i.e. magic potion.
154 **brazen towers** This is a reference to the bronze tower in which Danaë was incarcerated by her father Acrisius to try to prevent her giving birth to a son (Perseus) whom the oracle had foretold would kill his grandfather. Shirley uses this motif extensively in *The Bird in a Cage* (see Sanders 2002).
156 **loadstones** magnets.
157 **Customers** Purchasers of goods or services, often with a specifically sexual overtone.
159 **charge** expense.
161 **moved** affected by emotion, especially by anger.
167 **reveller** person who takes part in a revel, in this case a wedding.
167–8 **You'll...coranto** It would be expected that at the festivities following early modern marriage ceremonies the person giving away the bride would lead her in a dance, in this case a fast celebratory coranto (see Monahin 2019).
170 **How wife?** Why are you calling her wife?

---

163 SD1] *Gifford subst. (music.); not in* Q   163 what?] *this edn;* what, Q   164 Ha!] *Gifford;* Ha, Q
165 SD] *this edn; not in* Q   166 SD] *this edn; – Gifford; not in* Q   167–8] *lineation this edn;* How...Corranto. Q

136

THE CONSTANT MAID   5.3

COUSIN   'Tis upon record.   170
    I'll bring a parson that shall take his oath on't.
HORNET Give me my bond and money, Master Justice.
    [*Looking around for them*] Where? Where?
COUSIN [*Waving them at him*]   Here, here! But not to be recovered
    By law. I have a judgement, sir, against you.
HORNET You have conspired to rob, cheat, and undo me.   175
    I'll have you all Star-Chambered.
PLAYFAIR   Sir, be calm,
    And hear us.
HORNET   I'll hear nothing.
PLAYFAIR   Yes, you shall:
    It will be necessary. I am bold,
    Presuming on her favour, to demand
    A parcel of three thousand pound – the sum   180
    Belongs to me by virtue of a marriage
    And I must have it.
HORNET   Tell me of a marriage?
COUSIN I saw the priest conjoin 'em. He will deserve
    Your love.
PLAYFAIR   Perhaps you may continue
    A thousand or two thousand, for six months   185

170 **upon record** legal, official.
171 **parson** clergyman.
171 **take...on't** swear it is true.
173–4 **But...you** i.e. You won't be able to get them back by resorting to law. The magistrate will judge in my favour (because he witnessed the deal). The whole point of doing this in front of Justice Clement was to ensure that the exchange contract was legally binding and that Hornet could not get out of it.
176 **Star-Chambered** Brought before the Star Chamber (an English court of civil and criminal jurisdiction, trying especially those cases affecting the interests of the Crown).
178 **necessary** This word has legal force, as does 'must' at l. 182.
179 **Presuming...favour** Both presuming her willingness for me to ask, and taking the liberty because I am in her favour.
180 **parcel** (marriage) portion.
181 **by...of** in consequence of.
183 **conjoin 'em** join them together in marriage.
183–4 **He...love** He will be worthy of your approval (perhaps with a sense that Playfair will treat Hornet more respectfully in future).
184–6 **Perhaps...security** Playfair teasingly offers to lend some of the money back to Hornet at interest if he can produce security for it.

173] **SH** *omitted this edn*; Play. *Gifford; not in* 1661; Hart. Q   173 **SD**1] *this edn; not in* Q
173 **SD**2] *this edn; not in* Q   173 Here, here!] *this edn;* Here! here! *Gifford;* Here, here, Q
176–7] *lineation Gifford;* Sir...us. Q   183–4] *lineation this edn;* 'em: / He...love. Q
185 months] Q *subst.* (moneths)

137

5.3   THE COMPLETE WORKS OF JAMES SHIRLEY, VOLUME 7

Upon security –
HORNET Persecution!
CLEMENT   Faith sir, consider:
It is more safe to see her thus bestowed
Than trust a jury. If the doctor had
Given her too much opium or purged   190
Her soul away things might go worse. But I
Keep counsel.
HORNET   Ha' ye mortified me yet?
COUSIN For your own sake – and as you are true knight.
HORNET Now, ha' ye done?

      Enter MISTRESS BELLAMY, HARTWELL, FRANCES, *and* CLOSE.

The widow! Not a word more!
Take her: I'll pay you, sir, three thousand pounds   195
Tomorrow. Noble widow, you were in
The first list to be invited: my niece
I told you of is married to this worthy
Gentleman.
BELLAMY   You look like a bridegroom.
HORNET 'Tis in your power to make it good. What say you?   200
Shall we have issue? Now the word of comfort.
BELLAMY I will never marry.

---

187 Persecution This plays on the idea of usurers being represented as Jewish. Almost all the *OED* quotations for persecution from the seventeenth century have a religious import.

188 thus bestowed i.e. safely married to Playfair. The niece is described in terms of a chattel throughout much of the play.

189–91 If…worse Sir Clement reminds Hornet that if the case were to go before the jury of l. 189, there is evidence that Hornet had discussed murdering his niece with the doctor.

192 Keep counsel Observe secrecy (about Hornet's plan).

192 mortified almost killed; humiliated; brought my passion [for money] under control (see *OED*).

193 The cousin suggests piously that this is an act of kindness to Hornet, but then spoils it by mocking him about his 'knighthood'.

194 The…more Hornet does not want to look bad in front of Mistress Bellamy, whom he is still trying to court.

196–7 in…invited at the top of the guest list.

199 look…bridegroom Like a bridegroom, Hornet is wearing his finest clothes.

200 'Tis…good i.e. You could make that happen.

201 have issue i.e. come to an agreement. There is a glancing pun on 'issue' meaning children, deliberately comic in connection with Hornet who might be considered to be past that kind of issue.

---

187 Persecution!] *Gifford;* Persecution. Q   **194 SD**] *this edn; after l. 193* Q
194–9] *lineation this edn;* widdow; / Not…sir, / Three…widow / You…invited; / My…to / This…Gentleman. Q
194 widow!] *Gifford;* widdow; Q
194 more!] *this edn;* more? *Gifford;* more, Q
200 you?] *Gifford;* you, Q

138

THE CONSTANT MAID   5.3

HORNET You are resolved – why, so. Come hither, nephew –
    Shalt be my heir. I love thee for thy wit,
    But charm thy friends they do not laugh at me.   205
    I'll be a knight too, if I live, and build
    An hospital for twenty more o'th'order,
    Which I'll reduce myself out of the suburbs.
    It is a shame such men should lose their spurs
    In women's petticoats, and turn squires again   210
    To whores, or parasites to noblemen
    For want of fit provision.
CLEMENT   An excellent
    Foundation. But where's Startup?
CLOSE [*Aside*]   Sunk, I think.
HARTWELL Ne'er conjure for him! We are ingrateful to
    Our bliss, but wasting of these precious minutes   215
    Which are so many ages till the church
    Hath made us perfect.
HORNET   Is there any more
    Work for the priest? Then give you joy beforehand
    And let us celebrate the day together.
PLAYFAIR I'm glad of your conversion: ye are the first   220

---

203 resolved –] *this edn;* resolved? *Gifford;* resolv'd Q
203 nephew Hornet seems to have readily accepted Playfair as his kin, in keeping with the happy ending.
204 Shalt (Thou) shall.
205 charm persuade.
206–8 Hornet decides that if he survives long enough, he will found an order with a home in the suburbs for himself and some compatriot 'Knights', presumably of the same sort as the poor knights of Windsor mentioned at 3.2.98 (see note).
209–10 lose…petticoats become dependent on women; or turn away from manly pursuits in chasing after women.
210–11 squires…whores After graduating from being a squire to another knight, to being their own independent knight, Hornet imagines that in their old age such knights would again fulfil the role of service, but this time to 'whores'.
211 parasites…noblemen i.e. fulfil a demeaning role in a nobleman's service.
212 For…provision For lack of enough money.
213 Foundation Institution established with an endowment and regulations for its maintenance.
213 Sunk Disappeared; submerged (by circumstance).
214 Ne'er…him Don't try to summon him up.
214 ingrateful not feeling or showing gratitude.
215 but merely.
215–17 these…perfect i.e. every minute is precious and each will feel like an age until we are married.
217 perfect complete.
220 conversion i.e. accepting his fate and reforming his practice.

---

203 resolved –] *this edn;* resolved? *Gifford;* resolv'd Q
212–13] *lineation Gifford;* An…foundation. / But Q   **213 SD]** *this edn; not in* Q
214 him!] *this edn;* him; Q

139

5.3   THE COMPLETE WORKS OF JAMES SHIRLEY, VOLUME 7

Jew that in my remembrance has turned Christian.

CLEMENT Walk on to joys.

HARTWELL 'Twixt Love and Fortune now the accounts are even –
A chain of hearts and the first link in heaven.   [*Exeunt.*]

THE END

220–1 ye…Christian This inter-theatrical comment makes a joke about the plays which Shirley has reminded us of throughout *Constant Maid,* particularly of *MV.*

223–4 The play ends with a quasi *sententia* which celebrates the power of Love both earthly and heavenly. This is a finessing of Hymen's benevolent Elizabethan coupling of things in *As You Like It* (5.3), its metaphorics ('accounts'), and reversal of rhyme words ('even'/'heaven') grounding the aspirations of Shirley's work more emphatically in the pragmatism of the Caroline world from which it arises:

Then is there mirth in heaven,
When earthly things made even
Atone together.

---

224 SD1] *Gifford; not in* Q   **224** THE END] Q *subst. (*Finis.*)*

The Doubtful Heir

EDITED BY
Rebecca Yearling

THE
DOUBTFUL
HEIR.

A
Tragi-comedie,

AS
It was Acted at the private House
IN
BLACKFRIERS,
WRITTEN
By JAMES SHIRLEY.

Never Printed before.

LONDON,
Printed for *Humphrey Robinson* at the three Pigeons, and *Humphrey Moseley* at the Prince's
Arms in St. *Paul's* Church-yard.
1 6 5 2.

2. *The Doubtful Heir*, quarto title-page (1652), Cambridge University Library, Y.10.57.

General Introduction

CONTEXT

The Doubtful Heir was written during Shirley's four years in Ireland, 1636–40, and first produced by Ogilby's Men at the Werburgh Street Theatre in Dublin under the title *Rosania, or Love's Victory*. It was one of the Shirley plays that were produced by the Werburgh Theatre, coming after *The Royal Master* and before *The Gentleman of Venice*, *The Politician*, and *St Patrick for Ireland*, and was probably the first play that Shirley wrote specifically for an Irish audience.[1]

The play can be dated to *c.* 1638–9, given the Dublin prologue's references to two recent English plays, Thomas Killigrew's *Claricilla* (perf. *c.* 1636) and John Suckling's *Aglaura* (perf. *c.* 1637–8):

> "*Rosania*?" methinks I hear one say,
> "What's that? 'Tis a strange title to a play."
> . . . . Others that have seen
> And fashionably observed the English scene
> Say (but with less hope to be understood)
> Such titles unto plays are now the mood:
> *Aglaura, Claricilla . . .*
>
> (Dublin prologue, 1–2, 9–13)

Shirley's prologue implies a certain anxiety regarding whether his play—named after its heroine, in the currently fashionable English style—will find understanding among the theatregoers of Dublin. Nevertheless, the rest of the prologue suggests greater confidence in his Irish spectators' level of sophistication and civility. It reassures them that they and their supposedly delicate sensibilities are in safe hands, despite the martial overtones of the play's original subtitle, 'Love's Victory':

> You see, but can take in no shot; you are
> So far from danger in this amorous war.
> Not the least rude uncivil language shall
> Approach your ear or make one cheek look pale.
>
> (Dublin prologue, 25–8)

---

[1] It seems likely that *The Royal Master* was completed before Shirley left London. See Williams 2010, 173n.

THE COMPLETE WORKS OF JAMES SHIRLEY, VOLUME 7

When Shirley returned to London in April 1640, he brought back *The Doubtful Heir* with him, to be performed by his new company, the King's Men. The play was licensed as *Rosania* by Henry Herbert, the Master of the Revels, on 1 June 1640. However, the title had been altered by 7 August 1641, when the play appears on a list of sixty plays owned by the King's Men and protected by the Lord Chamberlain: it appears on that list as *The doubtfull heire*.[2] The play was then entered in the Stationers' Register on 4 September 1646 as *Doubtfull Heire, by Shirley*. It was first printed in 1652–3, as part of the volume *Six New Plays*.

The title page of the 1652–3 edition refers to the play as having been 'Acted at the private House / IN / *BLACKFRIERS*'. However, we have no record of any Blackfriars performance. What we do have is evidence that the play was put on at the King's Men's other playhouse, the Globe Theatre. *Six New Plays* features a prologue written by Shirley for a performance there, in which he comments that:

> Our author did not calculate this play
> For this meridian. The Bankside, he knows,
> Are far more skilful at the ebbs and flows
> Of water than of wit…
>
> (Globe prologue, 2–5)

This is confirmed by the title of a version of this prologue printed in Shirley's *Poems &c* (1646): '*A Prologue at the* Globe *to his Comedy call'd* The doubtfull Heire, *which should have been presented at the* Black-Friers'.[3] The claim on the play's title page that it was performed at the Blackfriars may thus be true (if there was an early performance there that is otherwise unrecorded), but may also be an error (perhaps reflecting the fact that Shirley originally assumed that the play would be performed at the Blackfriars). Either way, Shirley was clearly unhappy to have his play put on at the Globe. In the London prologue, he characterizes the Globe in the early 1640s as being associated with a more spectacular and sensationalist kind of entertainment than the private Blackfriars theatre. He goes on to explain that his play has none of the features that the average Globe playgoer might desire: it contains no dancing, no sword fighting, no devils, no clowns, no bawdry, and no ballads.[4] Instead, it has, 'But language clean, and, what affects you not, / Without impossibilities the plot' (11–12). Having implicitly insulted his audience, however, by implying that they are uninterested in sophisticated, witty theatre, Shirley tries to win them back, by appealing to the more civilized among his spectators:

> But you that can contract yourselves and sit
> As you were now in the Blackfriars pit,
> And will not deaf us with lewd noise and tongues
> Because we have no heart to break our lungs,

---

[2] The full list is available in transcription on the page 'Lord Chamberlain's List (1641)' at the Lost Plays Database, https://lostplays.folger.edu/Main_Page.

[3] See *Poems &c*, London (1646), Wing S3480; Thomason 165: E.1149[4], pp. 154–5 (D4v–5r).

[4] This is technically inaccurate: the play does, in fact, have two sword fights in Act 5, between the Captain and the two citizens of the subplot. Williams argues that this 'suggests that when the play was staged at the Werburgh Street Theatre it contained a fight scene, but for unknown reasons this did not translate to the London staging of the play' (Williams 2010, 205). However, it is also possible that Shirley simply forgot about, or disregarded, the existence of the fight scene when writing this second prologue.

146

THE DOUBTFUL HEIR: GENERAL INTRODUCTION

> Will pardon our vast stage and not disgrace
> This play – meant for your persons, not the place.
>
> (Globe prologue, 17–22)

In both prologues, therefore, Shirley advertises the play as being a polite, elegant drama, suitable for a refined audience.

PLOT, SOURCES, AND INFLUENCES

The Doubtful Heir may lack the kind of visual spectacle and sensationalism that early 1640s Globe audiences might have expected, but it is nevertheless a tightly structured and exciting drama. It tells the story of Olivia, the supposed queen of Murcia, whose right to the throne is challenged by the appearance of a young man claiming to be her cousin Ferdinand, the true heir. Ferdinand was thought to have died in infancy, but was in fact spirited out of the country to protect him from the malice of his protector, Olivia's father. Now returned, he attempts to claim the throne—but is instead sentenced to death for treason. Immediately afterwards, however, Olivia starts to fall in love with him and, breaking her own engagement to Leonario, Prince of Aragon, offers him a reprieve if he marries her. Ferdinand is already secretly engaged to Rosania, who has accompanied him to Murcia disguised as a page, Tiberio. Therefore, although he marries Olivia to save his own life, he avoids consummating the marriage. Olivia becomes jealous and attempts to seduce Tiberio in order to punish her husband, but soon afterwards discovers that Tiberio is a woman in disguise. Furious at the discovery of her husband's mistress, she once more imprisons Ferdinand, but he is saved by the arrival of Alfonso, Ferdinand's old guardian and Rosania's father, who confirms his identity as the true heir. Olivia gives up her throne and her husband, and instead marries her previous fiancé Leonario, while Ferdinand, in turn, reunites with Rosania and takes the throne of Murcia. Meanwhile, the play's action is interspersed with a comic subplot, featuring the adventures of two citizens who become first soldiers and then courtiers, under the instruction of a witty army captain.

The principal source for the main plot is Shirley's own 1635 tragicomedy, *The Coronation*, as both plays involve a female monarch who casts aside a previous suitor in order to marry a man who is, or later turns out to be, a challenger for her throne. Presumably what appealed to Shirley about the plot of *The Coronation* was the opportunity it offered for a series of surprising reversals and pathetic set pieces. In reworking his earlier play, Shirley attempts to streamline the action, conflating the two royal brothers, Leonatus and Demetrius, of *The Coronation* into one figure, Prince Ferdinand, and removing the character of the evil Lord Protector, Cassander. Indeed, one of the interesting things about *The Doubtful Heir* is the fact that there is no true villain. The supposed queen Olivia is portrayed as a headstrong woman who makes rash and misguided choices, but although she is proud and over-hasty, her actions do not take place out of pure malice. Shirley also turns Ferdinand into a more sympathetic character than the Demetrius of *The Coronation*. Demetrius wrestles a little with his

147

conscience when he realizes that he must give up his mistress, Polidora, in order to marry Queen Sophia, but reflects that:

> I dare not
> Turne rebell to a Princesse, I shall love
> Thy vertue, but a Kingdome has a charme
> To excuse our frailty, dearest Madam.
>
> (*Coronation*, 1640, F1r)

In other words, Demetrius is persuaded as much by the lure of the kingdom as he is by his fear of angering the queen. By contrast, although Ferdinand loves his country and wants to take his rightful position as head of it, he makes it very clear that he loves Rosania ''bove the crown' (5.2.65). His chief motivation in marrying Olivia is not his desire to become king but his desire to escape execution, in order that he may at some later point flee the kingdom with Rosania.

The main plot of *The Doubtful Heir* also bears some resemblance to that of Beaumont and Fletcher's tragicomedy *Philaster* (perf. 1608–10). Philaster is the son of the murdered King of Sicily, who falls in love with Arethusa, the daughter of his father's usurper. He is loved in turn by the noblewoman Euphrasia, who is accompanying him disguised as a page, Bellario. Like Rosania, Bellario is entered into the service of her lover's new mistress, leading—as in *The Doubtful Heir*—to rumours of an inappropriate relationship between mistress and page. However, in *Philaster* the disguised woman's true identity is only revealed to Philaster, and to the audience, at the play's conclusion. By contrast, in *The Doubtful Heir* Ferdinand knows Rosania's identity all along, and the audience knows from the beginning of the second act. Shirley is therefore able to play on the audience's knowledge of the deceit throughout, whereas in Beaumont and Fletcher the ridiculousness of the accusations against Bellario and Arethusa can only be appreciated in retrospect. Moreover, *Philaster*'s conclusion is somewhat different: Philaster loves Arethusa, not Euphrasia, and ends the play united with her, while in Shirley's play Ferdinand has loved Rosania all along, and ends by separating from Olivia and making Rosania his new queen. *Philaster* thus emphasizes Euphrasia's isolation and unrequited love, while in *The Doubtful Heir* the focus is more on the constancy and ingenuity of the two lovers, fighting against all odds to stay together.

There are other potential links between *The Doubtful Heir* and earlier drama. The main plot has similarities to that of Shirley's 1634–5 comedy *The Opportunity*, a play about a young man who is mistaken for an aristocrat, and who is wooed by the Duchess of Urbino, while himself falling in love with his own pretended sister, Cornelia. *The Opportunity*, in turn, was based by Shirley on the Spanish dramatist Tirso de Molina's 1613 play, *El Castigo Del Penséque* (Happé 2017, 53–4). Furthermore, the wooing scene between Olivia and the disguised Rosania in Act 4 recalls the wooing of the disguised Viola by another aristocratic Olivia in Shakespeare's *Twelfth Night* (perf. *c.* 1601–2). However, as Forsythe argues, it may be misguided to focus too much on finding specific sources for aspects of Shirley's plays. As he comments, they habitually draw upon elements of drama that were by this time 'stock or conventional', and so 'Shirley's true sources were, in perhaps the majority of cases, not single plays, incidents, or characters, but the aggregate, the sum total, of the similar plays, incidents, or characters, of earlier and contemporary playwrights' (Forsythe 1914, ix).

GENDER

As I noted earlier, the original Dublin prologue for *The Doubtful Heir* links the play to other contemporary works—Suckling's *Aglaura* and Killigrew's *Claricilla*—through its title. However, Lucy Munro suggests a further way in which *The Doubtful Heir* might be related to these two London plays. As she comments, *Aglaura* and *Claricilla* represented a popular sub-genre of drama at the time: that of 'she-tragicomedy', in which a central theme is 'the simultaneous chastity and desirability of their titular heroines'. However, in contrast to these plays, '*Rosania* focuses its anxiety on the body of the hero' (Munro 2007, 178–9). Whereas women's chastity is all-important in Suckling and Killigrew, in *The Doubtful Heir* it is Ferdinand's chastity—his ability to infinitely postpone the consummation of his marriage to Olivia in order to keep his faith to Rosania—on which the happy ending hinges. When Rosania sees him married to Olivia, she assumes that he is lost to her forever, commenting that "Tis as possible / To call past ages back' as it is to save the situation (3.1.305–6). However, when she learns from him that 'The queen's to me a stranger yet' (3.1.349), she realizes that there is still hope. The marriage is never consummated and so Ferdinand can leave his wife and return to his mistress at the play's end without shame. As Munro writes, Shirley's play is thus an ironic reworking of a common contemporary dramatic trope, as he suggests that male purity (in the form of fidelity to a betrothed, if not necessarily literal virginity) may be as important as female purity.

Shirley's interest in exploring and reversing traditionally male and female tropes continues throughout the play. In Act 2, when Ferdinand is found guilty of treason, he is initially stoical at the prospect of his own execution, but when he comes to say his farewells to the disguised Rosania before the queen and the rest of the court, he weeps:

> Come hither, boy, and let me kiss thee. [*He kisses Rosania.*] Thus,
> At parting with a good and pretty servant,
> I can, without my honour stained, shed tears.
> I took thee from thy friends to make thee mine
> ....
> And meant when I was king to make thee great,
> And shall I not, when I can live no longer
> To cherish thee, at farewell drop a tear?
> That I could weep my soul upon thee!
>
> (2.4.137–46)

It is at this moment that Olivia begins to feel the pangs of love towards him, remarking, 'What secret flame is this? Honour protect me!' (2.4.150). Public displays of emotion, including weeping, were commonly associated with femininity in this period (Vaught 2008, 1–2), and so are typically avoided by male romantic heroes. In Shakespeare's *Cymbeline*, for example, Posthumus resists crying when he is parted from Innogen: 'O lady, weep no more, lest I give cause / To be suspected of more tenderness / Than doth become a man' (1.1.94–6). By contrast, Ferdinand's tears apparently make him more enticing, not less: it is his emotional expressiveness and sensitivity that seems to attract the powerful queen, who promptly casts her former suitor Leonario aside.

Another interesting scene of gender role reversal occurs later in the play, when Olivia, seeking revenge for her new husband's emotional coldness, attempts to seduce 'Tiberio'.

'He' pretends not to understand the queen's meaning, and in response, the frustrated
queen attempts to engage in a role-play, in which she and Tiberio will swap places:

> OLIVIA I suppose you a lady all this while,
> And I the man. Our lips must meet again. [*Kisses her.*]
> Will this instruct thee nothing?
>
> ROSANIA   Gracious madam –
>
> ....
>
> OLIVIA .... This coldness
> Becomes no masculine habit. Come, we'll in
> And change our sexes. Thou shalt wear my clothes
> And I will put on these – help on with thine
> And I will dress thee handsomely – and then
> We'll act again.

$$(4.2.152-86)$$

Olivia is both conventional and deeply unconventional in the attitudes towards gender that she displays in this scene. Her belief that men should be passionate reflects
the traditional Galenic model of the sexes, in which males are characterized by their
greater bodily heat, which was believed to make them both more active and more capable of sustained desire, in contrast to women's relative passivity and 'coldness'
(Paster 1998, 421–32). However, Olivia's solution to the problem of inappropriate
male coldness is a less traditional one: she proposes that rather than trying to arouse
Tiberio's masculine assertiveness, she and he should more fully commit to the game
of gender exchange that she has initiated. Wooing was believed to be a man's task, not
a woman's: in Mary Wroth's *Loves Victorie* (*c.* 1619), Lissius claims that female wooing is 'The most unfittest, shamefullst thing to doo' (14r, l. 29). By swapping clothes,
therefore, Olivia and Tiberio will find themselves in apparel that more properly fits
the gender roles that they are currently performing: Tiberio will embrace his 'feminine' passivity in a woman's dress while Olivia will more comfortably play the traditionally masculine role of wooer while costumed as a man. Olivia thus shows her awareness
of traditional gender roles while simultaneously flouting them through her suggestion
that the *appearance* of conforming to social expectations is more important than
actually doing so.

Of course, the extent to which this scene reverses conventional norms of gender
behaviour is complicated by Olivia's status as queen. Christian Billing notes that, 'gender relations in the early modern period (as in ours) were inescapably also power relations' (2008, 104): women were typically seen as inherently inferior to men in both
their bodies and their minds, and this assumption was used to justify the greater power
that men typically held within society. However, female rulers might be seen as the
exception. Indeed, as Queen Elizabeth I had famously insisted, a female monarch
might be seen as symbolically male, being invested by God with a level of authority
that released her from the usual constraints upon female behaviour. Olivia's active
seduction of Tiberio—who is vastly her social inferior—might thus have been seen by
spectators as less transgressive than such behaviour would be from an ordinary woman,

THE DOUBTFUL HEIR: GENERAL INTRODUCTION

since she is already in a masculinized position by virtue of her rank, whereas he is in some sense effeminized by his subordinate role.

However, the idea that a woman might be considered male for political purposes was itself a potential source of anxiety. Some considered it 'unnatural, threatening established relations of hierarchy and degree' (McLaren 1999; 2004, 102)—and Olivia's scene with Tiberio in 4.2 does little to relieve such anxieties. The game that Olivia attempts to play might well be seen as perverse, given the way in which she uses her own power to exploit and manipulate an unwilling partner. Moreover, as Walen comments, Olivia 'pursues a more aggressive seduction than is typical in scenes with cross-dressed heroines'—and she notes also that the explicit stage directions to the couple to kiss are 'startling', given how infrequently such actions are actually carried out in early modern drama (2005, 89, 90–1). The fact that both parts were played by boy players does nothing to simplify the situation.

The play does not leave conventional gender roles and expectations behind entirely. Rosania may spend the majority of her time in male clothing, but she is a traditional woman in other respects, quietly bearing her sorrows and relying on Ferdinand to instruct and protect her. Like *Twelfth Night*'s Viola, there is 'no doubt in the audience's mind of her heterosexual sexual orientation or her properly "feminine" subjectivity' (Howard 1988, 431). Ferdinand is a sensitive and romantic hero, but he is also presented as a valiant warrior—prepared to die rather than willingly give up his crown again (5.4.91–3)—and a noble potential king. Meanwhile, Olivia's more aggressive aspects are tempered by the fact that her behaviour is seen as weak in a specifically feminine way. For example, Leonario comments of her fickleness in love that:

> There is
> A fire in Cupid's quiver that will scorch
> Through armour, and what's woman's flesh and blood
> To make resistance?
>
> (3.1.25–8)

Furthermore, the play's ending works to remove Olivia from her position of power and reinstall her in a more conventionally subordinate role. In the final act, her former fiancé Leonario, who has until this point been a somewhat passive character, abruptly reaffirms his manly agency, re-entering the play at the head of an army and announcing that he plans to take Olivia as his 'prize' (5.4.104). Leonario insists that the queen's previous marriage, being unconsummated, can be dissolved, and threatens her with the destruction of her kingdom if she resists. One might expect Olivia to protest at this treatment, but she meekly accepts, and while she is offstage, Ferdinand is recognized as the true king. By the end of *The Doubtful Heir*, therefore, Olivia has moved from being the most powerful person in the play to being simply a bride and a cousin to the true, male monarch. Nevertheless, despite the play's ultimate reaffirmation of traditional gender hierarchies, Shirley's overall portrayal both of female sexual desire (in the form of Olivia's attraction to Ferdinand) and masculine emotional expressiveness is not unsympathetic, suggesting that he was interested in questioning some of the conventional assumptions regarding what constituted acceptable masculine and feminine behaviour at the time.

POLITICS

The play's position within the unsettled political climate of the 1630s is an interesting one. Martin Butler notes that 'In play after play of this decade, politics is not just an occasional or ephemeral issue but is the basic, fundamental concern and the principal determinant of dramatic form' (Butler 1984, 281). *The Doubtful Heir* was written during the eleven years of King Charles I's period of personal rule, from 1629 until the recall of the Short Parliament in 1640, and it engages with political debates in its interest both in the personality of the monarch and the question of how far monarchical power needs to be circumscribed and limited. The supposed queen Olivia is impulsive, 'passionate and like / A sea tempestuous in her anger' (3.1.1–2) and throughout the play her courtiers express their anxiety regarding her growing sense of her own power:

> LEANDRO The queen grows mighty in her spirit,
> And this match with the prince [Leonario] would swell her state
> Too much.
>
> (1.1.155–7)

In her emotional unpredictability and her readiness to be guided by desire, jealousy, and anger rather than reason, Olivia is presented as a potential danger to the country. Moreover, she sees herself as being above the law. When she is confronted by her courtiers with the apparent proof of her attempt to break her own decrees concerning female chastity, she responds:

> By
> What power dare you take an account of me,
> That am above your laws, which must obey
> Me, as their soul, and die when I forsake 'em?
>
> (4.2.275–8)

At the same time, though, other aspects of Olivia's presentation suggest a more sympathetic view of her rule. As Jessica Dyson points out, after Ferdinand's initial invasion of Murcia he is given the chance to defend himself in the trial scene of Act 2, and it is made explicitly clear that 'this is a favour bestowed by the Queen and not a right' (Dyson 2013, 186). Leandro explains:

> LEANDRO Although the queen in her own royal power
> And without violating sacred justice – where
> Treason comes to invade her and her crown
> With open war – need not insist upon
> The forms and circumstance of law but use
> Her sword in present execution:
> Yet such is the sweet temper of her blood
> And calmness of her nature (though provoked
> Into a storm) unto the great'st offender
> She shuts up no defence, willing to give
> A satisfaction to the world how much
> She doth delight in mercy.
>
> (2.4.6–17)

Leandro's account of the 'calmness of her nature' is perhaps an exaggeration, given what we see of Olivia's behaviour elsewhere in the play, but the queen is certainly capable of acting justly. She is also capable of admitting her own mistakes, as she does when she learns that Ferdinand has a mistress in the court and acknowledges that she was wrong to choose him as a husband over Leonario: 'I have done ill / And find the penance here' (4.2.74–5).

The idea that Olivia's wilfulness and resistance to being curbed by her own laws might be seen as a critique of Charles is also mitigated by the fact that she is only the supposed queen and does not truly have a claim to the title. Although one could read the play as exploring the dangers of uncontrolled royal power, it could also be read from the opposite perspective, as a play which supports the idea of divine right and suggests that Olivia's weaknesses as a ruler show her lack of true title to the position. A true monarch, such a reading might argue, would be less fallible. Dyson suggests that this may also be the reason why Ferdinand avoids execution after his failed coup: '[Olivia's] decision to pardon him after hearing him speak [...] could be seen as Providential preservation of the rightful monarch' (Dyson 2013, 187). Shirley's play can thus be seen as engaging with contemporary debates about monarchical power, while also taking care not to commit itself too strongly to either side.

IRELAND

One of the central questions about *The Doubtful Heir* is whether it is a play that is specifically 'Irish' in its preoccupations. On the one hand, it was probably the first play that Shirley wrote while in Ireland and was originally intended for a Dublin audience. On the other, the fact that he brought it back to England with him so soon afterwards might suggest that he was writing with an eye on both locations. The issue is not helped by the fact that we do not know whether the play was revised between the Irish and English performances—although the epilogue to the Dublin production does hint at this possibility, in its comment that the play will be 'changed abroad' (epilogue, l. 8, as published in *Poems &c*; see collation).

Charles' period of personal rule was a subject that would have had been of broad popular interest at the time, being of concern to those both in Ireland and in England. However, it has been argued that the subplot, which involves the conflict between the Captain and the two citizens that he enlists as soldiers, was more specifically designed to appeal to Dublin theatregoers. La Tourette Stockwell writes that this plot is:

based on contemporary Dublin life and representing the long-standing feud between the 'castle-folk,' especially the army officers, and the Dublin tradespeople [...] These scenes are focused from the captain's point of view. Indirectly, they were also focused from the point of view of the Dublin audience, which included among its most enthusiastic members, the officers quartered at Dublin Castle.

(Stockwell 1968, 11)

It does seem very likely that Shirley wrote this subplot to appeal to a specific subsection of his Irish audience. As well as dramatizing the particular tensions between gentleman soldiers and the Dublin citizens (in the Captain's repeated refusal to pay his bills), the

THE COMPLETE WORKS OF JAMES SHIRLEY, VOLUME 7

play also spends some time depicting military life more generally—as, for example, in the Captain's long speech at the end of Act 1, which discusses the hardships of life in the trenches and on the march. As Stockwell writes, the subplot's scenes are told from the Captain's perspective, and he is presented as an essentially sympathetic character, who repeatedly outsmarts the vain, lazy, and cowardly citizens.

It also seems likely, therefore, that Shirley was more concerned to market his play to the British gentry than to the Irish citizens—and this idea might seem to be confirmed by the play's epilogue, in which the Captain explicitly aligns himself with the former. He addresses them genially, saying that he is sure that 'you o'the gentry, t'whom he owes / No money' will approve of the play (17–18). He then concludes the epilogue with a threat to the potentially more hostile citizen classes, identifying them with 'his city creditors' and threatening to 'send [. . .] to the wars' any of them who voice objections or dislike (20–1). That said, Shirley clearly did not want to alienate any citizens in his audience too much: he takes pains in the first act to emphasize that the two citizens with whom the Captain deals are exceptional characters – 'walking sicknesses, not citizens'—who are not representative of the mass of 'brave fellows' and 'noble souls' within the city more generally (1.1.124–9).

Beyond the fact that both deal with war, there seems little other obvious connection between the play's main plot and subplot, although there is a further loose thematic link. The main plot is concerned with concepts of manliness and femininity, given its interest in gender role reversal and the diametrically opposed types of woman represented by Olivia and Rosania. The subplot, meanwhile, deals with the Captain's attempt to make the citizens more 'manly': less petty and self-interested, less afraid of combat, and more willing to commit themselves to violent action when required. This culminates in Act 5, as the pair realize that they are no longer afraid to engage in duels, with the Second Citizen announcing, ''Tis not so hard to fight, I see, if a man be but desperate and give his mind to't' (5.3.153–4). The Captain celebrates their transformation, announcing, 'Let me hug ye, my brace of myrmidons' (5.3.156), comparing them to the warriors who supported Achilles during the Trojan War.

THE PLAY IN PRODUCTION

We do not know which actors took which parts in the original Dublin production, but it is possible that the cast contained some actors who had worked with Shirley in London previously. Four veterans of his former company, Queen Henrietta's Men— William Allen, Michael Bowyer, Hugh Clark, and William Robins—disappeared from the London theatre scene in around 1637, shortly after Shirley left for Ireland, and then reappeared in London in around 1640–1, when all four are listed as members of Shirley's new company, the King's Men. Stevenson speculates that they may have spent the interim at the Werburgh Street Theatre (1942, 151–8).[5] Meanwhile, the only actor from the King's Men who is definitely known to have acted in the London production is Stephen Hammerton, who played the part of Ferdinand. Hammerton, a former boy actor who later moved on to playing romantic leads, was popular enough

---

[5] Stevenson also suggests that Robins, who was known for his comic roles, may have played the Captain.

154

with audiences to be named directly in the play's London epilogue—'How did King Stephen do', the Captain asks the audience (12).

Shirley's plays in general do not seem to have met with any great success on the Irish stage. The Werburgh Street Theatre struggled to find audiences, and in a prologue written for Middleton's *No Wit, No Help Like a Woman's* Shirley complains:

> We are sorrie Gentlemen, that with all our paines
> To invite you hither, the wide house containes
> No more...
> When he [Shirley] did live in *England*, he heard say,
> That here were men lov'd wit, and a good Play;
> ....
> But they doe not appeare[.]
>
> (*Poems &c*, C5v-6r)

The Doubtful Heir clearly had enough potential, and enough cross-over appeal, to warrant the second production in London. However, the play seems to have no stage history after this production. It was not among the plays of Shirley's that were revived after the Restoration, and seems not to have been produced at any period since. Nevertheless, it has not been entirely forgotten. It was performed in a rehearsed reading at the Shakespeare's Globe theatre in London in 2008, as part of their 'Read Not Dead' series, and the programme note for that production emphasizes how effective the play still is on stage, due to 'the vigour of its language, its lively action and, above all, the skilful twists and turns of the constantly surprising narrative' (Williams 2008).

Textual Introduction

The Doubtful Heir was entered in the Stationers' Register on 4 September 1646 as *Doubtfull Heire, by Shirley*, and was first published as part of a collection of Shirley's plays in the octavo volume *Six New Plays* in 1652–3. The volume was published by Humphrey Robinson and Humphrey Moseley, and Greg has identified the printers as William Wilson and Thomas Warren (Greg 1939–59, 1124). The printers divided the work up between them on a play-by-play basis; *The Doubtful Heir* was printed by Warren, as were *The Cardinal* and *The Sisters*. However, as Elizabeth Yearling notes, he seems to have set the play 'from a different case or cases round which had accumulated a different set of ornaments' than those he used in the printing of his other plays in the volume: *The Doubtful Heir* uses an acorn ornament on A2 and A3 and an ornamental letter at the start of the dedication and the main text, neither of which are found in *The Cardinal* or *The Sisters*, though they do appear in other books set by Warren in the period 1652–3 (Shirley, ed. Yearling 1986, 32).

Each of the plays in *Six New Plays* has its own pagination, register, and title page, which would make it possible to sell them separately. Some copies of *The Doubtful Heir* bound alone survive. The title page reads:

THE / DOUBTFUL / HEIR. / A / Tragi-comedie, / AS / It was Acted at the private House / IN / *BLACKFRIERS*, / WRITTEN / By JAMES SHIRLEY. / [rule] / *Never Printed before*. / [rule] / *LONDON*, / Printed for *Humphrey Robinson* at the three Pi- / geons, and *Humphrey Moseley* at the Prince's / Arms in St. *Paul's* Church-yard. / 1652.

The play occupies gatherings A4, B–E8, F6 [$4 signed (- A1, A3, F4)]. A1r is the title page, with the verso blank. A2r–v has the dedication to Sir Edmund Bowyer. A3r gives the prologue; A3v gives 'The Persons of the Play' and identifies the scene. The text proper runs from B1r–F5v, and F6r gives the epilogue, with the verso blank. Page numbering begins on the second page of the text proper, and runs correctly pp. 2–74 (although with an uncorrected error on page 56, which has been set as 65). A1–4 was set by half-page imposition, and there is a blank leaf associated with quire A which in most surviving editions appears before the title page, but in a small number appears after A3.

This edition is based on a collation of twenty-two copies of the 1652 octavo text, seventeen of which were fully collated and five checked for known variants. The text is printed in roman type aligned to the left margin. Italics are used systematically for proper names, stage directions, entrances and exits, abbreviated speech headings, foreign words or phrases, and a *sententia* by Ferdinand on the last line of D6v. They are also used for the sign-off on the dedication (A2v), the main text of the prologue, for all

THE COMPLETE WORKS OF JAMES SHIRLEY, VOLUME 7

but the proper nouns in the cast list, and the main text of the epilogue (with the exception of the first word, 'Gentlemen,' which is also set on a line of its own, and the first,
oversize letter of the following sentence, 'I').

There are typically thirty-six lines on each page, excluding the headline and catch-
word, although sometimes this is affected by whether or not there are blank lines surrounding e.g. entrances. The first page of each act contains fewer lines, as the act
heading is given in larger font, and the initial stage direction of each act is also in larger
font with spacing surrounding it. Of the rest of the main text, every page has thirty-six
lines apart from B1v, B5r, B6r, C3r, C5r, C7r, C8r, D3v, F1v (all thirty-seven); B2v, C2v,
C8v, D2v, D7r, E3v, E5v, E6v, E7r, F3v, F4v (all thirty-five); D8v, E2r, E2v, D4r, F2r,
F2v, F3r (all thirty-four); D5r (thirty-three); and E4v (twenty-nine—although this is
because this page has the end of an act, and so finishes with a rule and blank space). B2v
also includes a blank line between lines 24 and 25. Overall, this shows that the casting
off was reasonably generous in the earlier quires and more conservative in the later ones.

The running headline, 'The Doubtfull Heir', first appears on B1v and continues on
every page until F5v. However, there are variants in the spelling of the second word
throughout the edition: in quire B it is written as 'Doubtfull'; however, quire C has
'Doubful' on C1r and then 'Doubtful' throughout the rest of the quire. Quire D similarly has 'Doubful' on D1r, and then 'Doubtful' on every page except D1v and D6v
where it is 'Doubtfull'. Quire E has 'Doubtfull' on E3r and E5v, and otherwise has
'Doubtful'. Quire F has 'Doubtful' throughout except on F4r where it is 'Doubtfull'.
This implies that the play was printed from C–D to E–F, with the spelling error being
caught between D and E. Quires D and E seem to have been set with one forme, while
either two formes were in use for F or else the inner former was printed before the
outer, with the outer representing the 'corrected' version of the headline.

It is not certain what the printer's copy-text was, but it is unlikely to have been the
theatre prompt-book, given the fact that there are some potentially confusing conventions employed regarding the naming of characters. The two citizens who appear in the
first act under the speech headings '1 *Cit.*' and '2 *Cit.*' are from the second act onwards
renamed '*Lieut.*' (for Lieutenant) and '*Ant.*' (for Ancient, meaning 'Ensign'), while two
other citizens who appear in the third act are in turn labelled '1. *Cit.*' and '2. *Cit.*',
despite being new characters, played by different actors. In a prompt-book, such label-
ling could cause confusion. I have simplified matters by renaming the latter pair 'Third
Citizen' and 'Fourth Citizen', and retaining the original nomenclature of the First and
Second Citizens in the speech headings throughout. For clarity I have also altered the
speech headings and stage directions referring to Olivia; in the original she is referred
to as Queen (or, more commonly in the speech headings, *Quee./Que./Qu.*) throughout.

Another aspect that suggests that the prompt-book was not the printer's copy-text is
the stage directions. These are often somewhat vague (B4r: '*Enter...Attendants, Ladies,
Gentlemen*'; F3v: '*Enter...Souldiers*'), and on occasion incorrect or insufficient. An exit
for the four citizens is missing on C8v. There is an '*Aside*' on E3v, which is placed next
to a speech of Olivia's where it does not seem to belong; it may belong to Ferdinand in
the speech that follows. There is some confusion on F3v l. 2 where a speech heading
(for '*Divers within*' to cry 'Help, help, quarter') is set instead as a marginal stage direction, and the line 'Help, help, quarter' appears to be given to Ferdinand. Such
moments of vagueness and occasional inaccuracy regarding the practicalities of stage

158

THE DOUBTFUL HEIR: TEXTUAL INTRODUCTION

movement suggest an author's copy: perhaps Shirley's own foul papers. This conjecture might also be supported by a substantive uncorrected error on B7r l. 22: the text reads 'no such thing / In Nature as a thirst,' but the immediately following reference to a 'Taylor' suggests that 'thirst' should read 'shirt'. A correction to this error has been made in the Folger text S3486: an unknown hand has crossed out 'thirst' and written 'shirt' in the margin. The thirst/shirt error is presumably the result of the compositor misreading messy handwriting. The possibility that the printed text has been influenced by stage production is raised by what appears to be a premature entrance in the instruction on F2r l. 22 to '*Enter Courtier*' (as the courtier does not speak and is not acknowledged for another thirteen lines of dialogue, despite the fact that he has come bearing urgent news). 'Predictive' or 'anticipatory' stage directions of this kind are often seen as originating in performance, as they provide backstage workers with advance warning of when actors are needed on stage. However, this is the only instance of a possible anticipatory stage direction in the text, so too much weight should not be placed on it; it is possible that it is simply a mistake made by the author or a scribe.

Entrances are typically centred, although on one occasion an entrance is fitted in to the end of a line of dialogue: on C2v, Ferdinand's line, 'We are interrupted' is followed on the same line by the stage direction '*Enter Keeper.*' In the first section of the play, the spacing is economical: there are no blank lines before or after entrance directions, other than in the initial entrances for each act. From C8v onwards, however, some entrances are printed with blank lines surrounding them, with this practice becoming increasingly common from D2v. This may be because the compositors realized that they had enough space to complete the printing without compressing the text quite so much.

Exits are usually set to the right of the page, and placed on the same line as the last line of the dialogue preceding—although sometimes they are on the line below if there are space constrictions. On E2v, the exit of Violinda and Rosania is set with a blank line above and below it, but this is the only place in the text where an exit has blank lines surrounding it. In three instances in quire B (B1v, B5r, and B5v) exits are centred, and in all of these cases *Exit* or *Exeunt* is abbreviated to *Ex.*, despite there being no constrictions of space. In the rest of the text, *Exit* or *Exeunt* is usual unless there are problems of space. An exit is also centred on E4v; it differs from the examples of this practice in quire B, though, because *Exeunt* here is not abbreviated, and the line also contains the instruction for Ferdinand, Rosania, and the Guard to *Manent* ('Remain'). Exits are usually set without brackets, but on B3v there is an exception: an exit printed over two lines in the right-hand margin as '[*Ex. Manent / [Rod, Ernesto.*'

Apart from entrances and exits, stage directions are relatively few. Important props such as letters and key details of costuming are often mentioned but sometimes not: for example, Rosania's clothing is specified (2.3.0 initial SD; 4.2.292 SD), but Alfonso's wearing and removing a false beard is not mentioned and must be deduced from the dialogue (5.4.180). Kisses and other stage actions such as kneeling are sometimes indicated, but not always (as in 2.4.137 SD, where a kiss is clearly necessary but not marked in the stage directions). Asides are similarly noted at some times and not at others, and in places this creates the potential for uncertainty: for example, on C3v and C5r, when Olivia is beginning to fall in love with Ferdinand, it is not clear how much of her speech

159

(e.g. 'By my blood, / He does talk bravely'; 'What secret flame is this? Honour protect me!') should be spoken aloud and how much aside (2.4.54-5; 150).

It seems likely that more than one compositor worked on the text, due to various features including inconsistencies in the speech headings. Speech headings are erratic throughout: the name of almost every character is given in multiple forms, so we have *Queen/Quee./Que./Qu./Q.*; *Rosa./Ros.*; *Ferd./Fer.*; *Er./Ern./Ernest.*; *Rod./Rodri.*; *Lean./Leand.*; *Leo./Leond.*; *Cap./Capt.*; *Viol./Vio.*; *Alfon./Alf.*; *1 Cit./1 Ci./1 C.*; *2 Cit./2 Ci./2 C.*; and *Lieut./Lieu.* Nevertheless, we may be able to discern some sense of pattern: Ernesto is always printed as *Er.* in quire B (with an exception on B1r where he is both *Er.* and *Ern.* and on B1v, where he is both *Ernest.* and *Er.*) and quire E, whereas he is printed as *Ernest.* consistently in quire C;[1] the Captain is more commonly consistently printed as *Cap.* in quire C, and as *Capt.* in quires B, D, E, and F; Olivia is known variously in quire C as *Queen*, *Quee.*, *Qu.*, and *Q.* but never as *Que.*, whereas in quires B, D, E, and F she is only printed as *Que.* (with an exception on E1r, where she is twice printed as *Quee.* and twice as *Que.*). These variations may suggest that a different compositor was responsible for quire C.

The inconsistencies in speech headings have led to one uncorrected error on E7r, where *Leand.* is instructed to speak. Leandro is not present in this scene, which is between Leonario and a soldier, so *Leon.* must be meant instead. A similar but more intractable problem appears on C3v, where there is an instruction for *Leond.* to speak. This abbreviation is clearly inaccurate, but it is not clear whether the text should properly read *Leand.* or *Leon.*; both characters are on stage, and the line might belong to either.

Other evidence for two or more compositors lies in the indentation of speech headings. In quires B and D they are consistently 4mm from the margin; but in quire C they vary from 2–6mm (often showing different practice on the same page), and on quires E and F they vary from 3–6mm.

There are also variations of spelling which may help identify different hands at work. For example, 'do' is spelled as 'doe' throughout quire B, with only two exceptions where it is spelled 'do', whereas after C1 'do' largely takes over, and 'doe' reappears only four more times in the whole text: on D1v, D5r, D6v, and E8r, plus one instance of 'undoe' on D8v. 'Again' is spelled as 'agen' throughout quire B (with one exception where it is 'again', on B3v l. 9) and quire D, whereas it is spelled only as 'again' throughout quire C, and as a mixture of predominantly 'agen' but occasionally 'again' in quire E. (The word does not appear in quire F). 'Blood' is spelled as 'blood' throughout quires C, E, and F, but in quire B it is once spelled as 'bloud' (B1v) and in quire D that spelling occurs three times (on D4r, D5r, and D8r). 'Money' is spelled as either 'mony' or 'money' throughout B, whereas in the rest of the text it is spelled as 'money', with one exception, on the final line of F1r, where the spelling may result from space constrictions.[2] These variations in spelling and speech prefix indentation might suggest that the same compositor worked on quires B and D.

It is difficult to draw definite conclusions on this matter, since there is also evidence for considerable inconsistency within the work of individual compositors, with variant

---

[1] He does not speak in quire F; and he speaks only twice in D, once as *Er.* and once as *Ernest.*
[2] The word 'money' does not appear in D in any form.

THE DOUBTFUL HEIR: TEXTUAL INTRODUCTION

abbreviations of speech headings, indentation of speech headings, and spellings often found on the same page of text. Meanwhile, punctuation offers little assistance, as question marks, exclamation marks, dashes, and semicolons are spread fairly evenly throughout. The text as a whole features very few possessive apostrophes; they are only found in E5r, F3r, F4v, and F5r, though even here they are not used systematically: for example, there is one on *Valentia's* in F4v l. 25, but not on *Arragons* on the next line. Tentatively, however, based on the evidence I have outlined above, I would suggest that at least three compositors worked on this text, with one setting quires B and D, one setting quire C, and one setting quires E and F.

The text has been proof-corrected, but in a rather cursory fashion: there are very few stop-press alterations, and a number of uncorrected errors: one in quire A, seven in B, eight in C, six in D, nine in E, and five in F. These errors include reversed or inverted letters and numbers (e.g. 'qulaity' for 'quality' on B3r; 'graut' for 'grant' on E1v); incorrect punctuation (e.g. 'the'ir' on B6v); and missing, shortened, or inaccurate catchwords. Stop-press corrections have been made in quire B (inner and outer), C (outer), and D (outer). Throughout the text, words are sometimes compressed together, with almost no space between them. I have not listed these instances as errors, although it should be noted that in one case, in C2v l. 19, the spacing has undergone a stop-press correction, with 'theeagain' being adjusted to 'thee again'.

Catchwords typically anticipate the first word on the following page (excluding headline), whether that be speech heading or speech, and match it in terms of typeface and size. However, there are variations and occasional errors within this: B2v gives only the initial letter of the following word ('A' for 'Afraid'); B4r has 'Abov' for 'Above'; C2v has '*Leand.*' for '*Lean.*'; C7v has '1 , *Cit.*' for '1. *Cit.*'; B2v has 'Take' where the actual first word of the next line is a speech heading '*Ros.*' (followed by 'Take'); E1v has *Rosa.* for *Ros.*; F2r again skips the speech heading ('*Que.*') and instead anticipates the first word of speech, 'I'; and F3r is missing its catchword, as is F5v. C5r departs from the usual pattern by having a two-word phrase as its catchword 'I not'. There are also variants between copies in terms of the placement of the catchword 'Only' on B5r: in some it is 12mm from the edge of the final line and in others it is 7mm (see stop-press collation notes). It is not clear whether this was a stop-press adjustment or whether the text simply shifted during the press-work.

All of the compositors seem to have had difficulties with the lineation. The scenes of the main plot are written in more-or-less regular iambic pentameter, but the lines of the subplot, involving the Captain and his dealings with the two citizens, are much more irregular, shifting between rough iambic pentameter and prose. There are many long or short lines in these sections, which have mostly been set as verse, although sometimes they have been set as prose with capitalization at the start of the line. The difficulty is compounded by the text's inconsistency in the marking of elisions. The most obvious occasion where the compositors ran into difficulty is in a confused section on E8r-v, in which a speech by the Captain shifts from prose to verse over the turn of a page. The speech starts set as prose on E8r, the page ending with the line 'worships face is a prognostication of preferment', but it is followed on E8v by a line set as verse, which repeats some of the words of the preceding line: 'is a Prognostication of preferment, where'. This might suggest that there was a change of compositors, or else an overnight break, between the setting of E8r and the setting of E8v.

When verse lines overrun the set space available, the overrunning text is usually placed with a round bracket to the right of the page, above or below the line to which it belongs. It is usually apparent which line the hanging text completes, but there is a problem of interpretation on E8v, where it is not clear whether the hanging word 'left' belongs to the line above ('I have but one Shirt') or the line below ('I have but half a one'). There is some variation within the text as regards the treatment of overrunning verse lines, though: in some cases the text is continued instead on the following line, but indented to show that it is intended to complete the previous line of verse, rather than being set as prose. This is the case with D7r l. 4; E6r l. 17; E6v l. 10; E7v l. 36; E8v ll. 12, 28, and 34; F1v ll. 16 and 27; and F5r ll. 6 and 9. On B7r l. 31 and E8v l. 30, meanwhile, the same thing occurs but the overhanging text is not indented. Typically, throughout the play text, each new speaker begins on a new line of the page, but in a handful of places a line of text is shared between two speakers. This occurs on B2r, B3v, B6v, B8r, C7r, and D6v. In some of these cases, the motive seems to have been to conserve space—and as with the lack of spacing surrounding entrances, it is notable that this practice occurs much more frequently in the more crowded first half of the text.

The prologue exists in three versions: one that was printed in *Six New Plays*, and two others that were printed in Shirley's 1646 *Poems &c*. One of these latter, entitled '*A Prologue at the* Globe *to his Comedy call'd* The doubtfull Heire, *which should have been presented at the* Black-Friers', is substantially the same as that in *SNP*, albeit with a handful of minor variations (listed in this edition's collation notes). However, the other—entitled '*To his own Comedy there, called* Rosania, *or* Loves Victory'—is an alternative version of the prologue that was used for the play's Dublin production. The differences between the Dublin and London prologues are discussed in the play's introductory essay, above. The epilogue, meanwhile, exists in two versions, substantially the same but differing in some details: one in *SNP* and the other in *Poems*. The latter is printed immediately after the prologue for the Globe, and is titled '*Epilogue to the same play there*'. The differences between these two texts are noted in the collation notes to the epilogue.

The Doubtful Heir was not published again until it appeared in the fourth volume of the Gifford/Dyce 1833 *The Dramatic Works and Poems of James Shirley*. Gifford's edition modernizes spelling and punctuation and attempts to tidy up some of the play's irregularities, most notably silently relineating and in places amending lines in order to smooth out the rhythms into more regular iambic pentameter. Gifford also adds scene divisions, which are lacking from the first edition, and numerous stage directions, many of which this edition has adopted. The play has not been re-edited since Gifford.

THE DOUBTFUL HEIR: TEXTUAL INTRODUCTION

THE DOUBTFUL HEIR—STOP-PRESS COLLATION
OF 1652 OCTAVO

Copies collated:

BRISTOL	Bristol Central Library, SR122 [play bound separately]
CAL	William Andrews Clark Memorial Library, PR3142 A1 1653
CARLISLE	Carlisle Cathedral
E	National Library of Scotland, H.3.d.5
F.1	Folger Shakespeare Library, S3466, Wing 2371:12 [play bound separately]
F.2	Folger Shakespeare Library, S3486 [Copy 3] (Woodward and McManaway/1134)
HD	Harvard University Library, 14433.30.28
HN.1	Huntington Library, 146309 pt. 1
HN.2	Huntington Library, 146316 pt. 1
HN.3	Huntington Library, 147760 [play bound separately]
L.1	British Library, G.18784
L.2	British Library, C.12.f.19(2.)
L.3	British Library, E.1226
L6.1	National Art Library (V&A), Dyce 9138, 25.E.37
L6.2	National Art Library (V&A), Dyce 9138, 25.E.38 [*Six New Playes* bound as part of a larger collection, incl. also *The Politician* and *The Gentleman of Venice*]
M	John Rylands Library, R56212
MEISEI.1	Meisei University, Tokyo, MR1420
MEISEI.2	Meisei University, Tokyo, MR1421
MEISEI.3	Meisei University, Tokyo, MR1422 [copy missing D1, D3, E2. Includes supplementary leaves bound before text, as follows: A1 (Meisei.3¹); A1, B1–6 (Meisei.3²)]
O6	Worcester College, Oxford, Plays.3.43 [bound A1, B1–F3, A2–3, F4–6]
O7	Wadham College, Oxford, A31.22
O9	All Souls College, Oxford, pp. 15.13 [bound *The Doubtful Heir* A1; *The Court Secret* B1–F7; *The Imposture* A1–4; *The Doubtful Heir* B–F3, A2–3, F4–6]

Variants by forme:

		State 1	State 2
B(i)			
B4r			
	cw	Abov	Above
B(o)			
B5r			

163

THE COMPLETE WORKS OF JAMES SHIRLEY, VOLUME 7

	cw	[7mm from edge of final line]	[12mm from edge of final line]
C(o)			
C1r			
	9	hand,	hand;
	13	honor	honors
C2v			
	19	theeagain	thee again
C6v			
	18	still.	still?
C7r			
	14	tamely, and expect me here;	tamely; and expect me here,
	17	now in revenge,	now, in revenge
D(o)			
D2v			
	14	*The*	*[The*
	15	*Ros.*	*Ros.]*

Distribution of variants:

	State 1	*State 2*
B(i)	CARLISLE [unclear], E, HD, HN.1, HN.2, L.1, L.2, L.3, L6.1, MEISEI.1, MEISEI.2, MEISEI.3, MEISEI.3², O6, O7	BRISTOL, CAL, F.1, F.2, HN.3, L6.2, M, O9
B(o)	CARLISLE, HD, HN.2, L.1, L.2, L.3, MEISEI.1, MEISEI.2	BRISTOL, CAL, E, F.1, F.2, HN.1, HN.3, L6.1, L6.2, M, MEISEI.3, MEISEI.3², O6, O7, O9
C(o)	MEISEI.3, O6	BRISTOL, CAL, CARLISLE, E, F.1, F.2, HD, HN.1, HN.2, HN.3, L.1, L.2, L.3, L6.1, L6.2, M, MEISEI.1, MEISEI.2, O7, O9
D(o)	BRISTOL, CAL, CARLISLE, E, F.1, F.2, HN.1, HN.2, HN.3, L.1, L.2, L.3, L6.1, L6.2, M, MEISEI.1, O6, O7, O9	HD, MEISEI.2, MEISEI.3

Uncorrected errors:

A3v, 9]	Alfonso's,
B2v, 24]	Blank line following
B2v, cw]	A [for Afraid]
B3r, 11]	qulaity [for quality]
B3v, 26–7]	Reversed SHs

164

THE DOUBTFUL HEIR: TEXTUAL INTRODUCTION

B6v, 17]	thei'r
B7r, 4]	to'th, field
B7r, 22]	thirst [for shirt]
C1r, rt]	*Doubful*
C1r, 8]	Coxbombs [for Coxcombs]
C3r, 9]	Ino [for Into]
C3v, 19]	*Leond.* [for either *Leon.* or *Lean.*—see Textual Introduction]
C5r, 3]	mean't
C7r, 8]	cheif
C7v, cw]	1,*Cit.* [for 1. *Cit.*—see Textual Introduction]
C8v, 23]	anorher
D1r, rt]	*Doubful*
D1r, 17]	atrend
D2r, 22]	I'st
D2r, 32]	you self
D2v, cw]	Take [for *Ros.*—see Textual Introduction]
D6r, 16]	these [for thee]
E1v, 8]	graut [turned n]
E1v, cw]	*Rosa.* [for *Ros.*—see Textual Introduction]
E3r, 30]	you selves
E3v, 28]	your [for you]
E4r, 27]	I'st
E7r, 11]	a gen
E7r, 29]	*Leand.* [for *Leon.*]
E7v, 10]	brought [for bought]
E8r-v, 36-1]	worships face is a prognostication of preferment / Is a Prognostication of preferment, where
F1r, 20]	yout [for your]
F1v, 12]	you selves
F2r, 33]	ha'? [for ha?]
F2r, cw]	I [for *Que.*—see Textual Introduction]
F3r]	missing catchword

165

The Doubtful Heir

TO THE MOST WORTHILY HONOURED
SIR EDMUND BOWYER

Sir,

Many years are vanished and a period not only of the scene, but more considerable revolutions have passed, since I had the happiness to be first known to you. I read excellent characters of you when you writ but a small letter, and though my observations, like seeds, were not cherished (by the fault of time) to a maturity, yet they begat 5 in me such great respect to your person, then budding with honour and expectation, that now, after so long absence, I find them not extinguished; and howsoever at the first complexion I may appear bold in this hasty interruption, yet your candour will be so far in my defence that I have presumed thus, rather to let you know that I can still

---

0 SIR EDMUND BOWYER Shirley's dedicatee may be Sir Edmund Bowyer (1613–81), of Camberwell in Surrey: an alleged Royalist who became a member of parliament in 1660 (Henning 1983, 1.696–7).

2 are vanished have gone by.

2 period...scene timespan that encompassed not only changing dramatic fashions (*OED*, Scene *n.* 6).

2–3 more...revolutions Presumably a reference to the recent English civil wars.

3–4 I read...letter A pun, based on the double meaning of character meaning 'alphabetical symbol' and character meaning 'personality' (*OED*, Character *n.* 3a; 12a). Shirley may mean that he could tell, from the smallest sample of Bowyer's writing, what the man himself must be like. Alternatively, he may mean that he first encountered Bowyer when the latter was a child (and so be punning on the idea that a child's writing is small). This latter interpretation may be supported by line 6's claim that when Shirley encountered Bowyer, the latter was 'budding with honour and expectation', a phrase suggesting considerable youthfulness. It is possible that Shirley encountered Bowyer as a pupil during his career as a schoolmaster. Shirley was master at St Albans School in *c.* 1620–5, and Bowyer's uncle (also Edmund) was an educationalist, acting as first governor of the free grammar school founded at Camberwell in 1615 (now Wilson's School).

4–5 though...maturity although my impression of you did not get a chance to develop. This is perhaps because Shirley did not manage to spend any more time in correspondence with Sir Edmund after their initial acquaintance or, if they knew each other personally, because their acquaintance was curtailed.

7 howsoever although.

7–8 at...complexion at first appearance.

8 hasty sudden, also with the sense of being rash or premature (*OED*, *adj.* 1a; 4).

8–9 your...defence Shirley means that Bowyer's fairness of mind will lead him to assume the best of Shirley himself (*OED*, Candour *n.* 3: 'openness of mind; fairness').

9 presumed acted without full authority or permission.

9–11 that...service Shirley is saying that although his dedication of his work to Bowyer may seem presumptuous, he would rather trust Bowyer to forgive his 'boldness' than let himself down ('unsatisfy myself') by neglecting to honour so excellent a gentleman.

---

0 BOWYER] O *subst.* (*Bowier*)

honour you than unsatisfy myself by neglecting the first opportunity of presenting my   10
service. Sir, it is a piece which perhaps you have seen in the active representment. The
estimation it gained from thence will be short of that grace it shall derive from your
acceptance, by which you will show how still you dare retain your nobleness and, by
renewing your smile upon me, encourage me to write myself –

Your humble servant,   15

JA[MES] SHIRLEY

11 **in...representment** i.e. on the stage.
12 **short of** less than.

16 JAMES] *Gifford subst.;* JA. O

THE DOUBTFUL HEIR

A PROLOGUE AT THE GLOBE TO HIS COMEDY CALLED *THE DOUBTFUL HEIR*, WHICH SHOULD HAVE BEEN PRESENTED AT THE BLACKFRIARS

All that the Prologue comes for is to say
Our author did not calculate this play
For this meridian. The Bankside, he knows,
Are far more skilful at the ebbs and flows
Of water than of wit – he did not mean   5
For the elevation of your poles this scene.
No shows, no dance, and – what you most delight in,
Grave understanders – here's no target fighting
Upon the stage, all work for cutlers barred.
No bawdry, nor no ballads – this goes hard –   10
But language clean, and, what affects you not,
Without impossibilities the plot.
No clown, no squibs, no devil in't. Oh, now,
You squirrels that want nuts, what will you do?
Pray do not crack the benches and we may   15
Hereafter fit your palates with a play.

0 This prologue exists in two versions: one in *O*, one in Shirley's *Poems &c* (1646). See *Poems &c*, Wing S3480; Thomason 165:E.1149[4], pp. 154–5 (D4v–5r). In *O* it is titled 'Prologue'.

2 calculate plan.

3 meridian This can mean either 'location' or, more specifically, 'the south' (*OED*, *n.* †5; †1). Shirley had originally expected the play to be performed in London at the indoor Blackfriars theatre which was to the north of the river Thames, rather than the larger, open-air Globe, which was to the south. The belief during the Caroline period that the Globe was more appropriate for coarse or populist entertainments than sophisticated theatre is discussed by Gurr (1970, 147–8).

3 The Bankside i.e. The people of the Bankside.

5–6 he…scene he did not mean this play to be staged in this location. The Globe's stage prominently featured two pillars or 'poles', which were not present at the Blackfriars, while the fact that the poles are described as elevated may be a reference to the Globe stage being higher off the ground than the Blackfriars stage. 'Elevation of your poles' is also a pun, referring to a technique of calculating latitude based on measuring the distance of a celestial object such as the pole above the horizon (*OED*, Elevation *n.* 9). Shirley thus continues the metaphor that he introduced with the word 'meridian', commenting on the fact that the play was due to be put on in one latitude (north of the river) but is being performed in another (south of the river).

8 understanders 1) groundlings; 2) those who comprehend.

8 target fighting displays of fighting. A target is a light, round shield. Despite Shirley's claim in this prologue, there are in fact two fights in the play: see Introduction.

9 cutlers In this context, makers of weaponry.

10 ballads light, popular songs. *O* has 'ballets' but *OED* comments that '*forms* [of the word 'ballad'] *with final -at , -ate , and -et are common until the 18th cent.*' (*OED*, Ballad *n.*).

11 what…not i.e. something you are not moved or impressed by.

13 squibs small fireworks.

14 squirrels a contemptuous term for a group of people (*OED*, Squirrel *n.* 1c).

15 crack break, with reference back to the previous image of bad spectators as squirrels who would like to be cracking open nuts.

0] *Poems subst.;* Prologue. O   1 All…say] *O subst.; Gentlemen*, I am only sent to say *Poems*
7 dance] O*; frisk Poems*   10 ballads] *Poems subst.; Ballets* O   11 But…clean] O*; The wit is clean Poems*

169

THE COMPLETE WORKS OF JAMES SHIRLEY, VOLUME 7

But you that can contract yourselves and sit
As you were now in the Blackfriars pit,
And will not deaf us with lewd noise and tongues
Because we have no heart to break our lungs,   20
Will pardon our vast stage and not disgrace
This play – meant for your persons, not the place.

17 **contract yourselves** 1) enter into an agreement with me; 2) reduce your physical presence, as if crammed into the smaller space of the Blackfriars theatre pit.

20 **break...lungs** i.e. by having to shout to be heard over the crowd noise.

22 **meant...place** The theatre is not what the author had in mind when writing, but the audience is perfectly suitable (so long as they can agree to behave decorously, like a Blackfriars audience).

19 and] O; or *Poems*   21 stage] O *subst.*; Scene *Poems*

170

THE DOUBTFUL HEIR

TO HIS OWN COMEDY THERE, CALLED
ROSANIA, OR LOVE'S VICTORY

"*Rosania?*" methinks I hear one say,
"What's that? 'Tis a strange title to a play."
One asks his friend, who late from travel came,
What 'tis, supposing it some county's name;
Who, rather than acknowledge ignorance,   5
Perhaps says 'tis some pretty town in France
Or Italy and wittily discloses
'Twas called Rosania for the store of roses –
A witty comment. Others that have seen
And fashionably observed the English scene   10
Say (but with less hope to be understood)
Such titles unto plays are now the mood:
Aglaura, *Claricilla*, names that may
(Being ladies') grace and bring guests to the play.
To save this charge of wit, that you might know   15
Something i'th'title which you need not owe
To another's understanding, you may see
In honest English there, *Love's Victory*.
Love maids do feel but warm in their first teens
And married once they know what t'other means.   20
Fear not the war; the victory is yours.

---

0 This prologue was written to be performed at the Werburgh Street Theatre in Dublin, and is printed only in Shirley's *Poems &c* (1646), pp. 148–9 (D1v–2r); it does not appear in O.

3 late recently.

10 English scene the English theatre.

11 but…understood Shirley implies that the Dublin audience may not understand or appreciate the current fashions of the English theatre scene.

12–13 Such…*Claricilla* There was a fashion in the late 1630s for plays named after women. *Aglaura* is a play by Sir John Suckling, first staged in 1637 by the King's Men at the Blackfriars Theatre and published in 1638. *Claricilla* is a tragicomedy written by Thomas Killigrew, which was performed in around 1636 by Queen Henrietta's Men at the Cockpit Theatre and published in 1641 (*OED*, Mood *n.*² †4: fashion, mode).

15 To…wit To avoid making you to puzzle over this.

17–18 you…*Victory* It was the custom on the English stage in the early modern period to have a board hung up on stage before the performance bearing the play's title. See, for example, Hieronimo's instruction to Balthazar in Kyd's *The Spanish Tragedy* to 'hang up the title' for the fifth-act play-within-a-play (K2v). It seems likely that this habit had been introduced on the Dublin stage, and that the speaker of Shirley's Dublin prologue brought a title board in with him which he gestured to at this point. For more on the title board tradition, see Chambers (1923, 3.126).

19 Young girls do not feel the first warmth of love until they enter their teens.

20 know…means know what victory in love means. Presumably referring to the 'victory' of sexual consummation, though it could also more broadly refer to the idea of being successful in love.

21 yours i.e. the audience's.

0] *Poems subst.*; PROLOGUE, / SPOKEN IN THE DUBLIN THEATRE. *Gifford*

The battle will be ended in two hours.
Wounds will be given and received, yet need
You fear no sigh or tear, whoever bleed.
You see, but can take in no shot; you are   25
So far from danger in this amorous war.
Not the least rude uncivil language shall
Approach your ear or make one cheek look pale.
The worst that can befall at this new play
Is we shall suffer if we lose the day;   30
For if you should traduce this poet's pen,
He'll be revenged and never write again.

22 two hours the traditional length of a play. Cf. *Romeo and Juliet*: 'the two-hours' traffic of our stage' (Prologue, 11).

25 You...shot The audience will be able to observe the 'amorous war' that the play depicts, but will not themselves be in danger of being shot or otherwise hurt.

30 we...day The worst that can happen is that the playwright and actors will suffer if the play is not well received.

31 traduce speak ill of, slander.

---

30 lose] *Gifford;* loose *Poems*

THE DOUBTFUL HEIR

THE PERSONS OF THE PLAY

LEONARIO, *Prince of Aragon*

FERDINAND, *King of Murcia*

RODRIGUEZ

ERNESTO } *noblemen attending on the court*

LEANDRO   5

ALFONSO [*a general of Valencia and*] *father to Rosania*

OLIVIA, *supposed Queen of Murcia*

ROSANIA, *Alfonso's daughter*

VIOLINDA [*Olivia's lady in waiting*]

CAPTAIN   10

[FOUR] CITIZENS

COURTIER

OFFICERS

SOLDIERS

[KEEPER OF A PRISON]   15

[SERVANTS]

[GUARD]

[ATTENDANTS, LADIES, *and* GENTLEMEN]

---

1 *Aragon* Region in the north-east of Spain.

2 *Murcia* Region in the south-east of Spain. In reality, Murcia was only briefly independent, between 1223 and 1243. For most of the time after this date it was incorporated into the kingdom of Castile.

6 *Valencia* Region in the south-east of Spain.

11 CITIZENS In O, the first two citizens are named '1 *Cit.*' and '2 *Cit.*' only in the first act, and are thereafter renamed 'Lieutenant' and 'Ancient'. Following Gifford, I am retaining the titles of 'First Citizen' and 'Second Citizen' to refer to these two characters throughout. In Act 3 two further citizens appear. In O these are named 1. *Cit.* and 2. *Cit.*, but for the sake of clarity (and, again, following Gifford) I have named these Third and Fourth Citizen.

---

6 *a...and*] *this edn; not in* O   9 *Olivia's...waiting*] *this edn; not in* O

11 FOUR] *Gifford; not in* O   15] *Gifford; not in* O   16] *this edn; not in* O

17] *this edn; not in* O   18] *this edn; Attendants, Ladies, Gentlemen, &c. Gifford; not in* O

173

I.I THE COMPLETE WORKS OF JAMES SHIRLEY, VOLUME 7

THE SCENE: MURCIA.

1[.1]

Enter RODRIGUEZ *and* ERNESTO.

RODRIGUEZ This turn was not expected; Prince Leonario
 Is much perplexed.
ERNESTO   I cannot blame his highness.
 So near an expectation of a blessing
 To be thus crossed!
RODRIGUEZ   The day of marriage set,   5
 With the applausive vote of both the kingdoms,
 By an unlooked-for war to be put off,
 Would vex a royal spleen.
ERNESTO   'Tis but deferred.
RODRIGUEZ I do not like the hope on't.
ERNESTO   I pity
 The princely lover, worthy (without blemish
 To the excelling virtues of the queen)   10
 Of as much goodness as her sex contains;
 So noble in his nature, active, bountiful,
 Discreet, and valiant, if we may believe
 What his young fame proffers to every knowledge.
RODRIGUEZ This character is not flattery, and yet   15
 The queen our mistress is not lost in this
 Just praise of him.
ERNESTO   I have no thought so impious.
 My duty never taught me to commend,
 But to obey. Her virgin sweetness makes me
 Her just admirer, but when I observe   20
 Her prudent manage of the state, a strength
 Would become many years, her pious laws,

---

0 The scene is set in the royal palace.
5 **applausive** loudly expressing approval and applause.
6 **unlooked-for** unforeseen, not expected, also with a sense of being unwelcome.
7 **spleen** Traditionally believed to be the seat of moroseness and irritability.
8 **hope** expectation.
9–10 **without...queen** Ernesto means that in praising the worthiness of her fiancée Leonario, he is not intending to deny the good qualities of the queen herself.
15 **character** description, delineation, or detailed report of a person's qualities.
16 **lost** forgotten.
18–19 **duty...obey** Ernesto feels bound to obey the queen but not to praise her.
21 **manage** management.
22 **Would...years** i.e. The queen's ability would be admirable even in someone much older and more experienced.

1[.1]] *Gifford subst. (*ACT I. SCENE I.*);* ACT. I. O

174

THE DOUBTFUL HEIR   I.I

But that without example, made to advance
Her sex's chastity, I forget all
Beside worth praise, though every least of her   25
Desert ask a volume. – 'Tis his Excellence.

    Enter LEONARIO [*and*] CAPTAIN.

RODRIGUEZ There's one not sorry for these wars.
ERNESTO   'Tis his
    Profession; soldiers batten in a tempest.
RODRIGUEZ And he deserves employment. Yet I think
    He'll never purchase with his pay.   30
LEONARIO [*To Captain*] Be confident;
    Your worth will plead alone. – The queen expects me.   *Exit Leonario.*
CAPTAIN Your highness' humble creature. [*Aside*] So, there's hope yet
    After a time of ease and surfeit we
    May cure ourselves by letting others' blood.   35
    [*To them*] My noble lords.
ERNESTO 'Morrow, Captain. You look blithe and bright.
CAPTAIN I'll put my sword to scouring that shall shine.
    I thank heaven my prayers are heard.
RODRIGUEZ   What prayers?
CAPTAIN That honest men may cut knaves' throats and bid   40
    Defiance to the hangman. Musk and civet
    Have too long stifled us; there's no recovery
    Without the smell of gunpowder.

    Enter two CITIZENS.

ERNESTO   But Captain –
FIRST CITIZEN 'Tis he; we must not lose him.
SECOND CITIZEN He has credit with the lords, it seems.   45
FIRST CITIZEN He has spied us.

---

23 But...example The precise meaning here is unclear, but Ernesto seems to intend, 'going beyond even the example set by the queen herself'.

28 batten A pun: *OED* gives two meanings of the verb 'to batten': 1) to thrive or improve in condition; 2) to fasten down and secure the fixtures of a ship in bad weather (*OED*, Batten $v.^1$ 1a; $v.^2$ 1).

30 purchase...pay become rich from his wages (*OED*, Purchase $v.$ 4†b: 'To acquire possessions; to amass wealth, become rich; to do well.').

32 Your...alone As an honourable man, the Captain requires no introduction.

38 that...shine in order that it shall shine.

40–1 That...hangman i.e. Soldiers will be allowed to mete out deadly justice and not be executed for murder (as they would in peace time).

41 Musk...civet Aromatic substances used as perfumes by courtiers. Cf. *As You Like It*: 'The courtier's hands are perfumed with civet' (3.2.61–2); *The Merry Wives of Windsor*: 'Yet there has been knights, and lords, and gentlemen, with their coaches; I warrant you, coach after coach, letter after letter, gift after gift; smelling so sweetly, all musk' (2.2.6–36).

42–3 no...gunpowder The complaint by militarists that peacetime corrupted men and sapped their masculinity was a common one throughout the Renaissance.

---

26 SD *and*] *Gifford; not in* O   **31 SD**] *this edn; not in* O   **32 SD**] O *subst. (Ex. Leon.)*   **33 SD**] *this edn;* O *marks an aside with a dash*   **36 SD**] *this edn; Gifford marks end of aside with a dash; not in* O

175

I.I   THE COMPLETE WORKS OF JAMES SHIRLEY, VOLUME 7

CAPTAIN My honest friends, welcome to court. My lords,
    Pray grace these honest gentlemen; they will
    Deserve to kiss your hands.
FIRST CITIZEN   Our business is
    To you, Captain.   50
CAPTAIN [*To lords*] Do you think what these brace of baboons come for?
RODRIGUEZ Not I.
CAPTAIN By this day, for money, moneys that I owe 'em.
ERNESTO Is't possible?
CAPTAIN [*To Citizens*] I ha' moved your suit, gentlemen.
FIRST CITIZEN What suit?   55
CAPTAIN Touching the masque which you two, in the name
    Of the whole city, offered to present
    At the town charges to congratulate
    The queen's intended marriage. I know
    This egg was long a-hatching and expected,   60
    But that your heads could not agree (they being
    Of several sizes, some upon the shoulders
    Of your long-winded officers whose purse
    Was made of the leather with their conscience).
FIRST CITIZEN Does he talk to us of a masque?   65
SECOND CITIZEN Good Captain, put your masque off and give us
    The money that you owe us.
CAPTAIN   Was't not meant nobly?
    But you, my good lords, know how much
    The queen and prince are sorry that so rare
    A precedent of their duty should not be   70
    Upon record. This villainous war distracts
    All civil mirth – but you will be remembered.
FIRST CITIZEN We know not what you mean; we have no antics
    In agitation. If your captainship
    Will pay your debts so: there is law and courses   75
    To be taken and you will find that Justice

51 **think** know.
54 **I...suit** I have put forward your request to the court.
56–64 **Touching...conscience** The Captain pretends that the citizens had intended to put on a show to celebrate the queen's wedding, and that he was responsible for proposing the idea to the court on their behalf. He suggests that the undertaking is taking a long time because they have had to negotiate with officials. These officials have
a conscience made of the same substance as their money-bags: a coarse leather, which will not allow them to feel
softer emotions.
58 **At...charges** paid for by the town.
59 **marriage** Pronounced as three syllables for the sake of the meter.
66 **put...off** set aside your tale of this masque. Also a pun on masque/mask, implying that the Captain is
disguising his true purposes under the cover of this invented story.
70 **precedent...duty** public demonstration or symbol of their virtue (*OED*, Precedent *n.* †3: 'A sign, an
indication of something; a token').
72 **remembered** favoured by the court, possibly with the sense also of being financially rewarded.
73–4 **we...agitation** we have no theatrical pageants in preparation.

51 SD] *this edn; not in* O   54 SD] *this edn; not in* O

176

THE DOUBTFUL HEIR   I.I

Can deal, sir, with the sword as well as balance.
CAPTAIN [*Aside*] The puppies talk philosophy. Nay, then,
   I must be plain. Would I could 'tice 'em to
   A little treason. They'll ne'er hang for felony.   80
   [*To them*] Why, whither do you think I am going now?
FIRST CITIZEN We care not whither, so you pay us first.
CAPTAIN [*Aside*] Let their own fathers swing, so they have money.
SECOND CITIZEN May be you are going to the wars.
CAPTAIN Yes, mongrels.   85
   To fight for your chamlet faces, while you stay
   At home and catch the cramp with telling money,
   Putting your guts to pension every day,
   And roots, until the wind cry out against you,
   And with your belching backwards stifle men   90
   That walk the street until the air be purged.
   Must we eat bullets without butter, whelps?
   Have our throats cut or drop like sheep by th'hundred
   O' the rot to buy your peace, you boding screech-owls?
   And ha' your consciences so coarse a nap   95
   To ask money of us?
FIRST CITIZEN   You had the conscience
   To take up our commodities.
CAPTAIN   Reason good;
   Should I go naked, leeches?
SECOND CITIZEN No, but there is reason
   That you should pay, good Captain, for your warmth.   100
CAPTAIN Pay you? For what? For clothes, such things as these?
   Your tribe is bound to keep us.

---

77 sword…balance The figure of Justice was traditionally pictured holding a sword as well as a set of scales, showing that Justice was powerful as well as impartial.

78 puppies foolish or impertinent young men (*OED*, Puppy *n*. 2a).

80 felony 'Formerly the general name for a class of crimes which may loosely be said to be regarded by the law as of a graver character than those called misdemeanours' (*OED*, *n*.¹ 4b).

83 Let…money They would let their own fathers be hanged so long as they could have money.

86 chamlet light, soft fabric. The Captain is referring to the unweathered and delicate nature of the citizens' skin.

88 Putting…day Making regular, small 'payments' of food to their stomachs. The metaphor may imply that the citizens are stingy even with their own diets, feeding themselves only a small 'pension' rather than a full 'salary' of food to live on.

89 roots The citizens will feed themselves on roots, an indicator of a poor (and perhaps implicitly beast-like) diet. Cf. *Timon of Athens*: 'Why, how shall I requite you? / Can you eat roots, and drink cold water?' (5.1.71–2).

90 belching backward farting.

91 until…purged until the wind trapped inside you is free.

92 eat…butter The Captain mingles a metaphor and a literalism: the idea of 'eating bullets' (being shot) and the idea of having butter—a luxury item—on one's food.

95 so…nap so rough a surface. The ungratefulness of civilians towards soldiers is a theme elsewhere in Shirley: see *The Cardinal*, 3.2.220–34.

102 tribe class of people, fraternity—sometimes used with a sense of contempt.

---

78 SD] *this edn; Gifford marks 79–80 'would…felony' as an aside; not in* O   **81 SD]** *this edn; not in* O
83 SD] *this edn; not in* O   **89** against] *Gifford;* agen O

177

1.1   THE COMPLETE WORKS OF JAMES SHIRLEY, VOLUME 7

FIRST CITIZEN How?
CAPTAIN Yes, and desire us to accept your wares
    To recompense our sufferings. 'Tis we,   105
    'Tis we that keep your worships warm and living
    By marching, fasting, fighting and a thousand
    Dangers. You o'er grown moths, you that love gold
    And will not take an angel sent from heaven
    Unless you weigh him. You that spend the day   110
    In looking o'er your debt-book and at night
    Can lap and lecher in your feather beds,
    Then snort and dream of four score in the hundred,
    Afraid of nothing but the gout – or, what
    Is a more just reward for your hard hearts,   115
    The stone, which puts you to the charge of physic
    To make you piss out your last usurer's gallon,
    Or of a surgeon to cut you for
    The pebbles, which (if you survive incision)
    You keep in penny boxes like dear relics,   120
    And show your friends when you intend to visit 'em
    And beg a dinner.
ERNESTO   Let not passion
    Make you too much abuse their quality.
    The city does contain brave fellows, Captain,
    As generous, as bountiful, discreet,   125
    And valiant too as any boast themselves
    In court or camp.
CAPTAIN   I grant you, my good lord,
    And honour all the noble souls within it.
    But these are walking sicknesses, not citizens;
    Two such prodigious things with crooked consciences,   130
    Though young, yet old in usury –
SECOND CITIZEN   All this, Captain,
    Wo'not pay us our money, which we must

---

108 moths are often used in the drama of the time as an example of parasitic and idle creatures. Cf. *Othello*: '[I]f I be left behind, / A moth of peace, and he go to the war, / The rites for why I love him are bereft me' (1.3.255–7).

109 angel…heaven A pun: an angel was also a gold coin, worth approximately 10 shillings during this period.

112 lap embrace (*OED*, *v.*² 3†c).

113 dream…hundred The citizens are imagined dreaming of an exceptionally high rate of return on their investments: 180 per cent.

116 The stone Gallstones.

117 usurer's gallon The sense of this is conveyed in Davenport's *A New Trick to Cheat the Devil* (1639): 'An Usurers Gallon, that's just halfe a pint' (C4v). Usurers were assumed to be stingy in all aspects of life. The Captain implies that the citizens will need medical help even to be able to produce that much urine.

122 passion Pronounced as three syllables.

124–7 The…camp Shirley may not wish to alienate the citizens in his audience by suggesting that these two citizens are representative of all.

---

109 will not] *Gifford;* wo'not O

178

THE DOUBTFUL HEIR   I.I

Have or petition for to your disgrace.
CAPTAIN Well, since there is no remedy, will you take
    These two noblemen's words for what I owe you?   135
FIRST CITIZEN With all our hearts.
RODRIGUEZ   That bargain is to make.
ERNESTO Good Captain, at this time you may excuse us.
CAPTAIN Why, do your lordships think I'd let you suffer?
    Come, you're my honourable friends; pass, pass
    Your word. I'll pay the money. [*Aside, to lords*] Hang 'em, dottrels: 140
    I'll not be beholden to 'em.
RODRIGUEZ We had rather you should, good Captain.
CAPTAIN No. Come hither, capons.
    Will money content you? Shall I walk the street
    Without a headache with your bawling for   145
    The debt when I ha' paid you?
SECOND CITIZEN   'Tis but reason.
CAPTAIN I'll fetch you money presently. You may follow
    If you please, but these noblemen shall see
    And witness what I pay you. I'll not trust
    Your memorandums.
FIRST CITIZEN   With all our hearts, sir.   150
SECOND CITIZEN We desire no more.
CAPTAIN I'll wait on you again.   *Exeunt [all but] Rodriguez and Ernesto.*

       Enter LEANDRO, *reading a paper.*

RODRIGUEZ   *Fortune de la guerre.*
    – My lord Leandro? What paper's that, he so intentively peruses?
LEANDRO [*Aside*] I like it and could willingly allow
    The change. The queen grows mighty in her spirit,   155
    And this match with the prince would swell her state
    Too much. [*To them*] My lords.

---

133 or…disgrace or we would be forced to make a formal written demand for the return of our loans, which would embarrass you.

136 That…make We haven't agreed to that.

139–40 pass…word give your promise. Cf. *Twelfth Night*: 'Sir Toby will be sworn that I am no fox, but he will not pass his word for twopence that you are no fool' (1.5.75–7). The Captain is trying to get the lords to act as his guarantors for the loan.

140 dottrels A dottrel is a species of plover that was famous for being easy to capture, as well as being a term for a fool, often with figurative reference to the first meaning. Also spelled 'dotterel' (*OED*, Dotterel *n.* 1, 2).

141 I'll…'em The Captain refuses to continue owing the citizens a debt.

143 capons 1) castrated cocks; 2) 'As a type of dullness, and a term of reproach' (*OED*, Capon *n.* 1a; 1c).

150 memorandums citizens' records of their financial transactions.

152 *Fortune…guerre* French for 'The luck of the war.' Rodriguez means that what happens in wartime is unpredictable and due only to chance. He is presumably referring to the fact that the citizens may or may not succeed in getting any of their money back from the Captain.

153 intentively intently, attentively.

---

140 SD] *this edn; not in* O   **150** With all] *Gifford;* Withall O
152 SD] *this edn; Exeunt Capt. and Citizens. Gifford; Ex. Manent Rod. Ernesto.* O
153 My…peruses] *lineation this edition;* that / He O   **154 SD**] *this edn; not in* O
157 SD] *this edn; Gifford marks end of aside with a dash; not in* O

179

I.I THE COMPLETE WORKS OF JAMES SHIRLEY, VOLUME 7

RODRIGUEZ We are yours.
LEANDRO See what dangerous papers have been scattered
    To wound the title of our royal mistress. 160
    My servant brought me this. Our enemy,
    Who calls himself Prince Ferdinand, would fain
    Have us believe him cousin to the queen,
    She an usurper of his crown.
ERNESTO We all know him dead. 165
RODRIGUEZ I'm sure I did attend his funeral.
ERNESTO I think I waited too.
LEANDRO This paper says he was conveyed away
    And so escaped his uncle's cruelty,
    To whose protection he was left an infant. 170
    He dying, we translated our obedience
    To his daughter, now our queen.
RODRIGUEZ   Here's an imposter.
LEANDRO Heaven aid the innocent, say I. He has
    Valencia's aid and comes not to invite
    But force a resignation. I wish things 175
    Were calm again.
ERNESTO Prince Leonario, if she prosper not,
    Is like to be a loser too.
LEANDRO   For him
    It matters not; we have more to think on now
    Than love and compliment. 180
RODRIGUEZ I thought he would be general
    'Gainst this pretended Ferdinand.
LEANDRO   What else?
    Her sweetheart, that gives Cupid in his crest.
    Alas! There needs no art nor strength of war
    To advance her cause. Justice will fight for her 185
    I'th'clouds, and Victory sent from heaven, without
    Her soldiers' sweat, will gloriously descend
    To crown his head with laurel.

---

167 **waited too** Presumably referring to having served some official function as an attendant at the funeral.
167–8 **SH** O has Leandro speak line 167 and Ernesto speak line 168, but this seems likely to be an error. Leandro is the one who has been reading the papers and knows their content, so it seems probable that the speech headings have been accidentally reversed.
170 **left…infant** left as an infant.
174 **Valencia's** Valencia was a Spanish kingdom on the eastern coast of the Iberian peninsula.
174–5 **not…resignation** not to request the queen's abdication but to enforce it.
180 **compliment** polite, flattering expressions (*OED, n.* 1b).
183 **gives…crest** Leandro ironically comments that Leonario, as a lover, will march into battle with Cupid as the emblem on his coat of arms.
188 **his** Leonario's.
188 **laurel** In ancient Rome, successful military commanders were crowned with laurel wreaths.

167–8 **SH**] *this edn;* O *reverses these speech headings, with Leandro speaking line 167 and Ernesto line 168; see commentary note*
180 compliment] O *subst.* (complement)

180

THE DOUBTFUL HEIR   I.I

ERNESTO   May it prove so.
LEANDRO I could say things would stagger your belief,
    But I forgot the queen sent for me. To   190
    You both a servant –   *Exit.*
ERNESTO I do not like my lord Leandro's winding.
    He has been faithful.
RODRIGUEZ Always honourable. – The queen.

    Enter QUEEN [OLIVIA], LEONARIO, CAPTAIN, LEANDRO, VIOLINDA,
    ATTENDANTS, LADIES, [*and*] GENTLEMEN.

LEONARIO I take this as the greatest honour, madam,   195
    You could confer. My name is young in war,
    But my affection to your royal person,
    Armed with the virtue of your cause, shall make me
    Do something worth your name.
OLIVIA   'Twas your request.
    Nor could we place our chief command but where   200
    'Tis equalled with your interest in us
    And your own merit.
LEONARIO   Sure my stars did mean
    This way to make you know how much my heart
    Dares in your service; and if Ferdinand –
    For so he calls himself – possess a soul   205
    Above the vulgar making, we shall spare
    The blood of many and conclude the war
    In single opposition.
LEANDRO With your highness' pardon,
    It not becomes you should engage your person   210
    And so great a cause so dangerously.
    It will be too much honour to th'impostor
    And, in the supposition of the world,
    A strength to his pretence to bring your birth
    So low to humble both your self and fortunes   215
    To his unworthy level: a thing grown
    Up in the night, a meteor hanging in
    The air, prodigiously, fed with vapour and

---

189 I...belief Leandro is referring, obliquely, to the fact that he knows the truth about the relative royal
statuses of Ferdinand and Olivia.
  190–1 To...servant I am servant to you both.
  192 winding devious or oblique ways or dealings (*OED n.*¹ 2a).
  201 interest financial and emotional investment.
  217–20 meteor...stars Meteors were traditionally thought of as ill omens. Cf. *1 Henry IV*: '[B]e no
more an exhaled meteor, / A prodigy of fear, and a portent / Of broachèd mischief to the unborn times'
(5.1.19–21). Here, Leandro implies also that meteors are deceptive and ambitious, resembling stars but
without being fixed and permanent.
───────
194 SD QUEEN OLIVIA] *this edn;* OLIVIA *Gifford;* Queen O   **194 SD** *and*] *Gifford; not in* O
199 SH] *this edn;* Oliv. *Gifford;* Olivia *has the speech heading* 'Que.' *and is referred to as* 'Queen' *in stage
directions throughout* O

181

I.I THE COMPLETE WORKS OF JAMES SHIRLEY, VOLUME 7

Black influence, ambitious to deceive
The world and challenge kindred with the stars. 220
It is too great a venture, sir.
ERNESTO Since there must be a war,
Let the armies meet in battle. There's more hope
After the worst to reinforce and prosper
Than when the kingdom's put upon one stake, 225
And one man's chance to assure it.
OLIVIA   I allow
Your counsel, lords, but have more argument
Convincing me not to run such a hazard
Of what must make Olivia rich hereafter.
A kingdom's loss may be repaired but your 230
Life, made a sacrifice to tyrant war,
May find a welcome to the other shades,
But no tears can invite you back to share
Or grief or joy with me. I'll have no duel.
LEONARIO 'Tis a command and my obedience 235
Shall meet it, though I fear 'twill be a sin
To be too careful of my self – but I
Shall still remember that I am your soldier
And this considered shall not make me rash,
But wisely teach me to deserve this title 240
Which lives but in your honour.
OLIVIA   I'll pray for you,
And not so much for what concerns the state
As what your merit hath already gained
Upon my heart.
RODRIGUEZ   Blessings upon 'em both.
A curse upon these wars that spoil their mirth. 245
OLIVIA My lord Leandro.

                    [*Olivia and Leandro talk apart.*]

LEONARIO There's your commission, Captain. I suppose
You have found ways to empty your exchequer?
CAPTAIN My bags are not brimful, my lord. I have

223–6 **There's...it** i.e. We have a better chance of success if we don't gamble the whole kingdom on one man's fortune in combat.

228–9 **not...hereafter** Olivia does not want to risk losing the life of Leonario, who will make her rich with his love after the battle.

242–4 **not...heart** Olivia says that she will pray for Leonario to do well, not only for the sake of her country, but also because of the extent to which she loves and values him.

248 **exchequer** At the time it was customary for army captains to be given all the wages for a company, and to distribute them among the ordinary soldiers. The Captain would thus be in charge of a considerable sum of money. See Cruickshank (1946, 143).

---

246 **SD**] *this edn; not in* O

182

THE DOUBTFUL HEIR   1.1

Defalked, and made an ebb for wine and women   250
And other things that keep poor men alive
To do their country service.
LEONARIO   Please you walk
With this gentleman, Captain. He shall pay you
Five hundred pieces that I owe you.
CAPTAIN Me? Your grace owes me nothing.   255
LEONARIO I could not pay the debt in better time, sir.
CAPTAIN Umh! I will take the money and allow the miracle.

                              Exeunt Captain and Gentleman.

ERNESTO [*Aside, to Rodriguez*] Did you observe the prince's nobleness?
Although the act become him, yet the manner
Takes me especially. Heaven preserve the Captain   260
From being mad.
              [*Olivia and Leandro rejoin the group.*]
LEONARIO   I prosper in your vote.
But shall I, madam – if that power, which crowns
With victory, guides me with fair success
In this your war, and triumph smile upon us –
Shall I at my return have that reward   265
My soul next heaven affects? Shall no delay
(Colder than frost to lovers' blood) afflict
My expectation of our marriage?
Although to doubt this be a sin, yet where
The ambition is so just, I shall but right   270
My heart to have it oft assured; nor can
It make your eye less rich in smiles when 'tis
Only my love encourages me to make
The busy, harmless question.
OLIVIA   It does please me.
Nor can you ask so often as I have   275
A cheerfulness to answer that I love you
And have propounded nothing dearer to me
Than that which perfects chaste affection
And chains two hearts. The priest with sadness will

---

250 Defalked Made subtractions or deductions from his exchequer (*OED*, Defalk *v.* †1: 'To reduce by deductions').
250 made...women The Captain says that he has spent some of the army wages on women and alcohol.
261 mad Ernesto's meaning is unclear. Rodriguez later describes the Captain as 'mad' in line 397 (in the sense of being 'madcap'—bizarre or zany), but that meaning does not seem to fit here. He may intend the word in the sense of 'foolishly imprudent', since Leonario has promised to repay the Captain's debts for him, which may result in the latter going off on another spending spree (*OED*, *adj.* 2).
261 I...vote I thrive in your good opinion.
274 busy anxious, eager, earnest (*OED*, *adj.* †4).
279 sadness steadfastness, constancy (*OED*, *n.* †3).

---

257 SD] O *subst.* (*Ex. Capt. & Gent.*)   **258 SD**] *this edn; not in* O   **261 SD**] *this edn; not in* O

183

I.I   THE COMPLETE WORKS OF JAMES SHIRLEY, VOLUME 7

Expect you safe again, but from this war   280
When you return he shall not in his register
Of lovers find one with more wing hath met
The bosom of her friend than glad Olivia
To make one soul with you.
LEONARIO   I have enough
And thirst for action in the field, from whence   285
I will bring harvest home or leave my self,
Happy in life or death to do you service.

       Exeunt [Olivia], Leonario, Leandro, Ladies, [and] attendants.

RODRIGUEZ Well, I'm afraid if Hymen should set up
His tapers now, they would not last to light
His priest, at their return, to say his office.   290
ERNESTO Hope fairly.
RODRIGUEZ   I allow his spirit, but
The prince hath not been practised in the school
Of war, where stratagems prevail above
All personal resolution.
ERNESTO He cannot want fit counsel to direct   295
His early valour. Besides, Ferdinand,
By computation as young as he,
May poise the scale.

      Enter CAPTAIN, *two* CITIZENS, *and a Soldier.*

            See, the Captain.
FIRST CITIZEN We always thought you noble, and we hope
You'll take no offence that our occasions   300
Prevailed above our modesty.
CAPTAIN   I know
You two are very modest. Well, I'm glad
I am furnished for you. My good lords, I must
Entreat you to be witnesses of what money
I pay these gentlemen that have trusted me.   305

---

282 wing speed (*OED*, *n.* 'on the wing' b(b) *fig.* (i): 'Moving or travelling swiftly or briskly').
288–90 Hymen…office Hymen was the Greek god of marriage. Rodriguez means that he fears there will be a long delay before the marriage between Olivia and Leonario can take place. If the god of marriage lit his candles now, in preparation for the nuptials, they would have burned out long before Leonario and his forces returned.
291 allow admit.
297 computation Pronounced as five syllables.
298 poise…scale balance the scale. Ernesto implies that as Ferdinand is also young and therefore perhaps just as inexperienced as Leonario, the battle may not be as one-sided as they fear.
300–1 our…modesty our needs overcame our politeness and reticence (*OED*, Occasion *n.*[1] 9b). Cf. *The Merchant of Venice*: 'My purse, my person, my extremest means / Lie all unlocked to your occasions' (1.1.138–9).

---

287 SD] *this edn; Exe. Oliv. Leo. Lean. Ladies, and Attendants. Gifford; Ex. Queen, Leon. Lean. Ladies, attendants.* O
296–7] *lineation Gifford;* besides / Ferdinand…he O   **298 SD]** *this edn; after* as he O

184

THE DOUBTFUL HEIR   I.I

SECOND CITIZEN And will again; command our shops.

CAPTAIN [*Aside to Ernesto*] No, sit there and starve – or if you like
    It better, take a swing at your own signpost.

ERNESTO [*To Captain*] Good words, Captain.

CAPTAIN [*To Ernesto*] They expect good money, and both good are too much.   310

FIRST CITIZEN We always loved you.

SECOND CITIZEN And do so still, most virtuously.

CAPTAIN It does appear.

FIRST CITIZEN And you shall find us ready –

CAPTAIN I'll make but one fair motion; it will be   315
    Sufficient trial of your honesty.
    I have five hundred pounds – you saw me tell it.
    Faith, make it up a thousand 'twixt you both
    Till I come back. You will be aldermen.

FIRST CITIZEN [*Aside*] Ne'er a whit the sooner.   320

SECOND CITIZEN Alas, sir, if it were at another time –

FIRST CITIZEN Hereafter, upon good occasion, you shall find –

CAPTAIN You both i'th'pillory, for selling copper lace
    By a wrong name. Well, there's no remedy.
    I'll keep my word; the money's ready for you.   325

FIRST CITIZEN You are noble, Captain.

SECOND CITIZEN May you kill all the queen's enemies.

CAPTAIN You would not 'scape, that cozen her liege people every day, then.

SECOND CITIZEN This payment, Captain, will come most seasonably.

FIRST CITIZEN And do us as much good as you had given us the sum twice told,   330
    another time.

CAPTAIN Before these noblemen, have you such want
    As you profess? You have no wives nor children.

---

308 take…signpost hang yourself from your own shop-sign (*OED*, Swing *v.*[1] 8, *slang or colloquial*: 'To be hanged').

310 expect…much The Captain refuses to both pay the citizens their money and be pleasant to them as well.

315 motion proposal.

317 tell count.

318–19 make…aldermen The Captain is asking the citizens to lend him a further £500, to be repaid when he comes home. In return, he promises to use both his money and influence to make them aldermen: members of the local council or, in London, the chief officers of a ward.

320 Ne'er…sooner The citizen agrees that he and his fellow citizen may at some point become aldermen, but suggests that this will not be due to any action of the Captain's (i.e. the Captain will not make it happen 'sooner').

323–4 copper…name ' "Lace", in this sense, was made by spinning gold or silver wire around a core of silk thread' (Jones and Stallybrass 2000, 25). Copper lace might be passed off by unscrupulous merchants as the more expensive gold lace. Cf. Hall (1650, 39): 'as if a man have sold you copper lace for gold; or alchymie-plate for silver'. See also the discussion of the players' use of copper lace as a stage stand-in for gold in Jones and Stallybrass (2000, 190–1).

---

307 SD] *this edn; not in* O   **307–8]** *lineation this edition;* starve, / Or … swing / At O
309 SD] *this edn; not in* O   **310 SD]** *this edn; not in* O   **317** saw] *Gifford;* see O   **320 SD]** *this edn; not in* O
323–4] *lineation this edition;* Copper / Lace … remedy O   **328]** *lineation this edition;* scape, / That O
330–1] *lineation this edition;* us / The O   **332]** *lineation this edn;* Before / These O

185

I.I   THE COMPLETE WORKS OF JAMES SHIRLEY, VOLUME 7

FIRST CITIZEN I protest upon my credit, I am to pay this day two hundred pound
     or be endangered to an arrest.   335
SECOND CITIZEN And I must go to prison, if before sunset –
CAPTAIN Then 'twill do you a pleasure?
BOTH Above expression.
CAPTAIN Here's twelve pence apiece for you. You're fit men to serve the queen.
BOTH How, Captain?   340
CAPTAIN Why, in the wars. Choose either pike or musket; you shall have that favour.
BOTH We are both undone.
LORDS Ha ha, but will you use 'em so?
CAPTAIN Ha' they not ready money? Why d'ye stare?
     No thanks for my protection?
BOTH   Protection?   345
CAPTAIN Did you not protest you should to prison else?
     Why, you unthankful sons of false light! Sergeant,
     Take 'em to their rendezvous.
FIRST CITIZEN Captain, a word. We are content –
CAPTAIN I'm glad on't. Why d'ye stay then?   350
FIRST CITIZEN – To abate half our money.
SECOND CITIZEN All, all good Captain. He shall have all, rather than be sent a-
     soldiering. D'ye know what 'tis? 'Tis no Artillery Garden, where you come
     off with 'As you were'.
RODRIGUEZ This was his project.   355
CAPTAIN Hmm, you will forgive me both your debts?
SECOND CITIZEN And pray heaven to forgive you, too.

   337 do...pleasure make you happy. The Captain is asking whether the repayment of his loan will be of help
to the citizens.
   339 twelve pence At the time, officers were permitted to forcibly conscript new recruits to the army or navy,
by giving them a fixed sum known as 'press money' (*OED*, Press money *n.* 3). If the citizens accepted this
money, they were then legally bound to serve. See Edelman (2000), 'press' and 'press-money'.
   341 pike...musket Two types of weapon—the former an eighteen-foot pole tipped with metal; the latter a
kind of heavy firearm. The Captain invites the citizens to take their choice whether to train as pikemen or mus-
ketmen in his regiment.
   347 false light A false light is one that leads men into danger or error, but in this context, the Captain is
referring specifically to the reputation cloth merchants had for cheating their customers by using 'false light':
deliberately keeping their shops dark in order to mislead potential buyers about the quality of their wares. See
Hentschell (2008, 139–41).
   351 To...money The First Citizen offers to reduce the Captain's debt by half, in exchange for being released
from the forced conscription.
   353 Artillery Garden The English army's practice ground, located at the time in Spitalfields in London.
   354 'As...were' A command given in army drill to instruct soldiers to return to their previous state. The
citizen is playing on this to suggest that after training in the Artillery Garden, the trainee soldier is left unharmed
by his experiences.
   355 project aim or scheme (*OED*, *n.* 2a).

334–5] *lineation this edition;* pay / This...indanger'd / To O
339] *lineation this edition;* Men / To O   341–2] *lineation this edition;* Musket, / You O
352–4] *lineation this edition;* rather / Than...'tis? / 'Tis...off / With O

186

THE DOUBTFUL HEIR   I.I

CAPTAIN My lords, bear witness:
    These two would bribe me to abuse the queen
    And the present service. Is this less than treason?   360
BOTH Oh!
ERNESTO Nay, nay, Captain.
CAPTAIN There are not two more able men i'th'army;
    I mean, for bulk. Ram me into a cannon
    If you shall buy yourselves with your estates   365
    From this employment. I'll not cozen you.
    Your money is good debt still; you may live
    And ask me for't again, and I may pay you.
RODRIGUEZ But shall they serve indeed?
CAPTAIN   That's at their peril
    When they come to th'field, but go they shall   370
    An they were my cousin-germans.
BOTH Good my lord, speak for us.
CAPTAIN You do not know, my lords, but a little suffering
    May save their souls and teach 'em, if they come
    Off with a quarter of their limbs, compassion   375
    To other men that venture their lives for 'em.
    Their consciences are tough and must be suppled.
    When they shall fast and march ten months in armour,
    Sometimes through rivers, sometimes over mountains,
    And not have straw at night, to keep their breech   380
    From growing to the earth, in storms, in heats;
    When they have felt the softness of a trench,
    Thigh-deep in water, and their dung to fatten it;
    When they shall see no meat within a month,
    But chew their match like liquorice and digest   385
    The bark of trees, like salads in the summer;
    When they shall live to think there's no such thing
    In Nature as a shirt, and wonder why
    A tailor was created; when they have

364 for bulk The Captain claims that the citizens are well qualified to be in the army, but only in terms of being able to provide bodily mass rather than any actual martial ability. There may also be an implied second meaning: *OED*, Bulk *n.*¹ 2†b: 'A dead body, carcase'. Cf. Falstaff's comment that bad soldiers will 'fill a pit as well as better' in *1 Henry IV* (4.2.66).

371 cousin-germans first cousins.

377 suppled softened and made gentle or pliable.

380 breech buttocks, rump. The Captain means that the citizens will have no protection between themselves and the ground when they lie down at night.

385 match A length of cord or thick paper designed to be used as a fire-lighter or a cannon-fuse. Soldiers would typically wear these tied around their waists. See Cruickshank (1966, 106).

388 shirt Following Gifford. The original reads 'as a thirst', but this makes little sense, and the reference to the tailor in the next line implies the correctness of Gifford's reading.

376 venture] *Gifford;* venter O   385 liquorice] Q *subst.* (Liquorish)
388 shirt] *Gifford;* thirst O*; see commentary note*

187

2.1   THE COMPLETE WORKS OF JAMES SHIRLEY, VOLUME 7

As much in ready shot within their flesh   390
As would set up a plumber or repair
A church with lead; beside ten thousand more
Afflictions, which they are sure to find,
They may have Christianity and not put
A soldier to the payment of his debts.   395
RODRIGUEZ 'Tis a mad captain. Come, my lord, let's leave him.   *Exeunt lords.*
CAPTAIN You shall have time and place to send for money
    Or make your wills. Set on. Who knows but you
    Hereafter may be honest and prove captains.
    You may have preferment in the wars for money,   400
    And so, my gentle creditors, march on.   *Exeunt.*

2[.1]

    Enter LEANDRO *with letters.*

LEANDRO The hope and care of many years are in
    One day destroyed. Hath heaven no stroke in war,
    Or is old Providence asleep? Leonario
    Is coming home with victory and brings
    Young Ferdinand, whom I expected to   5
    Salute a king, his prisoner; and the queen
    With her new conqueror, glorious in the spoils,
    By putting out this light will mix their beams
    And burn our eyes out with their shine. There is
    No talk but of this triumph, and the people,   10
    Whom I by art and secret murmurs had
    Made doubtful at the first noise of this conquest,
    As they had borrowed souls from fear and folly,
    Adore the rising star, and in the praise
    Of him and his great fate wonder that heaven   15
    Should hold a sun, and he so bright. Nor with
    This flattery content, but they condemn
    (As low as all their sins shall one day them)
    Him whom the chance of war hath made a prisoner.
    There is no trust to policy or time.   20

---

400 preferment...money The Captain implies that the citizens' wealth will bring them some advantage, as they will be able to buy themselves promotions.

0 The scene is set in the palace.
2 Hath...war Does heaven not have influence in war? (*OED*, Stroke *n.*[1] 3†d).
8 By...beams Olivia and Leonario, by extinguishing the 'light' of Prince Ferdinand's glory, have made their own combined glory shine brighter.
12 doubtful unsettled in opinion, uncertain about whom they wanted to win this conflict (*OED*, *adj.* 2).
14 the...star Leonario.
17 flattery adulation; pleasing delusion (*OED*, *n.* 1, 2).
20 There...policy There is no trusting strategy (or cunning).

2[.1]] *Gifford subst. (*ACT II. SCENE I.*); ACT. II. O

188

THE DOUBTFUL HEIR   2.2

The things of state are whirled by destiny
To meet their period. Art cannot repair 'em.

    Enter SERVANT.

SERVANT My lord, the queen hath sent for you.
  She is going forth to meet the prince and hath
  Commanded none be wanting to attend   25
  With all the state that may become her to
  Congratulate the triumph now brought home.   [*Exit.*]
LEANDRO I shall obey. I must attend this glory.
  It is not safe to wear a brow but what
  The queen's example first forms into smile.   30
  I here contract my knowledge and seclude
  My wishes, since they prosper not. I am
  Her chancellor. As great offices and high
  Employments do expose us to most danger
  They oft teach those possess 'em a state-wisdom,   35
  And by inherent virtues of the place
  Our fear to lose makes us secure ourselves
  By art more often than by conscience.
  But I may be endangered to suspicion.
  I like not things – but I delay my attendance.   *Exit.*

[2.2]

    Enter CAPTAIN, [FIRST CITIZEN, *now a*] *Lieutenant,* [SECOND CITIZEN,
    now an] *Ancient, and* SOLDIERS.

CAPTAIN Lieutenant.
FIRST CITIZEN Captain.
CAPTAIN Ancient, what think you of the wars now?

---

  22 To...period Until they come to their fated end.

  29–30 It...smile It is not safe to show any emotion other than that displayed by the queen: one must follow
her example and smile when she does.

  31 contract reduce, shrink, or restrict.

  31 seclude make secret (literally, to shut off or confine to prevent access from without).

  35 those possess those who possess

  36 by...place due to something inherent in the nature of the position (*OED,* Virtue *n.* 10a).

  37–8 Our...conscience Our fear of failure makes us protect ourselves by choosing our course of behaviour
based on craftiness rather than on knowledge of what is morally right.

  0 The scene is set in the street.

  0 SD *Ancient* Military rank: a contemporary corruption of the term 'ensign'. An ensign was the lowest rank
of commissioned officer. A lieutenant was the second-lowest ranked officer.

---

27 SD] *Gifford; not in* O

[2.2]] *Gifford subst. (*SCENE II.*); not in* O   **0 SD**] *this edn; Enter* Captain, *and* 1. *and* 2. Citizens, *dressed, the one
as a Lieutenant, the other as an Ancient, followed by Soldiers. Gifford; Enter Captain, Lieutenant, Antient and Soldiers.* O
2 FIRST CITIZEN] 1 *Cit. Gifford;* Lieu. O. *Throughout the rest of the play, the speech heading 'Lieu.' has been replaced
with 'First Citizen'*

189

2.2   THE COMPLETE WORKS OF JAMES SHIRLEY, VOLUME 7

SECOND CITIZEN We are come off with honour.

FIRST CITIZEN And our limbs, Captain.   5

CAPTAIN Is that all? Who made you a lieutenant?
  And you ancient? These titles were not born wi'ye.
  You did not wear these buffs and feathers in
  The memory of man when you received
  The binding twelve pence. It was otherwise.   10

SECOND CITIZEN But you received, if you remember, Captain,
  Beside what we released in honest debt,
  Sums for this great instalment. We ha' paid,
  I take it, for our names.

CAPTAIN   And it became you.
  Now you are gentlemen, my comrades of honour,   15
  And I dare walk and drink at taverns wi'ye.
  Your oaths become you now, and your splay feet.
  You looked before like maggots, city worms.
  I ha' made you both brave fellows, fellows to knights.
  You may be squires to ladies too.

SECOND CITIZEN   I think so.   20

CAPTAIN We are all now of a trade, for Mars is master of our company. Our shop
  is the field, resolution our stock, honour our purchase, and fire and sword the
  tools we work withal.

FIRST CITIZEN But now the wars are done, I think we may shut up our shop. There
  is no more pay, is there?   25

CAPTAIN Pox upon you! I see your souls bleat after profit still. A bullet in the right
  place would ha' knocked out this humour of getting money. But fear not: though
  you come off with more limbs than you deserve, you shall have pay.

SECOND CITIZEN Shall we, and not be troubled to fight for't?

---

4 **We…off** 'We have left the field of combat', although the citizen may mean this is a more metaphorical way:
'We have acquitted ourselves' (*OED*, Come *v.* 'to come off' 6a).

8 **buffs** thick leather coats, often worn by the military.

8 **feathers** worn as ornaments by soldiers.

12 **released…debt** The citizens have released the Captain from some of the debts he previously owed them.

13–14 **paid…names** The citizens took the Captain's advice from the previous act and bought their army
ranks and titles.

17 **splay feet** Splay feet are broad, flat feet that turn outwards, a condition that can make walking painful.
The implication is that the citizens have acquired such feet in the course of long marches in the army.

21 **Mars** Roman god of war.

21 **company** The Captain quibbles on two meanings of 'company': 1) a body of soldiers; 2) an organisational
body for a trade or profession (*OED*, *n.* 4b; 5a)

22 **purchase** 1) means of making a living; 2) something that is obtained or acquired.

27 **humour of** obsession with.

---

4 SECOND CITIZEN] 2 *Cit. Gifford; Ant.* O. *Throughout the rest of the play, the speech heading 'Ant.' has been
replaced with 'Second Citizen'*

21] *In* O, *from this line until the end of the scene is set as verse, but it seems to be intended as prose*

190

THE DOUBTFUL HEIR   2.2

CAPTAIN Yes, it will be necessary you fight. You will ha' your throats cut else   30
and be sent off like sheep. Do not fear payment: here be mandrakes that
will roar and cudgel you to your hearts' content. You sha'not walk the streets,
now you are officers, without a quarrel – pay enough.

FIRST CITIZEN A man had as good be no lieutenant as be beaten when he comes
home. What think you, ancient?   35

SECOND CITIZEN For my part, I can endure beating as well as another, if that be all.

CAPTAIN Will you to your shops again?

SECOND CITIZEN I have no mind to worsted stockings again and shoes that shine. I
would wear colours still.

CAPTAIN Well said, ancient. Come, I'll take your fears off. Do not confess you are   40
a lieutenant, or you an ancient, and no man will quarrel wi'ye. You shall be as
secure as chrisom children.

FIRST CITIZEN Shall we? They shall rack me ere I'll confess I am a lieutenant,
or ever see the wars.

SECOND CITIZEN Or I an ancient. I'll take't upon my death I was never a soldier   45
in my life.

CAPTAIN 'Tis well done. Now, because I love you and see you have an itch after
honour – so it may come without blows – let me advise you. You have moneys
at command?

FIRST CITIZEN And good debts too.   50

CAPTAIN You shall both turn courtiers.

SECOND CITIZEN Shall we?

CAPTAIN I say't, for, if my physiognomy deceive me not, you two are born to be –

---

31 **sent off** killed (*OED*, Send *v.*[1] 3c).

31 **mandrakes** unpleasant or unwanted people, associated with the poisonous, undesirable plant of the same
name (*OED*, Mandrake *n.* 1†b, 1a). Cf. *2 Henry IV*: 'Thou whoreson mandrake, thou art fitter to be worn in my
cap than to wait at my heels' (1.2.14–16).

32 **roar…content** Throughout the seventeenth century, off-duty or decommissioned soldiers had a reputation for trouble-making and causing social disturbances.

33 **quarrel** fight, violent altercation.

33 **pay** The Captain quibbles on 'pay', meaning both money given for services and in the sense of 'paying a
penalty', suffering negative consequences for one's actions. The quarrels the citizens engage in will be pay
enough for their services.

37 **Will…again?** Will you return to being shopkeepers?

38 **worsted** Also spelled 'worstead': a fine, knitted woollen fabric, often worn by the merchant classes. See
Fairholt (1885), 'worstead'.

39 **colours** coloured items worn to distinguish a soldier as a member of a particular army or company.

42 **chrisom children** Chrisom or chrism is a mixture of oil and balm, or a cloth anointed with oil and balm,
which was placed on the head of a child at baptism by the minister. The Captain presumably means that the
citizens will be treated in the same way as children so young that they could not be perceived as a threat or
danger to anyone.

43 **They…ere** They will need to torture me on the rack before.

50 **good debts** money owed to them by their debtors.

53 **physiognomy** The study of people's physical features, which was thought to indicate character. Gifford
amends this to 'skill in physnomy'.

---

53 physiognomy] *this edn;* phisnomy O

191

2.2   THE COMPLETE WORKS OF JAMES SHIRLEY, VOLUME 7

BOTH What?

CAPTAIN Coxcombs. I'll help to make you, too. You shall presently kiss the queen's   55
hand. You have moneys, you say. You shall never turn to your vomit of small
wares. I have friends at court. You may in time be great, and when I come with
a petition to your honours for moneys in arrear, or knocking out some rascal's
brains, such as you were when you wore a girt under your chops, you two
may stand between me and the gallows.   60

SECOND CITIZEN Hang us if we do not.

CAPTAIN You shall buy places presently. But stay —
Have you a mind to be officers to the queen
In ordinary or extraordinary?

SECOND CITIZEN Extraordinary, by all means.   65

FIRST CITIZEN We scorn to be ordinary courtiers.

CAPTAIN I commend your judgement. That will be more chargeable. But —

SECOND CITIZEN Hang't, we'll find money enough, but I resolve to be
extraordinary.

CAPTAIN I'll bring you to a court merchant presently. You will get infinite estates.   70

BOTH A-ha, Captain!

CAPTAIN And so command the ladies, if you be bountiful.

BOTH A-ha, boy!

CAPTAIN For I know you do love wenches. You will have all the business and
the country come tumbling in upon you like the tide after a month. You must keep   75
twenty men between you, night and day, to tell your money. Oh, 'tis unknown what

---

55 Coxcombs Fools or simpletons; showy, conceited persons (*OED*, Coxcomb *n*. 3a).

55 make...too i.e. make you into coxcombs, although the Captain also means that he will make them into courtiers.

56–7 turn...wares return to selling consumer goods. The Captain may have in mind the Biblical proverb, 'As a dog returneth to his vomit, so a fool returneth to his folly' (*Proverbs* 26.11).

57–60 when...gallows When the Captain gets into trouble for owing unpaid money or for killing someone unlawfully, the citizens will protect him from execution.

59 girt...chops piece of fabric worn around the neck, presumably as part of the dress of a merchant.

62 buy...presently The citizens will be able to buy places at court, just as they bought their promotions in the army.

64 ordinary...extraordinary A courtier in ordinary belonged to the regular class of courtier, and held a permanent position at court. A courtier in extraordinary was a courtier outside of the regular class, who might only be required on special occasions. (*OED*, Ordinary *adj.* 2b; Extraordinary, *adj.* 2). However, the citizens seem not to understand these terms in their technical sense, and instead assume that the Captain means 'extraordinary' in the sense of 'Of a kind not usually met with; exceptional' (*OED*, Extraordinary *adj.* 3). Given their response, they clearly associate ordinariness with cheapness; cheap, fixed-price meals of the kind available in taverns were known as 'ordinaries'.

67 chargeable costly, expensive (*OED*, *adj.* †4).

70 court merchant literally, legal court that presided over commercial affairs. The Captain puns on this, to suggest a person who sells places at court.

74–5 You...month As figures of importance at court, the citizens will be constantly petitioned by both businessmen and country landowners (who will, presumably, pay them handsomely for their services). There was belief at the time that tides reached their maximum amplitude once a month, so the image is of a greater-than-usual swell of water.

---

75 month] O *subst.* (moneth)

192

THE DOUBTFUL HEIR   2.3

will become on you if you be ruled and take this course. Had I moneys like you,
    I would be –

FIRST CITIZEN Come, we will lend thee moneys too hereafter.

CAPTAIN Will you? Come on, no more lieutenant now, nor ancient.   80

SECOND CITIZEN Do ye think we long to be beaten?   *Exeunt.*

[2.3]

      Enter FERDINAND, *in prison,* [*and*] ROSANIA, *like a page.*

ROSANIA Pray do not grieve for me. I have a heart
    That can for your sake suffer more, and when
    The tyranny of your fate calls me to die
    I can as willingly resign my breath
    As go to sleep.

FERDINAND   Can I hear this, Rosania,   5
    Without a fresh wound? That thy love to me
    Should be so ill rewarded! Th'ast engaged
    Thyself too much already. 'Tis within
    Thy will yet to be safe. Reveal thyself.
    Throw off the cloud that doth eclipse that brightness,   10
    And they will court thy person and be proud
    With all-becoming honour to receive thee.
    No fear shall rob thy cheek of her chaste blood.
    Oh, leave me to my own stars and expect,
    Whate'er become of wretched Ferdinand,   15
    A happy fate.

ROSANIA   Your council is unkind.
    This language would become your charity
    To a stranger, but my interest is more
    In thee than thus with words to be sent off.
    Our vows have made us one, nor can the names   20
    Of father, country, or what can be dear
    In nature bribe one thought to wish myself
    In heaven without thy company. It were poor then
    To leave thee here. Then by thy faith, I charge thee,
    By this (*Kisses him*) – the first and last seal of our love;   25
    By all our promises, when we did flatter
    Ourselves, and in our fancy took the world
    A-pieces, and collected what did like

  0 The scene is set in a prison.

  0 SD *in prison* Dessen notes that this is a relatively common type of stage direction in plays of the time, and
that 'a sense of prison was probably generated by one or more prisoners in chains/fetters' (Dessen 1999, 171).

  18 interest stake or involvement.

  28 like please.

[2.3]] *Gifford subst. (*SCENE III*); not in* O   **10** off] O *subst. (*of*)*
19 than] O *subst. (*then*)*   **25 SD**] *this edn; after* love. *in* O

193

2.3 THE COMPLETE WORKS OF JAMES SHIRLEY, VOLUME 7

Us best to make us a new paradise;
By that, the noblest ornament of thy soul,   30
Thy honour, I conjure thee: let me still
Be undiscovered. What will it avail
To leave me, whom thou lovest, and walk alone,
Sad pilgrim to another world? We will
Converse in soul, and shoot like stars whose beams   35
Are twisted, and make bright the sullen groves
Of lovers as we pass.
FERDINAND   These are but dreams
Of happiness. Be wise, Rosania.
Thy love is not a friend to make thee miserable.
Society in death, where we affect,   40
But multiplies our grief. Live thou, oh, live!
And if thou hast a tear when I am dead
But drop it to my memory. It shall,
More precious than embalming, dwell upon me
And keep my ashes pure. My spirit shall   45
At the same instant in some innocent shape
Descend upon that earth thou hast bedewed
And, kissing the bright tribute of thy eye,
Shall after wait like thy good angel on thee.
There will be none to speak of Ferdinand   50
Without disdain, if thou diest too. Oh, live
A little to defend me or at least
To say I was no traitor to thy love,
And lay the shame on death and my false stars
That would not let me live to be a king.   55
ROSANIA Oh, Ferdinand! Thou dost not love me now.
FERDINAND Not love Rosania?
If wooing thee to live will not assure thee,
Command me then to die and spare the cruelty
Of the fair queen. Not love Rosania?   60

---

35 Converse Keep each other company (*OED, v.* †2a).
36 twisted intertwined.
36–7 make...pass Woodland groves are traditionally the haunt of melancholy lovers. In Behn's *The Young King; or The Mistake*, one character remarks to another, 'I hear that you are grown retir'd of late, / And visit shady Groves, walk thus—and sigh / Like melancholy Lovers' (D2v). Rosania is saying that the example of the true love she and Ferdinand share will shine out to these miserable lovers as an example and an inspiration, as their souls journey together to heaven.
40 Society i.e. Company.
40 affect are emotionally involved. I.e. dying together is no comfort when your companion is someone you care about and do not wish to die.
44 embalming embalming fluid.

---

56 Ferdinand! Thou] *lineation this edition; Ferdinand,* / Thou O

194

THE DOUBTFUL HEIR

2.4

If thou wilt but delight to see me bleed,
I will at such a narrow passage let
Out life it shall be many hours in ebbing,
And my soul, bathing in the crimson stream,
Take pleasure to be drowned. I have small time   65
To love and be alive, but I will carry
So true a faith to woman hence as shall
Make poor the world when I am gone
To tell the story yonder. – We are interrupted.

    Enter KEEPER.

KEEPER You must prepare yourself for present trial.   70
  I have command to attend you to the judges.
  That gentleman, and all that did adhere
  To your conspiracy, are by the queen's
  Most gracious mercy pardoned.
FERDINAND   In that word
  Th'hast brought me more than life. [*To Rosania*] I shall betray   75
  And with my too much joy undo thee again.
  Heaven does command thee live. I must obey
  This summons. [*Aloud*] I shall see thee again, Tiberio,
  Before I die.
ROSANIA   I'll wait upon you, sir.
  The queen will not deny me that poor office.   80
  I know not how to leave you.
FERDINAND   Death and I
  Shall meet and be made friends, but when we part
  The world shall find thy story in my heart.   *Exeunt.*

[2.4]

    Enter OFFICERS *with bar, table, stools; then* ERNESTO, RODRIGUEZ, LEANDRO,
    [*and*] QUEEN [OLIVIA], *supported by* LEONARIO, FERDINAND, ROSANIA,
    LADIES, GENTLEMEN, *and* GUARD, *who set*[*s*] *Ferdinand to the bar.*

61–5 **If…drowned** Ferdinand extravagantly suggests the extent of his love for Rosania: if it would please her
to see him suffer and die, he would stab himself so as to bleed out over many hours, and his soul would embrace
this slow process of death in so good a cause.

70 **present** immediate.

72 **That gentleman** Rosania, in her disguise as Tiberio.

75 **betray** i.e. betray Rosania's true identity.

o The scene is set in a courtroom.

o **SD bar** The officers carry in a literal bar—a rail or barrier—to mark off where Ferdinand as prisoner will
be stationed.

68–9] *lineation this edn;* Make…tell / The O

75 than] O *subst.* (then)   75 **SD**] *this edn; Gifford marks the aside with a dash; not in* O

78 **SD**] *this edn; not in* O   83 **SD**] *Gifford; Exit.* O

[2.4]] *Gifford subst.* (SCENE IV.); *not in* O

o **SD** *and* QUEEN OLIVIA] *this edn; and* OLIVIA *Gifford; Queen* O   o **SD** *sets*] *this edn; set* O

195

2.4 THE COMPLETE WORKS OF JAMES SHIRLEY, VOLUME 7

OLIVIA Is that the prisoner at the bar?
LEONARIO He that pretended himself Ferdinand,
     Your uncle's son.
OLIVIA Proceed to his arraignment. My lord Leandro,
     You know our pleasure.   5
LEANDRO Although the queen in her own royal power
     And without violating sacred justice – where
     Treason comes to invade her and her crown
     With open war – need not insist upon
     The forms and circumstance of law but use   10
     Her sword in present execution:
     Yet such is the sweet temper of her blood
     And calmness of her nature (though provoked
     Into a storm) unto the great'st offender
     She shuts up no defence, willing to give   15
     A satisfaction to the world how much
     She doth delight in mercy. Ferdinand –
     For so thou dost pretend thyself – thou art
     Indicted of high treason to her majesty,
     In that thou hast usurped relation to   20
     Her blood and under name of being her kinsman
     Not only hast contrived to blast her honour
     With neighbour princes, but hast gathered arms
     To wound the precious bosom of her country
     And tear the crown, which heaven and just succession   25
     Hath placed upon her royal head. What canst
     Thou answer to this treason?
FERDINAND   Boldly thus:
     As I was never, with the height of all
     My expectation and the aid of friends,
     Transported one degree above myself,   30
     So must not Ferdinand – though his stars have frowned
     And the great eye of Providence seem to slumber
     While your force thus compelled and brought me hither
     With mockery of my fate to be arraigned
     For being a prince – have any thought beneath   35
     The title I was born to. Yet I'll not call
     This cruelty in you, nor in the queen

---

4 **arraignment** formal legal accusation and trial.
11 **execution** This might simply refer to the execution of justice, rather than necessarily a sentence of death. Pronounced as five syllables.
15 **She...defence** She allows the offender to defend himself any way he can.
16 **satisfaction** satisfying proof.
20 **usurped...to** made a false claim to be.
32 **great...Providence** all-seeing eye of God. In Renaissance iconography it was common to represent the Christian God as an eye looking down on the earth. See Walsham (1999, 10–11, 253–5).

196

THE DOUBTFUL HEIR

2.4

(If I may name her so without injustice
To my own right). A kingdom is a garland
Worth all contention, and where right seals not   40
The true possession, nature is forgotten
And blood thought cheap to assure it. There is something
Within that excellent figure that restrains
A passion here that else would forth like lightning.
'Tis not your shape, which yet hath so much sweetness   45
Some pale religious hermit might suspect
You are the blessed saint he prayed to. No,
The magic's in our nature and our blood,
For both our veins, full of one precious purple,
Strike harmony in their motion. I am Ferdinand   50
And you the fair Olivia, brothers' children.
LEONARIO What insolence is this?
OLIVIA   Oh, my lord, let him
  Be free to plead, for if it be no dream
  His cause will want an orator. By my blood
  He does talk bravely.
RODRIGUEZ   These are flourishes.   55
ERNESTO Speak to the treason you are charged with
  And confess a guilt.
LEONARIO   He justifies himself.
FERDINAND If it be treason to be born a prince,
  To have my father's royal blood move here;
  If it be treason in my infancy   60
  To have escaped by divine providence,
  When my poor life should have been sacrificed
  To please a cruel uncle, whose ambition
  Surprised my crown, and after made Olivia,
  His daughter, queen; if it be treason to   65
  Have been a stranger thus long from my country,
  Bred up with silence of my name and birth
  And not till now mature to own myself
  Before a sunbeam; if it be treason
  After so long a banishment to weep   70

40–2 where…it i.e. when a kingdom is possessed by a person who has no right to it, that person will forget
all gentleness and fight to keep power.

43 that…figure Olivia.

54 want need.

54–5 By…bravely This may be the first indication that the queen is becoming romantically interested in
Ferdinand.

55 flourishes parades of fine words or phrases; boasts (*OED*, Flourish *n*. 5; 5†b).

59 here i.e. within Ferdinand's own body.

64 Surprised Took possession unexpectedly or by force (*OED*, Surprise *v*. 2a, 2†b).

68–9 to…sunbeam to confess my identity openly (*OED*, Own *v*. 5a).

197

2.4　THE COMPLETE WORKS OF JAMES SHIRLEY, VOLUME 7

A tear of joy upon my country's bosom
And call her mine, my just inheritance
Unless you stain my blood with bastardy;
If it be treason still to love this earth
That knew so many of my race her kings,　　　　　　　　75
Though late unkindly armed to kill her sovereign
As if the effusion of my blood were left
To make her fertile; if to love Olivia,
My nearest pledge of blood, although her power
Hath chained her prince and made her lord her prisoner,　　80
Who sits with expectation to hear
That sentence that must make the golden wreath
Secure upon her brow by blasting mine;
If this be treason, I am guilty Ferdinand.
Your king's become a traitor and must die　　　　　　85
A black and most inglorious death.
ERNESTO　　　　　　　　　　You offer
At some defence but come not home. By what
Engine were you translated hence or whither
Conveyed? There was some trust deceived when you
Were carried forth to be preserved and much　　　　90
Care taken since in bringing of you up
And giving secret fire to this ambition.
FERDINAND　There wants no testimony here of what
Concerns the story of my birth and infancy,
If one dare speak and be an honest lord.　　　　　95
LEANDRO　How's that?
FERDINAND　Whose love and art secured me from all tyranny,
Though here my funeral was believed, while I,
Sent to an honourable friend, his kinsman,
Grew safely to the knowledge of myself　　　　　100
At last, till fortune of the war betrayed me
To this captivity.

77–8 effusion…fertile In ancient pagan belief, a barren land might be regenerated and made fertile by the spilling of the king's blood. Bolingbroke makes reference to this belief in Shakespeare's *Richard II* when he says, referring to the death of King Richard, 'I protest my soul is full of woe / That blood should sprinkle me to make me grow' (5.6.45–6).

79 pledge person given or held as security for the fulfilment of a promise or contract (*OED, n.* 1†b). Presumably Ferdinand means that Olivia, as his closest relative and next in line to the throne, held his place as monarch until he was able to claim it.

81 expectation Pronounced as five syllables.

86–7 You…home You make a gesture towards defending yourself, but don't get to the point.

88 Engine Ingenious plan or trick.

93–5 There…lord There is a nobleman present who could attest to the story's truth, if he dared to speak up.

88　whither] *Gifford;* whether O

THE DOUBTFUL HEIR   2.4

LEANDRO   I blush at thee,
  Young man, whose fate hath made thee desperate,
  And carest not what man's blood thou draw'st along
  In thy black stream, or what man's faith thou makest   105
  As hateful as thy crimes.
ERNESTO   That confederate
  Sure has some name. Declare him that he may
  Thank you for his reward and lose his head for't.
OLIVIA We always see that men in such high nature,
  Deformed and guilty, want not specious shapes   110
  To gain their practice friendship and compassion.
  But he shall feel the punishment. D'you smile?
FERDINAND A woman's anger is but worth it, madam,
  And if I may have freedom I must say –
  Not in contempt of what you seem, nor helped   115
  By overcharge of passion which but makes
  A fruitless noise – I have a sense of what
  I am to lose, a life, but I am so fortified
  With valiant thoughts and innocence I shall,
  When my last breath is giving up to lose   120
  Itself i'th'air, be so remote from fear
  That I will cast my face into one smile,
  Which shall, when I am dead, acquit all trembling
  And be a story to the world how free
  From paleness Ferdinand took leave of earth.   125
ROSANIA Alas, my lord, you forget me, that can
  Part with such courage.
FERDINAND   I forget indeed.
  I thought of death with honour, but my love
  Hath found a way to chide me. Oh, my boy,
  I can weep now.
LEONARIO   A sudden change: he weeps.   130
OLIVIA What boy is that?
FERDINAND I prithee, take thyself away.
OLIVIA   Your spirit
  Does melt, it seems, and you begin to think
  A life is worth preserving, though with infamy.

109–11 **We...compassion** i.e. It's always the case that arrogant, proud men know how to present themselves in attractive ways to win sympathy and friendship, even as they commit acts of treachery (*OED*, High *adj.*
and *n.*² 11; Practice *n.* 5†a).

113 **A...it** A woman's anger is too trivial to deserve more than amusement. The shallowness and changeabil-
ity of women's emotions was proverbial. See Dent (1984): 'a woman is a weathercock', W653; 'a woman's mind
is always mutable', W673.

116 **overcharge** an excess.

123 **acquit...trembling** clear me from any accusations that I was afraid.

2.4   THE COMPLETE WORKS OF JAMES SHIRLEY, VOLUME 7

FERDINAND Goodness, thy aid again, and tell this great   135
    Proud woman I have a spirit scorns her pity. –
    Come hither, boy, and let me kiss thee. [*He kisses Rosania.*] Thus,
    At parting with a good and pretty servant,
    I can, without my honour stained, shed tears.
    I took thee from thy friends to make thee mine.   140
    Is it not truth, boy?
ROSANIA Yes, my lord.
FERDINAND And meant when I was king to make thee great,
    And shall I not, when I can live no longer
    To cherish thee, at farewell drop a tear?   145
    That I could weep my soul upon thee! [*To the court*] But
    You are too slow, methinks. I am so far
    From dread, I think your forms too tedious.
    I expect my sentence.
OLIVIA   Let it stay a while.
    [*Aside*] What secret flame is this? Honour protect me!   150
    [*To lords*] Your graces' fair excuse. [*To Ferdinand*] For you – I shall
    Return again.   *Exit.*
FERDINAND   And I, with better guard
    After my silence in the grave, to meet
    And plead this cause.
ERNESTO   He is distracted, sure.
    His person I could pity but his insolence   155
    Wants an example. What if we proceed
    To sentence?
LEONARIO   I suppose the queen will clear
    Your duties in't.
LEANDRO   But I'll acquaint her.   *Exit.*
RODRIGUEZ My lord Leandro's gone.
ERNESTO   His censure will
    Be one with ours.

---

138 **pretty** Ferdinand deliberately chooses an ambiguous term. Presumably the court will understand 'pretty' in the sense of 'admirable, worthy' (*OED, adj.* 3a), but Rosania will recognize it as a compliment to her beauty (*OED, adj.* 2a).

148 **forms** methods of doing things; ways of behaving (*OED*, Form *n.* 14; 15).

152–4 **And...cause** The meaning here is uncertain. Ferdinand may mean that now he has returned from his supposed death (his 'silence in the grave') he will find a better guardian than Leandro, who will speak up on his behalf. However, he may also be implying that even if he is executed by Olivia, he will return from death (at the Day of Judgement?) to have his cause vindicated.

154 **distracted** mad.

156 **Wants...example** 'Needs to be made example of', but perhaps also 'has no example, is unprecedented'.

159 **censure** condemnatory judgement.

---

137 SD] *this edn; not in* O   146 SD] *this edn; Gifford marks the change of address with a dash; not in* O
150 SD] *this edn; Gifford marks the aside with a dash; not in* O
151 SD1] *this edn; Gifford marks end of aside with a dash; not in* O   151 SD2] *this edn; to Leo. Gifford; not in* O

200

THE DOUBTFUL HEIR   2.4

FERDINAND [*Aside, to Rosania*]   Yet shall I publish who   160
    Thou art? I shall not die with a calm soul
    And leave thee in this cloud.

       Enter [OLIVIA] *and* LEANDRO.

ROSANIA By no means, sir. – The queen.
OLIVIA Whose service is so forward to our state
    That when our pleasure's known not to proceed,   165
    They dare be officious in his sentence? Are
    We queen or do we move by your protection?
ERNESTO Madam, the prince –
OLIVIA   My lord, you have a queen.
    I not suspect his wisdom, sir, but he
    Hath no commission here to be a judge.   170
    You were best circumscribe our regal power
    And by yourselves condemn or pardon all
    And we sign to your will. The offence which you
    Call treason strikes at us, and we release it.
    Let me but see one curl in any brow.   175
    Attend the prisoner hither. – [*To Ferdinand*] Kiss our hand. –
    Are you so merciless to think this man
    Fit for a scaffold? You shall, sir, be near us,
    And if in this confusion of your fortunes
    You can find gratitude and love, despair not.   180
    These men that now oppose may find your title
    Clear to the kingdom too. Be, sir, collected,
    And let us use your arm.   *Exit, supported by Ferdinand.*
ROSANIA   What change is here?
LEANDRO What think you of this, lords?
RODRIGUEZ   I dare not think.
LEONARIO Affronted thus? Oh, my vexed heart.   *Exit.*   185
ROSANIA I'll follow still, and if this be no dream
    We have 'scaped a brook to meet a greater stream.   *Exeunt.*

---

164 forward presumptuous.
167 move…protection proceed under your guardianship.
169 I…wisdom I do not doubt his wisdom.
171 You were best 'It would be best if you'. Olivia is being ironic.
174 release it pardon it.
175 Let…brow I do not wish to see a single frown.

---

160 SD] *this edn; not in* O   **162 SD** OLIVIA] *Gifford; the* Queen O
176 SD] *this edn; Ferd. is brought to the state. Gifford; not in* O

201

3[.1]

Enter RODRIGUEZ [*and*] ERNESTO.

ERNESTO Though I believed her passionate and like
   A sea tempestuous in her anger, I
   Never thought she would marry him.
RODRIGUEZ   She's the queen.
   But with what honour she could quit the prince
   Who (without treason) did deserve her too,   5
   Comes not within my reach.
ERNESTO   If you consider,
   He has been valiant for her to great purpose
   And brought a prisoner home to mount his jennet:
   It was a pretty service!
RODRIGUEZ   How does he bear it?
ERNESTO He's here: you may enquire it.   10

Enter LEONARIO, *with letters, and a* SERVANT.

LEONARIO Be swift and faithful. Aragon bleeds here.
   Nothing but war can right my cause and honour.
SERVANT Expect an army great as your own thoughts,
   To cut the way to your revenge.   *Exit.*
LEONARIO   My lords
   Rodriguez and Ernesto.
BOTH   Your grace's servants.   15
LEONARIO A man may take the benefit of this garden
   Without a court offence. You have had the day
   Of triumph and the queen already teeming
   To bless the kingdom with an heir, and yet
   You see I walk like a poor neighbour prince   20
   And have my heart still.
RODRIGUEZ I am glad you bear it so.

---

0 The scene is set in the royal gardens.
5 **without treason** There are two possible meanings here. Rodriguez may be saying that he does not want to appear to be disloyally criticizing Olivia's decisions. Alternatively, he may mean that Leonario, unlike Ferdinand, is not a traitor to the queen.
6 **reach** capacity or power of comprehension (*OED*, *n*.¹ 7a).
8 **mount…jennet** A jennet is a pedigree Spanish horse, but Ernesto is making a sexual pun: Leonario has brought home a man who will replace him by 'mounting' his fiancée.
9 **pretty service** worthy or admirable act for his mistress. Ernesto is being ironic, as this outcome was clearly not what Leonario intended.
17 **court offence** offending against the court. Leonario may be punning on legal/royal courts.
18 **teeming** Leonario is making a snide comment about the queen's sexual infatuation with Ferdinand: she appears vibrantly fertile and ready to procreate.
21 **have…still** Leonario suggests that the loss of Olivia has not destroyed him: he still has his heart, and may love again in the future.

3[.1]] *Gifford subst.* (ACT III. SCENE I.)*;* ACT. III. O
0 **SD** *and*] *Gifford; not in* O   14–15] *lineation Gifford;* My … Ernesto. O   **15 SH**] *this edn; Ambo.* O

THE DOUBTFUL HEIR   3.1

LEONARIO   Nor have I a meaning
  To run myself into despair or strangle
  My better hopes out of pure melancholy.
  I praise the influence of my stars. There is   25
  A fire in Cupid's quiver that will scorch
  Through armour, and what's woman's flesh and blood
  To make resistance? Though I did not dance
  Upon the marriage night, I wished her joys
  I'th'morning.
ERNESTO   Her heart showed she was pleased   30
  With what she had done. She was as active as
  The air before she went to bed.
RODRIGUEZ   But I
  Observed a declination in the king,
  And as the night approached, which should have more
  Enlarged his mirth, he grew more melancholy.   35
LEONARIO Strange! And such a bride, that took him from
  So great a loss to place him in her bosom!
  But he was marked for the queen's thoughts and I
  By destiny to bring this pair of pigeons
  Together. I expect no more reward.   40
  The willow garland crowns me, but the prince
  Is here still.
ERNESTO   Your highness hath a noble temper.
RODRIGUEZ [*Aside, to Ernesto*] Howe'er he seem to cover it, his soul
  Hath a deep apprehension of the affront.
  Let's leave him. Our discourse may be displeasing.   45
  – We are servants to your grace.
LEONARIO   Y'have honoured me.   *Exeunt lords.*
  Think I am tame still? Let the inconstant queen

26–8 **A...resistance** Cupid's flaming arrow is a symbol of passion. Leonario implies that when a woman is hit by a passion so strong, any resistance is futile.

31–2 **active...air** Air is often used as a simile for lightness and quickness, in phrases such as 'as free as the air'. See Dent (1984), A88; A90; (?)A90.11.

33 **declination** a sinking of spirits.

38 **marked** Leonario implies that the union of Olivia and Ferdinand was preordained by fate.

39 **pigeons** Pigeons, like turtledoves, were believed to be amorous birds. Cf. *As You Like It*: 'As the ox hath his bow, sir, the horse his curb, and the falcon her bells, so man hath his desires; and as pigeons bill, so wedlock would be nibbling' (3.3.72–4).

41 **The...me** The willow tree is a traditional symbol of forsaken love, and wearing a crown made of its branches symbolizes Leonario's status as an abandoned lover. Cf. Claudio in *Much Ado About Nothing*: 'I offered him my company to a willow tree, either to make him a garland, as being forsaken, or to bind him up a rod, as being worthy to be whipped' (2.1.204–6).

41–2 **but...still** Leonario is playing on the idea that he has been 'crowned' after all, with the willow garland, yet is still a prince and not a king.

47 **tame** meek, lacking in boldness and anger.

---

43 SD] *this edn; not in* O   46 SD] *this edition; after* Grace. O

203

3.1　　THE COMPLETE WORKS OF JAMES SHIRLEY, VOLUME 7

Secure her thoughts and glory in my silence.
This heart is labouring a revenge.

　　Enter CAPTAIN.

Captain, what news? The court is merry still? 　　　　　　　　50
CAPTAIN　Not altogether so merry as it was hoped for.
LEONARIO　Can there be an eclipse already?
CAPTAIN　I have not read the almanac for this year,
　　But by my court astronomy I find
　　Our sun and moon are in no conjunction. 　　　　　　　　55
　　They take their fit by turns: the king was cold
　　And full of phlegm last night, and they that wait
　　Near both report the queen this morning looked
　　As she had wept.
LEONARIO　　　　　　Oh, tears of joy.
CAPTAIN　Of anger, rather, if you saw her sullenness. 　　　　60
　　She frowns on every man. She turned away
　　One of her servants but this morning for
　　Presenting her with verses that did praise
　　The king and wish her fruitful. Her own page
　　Was whipped for saying the king lay with the queen 　　65
　　And might, for aught he knew, get her with child ere morning.
LEONARIO　Thou art humorous.
CAPTAIN　And so are they.
LEONARIO　　　　　　This begins well. And what
　　Do people talk abroad of me and my
　　Affront?
CAPTAIN　　Why, they say they are sorry for you, 　　　　　70
　　Especially the women.
LEONARIO　　　　　　Thou art pleasant.
CAPTAIN　Some, that are chief in counsel, privately

---

48 Secure…thoughts Put her mind at ease (*OED*, Secure *v.* †2).
52 eclipse a loss of light or splendour.
53 almanac book containing a year's astronomical data, calculations and forecasts.
55 Our…conjunction Ferdinand, as Olivia's consort, is described as the moon to her 'sun'. In astronomy, a conjunction refers to the proximity of two planets, but the word can also mean a union in marriage (*OED*, Conjunction *n.* 3; 2†a). Picking up on Leonario's use of the word eclipse, the Captain punningly points out that the king and queen do not exist in a close or harmonious relationship.
56 fit capricious mood or humour, or outburst of emotion (*OED*, *n.*² 4e, 4f).
57 phlegm Believed to be one of the four humours that controlled human behaviour: a cold, wet humour, usually associated with lethargy and depression.
68 so…they The Captain deliberately misunderstands. Leonario means that he is being comical, but he interprets the remark as referring to a disorder of the bodily humours, which could lead to irrational, emotional behaviour.
69 abroad publicly.
71 pleasant jocular, light-hearted.
72–5 Some…not The Captain claims that some who might be thought to have insider knowledge believe that the separation of Leonario and the queen was a political stratagem on his part, as he had secretly discovered something about the queen—presumably, that she was not a virgin.

204

THE DOUBTFUL HEIR

3.1

Suspect it but a trick of state and that
You had discovered underhand the queen
Was not –

LEONARIO   Leave this mirth. Let me endear thy care   75
For my intelligence at court [*Gives him money.*] – I must
Not off so tamely – and expect me here
After a small dispatch. I have more to impart.   *Exit.*

CAPTAIN Your humble creature still, sir. 'Las, poor gent.
Were I as capable to be entertained now, in revenge   80
I would mount all the madams in the court.
There should be nothing like a woman in't
But I would touse and tumble. – Who are these?

    Enter [THIRD *and* FOURTH CITIZENS].

THIRD CITIZEN Save you, sir.
CAPTAIN It may be so.   85
FOURTH CITIZEN Pray, sir, take no offence. We have been enquiring about the
    court for two gentlemen.
CAPTAIN And cannot your four eyes see two gentlemen i'th'court?
THIRD CITIZEN Excuse us, sir, we have seen many. You may guess we have relation
    to the city, sir, and would be glad to meet two of our old acquaintances. A brace   90
    of our tribe, we hear, translated first out of the city to be sons o'th'sword, are
    since turned courtiers. Pray, d'ye know 'em?

    Enter [FIRST CITIZEN, *dressed as a courtier*] *and* VIOLINDA.

75–6 endear…court Gifford amends to 'endow thy care', but the emendation is not necessary if 'endear thy care' is taken to mean 'make precious (or valuable) your care (of me)'—i.e. 'Let me pay you for your information about the court' (*OED*, Endear *v.* †1, to render costly or more costly; †2a, to enhance the value of).

76 intelligence…court information about the court.

76–7 I…tamely I will not leave off in so meek a fashion. Leonario means that he will make use of the Captain for more than just information, and will employ him to play a more active part in his revenge.

77 expect…here wait for me here.

78 After…dispatch Leonario probably means that he needs to settle up some small business of his own (*OED*, Dispatch *n.* 5a) or to send a letter or a messenger off (Dispatch *n.* 1) before he returns.

80 Were…revenge Gifford thinks this is corrupt and suggests that half a line may be missing, between 'now' and 'in revenge'. However, the line seems to make sense as it is. The Captain is saying that if he were as attractive to the ladies as Leonario is, he would have sex with multiple other court women, to punish the queen.

82 in't in the court.

83 touse…tumble pull at or haul about, and have sex with.

85 It…so The Captain interprets the Third Citizen's polite formality—an abbreviation of the commonplace greeting, 'May God save you'—as a sincere wish.

90–1 brace…tribe two of our class or fraternity.

91 translated transported, transformed.

---

76 SD] *Gifford subst.; not in* O   **83 SD**] *this edn; Enter* 3 *and* 4 Citizens. *Gifford; Enter two Citizens.* O
84 SH] *this edn;* 3 *Cit. Gifford;* 1. *Cit.* O. *Throughout the rest of the play, the speech heading '*1. Cit.*' has been replaced with '*Third Citizen*'*
86 SH] *this edn;* 4 *Cit. Gifford;* 2. *Cit.* O. *Throughout the rest of the play, the speech heading '*2. Cit.*' has been replaced with '*Fourth Citizen*'*
92 SD FIRST…courtier] *this edn;* 1 Citizen, *dressed like a courtier, Gifford; Lieutenant*

3.1   THE COMPLETE WORKS OF JAMES SHIRLEY, VOLUME 7

CAPTAIN Yes, children of the gown, but their employment wo'not give them leave
to attend such vulgar conference. And here comes one of the mooncalves! Does
he look like a haberdasher? That's one of the maids of honour. The weasel loves   95
a hen's nest, and I have settled this persuasion, that no woman can hold out now
he is sworn a servant extraordinary.

THIRD CITIZEN Sir, do you know us?

FIRST CITIZEN No.

FOURTH CITIZEN We were your neighbours and of the same trade.   100

CAPTAIN [Aside] They'll make him sweat. How the rogue gloats upon 'em.

THIRD CITIZEN We were of your acquaintance when you sold garters.

FIRST CITIZEN Go hang yourselves.

FOURTH CITIZEN And statute lace.

VIOLINDA What are these?   105

FIRST CITIZEN Poor men that had some losses late by fire and would become
my clients to procure some letters patents to beg by. Alas, they are half distracted.

THIRD CITIZEN [Aside] He's proud. – I have a parcel of periwigs. Please you, for
old acquaintance, put 'em off for me among some friends of yours at court,   110
whose skulls are but thinly furnished. The hair is of a gentlewoman's
spinning.

CAPTAIN [Aside] I could love this citizen and owe him any money for his confident
abusing him.

[First Citizen gives something to Violinda.] Exit Violinda.

93 **children of the gown** professional people, such as lawyers, divines, etc., who wore long loose robes. Cf.
Fletcher, *The Bloody Brother* (1639): 'there is a reverence due, / From children of the Gown, to men of Action' (B2).
94 **vulgar conference** a discussion or meeting with ordinary, common people.
94 **mooncalves** Used of a person, 'mooncalf' may have several meanings: a fickle, unstable person; a born
fool, congenital idiot, or simpleton; a deformed creature or monster. Any or all of these derogatory terms could
be meant by the Captain to describe the citizens (*OED*, Mooncalf *n.* 2†a; 2c; †3). Trinculo and Stephano repeatedly refer to Caliban as a mooncalf in *The Tempest* 2.2.
95 **haberdasher** There is a double meaning here. Literally, the Captain means that the citizen is no longer
dressed in the clothes of his previous profession, those of a cloth merchant. However, 'haberdasher' is also often
used to mean a bawd or pimp, who deals in sexual 'wares': the Captain is commenting on the fact that the citizen
is accompanied by a woman. See Williams (1994), Vol. III, 'ware', 1501.
95–6 **weasel...nest** 'Weasel' is a common term for a lecher. Weasels are sleek, thin creatures, able to creep
into narrow places, and are also proverbially known for eating eggs. The idea of weasels 'sucking eggs', as they
would do in a hen's nest, is often used as a metaphor for lechery. See Williams (1994), Vol. III, 'weasel', 1509.
96 **I...persuasion** I have made him believe (*OED*, Settle *v.* 33e; Persuasion *n.* 3a). The Captain has convinced the First Citizen that courtiers are irresistible to women.
101 **gloats** looks furtively (*OED*, Gloat *v.* †1a).
104 **statute lace** lace of a size or measurement regulated by special decree (*OED*, Statute *n.*¹ †4).
107 **letters patents** legal documents in the form of open letters issued by nobility or government, granting
a monopoly, office, or right to some company or individual.
109 **periwigs** wigs often worn by courtiers or fashionable women.
110 **put...me** sell them for me (*OED*, Put *v.* 'to put off' 9†b).
113 **owe** pay.
113–14 **for his...him** for his boldness in abusing the First Citizen.

101 SD] *this edn; not in* O   109 SD] *this edn; not in* O   113 SD] *this edn; not in* O
114 SD *First...to Violinda.*] *this edn; not in* O

206

THE DOUBTFUL HEIR 3.1

He has bribed her absence with some ring or bracelet lest she should taste the 115
discovery now.

THIRD CITIZEN Methinks you need not be so proud.

FIRST CITIZEN I would have you know that I am an extraordinary–

CAPTAIN [*Aside*] – Proud coxcomb.

FIRST CITIZEN – Servant to the queen. What I was, I am willing to forget. What you 120
are is apparent. I defy the dunghill I came from, and it is *scandalum magnatum*
to be so saucy.   *Exit.*

THIRD CITIZEN I will not leave your worship so.   *Exit* [*in pursuit*].

CAPTAIN What will this rascal do with himself? Here comes the other fool to make
up the Gemini.   125

    Enter [SECOND CITIZEN] *with two petitions.*

SECOND CITIZEN Hmm. I will not know him. Let me see – [*Reading*] 'The humble
petition of . . .'

FOURTH CITIZEN Save you, master.

SECOND CITIZEN Prithee, fellow, do not trouble me. – 'Humbly praying . . .' The
queen shall sign it. Let me see this other –   130

CAPTAIN [*Aside*] Who the devil will bring him a petition? This whelp has discovered
him and now would pretend himself most busily employed about petitions to
the queen.

SECOND CITIZEN Hmm. 'Shall daily pray for . . .' – Hmm.

CAPTAIN [*Aside*] – More wit and money o' your side, for your extraordinary place 135
will not hold out.

FOURTH CITIZEN Sir, I have a suit to you.

SECOND CITIZEN Is it embroidered satin, sir, or scarlet? Yet if your business do
hold weight and consequence, I may deserve to wear your thankfulness in tissue

---

115–16 the discovery i.e. that the First Citizen is of mercantile origins.

121 *scandalum magnatum* a statute designed to protect peers from being slandered or defamed by commoners, from the Statute of Westminster in 1275. Such slander was considered a criminal offence.

125 Gemini reference to the mythological and astrological Gemini, the heavenly twins.

125 SD *petitions* formal requests for legal action. Individuals might give these to courtiers whom they felt
had power and influence at court.

126 Hmm . . . him The Second Citizen is seeking to avoid the Fourth Citizen, so he pretends not to know
him, and starts to read as if unaware of his presence.

131 whelp ill-conditioned young man (deriving from the term for a puppy).

131 discovered identified.

135–6 More . . . out Ironically completing the sentence that the Second Citizen was reading out, implying
that he will soon no longer be able to maintain his place at court.

138 Is . . . scarlet? The Second Citizen puns on the Fourth Citizen's reference to a legal suit as referring to a
suit of clothing.

138 scarlet heavy, expensive material, though not one typically associated with nobility.

138–9 Yet . . . thankfulness The First Citizen continues his conceit, suggesting that if he helps the Fourth
Citizen out with a particularly important matter, he should be rewarded with an unusual degree of gratitude—
implying also that a new suit would be an acceptable form of bribe.

139 tissue 'light silken fabric, sometimes shot with threads of gold or silver' (Fairholt, 1885, 'tissue').
Commonly associated with the nobility.

---

119 SD] *this edn; not in* O   **123 SD** *in pursuit*] *this edn; not in* O
125 SD SECOND CITIZEN] *this edn;* 2 Citizen *Gifford; Antient* O   **126 SD]** *this edn; not in* O
131 SD] *this edn; not in* O   **135 SD]** *this edn; not in* O

207

3.1 THE COMPLETE WORKS OF JAMES SHIRLEY, VOLUME 7

or cloth of bodkin. Ermines are for princes.   140

FOURTH CITIZEN Alas, my suit is not worth your wearing.

SECOND CITIZEN Good faith, sir, you must excuse me. At this time my attendance is expected at the counsel. Come to my chamber by five o'clock in the morning, four days hence, and you shall be sure to find me –

CAPTAIN [*Aside*] – Asleep.   145

FOURTH CITIZEN But do you not know me?

SECOND CITIZEN Hmm. Yes, I have seen your physiognomy: were you never in a conspicuous place called the pillory?

FOURTH CITIZEN How, the pillory?

CAPTAIN [*Aside*] A skirmish, an it be thy will.   150

FOURTH CITIZEN If it were not in the court garden, I would beat out thy brains.

SECOND CITIZEN Take heed, for I am an extraordinary –

FOURTH CITIZEN – Rat-catcher.

CAPTAIN [*To Fourth Citizen*] You may beat out his brains here as securely, sir, as if you met him i'th'market. Marry, if you do not kill him outright, it is but   155
the loss of your hand.

FOURTH CITIZEN I would it were but the loss of my left hand to beat one of thy eyes out. Are you an ancient?

SECOND CITIZEN Thank you for that, so I might deserve to be beaten. I am an extraordinary, sir.   160

CAPTAIN And deserves to be beaten accordingly. You may kick him without danger.

FOURTH CITIZEN May I?

> *Enter* [THIRD CITIZEN], *kicking the* [FIRST CITIZEN].

---

140 bodkin also known as baudekyn: an expensive silk cloth interwoven with gold threads. See Fairholt (1885), 'baudekyn'.

140 Ermines Garments made of or trimmed with ermine fur: commonly worn by peers of the realm and royalty. Ermine is the name given to the white winter fur of a stoat.

147 physiognomy See note to 2.2.55.

148 pillory Similar to the stocks, the pillory was a device that held a criminal fast by the hands and head, for public display and revilement.

150 skirmish minor battle or exchange of blows. The Captain is hoping for a fight to break out between the citizens.

150 an if.

154–5 You...market There were laws against striking a courtier within the royal grounds: in 1537, Henry Howard, Earl of Surrey, was imprisoned briefly for this offence (Casady 1938, 62–3). However, the Captain assures the Fourth Citizen that he will be able to act in safety here.

156 the loss...hand a waste of your effort.

157–8 I...out I would lose my left hand for the chance to beat one of your eyes out.

159 Thank...beaten The Second Citizen refuses to be trapped into the admission that he is an ensign, as that would give the Fourth Citizen a reason to be hostile towards him. (See note to 2.2.33).

159–60 I...sir *O* reads 'I am an extraordinary Sir', which creates ambiguity regarding whether the citizen is referring to himself as a 'sir', or using that term to refer to the Fourth Citizen.

---

145 SD] *this edn; not in* O   **147** physiognomy] *this edn;* phisnomy O   **150 SD]** *this edn; not in* O
154 SD] *this edn; not in* O
162 SD] *this edn; Re-enter* 3 Citizen, *kicking* 1 Citizen. *Gifford; Enter* 1. *Citizen kicking the Lieutenant.* O

THE DOUBTFUL HEIR   3.1

CAPTAIN Look, your friend will show you a precedent. He is acquainted with the
    court latitude.
THIRD CITIZEN This is no striking.   165
FIRST CITIZEN I know it is not.
CAPTAIN They are subtle knaves and know the law.
FIRST CITIZEN A pox upon 'em; I feel it.
SECOND CITIZEN At their peril, say I. These poor things do not believe we are
    extraordinary men. I shall know you another time, I shall.   170
CAPTAIN If you had known him now it had been better for your haunches.

            [*Exeunt First and Second Citizen, pursued by Third and Fourth.*]

    Well, I ha' not done with these whelps yet. Till they are undone I shall never be
    sufficiently revenged for their affront at court. The prince commanded me to
    expect his return here. I'll not leave the garden.

            Enter ROSANIA.

    Who's this? [*Withdraws.*]   175
ROSANIA Is perjury no sin? Or can heaven be
    So busy or asleep such crimes of men
    Pass with impunity? Let this wake your anger,
    This: Ferdinand is married, all his vows
    Scattered i'th'air, dispersed like withered leaves   180
    And hurried on the wings of some rude wind
    Whose pride was to deflower the spring. Oh, Ferdinand!
    Could'st thou, whilst yet thy breath was warm with love,
    With love of me, call back thy faith and tear
    Thy heart from mine to plant it in her bosom?   185
CAPTAIN [*Aside*] How's this?
ROSANIA What though she be a queen? Could any thirst
    Of present title flatter thy soul from me?
    I, that left all for thee and would have called
    Death for thy cause a triumph, now must live   190
    The scorn of my own thoughts, despised by thee.

---

164 **court latitude** extent of freedom allowed by the court.
165 **This…striking** The Third Citizen has found a way round the prohibition against striking courtiers by
kicking the First Citizen instead.
167 **subtle** shrewd, cunning.
170 **know you** recognize you.
171 **known him** acknowledged him.
171 **haunches** area round the hips and upper thighs: presumably the parts of the Second Citizen that are
currently being kicked.
173 **affront at court** The Captain is presumably referring to the 'affront' caused in Act 1 by the citizens
asking him to settle his bills with them, which they did in front of Rodriguez and Ernesto.
176 **perjury** violation of a solemn vow.
188 **flatter** beguile, charm away.

---

171 SD] *this edn; Exeunt* 1 *and* 2 *Cit. followed by* 3 *and* 4. *after* shall. *Gifford; not in* O
175 SD] *this edn; Retires behind a shrubbery. Gifford; not in* O   186 SD] *this edn; not in* O

209

3.1   THE COMPLETE WORKS OF JAMES SHIRLEY, VOLUME 7

CAPTAIN [*Aside*] Here's a new business. This obscures me quaintly.

     Enter LEANDRO.

LEANDRO The king commands you not to leave the garden.
    He espied you from the gallery window and
    Would have you here attend him.
ROSANIA   Sir, may I   195
    Without offence ask if the king be merry?
LEANDRO We are scarce yet acquainted with his nature
    But we observe no jubilee in his eyes.
    Nor is the queen so pleasant as our hopes
    Did promise, after marriage.
ROSANIA   Pray excuse   200
    This boldness.
LEANDRO   You'll expect his pleasure here?   *Exit.*
ROSANIA 'Tis my ambition once more to see
    And speak with him, and if his language
    Break not my heart, I'll take my leave. – The queen.

     Enter QUEEN [OLIVIA *and*] LEANDRO.

LEANDRO He is a servant to whom the king   205
    Was pleased to show affection when he had
    No expectation of your royal favour.
OLIVIA I do remember. I observed him once
    Use more than common passion to this servant
    And if we may build any confidence   210
    Upon a fair aspect, he may deserve it.
    Say we would speak with him.

     [*Leandro goes to Rosania. Olivia speaks aside.*]
               My heart's oppressed
    With melancholy. Something tells my spirit
    I am too tame. Have I advanced a thing
    Without a name to perch on the same cloud   215

    192 obscures me quaintly hides me cleverly (*OED*, Obscure *v.* 2b; Quaintly *adv.* †1a, †1b). The Captain continues to hide behind some object—perhaps a stage property such as a bush or a tree—to eavesdrop on Rosania.
    198 jubilee celebration.
    202 ambition Pronounced as four syllables.
    203 language Pronounced as three syllables.
    209 passion emotion, affection.
    210–11 if…aspect i.e. if Tiberio's exterior beauty can be trusted as an indication of his inner goodness. The Neoplatonic idea that inner and outer beauty were correlated was popular at court in this period, particularly among the circle associated with Charles I's wife, Henrietta Maria.
    214 tame weak, spiritless, or lacking in force. Olivia feels that she should be reacting to Ferdinand's betrayal in a more active, aggressive manner (*OED*, *adj.* 5a).

    192 SD1] *this edn; not in* O   **200–1**] *lineation Gifford;* Pray…boldness O
    203–4] *lineation this edition;* And…not / My O
    204 SD] *this edition; Re-enter* LEANDRO *with* OLIVIA. *Gifford; Enter Queen, Leandro. after* break not O
    212 SD] *this edn; not in* O

THE DOUBTFUL HEIR   3.1

With me – and for his sake slighted a prince,
My honour and his faith, transported with
My folly and his charms of tongue and person –
And dares he pay me with neglect and coldness?
Oh, my vexed soul! But he shall find I have   220
A sense of my dishonour. And yet open
Ways become trivial and poor revengers.
I will do something that shall sting him to
Repentance. – [*Leandro and Rosania approach.*]
                              My lord, you now may leave us.

                                                Exit Leandro.

Sir, of what country are you?
ROSANIA   Of Valencia.   225
OLIVIA Your name?
ROSANIA Tiberio.
My parents not ignoble, yet too hasty
I'th'apprehension of Prince Ferdinand.
His fortune (if I may yet call him so)   230
Gave me to be his page. I must confess
My diligence thrived so well since I came to him
That he did value me above his servant.
OLIVIA Yet I've not seen you wait since we were married.
ROSANIA It was no want of duty, madam. I   235
Had late some wrestling with a fever that
Compelled me to my chamber and disabled
Me for fit attendance.
OLIVIA   Why dost weep?
ROSANIA I, madam?
OLIVIA   I see the tears.
ROSANIA They are not sorrow, then, to see my master   240
Possessed of so much happiness in your love,
And I am confident, his soul so full
Of honour and regard to your great virtues
Will seal him worth your gracious favours, madam,
And the world's envy.
OLIVIA   I'll not blame him now   245
For loving thee, and so much hath thy faith
And innocence prevailed, thou shalt translate
Thy service and be mine. He shall consent.

  221–2 **open...revengers** open action only befits petty or incompetent revengers.
  228–9 **yet...Ferdinand** Gifford suggests there may be some words or lines missing in *O*, but the sense
seems to be that Tiberio's parents believed (too quickly) in Ferdinand's claims for his status.
  230 **if...so** i.e. *Prince* Ferdinand.

  224 SD1] *this edn; Lean. brings forward Ros. Gifford; not in* O   **224 SD2**] O *subst.* (*Ex. Leandro.*)
  236 wrestling] *Gifford;* wrestling O   **237–8**] *lineation this edition;* Compeld ... me / For O

211

3.1   THE COMPLETE WORKS OF JAMES SHIRLEY, VOLUME 7

ROSANIA I am to both most humble.
OLIVIA   Prithee, tell me:
    Making so much of thee, he does impart   250
    Sometimes the secrets of his bosom to thee.
    Tell me what fault he has, for thou know'st all.
ROSANIA 'Las, madam, I know none –
    Or if I did, it ill became the trust
    And duty of a servant to reveal 'em.   255
OLIVIA Thou wert his bedfellow?
ROSANIA   Gracious madam –
OLIVIA Does he not wanton in the night and talk
    Of mistresses?
ROSANIA   By truth, not to me, madam.
OLIVIA Dissemble not. I know he has a mistress.
ROSANIA If love were ever so unkind to him –   260
OLIVIA Unkind? Why, is't a sin to love? I shall
    Suspect thy youth has not been free. Thy looks
    Betray some seeds of love.
ROSANIA   By all that's good
    I never was in love but with my master.
CAPTAIN [*Aside*] Good!   265
OLIVIA He is not worth it.
ROSANIA Madam?
OLIVIA Be wise and govern well thy hopes. I'll help
    Thee to a mistress. Th'ast no mistress yet?
ROSANIA But yourself, madam.
OLIVIA   It shall be no other.   270
    Thy master is ingrateful.
ROSANIA   Goodness aid him.
OLIVIA And wisdom thee. Thou art a pretty youth.
    I will reward thee better if thou canst
    Be faithful and obey.
ROSANIA   In all things, madam,
    That shall become your creature.
OLIVIA   'Tis not safe   275
    To play with a queen's favours. You shall wait
    Near us. Forget thy master and be happy.   *Exit.*

---

  256 bedfellow…madam Olivia refers to the idea of two close male companions sharing a bed, but Rosania seems to misunderstand, assuming the queen has seen through her disguise and realized that she is Ferdinand's lover.
  257 wanton become carefree and expansive.
  262 thy…free 'Your young years have not been guiltless', or perhaps 'Despite your lack of years you have not been honest with me'.

259] *lineation Gifford;* not / I O   **265 SD]** *this edn; not in* O   **270** yourself] *Gifford;* you self O

212

THE DOUBTFUL HEIR   3.1

ROSANIA What clue can guide me in this labyrinth?
  I would when I had lost Ferdinand's heart
  I had lost my understanding. She returns.   280

     Enter QUEEN [OLIVIA].

OLIVIA The king is coming this way; now be free.
  Thou shalt have reason afterwards to bless
  Thy fate. [*Aside*] This cannot choose but vex him.

       The queen is pleasant with Rosania.

     Enter FERDINAND.

FERDINAND [*Aside*] The queen so pleasant? She has lost her sullenness,
  Plays with his hair and smiles.
ROSANIA   Madam, the king   285
  Observes us.
FERDINAND   Strokes his cheek, too. She does want
  A Ganymede. My poor Rosania,
  Art thou the path she walks on to revenge?
  All is not well within her heart, but mine
  Sinks with the heavy pressure. (*Exit* [*Olivia*].) She is gone.   290
  The queen does grace you much, Tiberio.
  Those favours are not common.
ROSANIA   She is pleased
  For your sake, sir, to cast some smile upon me.
  I know 'twas your request she should be kind
  To keep my heart alive.   295
FERDINAND Th'art not discovered?
ROSANIA   Did not you discourse
  My story to her?
FERDINAND   I?
ROSANIA   Take heed, yet this
  Will add but a thin feather to the scale
  Of my misfortune. She knows all and in
  The pity of my sufferings says you are   300
  Not worth my love and calls you most ungrateful.
FERDINAND We are both lost. Till now there was some hope
  How to repair thy sorrow.
ROSANIA   Do not mock me.
  'Tis a worse tyranny than to kill, to laugh

---

  283 SD *pleasant* friendly, playful. The nature of this pleasantry is clear from Ferdinand's following lines: the queen is touching Tiberio flirtatiously.

  287 Ganymede Male cup-bearer to, and lover of, Jupiter. 'Ganymede' was often used in this period as a term to describe a lovely androgynous youth, used as a sexual plaything. Cf. John Marston's *The Malcontent*, where Malevole abuses Ferrardo: 'Dukes *Ganimed* [...]: shadowe of a woman' (B).

  298 Will...scale Will add only a tiny amount to the weight.

---

280 SD] *this edn; Re-enter* OLIVIA.] *Gifford; Enter Queen.* O
283 SD1] *this edn; Gifford marks the aside with a dash; not in* O   **283 SD2** *Rosania*] O *subst.* (*Ros*)
284 SD] *this edn; not in* O   **290 SD**] *Gifford subst.; Exit Queen. after gone.* O

213

3.1   THE COMPLETE WORKS OF JAMES SHIRLEY, VOLUME 7

At what you have made wretched. 'Tis as possible   305
To call past ages back.
FERDINAND   Take heed, Rosania,
  And be not judge of what thou knowst not, dearest.
ROSANIA I know too much.
FERDINAND   That I am married.
ROSANIA There's no truth in man.
FERDINAND You are too rash, for there is truth in me,   310
  In Ferdinand, though in thy thoughts held black
  And stained prodigiously with breach of faith.
  I have not broke my vow. Do not compel me
  By thy unbelief to do a sin I hate
  As much as I love thee.
ROSANIA   Have you a soul?   315
FERDINAND Yes, and thy eye shall read it – be but calm –
  That soul thou once didst love, white with his first
  Simplicity and faith. I wo'not urge
  In my excuse the beauty of the queen,
  Enough to melt a Scythian into love,   320
  But call to mind my dear Rosania
  And do but put upon thee Ferdinand,
  So late forgotten by his stars, a prisoner,
  Slaved like a villain at the bar, expecting
  At every breath his sentence. Nay, admit,   325
  Rosania, the best part of his soul,
  Stood like a weeping fountain to take leave
  Of what she never must salute again.
  In this extreme, to preserve Ferdinand
  And save Rosania, wouldst thou scorn the breath   330
  Of mercy that did court thee from the lips
  Of a great queen? Couldst thou love Rosania,
  If thou wert Ferdinand, to lose thyself?
  Whom she would follow in a stream of tears,
  And when she had made an island of thy tomb,   335

305–6 'Tis...back Consoling Rosania would be as difficult as turning back time. She may be thinking specifically of the impossibility of reversing time to undo Ferdinand's marriage.

308 married Pronounced as three syllables.

320 Scythian Scythians—the tribe who inhabited the area around the Eurasian steppes in classical antiquity—were traditionally synonymous with brutal savagery. Cf. *King Lear*: 'The barbarous Scythian, / Or he that makes his generation messes / To gorge his appetite, shall to my bosom / Be as well neighboured, pitied, and relieved, / As thou my sometime daughter' (1.1.116–20).

322 put upon thee imagine yourself to be.

324 Slaved Reduced to a state of subjection.

328 she Rosania.

332–3 Couldst...thyself? i.e. Is it possible that Ferdinand could have truly loved Rosania if he had been willing to give up his life (knowing that such an act would kill her)?

THE DOUBTFUL HEIR

3.1

Striving to swim to thee, she could not choose
But drown herself in her own waves. I prithee,
Take reason to thee, and when th'ast considered –
ROSANIA Persuade me I am not Rosania
And I will say 'tis virtue, and that yet   340
Your heart may grow with mine. Is not the queen
Possessed of that which should have been my title,
A wife to Ferdinand?
FERDINAND   'Tis confessed the world
Doth think it so. I did consent to ceremony.
ROSANIA Call you enjoying of the queen but ceremony?   345
FERDINAND Pause there, and if thou hast but so much charity
To think I dare not blaspheme heaven, I'll call
That, and the angels, boldly to my witness:
The queen's to me a stranger yet.
ROSANIA   A miracle!
FERDINAND Retain but love, as thou preserv'st thy sweetness,   350
And that will teach thee to believe that Ferdinand,
Howe'er saluted king, is still thy subject,
And though her husband, in my faith to thee
The marriage-bed hath still our virgin sheets.
A brother might embrace a sister with   355
The heat I brought. That this is truth, the power
And name I have shall only serve to make
Our flight secure into another kingdom,
And when I part with these new shining glories
Thy faith will be confirmed, and thou acknowledge   360
I ventured much to keep my heart thy servant.
ROSANIA I know not what to say. Is not the queen
Displeased?
FERDINAND   She is, but cunningly disguiseth
Her passion to the world. But I forgot
What must enlarge my fears of her revenge –   365
If thou be known Rosania.
ROSANIA   Lose that fear.
I am still safe, and now I see the cause
Makes her repent her favours and thy greatness.
Forgive me, Ferdinand, and yet, I know not,

347 **blaspheme** speak irreverently about.
349 **stranger** someone with whom one is not intimate; not a family member. Ferdinand means that the marriage has not yet been consummated.
359 **new...glories** i.e. his status as Olivia's husband and consort.
367–8 **cause...repent** reason why she repents.

215

3.1   THE COMPLETE WORKS OF JAMES SHIRLEY, VOLUME 7

All is not well. There's poison in this balsam   370
Prepared for thee.
FERDINAND   From whom?
ROSANIA   Rosania.
FERDINAND   When she shall but consent to have me die,
She shall not trouble poison to send off
My despis'd life. My soul in just obedience
To her command will take a cheerful flight   375
In hope to serve her in the other world.
ROSANIA   You shall know more hereafter, and let this
Secure your thoughts: she yet believes me what
This shape presents, but without wise prevention
I fear I shall not live too long concealed.   380
I dare not say her honour is a-bleeding,
But a queen thus distasted may not find
That ice within her blood. – We are interrupted.

        Enter RODRIGUEZ.

RODRIGUEZ   Your pardon, sir. 'Tis the queen's pleasure this gentleman attend her
in the gallery.   385
FERDINAND   He shall wait her commands.   *Exit Rodriguez.*
I know not what to counsel. 'Tis not safe,
Sweet, to neglect her, yet my fears of some
Ill fate are round about me like a mist
And dark my understanding. Let a kiss   390
And silence teach our souls some new discourse. [*They kiss.*]
CAPTAIN   [*Aside*] Why, here's a volume of intelligence.
I'll stay no longer to expect the prince
But seek him out immediately. Disguises?
King, by your leave, I shall untruss your mistress.   *Exit.*   395
ROSANIA   I know not what I feel, nor what to fear.
If love e'er meant a tragedy, 'tis here.
FERDINAND   If we ne'er meet again, one more salute
Shall fortify our lives by joining breath. [*They kiss.*]
Nor shall our last hard fate deny us this   400
To change our faithful souls at our last kiss.   *Exeunt severally.*

370–1 There's…thee Rosania means that there is danger within the 'cure' that Ferdinand has invented for
his situation, since if the queen continues, in her anger, to pursue 'Tiberio' sexually, she may discover 'his' true
identity. At that point she will realise why Ferdinand has not consummated the marriage and become enraged.
370 balsam plant oil or resin, often used in the Renaissance as the basis for medicines and ointments.
373 trouble bother with.
379 prevention precautions.
382 distasted displeased, offended.
390 dark make dark or unclear (*OED*, *v.* †4).
395 untruss 1) reveal; 2) undress (*OED*, *v.* †5a; 4).
401 SD *severally* separately, at different doors.

384–5] *lineation this edition;* pleasure / This O   386 SD] O *subst. (Ex. Rodri.)*   391 SD] *this edn; not in* O
392 SD] *this edn; not in* O   395 SD] O *subst. (Ex.)*   399 SD] *this edn; not in* O

216

THE DOUBTFUL HEIR

4[.1]

Enter RODRIGUEZ, LEANDRO, [*and*] ERNESTO.

ERNESTO I know not what to think on't, but if I
    Have any sense, there is some new state madness
    Crept into court.
RODRIGUEZ   Are we not all asleep
    And these fine dreams perplex us?
LEANDRO   No, 'tis waking.
RODRIGUEZ Show me the tenth part of a reason why   5
    The queen did marry him.
LEANDRO   'Twas destiny.
ERNESTO Why since should he be melancholy?
RODRIGUEZ Or she so humorous?
ERNESTO Not lie together? Pray heaven the gentleman
    Be found with no defective title in him.   10
LEANDRO Observe her favours to that boy. He was
    His servant, now her minion. I like not
    These violent wheels. The whole frame may be soon
    Endangered, if these passions be not cured.
RODRIGUEZ New lodgings for him near her own, and he   15
    Given free access to the bedchamber.
LEANDRO   'Tis naught,
    Or will be so. I pity the good king.
    Though she have raised him to the highest glory
    Her power extended to, yet to make this height
    Her precipice and throw him into scorn,   20
    Nay, poison the best hopes he had of honour
    And love from her, and in his sight to court

---

0 The scene in set in the royal palace.

2 state madness This seems to mean madness or illogicality experienced by those in positions of government.

4 these...us i.e. these events which perplex us are elaborate dreams.

8 humorous given to changes of mood.

10 defective title In law, a title or position obtained through error or fraud. Ernesto is suggesting that Ferdinand may have deceived the queen in marrying her, because he is not able (presumably through impotence) to fulfil all the duties of a husband.

12 minion servile dependent of a powerful person, often one treated as a favourite. However, the word can be used in another sense—that of 'lover'—and this hangs uneasily in the background of Leandro's words (*OED*, *n.*[1] 1a; 1†b).

13 wheels changes or reversals of opinion or attitude (*OED*, Wheel *v.* 4b)—although 'wheels' may also imply a reference to fortune's wheel. Cf. *Henry V*: 'Fortune [...] is painted also with a wheel, to signify to you—which is the moral of it—that she is turning and inconstant' (3.6.30–2).

13–14 The...Endangered Leandro appears to be referring both to the 'frame' of society and to the queen's own bodily frame, suggesting in both cases that the situation may have dangerous repercussions. If the queen becomes mentally and emotionally erratic over her dealings with her husband and Tiberio, the country may be put at risk.

16 naught wicked or immoral (*OED*, *adj.* 2a).

4[.1]] *Gifford subst. (*ACT IV. SCENE I.*); ACT. IV. O
0 SD *and*] *Gifford; not in* O

4.1 THE COMPLETE WORKS OF JAMES SHIRLEY, VOLUME 7

A boy, his servant? It would vex the best
Of all our tempers, if we felt the sting on't.

Enter ROSANIA *and* VIOLINDA, *passing over the stage.*

ERNESTO He's here. That lady is the queen's cabinet.   25
LEANDRO They are merry about the mouth.
ERNESTO   Another summons?
'Tis possible the queen may marry him too.
LEANDRO There is some mystery we cannot reach.
If we do well remember, there's a law
Made by herself as soon as she was queen   30
To keep wives' pulses temperate and correct
The insolent blood of women that had husbands.
ERNESTO And men were not exempted.
LEANDRO   I say no more,
But heaven maintain the law and the law-makers
And conjure down that devil. –   35
'Tis the king and the smooth boy. Let's leave 'em.   *Exeunt lords.*

Enter FERDINAND *and* ROSANIA.

FERDINAND Was this the lady's message? Does the queen
Take thee into such favour?
ROSANIA   I tell truth,
And though it sound but ill on the queen's part,
Because she thinks me what I seem, my lord,
You need not wear one cloud upon your face   40
When you remember who I am. My fears
Are thick upon my heart how to secure
This shadow any longer.
FERDINAND   That afflicts
Me most, Rosania, for it pleases me   45
To hear she can affect thee, but what way
To keep her expectation high and thee,
My dearest, safe? Her passions may be violent.
ROSANIA They are already, sir, if I mistake not.
I wish to heaven that you were reconciled   50

---

25 **queen's cabinet** A cabinet is a council of high-ranking advisors. Ernesto is presumably using the phrase ironically, to imply that Olivia is currently confiding in, and taking advice from, her waiting woman, rather than from her actual ministers and counsellors.
26 **merry…mouth** smiling.
26 **Another summons?** Tiberio is being called to see the queen yet again.
31–2 **correct…husbands** i.e. keep married women from becoming lustful and rebellious against their husbands.
35 **that devil** presumably the 'devil' of lust and/or infidelity.
36 **smooth** beardless, but also perhaps in the sense of 'sycophantic, ingratiating' (*OED*, *adj.* 2a; 7b).
43–4 **how…longer** Rosania is concerned about how to keep up her disguise in the face of the queen's flirtatious probing.
47 **expectation** hopes of seducing Tiberio.

---

31 wives'] *Gifford;* Wifes O   41 need not wear] *this edition;* need not to wear O

218

THE DOUBTFUL HEIR   4.1

To do the office of a husband to her.
That peace would keep her bosom clear, and I
Should live to all the world except yourself
A stranger still.
FERDINAND   What language speaks Rosania?
There's death in every syllable. Should I   55
Obey what thou desir'st and do the office
Of a husband, ha?
ROSANIA   I'll wait upon you still
And hope you will vouchsafe me now and then
A harmless smile. Her beauty will deserve
Your whole heart and there's something in the memory   60
Of what she has advanced you to will help
To make you kind.
FERDINAND   Should I enjoy the queen?
Because the misery of my fate compelled
A ceremonious sin, shall I betray
The essence of my faith and leave a curse,   65
When thou art known, upon my name forever?
If thou hast taken new resolves against me,
Punish my heart some other way. Had she
More ornament than ever met in woman,
Mistress of more perfection than poets   70
Invented for the Queen of Love; to this,
Were the proud empire of the world her own,
And she would make me lord of her and these –
It would not buy me to the pleasure of
One night's embrace. My body shall not carry   75
My soul so far astray. The man condemned
To live in a perpetual snow hath not
A purer frost within his blood.
ROSANIA   This but
Engenders a new grief, although it bind
Rosania's heart. There is yet one way left   80
And that, ere I pronounce, you must forgive.
There is a trembling in my tongue, and I

---

62 **kind** generous or friendly towards Olivia, but also implying a willingness to engage sexually with her. See Williams, 'kind' (1994, 2.760–1).

64 **ceremonious sin** act that is not really a sin, only a transgression against ideal behaviour (*OED*, Ceremonious *adj.* 1, 3). Shirley may also be playing on the idea that the wedding ceremony that Ferdinand agreed to was the source of the sin.

69 **More...woman** More beauties or fine qualities than were ever united together in a woman previously.

70 **perfection** Pronounced as four syllables.

71 **Queen...Love** The goddess Venus.

78 **purer frost** The idea of a chaste individual having icy blood was commonplace.

4.1   THE COMPLETE WORKS OF JAMES SHIRLEY, VOLUME 7

Already feel such winter in my breath
My timorous lips do wither.

FERDINAND   Do not fright
My soul too much. There's something threatens me   85
So like a loss of thee that I am left
A piece of shaking earth. Death cannot look
To make me tremble so. Canst thou forsake me?

ROSANIA Not in my heart, but give my body leave
To seek some other place, my lord, to dwell in.   90
When I am gone into some wilderness
You will find ease at heart, and love the queen,
And perfect all. I'll pray you may live happy
And hold intelligence with some gentle winds
That shall convey my wishes and return   95
What joys do follow you. The purling rivers
I'll teach your name, and they which glide this way
Shall bring thee something, Ferdinand, of mine.
My tears I know will not be lost, which I
Will send thee daily by the courteous stream,   100
Clear pledges of my faith. Consent, my lord,
I may depart and you shall choose your way
To every blessing here.

FERDINAND   Not till we meet
With one embrace and take our flight together.
And I have thought a way to perfect it.   105
Observe, my sweet Rosania. The queen,
Thou sayst, affects thee. Cherish it, with all
The softness of her creature. If she allow,
Kiss her and promise what young lovers do.
Examine not, but by thy love to me   110
Be free in amorous language. If she have
Heat to a private meeting in her chamber,
Obey. This shall secure our love's ambition.
Enquire not, but resolve, and let me know
The time.

83–4 feel…wither Rosania feels chilled by what she is going to say, as if her vital spirits have been dried up and frozen.
86 thee Following Gifford. *O*'s 'these' makes no sense in this context.
87 earth i.e. dull, worthless matter, as if his soul had left his body (*OED, n.*[1] 14a, 14†b).
93 perfect accomplish.
94–6 hold…you The winds will act as a go-between for Ferdinand and Rosania, carrying her best wishes to him and bringing her back news of his happiness.
96 purling rippling, murmuring.
110 Examine not Don't question or inquire into it (*OED*, Examine *v.* 4a).
112 Heat to The strong desire for (*OED*, Heat *n.* 11a). Ferdinand may also be playing on the sense of heat meaning sexual excitement (*OED*, Heat *n.* 13).

---

86 thee] *Gifford;* these O

220

THE DOUBTFUL HEIR   4.2

ROSANIA   You will attempt no violence   115
    Upon the queen?
FERDINAND By this – (*Kisses her.*)
ROSANIA   What if she have commanded me
    This night?
FERDINAND To meet?
ROSANIA In her bedchamber.   120
FERDINAND Ha! Obey it.
ROSANIA At a late hour.
FERDINAND   It shall beget our comfort,
    If thou consent.
ROSANIA   But shall I not expose
    Myself to danger, if her love pursue
    Immodest ends, since you advise I should   125
    Apply myself to her desires?
FERDINAND   If she
    Take too much flame, by some soft art delay her
    Till I come to close all. Keep still thy person
    Secret. The least discovery will destroy
    Us both. The evening with much haste prepares   130
    Thy visit and our happiness.
ROSANIA   I'll obey,
    But be you sure to come.
FERDINAND   Lose thou no time
    Now to endear thee to her. Let us part.
    Love will find balm to cure the wounded heart.   *Exeunt severally.*

[4.2]

A table, and lights set out. Then enter QUEEN [OLIVIA] *and* VIOLINDA.

OLIVIA Was he not cheerful when he promised thee?
VIOLINDA He was, and he was not.
OLIVIA I have a strange apprehension, and this doth feed it.
VIOLINDA I told him 'twas an honour worth his joyful entertainment.
OLIVIA If it should prove successful, my revenge   5
    Were perfect. I'm resolute to pursue –

---

134 Love…heart This is italicized in *O*, as a *sententia*, and recalls the Biblical line from Jeremiah 8.22—'Is there no balm in Gilead?'—which has been interpreted as promising that divine love can heal all hurts.

134 SD *severally* See note to 3.1.401 SD.

0 The scene is set in Olivia's private rooms.

3 apprehension sense of apprehension.

4 entertainment consideration or acceptance (*OED*, *n*. 7b; †6).

6 Were perfect Would be complete.

[4.2]] *Gifford subst.* (SCENE II.); *not in* O
0 SD QUEEN OLIVIA] *this edn;* OLIVIA *Gifford;* Queen O

221

4.2   THE COMPLETE WORKS OF JAMES SHIRLEY, VOLUME 7

VIOLINDA It makes well
    For your contrivement that the king and you
    Do lodge at distance. – Stay, I hear a tread.
OLIVIA I hope 'tis he.   10

    Enter LEONARIO.

VIOLINDA Prince Leonario, madam.
OLIVIA What comes he for?
LEONARIO Although I have small expectation
    For my own sake that you can pardon, madam,
    This bold access, and at so dark an hour,   15
    Yet when you have heard my business, you will know
    Yourself so much concerned, I'll not despair
    To find your mercy.
OLIVIA   You prepare me for
    Something of consequence.
LEONARIO   Please you to dismiss
    Your lady. I have something to deliver   20
    Wo'not become her knowledge.
OLIVIA   Leave us.   *Exit Violinda.*
                      Now
    Our conference is free. Your grace's pleasure?
    It must be matter of much essence that
    Could not expect till morning, but you're welcome.
LEONARIO This time and darkness, madam, best becomes him   25
    Who for your sake blushes to see the day.
    But I came not to chide. My wrongs have learned
    A modest silence. My approach is not
    To name a suffering of mine, but to
    Discover what already is prepared   30
    Against your peace and honour.
OLIVIA   Is it treason?
LEONARIO It is, but threatens not your life. You may
    Live many years upon the wound.
OLIVIA   You fright me.
LEONARIO Lose not the beauty of your cheek so soon.
    Hide not beneath that cold and killing snow.   35
    One rosy blush and yet that pale would show
    Like innocence which you have lost. Oh, madam,

---

9 at distance at some distance from each other.
13 expectation Pronounced as five syllables.
24 expect wait (*OED*, *v.* †10).
30 Discover Uncover, expose.
33 upon after receiving.
34–5 Lose…snow Olivia goes pale at the thought of what she is about to hear.

8–9] *lineation Gifford;* For…do / Lodge O   **21 SD**] Q *subst. (Ex. Violinda.)*

222

THE DOUBTFUL HEIR   4.2

Had you not made a forfeit of your truth
To me no storm could shake you, but your soul
That made no change could know no fear. I come   40
To tell you what just providence hath done
In my revenge. Your breach of vow is punished
With loss of faith in him to whom you gave
The heart you promised me. The king, whose pride
You built on my dishonour, is as false   45
As you were.
OLIVIA   This is passion – but be
Not yet too rash in censuring him. Whom I
Have placed so near, I must defend, nor will
He need my strength to make their blood account
Who dare traduce his honour. He has a heart –   50
LEONARIO A false one. I was born without a fear
And dare upon his bosom (were he worth
The manly contestation) write him perjured.
OLIVIA I would this were not envy! But admit
He be thus guilty, 'tis a fault in him.   55
LEONARIO No, madam, it is yours. That sin that poisoned
The expectation of my joys in you
Hath made him false and will excuse his story
When you are named that broke your faith to me.
I can have no hope now to be repaired   60
But if it be worth memory to know
The triumph waits on innocence, the world
Shall say the queen deserved to meet a scorn
Deep as her wrongs to me.
OLIVIA   It cannot be.
LEONARIO Think so and help to make the revenge greater, 65
Till the winds catch the black report and multiply
The shame by scattering it about the kingdom.
Sit still, and careless of your fame encourage
His private lust – his mistress now in court.

46 **passion** a passionate speech.
49 **make ... account** make them answer for it with their blood (*OED*, Account *v.* †1).
50 **traduce** slander, speak ill of.
53 **contestation** conflict (*OED*, *n.* 5): Leonario says that Ferdinand is not worthy of being challenged by him to a fight.
54 **I ... envy** Olivia believes that Leonario's accusation is only made out of jealousy, and regrets it on his behalf.
54 **admit** if it were the case that.
61 **worth memory** worth remembering.
62 **triumph ... innocence** Leonario reflects that justice will always triumph and injured innocence be avenged.
65–7 **Think ... kingdom** If the queen refuses to believe the story, her punishment will become worse, as she will not act against Ferdinand, and reports of her humiliation will spread through the kingdom.

4.2   THE COMPLETE WORKS OF JAMES SHIRLEY, VOLUME 7

OLIVIA A mistress in the court?   70
LEONARIO Yes, madam, in the court,
    And may one day think any second place
    Too narrow to contain her greatness. She –
OLIVIA As you're a prince, no more. I have done ill
    And find the penance here. It does agree   75
    With his neglects and adds new flame to my
    Young jealousy. I feel a tempest rising.
    By all your goodness, leave me, sir. I cannot
    Now right you more than mourn and give belief to you.
    No more, I pray you, by all your love to honour.   80
LEONARIO I ha' done,
    And take my leave, my everlasting leave.
    'Tis time. How like the day that flattered us
    With cheerful light are my desires fled hence
    And left me here, a prodigy of darkness,   85
    A walking hearse hung round about with night,
    Whose wings must one day cover all. Farewell.
    If any star look forth, it is to call
    Me hence and light me to another world.
    Our lips are never like to meet again. (*Kisses* [*her*].)   90
    Farewell. [*Aside*] If I but stay, I shall forgive her.   *Exit.*
OLIVIA A mistress in the court? Something is busy
    About my heart.

        Enter VIOLINDA.

VIOLINDA   The prince is gone.
OLIVIA   No matter.   [*Exit Violinda.*]
    Affronted thus? But I forgot to ask
    Her name that rivals me. How this passion   95
    Befools our understanding and prevents
    The knowledge and the cure of what afflicts us!
    The morning will assure all, but shall this

---

75 agree fit, correspond.
78–9 I…to you The queen cannot right the wrong she has done to Leonario; she can only sorrow at her own actions and believe his accusations against Ferdinand.
85 prodigy extreme example (*OED*, *n.* 3b).
92–3 Something…heart My heart is agitated.
94 Affronted Insulted.
95 this passion this high temper.
96 Befools Makes a fool of.
98 assure all make everything clear or certain (*OED*, Assure *v.* 6). Presumably Olivia means that in the morning she will speak to Leonario again and find out the name of Ferdinand's mistress.

---

90 SD] *Gifford; Kisses* O   **91 SD1]** *this edn; Gifford marks the aside with a dash; not in* O
93 SD2] *this edn; Exit Vio. Gifford; not in* O

224

THE DOUBTFUL HEIR   4.2

Strike me to ashes? I may find a way
To my revenge.   100

    Enter VIOLINDA.

VIOLINDA Tiberio is come, madam.
OLIVIA Wait carefully.
VIOLINDA   I know my duty.   [*Exit Violinda.*]

    Enter ROSANIA; *kneels and kisses* [*Olivia's*] *hand.*

OLIVIA   Rise.
This meeting was not meant for ceremony.
There's something in this presence will deserve
We should put off all state and speak like friends.   105
You must be covered too. I'll have it so.
We are private now.
ROSANIA   These graces will
Undo a youth, whose birth and careless stars
Ordained him to be humble and with duty
Wait on your meanest servant.   110
OLIVIA Thou shalt soon have cause
To think thy stars are careful of thee, if
Thou canst be wise.
ROSANIA   Alas, my years are few.
OLIVIA Thy knowledge is not wanting to distinguish
Whose favours court thee and apply thyself   115
To understand and thank the kind bestower.
'Tis in my power to make thee great.
ROSANIA   You may
Advance this worthless walking shadow, madam,
And when you, like the free and bounteous sun,
Have blessed me with your rays, it is but like   120
His glorious warmth bestowed upon a piece
Of rude and barren earth, which takes not from
The lustre of your beams, but shows more clearly
By your own light what poverty you shined on.
OLIVIA This modesty becomes you not. Look in   125
My eye and read what's there.
ROSANIA   Something like anger,

102 **carefully** attentively.
104–5 **There's…friends** Olivia suggests that there is something special about this meeting that requires
that both of them speak openly and honestly.
106 **You…too** Olivia presumably means that Rosania should put her hat back on, which she would have
removed when she knelt to kiss Olivia's hand.
108 **careless** neglectful (*OED*, *adj.* 3).
112 **are…of** take care of.
114 **is…wanting** is sufficient.
126 **anger** It is not clear whether Olivia genuinely looks angry at this point or whether Rosania is mistaking a
look of lust for one of anger.

102 SD1] *this edn; Exit. Gifford; not in* O   102 SD2 *Olivia's*] *Gifford subst.; her* O

225

4.2 THE COMPLETE WORKS OF JAMES SHIRLEY, VOLUME 7

Enough to strike me dead.

OLIVIA   What now?

ROSANIA   A smile,
And such attending sweetness –

OLIVIA   Thus it shall
Invite thee still to gaze and love, Tiberio.
No frown shall point on thee. I find my eyes   130
Were meant for thee, and all they graced before
But objects of mistake. Here, here – oh, turn
Thy lovely face away, lest I be seen
To blush – my heart hath chose to place my love
And the reward. This would become thy tongue   135
A great deal better. Come, sit down, Tiberio.
What, still an infant's understanding? Think
I am the man, and learn a little better.
What beauty dwells upon this hand! [*Takes his hand.*] What softness!
How like the snow or innocence it shows,   140
Yet fires my heart with every gentle touch.

ROSANIA Dear madam. [*Aside*] Would the king would come!

OLIVIA This is a happiness that kings should sue for,
And yet there are poor comforts in these kisses.
Let hands preserve society with hands,   145
And with their change of whiteness and of balm
Make wealthy one another. But let what
Was meant for kisses meet and find out pleasure
By warm exchange of souls from our soft lips. (*Kisses* [*her*].)
Madam, how like you this?   150

ROSANIA 'Madam'?

OLIVIA I suppose you a lady all this while,
And I the man. Our lips must meet again. [*Kisses her.*]
Will this instruct thee nothing?

ROSANIA   Gracious madam –

OLIVIA And yet this recreation comes short,   155
Dear lady, of what love might well allow us.

---

132 **Here, here** Olivia presumably gestures at Tiberio, the object of her love.

134–5 **my...reward** Olivia's heart has given her love to Tiberio and rewards him with her bodily and worldly self.

135–6 **This...better** i.e. It would be more appropriate for Tiberio to woo Olivia than vice versa.

144–9 **these...lips** Olivia has been kissing Rosania's hands, but now wishes to move on to kissing her lips: the things that are 'meant for kisses'.

146 **change...balm** Olivia imagines two hands entwined, 'exchanging' sweat ('balm') from one to the other.

155 **recreation** Pronounced as five syllables.

---

139 **SD**] *this edn; not in* O   142 **SD**] *Gifford subst.; not in* O
151 **'Madam'?**] Madam. O   153 **SD**] *this edn; after* nothing? *Gifford; not in* O

226

THE DOUBTFUL HEIR 4.2

Admit you are a queen, you are not bound
To thin your royal blood with frost, but as
Your power, your pleasure should exceed. Nay, grant
You have a man (a man, said I) that can 160
Keep love alive and warm a yielding bosom,
Yet where from the invitement of your eye
And amorous choice I am become your servant,
You may be a little kinder.
ROSANIA Madam, I know not 165
How, with the safety of myself, my duty,
And your own name and power, to understand you.
[*Aside*] Yet this to some would need but little comment.
[*To Olivia*] Can you place such a value on a thing
That not deserves to breathe your name? Or should 170
I hope these charms of language you have spread
To catch my heart, which hath no wings but where
It can believe? For you transcend so much
In wonder of your love, a willing faith
Not easily can reach it. But, dear madam, 175
I know all this is but to try my duty,
And you have pleased to choose me forth to make
These silent hours more grateful by the mirth
My weak replies may raise you.
OLIVIA   Miracle!
I but imagined thee a woman. Now 180
I shall believe thee one indeed. This coldness
Becomes no masculine habit. Come, we'll in
And change our sexes. Thou shalt wear my clothes
And I will put on these – help on with thine
And I will dress thee handsomely – and then 185
We'll act again.

---

157 Admit Accept, acknowledge (*OED*, *v*. 2c). Alternatively, Olivia might be using the word in the conditional sense, as in 'grant (for the sake of argument) that...' (*OED*, *v*. 2†d).

158–9 but...exceed Royalty have power that exceeds the norm, so they should also enjoy more extreme pleasure than is permitted to ordinary people.

162 from as a result of.

170–3 Or...believe The precise meaning here is obscure: it is not clear whether Rosania is referring to her own heart or Olivia's language as potentially lacking wings. Regardless, she seems to be saying that Olivia may not be sincere in what she says, as she may be simply hoping to seduce 'Tiberio' using hyperbolic speech. She insists that she herself cannot love unless she trusts the sincerity of the speaker.

176 try test.

178 grateful pleasant, agreeable (*OED*, *adj*. 1).

182 habit clothing, outward appearance.

---

159 grant] *Gifford;* graut O; *O's reading is the result of a turned n*
168 SD] *this edn;* O *puts this line in parentheses, to mark it as an aside*   **169 SD**] *this edn; not in* O
170 breathe] O *subst. (*breath*)*

227

4.2   THE COMPLETE WORKS OF JAMES SHIRLEY, VOLUME 7

ROSANIA   Not for the world, dear madam.
    [*Aside*] Not yet come?
OLIVIA The world? [*Aside*] This confirms my jealousy.
    I'll search you to the soul. [*To Rosania*] Adonis, come.
    I'll call thee so and court thee with more charm   190
    Than Venus did, when in the Idalian Groves
    To buy a kiss she offered the proud boy
    Her flaming chariot and her doves of snow.
    'Tis in thy power to make thy fate and heart
    More happy, by consent to meet with mine.   195
    Tempt not the anger of a queen despised,
    Whose breath can like a whirlwind snatch thee up
    And drop thee in a wilderness, where with sorrow
    For thy neglect thou by degrees may'st sigh
    Thyself into a mist, which no sunbeam   200
    Shall pity or take up into a cloud.
    But love me, and compose thy heart to mine:
    We'll live with more delight than fancy can
    Enrich Elysium with. The soft hours shall stay
    Till we allow 'em wings, and while we kiss   205
    And on each other's lips breathe incense thus [*Kisses her*]
    We'll have ten thousand Cupids for our guard,
    Whose bows shall awe the destinies, and we write
    The king and queen of fate.

        Enter FERDINAND, LEANDRO, RODRIGUEZ, ERNESTO,
        CAPTAIN, [*and*] GUARD.

FERDINAND Will this deserve your faith?
LEANDRO   We must believe.   210

        Enter VIOLINDA.

VIOLINDA We are undone – the king!
                [*Olivia falls to the floor.*]

---

   188 This…jealousy Rosania's refusal to cooperate fuels Olivia's sense of rejection and anger, as she becomes suspicious that 'Tiberio's' heart belongs to another.
   189–3 Adonis…snow Olivia refers to the myth of Venus and Adonis, as recounted in Shakespeare's narrative poem of the same name, in which the goddess of love presses an unwilling youth to love her. Idalium is a mountain city in Cyprus, dedicated to Venus. Venus travels in a fiery chariot drawn by turtledoves.
   202 compose…mine arrange your feelings to fit mine (*OED*, Compose *v.* 1†b: 'To fashion, frame (the human body, etc.)').
   204 Elysium In Greek mythology, the dwelling-place of the blessed after death.
   204–5 The…wings Time will stand still until we allow it to pass.
   208–9 Whose…fate The destinies—the supernatural guardians of fate—will be kept from interfering by the guard of Cupids, and so will leave the lovers to choose their own destiny, unlike the situation of all other mortals who are under the control of exterior forces. '[W]e write' means something like 'allow us to be recorded as'.

   186–7] *lineation this edition;* Not…come? O
   187 SD] *Gifford subst.; not in* O   188 SD] *Gifford subst.; not in* O
   189 SD] *this edn; Gifford marks end of aside with a dash; not in* O   204 Elysium] O *subst.* (*Elizium*)
   206 SD] *Gifford; not in* O   209 SD *and*] *Gifford; not in* O   211 SD] *this edn; not in* O

THE DOUBTFUL HEIR   4.2

OLIVIA False keys?

ROSANIA [*Aside*] 'Twas time to come.

FERDINAND Had I not cause, my lords, to appear sad
  When I suspected this so great affront?
  My melancholy all this while was but   215
  A mourning for this shame. Look but, my lords,
  Into yourselves and make this suffering yours.

VIOLINDA [*Aside, to Olivia*] Madam, be raised again. I have an art
  To fetch you off with honour, and the youth too.   220
  I will persuade him there can be no cure
  In this extreme but to pretend himself
  A woman. I will dress him in your gown
  Before they can be 'ware on't. They all know
  This way he cannot fly. Meantime, put on   225
  A confidence, and let them know you are
  The queen, not to be shaken with their power.
  This will gain time.

OLIVIA   Prosper in this.

VIOLINDA   I will
  Redeem my fault or never sleep again.

                                      Exit with Rosania.

FERDINAND She blushes not.   230
  Were she not queen, what names could we bestow
  Upon this want of modesty?

LEANDRO   'Tis plain
  We came in time.

FERDINAND   Most happily to prevent
  Some further act of shame. Can she look on us
  Without a blush?

OLIVIA   I see no such attraction   235
  In your state faces that I should desire
  Much to look on 'em. Who made you king, I pray?

FERDINAND Your power (I dare not call it love), presuming
  That I was fit to be your property,
  Without a soul to see or have a sense   240

---

212 **False keys** Skeleton keys (*OED*, False *adj*. 13f).

213 **'Twas...come** i.e. It's about time! It is not clear whether Rosania says this to herself or mutters it as an aside to Ferdinand.

219 **art** stratagem or contrivance (*OED*, *n*.¹ 11b).

219–25 **I...fly** Violinda's plan is to take Tiberio offstage and disguise him as a woman, and then attempt to brazen it out with the lords by insisting that they were mistaken and that there are no men present in the queen's apartments. As plans go, this seems a very weak one: it relies on the lords' willingness either to believe that the queen was actually alone when they first entered or to believe that what they initially thought was the queen with a man was actually the queen with another woman.

229 **my fault** i.e. in allowing the pair to be discovered.

---

213 SD] *this edn; not in* O   219 SD] *this edn; not in* O

229

4.2   THE COMPLETE WORKS OF JAMES SHIRLEY, VOLUME 7

Of these dishonours. This rank heat of blood –
Madam, what penitence can make this clear?
Admit your thoughts were wanton and your flame
Too great to be suppressed: could you find none
For your adulterate embrace but one   245
That was my servant? My own hound devour me!
As if your lust had not enough of shame
And mischief to me but your malice must
Appear in't too. With what security
Can I expect to live when she begins   250
So soon to poison me?
LEANDRO   We heard her say
They two would write themselves the king and queen.
RODRIGUEZ So we did all.
FERDINAND   You may consider these.
LEANDRO 'Tis impious. Madam, with what grief
Do we remember now that law you made   255
After your coronation to preserve
The name of your sex chaste, which gave our hearts
Hope of your blessed progress. You made it death
To stain the marriage bed. Where shall we expect
The life of that good act, when you begin   260
A breach of chastity by so black example?
If the king urge an execution
Of what our vote, confirmed by yours, imposed
Upon the kingdom, you should prove yourself
More innocent or give us cause to mourn   265
This fall from virtue.
ERNESTO   Madam, we grieve for you.
OLIVIA So, so: have your great wisdoms said all yet?
I laugh at you, poor things, and am so far
From trembling at your thunder that I pity you,
And first I'll let you know yourselves. You are,   270
I take it, all my subjects? I will not
Exempt you, sir, since marriage takes not off

242 what...clear? How can the queen do anything to clear herself of this extreme of sinfulness?
243 Admit Even if we concede that.
253 these i.e. these pieces of evidence from the courtiers.
259–60 Where...act How shall we hope for the continued existence or efficacy of that law.
262–4 If...kingdom If the king desires to enforce the law of chastity that Olivia and her advisors imposed upon the land.
262 execution Pronounced as five syllables.
264–6 you...virtue Leandro means that, given the legal situation in which Olivia finds herself, she needs to either find a way to excuse her behaviour or else admit to her guilt and allow the courtiers to feel sorry for her fall.

254–5] *lineation this edition;* impious / Madam . . . we / Remember O   270 yourselves] *Gifford;* you selves O

230

THE DOUBTFUL HEIR   4.2

My interest and essence here, all strength
Flowing from me, and your derivative shine
Extinct, when I frown you to darkness. By   275
What power dare you take an account of me,
That am above your laws, which must obey
Me, as their soul, and die when I forsake 'em?
But I will reason coolly and admit
They live in force: 'gainst whom? Are you so shallow   280
To think we, that created and decreed 'em
For vulgar reformation, must be squared
And levelled by 'em, as we meant to lose
Our character and distinction and stoop
To th'common file of subjects? This were policy!   285
I speak not this with sense of any guilt,
So to decline it, for I here defy you,
And bring an innocence shall strike a blush
Upon your souls that sinned in my suspicion.
FERDINAND Where is the boy? Ernesto, take him to   290
Your custody, and bid him not despair.
I have contrived the rest.

    Enter ROSANIA, *like a woman, and* VIOLINDA.

ERNESTO   He's here.
VIOLINDA Take it upon you. If it come to searching,
We'll find a jury.

273 **interest…essence** title and intrinsic nature as monarch.

274 **derivative shine** Ferdinand's only power comes from his association with the queen; without her, he has no authority of his own.

279–80 **admit…force** Olivia appears to concede that the chastity laws are now in existence, independent of herself. However, there may be an implied 'if' here: '*If* I admit that these laws exist'. Olivia appears to be trying to work out what her own defence should be: is it that the laws do not apply to her, or is it that she did not break them?

282 **vulgar reformation** moral improvement of the common people.

282–3 **squared…'em** brought low, treated the same as ordinary people.

283–4 **as…distinction** as if we meant to lose our special status as monarch.

285 **file** catalogue, roll (*OED*, *n.*² 3†c).

285 **policy** prudent or shrewd behaviour. Olivia is being sarcastic, implying that it would be bad political strategy to allow herself to be treated like a normal offending subject.

286–7 **I…it** My words are not an admission of guilt, in order to justify it. Olivia means that although she has claimed that she is above the law, in this case she has not broken the law in the first place.

287 **So** So as.

289 In *O*, there is a stage direction—'*Aside*'—at this point, beside line 290, but this seems to be an error. Olivia's speech is directed at her subjects; none of it is intended as an aside. It is possible that the aside should be assigned to Ferdinand, for his following line.

293–4 **If…jury** Violinda presumably means that if the lords demand that Rosania's body be checked ('searched') to see whether she is actually female, she and the queen will find someone to do this check who will maintain that she is.

276 account] O *subst. (*accompt*)   289] O *marks 'Aside.' at the end of this line; see commentary note*

231

4.2   THE COMPLETE WORKS OF JAMES SHIRLEY, VOLUME 7

CAPTAIN   You are deceived, my lord,
    With your good pardon. He is not here.   295
ERNESTO Who is not here?
CAPTAIN   The he you do expect.
    And your officious ladyship might well
    Have spared your pains, to put on all this trim.
FERDINAND What means the fellow?
CAPTAIN   'Tis no news to you, sir.
    I could have told the queen before and you,   300
    My honourable lords, this was no boy,
    Though now he would but seem o'th'other sex.
    I knew her name.
ROSANIA   My name?
CAPTAIN   Are not you called
    Rosania?
FERDINAND Ha! Betrayed?
CAPTAIN Yes, indeed is she. You were present, sir,   305
    I'th'garden when this fine hermaphrodite
    Declared what sex was hid behind the breeches,
    And this I certified the prince before.
OLIVIA Now 'tis clear.
CAPTAIN There are some tokens too, I can remember,   310
    As kisses, and excuse for marrying with
    The queen, a virgin still, et cetera.
ALL A woman?
VIOLINDA But are you a woman indeed?
CAPTAIN And now, my lords, if you have hearts that are   315
    Honest and daring, come about again,
    For this is but a cunning piece of treason
    Against your faith and the queen's honour.
FERDINAND We are both lost, Rosania.
CAPTAIN 'Tis truth, or take my head off.   320
OLIVIA You do believe this transformation
    And know this lady, my good lord. I did
    Suspect before the cause of your neglects
    And meeting with some dark intelligence
    From the prince, to perfect this discovery   325

---

298 **trim** adornment.
308 **certified** formally informed.
310 **There...tokens** The Captain quibbles on the word 'token', which can mean a gift given as a mark of affection (*OED*, Token *n.* 9) but also a piece of evidence (Token *n.* 3a).
316 **come...again** change your opinion of the queen back to the way it was before.
321 **transformation** Pronounced as five syllables.

294–5] *lineation this edition;* You...pardon, / He O
299 you] *Gifford;* your O   303–4] *lineation this edition;* Are...Rosania? O   312 *et cetera*] O *subst. (&c)*
313 SH] *this edn;* Omnes O

232

THE DOUBTFUL HEIR   4.2

Did in my chamber woo with aptest forms
Of love, to try how long the sex would be
Concealed. You heard a part, and saw us kiss,
And came in time, with these wise noblemen,
To prevent further acts of shame.   330
RODRIGUEZ Is't possible?
ROSANIA [*To Ferdinand*] It was an ill contrivement to make me
      Proof of the queen's dishonour.
ERNESTO   An apparent plot
      Against the life and honour of the queen,
      Since he would urge that law maliciously   335
      Against her, knowing this to be a woman
      And his close strumpet.
RODRIGUEZ   The same law must be
      Their trial.
LEANDRO   What a change is here already.
OLIVIA You must not, lords, deny me justice.
RODRIGUEZ   'Tis
      Insufferable against a common person.   340
ERNESTO Let his first treason, if you think good, madam,
      Be urged in accusation.
LEANDRO   So, so.
OLIVIA You did us service, Captain.
CAPTAIN   I am bound to't.
      Here's more news for the prince.
OLIVIA   Use your pleasures.   *Exit [Captain]*.
RODRIGUEZ What need we circumstance? Let him die tomorrow.   345
OLIVIA Death will be mercy to so much ingratitude.
      Command them both to several custodies.
      The morning shall behold 'em dead.

327 **try** test.
332–3 **It...dishonour** Rosania reprimands Ferdinand for coming up with the scheme in the first place.
335 **that law** the chastity law.
337–8 **The same...trial** Ferdinand and Rosania must now be tried for having offended against the same law
of chastity, with their secret relationship.
339–40 **'Tis...person** The plot to trap the queen would have been unbearably wicked even if it was only set
to trap an ordinary person.
341–2 **Let...accusation** Ernesto suggests that at the trial, Ferdinand's attempt to usurp the crown in Act 1
should also be used as a charge against him. '[A]ccusation' is pronounced as five syllables.
343 **bound to't** obliged to do it (presumably by his duty to the crown).
345 **circumstance** provide details or consider contexts (*OED*, *v*. †3).

328 saw] *Gifford;* see O   332 SD] *this edn; not in* O
339–42] *lineation Gifford;* 'Tis insufferable / Against...person. / *Er.* Let...first / Treason...urg'd / In O
343–4] *lineation Gifford;* I...Prince. O   344 SD] *this edn; Exit.* O

233

5.1   THE COMPLETE WORKS OF JAMES SHIRLEY, VOLUME 7

ROSANIA Now more lost than ever.

Exeunt [all but Ferdinand, Rosania, and Guard].

FERDINAND   Pray, let's take
  Short leave of one another. 'Tis in vain   350
  To reason against providence or say
  We might ha' lived. Though I must die and after
  Be hid in my obscurest name and shade,
  I must declare whose blood they will profane
  In bleeding thee. Farewell. Our last, last kiss. [*They kiss.*]   355
  My heart would fain come to thee. I will make it
  My humble suit with my last breath it may
  Be quickly sent thee.
ROSANIA   We shall both meet when
  This dust falls off and our souls kiss again.   *Exeunt.*

5[.1]

Enter LEANDRO, RODRIGUEZ, ERNESTO, [*and*] SERVANTS *with lights.*

ERNESTO My lord, you tell us wonders. 'Tis high time
  To open such a mystery.
RODRIGUEZ   This change
  Will exceed all, and so convincing are
  The circumstances of this great discovery
  They do command our faith.
ERNESTO   And you shall steer us.   5
LEANDRO Then let us lose no time. Oh, my good lords,
  Did you but feel the torment of my bosom
  Till I discharge the duty which so long
  Hath slept in his concealment, you would call
  For wings to fly and think all motion tedious.   10
  For heaven's sake let's make haste that we prevent
  The morning, which will rise upon this knowledge
  With cheerful beams and put on all his glory.
ERNESTO Most gladly we attend.   *Exeunt.*

358–9 when...off when we shed our mortal bodies and our souls ascend to heaven.
0 The scene is set in the palace.
3 exceed all surpass all previous changes to the political fortunes of the country.
4 circumstances contextual details.
4 discovery revelation. Leandro has told the other lords his knowledge of Ferdinand's true identity.
11 prevent arrive or act before (*OED*, v. †1a; †5a.).

349 SD] *this edn; Exeunt all but Ferd. Ros. and Guard. Gifford; Exeunt. Manent. Ferd: Ros. & Guard. O*
355 SD] *this edn; not in O*

5[.1]] *Gifford subst. (*ACT V. SCENE I.*); ACT. V. O*
0 SD *and] Gifford; not in O*

234

THE DOUBTFUL HEIR   5.2

[5.2]

A table and taper set out. Enter FERDINAND, *with a book in his hand.*

FERDINAND I have no heart to think of anything
    But my Rosania. All devotion,
    When I remember her, flies off and leaves
    My soul no contemplation but her safety.
    They were too cruel to divide us. Night   5
    Itself looks now more black by this dim taper.
    Rosania's eyes would brighten all, but they,
    Weighed down with sleep and sorrow, are perhaps
    At rest. A thousand angels watch about 'em
    And let someone whose office is to wait   10
    On harmless love present me to her dreams.
    Oh, let her hear me often call upon her
    As I am led to death, and when the stroke
    Divides me from myself and from the world,
    My heart shall pay her tribute and my blood   15
    Do miracles, when every crimson drop
    My body bleeds shall not in vain be wept
    But fall into some letter of her name
    To keep alive our story.

    Enter two SERVANTS *with torches,* LEANDRO, ERNESTO, [*and*] RODRIGUEZ.

                  What lights are these?
    This place sure is not wont to be thus visited.   20
    They are spirits, ha! Yet if I have a memory,
    Those faces were but late familiar to me. (*They kneel.*)
    What mockery is this? If you be substances
    Of things I know, go tell the tyrant queen
    She might allow me death without this scorn,   25
    This jeering antimasque.
ALL   Long live the king.
FERDINAND What king?

  0 The scene is set in a prison.
  0 SD *a book* This is a bible or prayer book, given Ferdinand's subsequent references to the impossibility of
'devotion' at this time.
  10–11 someone…dreams It was commonly believed that angels could influence and inspire the dreams of
humans. See Rivière (2017, 11).
  23 mockery Ferdinand puns on the two meanings of this word: the mimicry or imitation of something
(*OED*, *n.* 3) but also the sense of 'derision' (*OED*, *n.* 1a).
  23 substances physical manifestations (*OED*, Substance *n.* 11a).
  26 antimasque An antimasque is a dramatic performance, usually comic or grotesque, that comes before a
masque. Ferdinand objects to the spectacle of his own death being preceded by another performance apparently
designed to mock or humiliate him.

  [5.2]] *Gifford subst. (*SCENE II.*); not in* O   **19 SD** *and*] *Gifford; not in* O
  26 SH] *this edn (and thus throughout remainder of scene);* Omnes. O

235

5.2   THE COMPLETE WORKS OF JAMES SHIRLEY, VOLUME 7

ALL Long live Ferdinand, King of Murcia.

FERDINAND A dream, a golden dream. What fancies wait
    Upon our sleep! And yet I wake. They are   30
    Apparitions. I'll shut my eyes and lose 'em.
    They wo'not vanish. – Leandro, Rodriguez, Ernesto?

ALL All your subjects.

LEANDRO Collect your scattered thoughts, my lord, and be
    Assured we now pay real duties to you.   35
    You are our king, and must be.

FERDINAND   Who says so?

LEANDRO I, whose cold fear and frailty,
    When fate of war had made you prisoner,
    Concealed the truth and justice of your title.
    'Twas I that saved you from your uncle's fury   40
    And sent you to Valencia, while I cozened
    The kingdom with your death till time might ripen
    Your challenge to the sceptre. If you can
    Find mercy to a treason great as this,
    I'll live and study how to merit pardon.   45

FERDINAND Rise, rise all,
    And if you be Leandro, pray come nearer.

        [*Leandro goes to Ferdinand. Rodriguez and Ernesto talk apart.*]

RODRIGUEZ Pray heaven this unexpected happiness
    Meet with no ecstasy. All senses are
    Not armed for such extremes of joy.

ERNESTO   The queen,   50
    When she finds this, will fall into a fever.
    By instinct her head must ache this very minute.

RODRIGUEZ And shake, too, for the crown is tottering.

FERDINAND Pardon? Thou shouldst divide the kingdom with me.
    But do all these believe it? Will you not   55
    When I make second claim deny me again,
    Call me impostor?

---

35 **real** It is possible that this is also a pun on 'royal'.

41–2 **cozened…death** tricked the kingdom with the account of your death.

48 **heaven** Pronounced as one syllable.

49 **ecstasy** The condition of being overpowered by strong emotion. It was believed that too strong an ecstasy could potentially cause death.

50–2 **The queen…minute** Ernesto suggests that it is Olivia, not Ferdinand, who will be made unwell by this alteration in circumstance. He imagines that, given the momentousness of the change, she will somehow feel it in her bones, even before she has been officially informed.

53 **shake…tottering** Rodriguez expands on Ernesto's conceit, suggesting that the queen will not only feel ill but will also feel her head and the crown upon it shaking, as she is about to be toppled by Ferdinand's rise.

54 **Pardon…me** Far from your needing to be pardoned, you deserve half my kingdom in reward.

---

35 real] O *subst.* (reall)   41 Valencia] O *subst.* (*Valentia*)   47 SD] *this edn; not in* O

236

THE DOUBTFUL HEIR 5.2

LEANDRO   Sir, forgive that first
    And I'll not ask heaven pardon for my next
    Denial, let death threaten all his stings.
    And I have satisfied these lords so well,   60
    They are confirmed in your just claim and person.
RODRIGUEZ AND ERNESTO We lay our lives and fortunes at your feet.
FERDINAND I may command you then. Fetch me Rosania.
    I'll be no king without her. Do not stay
    To hear how much I love her 'bove the crown   65
    And all the glories wait upon it – she
    That was my page, my fellow prisoner, Rosania.   *Exit Rodriguez.*
    'Tis that name next to heaven I bow to.
    Good my lord, follow him, and if she be
    Awake, oh, drop it gently by degrees   70
    (The joy is mighty; she a sad, weak virgin)
    That I shall live to make her queen.   *Exit Ernesto.*
    Stay you, and if I play too much the wanton with
    My fate or swell with expectation,
    Speak something to allay my hopes and say   75
    There may be crosses yet. The queen may want
    Faith or consent, or, put case, the people
    (A dangerous torrent to oppose) like not
    This innovation: where is the king then?
LEANDRO Doubt not their loves. You had their hearts before.   80
    Let nothing shake you.
FERDINAND   Th'art my better angel.
    Why then, if my Rosania will be queen,
    The kingdom's ours again.

          Enter ROSANIA, ERNESTO, [*and*] RODRIGUEZ.

                    – She comes, she comes.
    Thou make'st too little haste to be a queen.
    I am myself again. My name is found.   85
    I shall live too, thus [*Embracing Rosania*] to embrace Rosania

---

66 **wait** that wait.

66–7 **she…Rosania** Rodriguez may need to be reminded of who Rosania is, since for most of the play he has known her only as Tiberio.

70 **drop…degrees** inform her of the truth bit by bit, rather than telling her everything all at once. The fear is that too much intense emotion may overwhelm Rosania.

73–4 **if…expectation** if I become over-confident or excessively hopeful.

74 **expectation** Pronounced as five syllables.

76 **crosses** obstacles.

77 **put case** suppose the case to be that.

79 **innovation** new development.

81 **better angel** guardian angel.

62 **SH**] *this edn; Rod:Er.* O   67 **SD**] O *subst. (Exit Rodrig.)*
83 **SD**] *this edition; Enter Rosania, Ernesto, Rodriguez. after* shake you. O   86 **SD**] *this edn; not in* O

237

5.2   THE COMPLETE WORKS OF JAMES SHIRLEY, VOLUME 7

Without a fear. These lords are all thy subjects.
I am a king.

LEANDRO   You are.

FERDINAND   Then what must my
Rosania be?

ROSANIA   Happy, if this be more
Than dream. My tears and sufferings are all paid for   90
If this be true.

LEANDRO   Most true.

ROSANIA   What a strong arm
Hath heaven.

FERDINAND   See how the day hath made
Haste to salute Rosania, and to wait
Upon thy triumph blushes like a maid
When she is told she is in love. The stars   95
Are gone to tell the other world thy beauty,
Till now eclipsed with sorrow, hath thrown off
The imprisoning veil and shines above their brightness.
But how shall we, Leandro, now contrive
For our court entertainment where the queen's   100
Prepared to hear our tragedy?

LEANDRO   Leave me
To order your appearance – but first, sir,
We must secure this fort.

ERNESTO   The Captain is
My creature.

FERDINAND   Thou shalt be all our direction.
Come, my Rosania. Time hath turned again   105
Our glass and his keen scythe this comfort brings:
It cuts no sceptres down but to make kings.   *Exeunt.*

---

94 **blushes** i.e. the day blushes. Ferdinand is referring to the pinkness of the dawn light.

99–101 **how…tragedy?** The sense here is: 'How shall we arrange our acceptance into the court, given that the queen is awaiting our execution?' Ferdinand is punning on the two senses of 'entertainment'—a diverting or amusing activity or performance; reception or welcome by a host (*OED*, *n.* 10b; †5).

103 **fort** fortress, the city's main defensive structure, in which the prison is located.

104 **creature** servant; minion.

104 **Thou…direction** You will guide us in all things. Ferdinand is using the royal 'we'.

105–6 **Time…glass** Ferdinand refers to the traditional image of Father Time as a figure holding an hour-glass full of sand, which signifies the passage of human lives. Ferdinand and Rosania's lives seemed to be coming to an end, but now they have been reprieved from death and so the hourglass has been turned over.

106–7 **his keen…kings** The figure of Time is frequently conflated with that of Death, and so is also traditionally pictured with a scythe. Here, Ferdinand takes a cheerful view of the inevitable death of kings, as he points out that no ruler ever falls except to make way for another.

---

106 scythe] O *subst.* (sith)

238

THE DOUBTFUL HEIR 5.3

[5.3]

Enter LEONARIO, *reading a letter, and* SOLDIER.

LEONARIO So near?

SOLDIER   We heard before of your affront,
  My lord, and were prepared.

LEONARIO   It hath outstripped
  My expectation. These letters say
  Mendoza is their general, new returned
  With victory from the Moors. His fame I honour.   5
  My knowledge never reached his person.

SOLDIER   Sir,
  He brings old soldiers with him. The commanders
  Are such whose faith and valour in those wars
  Already tried, he durst name to the king
  To be employed here in your highness' cause.   10

LEONARIO We will to horse immediately. I long
  To salute the army.

SOLDIER   Which but wants your person,
  The soul of their design. You may soon reach 'em.

    Enter CAPTAIN.

LEONARIO I will.

CAPTAIN Your grace.   15

LEONARIO That we had wings! Away, to horse, to horse.

                    Exeunt Leonario [*and*] *Soldier.*

CAPTAIN Speed, an you be so hot o'th'spur! My business is but breath, and your
  design, it seems, rides post.

    Enter [FIRST CITIZEN] *and* [SECOND CITIZEN]. [*Captain remains apart.*]

---

  0 The scene is set outside, near the palace.

  3 expectation Pronounced as five syllables.

  5 Moors Between the eighth and fifteenth centuries CE, the Spanish Christians had waged a series of wars against the Moors—a loosely defined race of Muslim people who originally came from Northern Africa and the surrounding areas—in an attempt to drive them out of Spain. The Christians finally succeeded in bringing all of the Iberian Peninsula under Christian rule in 1492.

  6 My…person I've never met him in person.

  17 Speed…spur I hope you achieve your aim, given how forceful and energetic you're being (*OED*, Speed *v.* 1a; Hot, *adj.* 'hot on…the spur' †P3).

  17–18 My…post The Captain's business is clearly insubstantial and unimportant ('but breath') in comparison to Leonario's own plans, given how quick the latter is in his departure. The Captain may be punning on the idea that his 'business' is literally only 'breath', as he is employed by Leonario only to speak, to keep him up to date with court events.

  [5.3]] *Gifford subst.* (SCENE III.*); not in* O
  2–3] *lineation Gifford;* It…expectation, / These O   **6–7**] *lineation Gifford;* Sir…Commanders O
  16 SD] *Gifford subst.; Exeunt Leon. Sold.* O
  17–18] *lineation this edition;* business / Is O; *it is not clear whether* O *is set as verse or as prose with a capital at the start of the new line*   **18 SD**] *this edn; Enter* 1 *and* 2 Citizens. *Gifford; Enter Lieutenant and Antient.* O

239

5.3   THE COMPLETE WORKS OF JAMES SHIRLEY, VOLUME 7

The earth runs upon wheels – whom do I spy? My extraordinaries. I'll ha' sport
with them – but first observe them.   20
FIRST CITIZEN I see no profit in these offices that we ha' bought.
SECOND CITIZEN Not extraordinary, as the name did promise.
CAPTAIN [*Aside*] The rogues are poor, and now repent.
SECOND CITIZEN We were told by the cheating Captain that we should want men to
tell our money.   25
FIRST CITIZEN This 'tis to deal with *soldades*.
SECOND CITIZEN We should command the ladies, too, an we were bountiful. A
smallpox take their beauties. 'Tis the greater curse. I have undone myself in giving
away enamelled rings and bracelets.
FIRST CITIZEN Well, if I trust a captain again –   30
SECOND CITIZEN Or I.
CAPTAIN [*Aside*] I'm glad they are paid. I wo'not leave 'em. I feel my antipathy
strong yet.
SECOND CITIZEN I would venture half my soul to be revenged, if I knew how.
CAPTAIN [*Aside*] True rascals!   35
FIRST CITIZEN The ladies love him.
SECOND CITIZEN They all love men of war.
FIRST CITIZEN Would his poop were a-fire.
SECOND CITIZEN – And battles in bed, naturally.
FIRST CITIZEN Well, what ladies give him hereafter to buy new feathers, may his   40
body compel him to bestow upon a surgeon.
SECOND CITIZEN May diseases undermine his flesh like gunpowder and blow all his
skin up into blisters.

---

19 The…wheels The phrase 'the world goes (or runs) on wheels' was proverbial, meaning that events move
quickly. See Dent (1984, W893).

26 soldades Spanish for 'soldiers'. The word *soldado* originates from the Latin *solidus*, a coin: the citizen may
be punning on the idea that the Captain is preoccupied by money.

27 an if.

28 greater curse worse punishment. The Second Citizen implies that the worst thing you could do to hurt
a fashionable court lady is to spoil her beauty.

28 undone myself beggared myself.

29 enamelled i.e. as a cheap alternative to those set with gems.

32 are paid have been suitably punished (*OED*, Pay *v*.¹ 12b).

32–3 I…yet I feel their hostility towards me is still strong.

38 poop highest deck of a ship, located at its rear. The citizen may be using this term to refer wittily to the
Captain's backside.

40 ladies…feathers The Captain apparently has female admirers who give him money to buy things with
which to adorn himself, such as the feathers appropriate to a soldier. See note to 2.2.8.

42 May…gunpowder Undermining a building or encampment using gunpowder was a common siege
method. The attacking force would dig a hollow space under the foundation and then place gunpowder in the
hole to blow it up from below. The Second Citizen fantasizes about the Captain's skin being destroyed in this
way by venereal diseases from within, and 'blown up' into blisters.

19–34] *lineation this edn; in* O *much of this section is set as verse, but it seems to be intended as prose*
21 bought] *Gifford;* brought O   **23 SD]** *this edn; not in* O   **32 SD]** *this edn; not in* O
35 SD] *this edn; not in* O   **42–3]** *lineation Gifford;* Gunpowder, / And O

240

THE DOUBTFUL HEIR   5·3

FIRST CITIZEN May they that look for his nose go about for want of a bridge and
  let him wear no legs but what he buys from the carpenter.   45
SECOND CITIZEN May his face break out and undo him in taffeta and may the
  patches at the last be so many, till his skin be invisible and his goggle eyes look
  through a mask.
FIRST CITIZEN May he live to be as much coward as we ha' been and be beaten.
SECOND CITIZEN Abominably beaten; and may the miracle be on our side, that we   50
  may be valiant and be the men to do it. Oh, I would have no more mercy –
CAPTAIN [*Coming forward*] Save you, gallants. Save you, courtiers.
BOTH My noble Captain!
SECOND CITIZEN [*Aside, to First Citizen*] It may be he did not hear us.
CAPTAIN Hark you, what purchase have you two made lately?   55
BOTH Of what?
CAPTAIN Of lands and loggerheads – lordships, I would say. I know you are both
  rich, you cannot choose. But I will borrow no more o' you. Faith, be satisfied and
  leave off in time with the wealth you have.
FIRST CITIZEN Where is it, Captain?   60
SECOND CITIZEN Can you tell me where we may borrow as much money upon our
  extraordinary places as will set up shop again? For this court trade wo'not do.
CAPTAIN How?
FIRST CITIZEN No indeed, Captain. We ha' made little benefit since we came to be
  extraordinaries.
CAPTAIN Ye took not the right way then.   65
SECOND CITIZEN That may be.
CAPTAIN Why, cannot you lie and swear and pawn your souls for sixpence? The
  devil could not furnish the city with two more hopeful borachios. You have

---

44 for...bridge The venereal disease syphilis destroyed the nasal cartilage. The First Citizen puns on the
word 'bridge', playing on the idea that when a bridge over a river is missing, travellers will need to travel a longer
way around ('go about').

45 let...carpenter He hopes that the Captain will lose his legs and need wooden ones: another possible
result of venereal disease, as late-stage syphilis creates lesions in the bones.

46 undo...taffeta It was the fashion in the seventeenth and eighteenth centuries to hide the sores and scars
from diseases that damaged the skin by attaching small pieces of silk, velvet or taffeta cloth to the face (See
Yarwood 1980, 73). The citizen imagines the Captain having so many sores from venereal disease that the cost
of the taffeta will ruin him financially.

57 loggerheads literally, 'blockheads'. The Captain is ostensibly asking whether the citizens have bought any
lands or aristocratic titles for themselves, but 'accidentally' confuses the words 'loggerheads' and 'lordships'. He
may mean to suggest that all the citizens can actually purchase for themselves is a reputation as fools.

58 choose be otherwise (*OED*, *v.* 5a 'cannot choose' = 'have no alternative').

59 leave...time i.e. retire from your careers at an appropriate moment.

62 as...shop as will allow us to set up shops.

68 borachios drunkards, from the Spanish *borachoe* or *borrach'o*, a bottle made of pigskin, with the hair
inside, dressed with resin and pitch to keep the wine sweet. Possibly also a reference to the character Borachio
in Shakespeare's *Much Ado About Nothing*, who is a drunkard and also a devious and sycophantic rogue.

---

52 SD] *Gifford subst.; not in* O   **54 SD]** *this edn; not in* O
57–9] *lineation this edn;* say, / I know...choose, / But O *(the speech is set partially as verse and partially as prose)*
67–71] *lineation Gifford; in* O, *this speech is set as half prose, half verse. There is also an uncorrected error in* O, *so
that the text runs* 'your / worships face is a prognostication of preferment / Is a Prognostication of preferment,
where / Beside'

THE COMPLETE WORKS OF JAMES SHIRLEY, VOLUME 7

a carrot-coloured beard and that never fails; and your worship's face is a prognos- 70
tication of preferment where, beside dominical letters, you have all the conjuring
characters of the planets. But this is all your cunning to dissemble your estates.

FIRST CITIZEN By this empty pocket, I have but one shirt left.

CAPTAIN You jest, i'faith.

SECOND CITIZEN And by all my no money, I have but half a one.

CAPTAIN Come, come, you took up linen lately – I heard you did. 75

SECOND CITIZEN Ay – smocks.

CAPTAIN Why, they are in fashion with extraordinary courtiers. But if you be in
earnest, I can tell where you may furnish yourselves richly.

BOTH Where? Where?

CAPTAIN Why, in the shops for ready money – but you would save charges? 80

SECOND CITIZEN Aye, marry, Captain.

CAPTAIN Venture to rob a hedge. It is but hanging and what's that to men extraordinary? But if your wants be real, be not dejected. I'll set you up again myself.
I have been beholden to you two for your good words and wishes, gentlemen.

FIRST CITIZEN It pleases you to say so. [*Aside*] I begin to smell – 85

---

69 carrot-coloured beard Red hair and beards were associated both with representations of Judas Iscariot and with the stereotypical stage Jew. In *As You Like It*, Rosalind, speaking of Orlando, says 'His very hair is of the dissembling colour;' whereupon Celia replies, 'Something browner than Judas's' (3.4.6–7). The Captain presumably means that a man who looks so much like a stereotypical Jew cannot fail to be successful with money.

69–70 prognostication...preferment omen or promise of advancement or promotion.

70 dominical letters The letters A to G, used by the church to denote which days of the week were Sundays. This reference is somewhat obscure, but cf. a passage in *Love's Labour's Lost*, in which Rosaline teases Catherine that her face is 'my red dominical...O, that your face were not so full of O's!' (5.2.44–5). Dominical letters were often printed in red in almanacs; Rosaline seems to be saying that Catherine has red spots or scars on her face. This may be the Captain's meaning too.

70–1 conjuring...planets In astrology, the planets were believed to cast various kinds of influence, both negative and positive, over men's lives. The Captain seems to be suggesting that the citizen's face shows how all the planets are casting their influence in his favour. However, he may also be commenting that the spotty or pockmarked face itself looks like a map of the constellation.

71 to...estates to lie about the extent of your wealth.

75 took...linen bought new clothes (*OED*, Take *v.* 'to take up' 6a).

76 smocks loose shift dresses, typically worn by women, so the citizen may be making a bawdy pun, referring to the 'taking up'—i.e. raising—of women's smocks. However, it is possible that this is also a reference to the smock-frocks worn by labourers such as porters: the citizen may be referring to the fact that they can no longer afford fine clothes, only the cheap garments worn by manual workers. Cf. Middleton, *The Family of Love* (1608): 'I am of the bearing trade forsooth, you may see by my Smock—frock I wold say: I am (if it please you) of the spick & span new set vp Company of Porters' (F3r).

80 save charges avoid spending money.

82 rob a hedge steal clothes hung on hedges to dry. Cf. *1 Henry IV*: '[T]hey'll find linen enough on every hedge' (4.2.47–8).

82 It...hanging The penalty is only that of being hanged, with a pun on the fact that the linen is hanging on the hedges waiting to be taken.

85 I...smell The First Citizen's statement is unfinished, but presumably he is about to say that he smells a trick of some kind: he suspects that the Captain's apparent friendliness is not what it seems. 'To smell out' a knave was proverbial: see Dent (1984, SS558).

74] *Gifford adds a second 'left' at the end of this sentence; it is not clear from* O *where the hanging 'left' goes—with line 72 or 74*   **77–88]** *lineation this edition;* O *is set largely as verse but this still seems to be prose*   **85 SD]** *this edn; not in* O

242

THE DOUBTFUL HEIR 5·3

SECOND CITIZEN Not to us, Captain: we have been beholden to you.
CAPTAIN And it happens, as if fortune had made you miserable o' purpose to bless
   you both with such a preferment as wo'not be offered again in a coronation.
FIRST CITIZEN On, good Captain, for we are extraordinary miserable.
CAPTAIN Then observe: you are not ignorant how things go at court? The king is   90
   in prison.
SECOND CITIZEN So.
CAPTAIN And his wench with him, that walked in breeches. The queen resolves
   they shall both die.
SECOND CITIZEN Good.   95
CAPTAIN This morning, too. Now, in regard the king is a person of quality –
FIRST CITIZEN I think he be.
CAPTAIN – And the t'other a lady, as some imagine, you two may do very well to
   undertake now –
BOTH Anything.   100
CAPTAIN – to be a couple of hangmen. D'ye mark? To dispatch the queen's enemies
   in what horrid way her council shall think convenient. You will do service to the
   state and have extraordinary rewards besides the honour and reputation of your
   places. What say? 'Tis my pure love to make this first offer to you.
SECOND CITIZEN Do we look like a couple of hangmen?   105
CAPTAIN No, you ha'not so good a complexion – and now I think on't you sha'not
   live to have that preferment. Come, draw, you that wear your sword like a bum-
   bailey. Do as I bid you, and that quickly.
SECOND CITIZEN It wo'not come out, sir.
CAPTAIN [Drawing his sword] No? This shall in, then.   110
SECOND CITIZEN I will put more strength to't. [The Citizens draw.]

87 **to bless** 'in order that I (or fortune?) am able to bless' is implied.
88 **in . . . coronation** in the period of years for which a monarch rules.
101 **hangmen** Hangmen were traditionally hated in early modern society, and treated as social outcasts. In
Fletcher's *The Woman's Prize or, The Tamer Tamed*, Petruchio shows the extent of his desperation when he
pleads, 'I would do any thing below repentance, / Any base dunhill slavery; be a hang-man, / Ere I would be a
husband' (3.4, p. 113).
107–8 **bum-bailey** a minor sheriff's officer who arrests debtors. The implication is that a bum-bailey, being
so lowly an officer, would be unlikely to be experienced or skilled at combat.
109 **It . . . out** The Second Citizen is presumably wrestling with his sword, trying to remove it from the scab-
bard. This could be either an indication of his ineptitude or else a suggestion that his sword is so little used that
it has rusted.
110 **This . . . then** The Captain threatens the Second Citizen with his own sword if he fails to draw.

87 o' purpose] *Gifford;* A purpose O   93–4] *lineation Gifford;* Breeches; / The O
110 SD] *this edn; Draws his sword. Gifford; not in* O   111 SD] *this edn; They draw. Gifford; not in* O

243

5.3   THE COMPLETE WORKS OF JAMES SHIRLEY, VOLUME 7

CAPTAIN So. Now, d'ye mark – kill one other.

BOTH Kill one another?

CAPTAIN Yes, and do't religiously, with as much alacrity as you would devour an
orphan; and do't handsomely, that you may not be hanged when you are dead.   115
I'll see't done. He that is dull shall have my goad to quicken him.

(They fight.)

So, good! Good again! Well offered! They fight, by these hilts, furiously. Now
could I forgive 'em. So, enough.

FIRST CITIZEN This is very fine sport.

CAPTAIN Necessity has taught 'em the noble science. Come, if all fail you shall   120
fight challenges. There's money and broken pates to be got that way. You can
make legs and gape like gudgeons for benevolence, cut scurvy capers to show
your legs are well when your head bleeds. Farewell. Stay – you want money, I had
forgot. There is twelve pence apiece for you.

BOTH How, Captain? I hope not.   125

CAPTAIN [*Aside*] They are not hearty yet – they think I serve 'em with press-money
again. [*To them*] No, 'tis my pure bounty. Go, set up again and trust soldiers,
without impertinent asking for your debts. They'll pay you.

SECOND CITIZEN As you ha' done.

CAPTAIN I'll hearken how you behave yourselves. Farewell. When you are rich I'll   130
visit you again and borrow money.

FIRST CITIZEN Too much is too much. Hmm.

SECOND CITIZEN Now have I a great mind to fight with your captainship.

FIRST CITIZEN So have I, now my hand's in. Methinks 'tis nothing.

114–15 **devour…orphan** ruin an orphan financially. Cf. Jonson's *Volpone*: 'I turne no moneys, in the pub-
like banke; / Nor vsure priuate. […] nor deuoure / Soft prodigalls' (Bv). Cheating an orphan was held to be a
particularly contemptible act: the Captain implies that the two citizens are used to making money by defrauding
the innocent and helpless. Cf. his attack on them as resembling stereotypical Jewish usurers at 5.3.69.

115 **hanged…dead** The punishment for illegal duelling was to be hanged. The Captain presumably means
that if the citizens fight 'handsomely' enough, both will end up dead and so neither will face hanging.

116 **goad** something that spurs someone along—in this case, the Captain's sword.

117 **by…hilts** Swearing by the hilt—the handle—of your sword or dagger was common. The word is often
used in the plural even if it only refers to one weapon. Cf. Ford's *Tis Pity She's A Whore*: 'fight, or by these Hilts /
I'le kill thee' (B2v).

119 **This…sport** It is not clear whether the citizen is being ironic or sincere at this point. He may have
begun genuinely to enjoy the swordplay, as by 5.3.137–8 both citizens appear enthusiastic about continuing the
fighting.

120–1 **you…challenges** you will take on challengers in paid public fights.

122 **make legs** make an elaborate bow, stretching out one leg in front, as a gesture of deference.

122 **gape…capers** The citizens will humble themselves for the crowds, doing contemptible little dances
and poses for money. Gudgeons were a type of small fish commonly used as bait, although the term seems to
have transferred itself to refer to the kind of fish that were easily caught using bait because they would gape
hungrily for it. Dent gives, among other examples, the anonymous play *Capt. T. Stukeley*: 'Are not these English
like their country fish / Cald gudgeons? That will bite at every bate?' (Dent 1984, G472.11).

126 **hearty** warm and friendly, with the implication of being trusting.

---

126 SD] *this edn; not in* O   127 SD] *Gifford marks end of the aside with a dash; not in* O
130 yourselves] *Gifford;* you selves O   134 in.] *this edn;* in; *Gifford;* in, O

244

THE DOUBTFUL HEIR

5.4

CAPTAIN You are not desperate? 135

SECOND CITIZEN We are a little better. As good be hanged for killing of you, Captain, as live after the rate of our disgrace. I am resolved.

CAPTAIN Two mastiffs at once may worry me. I am put to't.

[The Citizens] fight [the Captain].

Must we have t'other bout?

SECOND CITIZEN This is enough at once. We may come to't in time. 140

CAPTAIN Why, now I love you – love you as well as you do law.

SECOND CITIZEN Upon good terms, we love you too.

CAPTAIN Let's shake hands. You sha'not to your vomit again. Now you dare fight, I'll tell you a hundred ways to get moneys. Come, we'll drink and divide fortunes. Run not back into cows again. 145

SECOND CITIZEN I'll be ancient now again.

FIRST CITIZEN And I lieutenant.

CAPTAIN Both my own boys.

SECOND CITIZEN 'Tis not so hard to fight, I see, if a man be but desperate and give his mind to't. 150

FIRST CITIZEN Pox o' cowards! Come, Captain.

CAPTAIN Let me hug ye, my brace of myrmidons, and drink a tun of wine to this conversion. *Exeunt.*

[5.4]

Enter QUEEN [OLIVIA *and*] VIOLINDA.

OLIVIA The prince so early met upon the way
This morning, sayest? And with a soldier?

VIOLINDA And in that haste, too, madam, I was told
The speed of wings was slow. Their fiery horse

---

135 **desperate** at the end of all other resources, reckless or violent.
136 **We...better** i.e. We are not quite desperate.
137 **live...disgrace** continue to live in the manner in which we have been disgraced.
138 **worry** attack; distress (*OED*, *v.* 5a; 6a).
138 **put to't** challenged; hard pressed.
140 **enough...once** enough for now.
141 **I...law** This is presumably a reference to the citizens' repeated claims earlier in the play that they have the law on their side in their financial dealings with the Captain.
143 **sha'not...vomit** Cf. the note to 2.2.58–9.
145 **Run...cows** The Captain urges the citizens to keep their new-found aggression, punning on the contemporary belief that the word 'coward' derived from 'cow-herd'.
151 **Pox** Curse.
152 **myrmidons** In Greek mythology, Achilles' band of fierce and loyal warriors.
152 **tun** large barrel.
0 The scene is set in the palace throne room.
3–4 **And...slow** In such hasty speed that in comparison flying would be considered slow.
4 **horse** horses.

---

138 SD] *this edn; They fight.* O

[5.4]] *Gifford subst. (*SCENE IV.*); not in* O
0 SD QUEEN OLIVIA *and*] *this edn;* OLIVIA *and Gifford; Queen* O

245

5.4   THE COMPLETE WORKS OF JAMES SHIRLEY, VOLUME 7

Bathing in foam yet fled as if they meant   5
To leave the wind and clouds behind 'em.
OLIVIA   Strange!
I could have wished him with less discontent
To have left us, but my stubborn fate designed it.
Having thus snatched away himself, it will
Become us to compose and make the best   10
Of our state game. I sent a messenger
With our command to th'governor of the fort
He should attend the king by the water gate
Leads to the garden. We do purpose conference.
If Ferdinand wisely consent to break   15
The magic that so chains his heart to that
Idol Rosania, we'll be reconciled,
And peace shall marry once again our hearts.
Methinks our lords are cold in their attendance.
Where be our train of ladies? – Nay, permit 'em.   20
A solitude becomes this sullen day
And our own thoughts. Methinks thou dost not look
With thy own face upon me.
VIOLINDA   Not I, madam.
OLIVIA My eyes have lost their virtue. All I look on
Have not the shape and colour they presented.   25
What whisper's that? Ha?
VIOLINDA   Here was none, madam.
OLIVIA I could be jealous of the wind, methinks,
And quarrel with the postures of those very
Shapes i'th'arras. Fie, Olivia, call home thy reason.

        Enter COURTIER.

5 yet nevertheless (*OED*, conjunctive *adv.* 9a).
8 designed it destined it to happen (*OED*, Design *v.* 9a).
10 compose 'ourselves' implied.
11 state game contest or intrigue for control of the state (*OED*, Game *n.* 6a, 7a).
13 water gate gate that provides access to or from a body of water.
19 cold negligent, unenthusiastic (*OED*, *adj.* 7a).
20 permit 'em leave them be.
21–2 A...thoughts Cf. Ernesto's prediction at 5.2.52 that the queen must instinctively sense that her position is under threat.
24 virtue efficacy.
24 All...on All the things that I look on.
25 presented originally appeared to have. '*Formerly* presented' is implied.
29 Shapes i'th'arras Pictures embroidered on the wall-hangings.

29 SD] *Gifford; after l. 18 in* O

THE DOUBTFUL HEIR   5·4

COURTIER Oh, madam!   30
OLIVIA What horror's in that voice? I see a treason
    In's looks.
COURTIER   Oh, madam, I beseech your pardon.
OLIVIA Why? Art a traitor?
COURTIER Not I, but there are practices, I fear,
    Against your royal person. The court gates   35
    Are shut. All's in confusion within,
    And I could hear abroad loud acclamations
    And triumph for the king, as he were new proclaimed.

        Enter CAPTAIN.

OLIVIA Which way comest thou?
CAPTAIN Over the wall, madam. The gates are shut.   40
    I'll tell you news: young Ferdinand, your husband,
    Is in all state attended and proclaimed
    King in his own right. He is proved to be
    What he did first pretend himself. Leandro
    And all the lords confirm't. The governor   45
    Hath given him up the fort, the wise city
    Her keys, and every officer on's knees
    Is praying and drinking the king's health.
OLIVIA Away and let thy face be seen no more
    But when the fatal noise of fire, some blood,   50
    Or burial calls thee forth!
CAPTAIN   This my reward
    For bringing news the king's alive? Take heed;
    Do not talk treason in your own defence. – Hark.

        Enter, in state, RODRIGUEZ, ERNESTO, LEANDRO, FERDINAND
        (who takes the throne), [*and*] ATTENDANTS.

OLIVIA From what an expectation am I fall'n!
ALL Long live Ferdinand king!   55
FERDINAND We thank you and will study to be worth
    Your prayers and duty. Madam, the chancellor
    Can clear and bring your faith to allow the wonder.

---

36 confusion Pronounced as four syllables.

53 Do…defence Olivia angrily dismisses the Captain, but he reprimands her: it is treasonous to show so little appreciation for the news that the true king is alive, even though she is doing it out of self-defence, in her wish to preserve her own status.

53 SD *in state* This implies entering 'in a procession with pomp and solemnity' (Dessen 1999, 215).

54 an expectation high hopes (*OED*, Expectation *n.* 1b).

58 allow accept.

58 wonder amazing event.

---

53 SD *and*] *this edn; not in* O   **55 SH**] *this edn; Omnes.* O

247

5.4   THE COMPLETE WORKS OF JAMES SHIRLEY, VOLUME 7

We are no impostor now nor need we borrow
A beam from you to make us shine, yet still   60
You are our cousin, fair Olivia.

     Enter ROSANIA *and* LADIES.

The 'husband' was a title long since due
To my Rosania. May it prosper here.
Our love and years grew up together, and
Our souls by holy contract tied when in   65
Alfonso's house – her father, and my guardian
(To whose trust I was sent an infant by Leandro) –
We plighted faith. It is no blemish
To fair Olivia still to be a virgin.
Though she have lost the queen, she is a princess   70
And hath now found a kinsman that shall study
What shall become his love, her blood and honour.
Upon your lip I print this fair assurance. [*Kisses her.*]

ROSANIA   And mine shall be to do you service, madam.

OLIVIA   If this be true, you must command my duty.   75

FERDINAND   We hear Prince Leonario is departed.

When he shall know the progress of our fortunes
He'll quit his stars, that hid their golden heads
To mock him with a small eclipse o' purpose
To light him with more glory to his happiness. (*Soft alarm* [*sounds.*])   80
Ha? What clamour's that? [*Alarm gets louder.*] The frightful noise increases.

     Enter GUARD.

GUARD   Fly and save yourselves! The fort's surprised by the Prince of Aragon,
whose troops have seized the city, reeling with wine and careless of their strength
in their joys for you, sir.

62–3 **The…Rosania** Ferdinand means that while Olivia will only get to call him 'cousin' from now on, he
will have the title of 'husband' to Rosania. However, the ambiguity of the phrasing suggests another possibility:
that Rosania herself should be called a husband. This may be a glance back at the fact that Olivia previously
wooed Rosania as a 'husband' when the latter was in disguise as Tiberio.

70 **the queen** the title of queen.

78–80 **He'll…happiness** He'll pardon his stars for his harsh view of them: they appeared to abandon him,
but they only did so temporarily in order to shine more brightly on his eventual triumph. The implication is that
Leonario will now be able to marry Olivia and have the happiness he hoped for all along.

80 SD **alarm** A sound from offstage—usually a drum but occasionally a trumpet or other instrument—
indicating a call to arms.

83–4 **city…sir** The citizens, drunkenly celebrating Ferdinand's accession, are in no fit state to defend their
city.

---

66 Alfonso's] O *subst. (Alfonzo's)*   73 SD] *this edn; Kisses Oliv. Gifford; not in* O
80 SD *this edn; Soft Alarum* O   81 SD1] *this edn; not in* O   81 SD2] *this edn; Enter first Guard.* O
82–4] *lineation this edn;* surpris'd / By…seiz'd the / City O; *it is not clear whether* O *is set as verse or as prose
with capitals at the start of some lines*

248

THE DOUBTFUL HEIR   5.4

FERDINAND The Prince of Aragon? The fates cannot   85
  Be so unjust, so envious of our blessing,
  To snatch it from us in a minute. Ha?
VOICES FROM WITHIN Help! Help! Quarter!
FERDINAND They are i'th'court already.
LEANDRO   We are all undone.
  Let's yield and ask conditions honourable.   90
FERDINAND Die he that dares but think so! Yield? No, Ferdinand
  Was here too late a prisoner. Let us sell
  Our lives at glorious rates. The evening puts
  A mask upon the horror. Follow me.   *Exit.*
LEANDRO – To certain death. Ladies, stay you. The danger   95
  Will meet us here too soon, and yet your persons
  In honour challenge safety.   *Exeunt lords [and Captain].*
OLIVIA Is there no end of my distractions?
  Or hath my folly yet deserved more vengeance?
ROSANIA It cannot be heaven will so soon destroy   100
  The blessing it bestowed. If thus you punish
  Whom you advance, who will believe your gifts
  Are more than flattery to betray our peace?

    Enter LEONARIO, ALFONSO [*in disguise as General Mendoza*], FERDINAND
    ([*as a*] *prisoner*), RODRIGUEZ, ERNESTO, [*and*] SOLDIERS.

LEONARIO This lady is my prize.
OLIVIA   How, sir? Your prize?
LEONARIO Mistake me not. There's no dishonour meant   105
  Your person, yet I boldly may pronounce
  You are and must be mine. I am not ignorant
  You are a virgin, all but name. Be wise
  As you are fair, and I forget what's past
  And take this satisfaction. If I meet   110
  Contempt, where I with honour once more court you,
  You will create a flame shall never die
  But in the kingdom's ashes. You were mine

---

88 Quarter Mercy.

93–4 The…horror Presumably referring to the fact that darkness is falling, which makes it harder to see the horrors of the attack (and, by implication, makes them less horrifying).

96–7 your…safety your gender and title will guarantee your safety (even if the enemy does penetrate the palace).

98 distractions sources of disorder or confusion. Pronounced as four syllables.

101–3 If…peace If heaven grants happiness only to snatch it away again, people will stop believing that its gifts are anything more than tricks.

109 I forget I will forget.

---

88 SH] *this edn; Within. Gifford; Divers within cry.* O. *In* O *this is set as a stage direction at the end of the line, rather than as a speech heading, which makes it appear as if* 'Help, help, quarter.' *(O) should be spoken by Ferdinand*
97 SD] *this edn; Exeunt Lords. Gifford; Ex. Lords.* O
103 SD] *this edn; Enter Leonario, Alfonso, Ferdinand, (Prisoner,) Rodriguez, Ernesto, Souldiers.* O

249

5.4   THE COMPLETE WORKS OF JAMES SHIRLEY, VOLUME 7

First by your own election, sealed above.
If I must lose what heaven bestowed upon me   115
The quarrel is not mine
But virtue's, whose right hand is armed with justice.

     Enter CAPTAIN [*behind*].

Punish not where you owe your heart, but let
Both our revenges meet in that impostor. [*Olivia approaches him.*]
I find your noble soul returns. Lord General,   120
While I retire with this fair queen – whom not
One violent accent shall affright, much less
A rude attempt – take hence that counterfeit
And cut his head off.
ROSANIA   Oh, my dearest lord.
LEONARIO The rest may, if they please, find mercy.   125
CAPTAIN [*Aside*] I were best be o' this side.
LEONARIO Away with him.
FERDINAND   Insulting prince, thou darest not.
LEONARIO How sir, dare not?
FERDINAND   I said it, thy better,
Being a king in my own right, without
Her charity, proclaimed and justified,   130
By birth a prince.
LEANDRO   All this is truth, sir.
LEONARIO You must not cozen thus my faith. Away!
Cut off his head.
ALFONSO   Dispatch you with the queen.
Let me alone to make his head secure.
LEANDRO Nay, take mine too. I'll wait on him in death.   135
It shall begin my service.
ROSANIA   Cruel prince.
OLIVIA What fate must I obey?
ROSANIA   My death will add
Some lines unto thy bloody chronicle.
Pray, let us die together.
LEONARIO   You shall speak
Her sentence, madam.

---

114 **election** choice.
114 **sealed above** ratified by heaven.
117 **SD** The Captain re-enters at this point but does not speak for some lines: he is presumably hanging back
and eavesdropping, to discover which way the political wind is blowing before he chooses a side.
118 **Punish...heart** Don't try to punish me, the man to whom you owe your heart.
118–19 **let...impostor** i.e. let both of us relieve our anger by punishing Ferdinand.

---

117 SD *behind*] *this edn; not in* O   119 SD] *this edn; not in* O   120 returns] *this edn;* return O
126 SD] *this edn; not in* O   128–30] *lineation this edition;* it, / Thy...right, / Without...justified O
137–40] *lineation Gifford;* My...lines / Unto...together. / *Leon.* You...Madam O

250

THE DOUBTFUL HEIR   5.4

OLIVIA   She must live, then.   140
LEONARIO To all we offer mercy but to
    Ferdinand. His doom is fixed. Come, madam.
OLIVIA Whither, sir?
LEONARIO   I know the way to your chapel.
    He that loves us make haste and bring the priest.
CAPTAIN That's I. I know her chaplains. They are my friends and all good fellows.   145
                            Exit [Captain, with Leonario and Olivia].
FERDINAND Pray, can you tell me where, or what, I am,
    Or what I must do next?
ALFONSO   Yes: you must die.
FERDINAND Let not that grieve you, gentlemen. 'Tis nothing
    To part with life, and if but my Rosania   150
    Would not weep methinks I could shake off this dust
    And leap to immortality without a guide,
    And in that cheerful flight prepare the blessed
    With so much praise and wonder of thy virtue
    They shall be more in love with thee than I,   155
    And double all their prayers to bring thee to 'em.
ROSANIA No, we will die together.
ALFONSO   You shall.
FERDINAND   How?
ALFONSO Both live and love, and bless my age the witness.
    D'ye know me? [*Pulls off his false beard.*]
ROSANIA   Father?
FERDINAND   Guardian!
LEANDRO Alfonso, my noble kinsman!
ALFONSO   How joys   160
    Flow in my heart to see this constancy.
FERDINAND How came you to be his?
ALFONSO   I have deceived
    The prince. Our forces are Valencia's,
    Not Aragon's, which he by letters sent for

---

153 the blessed the saints in heaven.
156 double...to'em Catholics and some Protestants believed that saints in heaven could intercede with God for a person's soul. Ferdinand says that the saints, impressed by Rosania's virtue, will work to ensure that she is brought to heaven after her death.
158 bless...witness bless the fact that I have lived long enough to see this.
159 SD The fact that Alfonso's disguise consists of a false beard is made clear in 5.4.180, where he shows the beard to Leonario.
162 his i.e. fighting on behalf of Leonario.

143–6] *lineation this edn;* I...us / Make...Priest. / *Capt.* That's...know / Her O
145 SD] *this edn; Exit.* O   **150–2]** *lineation this edn;* To...weep / Methinks...leap / To O
159 SD] *Gifford subst.; not in* O   **160–1]** *lineation this edition;* How...constancy! O
162–3] *lineation Gifford;* I...Valentia's O   **163** Valencia's] O *subst. throughout (Valentia's)*

251

5.4   THE COMPLETE WORKS OF JAMES SHIRLEY, VOLUME 7

In his revenge – but we met the intelligence   165
And arrived sooner, to pretend ourselves
The army he expected. You shall know more hereafter.
FERDINAND I want a knowledge where to begin my gratitude.
The joys you bring are mighty and overcome us.
Oh, my Rosania.   170
ROSANIA   This was beyond hope.

     Enter CAPTAIN.

CAPTAIN So, so. 'Tis done – he has mumbled up the ceremony.
A compendious priest may do much in few words.
They are fast enough. The queen was wise to take him.
[*To Ferdinand*] You are only like to be a loser, sir.
– They come.   175

     Enter LEONARIO [*and* OLIVIA].

ALFONSO All joys to the Prince of Aragon and the fair Olivia.
LEONARIO Why not 'the queen Olivia'?
ALFONSO Not while this gentleman's head is on, believe it.
LEONARIO Where is Mendoza?
ALFONSO   Hid within this bush. [*Shows the false beard.*]
But here's Alfonso, general of the army   180
Sent from Valencia to assist King Ferdinand
To his native right.
LEONARIO   Valencia?
ALFONSO My master, having failed in his first aids
To Ferdinand, intended not sit down
With so much loss, but raised another army   185
Which in our march consulted our security
By interception of all passages.
Your messenger by a party was surprised.
Him, stubborn to discover what he was,
Imperfect in his answer, we interpreted   190
Some spy and, searching, found your letters fraught

---

165 **met...intelligence** discovered the information.
168 **I...where** I don't know how.
171 **mumbled up** thrown together roughly and quickly (*OED*, Mumble *v.* †4).
172 **compendious priest** priest who is able to be pithy and succinct.
173 **fast** securely attached, i.e. married.
174 **You...sir** You are likely to be the only one who loses out.
184 **intended...down** did not intend to give up.
186 **consulted** took into consideration (*OED*, Consult *v.* 5a).
187 **passages** communications passing to and fro (*OED*, Passage *n.* 16).
189 **stubborn...discover** refusing to reveal.

---

174 SD] *this edn; Gifford indicates the change in addressee with a dash; not in* O
174–5] *lineation this edition;* You...come. O   175 SD *and* OLIVIA] *Gifford subst.;* Queen O
179 SD] *Gifford subst.; not in* O

252

THE DOUBTFUL HEIR   5.4

With mischief and revenge. These sent to our king,
We had command to hasten our design
And steer our course by sea to Cartagena.
How, after we arrived, we gained your faith   195
And purposes, your highness knows.
LEONARIO   Betrayed?
ALFONSO Sir, be a prince and just to your own honour,
    And, having perfected your fair desires
    With her, we hope you will account yourself
    Most happy that you missed a power to serve   200
    Further revenge upon a lawful prince.
    My soldiers will obey me now, although
    To help your marriage I appeared no friend
    To Ferdinand.
LEONARIO   – Who was the prince preserved
    By me and sent an infant to this lord,   205
    My noble kinsman.
ALFONSO   Him I bred till time
    And strength might arm him to return and claim
    His own.
LEONARIO Leandro denied this before.
LEANDRO To my dishonour. 'Twas a coward fear
    To lose myself unprofitably.   210
LEONARIO I apprehend with wonder.
FERDINAND If you repent not love and our alliance,
    She shall be worth your best embrace, and we,
    Forgetful of your passion, entertain you
    With all affection to our blood.   215
LEONARIO   I meet it
    And, satisfied in this story, joy I was
    Prevented. I congratulate your stars, sir.
    Nor is this treasure of less price to me
    Than when her temples were enchased with empire.

194 **Cartagena** a city and major naval port in the region of Murcia, in the southeast of the Iberian Peninsula.
209–10 **'Twas...unprofitably** It was the result of cowardly fear, which led me to err without creating any benefit (*OED*, Lose *v.*¹ 10a: 'To lose one's way, go astray. Also *figurative.*').
214 **passion** fit of anger, violent outburst.
214 **entertain** accept, welcome.
215 **I...it** I respond in kind to your affection.
218 **this treasure** Olivia.
219 **enchased** 1) ornamented; 2) enclosed or surrounded by (*OED*, Enchase *v.*² 1; †7). Leonario is making a reference to the crown or coronet worn by the king or queen to represent his or her status.

194 Cartagena] O *subst. (Carthagena)*

253

5.4 THE COMPLETE WORKS OF JAMES SHIRLEY, VOLUME 7

OLIVIA This love will give my soul another form.   220
FERDINAND Our story hath been full of change, but love
    Hath met a glorious victory and tied
    Our souls together with most firm embraces.
    My Lord Leandro, you shall to Valencia
    With our best thanks and greeting to the king.   225
    His army's charge is ours, beside what else
    We owe his royal bounty. Once more, welcome,
    Alfonso, now my father. Witness I
    Preserve my faith to my Rosania.
    I hear the priest call us to other rites.   230
    His altar doth expect another pair.
    Make haste to light his tapers with thine eyes
    And make our hearts each other's sacrifice.   *Exeunt omnes.*

THE END

---

226 **charge...ours** expenses will be paid by us.

233 THE END] Q *subst. (FINIS)*

THE DOUBTFUL HEIR

EPILOGUE, [SPOKEN BY THE] CAPTAIN

Gentlemen,
I am no epilogue. I come to pray
You'd tell me your opinion of the play.
Is the plot current? May we trust the wit
Without a say-master to authorise it? 5
Are the lines sterling? Do they hold conceit,
And every piece, with your allowance, weight,
That when you come abroad you'll not report
You are sorry to have given white money for't?
So, so – I know your meaning. Now pray tell 10
How did the action please ye? Was it well?
How did King Stephen do, and t'other prince?
Enough, enough – I apprehend, and since
I am at questions w'ye, tell me, faith,
How do you like the Captain? Ha? He saith – 15
I'll tell you, you're my friends – none here, he knows
(I mean you o'the gentry, t'whom he owes
No money) will enter a false action.
And let the rest look to't: if there be one
Among his city creditors that dares, 20
He hath vowed to press and send him to the wars.

THE END

4 **current** fashionable, modern, but also with the sense 'genuine, authentic', as opposed to being counterfeit (*OED, adj.* 7; †5).

5 **say-master** assay-master. The head of an assay-house: an officer appointed to assess the value of coin, gold, and silver plate, etc. The Captain continues the idea of wit being weighed up and assessed like precious metal.

6 **sterling** good quality. The Captain puns again on the idea that wit is like money (*OED, n.* 3: 'Genuine English money'; *adj.* 4: 'Thoroughly excellent, capable of standing every test').

9 **white money** silver coins.

12 **King Stephen** Reference to the actor Stephen Hammerton, who played Ferdinand in the London production. See Bentley (1941–68, 2.461).

18 **a...action** an unjust lawsuit.

0] *Gifford;* Epilogue, Captain. O; *Epilogue to the same play there* [*i.e. the Globe*]. *Poems*
2–3] O *subst.;* I am come again, what say? / Pray tell me your opinion of the Play. *Poems*
5 authorise] O *subst. (autorise)* 8 you come] O; 'tis chang'd *Poems*
11 please ye?] *Gifford; please ye,* O; please? Ha? *Poems*
13 Enough, enough -] O *subst.;* --Not a word more; *Poems*
16 you're] O *subst; y'are;* all *Poems* 22 THE END] Q *subst. (FINIS.)*

255

The Gentleman of Venice

EDITED BY
Lucy Munro

THE
GENTLEMAN
OF
VENICE

A

Tragi-Comedie

Prefented at the Private houfe in
Salisbury Court by her
Majefties Servants.

Written by
JAMES SHIRLEY.

LONDON,
Printed for *Humphrey Moseley* and are to be
fold at his Shop at the *Princes Armes* in St.
Pauls Church-yard. 1655.

3. *The Gentleman of Venice*, octavo title-page (1655), Library of St Catharine's College, Cambridge, Z.50.

General Introduction

The Gentleman of Venice is one of Shirley's less celebrated plays: it has a very limited stage history and has received remarkably little attention from scholars. Even one of its most supportive readers, Arthur Huntington Nason, bewails the 'repulsiveness' of one of its two interwoven plots and judges it 'most unfortunate' that it should be attached to the other, more decorous, narrative (1915, 306, 307). Yet *The Gentleman of Venice* is more than a dusty or scurrilous curio. It explores obsession, sexuality, social status, and inheritance through a potent combination of theatrical modes, and it offers some provocative contexts for thinking about performance and publication in the mid-seventeenth century. It is linked with two performance venues, the Werburgh Street playhouse in Dublin and the Salisbury Court playhouse in London, and—as I explore at greater length in the Textual Introduction—it was printed in two formats, octavo and quarto, apparently in order to enable readers to engage with it in different ways.

The play's first plot, which so distressed Nason, features Cornari, a Venetian gentleman, who despairs because he is unable to father a child with his wife, Claudiana. Faced with the prospect of his dissolute nephew Malipiero inheriting his fortune, he plots to have another man, the oddly-named English gentleman, Florelli, father his child for him. The second plot presents two young men: Thomazo, the disappointingly mediocre son of the Duke of Venice, and Giovanni, the surprisingly heroic son of the Duke's head gardener. It eventually transpires that Thomazo is really the son of the gardener and Giovanni the son of the Duke, and Giovanni's new status makes him worthy of marriage to the Duke's niece, Bellaura.

DATE AND AUSPICES

A number of uncertainties surround the composition of *The Gentleman of Venice*. In the late eighteenth century, the theatre historian Edmond Malone compiled a list of '[s]uch of the plays of Shirley as were registered by Sir Henry Herbert' for performance in London, which includes '*The Gentleman of Venise*, 30 Octob. 1639' (1790, 228–9). Herbert was awarded the office of the Master of the Revels in 1623 and served as the official theatrical censor throughout the Caroline period; Malone had apparently gleaned this information from Herbert's now-lost office-book (see Bawcutt 1996, 16–17). When *The Gentleman of Venice* was printed in 1655, its title page claimed that it had been 'Presented at the Private house in / *Salisbury* Court by her / Majesties Servants'. An attribution to this company and playhouse would fit a performance in 1639. Until 1636, Queen Henrietta Maria's Men operated at the Cockpit playhouse, where Shirley was their main playwright, but they lost their theatre during a severe outbreak of plague. By the time the playhouses reopened on 2 October 1637, the Cockpit had been taken over by a new company, Beeston's Boys, and Queen Henrietta Maria's Men had been reconstituted at Salisbury Court (Bentley 1941–68, 1.236–41). The new company included some of the actors from the earlier Queen Henrietta Maria's Men, such as Richard Perkins, Anthony Turner, William Sherlock, and William Wilbraham, and it is not unlikely that Shirley would have given them *The Gentleman of Venice* and *The Politician*, which is also ascribed to them on its 1655 title page.

Queen Henrietta Maria's Men may not, however, have been the first company to perform *The Gentleman of Venice*. Shirley left England for Ireland in November 1636 (Stevenson 1944, 19–22); he may have visited London in spring 1637 and spring 1638, but he appears otherwise to have remained in Dublin until around April 1640 (Stevenson 1944; Stevenson 1946). Malone lists *The Gentleman of Venice* between two plays that were first performed at the Werburgh Street playhouse in Dublin: *The Royal Master*, entered in the Stationers' Register on 13 March 1638 and licensed by Herbert for London performance on 23 April 1638, and *Rosania*, licensed for performance in London as *The Doubtful Heir* on 1 June 1640. Moreover, G. E. Bentley notes that *The Gentleman of Venice* and *The Royal Master* are the only Shirley plays known to have been licensed in London in 1636–9 (1941–68, 5.1113). It is therefore not unlikely that *The Gentleman of Venice* was written for performance at Werburgh Street, as Wilson F. Engel (1976, ix–xiii) and Justine Williams (2010, 219–21) have argued.

SOURCE MATERIALS

The search for the texts on which Shirley drew when composing *The Gentleman of Venice* has a long history. In the late seventeenth century, Gerard Langbaine wrote that 'the Intrigue between *Florelli*, *Cornari*, and *Claudiana*, is borrowed (as I suppose) from a Novel out of *Gayton's Festivous* Notes on *Don Quixote:* see Book 4. Chap. 6, 7, 8' (1691, 479). Unfortunately, Gayton's sprawling, theatrically allusive response to Cervantes was not published until 1654, before the publication of *The Gentleman of Venice* in 1655 but long after its first performance in the 1630s. A century later, Charles Dibdin stated that Shirley's source was *Don Quixote* itself, perhaps having in mind the 'Curious Impertinent' sequence, on which Gayton draws in the *Festivous Notes* (1800, 4.46; see Forsythe 1914, 231). The 'Curious Impertinent' features a husband, Anselmo, who attempts to test the chastity of his wife, Camila, by setting her up with his friend Lothario. The plot is adapted in other early modern plays (Clark 2002), but it does not appear to have exercised much influence on *The Gentleman of Venice*. Although Cornari and Anselmo both set up their wives with other men, Cornari's actions are not propelled by a desire to test his wife but by his conviction that he is infertile, and he has no pre-existing relationship with Florelli.

Although Shirley is unlikely to have drawn directly on Cervantes, he appears to have used another Spanish source. His use of untranslated plays such as Tirso de Molina's *El castigo del penséque* (a source for *The Opportunity*) and Lope de Vega's *Don Lope de Cardona* (a source for *The Young Admiral*) strongly suggests that he read Spanish, and

THE GENTLEMAN OF VENICE: GENERAL INTRODUCTION

scholars therefore looked into the vast canon of untranslated Spanish plays for a possible source for *The Gentleman of Venice*. As long ago as 1914, Robert S. Forsythe noted the similarity between the plot of Lope's *El hombre por su palabra*, printed in Madrid in 1625, and the narrative involving Bellaura and Giovanni (1914, 231). Forsythe drew on a German summary of Lope's plot by Wolfgang von Wurzbach (1899, 222–3) and he was unable to assess the connections between *El hombre por su palabra* and *The Gentleman of Venice* himself. However, in the late 1990s, this idea was finally investigated fully by Luciano García García (1998, 275–99). Comparing the narratives of *El hombre por su palabra* and *The Gentleman of Venice*, and examining a series of close textual interactions between the plays, García concludes that '*The Gentleman of Venice* está atravesada por un número tan considerable de coincidencias textuales con *El hombre por su palabra*, que es razonable pensar en una relación hipotextual entre ambas obras' ('*The Gentleman of Venice* is traversed by such a considerable number of textual correspondences with *El hombre por su palabra*, that it is reasonable to contemplate a hypotextual relationship between both works') (299). García's analysis demonstrates not only Shirley's debt to Lope but also his creative revision of the earlier play.

Lope's play focuses on King Lisandro of Macedonia, Alejandro (Lisandro's supposed nephew), Lucinda (Lisandro's daughter), Alberto the royal gardener, Federico (military hero and supposed son of Alberto), and Fieno (Federico's friend and servant). These characters correspond to Shirley's Contarini, Duke of Venice, Thomazo, Bellaura, Roberto, Giovanni, and Georgio. In addition to switching the relationships of Alejandro/Federico and Lucinda—making the lost child the Duke's son and the young woman his niece—Shirley takes Lope's Celia, the supposed sister of Federico, and turns her into Ursula, Giovanni's supposed mother and the real mother of Thomazo. Where Alberto in *El hombre por su palabra* confesses that he swapped the babies 'porque mi sangre reynara' ('in order that my blood will reign' [1625, 176v]), Ursula admits that she acted 'out of ambition / To see my own a great man' (5.4.84–5), leaving Roberto oblivious to the fact that he was bringing up another man's son (see García 1998, 292). In addition to these structural similarities, García (1998, 292–7) demonstrates that Shirley adapts closely some passages in *El hombre por su palabra*, notably the catalogue of the flowers in the King's garden (1625, 169v–170r; see *The Gentleman of Venice*, 2.1.78–100), Federico's praise of war as a source of honour (1625, 156r; *The Gentleman of Venice*, 3.2.37–57), and the introduction of forbidden love as a motivation for going to fight (1625, 155v–156r; *The Gentleman of Venice*, 3.2.77–124).

It is possible that the other plotline in *The Gentleman of Venice*, the story of Cornari, Claudiana, and Florelli, also had its roots in Spanish culture through the history of Henry IV of Castile (1425–74), known as 'Henry the Unable'. Henry's first marriage to Blanche of Navarre was annulled due to his sexual impotence, and although he claimed that he was under a curse and only unable to perform sexually with Blanche, rumours of his impotence lingered over his second marriage with Joan of Portugal. In the words of Edward Grimeston's 1612 translation of Louis Turquet de Mayerne's *The General History of Spain*:

the common rumor was, that not beeing able to endure that men should esteeme him vnapt for venereall acts, which he reputed a great and ignominious disgrace, hee dealt with the Queene his wife to receiue Don *Bertrand de la Cueua* into her bed, (his base and degenerate mind desiring and consenting that this Knight should lye with her, to the end shee might prooue with child by

263

him, and so by that meanes suppose an heire to the kingdome in his owne name, though vnlawfully begotten by another.)

(1612, 3T2v)

In Grimeston's resonant phrase, Beltrán de la Cueva, Duke of Alburquerque, was said to have 'acted the chiefe part in this Commedy' (3T6r) and fathered Joan's daughter, also called Joan.

As Matthew Steggle has demonstrated, a play listed as 'Henrye the vna…' in a badly damaged list of plays that were probably being considered for court performance by Prince Charles's Men around 1619 is likely to have been on the subject of Henry the Unable, drawing on sources such as Mayerne's *General History* or Pierre Matthieu's *History of Louis the Eleventh*, also translated by Grimeston. Steggle points out that '[t]he crux of the story, the incident that made Henry famous, is his forcing his wife into infidelity' (2010, 75). Thus, although Shirley does not appear to have begun his career as a playwright until 1625, he may nonetheless have been familiar with *Henry the Unable* and have recognized in the 'Commedy' of the impotent Spanish king and his desire to find a sexual substitute a narrative that he could turn to tragicomic purposes. Alternatively, it is possible that a hitherto overlooked Spanish play took the basic structures of the story of Henry the Unable and made them the stuff of fiction, and that Shirley in turn drew upon that play.

In either case, comparing Cornari with Henry of Castile reveals important similarities and differences between their stories. Like Henry, Cornari prizes succession over blood lineage—Cornari would rather have a virtuous child of Claudiana and another man succeed him than his own nephew, Malipiero. Yet Shirley departs from the 'Henry the Unable' narrative because he makes infertility, not impotence, the source of Cornari and Claudiana's reproductive failure. Although impotence and infertility are frequently conflated in early modern texts (see Evans 2014, 314–15), Cornari himself recalls to Claudiana 'with what religious flowing / Of chaste and noble love our hearts have met' (4.1.16–17), and the play does not suggest that he is without sexual feeling or is unable to satisfy his wife.

LITERARY CONTEXTS: TRAGICOMEDY

The description of *The Gentleman of Venice* on its 1655 title page as a 'Tragi-Comedie' opens up a series of literary, cultural, and political contexts for the play. Tragicomedy was a cross-cultural phenomenon in late-sixteenth- and early-seventeenth-century Europe, with dramatists in different countries grappling with the task of combining tragic and comic material in the same play, challenging classicizing literary cultures that often disdained such experiments as violating generic decorum. Crucial stress-points were identified not only in areas such as the provocation of laughter or sorrow, but also the kinds of characters and narratives that should feature in tragicomedy, given that tragedy was often thought paradigmatically to feature those of high status, true stories, and affairs of state, and comedy those of lower status, fictional narratives, and private matters.

Two dramatists who had a significant influence on Shirley's work—John Fletcher and Lope de Vega—offered commentaries on tragicomedy. In his address to the reader

THE GENTLEMAN OF VENICE: GENERAL INTRODUCTION

in the first edition of his pastoral tragicomedy *The Faithful Shepherdess*, issued around 1609, Fletcher adapts a set of key terms from the Italian dramatist and theorist Battista Guarini, arguing that:

A tragie-comedie is not so called in respect of mirth and killing, but in respect it wants deaths, which is inough to make it no tragedie, yet brings some neere it, which is inough to make it no comedie: which must be a representation of familiar people, with such kinde of trouble as no life be questiond, so that a God is as lawfull in this as in a tragedie, and meane [i.e. ordinary] people as in a comedie.

(Beaumont and Fletcher 1966–96, 2.497)

Fletcher follows Guarini (1601, 12; see Gilbert 1940, 504) in describing the emotional impact that tragicomedy can have on spectators, but he is more willing than Guarini to disturb them and to create a mixed emotional response. He is also willing to include in his tragicomedy not only 'persone grande' (great persons), as Guarini terms them (1601, 12), but also the everyday people of early modern comedy, a move that is reflected in the prominence that both Lope and Shirley give to their supposed gardener.

Around the same time as Fletcher was at work on *The Faithful Shepherdess* and its preface, Lope composed the *Arte nuevo de hacer comedias en este tiempo* (*New Art of Writing Plays in This Age*), printed in 1609, in which he declares:

> Lo trágico y lo cómico mezclado,
> y Terencio con Séneca, aunque sea
> como otro Minotauro de Pasife,
> harán grave una parte, otra ridícula,
> que aquesta variedad deleita mucho.
>
> (1971, 291–2)

> I mix the tragic with the comic
> and Terence with Seneca,
> even though the result be another Minotaur of Pasiphae.
> One part will be serious, another risible
> because this variety causes much delight.
>
> (Evans 2007, 60)

Lope is more willing than Guarini or Fletcher to countenance the idea that to write tragicomedy is to create a generic monster, referring explicitly to the classical myth of the bull-headed child to which Pasiphae, queen of Crete, gave birth after she was cursed by Poseidon and as a result had sex with a bull. His image of tragicomedy as a minotaur echoes Philip Sidney's description of 'mungrell Tragy-comedie' (1595, K2r), but, as Geraint Evans points out, it is used ironically: 'this is a form which is monstrous only to those who see through a lens of idealism or who wish to maintain a barrier between genres and, given the link between comedy and the lower orders, a barrier based on social rank' (2007, 61). Shirley may not have been familiar with Lope's treatise, but he knew his plays well enough to respond sensitively to their tragicomic dramaturgy.

The Gentleman of Venice deploys tragicomic conventions across its two plots. Both deal with questions surrounding social status and identity, exploiting tragicomedy's capacity to mix social groups in one play. In addition, both are concerned by questions of succession: the Duke and Cornari are alike in having unsatisfactory heirs, but the

265

THE COMPLETE WORKS OF JAMES SHIRLEY, VOLUME 7

Duke views Thomazo as 'Heaven's punishment' (1.3.34) whereas Cornari attempts to shape the future through his plot to procure a new heir. Characters in both plots are brought near to death, a key feature of Fletcherian tragicomedy: Thomazo is apprehended and charged with high treason for attempting to betray Venice to the Ottoman empire, while Florelli is threatened by a pistol-wielding Cornari. The Bellaura-Giovanni plot generally reflects the instruction of commentators such as Guarini that tragicomedy have a mixed and moderate tone. In contrast, the Claudiana-Cornari-Florelli plot is more disjunctive tonally, featuring as it does Cornari's tortured desire for an heir, the irreverent cynicism of Malipiero, and the bawdy comedy of Act 3, Scene 4, set in Rosabella's brothel. Nason describes the brothel scene and Malipiero's quarrel with Cornari in Act 1, Scene 1 as 'worthy of Restoration comedy at its best' (1915, 307), and Shirley's sexual realism and his depiction of the rake share with another play of the late 1630s, Richard Brome's *A Mad Couple Well Matched*, qualities that prefigure the work of Aphra Behn, George Etherege, and William Wycherley.

SOCIAL AND CULTURAL CONTEXTS: GENTILITY AND RANK

Questions of status and class, and their workings within a specific culture and locale, are encapsulated in the title of *The Gentleman of Venice*. An early reader of the Princeton University copy of the octavo annotated Marcello's comment that 'The helps of education [...] seldom / Do correct nature' (5.4.96–7) with a Latin proverb attributed to Theognis of Megara, 'Esquilla [n]o[n] Nascitur Rosa nec Hyacinthus' ('a rose or hyacinth never comes from a sea onion'), used by Theognis to describe the perceived inability of the child of an enslaved mother to become free but used by early modern writers to suggest that nobility is incompatible with common birth. However, Shirley's play is more equivocal in its approach to social rank than Marcello's comment or this gloss suggest. In early modern England, the gentry were the rank immediately below the nobility and, like the nobility, were entitled to have coats-of-arms and bear swords. Gentle status was often linked to the possession of land, but it could also inhere in other experiences or qualities. In the late sixteenth century, Thomas Smith claimed that:

whosoeuer studieth the lawes of the realme, who studieth in the vniuersities, who professeth liberall sciences, and to be shorte, who can liue idly and without manuall labour, and will beare the port, charge and countenaunce of a gentleman, he shall be called master [...] and shall be taken for a gentleman[.]

(1583, E2r)

To be a gentleman was to some extent dependent on an individual's ability to persuade others that he was a gentleman, whether or not he had the lineage, property, or education to back up his claim. Shirley himself plays with these ideas in *The Gamester*, set in London, in which Young Barnacle gains a reputation as a quarrelling gallant. Yet the idea of being a 'gentleman of Venice' was especially potent, as the English believed that the Venetians set great store by that title. As Peter Heylyn commented, '[t]he Gentlemen they haue in such respect, that to make a man a Gentleman of the city, is the greatest honour they can bestow vpon the best deseruer' (1625, N4r–v). It is perhaps unsurprising,

266

THE GENTLEMAN OF VENICE: GENERAL INTRODUCTION

therefore, that there are several characters in *The Gentleman of Venice* who might lay claim to that title. Cornari is described as '*a gentleman of Venice*' in the printed text's prefatory materials ('The Names', 2), and Malipiero exclaims, scornfully, 'You a gentleman of Venice?' (1.1.134) when Cornari refuses to lend him money. Thomazo is described repeatedly by Ursula as 'gentleman', in ways that draw satiric attention to his lack of gentlemanly virtue; in contrast, the Duke plans to elevate Giovanni to the rank of 'gentleman of Venice' (4.2.32) for his military service even before his noble status is revealed in the final scene. Of the other characters, Malipiero's ability to maintain his gentle status is dependent on inheriting his uncle's estate, while Florelli also becomes a 'gentleman of Venice' through his superlative displays at the academies.

The play consistently asks how social status is to be signalled or quantified. Giovanni's rise in status is marked first through objects associated with gentle or noble status, such as swords and armour. He grabs a sword during the fight with Malipiero and his companions, and Florelli attempts to give him money to buy a sword of his own, telling him, 'Thou hast deserved to thrive a nobler way / Than thy condition shows' (2.1.301–2), only for Giovanni to decline the gift as dishonourable. Giovanni finally appears with a sword of his own after he enlists to fight the Genoese (3.2.35), and Bellaura pays for his armour (3.2.137–8). His heroic actions in the war raise his status again. The Duke declares that Giovanni's 'early valour takes away / The prejudice of humble birth' (4.2.24–5) and is willing to create him 'gentleman of Venice' and to award him a 'noble pension [...] / To bear his title up' (4.2.32–4). Yet his social rise can only go so far. Bellaura responds scornfully to the Duke's proposal that she marry Giovanni, asking how he could conceive 'I can descend with such / Forgetfulness of myself, my birth or fortunes / To place my love on one so poorly born?' (4.2.154–6). It is only with the revelation that he is the Duke's son that Giovanni achieves sufficient status to marry Bellaura, who turns out to be his first cousin.

Like Giovanni, Bellaura is confined by her position in society. Her high rank gives her some agency, but—like the gentlewoman Claudiana—she is also treated as sexual property. Shirley treats Giovanni's request to marry Bellaura sympathetically, but he also seems to be aware of the pressure that is put on the young woman and he stresses her capacity to reject the Duke's proposal. She leaves the stage indignantly, telling Giovanni 'I ha' done wi'ye, sir' (4.2.160), and neither the Duke nor Giovanni make any attempt to change her mind. Yet there may also be an emotional cost to Bellaura in her actions. When Giovanni half-reveals his love for her in Act 3 she comments in an aside 'Poor Giovanni, / I pity thee but cannot cure' (3.2.124–5), and her response in the final scene to the revelation that Giovanni is the Duke's son is to exclaim 'My heart hath wings to meet him' (5.3.126). The part could be played, therefore, in a way that suggests that she goes against her own desires when she rejects Giovanni, trapped—as he is—by her own rank and status.

Charles R. Forker describes Giovanni's attraction to Bellaura as an 'instinctive drift toward a blood relation', commenting that 'a permissible incest—that is, marriage that threatens but never actually violates the carefully drawn boundaries of illicit consanguinity—becomes meritorious [...] and validates the time-honored aristocratic and romantic principle that blood will tell' (1989, 19). This is a fair assessment of the Bellaura-Giovanni plot, but the play also asks larger questions about what makes a gentleman and what constitutes 'gentle' behaviour. Malipiero believes that gentility is exhibited through conspicuous consumption, gambling, and whoring; Cornari is at

267

THE COMPLETE WORKS OF JAMES SHIRLEY, VOLUME 7

pains to tell Florelli 'I am a gentleman' (3.3.44) even though he has abducted him and is about to force him into sexual service; Florelli himself is described as a 'gentleman victorious for his parts' (4.1.98) through his victories in the trials of wit and action in the academies; and—as we have seen—Giovanni's conduct repeatedly transcends his presumed rank.

Through these means, Shirley complicates the correlation between noble birth and virtue that would seem to be central to the Bellaura-Giovanni plot. When Ursula confesses that the babies were swapped in their cradles, Marino tells the Duke,

> I shall believe your nobleness lived there
> In Giovanni, not suppressed in poverty,
> And their rude, coarse condition, notwithstanding
> The helps of education, which seldom
> Do correct nature, in Thomazo's low
> And abject spirit.

(5.4.93–8)

Such a statement reinforces the idea that lineage is all, but the play appears to be less convinced by this class ideology. Giovanni's accomplishments are not enabled purely by his noble lineage. Roberto willingly allows him to attend the academies and Ursula grumbles that he 'has cost you sweetly / To bring him up', asking 'What use had he of learning?' (1.2.14–15). Moreover, it is not only the degenerate behaviour of Thomazo that acts as a foil for the innate nobility of Giovanni, but the corruption of the high-born Malipiero. Thus, although Ira Clark briefly discusses *The Gentleman of Venice* as an example of Shirley's 'ascription of absolute royal prerogatives to nature' (1992, 121), the play itself is more equivocal about the relationship between birth, status, and virtue.

SOCIAL AND CULTURAL CONTEXTS: PLACE AND SPACE

Crucial to *The Gentleman of Venice* are three key locations: Cornari's palazzo; the academies, which are never represented on stage but are much talked about; and the Duke's garden. The first location that we encounter is Cornari's house, which—in contrast with the academies, or the open space of the garden, to which multiple characters have access—is a closed and claustrophobic space. Malipiero tries and fails to gain access to it in the opening scene, and all of the rooms that are represented on stage are either private ones or are made so. Its most symbolic moment comes at the start of Act 3, Scene 3, where a stage direction reads, '*The scene adorned with pictures, amongst the rest Claudiana's*' (3.3.0 SD). Florelli describes it as a 'fair and pleasant gallery' (3.3.2), and the scene draws heavily on the cultural associations of this kind of room.

Galleries in noble households were frequently used for the display of portraits demonstrating the family's wealth, prestige, and antiquity. In England they often included the portraits of monarchs and other important political figures, sometimes featuring Ottoman sultans alongside European kings and queens, Roman emperors, and figures from classical mythology in addition to portraits of past or present family members (Coope 1986, 62). As a backdrop to Cornari's unfolding scheme to father a child through Florelli, the '*pictures*' that were hung on the playhouse's *frons scaenae* could

THE GENTLEMAN OF VENICE: GENERAL INTRODUCTION

therefore have presented a complex image of what is at stake for Cornari: his own honour and that of his 'house', in the widespread early modern meaning of 'family' (*OED*, *n.* 10b), and the ability of his descendants to match the deeds of his ancestors.

Similar questions of rank and status are raised by the academies, which were a feature of European urban culture. An especially notable example in London was Francis Kynaston's Museum Minervae, which operated in Covent Garden between 1635 and 1639 (Howard 2007, 186–8; Zucker 2011, 130–5) and is satirized directly in Brome's *The New Academy* (1636) (Howard 2007, 188–91; Leslie 2010, paras. 2–3). In the *Constitutions* that he published for the Museum Minervae in 1636, Kynaston states that the academy offers training in subjects such as heraldry, '*Practicall knowledge of Deeds and Evidences*', '*Principles and Processes of common Law*', '*Knowledge of Antiquities Coynes, Medalls, Husbandry, &c.*', physiology, '*Anatomie, or any other parts of Physick*', astronomy, arithmetic, algebra and geometry, fortification, architecture, music, ancient and modern European languages, '*Skill at all weapons and wrestling*', riding, '*Dancing* and behaviour', painting, sculpture, and writing (A1v–A2r). Students are required to pursue just one intellectual and one corporal science at a time in order to 'avoid confusion', unless 'the capacitie of the scholler be extraordinary' (A1v). Offering a rationale for his enterprise, Kynaston states that '*hitherto no such places for the education, and trayning up of our own young Nobilitie, and Gentrie, in the practise of arms, and arts have been instituted here in* England, *as are in* Italy, France, *and* Germany', regretting that '*the noble and generous youth of this kingdome is sent beyond the seas*' as result (2¶1r). Florelli's attendance at the academies of Venice is, therefore, plausible, but the play's representation of them has as much in common with dramatic tradition as cultural fact.

As Jean E. Howard notes, there is a 'salacious overtone' to the ways in which plays of the 1630s depict the training offered by academies (2007, 192), and this extends in *The Gentleman of Venice* to their students. Florelli is the focus of attention and gossip through his feats of wit and activity, set up not only as a model for Thomazo to imitate but as a potential sexual partner for Claudiana. Having sent Claudiana to see the displays of prowess at the academy and pressured her into admitting that she likes Florelli best, Cornari tells her:

> Wert thou
> A virgin, Claudiana, thou wouldst find
> Gentle and easy thoughts to entertain
> So promising a servant. I should be
> Taken with him myself, were I a lady
> And loved a man.

(2.1.70–5)

Aware of his wife's chaste loyalty, Cornari asks her to imagine that she is unmarried, and he briefly puts himself in her position, rhetorically reworking the sexual substitution on which his plan depends. For Cornari, the academies offer a display of virile bodies and agile minds, presenting him with a showcase of men whom he might be able to exploit for their sexual capacity.

The play's most important location, the garden, also offers opportunities for display. Venice was known for its gardens, and many of them seem to have been viewed as semi-public spaces, as the Duke's garden is presented in the play. In *An Itinerary*

269

THE COMPLETE WORKS OF JAMES SHIRLEY, VOLUME 7

(1617), Fynes Moryson notes the 'great number' of gardens in the city, and their 'rare herbes, plants, and fruits, and water conduits, which with the carued Images and pictures, (out of the Gentlemens curtesie) may bee seene by any curious stranger' (1617, H3v). Two members of the Contarini family, whose name Shirley adopts for his Duke, were associated with gardens. Gasparo Contarini (1483–1542) built a house with a large garden, now known as the Contarini dal Zaffo, in the north of Venice, and Nicolò Contarini (1553–1631), who served as Doge in 1630–1, had extensive gardens near Verona.

The garden becomes a showcase for Giovanni, who displays virtuosity even in the act of gardening itself. Georgio describes the fantastic patterns that Giovanni makes in the hedges and turf, complaining:

> When I am digging, he is cutting unicorns
> And lions in some hedge, or else devising
> New knots upon the ground, drawing out crowns
> And the duke's arms, castles and cannons in 'em.
> Here galleys, there a ship giving a broadside;
> Here out of turf he carves a senator
> With all his robes, making a speech to thyme,
> That grows hard by, and twenty curiosities.
>
> (1.2.79–86)

Giovanni's designs for the garden unconsciously reflect his true status as the Duke's heir and the concerns with warfare and politics that such status would bring with it, but the play also debates whether he should be working at all. Roberto himself declares that it is beneath his status that his son should 'Live like a mole, or make it his last blessing / To plant, and order quickset' (1.2.12–13), and Bellaura asks Georgio, 'Why does / Your master, being rich, suffer his son / To work i'th'garden?'. Georgio blames Ursula: 'It is my mistress that commands him to't' (2.1.104–6, 108). Giovanni's status is contrasted sharply with that of Georgio, who complains that Giovanni expresses himself artistically 'but I do all the coarse work' (1.2.88).

As Jennifer Munroe writes, gardens are 'sites of ideological struggle, where one could conceive of renegotiating social position as much as one might imagine fitting in' (2008, 1–2). The Duke's garden is a space in which people of different social status meet and interact, and it is viewed by Giovanni as an 'academy' in which 'gentlemen and ladies [...] / Enrich my ear and observation / With harmony of language' (2.1.136–7, 39–40)—his own version of the city's schools of eloquence and deportment. The dual association of Florelli with the academy and—via his oddly floral-sounding name—the garden also reinforces the connection between the two locations.

Ideological questions connected with gardening and 'planting' are raised in the exchange between Thomazo and Malipiero in which they discuss their plans for what they will do with Venice when Thomazo is Duke. Having suggested dissolving the monasteries to make money, Malipiero ponders what should be done with their inhabitants, telling Thomazo:

> if you think 'em troublesome, it is
> A fair pretence to send 'em to some wild country
> To plant the faith and teach the infidels
> A way to heaven[.]
>
> (3.1.66–9)

270

The idea of 'plant[ing] the faith' resonates strongly in the context of the probable composition and first performance of *The Gentleman of Venice* in Dublin in the mid-1630s. The Lord Deputy, Sir Thomas Wentworth (later Earl of Strafford), for whom Shirley's *The Royal Master* was performed on New Year's Day 1638, actively pursued plantation and the settlement of Protestants from other parts of the kingdom in Ireland as a means of both increasing revenue for the Crown and creating 'a mechanism to bridle Irish recusancy' (Ó Hannracháin 2013, 306). As a Catholic, Shirley might have viewed the re-plantation of land occupied by the Catholic descendants of medieval settlers, known as the Old English, with some asperity, but he was also working in Dublin under Strafford's aegis. It is therefore hard to assess precisely where his sympathies lay, and to what extent he expected his audience to view the dispossession of the monks comically.

Shirley's decision to relocate the action of Lope's play from Macedonia to Venice enables him to bring together the palazzo, academies, and garden within one urban environment, and he also exploits the Venetian scene in other ways. The play includes explicit references to locations such as the Grand Canal (3.1.143), and features of the city such as its gondolas (1.1.178). It also acknowledges some of the distinctive aspects of Venice's social make-up in its references to the Jewish community, and its invocation of the casual anti-Semitism of the city's elite (3.1.43–9, 3.4.78–82, 151–5), and in its staging of the courtesan, Rosabella, whose conventional accomplishments are demonstrated in her dance and song (3.4.0 SD, 31 SD). Shirley refers in addition to the city's relations with its medieval and early modern political rivals: Venice fights a war against another Italian city-state, Genoa, and Malipiero and Thomazo plot to sell Venice out to the Ottomans. 'Venice,' Malipiero declares, 'is a jewel, a rich pendant, / Would hang rarely at the Great Turk's ear' (3.1.123–4), a statement that registers Venice's declining status as a Mediterranean power in the early modern period.

Shirley does not, however, create a realistic portrait of Venice or a coherent historical period for the play's action. The Dogeship of Andrea Contarini, whose name he uses for his duke, saw the last of a series of wars between Venice and Genoa, the War of Chioggia (1378–81), but the events of the play, in which the city of Treviso is taken by the Genoese, are unhistorical. Shirley elides, moreover, one of the most distinctive aspects of the Venetian political system: the fact that its rulers were elected for life and could not bequeath the city directly to their heirs. Instead, he appears to imagine Venice as a more conventional dukedom: Bellaura, the Duke's niece, refers to 'my dead father, the late duke of Venice' (4.2.153), while Thomazo fantasizes about the 'new laws' that he would make 'an I were Duke of Venice' (3.1.28). As a result, the character of the ruler's heir is a more pressing political problem than it would be in the historical Venice. Nonetheless, Shirley's references to the complex political make-up of Italy and tensions between Venice and the Ottoman empire place *The Gentleman of Venice* alongside plays such as Shakespeare's *Othello* as a depiction of both the status of the seventeenth-century city and its vulnerability.

Like *Othello*, *The Gentleman of Venice* also exploits contemporary English stereotypes about Italians. 'Beware of these Italians, / They are by nature jealous and revengefull' (1631, I4r), Captain Goodlack tells Spencer in the second part of Thomas Heywood's *The Fair Maid of the West* (*c.* 1631), while Fynes Moryson claims that Italians keep

271

THE COMPLETE WORKS OF JAMES SHIRLEY, VOLUME 7

their wives 'locked vp at home, and covered with vayles when they goe abroade, and [...] from any conversation with men' (1903, 409). Cornari transgresses both of these stereotypes, a fact to which Shirley draws attention when Claudiana describes him as 'no Italian, sure' (4.1.78). English stereotypes also inform the depiction of Rosabella, the courtesan, and Shirley presents his male characters as willing to blur the distinction between virtuous and sexually active women. Cornari suggests that Claudiana disguise herself as 'some pleasant *bona roba*' (4.1.116)—a term that has already been used of a prostitute by Malipiero (2.1.271)—and Claudiana strips away the euphemism, asking, 'Am I practised in those arts / Of sin that [Florelli] should take me for a courtesan?' (4.1.121–2). Part of the play's irony is that the normally jealous Cornari, whose name alludes to the metaphorical horns that cuckolds were supposed to wear, tries to force the chaste Claudiana to behave like a prostitute.

STAGE HISTORY

As already described, there are two early performance contexts for *The Gentleman of Venice*: the Werburgh Street playhouse in Dublin around 1637–9 and the Salisbury Court playhouse in London in 1639. In the prefatory material printed with the play in 1655, Shirley speaks as if he has seen the play performed, telling Sir Thomas Nightingale that it 'had once a singular grace and lustre from the scene when it enjoyed the life of action; nor did it want the best hands to applaud it in the theatre' ('Epistle Dedicatory', 3–4). The dramatist does not seem to have visited England in autumn 1639, when *The Gentleman of Venice* was licensed for performance at Salisbury Court, but he may have seen the play in Dublin or at Salisbury Court after he returned to London around April 1640 (Stevenson 1946). We do not know which performances the 1655 edition more accurately records. Shirley informs Nightingale that 'when [the play] had gotten strength and legs to walk, travelling without direction, it lost itself, till it was recovered after much inquisition and now, upon the first return home, hath made this fortunate address and application to your patronage' ('Epistle Dedicatory', 7–10). He probably means that the manuscript used in the playhouse was 'lost'—i.e. mislaid—after it was performed at Salisbury Court, a not unlikely event given the disruption that the outbreak of the Civil War in 1642 caused the playing companies.

The Werburgh Street playhouse, which was in operation by spring 1636, appears to have been an indoor playhouse on the London model of the Blackfriars, Cockpit, or Salisbury Court (Fletcher 2000, 20–1; Dutton 2006, 130–1; Munro 2007, 175–6). Alan J. Fletcher describes it as 'an upper-class enterprise, instigated by the Lord Deputy Sir Thomas Wentworth, and always run with an eye to the taste and requirements of the ruling classes resident in Dublin Castle' (2000, 21). The playhouse's managers selected plays from the repertoires of a number of the London companies, including Jonson's *The Alchemist*, Middleton's *No Wit, No Help Like a Woman's*, and plays by Fletcher that may have included *The Night-Walker* and *Wit Without Money*, revised by Shirley for Queen Henrietta Maria's Men in the earlier 1630s (Munro 2007, 177). Some of its plays appear to have been designed specifically for performance

272

in Dublin, such as Shirley's *St. Patrick for Ireland*; a lost play for which Shirley wrote a prologue, *The Irish Gentleman*; and *Landgartha*, written by Henry Burnell, a member of a Catholic Old English family, performed on St Patrick's Day, 1640. *The Gentleman of Venice* is less obviously tailored to performance in Dublin, although—as noted earlier—its references to land, inheritance, and 'planting' would have resonated there.

If we know little about the playhouse itself, some information has come down to us about the actors who performed there. 'Players' called Armiger and Rookes were buried in St Werburgh's church around October 1637 (Fletcher 2000, 331). 'Rookes' has not been identified but 'Armiger' may be Edward Armiger, a prominent member of a company that performed at the Red Bull and Fortune in the late 1620s and early-mid 1630s (Fletcher 2000, 552; Bentley 1941–68, 2.350). 'William Cooke ye player' features in a list of people assessed for a local tax in a nearby parish (Fletcher 2000, 333, 552); he had been sworn in as a Groom of the Chamber on 12 December 1635 as one of Prince Charles's Men, who performed at the Red Bull and Salisbury Court in the early 1630s (Bentley 1941–68, 2.413). 'Mr Perry at the play house' was assessed at five shillings in a poor relief levy of the parish of St Werburgh in the period between 25 April 1641 and 10 April 1642 (Fletcher 2000, 337, 553). This may be William Perry, who managed touring companies in the late 1620s and 1630s and was also associated with the Red Bull (Clark 1955, 27–8; Fletcher 2000, 553; Bentley 1941–68, 2.529–31), working at Werburgh Street in an acting or managerial capacity. I have also found new evidence in a later lawsuit that John Shank Jr, son of the famous comic actor of the same name, went to Ireland in summer 1638 and remained there for around four months.[1] Shank's brother-in-law William Birt, who brought the case against Shank and others, claims that the 'Company of Players' at the Fortune playhouse were 'many of them dispersed abroade' in 1639. This may mean that other players from this company, in addition to Armiger and Shank, were employed at Werburgh Street. Circumstantial evidence also suggests that some actors from the Cockpit—such as Michael Bowyer, William Robins, and William Allen—and Salisbury Court, such as Thomas Jordan, may also have travelled to Dublin (Stevenson 1942).

We know little about the roles taken by most of these actors. The best-known—such as Bowyer and Allen, who performed leading roles in Cockpit plays such as Massinger's *The Renegado* (1624–5), Shirley's *The Wedding* (1626), Heywood's *The Fair Maid of the West* (*c.* 1630), Davenport's *King John and Matilda* (*c.* 1634), and Nabbes's *Hannibal and Scipio* (1635) (Bentley 1941–68, 2.345, 386–7) or Robins, who played comic roles in *The Renegado*, *The Wedding*, and *The Fair Maid of the West*—are the least securely linked with Werburgh Street. However, the mixed backgrounds of the actors suggest that the company, like its repertoire, presented a hybrid of different London companies.

We are on slightly more secure ground with the play's performance at Salisbury Court in 1639. The Salisbury Court appears to have been the smallest of the indoor

---

[1] See William Birt v. Tobias Lisle, John Shank Jr, and Winifred Fitch, 1640, The National Archives, Kew, C 2/ChasI/B54/63.

playhouses (Wickham *et al.* 2000, 649–50). The plays associated with it suggest that it had two doors, a discovery space and above space, which both appear to have been able to fit three actors, and a central area of the *frons scaenae* that was hung with curtains (Stevens 1979; Astington 1991); its stage must have been able to fit around fifteen actors (Stevens 1979, 515), and it may also have had a stage trap (Astington 1991, 151–2). *The Gentleman of Venice* would not have been challenging to perform in this space. A stage direction in Act 3, Scene 3 describes Cornari '*Opening the hanging*' (77 SD), so that Florelli can walk into the fictional room behind it, and this scene also makes use of the *frons* for hanging portraits, as discussed earlier. The play does not, however, demand the use of a trap or the above space, meaning that it would have been easy to fit it to the capabilities of different playhouses.

The principal actors in Queen Henrietta Maria's Men in 1639 appear to have been the men listed in a lawsuit brought in February 1640, in which the playhouse's resident dramatist, Richard Brome, was sued for breach of contract: Richard Perkins, Anthony Turner, William Sherlock, John Young, John Sumner, Edward May, Curtis Greville, William Wilbraham, Timothy Reade, and William Cartwright Jr.[2] With the exception of Wilbraham, these names also appear in the manuscript annotations to the cast-list in a surviving copy of the 1640 edition of Brome's *The Antipodes*, first performed at Salisbury Court in 1638 (McEvilla 2012, 169). The annotations also assign roles to William Wintershall, a second actor called 'Turner', and three boy actors playing female roles, 'Ambrose', 'Chamberlain', and 'Watt'.

This was a capable and experienced group of players. Richard Perkins, their leading actor, was singled out for praise by John Webster for his performance in *The White Devil* in 1612 and by Thomas Heywood for his performance as Barabas in Christopher Marlowe's *The Jew of Malta* in 1633 (Bentley 1941–68, 2.525–8). His performances as the anguished patriarch Sir John Belfare in Shirley's earlier play *The Wedding* (Bentley 1941–68, 2.528) and the brooding Joyless in *The Antipodes* also suggest that he would have been well cast as Cornari. Another leading role in *The Gentleman of Venice*, Giovanni, may have been played by Edward May, who performed the role of Joyless's son, Peregrine, on whom the plot of *The Antipodes* centres. The leading comic actor in the company was Timothy Reade, who played various roles in the 'by-play' of *The Antipodes* and took the striking role of the 'changeling' Buzzard, a character who himself impersonates a person with severe learning difficulties, in Brome's *The English Moor* (*c.* 1637–8) (Steggle 2004, 120–1). If he played Thomazo in *The Gentleman of Venice*, Thomazo's comment to Giovanni, 'Thou lookest like a changeling' (2.1.246) would take on an additional force, reminding spectators of the actor's performance in the earlier play and raising the possibility that both Thomazo and Giovanni are 'changelings'.

There are no records of performances of *The Gentleman of Venice* between 1639 and 3 June 2007, when it was performed as part of Shakespeare's Globe's long-running series of staged readings of early modern plays, Read Not Dead. The coordinator of the reading was Yolanda Vazquez, and the cast was as follows:

---

[2] Richard Heton *et al.* v. Richard Brome, Court of Requests, 1640, The National Archives, REQ 2/622; Brome's answer is in REQ 2/723. See Haaker 1968, 297.

THE GENTLEMAN OF VENICE: GENERAL INTRODUCTION

The Duke of Venice	Chris Godwin
Cornari	Peter Forbes
Florelli	Ryan Kiggell
Malipiero	Edmund Kingsley
Giovanni	Alex Kerr
Thomazo	Daniel Crossley
Marino	Richard Hollis
Candiano	Richard Hollis
Roberto	Rupert Farley
Bernardo	Antonio Magro
Marcello	Owen Young
Georgio	Sam Alexander
Bellaura	Caroline Martin
Claudiana	Candida Benson
Ursula	Joyce Henderson
Rosabella	Caroline Martin

Vazquez asked the actors to 'pick up their cues and be swift', commenting that '[w]e talked of keeping the energy up and playing a heightened realism—any "everydayness" or "normality" about it and it seemed to fall flat'.[3] She also encouraged the actors to speak the play's many asides and soliloquies directly to the audience. Another aspect of the presentational style of the staged reading was a pre-show sequence in which each actor read the name of their character(s) and their descriptions from the dramatis personae printed in the programme. Kiggell's 'Florelli, *An English Gentleman*' drew laughter, and reading the descriptions also reinforced the idea that there is something suspicious about the backgrounds of Giovanni and Thomazo. This tactic reflected Vazquez's idea that 'Shirley expected us to know the sons had been changed and for us to enjoy being that little bit ahead of the other characters', a reading that is justified by the hints that are dropped throughout the play.

The reading brought out the comedy of the play and the emotional strains of the Claudiana-Cornari-Florelli plot. Forbes played Cornari with an intensity that meant that his comment to Claudiana, 'I shall be angry' (2.1.32), provoked laughter from the audience, and Kingsley's Malipiero had an air of concealed violence throughout. Giovanni and Thomazo were nicely differentiated, especially through Crossley's adoption of a slightly exaggerated upper-class drawl, and Henderson played Ursula with her own Scottish accent. Alexander had fun with Georgio's directness and his flights of fancy in his dialogue with Bellaura. Martin's doubling of the roles of Bellaura and Rosabella heightened the play's tendency to draw parallels between its female characters.

Some aspects of *The Gentleman of Venice* are very much of its time, such as its apparent conclusion that nobility cannot be taught, merely inherited. Yet Shirley seems himself to be aware of the ideological fissures created by the narrative that he adapts from

---

[3] Personal Communication, June 2007.

275

Lope, and he exaggerates these tensions by juxtaposing the stories of two 'lost' boys: the duke's concealed son, Giovanni, who was virtuous all along; and the nobleman's nephew, Malipiero, who has to learn to be virtuous through experience and punishment. The play presents a fascinating example of the ways in which Spanish drama could be refashioned for English audiences, not least through the double-plot structure that Shirley inherited from Shakespeare, Middleton, and others. Scholars have often viewed the Cornari plot as the play's subplot, yet in performance it is Cornari's anguish, not Giovanni's heroics, that make the more lasting impression. Moreover, looking beyond the 'gentlemen' to the women of Venice, and the social and emotional pressures to which they are subjected, opens up fresh angles on the play and its complex meditations on family, lineage, and character.

Textual Introduction

The Gentleman of Venice was entered in the Stationers' Register by Humphrey Moseley on 9 July 1653 (Eyre 1913–14, 1.423) and published in early 1655 in what Greg calls a 'simultaneous issue' (1939–57, 3.1124) of octavo (O) copies (Wing S3469) and quarto (Q) copies (Wing S3468). The play's publication history is closely entwined with that of *The Politician*, which was entered by Moseley in the Stationers' Register in a long list of plays on 9 September 1653 (Eyre 1913–14, 1.429) before being issued in octavo and quarto in 1655.[1] Both plays were published nearly twenty years after their original performances and both are linked to performance by Queen Henrietta Maria's Men at Salisbury Court and, possibly, the Werburgh Street playhouse in Dublin, in contrast with Moseley's other Shirley publication of the 1650s, the 1653 volume *Six New Plays*, which presents plays produced by the King's Men. In the case of *The Gentleman of Venice*, there are no clear signs that the manuscript on which O and Q were based had theatrical origins, such as the names of actors in stage directions or speech prefixes—as appears in Moseley's 1655 edition of Lodowick Carlell's *The Passionate Lovers* (D8r)—but there are also no textual confusions that absolutely preclude its use in the playhouse.

The title pages of the editions of *The Gentleman of Venice* and *The Politician* are similar, providing the title, a generic tag ('A / Tragi-Comedie' for *The Gentleman of Venice* and 'A / TRAGEDY' for *The Politician*), the play's theatrical auspices, and the author's name, the latter surrounded by rules. However, their formatting is not identical and where *The Gentleman of Venice* is described as 'Presented at the Private house in / Salisbury Court', *The Politician* is more simply described as 'Presented at *Salisbury* Court'. As Robert J. Fehrenbach (1971, 145) points out, some typographical features of the two plays are identical, such as the running title 'The Epistle Dedicatory' (A2v), the signature to the dedication, 'JAMES SHIRLEY', and the rules and type of the word '*FINIS*' at the end of each play; some identical ornaments appear in each. In addition, *The Gentleman of Venice* and *The Politician* both include 'The names with some small Characters of the Persons', consisting of a cast-list with detailed descriptions of each character, a feature that appears in no other printed editions of Shirley's plays, uniquely presenting 'psychological sketches' which reveal characters' 'ambitions, virtues, follies, and personal anxieties that would otherwise be revealed gradually through dramatic action' (Štollová 2017, 139). Wilson F. Engel supports the conjecture of Greg

---

[1] Moseley also adopted this unusual tactic in another 1655 publication, Lodowick Carlell's *The Passionate Lovers*, which appears to have been produced by a different print-shop to *The Gentleman of Venice* and *The Politician* (see Engel 1976, vii).

(1939–59, 3.1555, 4.1696) that the printer was William Wilson—who also appears to have been one of the printers who worked on *Six New Plays*—on the basis of similarities between Wilson's stock of ornaments and those used in *The Gentleman of Venice* and *The Politician* (1976, vii) and through the identification of individual pieces of damaged type (1978). He also cites C. William Miller's 'plausible case for Wilson's having two presses after 1653' (1976, vii; see Miller 1955), a set-up that could have helped with the production of both plays.

The quarto editions of these plays seem to have been intended to match earlier issues of Shirley's plays in single-volume editions, while the octavo format allowed *The Gentleman of Venice* and *The Politician* to be bound with Moseley's octavo edition of *Six New Plays*. Greg thought it probable that only the quartos of *The Politician* and *The Gentleman of Venice* were originally sold separately, and he treats the octavo issues of these plays as a collection (1939–57, 3.1124–5). His theory is supported by an advertisement that Moseley placed in *A Perfect Diurnal* in late January 1655, which lists Humphrey Robinson's *Schola Wintoniensis Phrases Latinae*, Gervase Markham's *The Perfect Horseman* and 'The Gentleman of *Venice* and the Politician, written by *James Shirley* Gent. All three printed for *Humphrey Mosely* at the Princes Armes in St. *Pauls* Churchyard' (Pecke 1655, 4142; McEvilla 2013, 28). Some surviving copies of the octavo editions are bound together (e.g. C11.1, HN.1, L.1, L6.2, PN.1), some with *Six New Plays* (e.g. L6.1, Mc.1, O.1).[2] Although we do not know precisely how readers consumed their copies of *The Gentleman of Venice*, these binding practices suggest that they picked up the cue of the matching octavo formats and that they may have approached the play as part of a broader set of works by Shirley rather than a text to be read in isolation.

This edition is based on a collation of sixteen copies of O and twenty-three copies of Q.[3] Given their similarity, there is some justification for viewing the octavo and quarto formats as different issues of the same edition. They were printed from a single typesetting, with changes only in the signatures, changes that were in fact imperfectly carried out. They seem to have been printed by forme, rather than seriatim, in order to ease pressure on the print-house's stock of type. As Fehrenbach notes of the printing of *The Gentleman of Venice* and *The Politician*,

it is unlikely that one size was printed entirely before the other size went to the press. It is more likely that a printer first imposed the type-pages in one forme and printed the sheets of the appropriate format; then he reimposed the type-pages in the other forme, made the necessary signature changes, and machined the sheets of the other size.

(1971, 146)

---

[2] C11.1, L6.2, HN.1, and PN.1 include the portrait frontispiece, dated 1646, also found with copies of *Poems* and *Six New Plays*; L.1 and HN.1 append to the plays a catalogue of '*Books Printed for* Humphrey Moseley'.

[3] The collations were carried out by Lucy Munro, Emily Hargreaves, and Alison Searle. Many thanks to Liza Blake (Library of Congress, Folger, Princeton, and University of Pennsylvania copies); Lucy Clarke (Bodleian copies); Melinda J. Gough (McMaster copies); Teresa Grant (Cambridge University Library copies); and Alexander K. P. Lash (Huntington copies) for their help with photographing and checking copies of O and Q. I am also grateful to the British Academy for a small grant that supported the first round of work on the collations.

The running titles of *The Gentleman of Venice* support this theory: a capital 'G' with a longer tail appears ten times in both the quarto and octavo, appearing twice in each octavo sheet except for sheet F, and occurring on the same page in each format; the misprint 'Veince' appears twice in each format, again on the same pages.[4]

Stop-press correction appears to have only been carried out during the printing of the octavo sheets. Other variants appear to have been caused by movement within the formes resulting in pulled type during the printing of the octavo sheets, or in the reimposition of the formes when the print-shop changed between the two different formats. The printing of the quarto sheets appears to have been more straightforward. Although there are some variants caused by pulled type, discussed below, no press corrections have been detected in the work for this edition or by earlier scholars who have worked on the printing of *The Gentleman of Venice*.

Much of the energy of previous commentators on *The Gentleman of Venice* has gone into trying to work out whether the sheets that made up O went through the press before those that made up Q (see Huberman 1937, Fehrenbach 1971, and Engel 1976). The following analysis revisits this question while also reassessing which variants in O are likely to be the result of stop-press correction. I will follow Engel's example and work through the editions by forme.

The inner forme of **sheet A** (A–B in Q) presents some evidence that O was printed first in the shape of the retention of the octavo signature reference A4 in Q, where it would not normally be numbered. This evidence is complicated, however, by changes in punctuation in the outer forme, in which full stops appear and disappear after the speech prefix '*Cor.*' (A4v, line 31) and the word 'yet' (A8v, line 30). All copies of O consulted have '*Cor*' and 'yet.', while all copies of Q consulted have '*Cor.*' and 'yet' (A4v and B4v). Thus, neither O nor Q has the 'correct' forms of '*Cor.*' and 'yet.'. It is possible that A4v was corrected during reimposition for the printing of Q, but the change on A8v/B4v was probably caused by an unintended shift in reimposition. Elsewhere, pulled type on the title-page (A1r) results in 'Humphrey' becoming 'H umphrey' (line 14), the latter appearing in all copies of Q examined. It also appears in the octavo and quarto editions of *The Politician*, which appears to have been printed after *The Gentleman of Venice*, the compositors having let the type for the imprint stand throughout the printing of both plays (Fehrenbach 1971, 146).[5]

The inner and outer formes of **sheet B** (C–D in Q) present evidence that O was printed first because Q's C1–3 are misnumbered as B, B2, and B3, the signature references having been retained from O. This suggests that other changes in the outer forme, in which 'your' (B1r, line 10) and '*Dukes*' (B2v, line 18) become 'you' and '*Duke*' in all copies of Q examined (C1r, C2v) were caused by pulled type rather than press correction.

---

[4] The long-tailed 'G' appears on octavo A4v (p. 2) (outer forme); A6v (p. 6) (outer); B1r (p. 11) (outer); B8r (p. 25) (inner); C6v (p. 38) (outer); C7v (p. 40) (inner); D6v (p. 54) (outer); D8v (p. 58) (outer); E6r (p. 69) (inner); E8v (p. 74) (outer); and on quarto A4v (p. 2) (outer forme); B2v (p. 6) (outer); C1r (p. 11) (outer); D4r (p. 25) (inner); F2r (p. 38) (outer); F3v (p. 40) (inner); H2v (p. 54) (inner); K2r (p. 69) (inner); K4v (p. 74) (outer). The misprint 'Veince' appears on octavo C4r (p. 33) (inner) and D5r (p. 51) (outer); and on quarto E4r (p. 33) (inner); H1r (p. 51) (outer).

[5] Further movement appears to have taken place between the printing of *The Gentleman of Venice* and *The Politician*, as the 'e' in 'be' is raised in the latter. See Fehrenbach 1971, 146.

THE COMPLETE WORKS OF JAMES SHIRLEY, VOLUME 7

Press correction was carried out in the outer forme of **sheet C** (E–F in Q) during the printing of O. The top line of C7r in two copies, LC and C11.1, reads 'Nothing is meant here but safety and here honor' where all other copies of O examined read 'Nothing is meant but safety here and honor'. All copies of Q examined have the corrected version.[6] An error in the signatures also suggests that O preceded Q for this sheet, as E4 (inner forme) in Q is numbered when it would usually be blank in quarto printing: the compositors seem to have changed C4 to E4 without removing the signature entirely. This suggests that other variants in the outer forme, in which 'cannot tumble' (C8v, line 36) appears as 'cannottumble' in all copies of Q consulted (F4v), and O's 'Through' (C5r, line 2) becomes 'Th rough' (F1r) in Q, were caused by shifts in reimposition. Q also has its own example of pulled type, with a shift from 'Didst' to 'Did st' (E2v, line 13) in some copies.

Stop-press correction also appears to have taken place in the outer forme of **sheet D** (G–H in Q). The final line of D4v seems to have been corrected, with 'if ye mingle not; and make' becoming 'if ye mingle not and make' in some copies of O and all copies of Q examined (G4v). This line is also misprinted in some copies of O, rendering the word 'mingle' almost illegible. Elsewhere in the outer forme, O's 'I'le' (D3r, line 4), appears as ''le' (G3r) in all copies of Q consulted. In two other probable examples of shifts in reimposition in the inner forme, the raised comma in O's 'laden'' (D2r, line 13) slips to its proper position in 'laden,' (G2r) and the catchword '*Cor.*' (O, D4r) loses its full stop (Q, G4r). This combined evidence suggests that O was printed first.

In the outer forme of **sheet E** (I–K in Q), pulled type seems to have caused 'of hine' (E2v, line 10), itself a misprint for 'of thine', to slip to 'o fhine' in some copies of O; it then slips further to 'ohine' in Q (I2v). Other changes, in which O's 'Be bold' (E1r, line 5) slips to 'Bebold' in Q (I1r), and spaces in 'hard ly' and 'm ind' (O, E8v, ll. 17, 23) are closed up in Q (K4v), appear to have been caused by shifts in reimposition. In the inner forme, variation in the catchword on E5v, which appears as 'This' in O and 'Thi' (K1v) in all copies of Q consulted, appears to have the same cause. It is also possible that misnumbering in Q's signature K, which reads K1, no signature, K3, K2 is a sign of rushed work during reimposition given that O's signatures are correct throughout.

In the inner forme of **sheet F** (L in Q), O's 'outward.' (F2r, line 28) slips to 'outward' in Q (L2r). Shifts in reimposition also appear to correct O's 'V enice' (F1r, rt) to Q's 'Venice' (L1r) and to restore a raised apostrophe in 'Hee's' in O (F2v, line 6) to its proper place in Q (L1v). In this forme, again, O appears to have been printed first.

This analysis suggests that O generally preceded Q as the formes went through the press, supporting the conclusions of earlier scholars.

In addition to the 1655 editions, another textual trace of *The Gentleman of Venice* may survive. In Act 3, Scene 4, Rosabella sings at Malipiero's request (see 3.4.31 SD in this edition). O and Q have a stage direction, '*Rosabella sings*' (C8r) but no lyric is provided. In 1986, John P. Cutts suggested that the first two stanzas of the lyric printed as 'Cupid's Call', the opening poem of Shirley's 1646 collection of *Poems* (B1r–v), which appear in one manuscript under the title 'The Curtizane' (see Beal 2017, s.v. 'James Shirley', ShJ 14), might have been originally written as the lyric for Rosabella's

---

[6] Engel (1976, xlviii) identifies another press correction in this forme, saying that 'And' (C3r, line 23) appears as 'An' in some copies of O. All of the copies examined for this edition have 'And'.

280

THE GENTLEMAN OF VENICE: TEXTUAL INTRODUCTION

song. These stanzas were extant by 1639, when they were printed anonymously in Samuel Pick's *Festum Voluptatis* (C3r–4r), which itself had been entered in the Stationers' Register on 17 October 1638 (see Rollins 1931, 204). An anonymous setting survives in New York Public Library Drexel MS 4257, no. 22 (reproduced in Jorgens 1987, XII; discussed in Cutts 1986, 24). Complicating matters, however, the verses printed as stanzas 3–4 of 'Cupid's Call' also circulated separately, again with the title 'Curtesan' or 'The Curtizan' (see Beal 2017, s.v. 'James Shirley', ShJ 1–7), and were also set to music. A setting probably composed by William Lawes survives in NYPL Drexel MS 4257, no. 12 (reproduced in Jorgens 1987, XII) and NYPL Drexel MS 4041, no. 73, f. 52r (edited in Callon 2002, no. 50; discussed in Cutts 1964, 184; Wood 1998, 39–40). Lawes regularly composed music for Caroline plays and masques (Wood 1998), including Shirley's *The Triumph of Peace* (1634), *The Duke's Mistress* (1636), and *The Cardinal* (1641), so it is not implausible that his setting of 'Cupid's Call' would have theatrical associations.

The song gives Rosabella an opportunity to display her skills as a singer and, possibly, musician, if she accompanies herself on the lute, as courtesans often do in early modern plays. As printed in Shirley's *Poems*, the lyric runs thus:

> HO! *Cupid* calls, come Lovers, come,
> Bring his wanton Harvest home:
> The West-wind blowes, the Birds do sing,
> The Earth's enamell'd, 'tis high Spring:
> Let Hinds whose soul is Corn and Hay,
> Expect their crop another day.
>
> Into Loves Spring-garden walk,
> Virgins dangle on their stalk,
> Full blown, and playing at fifteen:
> Come bring your amorous sickles then?
> See they are pointing to their beds,
> And call to reap their Maiden-heads.
>
> Hark, how in yonder shadie grove
> Sweet *Philomel* is warbling love,
> And with her voice is courting Kings,
> For since she was a Bird, she sings,
> There is no pleasure but in men,
> Oh come and ravish me agen.
>
> Virgins that are you[n]g and fair
> May kisse, and grow into a pair;
> Then warm and active use your blood,
> No sad thought congeal the flood:
> Nature no med'cine can impart
> When age once snows upon our heart.
>
> (1646, B1r–v)

Either set of verses could easily be incorporated into the scene, accentuating its bawdiness. Sung by Rosabella, these lyrics might present either an enthusiastic paean to the power of desire or a more cynical expression of women's submission to male force, signalled in the brutal reference to the reaping of maidenheads or the assertion that

THE COMPLETE WORKS OF JAMES SHIRLEY, VOLUME 7

Philomel—who was turned into a nightingale after she was raped by her brother-in-law Tereus—not only experiences desire in her new form but wishes to be subjected to further sexual violation.

The first post-seventeenth-century edition of *The Gentleman of Venice*, and the only modern-spelling edition, is in William Gifford and Alexander Dyce, eds, *The Dramatic Works and Poems of James Shirley* (1833). In addition to modernizing both spelling and punctuation, Gifford adds scene divisions, expands contractions (e.g. 'wo'not' becomes 'will not', 'shannot' becomes 'shall not', and 'ha'' becomes 'have'), regularizes metre, suggests alternative readings that he generally—although not always—places in square brackets, and tidies up and augments stage directions. Some of his emendations and additions have been followed in this edition, and my debts are recorded in the Textual Notes.

Two later editions have been produced as doctoral theses. The first is Engel's old-spelling edition, *James Shirley's The Gentleman of Venice*, originally produced as his University of Wisconsin-Madison PhD thesis and published by the Institut für Englische Sprache und Literatur, Universität Salzburg, in 1976. The second is Lieven Vermeulen's 'James Shirley's *The Gentleman of Venice*: A Textual Edition With Some Introductory Notes' (Rijksuniversiteit Gent, 1981), which remains unpublished. Engel and Vermeulen both produce conservative, old-spelling editions, making few textual interventions. Engel's edition is valuable primarily for his collation of eleven copies of O and twenty-five copies of Q, and his detailed commentary on the play's printing. He describes his text as 'very close to a diplomatic edition, since alterations have been made only where there are evident errors, inconsistencies, or hindrances to fluent reading in the copy' (1976, liii), but he nonetheless preserves a number of O's errors, such as 'of hine' (l. 2151) and introduces some mistranscriptions, such as 'whild' for 'while' (l. 865). In a stringent but not inaccurate review of Engel's edition, Charles R. Forker describes him as 'timid to amend' and his critical commentary as 'inexpert' (1979, 332). Vermeulen provides a fuller commentary than Engel, but his edition is more limited textually: he does not appear to have collated copies of O or Q and bases his edition on the Bibliothèque Nationale copy of Q (PARIS). I have consulted these editions throughout my work, but they have necessarily exercised little influence on my textual decisions.

THE GENTLEMEN OF VENICE—STOP-PRESS COLLATION OF 1655 OCTAVO AND QUARTO

Copies collated:

Octavo

BO	Boston Public Library, G.3976.51
C.1	University Library, Cambridge, Brett-Smith.876
C.2	University Library, Cambridge, Syn.7.63.383
C11.1	St. Catharine's College, Cambridge, Z.51
DUR (Bamb.)	Durham University Library, Bamburgh Q.7.29/1

282

THE GENTLEMAN OF VENICE: TEXTUAL INTRODUCTION

F.1	Folger Shakespeare Library, S3469
HD.1	Harvard University Library, GEN *EC65 Sh662 655gb
HN.1	Huntington Library, 645647a
L.1	British Library, Cup.404.b.4.(1.) [leaves C7–D5 mutilated]
L6.1	National Art Library (V&A), Dyce 25.E.38
L6.2	National Art Library (V&A), Dyce 25.E.39
LC	Library of Congress, PR3144.G4
Mc.1	McMaster University, B10203
O.1	Bodleian Library, Mal. 256 (7)
PN.1	Princeton University, 3930.3.372
Y.1	Beinecke Library, Yale, Ih Sh66 655

Quarto

BRISTOL	Central Library, Bristol, Bel.Lett.D.13.36 [K4–L2 mutilated]
C11.2	St. Catharine's College, Cambridge, Z.50
C11.3	St. Catharine's College, Cambridge, Z.59
F.2	Folger Shakespeare Library, S3468
HD.2	Harvard University Library, GEN *EC65 Sh662 655g
HN.2	Huntington Library, 146307
ILL	University of Illinois, Urbana, IUA11408
L.2	British Library, C.12.f.18.(6.)
L.3	British Library, C.34.e.4
L6.3	National Art Library (V&A), Dyce 25.C.98
L30	Senate House Library, University of London, [D.–L.L.] (XVII) Bc [Shirley] [A1 and L2 are modern reproductions]
LEEDS	Leeds University Library, Brotherton Lt d SHI
Mc.2	McMaster University, C2039
MEISEI.1	Meisei University, Tokyo, MR3075 [Missing A1, [C]2 (numbered B2)]
MEISEI.2	Meisei University, Tokyo, MR3076 [Missing A1, I2-3, L1 partial, L2]
O.2	Bodleian Library, Mal. 176 (1)
O.3	Bodleian Library, Mal. B 165 (9) [heavily cropped and cw or pag. mutilated C3r, C3v, D4v, E2v, L1r, L1v]
O.4	Bodleian Library, 4° S 3 Art.BS.
PARIS	Bibliothèque Nationale, Paris, YK–398
PEN	University of Pennsylvania, EC Sh655 655gb
PN.2	Princeton University, PR3144.G4 1655
TEX	University of Texas, Austin, Wh Sh66 655g WRE
Y.2	Beinecke Library, Yale, Eliz 212

Variants by forme:

There is some ambiguity about which variants in the octavo edition were caused by press correction and which by pulled type. This list includes only the strongest candidates for press correction; variants that appear to have been caused by pulled type or shifts in reimposition from O to Q are discussed above.

	State 1	*State 2*
A/AB(o)		
8° A4v / 4° A4v		
31	*Cor*	*Cor.*
C/EF(o)		
8° C7r / 4° F3r		
1	here but safety and here	but safety here and
D/GH(o)		
8° D4v / 4° G4v		
36	not;	not

Distribution of variants:

	State 1	*State 2*
A/AB(o)	BO, C.1, C.2, C11.1, DUR (Bamb.), F.1, HN.1, L.1, L6.1, L6.2, LC, Mc.1, O.1, PN.1, Y.1	BRISTOL, C11.2, C11.3, F.2, HD.2, HN.2, ILL, L.2, L.3, L6.3, L30, LEEDS, MEISEI.1, MEISEI.2, Mc.2, PEN, PN.2, PARIS, O.2, O.3, O.4, TEX, Y.2
C/EF(o)	C11.1, LC	BO, BRISTOL, C.1, C.2, C11.2, C11.3, DUR (Bamb.), F.1, F.2, HD.1, HD.2, HN.1, HN.2, ILL, L.1, L.2, L.3, L6.1, L6.2, L6.3, L30, LEEDS, Mc.1, Mc.2, MEISEI.1, MEISEI.2, O.1, O.2, O.3, O.4, PEN, PN.1, PN.2, PARIS, TEX, Y.1, Y.2
D/GH(o)	BO, C11.1, DUR (Bamb.), F.1, L6.1, Mc.1; LC	BRISTOL, C.1, C.2, C11.2, C11.3, F.2, HD.1, HD.2, HN.1, HN.2, ILL, L.2, L.3, L6.2, L6.3, L30, LEEDS, Mc.2, MEISEI.1, MEISEI.2, O.1, O.2, O.3, O.4, PEN, PN.1, PN.2, PARIS, TEX, Y.1, Y.2

THE GENTLEMAN OF VENICE: TEXTUAL INTRODUCTION

Uncorrected errors in both issues:

The compositors were often careless about the spacing between words, and they also crammed words around punctuation to fit more words to a line. It is therefore sometimes difficult to tell if a space has been left out in error or was a deliberate tactic. For this reason, the list below includes only examples where two words are run together without punctuation. Errors in the signatures of Q are discussed above.

8° A5r/4° B1r, 2]	hadly [for hardly]
8° A6v/4° B2v, 2]	'rather
8° A7r/4° B3r, 35]	Aademy
8° A7v/4° B3v, 18]	'poring
8° B1r/4° C1r, 21]	There'
8° B2v/4° C2v, 21]	I I
8° B6v/4° D2v, 1]	*Vrs.* [additional SP at the top of the page]
8° B6v/4° D2v, 22]	Barnardo [for Bernardo]
8° B6v/4° D2v, 35]	nses [turned u]
8° B8r/4° D4r, 34]	Brano's [turned u]
8° B8r/4° D4r, 36]	Herestill
8° C1r/4° E1r, 4]	Igrant
8° C2r/4° E2r, 23]	*Benardo*
8° C2v/4° E2v, 16]	doe's [for does]
8° C2v/4° E2v, 32]	pretheee
8° C3v/4° E3v, 22]	wo'me [for wi'me]
8° C4r/4° E4r, rt]	Veince
8° C4r/4° E4r, 20]	*Bel.* [for *Ro.*]
8° C5r/4° F1r, 2]	*iovanni*
8° C5v/4° F1v, 15]	it's [error for is't]
8° C6v/4° F2v, 28]	destine
8° C6v/4° F2v, 35]	Aud [turned n]
8° C8r/4° F4r, 27]	drpoping
8° D1v/4° G1v, 24]	heel [for he'll]
8° D2v/4° G2v, 2]	theDuke
8° D2v/4° G2v, 27]	e'm
8° D3r/4° G3r, 20]	*Caudiana*
8° D3r/4° G3r, cw]	*Cla.*
8° D3v/4° G3v, 1]	*Cor.* [additional SP at the top of the page]
8° D5r/4° H1r, rt]	Veince
8° D6v/4° H2v, 4]	theGarden
8° D8r/4° H4r, 6]	shouldthink

285

8° D8v/4° H4v, 8]	thingshandsomly
8° D8v/4° H4v, 14]	not?tis
8° E1v/4° I1v, 34]	new's
8° E2v/4° I2v, 14]	gotoo
8° E2v/4° I2v, 30]	Dukes [for Duke]
8° E3v/4° I3v, 11]	moreto fit [for more fit to]
8° E4r/4° I4r, 17]	Isalute
8° E5r/4° K1r, 18]	*Conrari*
8° E5r/4° K1r, 26]	seuse [turned n]
8° E5r/4° K1r, 31]	askyou
8° E5v/4° K1v, 17]	chice [for choice]
8° E6r/4° K2r, 29]	ss [for as]
8° E6v/4° K2v, 1]	*blindhim*
8° E6v/4° K2v, 13]	*ready* [for *reads*]
8° E7r/4° K3r, 1]	*Exeunts*
8° E7r/4° K3r, 13]	havea
8° E7r/4° K3r, 33]	Ring [for King]
8° E7v/4° K3v, 12]	this [for his]
8° E7v/4° K3v, 17]	*Cl.* [for *Co.*]
8° E8r/4° K4r, 3]	np [turned u]
8° F1r/4° L1r, rt]	V enice [O only; corrected during the reimposition of type for Q]

The Gentleman of Venice

A Tragicomedy

[THE EPISTLE DEDICATORY]
TO THE HONOURABLE
SIR THOMAS NIGHTINGALE, BARONET.

Sir,

The poem that approacheth to kiss your hand had once a singular grace and lustre from the scene when it enjoyed the life of action; nor did it want the best hands to applaud it in the theatre. But nothing of these is considerable to the honour it may receive now from your confirmation and acceptance.

I must acknowledge many years have passed since it did *vagire in cunis*, and when it had gotten strength and legs to walk, travelling without direction, it lost itself, till it was recovered after much inquisition and now, upon the first return home, hath made this fortunate address and application to your patronage, in which my ambition is satisfied.

5

---

0 **Thomas Nightingale** (d. 1702). Grandson of Sir Thomas Nightingale of Newport Pond, Essex, who was created Baronet 1 September 1628 and died in 1645 (Betham 1802, 2.2).

0 **Baronet** The lowest rank of British hereditary titles, instituted in England in 1611, in Ireland in 1619, and in Scotland in 1625 (*OED, n.* 2).

2 **poem** It was common for writers to refer to a play as a 'poem' in the early seventeenth century.

2 **kiss...hand** formal greeting offered by a person of inferior status to their superior.

2–3 **singular...action** i.e. a favourable reception and good reputation when it was brought to life on stage. See the Introduction for discussion of the play's performance contexts.

6 *vagire...cunis* wail in the cradle (Latin). Shirley imagines *The Gentleman of Venice* as a child, an image that appears in the prefatory materials of other literary works and plays, including his own prefaces to *Maid's Revenge* and *Grateful Servant*. In the latter he regrets that 'the Silken witts of the Time...are transported with many illiterate and prodigious births' (A2r).

7–8 **travelling...home** Shirley probably refers here to the loss of the manuscript playbook used by Queen Henrietta Maria's Men at Salisbury Court in 1639 in the period after the initial ban on commercial playing in 1642, when the property and goods of many of the playing companies were sold or dispersed.

8 **inquisition** investigation.

9 **fortunate** auspicious, lucky.

---

0 The Epistle Dedicatory] *this edn; on second page only (A2v) in* Q/O   0 THOMAS] *Gifford; THO.* Q/O

THE COMPLETE WORKS OF JAMES SHIRLEY, VOLUME 7

I know this nation hath been fruitful in names of eminent honour. But in these times 10
there be more lords than noblemen, and while you are pleased to smile upon this piece
I most cheerfully throw myself and it upon your protection, whose single worth to me
is beyond all the boasted greatness and voluminous titles of our age.

Be pleased to read what is presented to you, at an hour you will dedicate to recreation, and preserve the author in your memory, whose highest desires are to make good 15
the character of

Sir,

> The most humble among
> those that honour you,
>
> JAMES SHIRLEY

---

11 there...noblemen there are more men of aristocratic status than of true nobility. Shirley apparently
views Nightingale, a baronet, as an exception to this rule.
16 character reputation.

THE GENTLEMAN OF VENICE

THE NAMES WITH SOME SMALL
CHARACTERS OF THE PERSONS

[*Contarini,*] *the* DUKE *of Venice*

CORNARI, *a gentleman of Venice, of a great fortune, but having no child, contrives to have an heir from his wife, and against the nature and custom of the Italian endears an English gentleman to her affection and society*

FLORELLI, *the English gentleman, of a noble extraction and person, much honoured for his parts, by which he gained much reputation in the academies*　　5

MALIPIERO, *nephew to Cornari, a man of a violent spirit, and hated by his uncle for his debaucheries*

THE . . . PERSONS *The Gentleman of Venice* and *The Politician* were both printed in 1655 with unusual cast-lists that include alongside the names of the characters detailed descriptions of their personalities and roles in the play (see Štollová 2016). Although a modern edition would normally reorder the characters in order to avoid the early modern convention of ranking characters by gender and social status, the order presented in O and Q has been retained so as to preserve the style of the original.

CHARACTERS Descriptions.

PERSONS Dramatic characters.

1 **Contarini** The Contarinis were one of the twelve founding families of the Venetian republic. At the time when *The Gentleman of Venice* was composed and performed in the late 1630s, five members of this family had served as Doge of Venice, most recently Nicolò Contarini (1553–1631), doge from 1630 to 1631. Another member of the family, Carlo Contarini (1580–1656), was doge from 1655 to 1656, when the play was published. Given that the action of the play involves a war between Venice and Genoa, Shirley may have had in mind Andrea Contarini, whose service as doge from 1367 to 1382 saw the last of a series of wars between the two republics, the War of Chioggia (1378–81). Shirley also uses the name Contarini for Italian noblemen in *Humorous Courtier* and *Sisters*, both of which are set in Parma.

1 DUKE *of Venice* English writers frequently translated the Venetian 'Doge' as 'Duke' (the two terms have the same root in Latin *duc-* or *dux* [*OED*, Doge *n.* 1]). They were aware that the doge was elected for his lifetime, and that the office was not hereditary, but nonetheless sometimes represented him as a conventional duke. The disjunction is partly explained by the fact that Duke Contarini's original in *El hombre por su palabra* is Lisandro, King of Macedonia.

2 CORNARI The Cornari were a prominent family in early modern Venice. Giovanni Cornaro was Doge of Venice between 1625 and 1629, while Cardinal Federico Cornaro was Patriarch of Venice between 1631 and 1644. There is probably also a pun derived from *cornu*, the Latin for 'horn', since Cornari is seeking to give himself cuckold's horns.

2 *gentleman of Venice* This description suggests that Cornari is the 'gentleman of Venice' of the play's title, and Malipiero exclaims scornfully 'You a gentleman of Venice?' when his uncle refuses to lend him money (1.1.134). But the term is also used of Giovanni, who is created a 'gentleman of Venice' (4.2.32), and Ursula repeatedly refers to Thomazo as a 'gentleman'. For further discussion of this important term and its Venetian contexts see the Introduction.

3 *against . . . Italian* English commentators suggested that Italian men were especially jealous and protective of their wives.

5 FLORELLI It is not clear why the 'English gentleman' has an Italian name; it is possible that Shirley drew it from a source text that has not yet been identified. He uses the female name Florelia in *Imposture*.

5 *extraction* descent.

5 *person* bearing, appearance.

6 *parts* abilities, talents.

6 *academies* places of training or education. In the 1630s the term was used especially for places where specific skills (e.g. dancing, riding, combat) or general modes of behaviour and discourse were taught and displayed. Giovanni refers to them as 'schools / Of wit and action' (2.1.116–17).

7 MALIPIERO The surname of a prominent Venetian family. Pasquale Malipiero served as Doge of Venice between 1457 and 1462.

7 *spirit* character, disposition.

---

1 *Contarini*] *Gifford subst.; not in* Q/O

289

THE COMPLETE WORKS OF JAMES SHIRLEY, VOLUME 7

GIOVANNI, *supposed son of Roberto the duke's gardener, whose noble mind could not
be suppressed in his low condition, and in love with Bellaura* 10

THOMAZO, *the supposed son of the duke, whom no precepts, nor education at court,
could form into honourable desires or employments*

MARINO
CANDIANO } *courtiers of honour*

ROBERTO, *the duke's gardener, an humorous jolly old man* 15

BERNARDO
MARCELLO } *companions of Malipiero*

GEORGIO, *the gardener's servant*

[SERVANT *to Cornari*]

[FIRST GENTLEMAN] 20

[SECOND GENTLEMAN]

[THIRD GENTLEMAN]

[SENATORS]

[COURTIER]

BRAVOS 25

9 GIOVANNI His equivalent in *El hombre por su palabra* is Federico, supposed son of Alberto, the King of Macedonia's gardener.

9 *supposed son* The 1655 edition does not seek to conceal the twist at the end of the story.

11 THOMAZO His equivalent in *El hombre por su palabra* is Alejandro, supposed nephew of the King of Macedonia.

11 *precepts* rules for virtuous conduct.

12 *employments* activities, pursuits.

13–14 *of honour* 1) of high status or dignity; 2) holding a particular high-status office (*OED*, Honour *n.* 3a).

14 CANDIANO He is described in 1.3.0 SD as '*a senator*'.

15 ROBERTO His equivalent in *El hombre por su palabra* is Alberto, gardener to the King of Macedonia.

15 *humorous* 1) whimsical (*OED*, *adj.* 3a); 2) amusing (*OED*, *adj.* 4). This term also invokes the comedy of 'humours' developed by Jonson and Chapman in the late 1590s, which drew on the Galenic idea that the body was composed of four humours (black bile, blood, phlegm, and yellow bile), an imbalance of which affected an individual's personality.

15 *jolly* 1) cheerful (*OED*, *adj.* 1); 2) high-spirited (*OED*, *adj.* 3a); 3) convivial (*OED*, *adj.* 4).

18 GEORGIO His equivalent in *El hombre por su palabra* is Fineo, Federico's friend and servant. He refers to his 'prenticeship' (i.e. apprenticeship) (3.2.19), suggesting his youth as well as his subordinate position within Roberto's household.

19 SERVANT . . . *Cornari* Appears and speaks in two scenes (1.1 and 5.2) but does not appear in the 'Names' in O and Q.

20 FIRST . . . GENTLEMAN A group of 'Gentlemen' appear with Florelli in 1.3, one of whom is singled out as '1. *Gent.*' in O and Q; the others are given three mass speeches (1.3.54, 63, 64). Three 'Gentlemen' then meet Florelli in 5.3, when they are given the speech prefixes '*1.*', '*2.*' and '*3.*' in O and Q.

23 SENATORS A group of Senators appear in 1.3 and 5.4, one of whom speaks on each occasion. In 5.4 their number could include Candiano, if the actor was not required to double another character.

24 COURTIER Appears and speaks in 5.4 but does not appear in the 'Names'.

25 BRAVOS hired soldiers or assassins. The Bravos are required to speak in 2.1, but their lines are not divided up among them in O and Q.

19–24] *this edn; not in* Q/O

290

THE GENTLEMAN OF VENICE

ATTENDANTS

[OFFICERS]

BELLAURA, *the duke's niece, whom Giovanni passionately affected*

CLAUDIANA, *wife to Cornari, a lady of excellent beauty, ingratiated by her husband to Florelli, the English gentleman*   30

URSULA, *wife to Roberto, a froward woman, and who much doted upon Thomazo, her nurse-child*

ROSABELLA, *a courtesan*

---

26 ATTENDANTS Attending the Duke; one of them speaks in 4.2.

27 OFFICERS Appear in 3.4 but do not speak; these appear to be the 'Soldiers' listed in 'The Names' in O and Q, but I have followed the description of them as 'Officers' within the play itself (3.4.149 SD).

28 BELLAURA Her equivalent in *El hombre por su palabra* is Lucinda, daughter of the King of Macedonia.

28 *passionately affected* loved ardently.

29 *ingratiated* brought into favour, rendered agreeable. It is not clear whether the description means that Claudiana is persuaded to favour Florelli or that she is offered to him.

31 URSULA Her equivalent in *El hombre por su palabra* is Celia, Federico's sister, but Shirley changes both the relationship and her character.

31 *froward* bad-tempered, hard to please, ungovernable.

32 *nurse-child* Ursula was Thomazo's wet-nurse (i.e. the woman who breast-fed him as a baby).

---

27 OFFICERS] *Gifford; Souldiers* Q/O

I.I   THE COMPLETE WORKS OF JAMES SHIRLEY, VOLUME 7

THE SCENE: VENICE.

1[.1]

> *Enter* MALIPIERO, *who knocks at a door, to him* [*enters*] *a* SERVANT.

MALIPIERO Where is my uncle, sirrah?
SERVANT   Not within.
MALIPIERO Come hither; tell me truth.
SERVANT   He's gone abroad.
MALIPIERO He has commanded your officious rogueship
    To deny him to me.
>   *Malipiero kicks him.*
SERVANT   What do you mean, sir?
MALIPIERO To speak with my uncle, sirrah, and these kicks   5
    Shall fetch him hither.
SERVANT   Help!   *He runs in.*
MALIPIERO   Your howling will
    Be his cue to appear.
>   *Enter* CORNARI.

CORNARI   What insolence is this?
MALIPIERO No insolence: I did but correct your knave
    Because I would not lose my labour, sir.
    I came to speak wi'ye.
CORNARI   Shall I not be safe   10
    Within my house? Hence.
MALIPIERO   I ha' not done yet.
CORNARI You were best assault me, too.
MALIPIERO   I must borrow money,
    And that some call a striking; but you are
    My very loving uncle, and do know
    How necessary it is your nephew should not   15
    Want for your honour.
CORNARI   Hence. I disclaim
    And throw thee from my blood; thou art a bastard.

---

0 The scene is set on the doorstep of Cornari's house.
1 **sirrah** address to men or boys, indicating contempt or a reprimand, derived from 'sir' (*OED*, *n.* 1a).
3 **rogueship** derisive mock title, playing on 'worship'.
8 **knave** 1) manservant, especially one of low status (*OED*, *n.* 2); 2) rogue (*OED*, *n.* 3).
16 **Want…honour** i.e. go needy if you want to protect your reputation.
16–17 **I…blood** i.e. I reject all family ties with you.
17 **thee…thou** Cornari's shift from chilly 'you' (l. 12) to indignant 'thee' and 'thou' signals his anger.

1[.1]] *Gifford subst.* (ACT I. SCENE I.*);* Act. 1. Q/O   **0 SD** *enters*] *this edn; not in* Q/O
4 SD *Malipiero*] Q/O *subst.* (*Mal.*)

292

THE GENTLEMAN OF VENICE

MALIPIERO Indeed you do lie, uncle, and 'tis love
And reverence bids me say so. It would cost
Dear should the proudest gentleman of Venice 20
Have called my mother whore, but you shall only
By the disburse of fifty ducats take
My anger off, and I'll be still your nephew,
And drink your health and my good aunt's.
CORNARI Drink thy confusion.
MALIPIERO   Heaven forbid your heir should so 25
Forget himself and lose the benefit
Of such a fair estate as you have, uncle.
Shall I have gold for present use?
CORNARI   Not a zecchino.
MALIPIERO Consider but what company I keep.
CORNARI Things that lie like consumptions on their family 30
And will in time eat up their very name,
A knot of fools and knaves.
MALIPIERO   Take heed, be temperate;
A hundred ducats else will hardly satisfy.
The duke's own son, Signor Thomazo, wo'not
Blush to be drunk, sir, in my company. 35
CORNARI He is corrupted
Amongst diseases like thyself, become
His father's shame and sorrow, and hath no
Inheritance of his noble nature.
MALIPIERO   You
Were best call him bastard too. The money 40
I modestly demanded, and that quickly,
And quietly, before I talk aloud;
I may be heard to th'palace else.

19 **reverence** deep or due respect.
22 **disburse** payment.
22 **ducats** Venetian coins (*ducati*), issued in gold and silver. Shirley may have thought of them as equivalent to English crowns (coins worth 5 shillings), as he refers instead to crowns at 2.1.237; Florio in *Queen Anna's New World of Words* offers '*duckets, crownes*' as translations of *ducati* (1611, K3v).
25 **confusion** ruin, destruction.
28 **present** urgent, immediate.
28 **zecchino** a Venetian coin, another name for the gold *ducato*. Florio states that they are '*worth about seauen shillings and sixpence*' (1611, 3E7v).
30 **consumptions** sources of decay, destruction, wasting of the body, or needless expense.
32 **knot** gang, company.
32 **be temperate** keep calm, use restraint.
40 **The money** i.e. Produce the money.
43 **to** as far as.

25 Drink...confusion] *lineation this edn;* Drink thy / Confusion Q/O   28 zecchino] Q/O (Zechine)

293

I.I   THE COMPLETE WORKS OF JAMES SHIRLEY, VOLUME 7

CORNARI   Thou heard? I'll tell thee,
       Were treason talked I believe thy testimony
       Would hold no credit against the hangman. But   45
       I lose too-precious time in dialogue with thee;
       To be short, therefore, know –
MALIPIERO   Very well, to th'point.
CORNARI I will consume all my estate myself.
MALIPIERO You do not know the ways without instruction.
CORNARI I will be instructed, then.
MALIPIERO   I do like that;   50
       Let's join societies, and I'll be satisfied.
       Let me have part in the consuming of
       The money that does mould for want of sunbeams
       Within your musty coffers, I'll release you.
       You have no swaggering face, but I can teach   55
       Your very looks to make a noise, and if
       You cannot drink or game, we'll ha' devices.
       You may have whores. I that but live in hope
       After your death keep twelve in pension –
       They wear my livery. I'll resign the leverets;   60
       I can ha' more. I have a list of all
       The courtesans in Venice, which shall tumble
       And keep their buggle-boos for thee, dear uncle:
       We'll teach thee a thousand ways.
CORNARI   It sha'not need,
       I shall take other courses with my wealth   65
       And none of you shall share in't. I have a humour
       To turn my money into hospitals;

51 **join societies** form a partnership.
54 **coffers** chests, treasury.
55 **swaggering face** i.e. the demeanour of a loud, quarrelsome young man.
57 **game** gamble.
57 **devices** i.e. other schemes.
58–9 **but…death** i.e. can only maintain my present lifestyle because people think I will inherit your money.
59 **pension** board and lodging. The pronunciation 'pen-si-on' fills out the pentameter line, and Shirley similarly treats '-ion' as disyllabic elsewhere in the play.
60 **livery** 1) uniforms; 2) *fig.* the signs of venereal disease.
60 **leverets** 1) young hares; 2) whores, a usage alluding to the liveliness of leverets (Williams 1994, 2.805–6). Shirley uses the term in *Gamester* (1.1), *Imposture* (1.2), *Honour and Riches* (D1r), and *Honoria and Mammon* (1.2), and it also appears in his collaboration with William Cavendish, Duke of Newcastle, *Country Captain* (2.1).
62 **tumble** engage in sex.
63 **buggle-boos** private parts, vaginas (*OED*, Buggle-boo *n.* 1; Williams 1994, 3.166, both citing this play alongside other examples).
63–4 **thee…thee** Malipiero shifts to the intimate 'thee' as he gets increasingly excited about his plan.
66 **humour** fancy.
67 **hospitals** Cornari may refer to a range of charitable institutions that hosted travellers and pilgrims, looked after the needy, educated and maintained children, or tended to the sick; Malipiero understands the latter.

46 too-precious] *this edn;* too pretious Q/O   63 buggle-boos] Q/O *subst.* (bugle bowes)

294

THE GENTLEMAN OF VENICE   I.I

Your riots come not thither.
MALIPIERO   But we may:
Drink and diseases are the ways to that too.
But will you turn a master of this college   70
You talk of, uncle? This same hospital?
And lay out money to buy wooden legs
For crippled men of war, invite to your cost
Men that have lost their noses in hot service?
Live and converse with rotten bawds and bone-setters,   75
Provide pensions for surgery, and hard words
That eat like corrosives, and more afflict
The patient? But you'll save charges; I consider
My aunt, your wife –
CORNARI   How dar'st thou mention her
With thy foul breath?
MALIPIERO   May be excellent at composing   80
Of med'cines for corrupted lungs, impostumes,
At making plasters, diet-drinks, and in charity
Will be a great friend to the pox.
CORNARI   Thou villain!
MALIPIERO And you'll be famous by't. I may in time,
As I said before, if lust and wine assist me,   85
Grow unsound too, and be one of her patients,
And have an office after in her household
To prepare lint and cerecloths, empty veins,
And be controller of the crutches. Oh,
The world would praise the new foundation   90

74 lost…service i.e. suffered the effects of syphilis (which attacks the soft tissues of the nose) through their sexual promiscuity.
75 bone-setters 1) people (often without medical training) who treated dislocations and fractures (*OED*, Bone-setter *n.* 1); 2) people who treat venereal disease; 3) bawds (Williams 1994, 1.130–1).
77 corrosives 1) acid (*OED*, Corrosive *n.* 1); 2) caustic medicines (*OED*, Corrosive *n.* 2).
78 But you'll But if you wish to.
79 thou The reference to Claudiana appears to inflame Cornari's temper again.
81 impostumes swellings, abscesses.
82 plasters 1) medicines spread on bandages or dressings for application on the skin (*OED*, *n.* 1a); 2) soothing remedies (*OED*, *n.* 1b).
82 diet-drinks medicines.
83 pox syphilis.
86 unsound diseased (*OED*, *adj.* 1a), with a pun on morally corrupted (*OED*, *adj.* 2a).
87 after in later times.
88 lint material for dressing wounds.
88 cerecloths 1) plasters (*OED*, Cerecloth *n.* 1); 2) winding sheets (*OED*, Cerecloth *n.* 2).
88 empty veins i.e. draw blood in a medicinal procedure.
89 controller…crutches officer with the job of looking after the crutches that support the sick people. Malipiero also puns on 'crotches' (see *OED*, Crutches *n.* 8a), referring again to the sexual origins of the patients' maladies.

295

I.I THE COMPLETE WORKS OF JAMES SHIRLEY, VOLUME 7

Of such a pest-house, and the poor souls drink
Your health at every festival in hot porridge!
CORNARI Art thou of kin to me?
MALIPIERO   I think I am
As near as your brother's eldest son, who had
No competent estate from his own parents,   95
And for that reason by wise Nature was
Ordained to be your heir that have enough, uncle.
The Fates must be obeyed, and while your land
Is fastened to my name for want of males –
Which, I do hope, if my aunt hold her barrenness   100
You will never bang out of her sheaf – I may
Be confident to write myself your nephew.
CORNARI Thou hast no seeds of goodness in thee, but
I may find ways to cross your hopeful interest.
MALIPIERO You'll find no seeds in my aunt's parsley-bed,   105
I hope, and then I'm safe. But take your course.
Supply me for the present, for your honour –
The ducats, come.
CORNARI   You are cozened.
MALIPIERO   As you would not
Have me pull down this house when you are dead
And build a stews, the ducats, come.
CORNARI   Thou coward!   110
MALIPIERO Because I do not cut your throat? That were
The way to disinherit myself quaintly.
CORNARI Canst thou not steal and so deserve a hanging?

---

91 **pest-house** hospital for those suffering from infectious diseases.

92 **porridge** thick, savoury soup made with vegetables or meat and thickened with barley or pulses, often given to invalids.

94 **near** closely related.

95 **competent** adequate, appropriate.

99 **males** i.e. direct male descendants.

101 **bang…sheaf** A violent image of sex taken from the activity of threshing corn by beating it with a flail. It also appears in Fletcher's *Wit Without Money*, which Shirley may have revised in the 1630s, in which Vallentine asks his tenants 'Have you not thrashing [i.e. threshing] worke enough, but children / Must be bangd out oth' sheafe too?' (Beaumont and Fletcher 1966–96, vol. 1, 1.1.91–2).

103 **seeds** germs, latent signs.

104 **cross** thwart, debar.

104 **hopeful** expectant.

105 **seeds** offspring, stock. Malipiero assumes that Claudiana is infertile, but it later becomes apparent that Cornari is convinced that the problem lies with himself.

105 **parsley-bed** womb (*OED*, *n.* 2; Williams 1994, 2.994–5).

108 **cozened** deceived.

108 **As** i.e. If.

110 **stews** brothel, precinct full of brothels.

111 **cut…throat** Malipiero imagines murdering his uncle in revenge for his insults.

112 **quaintly** ingeniously (said ironically).

113 **so…hanging** i.e. because convicted thieves could be hanged.

THE GENTLEMAN OF VENICE   I.I

MALIPIERO Yes, I can, and am often tempted, but I wo'not
    Do you that mighty wrong, to let what you have   115
    So long and with so little conscience gathered
    Be lost in confiscation by my felony.
    I know a way worth ten on't, yet thus much
    I'll bind it with an oath: when I turn thief,
    Your gold shall be the first I will make bold with.   120
    In the meantime, lend me the trifling ducats
    And do not trouble me.
CORNARI   Not a mocenigo
    To save thee from the galleys.
MALIPIERO   No? The galleys!
    Must I shift still? Remember and die shortly?
    I'll live, I will, and rather than not be   125
    Revenged on thy estate, I will eat roots –
    Coarse ones, I mean – love and undo an herb-wife
    With eating up her salads, live and lap
    Only in barley-water. Think on't yet:
    I am now for wine; you know not what that heat   130
    May do, the injury being so fresh. I may
    Return, and you'll repent.
CORNARI   'Tis more than I
    Can hope of thee. Go to your rabble, sir.

115–16 what…gathered Suggests that Cornari has gained his wealth through trade or subterfuge rather than purely through inheritance.

117 lost…felony i.e. legally seized as a punishment for his murder of Cornari. In early modern English common and statute law, a felony was a crime more serious than a misdemeanour, and one typically involving the forfeiture of lands and goods.

118 on't of it.

120 make bold take a liberty, presume.

121 trifling insignificant, of little value.

122 mocenigo Venetian silver coin introduced under Pietro Mocenigo (Doge of Venice 1474–6) and issued until 1575.

123 galleys boats used to take people and goods around the Mediterranean; the oarsmen were usually enslaved people or condemned criminals.

124 shift provide for myself, continue to cheat for a living.

124 Remember i.e. Reflect on my sins.

126–31 Malipiero imagines himself living a humble but healthy life in order to survive Cornari, but he immediately undercuts this threat with another one, that he will go drinking and return in an inebriated fury.

127 herb-wife woman who sells herbs.

128 lap drink in the style of an animal.

129 barley-water drink made from pearl barley, used as a soothing medicine (*OED*, *n.*).

130 heat inflamed state (here caused by drunkenness).

---

122 mocenigo] Q/O *(Muccinigo)*   **127** Coarse] *Gifford;* Course Q/O

297

I.I   THE COMPLETE WORKS OF JAMES SHIRLEY, VOLUME 7

MALIPIERO You a gentleman of Venice? But remember –
    A pox o' your wealth! I will do something   135
    To deserve the halter, that I may disgrace
    The house I came on, and at my execution
    Make such a speech as at the report thou shalt
    Turn desperate, and with the remnant of
    My cord go hang thyself, and that way forfeit   140
    All thy estate when I am dead. I'll do
    Or this, or something worse, to be revenged.   *Exit Malipiero.*

      Enter SERVANT.

CORNARI He's lost! This doth new fire my resolution.
    [*To Servant*] See if your mistress be yet ready, sirrah;
    Say I expect her.   *Exit Servant.*   145
    My blood is almost in a fever with
    My passion, but Claudiana may cure all,
    Whom I have wrought with importunity
    To be spectator at the exercise
    This day i'th'Academy. Here she comes.   150

      Enter CLAUDIANA.

    Art ready?
CLAUDIANA   Ever to obey you, sir,
    But if you would consider yet, you may
    Be kind and let me stay. I dare not think
    You are less careful of my honour, but
    You gave once command, with my consent too,   155
    Not to be seen too much abroad.

---

134 **You** i.e. Are you.
135 **A pox o'** An oath meaning literally 'a plague on'; a modern oath with similar force would be 'damn'.
136 **halter** noose.
137 **The...on** My family.
139 **Turn desperate** Despair.
140–1 **forfeit...estate** The land and goods of people who committed suicide were forfeit to the state.
142 **Or...or** Either...or
143 **lost** ruined, damned.
143 **new...resolution** i.e. make me even more determined.
147 **passion** outburst of emotion.
148 **wrought** persuaded.
148 **importunity** persistence.
149 **exercise** displays of martial or intellectual skill.
153 **Be kind** 1) Act in an affectionate, benevolent, or noble manner (*OED*, Kind *adj.* 7b, 10, 6b); 2) Behave in a manner suitable to a husband or an Italian (see *OED*, Kind 7a, 4a).
153 **stay** i.e. remain at home.
154 **are** i.e. have become.

---

134 remember –] *this edn;* remember, Q/O   135 o'] *this edn;* 'a Q/O
142 **SD**1 *Malipiero*] Q/O *subst. (Mal.)*   144 **SD**] *Gifford subst.; not in* Q/O

THE GENTLEMAN OF VENICE

CORNARI   I did.
I must confess, Claudiana, I had thoughts
And scruples which thy innocence hath cleared,
And though our nice Italian everywhere
Impose severely on their wives, I should   160
Be unjust to make thee still a prisoner to
Thy melancholy chamber. Take the air,
'Tis for thy health, and while I wait upon thee
Thou art above the tongue and wound of scandal.
CLAUDIANA I know your presence takes off all dishonour,   165
But –
CORNARI   No more, I charge thee by thy love,
And to convince all arguments against it
I have provided so thou shalt observe
Unseen the bold contentions of art
And action.
CLAUDIANA   I'm not well.
CORNARI   I shall be angry   170
If my desires be played withal. Pretend not
With purpose to delude me; I have blessings
Stored in thy health, but if you practise any
Infirmity to cross my will that aims
At the security of thy health and honour –   175
CLAUDIANA Sir, you shall steer me.
CORNARI   This becomes Claudiana;
I will thank thee in a kiss. [*Kisses her then calls offstage.*] Prepare
The gondola!
SERVANT (*Within*) It waits.
CORNARI [*To Claudiana*] And I on thee,
The treasure of my eyes and heart.   *Exeunt.*

---

158 scruples doubts.
159 nice strict, over-careful.
162 melancholy chamber Evokes the oppressive atmosphere of Cornari's household.
171 withal with.
172–3 I…health The value that Cornari places on Claudiana's health is apparently not merely a product of his love for her, but his desire for her to be able to give him an heir.
173 practise i.e. counterfeit.
174 that i.e. Cornari's 'will'.
176 becomes suits.
178 waits 1) is waiting (as the Servant intends); 2) offers service, watches (in Cornari's pun in l. 178).

---

177 SD] *this edn; not in* Q/O; *goes to the door Gifford*   **178 gondola**] *Gifford; Gundelo* Q/O
178 SD2] *this edn; not in* Q/O

[1.2]

Enter ROBERTO, URSULA, [*and*] GEORGIO.

ROBERTO Where is my son Giovanni, sirrah?

GEORGIO He went two hours ago to the Academy
To see the exercise today.

URSULA   How's that?
What business has he there, pray, 'mongst gentlemen?
He does presume too much.

ROBERTO   Patience, good Ursula.   5

URSULA You give him too much rein; 'twould become him
To follow his profession and not look after
Those gentlemanly sports.

ROBERTO   No tempest, wife;
No thund'ring, Ursula. Am not I the duke's
Chief gardener, ha? And shall I make my son   10
A drudge, confine him here to be an earthworm,
Live like a mole, or make it his last blessing
To plant, and order quickset? Let him walk
And see the fashions.

URSULA   He has cost you sweetly
To bring him up. What use had he of learning?   15
What benefit but to endanger us,
And with his poring upon books at midnight
To set the house on fire? Let him know how
To rule a spade, as you ha' done.

ROBERTO   He does so,
And knows how to inoculate, my Ursula,   20
My nimble tongue. No more. Because he read
The story of Xanthippe t'other night,

---

0 The scene appears to be set in the Duke's garden.

6 rein freedom (referring to the long straps attached to the bridle of a horse).

7 profession i.e. that of gardener.

8–9 tempest...thund'ring i.e. outbursts of emotion.

11 drudge servile worker.

12 blessing gift from God (said ironically) (*OED*, *n.* 4a).

13 quickset hedges (*OED*, *n.*¹ 2).

14 sweetly i.e. a great deal.

18 set...fire i.e. with the candles that he uses to read by.

19 rule wield, hold authority over.

20 inoculate propagate, encourage. An image from horticulture, meaning to 'set' or insert a bud or cutting into another plant for cultivation (*OED*, *n.* 1a); Roberto apparently means that Giovanni gives him the conversational prompts that he needs to be witty.

22 Xanthippe Legendarily bad-tempered wife of the philosopher Socrates.

[1.2]] *Gifford subst. (*SCENE II.*); not in* Q/O   **0 SD** *and*] *Gifford; not in* Q/O

300

THE GENTLEMAN OF VENICE

I.2

That could out-talk a drum and sound a point
Of war to her husband, honest Socrates,
You took a pet. He shall abroad sometimes,   25
And read and write till his head ache. Go to.
URSULA So, so, the duke's garden shall be then
Well looked to! He deserves a pension
For reading *Amadis de Gaule* and *Guzman*
And *Don Quixot*? But I'll read him a lecture –   30
ROBERTO You will? Offer but to bark at him,
And I will send him to the university
To anger thee. Nay, he shall learn to fence, too,
And fight with thee at twenty several weapons
Except thy two-edged tongue. A little thing   35
Would make me entertain a dancing-master.
Peace, or I will destroy thy kitchen, Ursula,
Disorder all thy trinkets, and instead
Of brass and pewter, hang up viol da gambas.
I'll set an organ up at thy bed's head,   40
And he shall play upon't. What, tyrannical

23–4 sound…war make a noise like the trumpet call that signalled the beginning of a skirmish (see *OED*, Point *n.* 28; Falconer 1965, 58).

24 Socrates Ancient Athenian philosopher (*c.* 470–399 BCE). He is supposed to have married the younger Xanthippe when he was in his fifties.

25 a pet offence.

26 Go to An expression indicating impatience (compare 'get away', 'away with you').

28 look'd to taken care of.

29–30 Amadis…Quixot These three Spanish works were popular throughout Europe, but they may also nod to the fact that Shirley adapts a Spanish source in the Giovanni-Bellaura plot. As García (1998, 195) notes, they also represent the three 'géneros dominantes' (dominant genres) of Spanish literature as it circulated in England.

29 Amadis de Gaule Famous chivalric romance probably dating from the fourteenth century, which may have originally been written in Spanish or Portuguese. The earliest extant version, *Amadís de Gaula*, by Garci Rodríguez de Montalvo, was published in Spanish in 1508. It was translated into English from the French by Anthony Munday around 1590 but was well-known in England at a much earlier date.

29 Guzman *Guzmán de Alfarache*, a Spanish picaresque work by Mateo Alemán, published in two parts in 1599 and 1604. An English translation by James Mabbe was published in 1622.

30 Don Quixot Miguel de Cervantes's novel *El ingenioso hidalgo Don Quijote de la Mancha*, published in two parts in 1605 and 1615. English translations by Thomas Shelton were published in 1612 (Part 1) and 1620 (Part 2).

30 read…lecture i.e. teach him a lesson.

34 several different.

35 two-edged often used of a sword with two cutting edges.

35 A…thing i.e. The least provocation.

36 entertain employ.

37 Peace Be quiet.

38 trinkets small drinking vessels.

39 brass and pewter i.e. kitchen implements.

39 viol da gambas large string instruments held between the legs.

---

30 *Quixot?*] *this edn; Quixot,* Q/O   **30** lecture –] *this edn;* lecture. Q/O
39 viol da gambas] Q/O *(Violl de Gambos)*

I.2   THE COMPLETE WORKS OF JAMES SHIRLEY, VOLUME 7

To thy own flesh and blood? To Giovanni?
My heir? My only boy? Fetch me a tailor;
He shall have new clothes and no more be warm
With the reversion of your petticoats.   45
Do not provoke me. What, imperious?
Get you in, or I will swinge you. Go and weed.

URSULA Now for vexation could I cry my heart out.   *Exit.*

ROBERTO Sirrah, stay you. And is Giovanni gone
To th'Academy, say'st?

GEORGIO   Yes, sir. They say   50
There is an English gentleman that wins
The garland from 'em all at every exercise.
One of the court told my young master on't,
As he enquired of every gentleman
Comes into th'garden, 'What's the news abroad?'   55

ROBERTO And does he not tell thee tales and dainty stories
Sometimes?

GEORGIO   Oh, of Tamburlaine, and the Great Turk, and all
His concubines; he knows 'em to a hair.
He is more perfect in the chronicles
Than I am in my prayers.

ROBERTO   I do believe't.   60

GEORGIO And talks a battle as he were among 'em;
He tickles all your turbans, and, in a rage,
Wishes he had the cutting of their cabbages
To show what house he came on.

ROBERTO   Ha, my boy!

---

45 **the...petticoats** i.e. garments made out of Ursula's old clothes.

45 **reversion** right to succeed to (a legal term).

46 **What, imperious?** Are you trying to domineer over me? Ursula may gesture or pull faces to provoke this reaction; Shirley frequently uses dialogue to indicate the action and emotions of non-speaking characters.

47 **swinge** 1) beat (*OED*, *v.* 1a); 2) *fig.*, chastise (*OED*, *v.* 1.b).

52 **garland** wreath given to the victor in a contest. The usage here may be figurative.

57 **Tamburlaine** Central Asian conqueror Timur (1336–1405), known as 'Timur the Lame'; he is the central character in Marlowe's play *Tamburlaine the Great* (1587), and Shirley probably exploits spectators' knowledge of this play.

57 **Great Turk** Ottoman Sultan. At the time that the play was written and performed the Sultan was Murad IV (1612–40), who ruled from 1623 to 1640. English commentators frequently referred to the Ottoman empire as 'Turkey' even though it covered a large territory in north Africa, western Asia, and southeast Europe.

58 **to...hair** in every detail.

62 **tickles...turbans** i.e. defeats the imaginary Ottoman soldiers.

63 **cutting...cabbages** An appropriately horticultural metaphor for beheading enemies, but Georgio may also continue a line of thought from 'turbans' as 'cabbages' were also offcuts of cloth that tailors and dressmakers kept as a perk of their trade (see *OED*, Cabbage *n.*³ 1).

64 **what house** i.e. that of a gardener.

---

62 turbans] Q/O *(turbants)*

302

THE GENTLEMAN OF VENICE   I.2

GEORGIO Oh, sir, he has a pestilent memory.   65
    He told me t'other day there was another
    World in the moon, and that the world we live in
    Shines like to that to people that live there,
    How many miles it is about the earth,
    How many to the stars. I fear he will   70
    Be mad if he read much, 'tis just like ravening,
    And such hard words would choke me to repeat 'em.
ROBERTO He never tells me this.
GEORGIO   We are familiar.
    You are his father, and he dares not lie
    To you; to me he may talk anything,   75
    He knows my understanding to an inch.
    Would you would speak to him, though, to take a little
    More pains? 'Tis I do all the droil, the dirt-work.
    When I am digging, he is cutting unicorns
    And lions in some hedge, or else devising   80
    New knots upon the ground, drawing out crowns
    And the duke's arms, castles and cannons in 'em.
    Here galleys, there a ship giving a broadside;
    Here out of turf he carves a senator
    With all his robes, making a speech to thyme,   85
    That grows hard by, and twenty curiosities.
    I think he means to embroider all the garden
    Shortly, but I do all the coarse work. Here's
    My mistress again.

        Enter URSULA.

66–8 another...there The idea that the moon might be habitable was a current subject of debate in the late
1630s, with John Wilkins's *The Discovery of a World in the Moon*, which drew on the theories of Galileo and
Kepler, and Francis Godwin's *The Man in the Moon, or Discourse of a Voyage Thither* both published in 1638.
Burton writes in the preface to *The Anatomy of Melancholy*, 'Copernicus is of opinion the earth is a plannet,
moues and shines to others, as the Moone doth to vs. *Digges, Gilbert, Keplerus* and others defend this Hypothesis
of his in sober sadnesse, and that the Moone is inhabited; if it be so, that the Earth is a Moone, then are we all
lunaticke within it' (1621, c8r).
    73 **familiar** close friends (*OED, adj.* 3a).
    76 **to...inch** i.e. precisely.
    77–8 **take...pains** put in a bit more effort.
    78 **droil** drudgery.
    78 **dirt-work** dirty work.
    81 **knots** flower-beds with intricate designs (*OED*, Knot *n.*[1] 7).
    83 **broadside** discharge of all its artillery on one side (*OED, n.* 2).
    85–6 **making...by** Giorgio offers an image of a senator orating on a lofty subject, perhaps with appropriate
rhetorical gestures, and then undercuts it by activating the pun on 'thyme/time'. The pun is evident in O and
Q, where 'thyme' is spelled 'Time'.
    86 **twenty curiosities** i.e. many more strange and ingenious devices in addition to the senator.

85 thyme] *this edn;* Time Q/O   88 coarse work] *Gifford;* course-worke Q/O

303

I.2   THE COMPLETE WORKS OF JAMES SHIRLEY, VOLUME 7

ROBERTO   What, is the storm laid?

URSULA [*Aside*] I must be patient. – Your son's not come yet.   90

ROBERTO Why, now thou art Ursa Major! Love thy whelp
   And we are friends.

URSULA   Was not the duke's son here?
   I fear he is sick that I have not seen him
   These two days in the garden.

GEORGIO   There's a gentleman.

URSULA Aye, there's a gentleman indeed;   95
   I dreamt on him last night. Pray heaven he be
   In health; I prithee make enquiry.
   There's a gentleman, an you talk of a
   Gentleman.

GEORGIO   Signor Thomazo?

ROBERTO   Where is he?

GEORGIO I know not, but my mistress would send me   100
   To know the state of his body.

ROBERTO Why, how now, Ursula? [*To Georgio*] Sirrah, about your business,
   And spare that inquisition. – What hath
   Your impudence to do with the duke's son?

URSULA Have not I to do that gave him suck?   105
   I hope I was his nurse, and it becomes me
   To enquire of his health. He is the very pearl
   Of courtesy – not proud, nor coy, I warrant you,
   But gentle as my Sunday muff.

ROBERTO   Your coney-skin.

URSULA I am the better when I look upon him –   110
   There's a gentleman, an you talk of a gentleman –

89 **laid** subsided.

91 **Ursa Major** Great Bear (punning on the name of the constellation also known as the Plough or Big Dipper and Ursula's name, which means 'little bear').

91 **whelp** child (a term generally used of animals).

93 **that** i.e. because.

98–9 **There's…Gentleman** This statement becomes Ursula's catchphrase in the play; it suggests her investment in Thomazo and ironically points up his less-than-gentlemanly conduct.

98 **an** i.e. if.

102 **how now** i.e. what is the matter with you (short for 'how is it now').

105 **gave…suck** breast-fed him.

106 **becomes** is suitable for.

107–8 **pearl…courtesy** height of good manners.

109 **my…coney-skin.** Ursula refers to the coverings worn on the hands in winter for warmth, which were made of rabbit-fur; Roberto picks up the image and turns it into an insult, which might be said in aside or under his breath.

109 **coney-skin** rabbit-skin.

90 SD] *Gifford subst.; not in* Q/O   98–9] *lineation this edn;* There's…of a Gentleman. / Signior Q/O
98 an] *Gifford;* and Q/O   102 SD] *Gifford subst.; not in* Q/O   102 your] O; you Q
111 an] *Gifford;* and Q/O

304

THE GENTLEMAN OF VENICE   1.3

So complete, so affable; a scholar, too,
If I could understand him. Prithee, sweetheart,
Get me with child that I may long a little.
ROBERTO For a piece of the duke's son?   115
URSULA I shall ne'er forget how prettily
He took the nipple, and would play, and prattle himself
Asleep, I warrant you. But he's now a man,
A great man, and he remembers me still.
There's a gentleman, an you talk of a gentleman.   120
ROBERTO The woman dotes.   *Exeunt.*

[1.3]

   Enter MARINO *meeting* CANDIANO, *a senator.*

MARINO Whither so fast?
CANDIANO   To the Academy.
MARINO   Spare
Your haste; all's done.
CANDIANO   Who has the vote today?
MARINO The English gentleman is still victorious.
All praises flow upon him; he has deposed
Our city, which hath now resigned her laurel.   5

   Enter FLORELLI *and other* GENTLEMEN.

CANDIANO Is not this he?
MARINO   The same, in's face the promise
Of a most noble nature.
FLORELLI   Gentlemen,
Pray give me leave to understand your language,
For this, so much above me, scarce will be –
When I'm less ignorant – worth my thanks.

112 **complete** accomplished.
114 **Get...little** Make me pregnant so that I can indulge my imagination.
115 **piece...son** i.e. a baby that looks like Thomazo. Roberto thinks that Ursula is talking about the belief that women could give birth to babies that looked like something they looked at repeatedly or imagined during pregnancy. (If Ursula did have another child it might well look like Thomazo, given that she and Roberto are his natural parents.)
121 **dotes** is infatuated, is talking foolishly.
0 The scene is set on a Venetian street.
1 **Whither...fast?** i.e. Where are you going in such a hurry?
4–5 **deposed...city** i.e. beaten all the Venetians.
6 **in's** in his.
8 **your language** the style in which you are speaking (i.e. with so much praise). The play never suggests that Florelli does not speak Italian.
9 **this** i.e. the honour of being selected as the most accomplished.

---

120 an] *Gifford;* and Q/O   121 **SD]** *Gifford subst.; Exit.* Q/O
[1.3]] *Gifford subst.* (SCENE III.); *not in* Q/O

305

1.3 THE COMPLETE WORKS OF JAMES SHIRLEY, VOLUME 7

FIRST GENTLEMAN This is, 10
We know, pretence of modesty; we must
Congratulate your triumph.

FLORELLI For this time
I'll be content your praises shall abuse me.
Who are these?

MARINO Friends and honourers of your worth.

FLORELLI I see that courtesy is native here; 15
All the reward I can return must be
To speak abroad the nobleness of Venice
For so much grace to an unworthy stranger.

CANDIANO [*Looking offstage*] The duke himself!

Enter DUKE, THOMAZO, SENATORS, [*and*] MALIPIERO.

DUKE We must resolve to send new forces, 20
And speedily; the flame will else endanger
Venice itself.

SENATOR This town lost will encourage
The insulting Genoese.

DUKE Thomazo!

THOMAZO Sir.

DUKE I look when you will ask me leave to trail
A pike, and purchase honour in these wars. 25

THOMAZO I have not been well since I was last
Let blood, and therefore, if you please, I would
Be excused till the next wars, and then have at 'em;
By that time I shall be a better rapier-man.

DUKE [*Aside*] This fool is the dishonour of my blood. 30
He declines all that's noble and obeys

---

13 **abuse me** i.e. make me believe in flattery.

14 **these** Marino and Candiano.

18 **grace** favour, kindness.

20–2 **We…itself** Although no fighting occurs onstage, the narrative takes place in the context of a struggle between Venice and its trading rival Genoa, another Italian republic. Historically, a series of wars between Venice and Genoa took place in the period between 1256 and 1381. In *El hombre por su palabra*, Macedonia and Dalmatia are at war.

22 **This town** i.e. Treviso: its identity is revealed in 4.2.

24 **look** am awaiting the time (*OED*, v. 8a).

24–5 **trail…pike** i.e. go into battle. To 'trail' meant to carry a pike (a long wooden shaft with a pointed steel head) or similar weapon 'in the right hand in an oblique position with the head forward and the butt nearly touching the ground' (*OED*, v.¹ 2a). Pikes were used by the infantry, so the Duke perhaps picks a deliberately inglorious image.

25 **purchase** obtain.

26–7 **was…blood** last had blood drawn for medicinal purposes. There is irony in the fact that Thomazo is only willing to shed blood in order to improve his own health.

29 **rapier-man** someone skilled in using a rapier (a long, thin, sharp-pointed sword).

30 **blood** 1) family, kindred (*OED*, n. 5a, 8); 2) 'good' family, gentility (*OED*, n. 9a).

---

10 SH] Q/O *subst.* (*1. Gent.*)   19 SD1] *this edn; not in* Q/O
19 SD2 *and*] *Gifford; not in* Q/O   30 SD] *Engel susbt.; not in* Q/O

306

THE GENTLEMAN OF VENICE   I.3

A base and vulgar appetite; he dwells
Like a disease within my name. But 'tis
Heaven's punishment. – What are they?
MARINO   All strangers,
But among them one in whom you may read   35
Something worth your grace: an English gentleman.
DUKE He to whom fame gives the honour of our
Exercises. [*Aside*] Nature with such an active heat
Might have built up my son, but he's cursed to live
A shadow.
                    Marino fetches Florelli to kiss the Duke's hand.
          Welcome, sir, to Venice.   40
THOMAZO He shall kiss my hand too; I am the duke's son.
FLORELLI You honour me. [*Kisses his hand.*]
DUKE   Thomazo, give that gentleman
A box o'th'ear.
THOMAZO   He wo'not take it kindly,
He is one –
DUKE   Will strike again, is not that it?
THOMAZO I would not use a stranger so discourteously, or else –   45
DUKE Embrace him, then, and make yourself worthy of
His friendship and converse; you'll gain more honour
Than the empty title of your birth can bring ye.
[*To Senators*] But to the great affair, the war: your counsels.
                    Exeunt Duke, Senator[s, Candiano] and Marino.
THOMAZO My father bids me embrace you, sir.
FLORELLI   I shall   50
Be proud when I can do you any service.
THOMAZO Gentlemen, pray know me, everyone.
I am the duke's son. My name's Signor Thomazo.
GENTLEMEN You do us too great honour.
MALIPIERO [*To Florelli*] We had no object worth our envy, sir,   55

33 **name** 1) family name (*OED*, *n.* 4a); 2) honour, reputation (*OED*, *n.* 8).
34 **they** i.e. Florelli and the 'other gentlemen'.
34 **strangers** 1) unknown persons; 2) foreigners, people not native to Venice (*OED*, Stranger *n.* 1a).
40 **shadow** hollow imitation.
40 SD **kiss...hand** a respectful greeting to a social superior.
43 **He...kindly** i.e. He won't like that, he won't put up with that.
47 **converse** conversation.
49 **your counsels** i.e. we need to leave so that I can get your advice.
55 **object** person who attracts admiration.

34–40] *lineation this edn; they? / All...one / In...grace, / An...Gentleman. / He...fame / Gives...nature /
With...up / My...shadow, / Welcome Q/O*   38 SD] *Engel susbt.; not in Q/O*
42 SD] *this edn; not in Q/O*   49 SD1] *Gifford subst.; not in Q/O*
49 SD2] *this edn; Exeunt Duke, Senatour and Marino. Q/O*   55 SD] *this edn; not in Q/O*

307

2.1   THE COMPLETE WORKS OF JAMES SHIRLEY, VOLUME 7

Till you arrived; you have at once dishonoured
And made our Venice fortunate.
THOMAZO   Malipiero,
Let's bid 'em welcome in rich wine.
MALIPIERO   I attend you, sir.
[*Aside*] This fellow must not live to boast his trophies;
He may supplant me, too, if he converse   60
Too freely with Thomazo, whose coarse wit
Is all the stock I live by. – Please you, gentlemen,
To walk?
GENTLEMEN We follow.
THOMAZO   I would not have the way,
But that you are a stranger.
GENTLEMEN   It becomes you.   *Exeunt omnes.*

2[.1]

Enter CORNARI *and* CLAUDIANA, *as in the Duke's garden.*

CLAUDIANA I have obeyed you, sir.
CORNARI   Thou hast done well,
My Claudiana, very well. Who dare
Traduce thee for't? Am I not careful of thee?
I prithee give me thy opinion:
Who deserved best of all the gentlemen?   5
CLAUDIANA I have not art enough to judge.
CORNARI   But thou
Hast fancy, and a liberal thought that may
Bestow thy praise on some or other; tell me,
If thou hadst been to give the garland, prithee

63–4 have...stranger Thomazo appears to say that he leads the way despite Florelli's status as the victor in the academies, which might otherwise give him precedence, because Florelli is a foreigner.

o SD *as...garden* This direction may indicate that Cornari and Claudiana are wearing outdoor clothes, but it is possible that prop trees and/or bushes were used to indicate the setting. At the beginning of 5.1 Giovanni's armour is '*hung upon several trees*' (o SD) and, if trees appeared here, these may also have been used in earlier scenes set in the garden. The list of the properties of the Admiral's Men in Henslowe's *Diary* includes 'j baye tree' and 'j tree of gowlden appelles' (Foakes 2002, 319, 320), the latter probably used in Dekker's *Old Fortunatus*.
   3 Traduce Slander, censure.
   6 art ability acquired through study, trained discernment.
   7 fancy individual taste, critical judgement.
   7 liberal 1) noble, superior (*OED, adj.* 2); 2) unobstructed (i.e. by Cornari) (*OED, adj.* 3b); 3) free from bias (*OED, adj.* 4a).

57–8] *lineation this edn;* fortunate. / *Malipiero...wine.* / I Q/O   **59 SD**] *Gifford subst.; not in* Q/O
61 coarse] *Gifford;* course Q/O
2[.1]] *Gifford subst. (*ACT II. SCENE I.*);* Act. 2. Q/O   **o SD** *Duke's*] *this edn;* Duke Q/O
1 I] *Gifford;* I I Q/O

308

THE GENTLEMAN OF VENICE   2.1

Whose head should wear it? Though we ha' not judgement   10
To examine and prepare our justice, yet
Where men contend for any victory
Affection may dispose us, and by some
Secret in nature we do still incline
To one and guard him with our wishes.
CLAUDIANA   I hope   15
This is but mirth.
CORNARI   By my regard to thy
Fair honour, nothing else. It sha'not rise
To a dispute. Who has the vote today
Of all the gentlemen? I must know.
CLAUDIANA   They are
To me indifferent.   20
CORNARI So is my question, but I must have more.
It cannot be but some man must deserve
More print and poise in thy opinion.
Speak, as thou lov'st me, Claudiana.
CLAUDIANA   Sir,
Your inquisition is not without change   25
Of looks upon me, and those smiles you ask with
Are not your own, I fear.
CORNARI   Nay, then you dally,
And undo that obedience I so much
Commended.
CLAUDIANA   Dear Cornari –
CORNARI   Yet again?
The man; tell me the man.
CLAUDIANA   What man?
CORNARI   The gentleman   30
That best deserves in thy opinion.
I shall be angry. What, deny to give me

10–11 **Though…justice** i.e. Although we are not appointed to judge; although we don't have enough legal experience to judge.

13 **Affection** 1) Goodwill (*OED*, *n.* 2a); 2) Partiality (*OED*, *n.* 6).

13 **dispose** 1) incline (*OED*, *v.* 6a); 2) prepare (*OED*, *v.* 5a).

16–17 **By…honour** Cornari swears an oath on Claudiana's chastity.

20 **To…indifferent** i.e. All the same to me. In his reply Cornari picks up an alternative meaning of 'indifferent': disinterested, neutral (*OED*, *adj.* 1.a).

23 **More…poise** i.e. To be more strongly imprinted and significant (see *OED*, Print *n.* 2b, Poise *n.*[1] 2a).

25–7 **change…own** Cornari apparently smiles in an uncharacteristic manner as he questions Claudiana.

27 **dally** 1) amuse yourself, refuse to take things seriously (*OED*, *v.* 2a–b); 2) trifle with me (*OED*, *v.* 3a); 3) delay (*OED*, *v.* 5).

---

29 Cornari –] *this edn;* Cornari. Q/O

309

2.1   THE COMPLETE WORKS OF JAMES SHIRLEY, VOLUME 7

This trivial satisfaction? The expense
Of a little breath? Why do you tremble so?

CLAUDIANA Alas, I know not what to answer, this   35
Must needs engender fears in my cold bosom
That my poor honour is betrayed, and I
Stand in your thoughts suspected of some guilt
I never understood. If the report
Of malice have abused me to your ear,   40
For by yourself I am all innocent –

CORNARI What do you mean, Claudiana?

CLAUDIANA   Sir, your question
Hath frighted me; 'tis strange, and killing to
My tender apprehension.

CORNARI   You're a fool
To be thus troubled and, but that I know   45
The purity of thy faith to me, this language
Would make me jealous. 'Tis an ill-dressed passion,
And paleness, that becomes not Claudiana
To wear upon her modest cheek. I see
Thy heart sick in thy eyes; be wise and cure it.   50
My question was but mirth, without the sense
Of the least scruple in myself, or meaning
To discompose one cheerful look.

CLAUDIANA   Your pardon.

CORNARI And you as safely might have answered me
As I had casually asked the time o'th'day,   55
What dressing you delight in, or what gown
You most affect to wear.

CLAUDIANA Once more I ask you pardon. You restore me,
And I am now secured by your clear goodness
To give my weak opinion –

CORNARI   Of the man   60
That did appear in thy thoughts to deserve
Most honour.

---

34 **Why…so?** The dialogue again suggests a particular effect in performance.
36 **engender** create, give rise to.
36 **cold** free from sexual passion (*OED*, *adj.* 7c); fearful.
41 **by yourself** a mild oath. It may be a sign of Claudiana's panic that she swears at all.
43 **killing** oppressive, fatal.
46 **faith** sexual loyalty.
47 **ill-dressed** inelegant, disorderly.
53 **discompose** disturb, unsettle.
56 **dressing** elegant clothing or adornment.
59 **clear** 1) evident (*OED*, *adj.* 9a); 2) innocent (*OED*, *adj.* 15a); 3) absolute (*OED*, *adj.* 17).

---

41 innocent –] *this edn;* innocent) Q/O; innocent) – *Gifford*

THE GENTLEMAN OF VENICE   2.1

CLAUDIANA   You'll excuse a woman's verdict;
    My voice is for the stranger, sir.
CORNARI   Why, so!
    You like him best. What horror was in this
    Poor question now? You mean the Englishman?   65
CLAUDIANA The same, most graceful in his parts and person.
CORNARI 'Tis well, I'm satisfied, and we both meet
    In one opinion, too; he is indeed
    The bravest cavalier. What hurt's in all
    This now? I see you can distinguish. Wert thou   70
    A virgin, Claudiana, thou wouldst find
    Gentle and easy thoughts to entertain
    So promising a servant. I should be
    Taken with him myself, were I a lady
    And loved a man.
CLAUDIANA   How's this? My fears return.   75

        Enter BELLAURA *and* GEORGIO.

CORNARI Madam Bellaura, the duke's charge, is entered
    The garden; let's choose another walk.   *Exeunt [Cornari and Claudiana].*
BELLAURA Why, you are conceited, sirrah; does wit
    Grow in this garden?
GEORGIO Yea, madam: while I am in't I am a slip   80
    Myself.
BELLAURA Of rosemary or thyme?
GEORGIO   Of wit,
    Sweet madam.
BELLAURA   'Tis pity but thou shouldst be kept
    With watering.

---

63 Why, so! An exclamation with a similar force and meaning to 'There!'.
66 parts abilities, talents.
66 person 1) personality (*OED*, 3a); 2) outward appearance (*OED*, *n.* 4b).
69 cavalier gentleman, especially one with military training.
70 distinguish exercise discernment, make a distinction between things.
71–2 thou … entertain i.e. you would willingly receive attention from. 'Easy' carried hints of sexual availability in this period (*OED*, *adj.* 12a).
73 servant lover.
76 charge ward.
78–101 Why … Giovanni? García (1998, 292–3) notes that there is a similar catalogue of flowers in *El hombre por su palabra*, Act 2, Scene 9 (Lope 1625, 169v–170r), although in Lope the conversation is between Lucinda and Federico, the counterparts of Bellaura and Giovanni.
78 Why … sirrah Bellaura and Georgio enter mid-conversation.
80 slip twig, cutting (*OED*, *n.* 1a).
82–3 'Tis … watering i.e. It would be a pity if you should not be maintained by being watered. The word 'but' here means 'if … not' (*OED*, But *conj.* 8b(a)). Bellaura builds on the image of Georgio as a 'slip' of wit that is growing in the garden, which needs to be nourished properly by being watered.

---

77 SD] *this edn; Exeunt Cor. and Claud. Gifford; Ex.* Q/O
81–4] *lineation this edn;* My self / Of … time? / Of … Madam. / 'Tis … watering. / There's … it. / I Q/O

311

2.1 THE COMPLETE WORKS OF JAMES SHIRLEY, VOLUME 7

GEORGIO   There's wit in every flower
   If you can gather it.
BELLAURA   I am of thy mind.
   But what's the wit, prithee, of yonder tulip?   85
GEORGIO You may read there the wit of a young courtier.
BELLAURA   What's that?
GEORGIO Pride and show of colours, a fair promising,
   Dear when 'tis bought, and quickly comes to nothing.
BELLAURA The wit of that rose?
GEORGIO   If you attempt, madam,
   To pluck a rose I shall find a moral in't.   90
BELLAURA No country-wit?
GEORGIO That grows with pot-herbs, and poor roots, which here
   Would be accounted weeds, coarse things of profit,
   Whose end is kitchen-physic and sound health,
   Two things not now in fashion.
BELLAURA   Your wit dances.   95
   Where learned you all these morals?
GEORGIO   I but glean
   From my young master, Giovanni, madam.
   He'll run division upon every flower; ·
   He has a wit able to kill the weeds
   And ripen all the fruit in the duke's orchard.   100
BELLAURA Where is Giovanni?
GEORGIO He went betimes to th'Academy.
   He is at all the exercises; we
   Shall ha' such news when he comes home.
BELLAURA   Why does
   Your master, being rich, suffer his son   105
   To work i'th'garden?

---

87 colours 1) the coloured petals of the tulip; 2) heraldic colours indicating high status; 3) brightly coloured (and therefore expensive) clothes.

88 Dear 1) Highly valued (*OED*, *adj.* 4a); 2) Expensive (*OED*, *adj.* 6a).

90 pluck...rose Literally refers to picking a rose, but 'pluck a rose' was a slang term for a woman urinating or defecating (*OED*, Pluck *v.* 7; Tilley R184) and it may also allude to the 'plucking' of Bellaura's virginity by a lover.

91 country-wit unsophisticated humour. Given the possible meanings of 'pluck a rose', there may also be a bawdy pun here: compare Hamlet's comment after he asks Ophelia to 'lie in your lap' and she demurs: 'Do you think I meant country matters?' (*Hamlet*, 3.2.111). The question mark here follows the punctuation in O and Q; an alternative would be to use an exclamation mark, making Bellaura's response indignant rather than teasing. Question marks and exclamation marks are used relatively interchangeably in seventeenth-century texts.

93 coarse...profit i.e. valued only for their medicinal uses rather than their beauty.

94 kitchen-physic 1) food for invalids (*OED*, *n.*); 2) homely remedies (Engel). Compare Tilley P260: 'Kitchen physic is the best physic'.

98 run division speak at length. An image from music, referring to the 'execution of a rapid melodic passage' in which long notes are divided into short ones (*OED*, Division *n.* 7).

89–90] *lineation this edn;* attempt / Madam...in't Q/O   93 coarse] *Gifford;* course Q/O

312

THE GENTLEMAN OF VENICE   2.1

GEORGIO My master? He's an honest mortal man, madam.
   It is my mistress that commands him to't;
   A shrew, and loves him not, but 'tis no matter.
   I ha' the better company. He's here.   110

     Enter GIOVANNI.

   I'll leave him to you, madam – I must now
   Water my plants.   *Exit.*
BELLAURA Why, how now, Giovanni? You frequent, I hear,
   The academies.
GIOVANNI   When I can dispense,
   Madam, with time and these employments, I   115
   Intrude a glad spectator at those schools
   Of wit and action which, although I cannot
   Reach, I am willing to admire and look at,
   With pity of myself lost here in darkness.
BELLAURA By this expression I may conceive   120
   How much you have improved, and gained a language
   Courtly and modest.
GIOVANNI   Madam, you are pleased
   To make my uneven frame of words your mirth.
   I profess nothing but an humble ignorance,
   And I repent not if by any way –   125
   My duty and manners safe – it may delight you.
BELLAURA Indeed, Giovanni, I am pleased, but not
   With your suspicion that my praises are
   Other than what become my ingenuous meaning;
   For if I understand, I like your language,   130
   But with it I commend your modest spirit.
GIOVANNI It is an honour, madam, much above
   My youth's ambition, but if I possess
   A part of any knowledge you have deigned
   To allow, it owes itself unto this school.   135
BELLAURA What school?
GIOVANNI   This garden, madam. 'Tis my academy,
   Where gentlemen and ladies – as yourself,
   The first and fairest, durst I call you mistress –
   Enrich my ear and observation

---

109 shrew bad-tempered woman.
115 these employments i.e. his work in the garden.
123 uneven...words inelegant manner of speaking.
126 duty...safe 1) without harming my work; 2) without a breach of decorum.
129 ingenuous 1) noble, generous (*OED, adj.* 2a); 2) straightforward, innocent (*OED, adj.* 4a–b).
138 durst I if I dared.
138 mistress 1) patron, inspirer of virtue (*OED, n.* 3a); 2) sweetheart (*OED, n.* 5a). Giovanni appears to mean the former sense, but the word carries with it his so-far unarticulated desire for Bellaura.

313

2.1   THE COMPLETE WORKS OF JAMES SHIRLEY, VOLUME 7

With harmony of language, which at best   140
    I can but coldly imitate.
BELLAURA   Still more courtly!
    Why, how now, Giovanni? You will be
    Professor shortly in the art of compliment;
    You were best quit the garden and turn courtier.
GIOVANNI Madam, I think upon the court with reverence.   145
    My fate is to adore it afar off;
    It is a glorious landscape, which I look at
    As some men with narrow optic glasses
    Behold the stars and wonder at their vast,
    Though unknown, habitable worlds of brightness.   150
    But were my eye a nearer judge, and I
    Admitted to a clearer knowledge, madam,
    Of the court life, there I might find the truth
    Of man's best ideas, and enjoy the happiness
    Now only mine by naked speculation.   155
    I think how there I should throw off my dust
    And rise a new creation.
BELLAURA   The court
    Is much beholding to you, Giovanni.
GIOVANNI It is a duty, madam, I owe truth.
BELLAURA A truth in supposition all this while.   160
GIOVANNI I should be sad if any experience should
    Betray an error in my faith, and yet
    So soft and innocent a trespass, madam,
    Might well expect a pardon.
BELLAURA   Some that have
    Freely enjoyed the pleasures, or what else   165
    You so advance in court, have at the last

---

143 **Professor** Expert or someone able to give expert tuition to others (see *OED*, *n.* 5a, 4a).

143 **compliment** formal politeness or courtesy.

146 **afar off** from far away.

148–50 **As...brightness** Recalls Georgio's comment about Giovanni's interest in astronomy and the possibility of life on other worlds at 1.2.66–70; he may have in mind such astronomers as Tycho Brahe (1546–1601), Johannes Kepler (1571–1630), and Galileo Galilei (1564–1642).

148 **optic glasses** telescopes.

151–3 **were...life** i.e. if I were able to scrutinize the court's customs more closely and understand them better.

155 **naked** mere (*OED*, *adj.* 19a), with the naked eye.

155 **speculation** observation. The term was often used in relation to astronomy, continuing the speech's governing image.

156–7 **throw...creation** shake off the dust of the garden (i.e. the circumstances in which I was born or the conditions in which I live) and be reborn. The terms 'dust' and 'creation' recall the Biblical story of the creation of Adam from 'the dust of the ground' [Genesis 2.7].

158 **beholding** indebted (i.e. for this rosy picture of its virtues).

160 **in supposition** uncertain, doubtful.

THE GENTLEMAN OF VENICE   2.1

Been weary and accused their gay condition,
Nay, changed their state for such an humble life
As you profess, a gardener.
GIOVANNI   I despise not
What I was born to, madam, but I should   170
Imagine the disease lay in the mind,
Not in the courtier, that would throw away
So spacious a blessing to be servile.
BELLAURA You know not, Giovanni, your own happiness,
Nor the court sins; the pride and surfeits there   175
Come not within your circle. There are few
Pursue those noble tracts your fancy aims at.
It is a dangerous sea to launch into,
Both shelves and rocks you see not, aye, and mermaids.
GIOVANNI What are they, madam?
BELLAURA   You have heard of mermaids.   180
GIOVANNI You mean not women, I hope, madam?
BELLAURA   Yes.
GIOVANNI Oh, do not by so hard an application
Increase the poet's torment that first made
That fabulous story to disgrace your sex!
You're firm, and the fair seal of the great maker,   185
A print next that of angels.

167 **gay condition** splendid or showy way of life.
168 **state** occupation, profession (*OED*, *n.* 19); (high) position in society (*OED*, 14a, 15).
169 **profess** make your profession.
171–2 **lay...courtier** i.e. came from an individual's psychological problems rather than holding the office of the courtier.
173 **spacious** great.
175 **surfeits** overindulgences.
176 **Come...circle** i.e. Are out of your experience, are above your social station. The term 'circle' can also refer to the orbit of a planet (*OED*, *n.* 4b).
177 **tracts** courses of action, paths.
178 **It** i.e. The court.
179 **shelves** sandbanks.
179 **mermaids** mythical creatures often conflated with sirens, which were thought to lure sailors to their deaths; refers in an extended sense to alluring or deceiving women and prostitutes (*OED*, Mermaid *n.* 3a). Shirley uses a similar image in *Love's Cruelty*, in which Eubella declares that the Duke's 'mermaids cannot winne me with their songs / Nor all his tempests shake me' (4.2).
182 **application** 'practical lesson or moral of a fable, parable, *etc.*' (*OED*, *n.* 4a).
184 **fabulous** absurd, ridiculous.
185–6 **You're...angels** i.e. You are constant in your goodness, and a sign of God's creation/purpose for us, a sign of his workmanship that is almost as perfect as the angels.
185 **firm** steadfast, constant.
185 **seal** sign of authenticity or authority.
185 **the great maker** i.e. God in his role as creator of the universe.

184 sex!] *this edn.* sex. Q/O

315

2.1   THE COMPLETE WORKS OF JAMES SHIRLEY, VOLUME 7

BELLAURA   We are bound t'ye.
If our cause want a flourish you have art
To make us show fair.
GIOVANNI   And you are so.
'Tis malice dares traduce you, or blind ignorance
That throws her strains, which fall off from your figures,   190
For those which weaker understandings call
Your spots are ermines, and can such as these
Darlings of heaven and nature, women, shoot
At court an influence like unlucky planets?
They cannot, sure. Why, you live, madam, there,   195
That are enough to prove all praise a truth
And by a sweet example make 'em all
Such as you are: objects of love and wonder.
Oh, then how blessed are they that live at court,
With freedom to converse with so much virtue   200
As your fair sex embraceth!

        Enter URSULA.

BELLAURA   Here's your mother.
GIOVANNI She was too hasty.
URSULA   Madam, I hope you'll
Pardon my son's rudeness to hold discourse
With your ladyship.
BELLAURA   'Tis a courtesy,
And he talks well to pass away the time,   205
Exceeding well. But I must to my guardian,
The duke –   *Exit.*
URSULA   Happiness attend your ladyship.
[*To Giovanni*] Now, sir, what are you thinking of?
GIOVANNI   Your pardon, nothing.

---

187 **want...flourish** needs rhetorical embellishment.

189–90 **malice...figures** i.e. only malicious people vilify you, or ignorant people use vicious language towards you. 'Strains' here refers to streams of ungoverned language (*OED*, *n.*³ 13c).

190 **fall...figures** i.e. don't leave a mark on you. There may also be a pun on rhetorical figures, building on the references to purposeful language in this part of the exchange.

191–2 **those...ermines** i.e. the characteristics or behaviours that ignorant people call faults or sins are marks of high status. The fur of the ermine or stoat changes to white with a black tip on its tail in winter, and these winter furs were made into robes for judges and the hereditary nobility (*OED*, Ermine *n.* 3), leading to the use of 'ermine' in heraldry to refer to a white field with black spots (*OED*, Ermine *n.* 4).

193–4 **shoot...planets** i.e. have a malign influence. 'Planets' here refers to comets, the appearance of which was thought to be a bad omen.

202 **was too hasty** has arrived too soon (i.e. because she is interrupting Giovanni's conversation with Bellaura).

203 **rudeness** bad manners, uncouthness.

208 **Your pardon** Excuse me.

202–4] *lineation this edn;* hasty. / Madam...rudeness / To...Ladiship. / 'Tis Q/O
208 SD] *Gifford subst.; not in* Q/O

316

THE GENTLEMAN OF VENICE   2.1

URSULA Nay, stay. I must talk with you myself,
  But first what talk had you with my lady?   210
GIOVANNI She was pleased to ask some questions.
URSULA   What were they?
GIOVANNI I ha' forgot.
URSULA   You ha' forgot? You're a lewd
  And saucy boy. Go to! Your father spoils you,

      Enter ROBERTO [*and* GEORGIO].

  But if you use me, sirrah, o' this fashion
  I'll break your pate, I will. The duke's own son –   215
  My blessing upon him – would not answer me
  With 'I ha' forgot', I warrant you, but you –
ROBERTO Why, how now, Ursula? What? Perpetual clamours?
URSULA Oh, here's your stickler.
GIOVANNI   Nothing unkind to me.
  She was angry with your servant Georgio,   220
  And threatened to break his head. [*To Georgio*] Away –
GEORGIO   My head? Come, heels –
                                                Exit.

ROBERTO Was it but so? She shall. She shall do that,
  With all my heart, and I will break it too.
URSULA Nay, then, I will be friends with him.
ROBERTO   Where's the knave?
URSULA I wo'not be compelled to break his head   225
  An you were twenty husbands. Fare you well. [*She goes to leave.*]

---

  212 lewd 1) ignorant, ill-mannered, bungling (*OED, adj.* 4); 2) bad, unprincipled, worthless (*OED, adj.* 5); 3) lascivious (*OED, adj.* 7).
  213 saucy 1) insolent (*OED, adj.*[1] 2a); 2) lascivious (*OED, adj.*[1] 2b).
  213 SD The placing of this stage direction, which follows Q/O, means that Ursula speaks on for four lines before Roberto interjects.
  214 O and Q have an extra speech prefix for this line, which appears at the top of sig. B6v.
  214 o' this fashion in this way.
  215 pate head.
  218 clamours outcries, expressions of feeling.
  219 stickler supporter.
  220–1 She…head Giovanni apparently lies to protect Ursula from Roberto's anger.
  221 Come, heels i.e. Let's get out of here.
  222–3 She…too An example of the way in which violence against a servant is often treated as comic in early modern plays.
  224 Nay…him Ursula characteristically shifts her position to oppose her husband.
  226 An If.
  226 SD Giovanni's comment 'She comes again' (l. 229) indicates that Ursula moves away from Roberto and Giovanni but does not leave the stage.

---

  212 forgot?] *this edn;* forgot! *Gifford;* forgot Q/O   **213 SD** *and* GEORGIO] *Gifford subst.; not in* Q/O
214] *no SH Gifford; Vrs.* Q/O   **214** o' this] *Gifford;* 'oth this Q/O
219–21] *lineation Gifford;* stickler. / Nothing…angry / With…break / His…away – / My Q/O
221 SD1] *Gifford subst.; not in* Q/O   **226** An] *Gifford;* And Q/O   **226 SD**] *this edn; not in* Q/O

2.1   THE COMPLETE WORKS OF JAMES SHIRLEY, VOLUME 7

ROBERTO 'Tis such a wasp, but she sha'not wrong thee.

GIOVANNI I know she wo'not, sir, she is my mother.
  She comes again.

  Enter THOMAZO, MALIPIERO, BERNARDO, *and* MARCELLO.

URSULA [*To Thomazo*] My heart does leap to see you.

ROBERTO [*Aside*] The duke's son and a troop of gallants, but   230
  I always have sore eyes to see one there,
  That Signor Malipiero. He does owe me
  Already forty crowns, and I forgive him.

MALIPIERO Signor Roberto, remember that I owe
  You forty crowns.

ROBERTO   Pray, do you forget 'em.   235

MALIPIERO I never pay till it come to a hundred.

ROBERTO Never pay! It is no matter, signor.
  [*Aside*] I were best be gone before he borrow more;
  It is a trick he uses to put on
  With his rich clothes. I'll vanish.   *Exit.*   240

MALIPIERO [*To Bernardo and Marcello*] Strange this Englishman appears not.

URSULA [*To Thomazo*] I was afraid you had been sick, my lord.

THOMAZO I was never sick in my life but when
  I had a fever or some other infirmity.
  I'll call thee nurse still. Giovanni!

GIOVANNI   Sir.   245

THOMAZO Thou lookest like a changeling.

GIOVANNI   The more's my misfortune.
  You are the duke's son.   *Exit.*

THOMAZO   Who can help it? Nurse –

---

227 wasp irascible and petty individual.

229 My…you Ursula's fondness for Thomazo again contrasts with her lack of feeling for Giovanni.

231 I…see i.e. it pains me to look at.

233 crowns English coins worth 5 shillings. Characters generally refer to Venetian coinage in the play, so this may be a mistake, but lower-class characters are sometimes more 'English' in their range of reference in early modern plays.

234 Signor Roberto Malipiero's exaggerated politeness is directly related to the fact that he owes Roberto money.

239–40 It…clothes i.e. he is as likely to borrow money as he is to wear expensive clothes.

239 uses is accustomed.

242 SD Ursula and Thomazo have probably been conversing throughout the exchange between Roberto and Malipiero.

244 infirmity illness.

246 changeling child substituted for another in the cradle. Thomazo means that Giovanni looks out of place in the garden (perhaps because of his manner and bearing), but the play again hints at the mystery surrounding the two young men.

---

229 SD1 BERNARDO] Q/O *subst.* (Barnardo)   **229 SD2**] *this edn; not in* Q/O
230 SD] *this edn; not in* Q/O   **238 SD**] *Gifford subst.; not in* Q/O   **241 SD**] *this edn; not in* Q/O
241 not.] *Gifford;* not? Q/O   **242 SD**] *this edn; not in* Q/O
247 Nurse –] *this edn;* nurse, Q/O

318

THE GENTLEMAN OF VENICE   2.1

URSULA He was never courteous to women.
  Here's a gentleman, an they talk of a gentleman;
  Now could I weep for joy. I must take my leave, sir.   250
THOMAZO I must make bold with my nurse.   [*He kisses her.*]
URSULA Blessings upon thy heart! How sweetly he kisses;
  Here was a touch for a lady.   *Exit.*
THOMAZO   Go thy ways;
  An admirable twanging lip; pity thou art
  A thought too old! Ha, wagtail!   255
BERNARDO [*To Malipiero*] Does he come alone?
MALIPIERO   Alone. Be you resolute:
  When you see me draw, shoot all your points
  Into his heart.
BERNARDO   Be confident.
MARCELLO   Unless
  He be steel-proof, he sha'not boast abroad
  Much victory in Venice.   260

      Enter FLORELLI *and* GIOVANNI.

GIOVANNI Signor Thomazo, sir, is there.
FLORELLI   I thank you.
GIOVANNI You pay too much, sir, for no service.
THOMAZO   Here he is.
  We were wagering thou wouldst not keep thy promise.
FLORELLI I durst not make that forfeit of your grace;
  I most consult my own, when I am careful   265
  To wait upon your honour.
MALIPIERO   You are noble.
FLORELLI Your humble servant, gentlemen.

  248 He i.e. Giovanni.
  251 make bold take liberties.
  252–3 Blessings...lady Part or all of this speech might be delivered as an aside.
  254 twanging exceptionally fine (*OED, adj.* b). Compare Massinger, *A New Way to Pay Old Debts*: 'That kisse / Came twanging off' (1976, II, 3.2.180–1).
  255 A thought A little.
  255 wagtail A familiar way of addressing a young woman, applied more incongruously to Ursula.
  256 he i.e. Florelli.
  257 shoot rush, speed (*OED, v.* 1a).
  257 points swords (*OED*, Point *n.* 19c), or the points of those swords.
  262 You...service Giovanni probably means that Florelli's thanks are excessive; given that he rejects the Englishman's money later in the scene (see ll. 300–4) he would presumably react less mildly if it was offered here.
  264 I...grace i.e. I wouldn't make you lose your bet and pay a forfeit. Florelli gracefully assumes (or pretends to assume) that Thomazo has bet that he would keep his promise.
  265 I...own i.e. I take my own honour into consideration.

  249 an] *Gifford;* and Q/O   **251 SD**] *Gifford subst.; not in* Q/O
  256 SD] *this edn; not in* Q/O

319

2.1 THE COMPLETE WORKS OF JAMES SHIRLEY, VOLUME 7

THOMAZO   Where didst sup?

FLORELLI I was not willing to engage myself
  Abroad, lest I might trespass on your patience.

THOMAZO What shall's do this evening?

MALIPIERO   Walk a turn,   270
  And then to a *bona roba*.

BERNARDO   A match.

THOMAZO   Giovanni!
  Thy spade, and hold my cloak.

MALIPIERO   What's the device?

THOMAZO I have great mind to dig now. Dost think I cannot
  Handle a spade? I'll make a bed with my gentlemen now
  For a hundred ducats.

MALIPIERO   'Tis a base employment,   275
  Fit for such a drudge as Giovanni.

GIOVANNI   Sir!

MALIPIERO   A drudge, I said!
  D'ye scorn your little dunghill breed?

GIOVANNI This is not noble.

MALIPIERO [*Drawing his sword*] How, mole-catcher?

FLORELLI   Forbear, he is not armed.

MALIPIERO You were best be his champion.

THOMAZO   Are you good at that?   280
  I do not love to wear my doublet pinked.   *Exit.*

GIOVANNI Three against one?

  [*Malipiero, Bernardo and Marcello attack Florelli, who defends himself.*]
  Giovanni recovers a sword, having first used his spade to side with the Englishman.
  Bernardo having lost his weapon flies.

---

  267 sup eat (supper). Supper was a meal eaten in the early evening, between around 5pm and 8pm, not the late-night snack that it became in later periods.
  270 shall's shall us, i.e. shall we.
  271 *bona roba* courtesan, from Italian *buonaroba*, translated by John Florio as '*good stuffe, a good wholesome plum-cheeked wench*' (*A World of Words* (London, 1598), E2r). In *Humorous Courtier* Shirley refers to 'an *Italian / Bona Roba*, a plumpe Lady, that fils / Her gowne' (2.2).
  272 device plan, scheme.
  274–5 I'll...ducats i.e. I bet you 100 ducats that I and my followers can dig a flowerbed.
  275 base menial, degrading.
  279 Forbear...armed The fact that Giovanni does not wear a sword is a sign that he does not have the status of a gentleman, and his lack of status is one of the reasons why his comment 'This is not noble' provokes the snobbish Malipiero.
  281 pinked cut so as to display a contrasting lining or undergarment (*OED*, Pink *v.* 1).
  282 Three...one? Bernardo and Marcello may draw their swords before or after Thomazo's hasty exit, or they may move threateningly to back up Malipiero.

  276 drudge, I said!] *this edn; drudge*, I said. *Gifford;* drudge? I said, Q/O
  278 SD] *this edn; Mal. Ber. and Marc. draw their swords; Florelli stands on his defence. after* 'champion.' *l. 280 Gifford; not in* Q/O   **282 SD** *Malipiero...himself.*] *this edn; not in* Q/O
  282 SD *Giovanni...flies.*] Q/O *subst. (in margins of ll. 282–3)*

THE GENTLEMAN OF VENICE   2.1

MALIPIERO   Hold!
GIOVANNI   I am no drudge, you'll find,
   To be commanded, sir. You painted flies,
   And only fit for trouts!
FLORELLI   Let's give 'em play and breath.
MALIPIERO Lost our advantage? Is Thomazo fled?   285
MARCELLO And Bernardo. We were best retire; that gardener
   Will stick me into ground else for a plant.   *Exit.*
MALIPIERO Expect we'll be revenged.   *Exit.*
GIOVANNI   Let's prevent 'em.
FLORELLI They are not worth it, Giovanni, so
   I heard you named.
GIOVANNI   My name is Giovanni.   290
FLORELLI Thou hast relieved and saved my life. I find
   Their base conspiracy; what shall I pay
   Thy forward rescue?
GIOVANNI   'Tis but what I owe
   To justice, with the expense of blood and life
   To prevent treachery; reward I have   295
   Received i'th'act, if I have done you service.
   But 'twas your innocence, that made such haste
   To your own valour, not my sword, preserved you.
   I am young and never taught to fight.
FLORELLI   I prithee
   Accept this trifle. [*Offers him money.*] Buy a sword and wear it;   300
   Thou hast deserved to thrive a nobler way
   Than thy condition shows.
GIOVANNI   Though some would call
   This bounty, urge it not to my disgrace.
   I scorn to sell the motion of my arm!
   I fear you are not safe yet; there may be   305
   Danger in following them, and it grows dark.
   Have patience while I fetch a key that shall

---

283 painted 1) artificial (*OED, adj.* 1b); 2) brightly or gaudily dressed (see *OED, adj.* 3).
283 flies artificial flies made of feathers, silk, etc., placed on a hook to attract fish.
284 play freedom of movement.
284 breath time to breathe.
285 Lost i.e. Have we lost.
291 find become aware of.
293 forward prompt, eager, zealous.
300 trifle insignificant thing, here used specifically to refer to a small amount of money (*OED, n.* 5a).
302 condition current status.
304 motion action, exertion.

300 SD] *this edn; Offers him money. after 'shews.' l. 302 Gifford; not in* Q/O

2.1 THE COMPLETE WORKS OF JAMES SHIRLEY, VOLUME 7

Befriend you with a private way. *Exit.*

FLORELLI   Thou'rt noble.
Though I am careless where the terms of honour
Engage my life, 'tis wisdom not to lose it   310
Upon their base revenge. But I must study
Some other payment for this young man's courage.
Howe'er his body suffer in a cloud,
His spirit's not obscure, but brave and active.

  Enter CORNARI *and* BRAVOS *armed.*

CORNARI If my intelligence fail not, he must be   315
Here still. This evening hath put on a vizard
To conspire with me. [*To Bravos*] There he walks – surprise him!

  They seize upon [*Florelli*], *bind his arms and feet, and blind him with a bag.*

FLORELLI Villains! Cowards! Slaves! My sword!
BRAVOS If you be loud we'll strangle you.
CORNARI   Dispatch!
BRAVOS We ha' done, sir. Is he for the river now?   320
CORNARI No, follow me.   *Exeunt.*

  Enter GIOVANNI.

GIOVANNI   These show like officers.
Alas, he's apprehended on their base
Complaint. I cannot help; thy cause and innocence
Must now befriend thee! Base world! Yet I may
Injure the parts abroad – 'tis only Venice   325
Is sick with these distempers. Then I'll leave it,
And instantly pursue some other fate
I'th'wars. It may cure something too within me
That is denied all remedy at home.
Some bodies, for their physic, are designed   330
To change of air; I'll try't upon my mind.   *Exit.*

---

308 **private way** i.e. a secret way out of the garden.
309 **careless** reckless.
311 **study** consider, work out.
313 **suffer...cloud** i.e. is concealed in obscurity.
316–17 **This...me** i.e. The darkness will conceal my actions.
319 **Dispatch** Hurry.
321 **These** i.e. the Bravos.
326 **distempers** disorders, disturbances.
328–9 **something...home** i.e. his love for Bellaura.
330–1 **designed...air** i.e. recommended to move to a new climate.

---

308 Thou'rt] *Gifford;* Th'art Q/O   317 SD1] *Gifford subst.; not in* Q/O
317 SD2 *Florelli*] Q/O *subst.* (him)   331 SD] Q/O *subst.* (Ex.)

322

THE GENTLEMAN OF VENICE   3.1

3[.1]

Enter MALIPIERO *and* THOMAZO.

THOMAZO Not this Englishman to be found?

MALIPIERO   He's not above ground
Where I could suspect him in the city –

THOMAZO Let him go. Maybe his haste toppled him
Into the river, and we may eat his nose
In the next haddock.

MALIPIERO   Wherefore did you fly?   5

THOMAZO Dost think 'twas fear?

MALIPIERO   'Twas something like a will
To keep your skin from eyelet holes.

THOMAZO   I grant you.
What had I to do to bring up a fashion?

MALIPIERO We might ha' gone a sure and nearer way
To ha' killed him in a right line with a bullet.   10
But let him go, so he quit Venice anyway.

THOMAZO He would spoil our mirth. But I much wonder
Bernardo is not come yet, whom I sent
Ambassador for money to the merchants.

MALIPIERO Nor Marcello, whom I employed to the same end   15
To my most costive uncle for some goldfinches.

THOMAZO Why should the state have an exchequer and
We want?

MALIPIERO   For pious uses, too, to drink their health
And see the commonwealth go round
In mutual commerce of mirth and spirit,   20

---

0 The scene is set on a Venetian street.

1 **Not…found?** Can't this Englishman be found?

2 **suspect** imagine; expect.

5 **fly** flee.

6–7 **'Twas…holes** i.e. It looked as if you wanted to keep your skin whole.

7 **eyelet holes** 1) holes for laces (*OED*, Eyelet *n.* 1a); 2) *fig.* wounds (*OED*, Eyelet hole *n.* 1b), a similar image to that at 2.1.281.

7 **I…you** i.e. I admit it.

8 **What…fashion?** Why would I want to start a fashion?

9 **nearer** more direct.

10 **right line** direct route.

16 **costive** 1) miserly (*OED*, *adj.* 2a); 2) *lit.*, constipated (*OED*, *adj.* 1a).

16 **goldfinches** *fig.* gold coins.

17 **exchequer** treasury.

18 **want** i.e. lack money

18 **to…health** i.e. to buy wine to toast the merchants and others who contribute to Venetian trade and fill its treasury.

19 **commonwealth** state, republic.

3[.1]] *Gifford subst. (*ACT III. SCENE I.*);* Act. 3. Q/O   7 eyelet holes] *this edn;* oilet-holes Q/O

323

3.1 THE COMPLETE WORKS OF JAMES SHIRLEY, VOLUME 7

Which phlegm and usury hath almost stifled.
Sobriety and long gowns spoil the city;
'Tis we would keep the body politic
From stinking, ulcered with long obligations
And notaries which now stuff the Rialto   25
And poison honest natures that would else
Live freely and be drunk at their own charge.

THOMAZO I would make new laws an I were Duke of Venice.

MALIPIERO We would not sit i'th'chimney corner then
And sing like crickets.

THOMAZO   We would roar like trumpets   30
And deaf the senators with 'Give us your monies –'

MALIPIERO Theirs? Give us our own, their states, their wives
And wardrobes, Scanderbeg.

THOMAZO   And their pretty daughters,
My valiant Turk, who should feed high o' purpose –

MALIPIERO To keep the wanton blood in titillations.   35

THOMAZO It should be a law no maid should be in fashion.

MALIPIERO Yes, let 'em be in fashion, but not hold.

THOMAZO Not after fourteen be it then enacted.

---

21 phlegm One of the four humours in ancient and early modern medicine, thought to cause apathy and sluggishness if it predominated in the body.

22 long gowns i.e. the unfashionable garments worn by older men in Caroline England.

23 body politic state (imagined as a human body).

24 obligations 1) financial agreements, bonds (*OED*, Obligation *n.* 1); 2) duties, commitments (*OED*, Obligation *n.* 3b).

25 notaries people authorized to process legal formalities.

25 Rialto Mercantile district and marketplace in Venice, adjoining the Rialto Bridge. Shirley follows Shakespeare in *The Merchant of Venice* (e.g. 1.3.19, 36) in naming key Venetian locations such as the Rialto explicitly. For detailed discussion of the representation of Venice in the play see the Introduction.

29–30 We…crickets Crickets were thought to cluster in warm parts of the house such as the chimney; cf. Dekker, *The Second Part of The Honest Whore*: '*England* they count a warme chimny corner, and there they swarme like Crickets to the creuice of a Brew-house' (Dekker 1953–61, II, 1.1.28–9). Malipiero uses the image as one of poverty.

32–3 Give…wardrobes Malipiero seems to say that the senators should give himself and Thomazo the money that they are in line to inherit, and then hand over in addition their property, wives, and rich clothing.

33 Scanderbeg George Kastrioti (1405–68), an Albanian warrior known as Scanderbeg (from Turkish *İskender Bey*), renowned for fighting against the Ottoman forces (see *OED*, *n.*).

34 valiant Turk Thomazo picks up Malipiero's image: if he is Scanderbeg, Malipiero is an Ottoman warrior.

34 feed high be supplied with rich food.

35 wanton lustful.

35 titillations a state of sexual arousal.

36 no…fashion i.e. virgins should be out of fashion.

37 let…hold i.e. virgins should be all the rage, but they should not keep their virginity for long.

38 Not…enacted i.e. There should be a law that no girl should remain a virgin after the age of fourteen.

38 fourteen The age of consent for girls for most of the seventeenth century was twelve, but fourteen is more often treated as a point of sexual maturity in plays. Cf. the discussion in *Romeo and Juliet* of whether Juliet is fourteen (1.3.11–24) and Antigonus's declaration in *The Winter's Tale* that if Hermione turns out to be unfaithful he will 'geld' his daughters so that 'fourteen they shall not see / To bring false generations' (2.1.149–50).

---

28 an] *Gifford;* and Q/O

324

THE GENTLEMAN OF VENICE   3.1

MALIPIERO We would banish all the advocates that refused
　　To pimp and prove it civil law.
THOMAZO　　　　　　　　　No scribe   40
　　Should dare to show his ears in our dominions.
MALIPIERO Hang 'em, they are labels of the law and stink
　　Worse than a fish-shambles in Lent. No Jew
　　Should turn a Christian upon peril of
　　A confiscation.
THOMAZO　　　　Why?
MALIPIERO　　　　　　　The slaves are rich.   45
　　To turn 'em Christians were to spoil their conscience
　　And make 'em hide their money; 'tis less evil
　　In state to cherish Jews than Christian usurers.
THOMAZO I will have every citizen a Jew then.
MALIPIERO We have built no seraglio yet.
THOMAZO　　　　　　　　　　That's true;   50
　　What think you of the universities?
　　Would not they serve?
MALIPIERO　　　　　　Oh, excellent!
　　They have several schools for several games.

39 **advocates** lawyers, barristers (*OED*, Advocate *n.* 2a).
40 **To pimp** To arrange for the sale of women for sex.
40 **prove…law** i.e. argue that it is legal.
40 **civil law** the branch of the legal system that dealt with private relations between individuals.
40–1 **No…dominions** Recalls Jack Cade's treatment of the Clerk in *2 Henry VI* (4.2.86–109).
42 **labels** 1) narrow strips of fabric attaching a seal to a document (*OED*, Label *n.*¹ 3c); 2) supplementary notes, codicils (*OED*, Label *n.*¹ 7). An alternative meaning would be ribbons, tassels (*OED*, Label *n.*¹ 3b), specifically the long, thin ribbons worn as earrings. See Rowley, *All's Lost By Lust*, 'Your Ieweller has new devices for yee, / Fine labels for your eares, bracelets for wrists' (1633, B4r). If this is the intended sense, Malipiero may mean that scribes are ornaments of the law; he may also mean that they are 'thin' men—and therefore out of place in his excessive new world—like the 'thin religious men' at l. 61.
43 **fish-shambles** fish-market.
43–8 **No…usurers** Malipiero's cynical and racist attitude towards Jews in some respects echoes official Venetian policy, which needed Jewish capital because Christians were technically forbidden by biblical law to lend money at interest to other Christians (see Exodus 23.24, Leviticus 25.35–8, and Deuteronomy 23.20–1). Compare the debate over usury between Antonio and Shylock in *The Merchant of Venice* (1.3.59–139); Shirley may also be remembering the climax of Shakespeare's play, in which Shylock is forced to convert to Christianity, and the machinations of Barabas, the title character of Marlowe's *The Jew of Malta*, first performed around 1589 but revived at the Cockpit in the early 1630s by Queen Henrietta Maria's Men, the company for which Shirley was then writing.
45 **confiscation** i.e. confiscation of their goods.
50 **seraglio** Italian term for the apartment in the palace of a high-ranking Muslim man in which women were secluded, a harem. Malipiero actually has in mind a brothel, and his line of thought follows a common connection that was drawn between usury and prostitution.
52 **serve** be suitable.
53 **schools** buildings or rooms belonging to particular departments or faculties of a university.
53 **games** sexual activities.

40–1] *lineation Gifford;* To…Law. / No…Dominions Q/O   **52** excellent!] *this edn;* excellent, Q/O

325

3.1   THE COMPLETE WORKS OF JAMES SHIRLEY, VOLUME 7

THOMAZO   And scaffolds
  For the spectators when we keep our acts.
MALIPIERO The college rents would find the wenches petticoats,   55
  And the revenues of a score of abbeys
  Well stripped would serve to roll 'em in clean linen
  And keep the toys in diet.
THOMAZO   Excellent!
  But when we have converted to the use
  The monasteries, where shall we bestow   60
  The friars and the thin religious men?
MALIPIERO   You may
  Keep them with little charge. Water is all
  The blessing their poor thirst requires, and tailors
  Wo'not be troubled for new clothes; a hair-shirt
  Will outwear a copyhold and warm four lives.   65
  Or, if you think 'em troublesome, it is
  A fair pretence to send 'em to some wild country
  To plant the faith and teach the infidels
  A way to heaven, for which they may be burned
  Or hanged, and there's an end o'th'honest men.   70
  There be a thousand ways to quiet them.
THOMAZO My admirable counsellor, thou shouldst be
  My supreme officer to see justice done.
MALIPIERO You cannot honour men of worth too much.
THOMAZO We'll ha' the bridges all pulled down and made   75
  Of silver.
MALIPIERO Dross! Gold is our orient metal.

        Enter BERNARDO.

  Here is Bernardo. Welcome, where's the money?

---

53 scaffolds platforms, stages (*OED*, Scaffold *n.* 3, 4). Thomazo probably refers to the tiered seating in medieval and early modern lecture theatres.
55 rents properties owned by the colleges and yielding them income.
55 find...petticoats provide money to pay for clothes for the prostitutes.
56–7 revenues...stripped Probably refers to expropriating the monasteries' real estate, as 'revenue' most often refers to a regular income, especially one gained from property or land (*OED*, *n.* I).
57 linen 1) undergarments; 2) bed-linen.
58 toys playthings, referring to the prostitutes.
64 hair-shirt shirt made of hair, worn by an ascetic or penitent.
65 outwear...copyhold Malipiero likely has in mind copyhold of inheritance, in which the lease of land usually passed to the heirs of the original tenant.
67 pretence pretext.
67–8 wild country...plant terms with particular resonance in a Dublin performance: see the Introduction.
76 Dross 1) 'Extraneous matter thrown off from metals in the process of melting' (*OED*, *n.* 1a); 2) Rubbish (*OED*, *n.* 4).
76 orient resplendent, radiant (*OED*, *adj.* 1b). The fact that 'orient' refers to the east (*OED*, *adj.* 2) also links the image with the Ottoman empire.

67–8] *lineation this edn;* A...wild / Country...infidells Q/O

326

THE GENTLEMAN OF VENICE

3.1

BERNARDO Not a *gazet*. The merchants are all sullen
  And say you owe too much already.

MALIPIERO These are dogbolts. 'Tis time we had new laws   80
  An they wo'not trust.

THOMAZO   But we must build
  No golden bridges at this rate with sunbeams.

MALIPIERO They were best content themselves with honest stone,
  Hard as the heart of your ungodly merchants.

THOMAZO Prithee, let's leave our dream of frighting sailors   85
  And say what hope hast thou of getting money
  For this day's mirth?

MALIPIERO Some hope there is, if my uncle have but faith
  Enough to credit what I never mean –
  Thrift and submission, and holy matters –   90
  'Tis all the ways are left to cozen him
  And creep into his nature. I have pawned
  All my religion that I'll turn friar.

THOMAZO Hast pawned thy religion? Much good do him;
  Let him take the forfeit, so he send thee money –   95

MALIPIERO For present use, and howl, and hang himself.
  I care not – Oh, here's Marcello.

     Enter MARCELLO.

                    Did'st speak with him?

MARCELLO Yes.

MALIPIERO That's well.

MARCELLO He does commend him to you, and with it this –   100

MALIPIERO I knew 'twould take his tender conscience.

---

78 gazet Venetian coin (*gazeta*) of little value (*OED*, *n.*). In Brome's *The Novella*, Pedro offers Paulo 'a piece of four gazetts' to which Borgio responds 'That's three-pence sterling: you are bounteous, sir' (Brome 2010, *The Novella*, 3.1; 1277.). References to a range of Venetian coins are one of the means through which Shirley reinforces the play's setting.

80 dogbolts wretches, menial individuals (*OED*, *n.* 1).

88–9 have...mean i.e. is sufficiently trusting to believe the promises I have no intention of keeping. 'Credit' offers a pun on 'offer a loan on the security of'.

90 Thrift...matters frugality and humility, and other religious virtues.

91–2 'Tis...nature i.e. These are the only options I have if I want to deceive him (that I have reformed) and regain his affection.

92–3 pawned...friar i.e. I have sworn by everything that's holy that I will become a priest. 'Pawned' literally refers to a pledge (*OED*, Pawn *v.* 1) or something given as security for a debt (*OED*, Pawn *v.* 2a); this is the sense that Thomazo picks up in l. 94.

94 Much...him i.e. 'Much good do it him' or 'Much good do him with it': Thomazo comments that Cornari wouldn't benefit much from a bargain involving Malipiero's religion. It is possible that a word has been omitted ('do' should perhaps be 'do't', which would fit the metre) or 'with it' is elided.

95 forfeit i.e. Malipiero's religion.

95 so...money as long as he sends you money.

---

81 an] *Gifford;* and Q/O   97 Oh,] *Gifford;* oh– Q/O

327

3.1   THE COMPLETE WORKS OF JAMES SHIRLEY, VOLUME 7

THOMAZO Hast thou prevailed?
MARCELLO [*Taking out a rope*] This halter. He has tied the knot himself,
    And says next the philosopher's stone he knows not
    What thing of nobler value to present you.   105
    And rather than you should delay for want
    Of a convenient – you know what, you should
    Once more peruse his orchard. There's one tree
    He would have bear no other fruit.
MALIPIERO   I thank him
    For his fine noose. Would I had his neck in't,   110
    The devil should not conjure him from this circle.
    Is this the end of all?
THOMAZO   No, not of all.
MALIPIERO I prithee try how it will hold – D'ye hear?
    Let's lay our heads together. Which of you
    Is best acquainted with the Turk?
THOMAZO   What Turk?   115
MALIPIERO The great and mighty sultan, the Grand Signor.
    Or have you but a Christian correspondence
    With any of his heathen officers?
THOMAZO   What to do?
MALIPIERO No rogue that lies perdu here for intelligence?
BERNARDO What then?   120
MALIPIERO I would make a bargain with him now, and sell
    This city to the pagan instantly.
    Venice is a jewel, a rich pendant,
    Would hang rarely at the Great Turk's ear.
THOMAZO   No doubt.
MALIPIERO Or at one horn of his half-moon.
MARCELLO   I think so.   125

---

104 **philosopher's stone** mythical substance sought by alchemists, which was supposed to turn base metals into gold.

107 **convenient –** This follows the punctuation in O and Q, which suggests that Marcello pauses here.

107 **you know what** i.e. tree on which to hang yourself.

111 **The...circle** i.e. even the devil would not be able to rescue him. The image is of the necromantic circle in which a magician would attempt to summon a devil, as represented on the title page of the 1616 edition of Marlowe's *Doctor Faustus*.

113 **hold –** This again follows the punctuation in O and Q, which suggests that Malipiero begins a thought and then interrupts himself with 'D'ye hear?', which introduces the new idea for another plan to get money.

116 **great...Signor** i.e. the Ottoman Sultan.

119 **perdu** hidden from view.

121–4 **I...ear** Shirley may again recall Marlowe's *The Jew of Malta*, in which Barabas conspires with the Ottoman forces to overthrow the city of Malta.

125 **half-moon** the crescent symbol of the Ottoman Empire.

---

103 **SD**] *this edn; not in* Q/O   103 halter.] *this edn;* halter— Q/O; halter; *Gifford*

328

THE GENTLEMAN OF VENICE   3.1

MALIPIERO I would betray, if I knew how, the state,
    Or anything for half a hundred ducats
    To make one merry night, though after I
    Were broke upon a wheel or set upright
    To peep through a cleft tree like a polecat   130
    In the highway – No money from the mongrels?
    Well, if I live, I will to Amsterdam
    And add another schism to the two hundred
    Fourscore and odd.
    I am resolved.
THOMAZO   What?
MALIPIERO   To cry down all things   135
    That hang on wit, truth or religion.
THOMAZO Come, thou art passionate. Is there no trick?
    No lewd device? Let me see – I have thought
    A way to raise us, my dear Tully, a project
    Shall raise us, or I'll venture –
MALIPIERO   What?
THOMAZO   My neck,   140
    For hanging is the end of my device
    Unless I thrive in't. Go to the rendezvous,
    To Rosabella's o'th'Grand Canal,
    Kiss her and call for wines, my bully-rooks,
    A dish of dainty fiddlers to curvet to,   145

---

129 broke…wheel a form of torture in which suspects or criminals were tied to a wheel or a frame shaped like a wheel and their limbs broken.

129–31 set…highway May refer to an ad-hoc punishment inflicted on prostitutes or promiscuous women, to whom the term 'polecat' could be applied (see *OED*, Polecat, *n.* 2). Compare Beaumont and Fletcher, *The Scornful Lady*, 'Ile make you take a tree whore, then with my tyller bring downe your *Gibship*' (Beaumont and Fletcher 1966–96, II, 5.1.90–1), 'gib' being a synonym for 'cat'.

131 highway This again follows the punctuation in O and Q, which suggests that Malipiero interrupts himself to begin a new thought.

132–4 I…odd Refers to a series of English separatist churches that established themselves in Amsterdam in the late sixteenth and early seventeenth centuries.

137 passionate angry.

139 Tully Thomazo compliments Malipiero's powers of persuasion or intellect by referring to him by the nickname of Marcus Tullius Cicero (103–43 BCE), a Roman politician, orator, lawyer, and philosopher.

141 is the end will be the result.

143 Grand Canal The most important waterway in Venice.

144 bully-rooks comrades, drinking buddies (*OED*, Bully-rook *n.* 1).

145 dish i.e. band. Thomazo imagines them as food to accompany the wine.

145 dainty 1) excellent (*OED*, *adj.* 1); 2) delicious, choice (*OED*, *adj.* 3).

145 curvet leap about, prance (*OED*, *v.* 2). In horsemanship a curvet is 'a leap in which a trained horse rears up and jumps forward on its hind legs without its forelegs touching the ground' (*OED*, *n.* 1).

---

139 A way] *Gifford;* Away Q/O   **142** rendezvous] Q/O *subst.* (randevouz*)*
143 o'th'] *this edn;* O' the Q/O; on the *Gifford*
143 Grand Canal] *this edn;* Gran Canale *Gifford;* grand Cavale Q/O
145 curvet to] *Gifford;* curvet too Q/O

329

3.2   THE COMPLETE WORKS OF JAMES SHIRLEY, VOLUME 7

And drink a health that I may prosper. Tumble
And shake the house. I'll fetch you off.
MALIPIERO   But signor –
THOMAZO No more words. Cannot you be gone? Be drunk,
And leave me to the reckoning; I'll return
With Indian spoils like Alexander.   *Exit.*
MALIPIERO   Spoken   150
Like a true Macedonian. We are gone.
He's right, and may in time and our good breeding
Be brought to something may deserve the galleys.
Follow your leaders, myrmidons.
BERNARDO *and* MARCELLO   We attend.   *Exeunt.*

[3.2]

> *Enter* GIOVANNI [*wearing a sword*] *and* GEORGIO.

GEORGIO But will you venture, Signor Giovanni,
Your body to the wars indeed?
GIOVANNI   I mean so.
GEORGIO And leave me to be lost or thrown away
Among the weeds here!
GIOVANNI   Try thy fortune wi'me.
GEORGIO Yes, and come hopping home upon one leg.   5
Will all my pay then buy a handsome halter

146 **Tumble** Dance, leap about.
147 **fetch you off** deliver you.
149 **leave...reckoning** let me pay the bill (*OED*, *n.* 5a). The term 'reckoning' also refers to the idea of
accounting to God for one's actions in life (*OED*, *n.* 1a) or of comeuppance more broadly, both of which are
appropriate given the eventual failure of Thomazo's scheme.
150 **Indian...Alexander** Refers to the campaign of Alexander the Great of Macedonia (356–323 BCE) in
what is now Pakistan and northern India, which ceased at the Beas River when his troops mutinied. Thomazo
does not appear to realize that Alexander's campaign was a failure.
151 **Macedonian** Inhabitant of Alexander's kingdom.
152 **right** upright, righteous (*OED*, *adj.* 4), said ironically. Malipiero appears to mean that Thomazo is faith-
fully following the corrupt path laid out for him by his friends.
152 **good breeding** i.e. tuition, education.
154 **myrmidons** i.e. Thomazo's followers or gang. The term derives from the warlike people of the ancient
Greek kingdom of Thessaly, who followed Achilles to the siege of Troy in Homer's *Iliad*.
0 The scene is set in the Duke's garden.
0 SD Bellaura's comment at l. 35 indicates that Giovanni enters wearing a sword, in contrast with his previous
appearances, but he may not be in full military garb, as Gifford indicates in his stage direction '*dressed as a
soldier*'.
1 **venture** risk.
2 **mean so** intend to do so.
6 **halter** i.e. sling.

---

154 **SH**] *this edn; Both.* Q/O
[3.2]] *Gifford subst.* (SCENE II.*); not in* Q/O
0 SD *wearing a sword*] *this edn; dressed as a soldier Gifford; not in* Q/O   4 wi'me] *this edn;* wo'me Q/O

330

THE GENTLEMAN OF VENICE

To hang my arm in, if it be but maimed?
Yet I endure a battle every day:
My mistress hath a mouth carries whole cannon,
And if you took that engine to the wars,　　　　　　　　10
You would find it do rare service.
GIOVANNI　　　　　　　　　What?
GEORGIO　　　　　　　　　　　Her tongue.
Make her but angry and you'll need no more
Artillery to scour them with a breach.
What spoil her breath would make in a market place!
GIOVANNI　Be less satirical.　　　　　　　　15
I must not hear this; she is my mother.
GEORGIO　She is my mistress, and that's worse. But I'm resolved;
I'll to the wars wi'ye. Do not tell her on't.
My prenticeship is worse than killing there.
My hand, I'll wi'ye.　　　　　　　　20
GIOVANNI　In the meantime buy ye a sword, and belt,
And what is fit.

　　　　　　　　　Gives him money.

GEORGIO　　　　　No more. I'll be a soldier
And kill according to my pay. This will
Suffice to vamp my body; I may rise
If I grow rich in valour. That will do't:　　　　　　　　25
Money and a tilting feather make a captain.　　　　*Exit.*
GIOVANNI　There is no other way to quiet the
Afflictions here; beside, 'tis honourable,
And war a glorious mistress.

　　　　　Enter BELLAURA *and* ROBERTO.

'Tis Bellaura and my father.　　　　　　　　30
ROBERTO　I know, madam, you may break his resolution;
If you be pleased, you may command. He's here.

10　**engine**　large machine used in warfare, such as a battering ram, catapult, or cannon (*OED*, 4a).

13　**Artillery**　Heavy weaponry, i.e. mounted guns, cannons, mortars, *etc.* (*OED*, *n.* 2b).

13　**scour**　1) clear out, drive out (*OED*, *v.*² 8a, 11b); 2) beat, scourge (*OED*, *v.*² 9); 3) take command of a military position (*OED*, *v.*² 10).

13　**breach**　a gap made by an artillery attack (*OED*, breach *n.* 7c).

14　**spoil**　devastation, a work of destruction (see *OED*, *n.* 7a, 8a).

19　**My...there**　i.e. My apprenticeship here is worse than being killed in the wars.

20　**My hand**　Georgio offers to shake hands to seal the bargain.

24　**vamp**　renovate, patch up (*OED*, *v.*¹ 1a).

26　**tilting feather**　1) a hat with a swaying feather (see *OED*, *adj.* 1); 2) a feather of the kind worn on the helmet of a combatant in a tilt or joust.

28　**here**　1) in my (Giovanni's) heart; 2) that I feel when I am here in Venice.

31　**resolution**　determination, fixed intention, firmness of purpose.

14　place!] *Gifford subst.;* place? Q/O　　31　SH] *Gifford subst.; Bel.* Q/O

331

3.2   THE COMPLETE WORKS OF JAMES SHIRLEY, VOLUME 7

BELLAURA I'll try my skill.
ROBERTO   Blessings attend your ladyship.
    I'll wait for the success.   *Exit.*
BELLAURA   How now, Giovanni?
    What, with a sword? You were not used to appear   35
    Thus armed; your weapon is a spade, I take it.
GIOVANNI It did become my late profession, madam,
    But I am changed.
BELLAURA   Not to a soldier?
GIOVANNI It is a title, madam, will much grace me,
    And with the best collection of my thoughts   40
    I have ambition to the wars.
BELLAURA   You have?
GIOVANNI Oh, 'tis a brave profession, and rewards
    All loss we meet with double weight in glory,
    A calling princes still are proud to own,
    And some do willingly forget their crowns   45
    To be commanded. 'Tis the spring of all
    We here entitle Fame to – emperors
    And all degrees of honours owing all
    Their names to this employment – in her vast
    And circular embraces holding kings   50
    And making them, and yet so kind as not
    To exclude such private things as I, who may
    Learn and commence in her great arts. My life
    Hath been too useless to myself and country;
    'Tis time I should employ it to deserve   55
    A name within their registry that bring
    The wealth, the harvest-home of well-bought honour.
BELLAURA It is an active time, I must confess,
    And the unhappy scene of war too near us.
    But that it should inflame you on the sudden   60

36 **is** 1) is usually; 2) would more suitably be.
37–57 **It…honour**. García (1998, 294–5) notes a similar passage in an exchange between Federico and
Lucinda in *El hombre por su palabra*, 1.2 (Lope 1625, 156r).
40 **collection** deduction, conclusion (*OED, n.* 5).
43 **double weight** twice as much.
44 **own** call their own.
46 **spring** source, origin.
47 **entitle** give a rightful claim to.
48 **degrees** ranks.
53 **commence in** be admitted to.
56 **registry** register, book of honour (*OED, n.* 1).
57 **harvest-home** bringing home of the last of the harvest (*OED, n.* 1a), i.e. the 'harvest' or spoils of war.
58 **active** 1) busy, lively (*OED, adj.* 4a); 2) characterized by outward action (*OED, adj.* 1a).
60 **inflame you** inspire you, make you desire.

59 near] *Gifford;* nere Q/O

332

THE GENTLEMAN OF VENICE   3.2

To leave a calm and secure life, is more
Than commonly it works on men of your
Birth and condition. Besides, I hear
Your father is not willing you should leave him
To engage yourself in such apparent danger;   65
Here you will forfeit your obedience
Unless you stay.
GIOVANNI   I cannot despair, madam,
Of his consent, and if by my own strength
Of reason I incline him not, it was
In my ambition to address my humble   70
Suit to your ladyship to gain it for me.
At worst it is no breach of duty, madam,
If I prefer my country and her cause,
Now bleeding, before any formal ties
Of nature to a soft, indulgent father.   75
For danger, let pale souls consider it,
It is beneath my fears.
BELLAURA   Yet I can see
Through all this resolution, Giovanni!
'Tis something else hath wrought this violent change.
Pray let me be of counsel with your thoughts   80
And know the serious motive. Come, be clear.
I am no enemy and can assist
Where I allow the cause.
GIOVANNI   You may be angry,
Madam, and chide it as a saucy pride
In me to name or look at honour, nor   85
Can I but know what small addition
Is my unskilful arm to aid a country.

61–2 more…works i.e. is a greater than usual effect.
66 Here In this case.
67–8 despair…Of lose hope of gaining.
69 incline him make him agree.
69–71 it…me Roberto and Giovanni have had the same idea of asking Bellaura to intercede for them, albeit with opposite intentions.
71 Suit Petition.
72 duty i.e. his duty to his father as his son.
75 soft gentle, compassionate, merciful.
75 indulgent lenient.
76 pale feeble, timorous.
77–124 Yet…apprehensions García (1998, 295–7) notes parallels between this exchange and an extended speech in *El hombre por su palabra* 1.2 (Lope 1625, 155v–156r) in which Federico justifies himself to Lucinda against the accusation that he is abandoning his ageing father to go to war.
83 allow…cause approve of the business or the case that is being made.
85–6 nor…know i.e. I cannot help but know.

78 Giovanni!] *this edn;* Giovanni; *Gifford; iovanni?* Q/O

333

3.2   THE COMPLETE WORKS OF JAMES SHIRLEY, VOLUME 7

BELLAURA I may therefore justly suspect there is
   Something of other force that moves you to
   The wars. Enlarge my knowledge with the secret.   90
GIOVANNI At this command I open my heart, madam.
   I must confess there is another cause,
   Which I dare not in obedience
   Obscure since you will call it forth, and yet
   I know you will laugh at me.
BELLAURA   It would ill   95
   Become my breeding, Giovanni.
GIOVANNI   Then
   Know, madam, I'm in love.
BELLAURA   In love with whom?
GIOVANNI With one I dare not name, she's so much
   Above my birth and fortunes.
BELLAURA   I commend
   Your flight; but does she know it?
GIOVANNI   I durst never   100
   Appear with so much boldness to discover
   My heart's so great ambition; 'tis here still,
   A strange and busy guest.
BELLAURA   And you think absence
   May cure this wound.
GIOVANNI   Or death.
BELLAURA   I may presume
   You think she's fair.   105
GIOVANNI I dare as soon question your beauty, madam,
   The only ornament, and star of Venice.
   Pardon the bold comparison, yet there is
   Something in you resembles my great mistress.
   [*Aside*] She blushes. –   110
   Such very beams disperseth her bright eye,
   Powerful to restore decrepit nature,
   But when she frowns, and changes from her sweet
   Aspect – as in my fears I see you now
   Offended at my boldness – she does blast   115

96 **breeding** training, good manners.
100 flight 1) hasty departure (*OED, n.*² 1a); 2) ambition (i.e. in loving a social superior) (*OED, n.*¹ 3a).
102 here i.e. concealed within my heart.
103 strange 1) unfamiliar, surprising (*OED, adj.* 10); 2) introduced from outside, foreign (*adj.* 5).
  103 busy 1) active (*OED, adj.* 3.a); 2) anxious, uneasy (*OED, adj.* 4); 3) meddlesome, interfering (*OED, adj.* 6).
  111–12 beams…nature Giovanni echoes the Platonic theory that eyesight worked through extramission, in the shape of invisible beams of light emitted by the eyes, but he reworks it so as to imagine Bellaura's eyebeams as a positive force.

93 in obedience] Q/O*; in [my] obedience *Gifford*   110 SD] *Gifford subst.; not in* Q/O

334

THE GENTLEMAN OF VENICE   3.2

Poor Giovanni thus, and thus I wither
At heart, and wish myself a thing lost in
My own forgotten dust. But is't not possible
At last, if any stars bless but high thoughts,
By some desert in war and deeds of honour –   120
For mean as I have raised themselves to empire –
That she without a blush to stain her cheek
May own me for a servant – I am lost
In wand'ring apprehensions.
BELLAURA [*Aside*]   Poor Giovanni,
I pity thee but cannot cure. – I like   125
Thy aspiring thoughts, and to this last of love
Allow the wars a noble remedy.

    Enter ROBERTO *and* URSULA.

I have argued against your son's resolve, but find
His reasons overcome my weak dispute,
And I must counsel you to allow 'em too.   130
URSULA Nay, I was never much against it, madam.
ROBERTO She loves him not. But does your ladyship
    Think fitting he should go?
BELLAURA   Yes, yes, 'tis honourable.
And to encourage his forward spirit,
The general is my kinsman, Giovanni,   135
What favours he can do you, you shall have
My letters to entreat, and at my charge
You shall be furnished like a gentleman.
Attend me at my lodgings.

---

119 **stars** i.e. astrological forces.
119 **high** aspiring, ambitious.
120 **By…honour** 1) through valiant military action and honourable actions (*OED*, *n.*[1] 2b); 2) by way of reward earned in the war and honourable actions.
121 **mean** 1) humble, inferior in rank (*OED*, *adj.*[1] 2a); 2) poor (*OED*, *adj.*[1] 2c).
122 **a…cheek** i.e. shame.
124 **wandering** 1) restless (*OED*, Wandering *adj.* 2b); 2) erring (*OED*, Wandering *adj.* 3.a). It is probably pronounced as two syllables, as the spelling in O and Q ('wandring') suggests.
124 **apprehensions** 1) notions; 2) anticipations, fears.
124–5 **Poor…cure** Bellaura apparently realizes that Giovanni is in love with her.
126 **last** i.e. the last of Giovanni's 'aspiring thoughts'. Alternatively, 'last' can refer to a thing of lowest importance (*OED*, *n.*[2] 2a) or the 'worst or most extreme instance' (*OED*, *n.*[4] 6).
133 **Think fitting** Consider it appropriate.
134 **forward** eager, zealous.
137 **charge** 1) expense; 2) instruction.
138 **furnished** equipped.

---

118 is't] *Gifford;* it's Q/O   124 SD] *Gifford subst.; not in* Q/O

335

3.3   THE COMPLETE WORKS OF JAMES SHIRLEY, VOLUME 7

GIOVANNI   You bind all
  My services. Why, this will make a show yet.   140
ROBERTO Nay, then, take my consent and blessing too.
URSULA And mine. [*Looking offstage*] The duke!

                             Exeunt [*Roberto, Ursula, and Giovanni*].

    Enter DUKE *and* MARINO.

DUKE Bellaura, I must speak to you.
BELLAURA   I attend.
DUKE [*To Marino*] You have my purpose, and return me clearly
  How he bestows himself, and what society   145
  Withdraws him from his duty thus.
MARINO   I shall
  With my best care.
DUKE   I fear that Malipiero –
  But let me find your diligence.   [*Exit Marino.*]
                Bellaura.   *Exit with Bellaura.*

[3.3]

    The scene adorned with pictures, amongst the rest Claudiana's.

    Enter BRAVOS *with* [FLORELLI, *bound*].

                They unbind him and exeunt [*leaving him*].

FLORELLI I am all wonder. Shall I trust my senses?
  A fair and pleasant gallery. Was I
  Surprised for this? Or do I dream? I did
  Expect the end of my conveyance should
  Have been more fatal.   5
  No tract appears, or sign of those that brought me.

---

140 make...show give a good impression, appear impressive.
144 return me report to me.
145 How...himself 1) How he spends his money (*OED*, Bestow *v.* 5b); 2) How he behaves himself (*OED*, Bestow, *v.* 5c); 3) Where he is staying (*OED*, Bestow *v.* 3a).
145 he i.e. Thomazo.
148 find...diligence i.e. see you apply your industry to this task.

o The scene is set in a room in Cornari's house.
o SD *scene* A painted hanging covering part of the *frons scenae* or the *frons* itself; it is intended to look like the picture gallery of a noble household.
1 wonder 'astonishment mingled with perplexity or bewildered curiosity' (*OED*, *n.* 7a).
3 Surprised Taken prisoner.
4 end...conveyance purpose for which I was transported here.
6 tract 1) footprint (*OED*, *n.* 10a); 2) 'mark remaining where something has been' (*OED*, *n.*³ 11).

---

142 SD1] *this edn; not in* Q/O   **142 SD2**] *Gifford subst.; Exeunt.* Q/O   **144 SD**] *this edn; not in* Q/O
147 Malipiero –] *this edn; Malipiero,* Q/O; *Malipiero; Gifford*   **148 SD1**] *this edn; not in* Q/O
[3.3]] *Gifford subst. (*SCENE III.*); not in* Q/O
o SD2 FLORELLI, *bound*] *this edn;* FLORELLI *Gifford; the Englishman* Q/O
o SD3 *leaving him*] *this edn; not in* Q/O; *uncover and (before 'unbind') Gifford*

THE GENTLEMAN OF VENICE   3.3

The place is rich in ornament. Sure, these
Are pictures, all things silent as the images,
And yet these speak. Some do inhabit here;
This room was not ordained only for air   10
And shadows. 'Tis some flattering prologue to
My death, some plot to second the affront
Of Malipiero with more scorn to ruin me.

 Enter CORNARI *with a case of pistols.*

What art?
CORNARI A friend.
FLORELLI   That posture and presentment
Promise no great assurance, yet there's something   15
Within that noble frame would tempt me to
Believe thou art –
CORNARI [*Aiming the pistols at him*] What?
FLORELLI   A black murderer.
Point not thy horrid messengers of death
Upon a man disarmed; my bosom is
No proof against those fiery executioners.   20
How came I to deserve from thee unknown
So black a purpose as thy looks present me?
I never saw thy face, nor am I conscious
Of any act in whose revenge thou hast
Put on this horror. Let me know my guilt   25
Before I die. Although I never lived
At that poor rate to fear a noble death,
Yet unprepared, and thus to die, doth something
Stagger my soul, and weaken my resolve

---

7 ornament furniture, decorations.
12 second 1) support (*OED*, *v.*¹ 1a); 2) follow, accompany (*OED*, *v.*¹ 1b); 3) succeed (*OED*, *v.*¹ 2c).
13 SD *case* pair.
14 posture 1) pose (*OED*, *n.* 1a); 2) position of your weapon (*OED*, *n.* 2b); 3) 'condition of armed readiness' (*OED*, *n.* 3).
14 presentment appearance, display.
15 assurance guarantee of safety.
16 frame body, physique.
17 black wicked, hateful. The Cornari/Claudiana/Florelli intrigue consistently employs binaries around 'black' and 'white'.
18 thy…death i.e. the pistols.
20 No…against Not able to withstand.
21 unknown i.e. a stranger to me.
22 as…me i.e. as your appearance makes me think.
27 At…death i.e. in such an unworthy manner that I am afraid to die. Cf. *Honoria and Mammon*: 'I ha' not liv'd / After the rate to fear another world' (5.2).
28 unprepared i.e. unprepared for death, without having made confession.
28–9 doth…soul i.e. makes me hesitate or waver, makes me afraid of what will happen to my soul after death.

---

17 SD] *this edn; not in* Q/O

337

3.3   THE COMPLETE WORKS OF JAMES SHIRLEY, VOLUME 7

To meet thy execution. Thou hast   30
Too good a face to be a mercenary
Cut-throat, and Malipiero would become
The hangman's office better.
CORNARI   You believe, then,
How easily I can command your destiny.
I have no plot with any Malipiero,   35
And thus remove thy fears.

He carries in the pistols.

FLORELLI   Is he gone?

[CORNARI *returns.*]

CORNARI   You're still within
My power, but call yourself my guest, not prisoner,
And if you be not dangerous to yourself
Nothing is meant but safety here and honour.
FLORELLI This does amaze me more; but do Italians   40
Compel men to receive their courtesies?
CORNARI I must not give you reasons; yet for your
Surprise you may receive a timely knowledge
And not repent. I am a gentleman,
And by that name secure thee. If you can   45
Fancy a peace with this restraint, 'tis none
But something that may please you above freedom;
If your unruly thoughts tempt a resistance
Death is let in at everything you look at.
FLORELLI I'll leave my wonder and believe. What now   50
Must I obey?
CORNARI   First, walk away your fright.
FLORELLI 'Tis off.
CORNARI   How do you like this gallery?
FLORELLI 'Tis very handsome.
CORNARI   And these pictures?

---

30 thy execution i.e. my execution at your hands.

33 office 1) position; 2) duty.

33 You Cornari generally uses the respectful 'you' to Florelli in this scene even though Florelli has been addressing him as 'thou'; the characters' pronoun use suggests the complex power dynamic between them: Cornari is ostensibly in control of his captive, but he also needs something from him.

42–4 for...repent i.e. I will soon explain why you have been abducted and you will not regret it. 'Knowledge' can also mean 'personal acquaintance; friendship, intimacy' (*OED*, *n.* 3b) or sexual intimacy (*OED*, *n.* 3c), which may colour Cornari's choice of words.

46 Fancy...restraint i.e. Reconcile yourself to your captivity.

48 If...resistance i.e. If you are tempted to resist.

51–2 walk...off It is not clear from the dialogue whether Florelli obeys Cornari's instruction or simply declares that he is not frightened. Galleries were popular spaces for indoor walking in the period, so there is a grotesque aspect to the way in which Cornari attempts to force Florelli into a parody of conventional behaviour.

---

34 destiny] *Gifford;* destine Q/O   **36 SD1–2**] Q/O *subst. (He carries in the Pistolls and returnes.)*
39 but...and] Oc/Q; here but safety and here Ou

338

THE GENTLEMAN OF VENICE

3.3

FLORELLI Well.

CORNARI Your eyes are yet too careless, pray examine 'em.

FLORELLI They cannot answer.

CORNARI Now your opinion. 55

FLORELLI Very good faces.

CORNARI Have your eyes ever
Met with a substance that might reflect
On any of these shadows, sir, in Venice?

FLORELLI Never.

CORNARI Look a little better. Is there nothing
Of more than common curiosity 60
In any of these beauties?

FLORELLI I have seen
Fair ones. [*Aside*] What should this mean?

CORNARI But pray tell me,
Of these – which some have praised for handsomeness –
Which doth affect you most? I guess you have
By frequent view and the converse with ladies 65
Arrived at excellent judgement.

FLORELLI I did not
Expect this dialogue, yet I'll be free.
I profess stranger to 'em all, but this (*Pointing to* [*the picture of*] *Claudiana*)
I should elect the fairest and most worthy
A masculine embrace. I build upon 70
The promise of your honour; I should else
Be nice in my opinion.

CORNARI You are just,
And I prefer that too. What will you say
To call that lady mistress and enjoy her?
She's noble, to my knowledge – But enough 75
At this time. I must pray your kind excuse
If whilst you walk into this room – (*Opening the hanging.*)

FLORELLI A fair one.

---

53 **Well** i.e. I like them very much.
54 **careless** inattentive.
55 **They...answer** This line might be spoken as an aside.
57–8 **substance...shadows** i.e. a real person who resembles one of these pictures.
64 **doth...most** do you like most.
68 **I...all** i.e. I acknowledge that I know none of them.
71–2 **else...opinion** i.e. otherwise be too careful or polite to express such views.
72 **just** 1) honest, impartial; 2) accurate, careful.
77 **SD** i.e. Drawing back the curtains at the back of the stage to reveal a door or discovery space.

---

62 **SD**] *Gifford subst.; not in* Q/O   68 **SD**] Q/O *subst. (pointing to* Claudiana) *(in margins of ll. 68–70)*
75 knowledge –] *this edn;* knowledge, Q/O; knowledge.– *Gifford*
77 room –] *this edn;* room Q/O; room.– *Gifford*

339

3.4 THE COMPLETE WORKS OF JAMES SHIRLEY, VOLUME 7

CORNARI Which is designed your lodging, I become
   Your jailer and make sure this gallery
   Till my return. Be constant to your temper;   80
   There shall be nothing wanting to procure
   You safe and pleasant hours.
FLORELLI   Distrust falls off.
   I will expect to find you noble, though
   My faith bind not to all, and enter.   *Exit.*
CORNARI   So.
   I tread a maze too, but must not resign   85
   My office till I perfect my design.   *Exit.*

[3.4]

> *Enter* MALIPIERO *with* ROSABELLA, *dancing,* [*and*] BERNARDO
> [*and*] MARCELLO.

BERNARDO Active Malipiero!
MARCELLO   Excellent!
   They move as they had nothing else but soul.
MALIPIERO So, drink. We are not merry. Here's a health
   To my hen-sparrow!
MARCELLO   Let it walk round.
BERNARDO What, Rosabella's health? Before the state's?   5
MALIPIERO Hang states and commonwealths! We will be emperors,
   And laugh and drink away whole provinces.
   Shall we not, didapper?

---

79 make sure secure (i.e. by locking the door).
80 Be...temper i.e. Remain calm.
81–2 procure...hours i.e. give you a secure and enjoyable time.
83–4 I...all i.e. I will assume that you mean no harm, but my trust will only go so far.
85 tread...maze walk through a labyrinth (i.e. must progress carefully).
86 till...design i.e. until I have achieved my aims.

0 The scene is set in Rosabella's brothel, and the opening stage direction establishes it as a place for riotous behaviour. The dancing might constitute an extended piece of stage spectacle in performance.
1 Active Lively.
2 They...soul i.e. They move as if they have transcended the limitations of their physical bodies.
3 health toast
4 hen-sparrow courtesan. Sparrows were sacred to Venus in Roman mythology, and were proverbially lustful (Tilley S715; Williams 1994, 3.1279–80).
4 Let...round i.e. Let the cup be passed from person to person so that everyone can drink the health.
5 Before...states To drink a health to ruler or state could be a public show of loyalty; Bernardo is apparently shocked that Malipiero should propose a toast to Rosabella before he has paid tribute to the Venetian state.
8 didapper small diving water-bird. The term is often used to refer to a sexually available woman.

[3.4]] *Gifford subst.* (SCENE IV.); *not in* Q/O
0 SD] *this edn; Enter* Malipiero *with* Rosabella *dancing,* [*Dance*] Bernardo, Marcello. Q/O
5 state's?] *Gifford subst.;* states— Q/O

340

THE GENTLEMAN OF VENICE   3.4

ROSABELLA   What you please, but will Signor
Thomazo be here presently, and bring –
MALIPIERO The Golden Fleece, thou Lady Guinevere,   10
And he shall mount thy little modesty
And ride like Agamemnon, and shall pay for't,
While we, like valiant Greeks, in lusty wine
Drench the remembrance that we are mortal.
More wine, my everlasting marmoset!   15
BERNARDO Brave Malipiero still! Our grand signor's health: (*Drinks.*)
Signor Thomazo!
MALIPIERO   Let it come, squirrels,
And then a song. My pretty Rosabella,
Which of the senators were here last night
To court thee with a draught of dissolved pearl?   20
Be supple to thy friends, and let thy men
Of state – who hide their warped legs in long gowns
And keep their wisdom warm in furs, like agues,
Most grave and serious follies – wait and want

10–14 Malipiero mixes various mythologies and mythological narratives, two of which involve female adultery and two of which involve voyages in pursuit of a valuable prize.

10 Golden Fleece In Greek mythology, a golden sheep's fleece consecrated to Ares by King Aeëtes and stolen by Jason and his Argonauts.

10 Guinevere Wife of King Arthur; her affair with Lancelot is probably alluded to here.

11 mount…modesty i.e. have sex with you.

12 ride 1) ride in triumph; 2) ride a horse on a military campaign (*OED*, *v.* 1e, 2a); 3) have sex (*OED*, *v.* 20a; Williams 1994, 3.1154–5).

12 Agamemnon King of Argos and Mycenae in Greek mythology. He extended his kingdom by waging war with his neighbours and led the Greek forces in the pursuit of his sister-in-law, Helen, to Troy after her abduction by Paris.

12 pay for't 1) meet the financial expense for his sexual encounter; 2) get his just deserts. There is a possible allusion to the eventual fate of Agamemnon, who was murdered by his wife Clytemnestra in part because she was jealous of Cassandra, a Trojan princess and prophet who had been enslaved as a concubine to Agamemnon after the fall of Troy.

13 valiant Greeks i.e. the Greek soldiers who conquered Troy.

15 marmoset small monkey, used as a term of endearment (*OED*, *n.* 3b). Monkeys were also symbols of lust (Williams 1994, 3.900–1), and a prostitute is referred to as a 'she-marmaset' in Brome's *Covent Garden Weeded* (Brome 2010, 4.1; 701).

16 Brave 1) Courageous, intrepid (*OED*, *adj.* 1a); 2) splendid, showy (*OED*, *adj.* 2); 3) worthy, excellent (*OED*, *adj.* 3).

16 grand signor Refers to Thomazo's status as heir to the Duke of Venice, but it also echoes the earlier reference to the Grand Signor, the Ottoman sultan (3.1.116).

17 squirrels a cheerful insult to comrades (see *OED*, squirrel *n.* 1c).

20 draught…pearl Cleopatra is said to have drunk wine into which a pearl had been dissolved; such a drink is used as a symbol of luxury in early modern texts. Compare *Hamlet*, 5.2.218–21: 'The King shall drink to Hamlet's better breath, / And in the cup an union [pearl] shall he throw / Richer than that which four successive kings / In Denmark's crown have worn'.

21 supple (sexually) yielding, compliant.

23 agues fevers, fits of shivering.

341

3.4   THE COMPLETE WORKS OF JAMES SHIRLEY, VOLUME 7

The knowledge of thy fiddle, my dear Dowsabel.   25
ROSABELLA What hath advanced your brain thus, Malipiero?
    You were not wont to talk at such a height.
    There is some mighty fortune dropping; is
    Your uncle sick whose heir you hope to be?
MALIPIERO Hang uncles; there's a damp in's very name.   30
    Wine, or I sink – So now, thy song; come, sit.
                  Rosabella sings.

        Enter THOMAZO *with* MARINO.

THOMAZO [*To Marino*] Nay, you shall enter. – Gentlemen, my friend.
    Salute him, Malipiero. He is one
    May do us service.
MARINO   Sir! I'll take my leave.
THOMAZO That were a jest; you shall stay, by this hand.   35
    Who has the wine? Drink to my noble friend
    Whilst I embrace my Queen of Carthage.
ROSABELLA   Welcome.
              [*They embrace.*]

MALIPIERO [*To Thomazo*] I have seen this gentleman wait near your father.
THOMAZO [*To Malipiero*] Right, in his bedchamber – a sober coxcomb.
    We met by chance. Let's make him drunk; I have   40
    The brave devices here, boy.
              [*He takes out bottles of wine.*]

MALIPIERO Good. [*To Marino*] You're welcome.
    [*To Thomazo*]   Fill me a tun of wine.
MARINO How, signor!
MALIPIERO   It is too, too little for a friend.

---

25 fiddle euphemism for the female genitals (Williams 1994, 1.478).
25 Dowsabel Sweetheart, an English form of the name Dulcibella, common in pastoral songs and poems (*OED, n.*).
27 at...height i.e. in such a high-blown style.
30 damp 1) depression of the spirits; 2) discouragement (*OED, n.*[1] 5–6).
31 SD1 *Rosabella sings* O and Q include the cue for a song but not the lyric. Cutts (1986) suggests that the Shirley lyric, 'Cupid's Call', which presents women as sexually active and available, may have been used here. See the Textual Introduction.
35 by...hand a mild oath, used as an intensifier.
37 Queen of Carthage Dido, Queen of Carthage, whose love affair with the Trojan Aeneas is most famously narrated in Virgil's *Aeneid*.
39 coxcomb fool, from the hat in the shape of a cock's comb worn by jesters.
41 devices i.e. bottles of wine, means with which to get Marino drunk.
42 tun large cask or barrel, used figuratively to refer to a vast amount.
43 How Exclamation indicating surprise or disgust.

---

32 SD] *Gifford subst.; not in* Q/O   **37 SD]** *this edn; not in* Q/O   **38 SD]** *this edn; not in* Q/O
39 SD] *Gifford subst.; not in* Q/O   **41 SD]** *this edn; not in* Q/O   **42 SD1]** *Gifford subst.; not in* Q/O
42 SD2] *Gifford subst.; not in* Q/O

THE GENTLEMAN OF VENICE

3.4

MARINO [*Aside*] They'll drown me; here's a precious knot!

THOMAZO [*To Rosabella*] I hug thee, Cleopatra. – Gentlemen,   45
    Am not I behind half-a-score glasses? Fill;
    Come, charge me home. I'll take it here.

He takes the bottle [*and drinks*].

MARINO [*Aside*] What will become of me? They mean to drench
    Me for the sullens; I am like to have
    A very fine time and employment here.   50

THOMAZO But ha' you ne'er a banquet?

ROSABELLA   'Tis preparing.

THOMAZO Let it be as rich as the Egyptian queen
    Made for Mark Antony. In the meantime,
    What limb of wantonness have you ready for
    My noble friend here? Get him a fine flesh-saddle!   55
    Or where's thy mother? Now I think upon't,
    He loves to ride upon a pad.

MARINO   Not I, sir.

MALIPIERO Oh, by all means, signor! He shall go to
    The price of any lady-ware.

MARINO   Who, I?
    Alas, my tilting days are done. Nay, nay, then,   60
    I'll drink wi'ye, gentlemen, but I cannot tumble.

THOMAZO Why, then, here's to thee.

[*He drinks.*]

---

44 precious knot 1) costly problem (*OED*, Precious *adj.* 2; Knot *n.*¹ 10); 2) worthless group (*OED*, Precious *adj.* 4b, Knot *n.*¹ 18). 'Precious' could also mean fastidious or over-refined, if used sarcastically (*OED*, *adj.* 3).

45 Cleopatra Cleopatra VII (69–30 BCE), last Ptolemaic ruler of Egypt, already invoked at l. 20.

46 half-a-score ten.

47 charge…home i.e. fill me up. The word 'charge' was often used of a violent or impetuous attack.

48 drench Me 1) force me to drink (see *OED*, Drench *v.* 1); 2) force me to take medicine (used especially of animals) (*OED*, Drench *v.* 1); 3) drown me (*OED*, Drench *v.* 6). A similar sequence features in *Politician*, 3.2.

49 for…sullens to cure me of my gloominess (see *OED*, sullen *n.*).

51 banquet course of sweetmeats, fruit, and wine, served as a separate course after a meal.

52–3 Let…Antony Refers to the opulent entertainments laid on by Cleopatra for the Roman general and politician Mark Antony (83–30 BCE), later her lover, on board her ship on the river Cyndus at Tarsus in present-day Turkey. They are famously remembered by Enobarbus in Shakespeare's *Antony and Cleopatra* (2.5.193–233).

54 limb…wantonness i.e. prostitute.

55 flesh-saddle i.e. prostitute, alluding to sexual 'riding' (see Williams 1994, 3.1187–9). Similar images appear in *Grateful Servant* (5.1) and *Love's Cruelty* (2.3).

57 pad horse that is easy to ride (*OED*, *n.*³ 2); sexually experienced woman.

59 lady-ware female genitals (i.e. the part of the woman 'sold' by a prostitute).

60 my…done Marino suggests that he is too old both for jousting on horse-back in a courtly tournament and for sexual activity. Shirley uses a similar image in *Gamester*: 'I doe not come / Awooing for my selfe, I am past Tilting' (3.2).

61 tumble roll around in a bed, engage in sexual activity (see Williams 1994, 3.1435–6). Shirley uses the phrase 'touse [i.e. pull about roughly] and tumble' in *Doubtful Heir* (3.1.83).

---

44 SD] *Gifford subst.; not in* Q/O   **45 SD**] *Gifford subst.; not in* Q/O
47 SD] *Gifford subst.; He takes the bottle.* Q/O *(in margins of ll. 46–7)*   **48 SD**] *Gifford subst.; not in* Q/O
58–60] *lineation this edn;* Oh…Signior. / He…Ladyware. / Who…then Q/O   **62 SD**] *this edn; not in* Q/O

343

3.4   THE COMPLETE WORKS OF JAMES SHIRLEY, VOLUME 7

MARINO [*To Rosabella*] No lady-ware for me, sweet mistress;
    I blush to say I cannot mount at this time.   [*Exit Rosabella.*]
    [*Aside*] Would I were off again. Polecats for me?   65
THOMAZO Now, gentlemen, wipe your eyes.

                      [*He*] *shows a cabinet.*

MARINO A cabinet of rich jewels!
THOMAZO   And how, and how show things?
    Is't fit we want to revel, while my father
    Has these toys idle? We grope in the dark
    And lose our way, while such bright stars as these   70
    May light us to a wench?
MARCELLO   There is no conscience in't.
    But what shall we do with 'em? There's a lustre
    Hath struck me into a flame.
MALIPIERO   Drink half
    And tumble out the rest in featherbeds.
THOMAZO Where's Rosabella, to lend money?
MARINO   Stay, sir.   75
    She never can disburse to half their value;
    Beside, I know their sly and costive natures.
    I am acquainted with a Jew – are we
    All faithful? Are there no traitors here?
    I am acquainted with a Jew shall furnish you   80
    To purpose and transport these where they sha'not
    Betray from whence they came. Trust her? 'Tis dangerous,

---

64 mount have sex, 'rise' to the occasion.
65 off away from here.
66 SD *cabinet* portable case.
67 And . . . things And how do things look? The repetition of 'And how, and how' is probably intended to represent the drunken disorder of Thomazo's thoughts; compare 'double, double' at l. 136.
68 want lack resources.
69 toys trifles, knick-knacks (*OED*, *n.* 7a).
71 light us light our way, procure us access.
71 There . . . in't i.e. There is no justice in your father's miserliness.
72 'em i.e. the jewels.
76 disburse pay out.
78–82 The reference to a Jew as a handler of illicit goods again reflects the ambiguous position of Jews within the Venetian state.
80–1 furnish . . . purpose supply you in the manner you desire (i.e. by paying the true value of the jewels) (see *OED*, Purpose *n.* P7c).
82–4 'Tis . . . son This is a confusing sentence. It may mean 'It's dangerous to trust Rosabella and to do so will mean that your mirth is dispelled when you are cheated by a usurer', but it is also possible that it is incomplete or defective. Gifford prints "'tis dangerous; / Besides the scanting of your mirth, by a / Penurious—So!' Another option would be to print 'soul' instead of 'son' so that the 'penurious' individual is Rosabella herself.

---

63 SD] *this edn; not in* Q/O   **64 SD**] *Gifford subst.; not in* Q/O   **65 SD**] *Gifford subst.; not in* Q/O
66 SD] Q/O *subst.* (*Shewes a Cabinet.*) (*in the margins of ll. 66–7*)   **71 SH**] *Gifford subst.;* Mari. Q/O
73–4] *lineation Gifford;* Hath . . . flame. / Drink . . . rest / In Q/O   **78** Jew –] *Gifford;* Jew, Q/O

344

THE GENTLEMAN OF VENICE 3.4

Besides the scanting of your mirth by a
Penurious son. Give me the cabinet –
You're sure all these are friends and will say nothing? 85
THOMAZO I warrant thee. What luck had I to meet him!
MALIPIERO Will you trust him?
THOMAZO He's one of us. Make haste, a mighty sum –
MARINO I'll bring a storm of ducats instantly.   *Exit [with the cabinet].*
THOMAZO So, so, to th'wine again. 90

                    [*He drinks.*]

MALIPIERO You need not spend the total here; I have use
    For forty of those ducats.
THOMAZO   Shalt have fifty.
MALIPIERO These gentlemen are out of fig-leaves too;
    Some fresher robes would show well.
THOMAZO   They shall have
    New skins, my Holofernes.
MALIPIERO   I'll have half. 95
BERNARDO AND MARCELLO A match!
MALIPIERO   Wine! To our generalissimo!

                    [*He drinks.*]

THOMAZO That's I! I understand the metaphor;
    It shall have law. Oh, for some trumpets now!
MALIPIERO Tantararara, boys! Out-roar the winds
    And drink the sun into eclipse. Hang mitching! 100
    But where's my wanton pinnace?

83–4 **scanting…son** Marino may allude to the proverb 'To speak of a usurer at the table mars the wine' (Tilley U27; see Engel, 75).
84 **Penurious** Stingy, usurious.
86 **warrant** assure, promise.
93 **fig-leaves** i.e. clothes.
95 **new skins** Cf. *Opportunity*: 'Snakes goe cast your coates / Here's earnest for new skins' (1.1).
95 **Holofernes** Teacher. A name used of teachers in Rabelais's *Gargantua and Pantagruel* and Shakespeare's *Love's Labour's Lost*, originally the name of the enemy general slain by Judith in the Old Testament book of Judith 2.4.
96 **generalissimo** military commander. The term was probably a relatively unfamiliar Italian loan-word in the 1630s.
98 **Oh…now!** Thomazo continues the metaphor by referring to the trumpets used on the battlefield.
99 **Tantararara** Imitation of the sound of a trumpet (*OED*, Tanara *int.*).
100 **mitching** skulking, stealing (*OED*, *n.* 1).
101–6 **But…all** Malipiero sets off a line of nautical imagery in which Rosabella is figured as a small boat and her other clients as pirates that try to 'board' her; in ll. 104–6 he imagines a violent response to such an attack.
101 **wanton** 1) free, unrestrained (*OED*, *adj.* 4c); 2) lascivious (*OED*, *adj.* 2a); 3) merry, playful (*OED*, *adj.* 4a).
101 **pinnace** 1) small, light sailing vessel; 2) *fig.*, whore (Williams 1994, 2.1035–6).

88 sum –] *this edn;* summe. Q/O   89 SD *with the cabinet*] *Gifford; not in* Q/O   90 SD] *this edn; not in* Q/O
92 Shalt] *Gifford;* S'hat Q/O   96 SH1] Q/O *subst.* (*B. M.*)   96 SD] *Gifford subst.; not in* Q/O
99 Tantararara] *this edn;* Tantarra rara Q/O

345

3.4　　THE COMPLETE WORKS OF JAMES SHIRLEY, VOLUME 7

BERNARDO　　　　　　　　　　　　Boarded by
　　Some man-of-war by this time.

MARCELLO　　　　　　　　　　She is spooned away.

MALIPIERO　My top and topgallant gone? Ha! Are there pirates
　　Upon these coasts? Give fire upon the water-rats
　　And shoot pell-mell; fight as a whirlwind flings,　　　　　　　　105
　　Disordering all! What man of menaces
　　Dare look awry upon my catamountain?

THOMAZO　Not I. [*To Bernardo*] Now he's got rampant, he'll kill somebody.

BERNARDO　You must not be affrighted. T'other lift,
　　And be a giant eke, and talk of terrors　　　　　　　　　　　　110
　　With words Olympus-high.

THOMAZO　Will that do't?

BERNARDO　　　　　　　　Oh, sir!

THOMAZO　　　　　　　　　　Give me the bottle, then!

　　　　　　　　　　　　　[*He drinks.*]

MALIPIERO　[*To Marcello*] Suppose thou wert my uncle now. Come hither;
　　Hold thy head fair, that I may whip it off.

MARCELLO　Mine's nothing like. Bernardo has been taken　　　　　115
　　For your uncle, signor.

MALIPIERO　[*To Bernardo*] How dare you be like
　　The rogue, my uncle, sirrah?

---

101 Boarded 1) Assailed; 2) Sexually encountered (see Williams 1994, 1.122–3).

102 man-of-war 1) warship; 2) *fig.*, another client.

102 is…away 1) has been moved in on rapidly by another vessel (see *OED*, Spoon $v.^1$ 2); 2) is having sex with another man (see Williams 1994, 3.1291).

103 top…topgallant the uppermost sails on a ship (see *OED*, Top $n.^1$ 9c). The phrase often means 'in full array', as *OED* notes, but here it seems to refer to the ship as a whole. Dekker and Chettle give a drunken beggar in *Patient Grissil* the ranting lines 'helter skelter here roagues, top and top gallant, pell mell, huftie tuftie, hem, God saue the Duke, and a fig for the hangman' (Dekker 1953–61, III, 4.3.35–6).

104 water-rats pirates. Shirley echoes *The Merchant of Venice*: 'There be land rats and water rats, water thieves and land thieves – I mean pirates' (1.3.22–3).

105 pell-mell without order, in a rush (*OED, adv.* 1c, 2).

107 awry 1) with distrust (*OED, adv.* 1b); 2) improperly (*OED, adv.* 2a).

107 catamountain 1) leopard, panther (*OED, n.* 1); 2) *fig.* a spirited woman or whore (Williams 1994, 1.217–18).

108 rampant 1) violent, unrestrained (*OED, adj.* 2b); 2) lustful (*OED, adj.* 3).

109 T'other The other (bottle).

110 eke also (a poetic archaism, used in imitation of Malipiero's bombastic style).

111 Olympus-high Grand enough to reach Mount Olympus, the home of the gods in Greek mythology.

114 fair unobstructed (*OED, adj.* 16), at the right angle.

115 nothing like i.e. nothing like Cornari's.

115 taken mistaken.

---

102 spooned] Q/O (spoon'd); spoom'd *Gifford*　　**108 SD**] *Gifford subst.; not in* Q/O
108 he'll] *Gifford;* heel Q/O　　**109** T'other] *Gifford subst. (*t' other*);* to'ther Q/O
112 then!] *this edn;* then? Q/O　　**112 SD**] *Gifford subst.; not in* Q/O　　**113 SD**] *this edn; not in* Q/O
116 SD] *this edn; not in* Q/O

THE GENTLEMAN OF VENICE

3.4

BERNARDO   I, sir? 'Tis
Signor Thomazo that he means, and see
For very fear his head falls off.

> *Thomazo was drinking and here sets down the bottle.*

MALIPIERO   Reach it me.
I'll drink a health, then, in his skull.   120

> [*He takes the bottle and drinks.*]

THOMAZO Who talks of me? Who dares mention
A thought of me? Where be the dainty ducats?

> *Enter* MARINO.

MARINO The money's coming, sir. Six men are laden
And will be here immediately.

MALIPIERO   Thou shalt drink
A health! Kneel, venerable sir.

THOMAZO   Be humble,   125
Thou man of mallecho, or thou diest.

MARINO   I do, sir. (*Kneels.*)

MALIPIERO To the town – afire!

> [*He drinks.*]

MARINO   What d'ye mean, signor?

THOMAZO He has a very good meaning, never doubt it.

MALIPIERO That you shall pledge, or forfeit your sconce to me;
None shall have the honour to pledge this health   130
But this whey-bearded signor.

THOMAZO Now do my brains tumble, tumble, tumble –

MALIPIERO Give it him –
And drink it with devotion as I did.

> [*Marino is given the bottle and drinks.*]

---

119 For…off One way of staging this moment would be that the actor leans his head all the way back so that it cannot be seen, meaning that the bottle momentarily takes its place.

119 Reach…me i.e. Pass me the bottle.

120 his skull i.e. the bottle. Skulls made into drinking bowls feature in two revenge tragedies, Middleton's *The Witch* (Middleton 2007, 1.1.109–44) and Davenant's *Albovine* (1629, D2v–3r).

122 dainty precious (*OED*, *adj.* 2).

126 man…mallecho wicked man (*OED*, Mallecho *n.*, from the Spanish *malhecho*, 'wrongful act'). Compare *Hamlet*, 3.2.131: 'Marry, this is miching *malhecho*. That means mischief'; it is notable that Shirley uses the term 'mitching' at l. 101. O and Q print '*Malligo*', which appears in no other early modern texts. Engel instead reads 'Malaga', a city in Andalusia, Spain.

127 To…afire! The drinking of a health is again misused, as Malipiero appears to toast Venice itself, and then instead celebrates its potential destruction. The toast and Thomazo's response (l. 128) suggest that spectators are intended to remember Malipiero's threat to betray the city to the Ottomans (3.1.121–5).

129 sconce head.

131 whey-bearded white-bearded (i.e. old).

---

119 falls] *Gifford;* fales Q/O   119 SD] Q/O *(in margins of ll. 119–20)*   120 SD] *this edn; not in* Q/O
126 mallecho] *Gifford; Malligo* Q/O; Malaga *conj.* Engel
127 To…afire!] *this edn;* To the Town, a fire. Q/O; To the town a-fire! *Gifford*
127 SD] *this edn; not in* Q/O   134 SD] *Gifford subst.; not in* Q/O

347

3.4 THE COMPLETE WORKS OF JAMES SHIRLEY, VOLUME 7

THOMAZO I long to see these double-double – (*Hiccups.*) 135
But where's the cockatrice, this whirligig?
Is my head fast?

MARCELLO The screw is firm, suspect not.

MARINO [*Aside*] I dare not pray nor ask forgiveness here.

THOMAZO Do not my brains now turn upon the toe?

MALIPIERO Do you hear, my doughty Signor Thomazo, 140
Wo'not you kill the duke, your graceless father, now?

THOMAZO Yes, marry will I.

MALIPIERO [*To Marino*] You shall let him into
The chamber one night, where he shall strangle him.

THOMAZO Oh, I can play upon his windpipe rarely.

MALIPIERO We'll set (d'ye mark) some corner of the palace 145
Afire at the same time, and in that hurry
Break into the treasury, take what we think fit,
And steal away by sea into another country.

MARINO Most admirably contrived! [*Aside*] The men are come.

Enter OFFICERS.

THOMAZO Hey, the money, boys?

MARINO Disarm the traitors. 150

MALIPIERO Plots, ambuscados! Are these your Jew-tricks?

MARINO [*To Thomazo*] I'll wait till you have slept away your surfeit
Here in the house.

---

135 double-double four times. Thomazo appears to cut himself off with hiccupping (O and Q read '——hickets' at the end of the line) before he can say the full amount of money he wants. Cf. Georgio's recommendation that Giovanni 'ask quickly / A hundred thousand double-double ducats' from the Duke (4.2.71–2).
136–7 cockatrice...fast Thomazo refers to Rosabella twice in l. 136, but the image of the 'whirligig' appears to then make him think of his own spinning head.
136 cockatrice 1) basilisk (a monstrous serpent said to kill with its gaze); 2) *fig.* whore.
136 whirligig 1) spinning toy (*OED*, *n.* 1a); 2) fickle or giddy person (*OED*, *n.* 3b).
139 turn...toe spin in the manner of a dancer, used in the context of drinking in Porter, *The Two Angry Women of Abingdon*: 'if I cannot drink it down to my foot ere I leave, and then set the tap in the midst of the house, and then turn a good turn on the toe on it, let me be counted nobody' (1599, D3v).
140 doughty worthy, valiant.
141 graceless wicked, ungodly (*OED*, *adj.* 1a), with a pun on 'grace', the courtesy title given to dukes and other high-ranking nobility (*OED*, Grace *n.* 16b).
142 marry...I I certainly will.
143 chamber bedchamber.
144 rarely remarkably well.
151 ambuscados 1) ambushes (*OED*, Ambuscado *n.* 1); 2) troops lying in ambush (*OED*, Ambuscado *n.* 2).
151 Jew-tricks i.e. Jewish tricks, a term that draws on anti-Semitic cliché to describe a crafty or cheating action.
152 surfeit excessive intake of drink.

---

135 SD] *Gifford;* hickets Q/O   **138 SD**] *Gifford subst.; not in* Q/O   **142 SD**] *Gifford subst.; not in* Q/O
142–3] *lineation this edn;* I. / You...night, / Where Q/O   **149 SD1**] *Gifford subst.; not in* Q/O
152 SD] *this edn; not in* Q/O

348

THE GENTLEMAN OF VENICE   3.4

THOMAZO   Which is the Jew of all these?
MALIPIERO We are cheated by a court–nap.
THOMAZO My friend, are you the Jew? Where be the jewels?   155
MARINO Truth is, I have sent the jewels to your father
    And he will lend no money.
THOMAZO   No money?
MALIPIERO But must we go to prison?
THOMAZO I'll to prison with 'em, spite o'your teeth!
MARINO Not till you have slept. This way.   *Exit with Thomazo.*   160

    Enter ROSABELLA.

ROSABELLA The banquet's ready, gentlemen.
MALIPIERO   A rescue!
    We are snatched up for traitors; we are betrayed
    And going to prison.
ROSABELLA Who pays for the wine and banquet?
MALIPIERO Why, any living body that has a scruple   165
    In's conscience for the loss of thy dear comfits
    And caraways. [*To Officers*] Away! Lead me, ye rogues,
    I'll not march else, and let us make a show,
    My fine officious rascals. On afore;
    I follow in fit state. [*To Rosabella*] So farewell, firelock.   170
ROSABELLA I shall be undone.
MALIPIERO   Undoing is thy trade.
    [*To Officers*] March on, I say.   *Exeunt.*

---

153 Which...Jew Shirley parodies Portia's question in *The Merchant of Venice*: 'Which is the Merchant here, and which the Jew?' (4.1.171).

154 court–nap officer of the court (see *OED*, Court *n.*¹ C2). This is *OED*'s only citation, but to 'nap' is to seize or arrest: see *OED*, Nap *v.*³ 1; Dekker and Webster, *Westward Ho*: 'Ile nap some of them' (Dekker 1953–61, III, 4.2.183).

159 spite...teeth in spite of you.

166 comfits sweetmeats made from fruit, seeds, or nuts, preserved in sugar.

167 caraways sweetmeats containing caraway seeds.

170 in...state Malipiero's comment may suggest that his hands have been tied, or he may complain generally about the indignity of arrest.

170 firelock mechanism of a gun that produces sparks to ignite the powder (*OED*, *n.* 1), or a gun with such a mechanism (*OED*, *n.* 2). Images of fire and explosions are often used in relation to prostitutes and their activities (see Williams 1994, 1.486–9, 490).

171 undone ruined.

171 Undoing 1) Destroying, esp. ruining by seducing (*OED*, Undo *v.* 8a, 8c); 2) Unfastening clothing (*OED*, Undo *v.* 3b).

---

160 SD1 *Thomazo*] Q/O *subst.* *(Tho.)*   **167 SD**] *Gifford subst.; not in* Q/O
170 SD] *this edn; not in* Q/O   **172 SD**1] *Gifford subst.; not in* Q/O

349

4.1 THE COMPLETE WORKS OF JAMES SHIRLEY, VOLUME 7

4[.1]

   Enter CORNARI, *after him* CLAUDIANA.

CLAUDIANA Your pleasure, sir; you did command my presence.
CORNARI Are you come? You and I must not be
 Interrupted, Claudiana.
CLAUDIANA Why do you shut your chamber?
CORNARI   We must be private.
 How does my life?
CLAUDIANA   Well, sir, if you be so.   5
CORNARI I have a suit to thee, my best Claudiana.
CLAUDIANA To me? It must be granted.
CORNARI   That's well said,
 But 'tis a business, sweet, of mighty consequence,
 More precious than my life.
CLAUDIANA   Goodness forbid
 I should not give obedience to the least   10
 Of your commands, but when your life requires
 My service I should chide my heart and thoughts
 Unless they put on wings to show their duty.
CORNARI Nay, 'tis a business, sweet, will speak thy love.
 Thou know'st how many years since the priest tied 15
 Our holy knot, with what religious flowing
 Of chaste and noble love our hearts have met,
 How many blessings have I summed in thee.
 And but in thee – for unto this heaven gave not
 That which indeed doth crown all marriage,   20
 Children. Thou hast been fruitful, Claudiana,

---

0 The scene is set in a room in Cornari's house.
1 **Your pleasure** i.e. I am at your disposal.
2–4 **You…chamber?** Gifford adds a stage direction, '*Makes fast the door*' at l. 3.
5 **my life** i.e. Claudiana. A term of endearment that also suggests excessive affection or possessiveness.
8 **sweet** darling, sweetheart.
13 **put…wings** make haste.
14–15 O and Q present the speech prefix '*Cor.*' on lines 14 and 15, which come on either side of a page break (from p. 47 [sig. D3r] to p. 48 [sig. D3v]), and the catch-word at the bottom of p. 47 is '*Cla.*' even though the speech as it stands is entirely Cornari's. The simplest explanation may be that a line of Claudiana's was accidentally cut from the top of p. 48. Alternatively, the print shop may have had other problems during the preparation of the type for these lines, or there may have been some confusion or ambiguous placement of speech prefixes in the manuscript on which O and Q were based.
14 **speak** manifest, show.
15–16 **the…knot** i.e. we were married.
18 **summed** counted up.
21 **fruitful** fertile, abundant.

4[.1]] *Gifford subst.* (ACT IV. SCENE I.*); Act. 4. Q/O
15] *no SH Gifford; Cor.* Q/O (*Q/O also have catch-word Cla.*)

350

THE GENTLEMAN OF VENICE   4.1

In all that's good, but only fruitfulness.
And when I think who, in my want of that
Great blessing of thy womb, must be my heir –
A base and impious villain, to possess   25
And riot in my spacious fortunes – I
Forget that other happiness in thy person
And let in a vexation to consume me.
CLAUDIANA I know not what to fear. It is heaven's will
And not my fault.
CORNARI   Oh no, the fault is mine,   30
All mine, Claudiana, for thou art not barren.
'Tis I, a man prodigious and mulcted
By nature, without faculty of man
To make our marriage happy and preserve
This fair, this lovely figure. Be at peace   35
And let me blush, a thing not worth the love
Of such a bounteous sweetness.
CLAUDIANA (*Kneel*[*ing*])   Let me fall
Beneath that which sustains me, ere I take
In a belief that will destroy my peace,
Not in the apprehension of what   40
You frame to accuse yourself, but in fear
My honour is betrayed to your suspicion.

22 **but only** with the exception of.
22 **fruitfulness** becoming pregnant.
23–4 **in…womb** i.e. because we do not have a child.
27 **that…person** i.e. the happiness that you bring me in yourself.
28 **vexation** troubling emotion, source of affliction.
29 **I…fear** These words could be spoken as an aside.
30 **the…mine** It is unusual for a couple's infertility to be presented as the man's 'fault' in early modern drama, and it was probably more likely that the woman would be blamed in real life. However, as Evans points out, 'even in medical literature that focused on the failures of the female body, male infertility was not absent' (2014, 314), and certain tests were recommended for assessing male fertility, e.g., 'let him pisse in a pot, and let the urine stand awhile, if worms grow therein, then is that urine barren' (Wirsung 1605, T4v; see Evans 2014, 316–17).
32 **prodigious** 1) appalling (*OED*, *adj.* 2a); 2) unnatural, freakish (*OED*, *adj.* 3).
32 **mulcted** punished.
33 **faculty…man** virility, the capacity to father children.
34 **preserve** keep alive (i.e. through children who would look like Claudiana).
35 **Be…peace** Do not worry.
37 **bounteous** generous, abundant.
38 **that…me** i.e. the earth.
38 **ere** before.
40 **apprehension** 1) ability to understand (*OED*, *n.* 8); 2) dread (*OED*, *n.* 12).

37 SD] Q/O *subst.* (*Kneeles*)

351

4.1   THE COMPLETE WORKS OF JAMES SHIRLEY, VOLUME 7

O kill me, sir, before I lose your thought,
Your noble thought.
CORNARI   Rise. With thy tears I kiss
Away thy tremblings. [*Kisses her.*] I suspect thy honour?   45
My heart will want faith to believe an angel
That should traduce thy fair name. Thou art chaste
As the white down of heaven, whose feathers play
Upon the wings of a cold winter's gale,
Trembling with fear to touch the impurer earth.   50
How are the roses frighted in thy cheeks
To paleness, weeping out of transparent dew
When a loose story is but named? Thou art
The miracle of a chaste wife, from which fair
Original, drawn out by heaven's own hand,   55
To have had one copy I had writ perfection
To all my wishes here, but 'tis denied me.
Nor do I mock thee with a fable while
I miserably complain, convinced and lost
In my own masculine defect, but yet   60
I love thee, Claudiana – dost not think so? –
And after so much injury I bring
Not my repentance only, but a just
And noble satisfaction.
CLAUDIANA   You oppress
My senses with the weight of new amazement.   65
CORNARI I must be clear: thou must embrace another –
Another in my bed, whom from the world
I have made choice to know thee. Be not frighted,
This way is left, and this alone, to recompense
My want and make both happy.

---

43 thought 1) opinion (of me), belief (in my virtue) (*OED*, Thought *n.* 10); 2) care (of me), consideration (of my welfare) (*OED*, Thought *n.* 4a). Cf. *Cardinal*, 'If I then be happy / To have a name within your thought' (1.2).
44 noble thought 1) good opinion (of me), strong belief (in my virtue), good care (of me), with 'noble' used as an intensifier; or 2) magnanimous judgement (see *OED*, Noble *adj.* 5), with 'noble' defining the quality of Cornari's 'thought'.
46–7 My…name i.e. I wouldn't be able to believe even an angel if they slandered you.
48 white…heaven i.e. snow. In acts 4 and 5 Claudiana is repeatedly described as 'white', a term linking ideologies of race, sex and class.
51–3 How…named? Cornari says that Claudiana goes pale and sweats nervously if anyone talks about sex.
56–7 I…here i.e. I would have had everything I wanted in this life.
58 a fable 1) a foolish story, idle talk; 2) a fabrication.
59 convinced 1) overcome by (*OED*, *v.* 1); 2) firmly persuaded of (*OED*, *v.* 3a).
64 satisfaction act of compensation (*OED*, *n.* 1b). 'Satisfaction' also refers to the performance of an action of penance enjoined by a confessor in Roman Catholic practice (*OED*, *n.* 2) and the atonement made by Christ for the sins of the world (*OED*, *n.* 3); these senses may underlie Cornari's statement.
70 want defect.

---

45 SD] *this edn; not in* Q/O   **56** writ] *Gifford;* write Q/O

352

THE GENTLEMAN OF VENICE   4.1

CLAUDIANA   I embrace   70
Another in your bed?
CORNARI   Dost think I would
Attempt, or wish thee to't, without a care
In every circumstance to both our fames?
CLAUDIANA Fame? Are you master of your reason? Dare you
Provoke heaven thus?
CORNARI   Heaven only shall be witness,   75
Whose secrecy I'll trust but not another's,
Beside the principal agent, to get heaven.
CLAUDIANA You're no Italian, sure.
CORNARI   Yes, and thy husband,
A just one to thy memory, that would
Cancel his faith rather than be a strict   80
Idolater of words and severe laws,
To the destroying of so sweet a figure.
I would not have thee fly like birds i'th'air,
Or ships that leave no tract to say here was.
So rich a blessing, rather, like a plant   85
Should root, and grow, and bloom, and bear forever.
CLAUDIANA I'm lost forever.
CORNARI Be wise and meet my wishes. 'Tis my love
That hath o'ercome all nice considerings
To do thee justice. Nor will I intrude   90
Upon thy bosom one shall be unwelcome;
He's honourably born, of comely person,
But has a soul adds glory to 'em both.
A boy from him, born to my name and fortunes
Leaves not another wealth to my ambition.   95
To raise thy free consent, my Claudiana,
'Tis he whom thou dost think worth thy own praise:
The gentleman victorious for his parts

73 **fames** public reputations.
75 **heaven** the power of heaven, God.
77 **the…agent** i.e. Florelli.
77 **heaven** 'a state of supreme bliss' (*OED*, *n.* 6b).
79 **A…memory** i.e. Someone who is taking care of how you will be remembered.
88 **meet** i.e. agree to, conform to.
89 **nice** A range of meanings are available here: 1) foolish (*OED*, *adj.* 1b); 2) scrupulous (*OED*, *adj.* 3a); 3) strict (*OED*, *adj.* 3c); 4) refined, cultured (*OED*, *adj.* 3d); 5) cowardly, unmanly (*OED*, *adj.* 4a); 6) strange, extraordinary (*OED*, *adj.* 5); 7) coy, '(affectedly) modest' (*OED*, *adj.* 6a).
89 **considerings** points of consideration, scruples.
90 **intrude** force.
91 **one shall** i.e. someone who will be.
92 **comely** handsome.
93 **'em** i.e. his birth and appearance.
95 **not…ambition** nothing else that I could wish to achieve.

353

4.1   THE COMPLETE WORKS OF JAMES SHIRLEY, VOLUME 7

So late in Venice, the English cavalier.

CLAUDIANA I am undone.   100

CORNARI To be short,
I have surprised his person for this use.
He hath been many days an obscure guest
Within the lodgings next the garden, for
I must confess I have had strugglings in   105
My nature, and have sat in council 'gainst
Myself sometime touching this great affair.
But I have answered everything opposed it,
And took this time to acquaint thee.

CLAUDIANA Good sir, kill me.   110

CORNARI I will,
And him too, if ye mingle not and make
The project as I cast it. Be not obstinate.
Why, he shall ne'er discover who thou art,
If thou be faithful to thyself; thou may'st   115
Pretend thyself some pleasant *bona roba*,
Or take what name and shape thou wilt.

CLAUDIANA   There's none
Can hide my shame or wash the stain away.

CORNARI What shame or stain is in't when it is kept
A secret darker than the book of destiny   120
From mankind?

CLAUDIANA   Am I practised in those arts
Of sin that he should take me for a courtesan?
Nay, rather let me be known your wife,
It will oblige him more to use me well
And thank your loving pains that brought me to him.   125
If I must be a whore, and you a –

CORNARI   Stay.
And I a – what? I bleed within me.

---

103 **many days** Suggests that a period of time has passed between the end of Act 3 and the beginning of Act 4.
103 **obscure** hidden, secret.
106–7 **sat…Myself** i.e. advised myself.
112 **ye…not** i.e. you don't have sex.
113 **cast** intend, design.
115 **If…thyself** i.e. If you do not give yourself away, if you put faith in your own virtue.
116 **pleasant** amiable, merry, delightful.
119–21 **kept…mankind** i.e. concealed even more securely than the knowledge of future events is from humanity.
125 **pains** 'careful and attentive effort' (*OED*, Pain *n.* 5b).
126 **a –** Cornari interrupts Claudiana before she can say the word 'cuckold', 'bawd', 'pimp', or 'pander'.
127 **I bleed…me** Gifford marks these words as an aside.

---

106 sat] *this edn;* sate Q/O   126–7] *lineation Gifford;* If…a — / Stay…me. Q/O

354

THE GENTLEMAN OF VENICE   4.2

This key will make the chamber free. [*Gives her a key*.] I follow.
CLAUDIANA Consider, sir, I'm else undone forever.   *Exit.*
CORNARI Why, if he know me for her husband, 'tis   130
   Without a name; I can secure my honour
   And send him quickly to eternal silence.
   I'm resolved they must obey. Proceed;
   A little blood will wash away this deed.   *Exit.*

[4.2]

    Enter DUKE, SENATORS [*including* CANDIANO *and*] ATTENDANTS;
    letters upon a table.

DUKE Our city, drooping with the wounds so late
   Received, is now to study with what joys
   To entertain so great a victory.
   Treviso is returned to our obedience
   Almost without a loss; how many fell   5
   On the adverse part those papers signify
   And must enlarge our triumph. But is't not
   Strange what our general writes of Giovanni,
   Whose spirit he admires, and forward valour,
   Referring to his bold attempt, our conquest?   10
   That he advanced his head and sword first on
   The enemy's walls, which inflamed our army
   To second him with courage, and that after
   With his own hands he slew their general,
   Whose fall shot death and trembling through their army.   15

128–9 As Gifford was the first to notice, the speech-headings appear to be out of place in O and Q, with *Cla.* at l. 128, and no speech heading at l. 129.

130–1 Why…name i.e. He may know that I am her husband but he does not know who I am.

131–2 I…silence i.e. I can preserve my reputation by murdering him.

134 A…deed Echoes and reverses *Macbeth*, 2.2.65: 'A little water clears us of this deed'.

0 The scene is set in the Duke's palace.

0 SD *letters…table* This direction, retained from O and Q, allows for the letters to be placed on a table before the actors enter or be brought in after them.

1–7 Our…triumph Historically, none of the struggles between Genoa and Venice, which were largely fought at sea, resulted in triumph for Venice.

2 study deliberate upon, try to work out.

3 entertain i.e. celebrate.

4 Treviso A city in the Veneto, 19 miles north of Venice. There is no record of it having been taken by the Genoese, but it was taken by the Duke of Austria and the Carraresi, the ruling family of Padua, in the 1380s, returning to Venice in 1388.

4 obedience jurisdiction, rule.

6 adverse part i.e. the opposing side.

128] *no SH Gifford; Cla.* Q/O   **128 SD]** *Gifford subst.; not in* Q/O
129 SH] *Gifford subst.; not in* Q/O   **129 SD]** Q/O *subst. (Ex.)* **134 SD]** Q/O *subst. (Ex.)*
[4.2]] *Gifford subst. (*SCENE II.*); not in* Q/O
0 SD *including* CANDIANO *and*] *not in* Q/O; *Enter Duke,* CANDIANO, *Senators, and Attendants. Gifford*

355

4.2   THE COMPLETE WORKS OF JAMES SHIRLEY, VOLUME 7

CANDIANO Where is Giovanni?
DUKE He is by direction of our general
    Now marching hither. To his only conduct
    The captives are remitted, and his act
    By us to be considered, but we have   20
    Sent order for the placing of his prisoners
    Securely, and commanded he should here
    Attend our pleasure.
CANDIANO   The young gardener?
DUKE The same, whose early valour takes away
    The prejudice of humble birth, and ought   25
    To be encouraged nobly.
CANDIANO   'Tis but justice.
    Is't possible the gardener's son should so
    Behave himself in war?
    He will deserve some honour for't.
DUKE   Why, may not
    Our power dispense and, though his low condition   30
    By our rule exempt him, for his gallant service
    Done now create him gentleman of Venice,
    With a noble pension from our treasury
    To bear his title up?
CANDIANO   We give it strangers
    Whose birth we not examine. He deserves it.   35

    Enter MARINO [*who whispers to the Duke*].

DUKE   Let him receive no favour
    For his relation to me, but take
    His place and punishment with the rest. Away.
    I cast him from my thought.   *Exit Marino.*

18 **only conduct** sole custody.
19 **remitted** assigned, discharged.
19 **act** i.e. his decisive actions during the taking of Treviso.
24 **early** youthful.
26 **To…justice** Marino enters after l. 26 in O and Q, and he also has an extra entrance at l. 45 and then no
exit before his entrance with Bellaura at l. 135. I have followed Gifford, who moves Marino's entrance to l. 35
(when he makes his intervention by whispering with the Duke) and deletes the second entrance.
26 **but** only.
30 **dispense** grant a dispensation, make an exception.
30–1 **though…him** i.e. although his humble status would normally prohibit him.
34 **bear…up** i.e. support his claim to gentility.
35 **we…examine** we do not pry into.
36 **him** i.e. Thomazo.

35] *lineation Gifford;* examine, / He Q/O
35 SD] *this edn; Enter* MARINO, *and whispers the Duke. Gifford; Enter* Marino. *after l. 26* Q/O

356

THE GENTLEMAN OF VENICE   4.2

CANDIANO   Why comes not
  Our general himself?
DUKE   Reasons of war   40
  May yet compel his stay. He's to repair
  Some breaches which our soldiers made, and wisely
  By some new fortification secure
  The town if the enemy should reinforce.
      [*Enter an* ATTENDANT.]
ATTENDANT Signor Giovanni waits.
DUKE   Hath he disposed   45
  By our direction those prisoners were
  Sent by our general?
ATTENDANT He hath, an please Your Excellency.
DUKE   Admit him.
      Enter GIOVANNI *plumed and brave,* [*and*] GEORGIO *his servant.*

GIOVANNI All health and honour to the duke and senate.
DUKE We thank thee, Giovanni, and will spare   50
  Your trouble to relate what we have gained
  I'th'war. Our general writes how much our Venice
  Doth owe to you, whose maiden yet bold valour
  Hath wrought our safety and suppressed the late
  Insolent Genoese.
GIOVANNI   Your bounty makes   55
  That mine which I want merit, sir, to challenge.
  But if my will to serve my country – for
  Beside that name and warm desires, I dare
  Call nothing mine – you're pleased to accept and cherish
  A young man's duty, you will teach me in   60
  The next employment to deserve indeed.
  Till when, you lose not to have built upon

48 **an** i.e. if it.
48 **SD** *plumed* i.e. wearing a helmet with feathers.
48 *brave* finely dressed.
53 **maiden** untried in combat.
55 **bounty** munificence, abundant generosity (*OED, n.* 4a).
55–6 **makes…challenge** 1) makes you give me more praise than I deserve; 2) makes you praise me excessively but I do not have sufficient status to dispute with you.
57 **will** willingness.
58 **name** reputation.
58 **warm** 1) ardent, keen (*OED, adj.* 10a); 2) full of gratitude (*OED, adj.* 12a).
58 **desires** i.e. willingness to serve, longing to succeed.
61 **employment** task.

44 SD] *Gifford subst.; not in* Q/O   45] *no SD Gifford; Enter* Mar. *after 'waites.'* Q/O
48 an] *this edn;* and Q/O   48 SD *and*] *this edn; followed by Gifford; not in* Q

357

4.2　　THE COMPLETE WORKS OF JAMES SHIRLEY, VOLUME 7

This humble pile a monument of your goodness,
To tell the world, although misplaced on me,
You love a growing virtue.
DUKE　　　　　　　　This Giovanni?　　　　　　　　　65
His words taste more of courtier than the garden.
To show we understand, and to that knowledge
Have will to recompense the desert, Giovanni,
The senate bids you ask what in your power
Your thought can aim at to reward your service,　　　70
And you shall soon possess it.
GEORGIO [*Aside to Giovanni*]　　Ask, ask quickly
A hundred thousand double-double ducats.
'Twill serve us both. Do't, beggars must be impudent.
GIOVANNI　Now you destroy what else might live to serve you.
This grace will make me nothing when I call　　　75
My airy worth to balance; keep those glorious
Rewards for men born and brought up in honour,
That may be great and able columns to
Your ever-envied state. Alas, I rise
Like a thin reed beneath this commonwealth,　　　80
Whose weight an Atlas must sustain like heaven.
This favour is too mighty, and if you
Command me ask a just reward, 'tis nothing.

63 **pile** pointed stake or post driven into water or marshy ground to support the foundations of a building or other structure. The metaphor is appropriate to the play's Venetian setting.
64–5 **To...virtue** i.e. To make known that you support the development of valour, even though you are mistaken in believing me valiant.
65 **virtue** valour, courage.
65 **This** i.e. Is this.
66 **taste...of** i.e. are more appropriate to.
67–8 **To...desert** i.e. In order to demonstrate that we comprehend your worth and want to reward it.
69–70 **what...at** i.e. whatever you can think of. The Duke's phrasing suggests that he is urging Giovanni to think of the richest possible reward, perhaps thinking that he would otherwise limit himself to what he thinks appropriate to his social rank as a gardener.
72 **hundred...ducats** i.e. 400,000 ducats. This is an incredible sum, with a spending power roughly equivalent to £12 million in 2017.
75–6 **This...balance** i.e. This good fortune will reveal my insignificance when it is weighed against my insubstantial virtues. Giovanni imagines the scales ('balance') held by Justice, or Fortune in some traditions, in which his flimsy heroism is weighed against the Duke's reward and found wanting. Compare *Brothers*, in which Francisco pleads with Don Carlos, 'let me not be lost for want of that [i.e. money], / Deserves not to be nam'd to fill the ballance / Against true honour' (1.1).
78 **columns** supports.
80 **thin reed** i.e. something insubstantial compared with the 'great and able columns'.
81 **Atlas** In Greek mythology, a Titan who was sentenced to hold up the sky for eternity after the war between the Titans, led by Chronos, and the Olympian gods, led by Chronos's son, Zeus.
82 **mighty** great.
83 **just** correct, appropriate.

71 SD] *Gifford subst.; not in* Q/O

THE GENTLEMAN OF VENICE   4.2

GEORGIO [*Aside to Giovanni*] You had as good ha' said nothing;
      I blush for you. You know many soldiers   85
      So modest to refuse pay or preferment?
      They cannot have it sometimes after many
      Petitions to the state. And now their minds
      Are soluble and apt to pour out favours,
      You to be so maidenly –
GIOVANNI   May I credit,   90
      With pardon of your wisdoms, that you mean
      To encourage thus the low-born Giovanni?
GEORGIO [*Aside*] Now he makes question of their honesty too.
      Oh, simple soldier!
DUKE We look not at thy root but at thy blossom,   95
      And as a preserver of our country
      We offer up a gratitude; consult
      With thy best judgement. (*Aside*) Though beside this act
      Of his abroad I can give no account
      Why I should love this young man, or prefer him,   100
      I know not by what mystery I have
      Had thoughts to wish him more than common fortune,
      And this occasion of his merit offered
      I will pursue.
GEORGIO [*Aside to Giovanni*] Do as I counsel you, and remember I   105
      Have left my fortunes and my trade to serve you.
GIOVANNI Call it not pride if I be willing to
      Believe Your Excellence, that I have done
      Something your goodness prompts you to reward,
      And the grave senate. I have thought –

85 **You** i.e. Do you.
88 **their** the Senate's.
89 **soluble** pliable, open to requests (*OED*, *adj.* 4). The earliest senses of the word appear to relate to relaxation of the body, specifically the bowels, meaning free from constipation or laxative (*OED*, *adj.* 1a–b), which may inform Georgio's use of 'pour out' later in the line.
90 **You...maidenly** i.e. You are behaving so coyly.
91 **With...wisdoms** i.e. Begging your pardon, wise sirs. 'Wisdoms' is used here as a title of respect (*OED*, wisdom *n.* 1e(a)).
93 **makes...of** calls into question.
95 **We...blossom** i.e. We are not interested in your background but in your deeds.
97–8 **consult...judgement** i.e. think carefully.
99 **abroad** i.e. in the war against the Genoese.
99 **can...account** cannot explain.
103–4 **this...pursue** i.e. 1) I will pursue the opportunity (to advance his status) that his valour presents; 2) I will continue to urge him to claim his reward.

84 **SD**] *Gifford subst.; not in* Q/O   84–5] *lineation this edn;* You...you, / You Q/O
93 **SD**] *Gifford subst.; not in* Q/O   96 as a] Q/O; as [to] a *Gifford*   98 **SD**] Q/O *subst. (after l. 99)*
105 **SD**] *this edn; not in* Q/O   110 thought –] *Gifford;* thought. Q/O

359

4.2   THE COMPLETE WORKS OF JAMES SHIRLEY, VOLUME 7

DUKE   Be free.   110
GEORGIO [*Aside*] Now do I expect to be half a senator at least.
GIOVANNI And since you raise my act to such a merit
    I will not ask a thing too much beneath it –
GEORGIO [*Aside*] Well said, 'Vanni.
GIOVANNI   And shame your bounty.
    Yet I may fear you will not grant –
GEORGIO [*Aside*]   Again?
DUKE   Name it   115
    With confidence.
GIOVANNI   I look at no reward of gold –
GEORGIO [*Aside*] How's that? He's out on's part.
GIOVANNI   I know not
    By what fate I contemn it, nor at titles
    Of honour, or command, or what can trench
    On state or wealth –
GEORGIO [*Aside to Giovanni*] I thank ye heartily;   120
    I must to dig again.
GIOVANNI   Employ such gifts
    To pay some slight and mercenary souls
    That make their end of good reward and not
    Itself. But since you have imposed I should
    Make choice of somewhat, know my ambition aims –   125
DUKE At what?
GIOVANNI   It is too great a happiness, but I now
    Consider I have prattled to the wind.
    What I desire is not within your power,
    And what you may command not in my wishes,
    For I would ask Bellaura. Can you make   130
    Me fit for such a blessing? No, you cannot
    Unless I were unborn and should again

---

110 **Be free** i.e. Speak freely.
117 **He's...part** i.e. He has forgotten his lines.
117–18 **I...it** i.e. I don't know what makes me reject or disdain it (i.e. the 'gold' of l. 116).
119–20 **trench On** have a bearing upon (*OED*, *v.* 7c).
121 **to dig** i.e. take up digging, go and dig.
122 **slight** unworthy.
123–4 **make...Itself** i.e. accomplish their purpose by being rewarded financially, not through completing the task itself.
129 **in...wishes** what I want.
131 **fit for** deserving of.

---

111 SD] *Gifford subst.; not in* Q/O   113 it –] *this edn;* it. Q/O; it,– *Gifford*
114 SD] *Gifford subst.; not in* Q/O
114–16] *lineation this edn; Vanni*j. And...fear / You...grant — / Agen? / Name...confidence. / I Q/O
115 SD] *Gifford subst.; not in* Q/O   116 gold –] *this edn;* gold. Q/O; gold,– *Gifford*
117 SD] *Gifford subst.; not in* Q/O   120 wealth –] *this edn;* wealth. Q/O; wealth,– *Gifford*
120 SD] *Gifford subst.; not in* Q/O

THE GENTLEMAN OF VENICE   4.2

Come forth, not Giovanni, but the son
Of some bright name and this world-taking honour.
DUKE Bellaura? Strange request.

    Enter MARINO *and* BELLAURA.

MARINO   Madam, I dare not   135
Be seen. If you prevail, I shall attend
And put his mercy into act.   *Exit.*
DUKE   She's here.
BELLAURA I have a suit to your highness.
DUKE   Me, Bellaura?
BELLAURA About your son, whom men to your dishonour
Lead like some base offender.
DUKE   I must speak   140
The cause into your ear.
                  [He] whispers to her.
GIOVANNI   I was too blame
To mention her so public, but my heart
Grew sick with silence and their proposition
To ask what I desired most prevailed
Against my reason.
DUKE   Leave him to me, Bellaura.   145
Do you observe that gentleman?
BELLAURA   'Tis Giovanni.
He does become the soldier.
DUKE   He has done wonders
Abroad, and quit our gratitude, to be
Only by you rewarded. Can you love him?
BELLAURA I understand you not.
DUKE   And marry him?   150
BELLAURA How have I lost myself since I became
Your charge, a legacy bequeathed your care
By my dead father, the late duke of Venice,
That you should think I can descend with such

---

134 **world-taking** 1) all-encompassing; 2) worthy of someone able to conquer the world.
140 **Lead** i.e. escort to prison.
141 **too blame** too much at fault.
142 **public** publicly, openly.
143 **proposition** offer to me.
145 **him** i.e. Thomazo.
147 **He…soldier** i.e. Being a soldier suits him, he has truly become a soldier.
148 **quit…gratitude** i.e. he has rejected our reward.
151 **myself** my status, my identity.

141 SD *He] this edn; not in* Q/O

361

4.2   THE COMPLETE WORKS OF JAMES SHIRLEY, VOLUME 7

Forgetfulness of myself, my birth or fortunes   155
To place my love on one so poorly born?
DUKE   You blush.
BELLAURA 'Tis anger in my blood to hear him named.
　(*To Giovanni*) You pay me coarsely for my charity.
　Learn modesty hereafter to be grateful.
　I ha' done wi'ye, sir.   *Exit.*   160
GEORGIO [*Aside to Giovanni*]   Do you hear the tit? Be wise, and look at
　Ready money; 'tis a better commodity
　Than any lady in Christendom.
GIOVANNI   Pray dismiss
　And pardon Giovanni. I am satisfied.
　For your own honour let not my ambition   165
　Be told abroad; I'll check and punish my
　Aspiring thoughts hereafter.
DUKE   You have leave.
　Come, gentlemen.
CANDIANO   He is in love.
DUKE   I pity him.   *Exeunt Duke and Senator[s].*
GEORGIO What shall become of us now by your folly?
GIOVANNI We'll to the garden, George, and there begin   170
　Another growth, for what we have's despised.
GEORGIO I knew I should return to my dear dunghill.
GIOVANNI I prithee see the armour which Bellaura
　Bestowed on me brought home.

155 **birth** noble lineage, high social rank.
158 **coarsely** rudely, in an unrefined manner.
159 **modesty** i.e. sufficient modesty.
160 **I…wi'ye** i.e. I am finished with you.
160 **tit** young woman (*OED*, *n.*⁴ 2a).
162 **Ready money** Money in the form of banknotes or coins rather than in bonds, property, promises, etc.
166 **told abroad** repeated publicly.
166 **check** 1) reprimand (*OED*, *v.* 11); 2) restrain, repress (*OED*, *v.* 13); 3) control (*OED*, *v.* 14a).
167 **leave** permission to depart.
167–8 **You…him** O and Q put each of the statements in these lines on a separate line, with two speech-headings, '*Du.*', before 'You' and '*Du.*' again before 'I pitty'. Gifford treats it as a single speech, arranging 'Come…him' as a single line and deleting the second speech-heading. It seems more plausible, however, that the compositor simply omitted a speech-heading before 'He is in love', and Candiano is the most likely person to speak that line given his sympathy for Giovanni earlier in the scene (ll. 34–5).
169 **by** as a result of.
170–1 **begin…growth** i.e. 1) take up a new gardening project; 2) find another way to progress.
171 **what we have's** i.e. the state we have reached so far is.
172 **dunghill** 1) pile of animal dung, straw, *etc.*, to be rotted down for manure (*OED*, *n.* 1); 2) *fig.*, state of poverty (*OED*, *n.* 3a).

158 SD] Q/O *(in right-hand margin of l. 157)*   158 coarsely] *Gifford;* coursely Q/O
161 SD] *this edn; not in* Q/O
161–3] *lineation this edn;* wise, / And…better / Commodity…Christendom; / Pray Q/O
168 SH1] *this edn; not in* Q/O   168 SD *Senators*] *Gifford; Senator* Q/O

362

THE GENTLEMAN OF VENICE   4·3

GEORGIO   Your armour? Yes,
We might have worn soft-natured silk an you had   175
Been ruled by me; a pox of love for my part,
'Tis good for nothing but to make things dear.
GIOVANNI I'll be revenged upon my stars that made
Me poor, and die forgotten in my shade.   *Exeunt.*

[4·3]

    A table prepared, two tapers. Enter FLORELLI.

FLORELLI I find no great devotion in this
Monastic life. The major-domo promised
A mistress here of that complexion,
But I like not this solitude
And tedious expectations.   5
I shall ne'er do things handsomely.
Give me freedom and fair play,
And turn me to a harpy, but to be thus
Compelled to an embrace – for that's the meaning
Of my sly signor, if it be not worse –   10
Fed high to encounter with an Amazon
I know not? 'Tis not well, nor conscionable
In my opinion. I hear some busy
About the lock.

    Enter CORNARI.

175 soft-natured fine, luxurious, attractive.
175 an if.
177 dear expensive.
178 my stars fate, destiny, the astrological forces.
179 shade obscurity (*OED*, *n.* 1c), with a pun on the shade cast by the trees in the garden, which might obscure the stars from view.
0 The scene is set in a room in Cornari's house.
0 SD *tapers* i.e. wax candles (on the table).
1 devotion 1) purpose (*OED*, *n.* 7); 2) feeling of devout reverence (*OED*, 1c).
2 major-domo 'chief official of an Italian or Spanish princely household' (*OED*, *n.* 1).
3 that complexion This reference suggests that Florelli may still be in the gallery of 3.3, and that the '*scene*' is again '*adorned with pictures*' (3.3.0 SD).
5 expectations periods of waiting (*OED*, Expectation *n.* 2a).
6 handsomely 1) skilfully (*OED*, *adv.* 2a); 2) elegantly, neatly (*OED*, *adv.* 3a); 3) readily (*OED*, *adv.* 4).
8 turn…harpy i.e. then you could turn me over to a (sexually) rapacious person (see *OED*, Harpy *n.* 2).
8 harpy The harpies in Greek mythology were monsters with the face and torso of a woman and a bird's wings and claws.
11 Fed…encounter i.e. Pampered with luxurious food in order to prepare me to have sex.
11 Amazon 1) female warrior; 2) sexually audacious woman (Williams 1994, 1.16–17). In Greek mythology the Amazons were a nation of warlike women.
12 conscionable equitable, fair, reasonable.

---

175 an] *Gifford;* and Q/O
[4·3]] *Gifford subst. (*SCENE III.*); not in* Q/O   **13 some busy]** Q/O; some [one] busy *Gifford*

363

4·3   THE COMPLETE WORKS OF JAMES SHIRLEY, VOLUME 7

My jailer? What now follows?
Sir, if I must ha' my throat cut – as much   15
Better I do not hope, though I deserve not
That bounty from your hands, I live so dully –
I would request you set a time, and't be
A day or two, to pray and think of matters,
And then turn me loose to the other world!
CORNARI   Read that.   20

Gives him a paper.

[*Aside*] He sha'not see my blushes. I must pity
Thee, Claudiana, but my stubborn fate
Will have it so. It is to make thee live
Although we both must suffer, and I, like
A father thus whose child at play upon   25
A river's bank is fall'n into the stream,
Leap in and hazard all to save a little.
But I must on.   *Exit.*
FLORELLI   Amazement circles me;
Such wonders are not read in every marriage.
What shall I do? Madness to question it.   30
I must resolve or die. Since there's no help,
'Tis something if she be but like that face
To comfort my proceeding.

Enter CORNARI *leading his wife* [CLAUDIANA] *veiled.*

---

17 **dully** i.e. without the opportunity to do anything to offend.
18–19 **set...matters** i.e. appoint a time for my death, giving me a day or two to put my soul in order.
20 **turn...world** i.e. kill me.
20 **SD** Cornari has apparently set out his scheme on paper so that he does not have to speak it out loud and embarrass himself.
23 **to...live** to immortalize you (i.e. by giving you the opportunity to have a child).
24–7 **like...little** Cornari's image is strangely vivid and disturbing given his longing for a child.
27 **hazard** risk losing.
28–9 **Amazement...marriage** This is Florelli's reaction to the '*paper*', which he has been reading while Cornari has been speaking in aside.
30 **Madness** i.e. It would be mad.
30 **question** 1) doubt (*OED*, 5a); 2) challenge (*OED*, 6a).
31 **there's...help** i.e. nothing can be done about it.
33 **comfort...proceeding** i.e. to make sex with her tolerable and/or enjoyable.
33 **comfort** 1) encourage, incite (*OED*, *v.* 1a–b); 2) invigorate (*OED*, *v.* 4); 3) gladden (*OED*, *v.* 5); 4) relieve, assist (*OED*, *v.* 6).
33 **SD** *veiled* Venetian women in the early seventeenth century wore long veils or *veléta*, which covered their heads and faces and reached nearly as far as the ground; respectable unmarried women (and prostitutes, who imitated them) wore white veils, while wives and widows wore black ones (Johnson 2011, 107). The colour of Claudiana's veil might therefore indicate something of her status to Florelli and/or the playhouse audience. Veils would normally have been worn only in public, so the fact that Claudiana wears a veil also suggests the extent to which the norms of Cornari's household are being transgressed.

---

14 follows] *Gifford;* fellowes Q/O   21 **SD**] *Gifford subst.; not in* Q/O   33 **SD** CLAUDIANA] *Gifford subst.; not in* Q/O

364

THE GENTLEMAN OF VENICE   4.3

CORNARI Be bold, and take as lent this treasure from me;
   I must expect it back again with interest.   *Locks the door and exits.*   35
FLORELLI [*Aside*] The door is fast again. Here is a precedent
   For husbands that want heirs to their estate!
   A goodly person. – Please you, lady, to
   Unveil? (*She unveils*) [*Aside*] A rich and most inviting beauty;
   I am all flame! – Shall I take boldness, after   40
   My duty paid your white hand, to aspire
   And touch your lip? (*He kisses* [*her.*]) [*Aside*] Now could I wish to dwell here. –
   Can you read, lady?

                 She takes the paper and turns.

   [*Aside*] She turns away her face. I hope my signor
   Has taken pains to bring her to the business   45
   And not left me to break her. Can she speak? –
   Those lines – I know not how you like 'em, madam –
   Were none of my invention; the character
   I guess to be your husband's. I am here
   A prisoner to his will, to which unless   50

34–5 take . . . interest The image of Claudiana as 'treasure' sets up an uneasy relationship between Cornari's refusal to lend Malipeiro money and his willingness to lend out Claudiana in order to acquire a new heir, and it is repeated at 5.2.86, where it has a directly sexual meaning.

36 fast locked.

36 precedent model, exemplar. O and Q read 'president', which was an alternative spelling for 'precedent' in early modern English. 'Precedent' fits the context, and Florelli's amazement, better, but if 'president' were retained, Florelli would be saying that Cornari is the appointed leader of husbands who lack heirs (*OED*, President *n.* 2, 4).

38 goodly person attractive physique (see *OED*, Goodly *adj.* 1a; *OED*, Person *n.* 4b).

38 Please you Would you be pleased; would you be willing.

40 flame desire, passion.

40 take boldness i.e. be so bold, take such a bold action.

40–1 after . . . paid i.e. after I have kissed.

41 white 1) fair (in the senses of 'pale', 'beautiful' and 'refined' because it implies that the owner does not do manual work and avoids getting tanned) (see *OED*, *adj.* 2a); 2) innocent (*OED*, *adj.* 7a).

42 SD1 The dialogue implies that Florelli kisses Claudiana's hand and then her lips; in performance these actions could take place at different points during the speech, although the position of the stage direction here follows O and Q.

43 Can . . . read Female literacy was higher in London than in other parts of England in the early modern period, and high-status women were more likely to be able to read and write, but even some relatively elite women were illiterate or only partially literate, depending on their families' views about women's education. However, Florelli may simply mean 'Will you read this?', the sense in which Ursula uses this formulation at 5.4.10.

45 taken pains made an effort.

45 bring . . . business i.e. make her understand what is required of her, persuade her to accept what he wants her to do.

46 break her tame her, break her in (in the manner of a horse being trained to be ridden) (*OED*, Break *v.* 14a). As Williams (1994, 1.146–7) points out, to 'break' in sexual slang often means to rupture the hymen, i.e. to take a woman's virginity. Here, in contrast, Florelli hopes that Cornari has prepared Claudiana emotionally for the sexual encounter that he has planned.

48 character handwriting.

---

34 Be bold] Q/O; Behold *Gifford*   **35** SD] *this edn; locks the door and Ex.* Q/O *(in margins of ll. 35–6)*
36 SD] *Gifford subst.; not in* Q/O   **36** precedent] *Gifford;* president Q/O   **39** SD1] Q/O *subst. (in margin)*
39 SD2] *this edn; not in* Q/O   **42** SD1] Q/O *subst. (he kisses) (in margin)*
42 SD2] *this edn; not in* Q/O   **43** SD] Q/O *subst. (in margins of ll. 43–4)*
44 SD] *Gifford subst.; not in* Q/O

365

5.1　　THE COMPLETE WORKS OF JAMES SHIRLEY, VOLUME 7

You give obedience I have took leave
Of day forever, destined by his vow
To an eternal shade.　　　　　　　　　　　　　　　*Exit Claudiana.*
　　　　　　　She leads the way.
Conscience be calm, no grumblings now of piety.　　　　*[Exit.]*

5[.1]

> *[Enter]* GIOVANNI. *[He hangs] the pieces of armour upon several trees.*
>
> *[Enter]* ROBERTO *[and]* URSULA.

GIOVANNI　These were the excellent Bellaura's gift,
　Of no use now to me but to keep fresh
　The memory of my dreams and that I loved her.
　I see how passion did blind my reason,
　And my prodigious hopes, vanished to air,　　　　　　5
　Have left me to contemplate my own vanity.
ROBERTO　I know not, but if I may credit Georgio,
　That did wait on thee to the senate, thou
　Hast lost an opportunity that might
　Have made us all *clarissimos*, Giovanni.　　　　　　10
　I might have kept my reverend mules and had
　My crupper worshipped by the plebeians,
　And Ursula here been Madam Heaven-knows-what.
　And did you wisely to refuse?
URSULA　　　　　　　　　　Nay, nay, I know
　He was not born to do us good. Not stoop　　　　　　15
　To take preferment from the duke and senate?

53　**eternal shade** i.e. death.
0　The scene is set in the Duke's garden.
0　SD　Georgio has apparently done as Giovanni asked him and 'brought [the armour] home' (4.2.174). The stage direction in O and Q suggests that Giovanni hangs the armour, and that he steps back to look at it as he speaks his opening lines. Gifford adopts a different approach: his stage direction, '*Giovanni's armour hung upon several trees*', indicates that stage-hands hang the armour before Giovanni, Roberto, and Ursula enter.
5　**prodigious** unnatural (*OED, adj.* 3), excessive (see *OED, adj.* 4).
5　**to air** i.e. into nothing.
7　**credit** believe.
10　*clarissimos* grandees, magnificos (a term for the Venetian elite).
11–12　i.e. I would have been the same person and yet been treated as one of the elite.
11　**reverend** old.
11　**mules** hybrid animals that result from crossing a male donkey with a female horse.
11　**and had** and yet had (i.e. because he would be a *clarissimo* and therefore deemed worthy of respect).
12　**crupper** 1) leather strap buckled under a horse's tail to prevent the saddle slipping (*OED, n.* 1); 2) buttocks, bum (*OED, n.* 3a).
15　**Not stoop** i.e. Is he too proud, is he not humble enough.

---

54 SD] *Gifford subst.; not in* Q/O
5[.1]] *Gifford subst.* (ACT V. SCENE I.*)*; Act. 5. Q/O
0 SD] *this edn; Giovanni. The pieces of Armour hung upon severall trees* Roberto, Ursula. Q/O
10　*clarissimos*] Q/O (*Clarissimo's*)

366

THE GENTLEMAN OF VENICE

5.1

ROBERTO Well, 'twas his modesty.
URSULA   He learned it not from me.
ROBERTO No more –
URSULA You will be always taking his part against me,
But I know what I know, and that's a secret.   20
Here comes the tother dunderhead.

     Enter GEORGIO.

GEORGIO The armour is hung up already. This
We must all come to.
ROBERTO   What, to the gibbet, Georgio?
GEORGIO Master, look here. (*Pointing to the helmet.*)
If you had but this hole to put your head in   25
It would be a great preservative to your hearing
And keep out all the noise of my dame's culverin.
Within this fortification, well locked up,
You would think her loudest scolding a mere whisper.
URSULA What's that you talk of your dame, sirrah?   30
GEORGIO Oh, dame, I have news for you.
URSULA For me? What is't? Whom does your news concern?
GEORGIO One that you love with all your heart.
ROBERTO   Who is't, knave?
GEORGIO Knave? Call your word in, and eat it. I'll advise;
You may fare worse. You do not hear the news, then?   35
URSULA I shall when you'll find utterance.
GEORGIO   The news –
We are all of one religion?
ROBERTO   Out with it.
GEORGIO Everything is not to be talked on.
ROBERTO So it seems, by your concealment.

---

20 But…secret Shirley again drops a hint that there is something mysterious about Giovanni.

21 the tother i.e. the other (*OED*, Tother *pron.* 1). While 'tother' means 'the other', it is often preceded by 'the' in early modern texts. Shirley gives this construction to people of a range of social ranks in his plays.

21 dunderhead idiot, fool (*OED*, *n.*).

27 culverin 1) a large cannon (*OED*, *n.* 1b); 2) 'volleys of oaths' (*OED*, *n.* 1c), violent speech. Shirley uses the term in a similar way in *Honour and Riches*, in which the Soldier claims to 'imitate the Drum / Bold Artillery' and Honour reproves him, at which point Ingenuity comments, 'She has quash'd his Culvering'. 'Culvering', also found in O and Q, is a variant spelling.

30 talk say.

30 dame mistress.

36 you'll…utterance you will tell me.

37 We…religion i.e. Can everyone here be trusted. This phrase would have additional impact in the context of religious controversy in early modern England, where different Christian sects were frequently at odds, and it would be especially resonant for a spectator or reader who shared Shirley's Roman Catholic faith. The same phrase appears in *Country Captain*, 3.1.

---

24 SD] Q/O *subst. (in margins of ll. 23–4)*

367

5.1　　　THE COMPLETE WORKS OF JAMES SHIRLEY, VOLUME 7

URSULA　　　　　　　　　　　　Shall we hear it?
GEORGIO　Yes. Signor Thomazo –
URSULA　　　　　　　　　What of him?　　　　　　　　　　　40
GEORGIO　There's a gentleman, an you talk of a gentleman.
URSULA　What of Thomazo? Now am I longing.
GEORGIO　I heard, as I came hither –
URSULA　　　　　　　　　What?
ROBERTO　　　　　　　　　　　　Let us hear too.
URSULA　What? Be brief.
GEORGIO　　　　　　　That he is to lose his head, mistress –
URSULA　Now a thousand blisters upon that tongue!　　　　45
GEORGIO　But you do not know for what, mistress! There's it;
　　You are so angry still at half a business.
URSULA　For what is he to suffer? Oh, my heart!
GEORGIO　For nothing but high treason.
ROBERTO　How?　　　　　　　　　　　　　　　　　　　50
GEORGIO　You ha' not patience to hear a story out.
ROBERTO　High treason, said he? That's a shrewd business.
URSULA　Thomazo lose his head?
ROBERTO　　　　　　　　　So it seems.
URSULA　Better thy generation were headless.
GEORGIO　I told you but in good will, because I knew　　　55
　　You loved him. I ha' done.　　　　　　　　*Exit.*
URSULA　Passion! O my dear heart! I'll to the duke
　　Myself and beg his pardon.
ROBERTO　　　　　　　　You'll make
　　Yourself a party in the treason, will you?
　　You'll beg his pardon? You'll beg a halter,　　　　60
　　And sooner 'twill be granted.
URSULA　　　　　　　　Giovanni,
　　Sweet Giovanni: there's a sunshine word.
　　Dear child, go with us.
ROBERTO　　　　　　　Us? Dost think I'll go

---

41 **There's…of a gentleman** Georgio mockingly repeats Ursula's catchphrase.
45 **thousand…tongue** A proverbial curse on a liar or tell-tale: see Tilley R84, 'Report has a blister on her tongue'.
47 **still…business** i.e. when I have only told you half of the story (see *OED*, business *n*. 15a).
52 **shrewd** dangerous (*OED, adj.* 4).
54 **generation** descendants, posterity (*OED, n.* 1a), i.e. Giovanni.
56 **SD** *Exit* Georgio seems to exit discreetly, as Ursula does not realize that he has gone until l. 79.
59 **party** participant, accomplice.
62 **sunshine** cheering.

41 an] *Gifford subst.;* and Q/O

368

THE GENTLEMAN OF VENICE   5.1

And run my head into the hemp?
URSULA   Best honeysuckle!
One word of thine will strike the pardon dead.   65
GIOVANNI I'd rather go a-pilgrimage.
URSULA Thou shalt go a-pilgrimage another time,
  To the world's end. I charge thee on my blessing,
  And husband you must go too.   [*Giovanni sneaks out.*]
ROBERTO   No, no, not I.
  I thank you, Ursula, I'll not have my foot   70
  Nor hand in any treason.
URSULA Is it so much to kneel? You shall say nothing
  Unless you please; leave all the talk to me.
ROBERTO I wo'not go, though the duke send for me.
URSULA How? That's a piece o'treason.
ROBERTO   So, if I go not,   75
  She'll betray me too. Well, Giovanni shall go too.
  Where is he?
URSULA   Let me alone to conjure him.
  Shall we go presently? Delays are dangerous.
  [*She looks around.*] The rascal George is gone too! All forsake me
  In my distress.
ROBERTO   What will you say, Ursula,   80
  When you come there? What will the duke think on you?
  Or who shall suffer for your impudence?
  And what? That is considerable. I have
  No mind to go again.

---

64 the hemp i.e. a noose.

64 Best honeysuckle i.e. Darling.

65 strike...dead Ursula appears to mean that Giovanni's support will give her plea for a pardon for Thomazo additional force (see *OED*, Strike *v.* 31a; Dead *adv.* 2a), but the phrase would more normally imply that the attempt would be ruined (see *OED*, Strike *v.* 45, 46). The possibility that Giovanni's intervention might save Thomazo appears to be the cause of Ursula's sudden outburst of affection for him.

68 To...end Despite her attempts to ingratiate herself with Giovanni, Ursula's anger may rise again here.

68 charge...blessing i.e. I order you as your mother. Ursula alludes to the practice of a child kneeling to receive a parent's blessing. Compare Marlowe, *The Jew of Malta*, 'I charge thee on my blessing that thou leave / These devils and their damned heresy' (Marlowe 2009, 1.2.343–4).

69 SD There is no exit direction in O or Q, but Giovanni must leave the stage before l. 77, when Roberto notices he has left, and he could take advantage of Ursula turning her attention to Roberto to make his escape.

72 to kneel i.e. to kneel before the Duke to beg Thomazo's pardon.

75–6 So...me too These lines might be spoken as an aside to the audience.

77 Let...alone i.e. Leave it to me.

77 conjure him 1) entreat him (see *OED*, Conjure *v.* 4a); 2) make him do my bidding (in the manner of a magician summoning a devil) (*OED*, Conjure *v.* 5a); make him reappear (see *OED*, Conjure *v.* 8, 9c).

78 presently now, at once.

83 considerable worthy of consideration, important (*OED*, *n.* 3).

83–4 I...again i.e. I have again decided not to go.

---

65 of thine] *Gifford;* of hine O *(earlier states);* o fhine O *(later states);* ohine Q
69 SD] *this edn; Exit. after l. 66 Gifford; not in* Q/O
75 o'treason] *this edn;* of treason *Gifford;* a treason Q/O
79 SD] *this edn; not in* Q/O   **81** duke] *Gifford;* Dukes Q/O

5.1   THE COMPLETE WORKS OF JAMES SHIRLEY, VOLUME 7

URSULA   Then I'll spoil the garden,
    Break up the hedges and deface the works   85
    Your darling Giovanni made. I'll let in
    A regiment of swine and all their officers
    To undermine the castle he made last,
    And fortified with cannon, though I die for't.
ROBERTO More treason. Well, I will go, but I hope   90
    You wo'not trudge this evening. If we must
    Resolve upon't let us do things discreetly.
URSULA That was well said! Nay, I am for discretion
    For all my haste.
ROBERTO   I think it most convenient
    To wait his business coming forth his chamber   95
    Tomorrow morning, Ursula, and then let
    Good natures work. Tonight's no time.
    We must consult our pillows what to say
    And how to place our words.
URSULA   Now 'tis my best
    Pigeon; let's home instantly.   100
ROBERTO A sober pace goes far. Not too fast, Ursula,
    Remembering the proverb and what follows.
    We should march slow to save me from the gallows.   *Exeunt.*

---

85 works 1) creations, handiworks (*OED*, Work *n.* 11a); 2) architectural structures (*OED*, Work *n.* 13a); 3) fortifications (*OED*, Work *n.* 14).

87 regiment...swine herd of pigs. Ursula chooses the word 'regiment', which literally refers to a large body of soldiers, in order to continue a line of imagery from 'works' and imagine an attack on the 'castle' and 'cannon' that Giovanni has created in the flower-bed with elaborate planting (see 1.2.83).

88 undermine dig beneath as part of a military operation (*OED*, *v.* 1a).

91 trudge i.e. go to the palace (*lit.*, walk laboriously, go on foot [*OED*, *v.* 1a]).

92 Resolve upon't Decide to do it.

94 convenient appropriate.

95 wait...chamber i.e. attend him when he emerges from his private rooms to conduct his public affairs.

97 Good natures i.e. 1) our willingness to please, our obliging dispositions; and/or 2) the Duke's benevolence.

97 work 1) strive to achieve our purpose (see *OED*, *v.* 11a); 2) be put to work.

100 Pigeon Sweetheart. The word also means a naïve or gullible person, a sense that Ursula may also intend.

101 A...far A version of the proverb 'soft pace goes far' (Tilley P3), as Roberto acknowledges in the next line.

101 sober sedate, unhurried.

103 me This is the reading in O and Q, and it makes sense if it is read in terms of Roberto's reluctance to put himself in danger; it is also possible that it could be spoken as an aside. An alternative reading would be 'men', which would mean that Roberto refers to the threat to Thomazo, or to a general threat, rather than solely the danger that he is in. This possibility would involve just a dropped letter, and it would add to the sententious quality of Roberto's speech. Gifford's suggestion, 'us', would require a more serious mistake in the print-shop.

---

103 me] Q/O*;* men *this edn conj.;* [us] *Gifford*   **103 SD**] *this edn; Exit* Q/O

370

[5.2]

THE GENTLEMAN OF VENICE   5.2

Enter CORNARI *with a pistol and a rapier* [*and*] FLORELLI.

CORNARI   You have had your time of pleasure. Can you pray?

FLORELLI   Pray? What do you mean, signor?

CORNARI   The lady whom you have enjoyed commanded
    I should present one of these two, or both,
    In token of her gratitude.

FLORELLI   This cannot   5
    Be earnest, sir.

CORNARI   These are the jewels
    Which you must wear, sir, next your heart. How d'ye
    Affect the lustre of this toy? 'Tis bright,
    But here's a thing will sparkle.

FLORELLI   I am lost.
    Is this the promise of my safety?

CORNARI   Yes,   10
    This will secure all, thou dull islander.
    'Cause you can dance, and vault upon a hobby-horse,
    D'ye think to mount madonnas here and not
    Pay for the sweet career? Fool, to thy prayers,
    For when these messengers salute thy heart   15
    Thy soul shall find I'm an Italian,

---

0 The scene is set in a room in Cornari's house.

4 these two i.e. the pistol and rapier.

6 earnest serious, sincere.

7–9 How…sparkle It seems likely that Cornari gestures first to the rapier and then to the pistol, which could 'sparkle' in the sense of sending out sparks (*OED*, *v.*¹ 2a) and also in the sense of issuing small particles (*OED*, *v.*¹ 1), i.e. bullets.

8 Affect Like.

8 lustre sheen, shininess.

11 islander i.e. inhabitant of Britain. Given that Venice is made up of islands, Cornari's emphasis may be on 'dull'.

12 vault…hobby-horse Literally refers to the gymnastic activity of vaulting, but figuratively to the action of having sex because 'hobby-horse' was a slang term for a lustful woman or prostitute (Williams 1994, 2.669–70).

13 mount 1) get onto the back of (developing the image of riding from l. 12) (*OED*, *v.* 13a); 2) have sex with (*OED*, *v.* 14a; Williams 1994, 2.914–15).

13 madonnas women. This is a respectful, or mock-respectful, way of addressing a woman, often an Italian woman (*OED*, *n.* 1a), but it was also used to refer to lustful women or prostitutes (*OED*, *n.* 1b).

14 career 1) gallop at full speed (as of a horse), charge (as in a tournament) (*OED*, *n.* 2a); 2) frisk, gambol (as of a horse) (*OED*, *n.* 2b); 'sexual bout' (Williams 1994, 2.204). The sexual usage also appears in *Witty Fair One*—''tis not that I stand upon a cariere, but I wo'not be compeld to lye with any Whore in Christendome' (4.4)—and *Country Captain*, 4.2.

15 these messengers i.e. the pistol and rapier.

15 salute 1) greet, honour, address (*OED*, *v.* 1a, 1d, 1e, 2a); 2) assail (*OED*, *v.* 2g). The latter is an ironic usage: *OED* quotes Rowlands, *Guy, Earl of Warwick*: 'So drawes his swoorde, salutes him with that same / About the head, the shoulders, & the side' (1609, M2r).

[5.2]] *Gifford subst.* (SCENE II.)*; not in* Q/O   **0 SD** *and*] *this edn; not in* Q/O

5.2 THE COMPLETE WORKS OF JAMES SHIRLEY, VOLUME 7

And wo'not trust a life to him whose tongue
Commands my honour.

FLORELLI   Art a Christian?

CORNARI As much as comes to a Venetian's faith,
That believes no man is more fit to die   20
Than he that has been capering with my wife.

FLORELLI Ye cannot, sir, forget I was betrayed;
Awake thy conscience and let that answer.
I have obeyed a dire necessity,
And was brought hither by a stratagem.   25

CORNARI 'Tis all one, signor. I presume you gave
Consent to the dear matter of delight,
Which is not held convenient you should talk of.

FLORELLI Hold.

CORNARI   Hope not to breathe ten minutes. Gather up
Those thoughts you would have wait upon you to   30
Another world.

FLORELLI   Then 'tis high time to think
Of other matters. Though you have cruelly
Resolved there is no safety for your fame
To let me still be numbered with the living –
Which if your scattered reason were collected   35
I could refute, but I'll not hope it now –
Since most ignobly 'gainst the rules of honour,
And faith already forfeit, you will make

17–18 **wo'not...honour** i.e. will not allow a man to carry on living if he could say something to dishonour me.

18 **Art** i.e. Art thou, are you.

19 **As...faith** i.e. Insofar as I am a Venetian, with their ideas about morality.

21 **capering** 1) dancing, leaping, skipping; 2) having sex with (Williams 1994 1.202). Shirley uses this term in a similar way in *Example*, 3.1.

24 **dire** dreadful, evil.

24 **necessity** 1) constraint, compulsion; 2) something under another's control.

25 **stratagem** 1) trick (*OED*, *n.* 2a); 2) act of violence (*OED*, *n.* 3).

26 **'Tis...one** i.e. That's as may be, that is no concern of mine.

27 **dear...delight** i.e. the act of having sex with Claudiana.

28 **is...of** i.e. it is not appropriate that you should discuss.

29–31 **Gather...world** i.e. Prepare yourself to make a good death by thinking appropriately virtuous thoughts.

33 **fame** public reputation, honour.

35 **if...collected** i.e. if your mental faculties were put in order, if you were able to think rationally.

36 **I'll...now** i.e. I could not hope to succeed given your present state.

37 **ignobly** dishonourably.

38 **faith...forfeit** having already broken your promise.

---

20 more fit to] *MS emendation in Folger S3468; Gifford;* moreto fit Q/O   29 breathe] *Gifford;* breath Q/O

372

THE GENTLEMAN OF VENICE   5.2

This undefenced pile your sacrifice,
Yet do not kill me twice.
CORNARI   Twice?
FLORELLI   Such a rage   40
Were infinite. Practise not cruelty
Upon my second life by murdering my
Eternity: allow to my last breath
Leave to discharge the weight of many sins
Into the bosom of some confessor.   45
CORNARI This may be granted; 'tis not much unreasonable.
FLORELLI Your charity will think it fit to allow
Some minutes to collect myself.
CORNARI   To show
My design has no malice in't, I'll do
Your soul that office, though our bodies must not   50
Enjoy this air together many hours.
I'll send one to you.   *Exit.*
FLORELLI   The innocence of a saint
Would not secure his life from an Italian
When his revenge is fixed. In what black hour
Did I salute the world, that I am thrown   55
Upon so hard a fate? It is not fit
To expostulate with heaven, or I could say
Something in my defence, as I am man,
To keep this mighty rock from falling on me.

39 undefenced undefended.

39 pile 1) stronghold (*OED*, *n.*³ 1); 2) *fig.*, Florelli's body. The term could also refer to the pyre on which a sacrifice was burned, a usage which may inform Florelli's use of 'sacrifice' later in the sentence (*OED*, *n.*⁵ 1c).

41 infinite without limit.

41–5 Practice...confessor Florelli pleads with Cornari not to kill him without having given him the opportunity to absolve his sins through sacramental confession because to do so would be to put at risk Florelli's hope of an eternal 'second life' in heaven. Confession was abolished as a sacrament by the protestant Church of England in 1548, but English Catholics such as Shirley—and, apparently, Florelli—continued to believe that it was necessary to confess and be absolved of mortal sins such as adultery before death or face damnation.

46 'tis...unreasonable i.e. it isn't that much to ask.

47 Your...allow i.e. Since I know you to be charitable I am sure you will allow.

50 office 1) duty (*OED*, *n.* 3a); 2) moral obligation (*OED*, *n.* 3c); 3) act of kindness (*OED*, n. 5); 4) religious or ceremonial duty, performance of rites for the dead (*OED*, *n.* 9).

50–1 our...hours A very convoluted way of saying 'one of us will soon be dead', suggesting the mental contortions that Cornari undergoes in this scene.

52 SD Cornari clearly takes the pistol and rapier with him when he leaves, as Florelli later refers to himself as 'disarmed' (l. 97).

52–4 The...fixed Refers to the widespread believe that Italians were especially liable to take violent revenge for slights against them. In *Love's Cruelty*, Hippolito declares 'such mercie / Becomes not an *Italian*' (4.1).

54 black unhappy, calamitous (*OED*, *adj.* 11a).

55 Did...world i.e. Was I born.

57 expostulate...heaven argue with God, dispute the fate that God has set out for me.

57 or i.e. if it were.

373

5.2 THE COMPLETE WORKS OF JAMES SHIRLEY, VOLUME 7

My tutelar-angel be at counsel with   60
My thoughts, and if there be a path of safety
Direct my trembling steps to find and taste it.

    Enter CORNARI *in a friar's habit.*

H'as kept his word, and 'tis no time to trifle.
[*To Cornari*] As you're a priest and by that sacred order
And scapular you wear, not only hear me   65
But use your pious art to save from ruin
A man condemned for that which heaven and you
Call virtue, for not doing a black deed
Would damn three souls at once. And if your power
Cannot prevail for mercy to my life,   70
I challenge you when I am dead to be
A witness of my innocence.
CORNARI   This has
No shape of a confession.
FLORELLI   Nor do I
Under that holy seal discourse a story.
Yet, Father, I must throw myself upon   75
Your charity. Know, therefore, I am betrayed,
And by the plot of him that owes this palace –
Whose name is never like to meet my knowledge –
Snatched up one fatal evening, and forced hither

60 **tutelar-angel** guardian-angel.
60–1 **be…thoughts** i.e. advise me, offer me counsel.
62 **taste it** 1) put it to the test (*OED*, Taste *v.* 12a); 2) feel it, experience it (*OED*, Taste *v.* 12c).
62 SD *in…habit* Cornari's identity is concealed from Florelli by this disguise, but his speeches during this part of the scene, and especially his exclamation, 'Ha!' (l. 91), suggest that spectators are intended to know who he is.
63 **H'as** He has.
63 **'tis…trifle** i.e. there is no time to waste.
64 **sacred order** i.e. office of priest.
65 **scapular** 'A short cloak covering the shoulders…adopted by certain religious orders as a part of their ordinary costume' (*OED*, *n.* 1a).
68 **black** wicked.
69 **three souls** i.e. those of Cornari (for prostituting his wife) and Claudiana and Florelli (for adultery).
70 **prevail…life** i.e. preserve me from death by interceding with Cornari.
71 **challenge** demand, call on.
72–3 **This…confession** i.e. This isn't the proper form in which a confession should come, this doesn't sound like a confession.
73–4 **Nor…story** i.e. I am not going to abuse the seal of confession by telling a story/making a groundless assertion (see *OED*, Story *n.* 6a). The 'holy seal' obliged a priest to keep the penitent sinner's confession secret (see *OED*, Seal *n.*² 2b).
77 **owes** owns.
78 **like** likely.

---

64 SD] *Gifford subst.; not in* Q/O

374

THE GENTLEMAN OF VENICE
5.2

By some dark ministers he had employed – 80
I know not which way – to this fatal chamber.
I shudder but to name what impious act
Against his own and his dear lady's honour
He had designed for me. Her chaster soul
Should have been stained in his distrust of heaven 85
To bless him with an heir, and her white treasure
By me a stranger rifled, had not providence
Chained up our blood, so that the hours he gave
To serve his black ambition, and our lust,
We only spent in prayers for his conversion. 90
CORNARI Ha!
FLORELLI This yet he knows not, and it is not safe
To appear in our own virtue, since the justice
We did our peace in crossing his expectance
May improve his rage to both our ruins. This
Sad story frights you. There is horror in't, 95
But 'tis an hour, the last, without some miracle,
To rescue me – a man disarmed – from violence.
Nor dare I mock heaven now, or hang upon
My soul the burden of a lie, when 'tis
Taking her last eternal flight. It is not 100
A fear to die afflicts me, with my faith
And innocence about me – I have looked
Death in the face, and be it thought no boast

---

80 dark 1) wicked; 2) secret.
80 ministers 1) servants, attendants (*OED*, Minister *n.* 1b); 2) underlings (*OED*, Minister *n.* 1d).
84 chaster purer, more virtuous.
85–6 in...bless i.e. because he did not believe that God would provide.
86 white treasure innocent body, chastity. 'Treasure' can refer to the female genitals, virginity, and chastity (see Williams 1994, 3.1419–20); Cornari has already referred to Claudiana as 'The treasure of my eyes and heart' (1.1.180) and 'this treasure' (4.3.34). In Shakespeare's *Titus Andronicus*, Aaron invites the rapists Chiron and Demetrius to 'serve your lust...And revel in Lavinia's treasury' (2.1.130–1).
87 providence protective care of God, divine guidance.
88 blood sexual appetites (*OED*, *n.* 13; see also Williams 1994, 1.115–16).
91 Ha! An exclamation indicating surprise.
92 appear...virtue i.e. reveal that we have preserved our chastity.
92–3 justice...expectance i.e. the righteous way in which we preserved our mental and spiritual tranquillity by thwarting his expectations. 'Justice' can also mean the observation of divine law (see *OED*, *n.* 8).
94 improve intensify, make worse (*OED*, *v.*² 3b).
94–5 This...you Florelli may be responding to Cornari's 'Ha!' or to physical signs of discomfort.
96 'tis...last i.e. this is the last moment.
97 To i.e. At which it would be possible to.
98 mock heaven attempt to fool God.
98–9 or...lie Florelli refers to the 'lie' that he has told by letting Cornari think that he and Claudiana have had sex; this is a sin to which he might have confessed formally if was actually making a confession to the man he thinks is a priest, rather than begging him for help.
100 last...flight final ascent to heaven and eternal life.
103 be...boast i.e. do not think I am boasting.

5.2   THE COMPLETE WORKS OF JAMES SHIRLEY, VOLUME 7

To say I have taught others by example
To march up to the ugliest face of danger. 105
But to die thus dishonourably, to be
Sent out o'th'world i'th'dark, without a name
Or any account to those to whom I owe
My blood and birth, persons that carry names
Of honour in my country? This doth stagger me 110
To quit my life and may excuse my address
To you, who have authority from heaven
To take his fury off whom otherwise
I expect my violent executioner.
I have some tremblings for his lady, whose 115
Most holy tears streamed through my soul compassion
And charmed my blood; tears, if he durst have patience,
Were powerful enough to beg from heaven
That blessing which he fondly thinks to hasten
With loss of his eternity.

CORNARI   No more.   *Exit Cornari hastily.* 120

Having thrown off the habit, enter [CORNARI] *again with* CLAUDIANA.

Forgive me, O forgive me, Claudiana!
And if my sin of forcing thy obedience
Beyond the rules of honour and of marriage
Have not quite murdered thy affection,
Wish me a little life for my repentance. 125

CLAUDIANA I joy to hear this from you.

CORNARI There's work within me, and so deep a sense
Of my own shame and sorrow that I feel

---

107 **i'th'dark** secretly.

107–9 **without...birth** i.e. denied my reputation or the facts of my death being made known to my family. Florelli may also imply that his death will go unrecorded.

110–11 **doth...life** i.e. makes me reluctant to die.

111 **address** appeal.

115 **tremblings** fears, apprehensions.

117 **charmed...blood** subdued my lust. Compare *Country Captain*: 'There is a blessing falne upon my bloud: your only thoughts charme had power to make my thoughts wicked, and your conversion disenchants me' (5.3).

117 **tears** i.e. these (i.e. Claudiana's) tears.

117 **durst** dared to have the courage to.

118–19 **to...blessing** i.e. to persuade God to provide him with an heir.

120 **eternity** salvation, eternal life in heaven.

124 **thy affection** your love for me.

125 **Wish...repentance** i.e. Give me enough time to show how repentant I am.

126 **I joy** I am overjoyed.

127 **work** distress, affliction (*OED*, *n.* 24); a process of transformation (see *OED*, *v.* 33a).

---

120 **SD**] *this edn; Exit Conrari hastily, having thrown off the habit / Enter again with Claudiana.* Q/O
127 **SH**] *Gifford subst.; Fl.* Q/O

376

THE GENTLEMAN OF VENICE   5.2

My heart already weeping out a bath
To make thee white again.
CLAUDIANA   Sir, in what best   130
I understand, I must ask you forgiveness.
CORNARI Ha, mine? For what? Betraying thee to darkness?
CLAUDIANA For disobeying your command.
CORNARI   Thou didst
The impious act by my design, which takes
Thy guilt away and spreads the leprosy   135
Upon myself.
CLAUDIANA   Although you kill me, sir,
I must remove the cloud, and let you see
Me as I am, not changed from my first innocence.
CORNARI Is't possible?
CLAUDIANA   Most easy, where there is
A chaste resolve. And I must tell you, sir,   140
Although I wanted courage to oppose
Your passion, when your reason and religion
Were under violence of your will, my heart
Resolved to try my own defence, and rather
Than yield myself a shameful spoil to lust,   145
By my own death to quit my name from scandal.
But providence determined better for me
And made me worth a stranger's piety,
Whom your choice meant the ruin of my honour.
If this want entertainment in your faith,   150

129–30 weeping…again i.e. crying sufficient tears to wash off the stain of my sinful plans. The image recalls the Christian sacrament of baptism, in which candidates are immersed in water or have water poured or sprinkled on them.

130–1 in…understand i.e. as far as I understand it.

132 mine i.e. my forgiveness.

133–6 Thou…myself Cornari appears not to be listening to Claudiana properly, and not to have fully taken in Florelli's assertion that they did not have sex.

135 leprosy 1) disease (referring to the debilitating disease caused by infection with the bacterium *mycobacterium leprae* [*OED*, *n.* 1]); 2) *fig.*, tainting effect (*OED*, *n.* 2).

137 cloud affliction, state of confusion.

140 resolve firm intention.

142–3 your…will i.e. your ability to think properly and your religious faith were repressed by your desires.

145 spoil property seized by force.

146 By…scandal i.e. To kill myself in order to preserve my reputation. Christian belief held that suicide was a mortal sin leading to damnation, but English literary culture was often more positive towards it, especially when it involved women who were subjected to sexual crimes or threatened with them. Claudiana places herself in the tradition of the classical Lucrece, who killed herself after she was raped by Tarquin, and figures from earlier English plays, such as the Lady in Middleton's *The Second Maiden's Tragedy*, who kills herself to avoid being raped by the Tyrant.

148 piety 1) pity, compassion; devotion to God.

149 Whom…meant i.e. Whom you intended to be.

150 If…faith i.e. If you are unable to believe this to be true.

150 entertainment positive reception.

139 Is't] *this edn; not in* Q/O

5.2   THE COMPLETE WORKS OF JAMES SHIRLEY, VOLUME 7

'Tis peace to my poor heart that I have many
White witnesses in heaven.
CORNARI   You have done no feats, then?
My wife is chaste?
FLORELLI   I cannot, sir, engage
My last breath to a nobler truth.
CORNARI   'Tis so –
You may withdraw, Claudiana.   *Exit Claudiana.*
                         By what   155
Has been expressed, though I am satisfied
You are not guilty in the fact, as I
Expected, 'tis not safe, when I consider
My own fame in the story, that you live, sir.
I must not trust you longer with a secret   160
That by my tameness may hereafter spread
The infamy abroad. There's no avoiding –
FLORELLI Then I must die.
CORNARI   Perhaps you have some hope
This engine may deceive me, and my fortune,
Not coming better armed, give you the advantage   165
To use your strength upon my single person.
I know you are active, but I'll make sure work.   *Exit.*
FLORELLI Till now I did not reach the precipice.
My heart would mutiny, but my hands are naked
And can do nothing.   170

        Enter CORNARI *with* BRAVOS *armed.*

152 **White** Morally pure.
152 **feats** sexual deeds (Williams 1994, 1.470). Shirley uses the word in a similar way in *Constant Maid* (3.1.78–82): 'if he have not art to / Persuade her to the feat with him, yet there / Be tricks…she may be compelled to marry him in / Her own defence'.
153 **engage** pledge, offer as a guarantee.
154 **'Tis so**—The dash appears in O and Q, suggesting that Cornari cuts himself off as he realizes that he does not want to speak in front of Claudiana.
157 **fact** evil deed, crime.
159 **My…story** i.e. How my reputation will suffer if these events become known.
161 **tameness** 1) lack of courage; 2) unwillingness to take action.
164 **This…me** Cornari probably draws his pistol on Florelli again here, and refers to the possibility that the weapon ('this engine': see *OED*, Engine *n.* 4a) may let him down, as early modern firearms were notoriously unreliable.
164 **fortune** misfortune.
167 **active** energetic, alert.
167 **make…work** carry out this task, deal with you effectively (*OED*, *n.* P2 d(a)).
168 **precipice** 1) abyss; 2) *fig.*, point of greatest danger.
169 **my…naked** i.e. I am unarmed.

153 chaste?] *this edn;* chast. Q/O   155 SD] Q/O *subst. (Ex. Cla.) (in the margin of l. 154)*
167 SD] Q/O *subst. (Ex.)*

378

THE GENTLEMAN OF VENICE

5.2

A knot of murderers! Arm me with a sword
And let me die fighting against you all;
I'll say you're noble hangmen and not throw
One curse among you.

CORNARI   I've one word to say, sir.
[*To Bravos*] Let none approach. –   175
The fatal doom I threatened is reversed.
Throw off your wonder, and believe you may
Live long, if not in Venice, and your safety
Is more confirmed at distance. You are noble,
An honour to your nation. Here is gold. [*Offers him a purse.*]   180
I know not how you may be furnished, sir,
For travel hence; bills of exchange may fail.
These will defray a present charge. Betray
No wonder. Take it.

FLORELLI   I'll accept your bounty,
And will not ask to whom I owe all this.   185
Forgive me that I thought you not so honourable.
So, when you please, I'll take my leave.

CORNARI   Not yet.
By such attendants as you came to me,
I have provided, sir, for your departure.
[*To Bravos*] Your duties, gentlemen. You know my purpose.   190

        The Bravos blind him and bind him as before.

                Exeunt [Bravos with Florelli].

Enter CLAUDIANA.

173–4 not…you i.e. I will not curse you (since you let me die nobly).
176 fatal doom sentence of death.
178–9 your…distance i.e. you will be safer the further you go from Venice.
180 Here…gold Cornari may hand the money to Florelli or throw it down.
181 furnished provided for.
182 bills…exchange written orders directing that a person named should be paid a sum of money (*OED*, Bill *n.* 9a), the forerunners of cheques.
183 defray pay, meet.
183 present immediate, urgent.
183 charge expense.
185 will…this a reminder that Florelli does not know Cornari's identity.
187 So Thus, In this manner.
188 as i.e. by means of which.

---

175 SD] *Gifford subst. (To the Bravos.); not in* Q/O
180 SD] *this edn; Gives him money. Gifford (after 'it.' l. 184); not in* Q/O
190 SD1] *Gifford subst.; not in* Q/O   **190 SD3** *Bravos with Florelli] this edn; not in* Q/O

379

5.2   THE COMPLETE WORKS OF JAMES SHIRLEY, VOLUME 7

CORNARI Resume thy place within my soul, Claudiana.
When I have done my sorrow for what's past
We'll smile and kiss forever.

Enter a SERVANT.

SERVANT A letter, sir.
CORNARI   From whence?
SERVANT   Your nephew, now
A prisoner.
CORNARI   Let him rot, and give 'em back   195
The paper kite.
SERVANT   The messenger is gone.
CORNARI Then he expects no answer.
CLAUDIANA   You may read it.
CORNARI [*Reads.*] 'Sir, I send not to you for relief, nor to mediate my pardon.
I have not lived after the rate to deserve your bread to feed me, nor your breath
to save me. I only beg that you would put me into your prayers and forgiveness,   200
and believe I do not wish life but to redeem myself from past impieties and
satisfy by a repentance the dishonours have been done to you by the worst of men.
Malipiero.'
This is not his usual style.
CLAUDIANA This miracle may be.
CORNARI   I do want faith.   205
CLAUDIANA And sent a blessing to reward our penitence.
Heaven has a spacious charity.
CORNARI   Thou art all goodness.   *Exeunt.*

195 **'em** i.e. those who delivered the letter.
196 **paper kite** i.e. the letter.
205 **This...be** i.e. This miraculous thing may actually be true.
206 **sent** i.e. sent as.
207 **spacious** great, far-reaching (*OED, adj.* 3a).

193] *Exeunt. in margin* Q/O; *not in Gifford*
194–6] *lineation this edn;* A...sir. / From whence? / Your...Prisoner. / Let...paperkite. / The...gone. Q/O
197] *Cor. ready* Q/O *(after 'answer.'); not in Gifford*   198 SD] *Gifford subst.; not in* Q/O
198–203] *lineation Gifford;* Sir...nor to / Mediate...after / The...me, / Nor...beg / That...prayers, /
And...life, / But...impieties, / And...dishonors / Have...men. / *Malipiero.* Q/O
207 SD] Q/O *subst. (Ex.)*

380

THE GENTLEMAN OF VENICE

[5.3]

Enter the BRAVOS [*with* FLORELLI].

> *They* [*unbind him,*] *lay him down, and exeunt.*

> *Florelli recovers.* [*He takes the bag off his head and discovers the purse.*]

FLORELLI Sure, this is gold.

> *Enter three* GENTLEMEN.

GENTLEMEN Florelli!

FLORELLI The same.

FIRST GENTLEMAN Thy looks are wild.

SECOND GENTLEMAN Where in the name of wonder hast thou been?

FLORELLI I am dropped from the moon.

THIRD GENTLEMAN The moon?

FLORELLI I was snatched up in a whirlwind, 5
  And dined and supped at Cynthia's own table,
  Where I drank all your healths in nectar, gentlemen.
  Do ye want money? If you have a mind
  To return viceroys, let's take shipping instantly.

FIRST GENTLEMAN And whither then?

FLORELLI For new discoveries. 10
  A cloud will take us up at sea.

SECOND GENTLEMAN 'Tis morning.

FLORELLI To drink, and then aboard, no matter whither.
  I'll keep this for a monument.

THIRD GENTLEMAN That bag?

---

0 The scene is set on a Venetian street.

2 Thy...wild You look distracted. Hoenselaars argues that Florelli undergoes a change of character 'from a serious, brave, and loyal cavalier to [a] comic, mad Englishman' (1992, 234), but it is likely that Florelli feigns distraction to avoid explaining what has happened to him and account for his abrupt departure from Venice.

6 Cynthia A name for the classical goddess Artemis/Diana. Like many writers, Shirley conflates Cynthia with the moon goddess Selene: Florelli imagines that he has been taken up by Cynthia, like Selene's mortal lover Endymion (named at l. 14). Cf. *Traitor*, in which the Duke describes Amidea's effect on him: 'methought I could have flowne / And kiss'd the cheeke of *Cynthia*' (4.1).

7 nectar The drink of the gods in classical mythology.

9 viceroys Governors of a country or province. Florelli implies that the Gentlemen will gain money and/or status by travelling with him.

10 whither where to.

11 A...sea Florelli probably means that they will be swept up in a cloud to visit Cynthia again, or that they will be taken up by another god.

13 monument token, evidence of events (*OED, n.* 5a).

[5.3]] *Gifford subst.* (SCENE III.); *not in* Q/O
0 SD] *this edn; Enter the Bravos, they lay him down, and Exeunts / Florelli recovers.* Q/O; *Enter Bravos with* FLORELLI; *they lay him down, uncover and unbind him, and exeunt; Florelli rises. Gifford*
2 SH1] *this edn; Omnes.* Q/O **2 SH3**] Q/O *subst. throughout scene* (*1.*)
3 SH] Q/O *subst. throughout scene* (*2.*) **5 SH1**] Q/O *subst. throughout scene* (*3.*)

381

5.3 THE COMPLETE WORKS OF JAMES SHIRLEY, VOLUME 7

FLORELLI Do not profane it, 'twas Endymion's pillow,
 Stuffed with horn-shavings of the moon. It had   15
 The virtue when she clapped it o'er my head
 To bring me thence invisible through the air.
 The moon does mobble up herself sometime in't
 Where she will show a quarter face and was
 The first that wore a black bag.
FIRST GENTLEMAN   But dost hear?   20
FLORELLI No inquisitions. If you will leave Venice
 Let's drink and spoon away with the next vessel
 A hundred leagues hence. I may tell you wonders.
 Here is a chime to make King Oberon,
 Queen Mab and all her fairies turn o'th'toe, boys.   25
SECOND GENTLEMAN He's mad, I think.   *Exeunt.*

---

14 Endymion's pillow Selene asked Zeus, the king of the gods, to give Endymion immortal life; in response, Zeus put him into an eternal sleep.

15 horn-shavings matter shaved off a horn when it was shaped into a drinking vessel, the tip of a staff or another object. Florelli imagines shavings from the 'horns' of the crescent moon being used to stuff Endymion's pillow.

16 she i.e. Cynthia.

18 mobble muffle (*OED*, *n*.).

19 show...face i.e. appear as a crescent moon, with much of her face hidden.

20 black bag A fashionable item of head-gear which could hide the face and function as a veil, like those worn in one of Wenceslas Hollar's engravings in *Ornatus Muliebris Anglicanus* (London, 1640), n.p. *The Resolution of the Women of London to the Parliament* refers to 'the women of London...from the blacke-bagge to the Oyster-wench' (1642, A2r).

22 spoon away move rapidly, scud (see *OED*, Spoon *v*.¹ 1).

23 leagues units of distance equivalent to three nautical miles.

24 chime tune.

24–5 King...Mab King and Queen of the Fairies, who feature in a number of literary and dramatic texts. The earliest surviving allusion to Queen Mab appears to be in Shakespeare's *Romeo and Juliet* (1.4.53–95), but King Oberon appears in earlier texts, such as the thirteenth-century romance *Huon of Bordeaux*. Shirley also refers to them in *Ball*: 'and Sr. *Ambrose* were / Knight of the Sunne, King *Oberon* should not save him, / Nor his Queene *Mab*' (1.1).

25 turn o'th'toe dance.

---

24 King] *Gifford subst.;* Ring Q/O

THE GENTLEMAN OF VENICE   5.4

[5.4]

    Enter URSULA, ROBERTO, [*and*] GIOVANNI.

URSULA I could not sleep all this night for dreaming
  O' my poor suckling.
ROBERTO   Peace, I say, and wait
  In silence, Ursula.
GIOVANNI   You may excuse me yet;
  I would not see His Excellence.
URSULA   'Tis not
  My meaning, boy, thou shouldst appear unless   5
  There be necessity. You may stay i'the next chamber.   [*Exit Giovanni.*]

    Enter a COURTIER.

I beseech you, signor, is His Grace coming forth?
COURTIER Not yet.
URSULA   I have an humble suit; I must
  Deliver a paper to His Grace's own hand,
  I hope His Grace can read.   *Exit* [*Courtier*].   10
ROBERTO Why, how now, bagpiper?
URSULA Nay, there's no harm in't.
ROBERTO What if he can?
URSULA You will be talking.
  Did not I say I would speak all myself?   15
ROBERTO But Urs, what do you think now will become on's
  When you have told your tale? Though I am innocent
  It will be no great credit nor much comfort

  0 The scene is set in an antechamber in the Duke's palace.
  2 suckling i.e. child for whom I was a wet-nurse.
  3 excuse me let me depart.
  10 I...read. 'That' is implied before 'I'. Ursula means she is delivering a paper which she hopes the Duke will make time to read.
  11 bagpiper This may be a misprint for 'bagpipe', an insulting term used for someone who cannot discipline their speech (*OED*, Bagpipe *n*. 4a).
  12–15 Nay...myself O and Q print this as one speech by Ursula, but the exchange makes more sense if she continues to ruminate with 'Nay, there's no harm in't', only to be interrupted by Roberto with 'What if he can?' (responding for a second time to 'I hope his grace can read' and perhaps deliberately misunderstanding it), at which point she turns on him with 'You will be talking'.
  16 Urs A diminutive of 'Ursula', which also fits the metrical line.
  16 on's on us, i.e. of us.
  18–40 It...unity In his fevered speculation about how he and Ursula might be punished for a crime of which he is ignorant, Roberto runs through various punishments for prostitution, theft, sedition, fraud, and treason.
  18 credit source of honour.

  [5.4]] *Gifford subst.* (SCENE IV.*); not in* Q/O   **0 SD** *and*] *Gifford; not in* Q/O
  4–6] *lineation this edn;* excellence. / 'Tis...appear / Unlesse...Chamber. Q/O
  6 i'the] *Gifford subst.;* ith'e Q/O   **6 SD1**] *Gifford subst.; not in* Q/O
  7] *no SH Gifford;* Vrs. Q/O   **7** His] *Gifford subst.;* this Q/O
  8–9] *lineation this edn;* Not yet. / I...deliver / A Q/O   **10 SD**] *Gifford subst.* (Exit Cour.*);* Ex.Cl. Q/O
  13 SH] *this edn; not in* Q/O   **14 SH**] *this edn; not in* Q/O   **14–15**] *lineation Gifford;* You...say / I Q/O

383

5·4   THE COMPLETE WORKS OF JAMES SHIRLEY, VOLUME 7

To see you whipped, my Ursula. I would
Be sorry for my part to peep through a pillory   20
And have an even reckoning with my ears,
Having no more hair to keep warm and hide
The poor concavities.
URSULA   Never fear it, husband.
ROBERTO I will so curse you, Ursula, and once
A day bind your body to a pear tree   25
And thrash your haunches till you stink again.
For aught I know thou hast committed treason.
Look to't, and bring me off with all my quarters;
If I be maimed or cropped, I'll flay thee, Ursula,
And stuff thy skin with straw, and hang thee up   30
To keep the fruit from crows, and after burn it
To kill the caterpillars. Come, be wise in time,
And let Thomazo quietly be hanged
Or headed yet, and talk no more. He is
But one and has a young neck to endure it.   35
We are old and sha'not show with half the grace
Without our heads. 'Twill be a goodly sight

19 **whipped** i.e. publicly whipped, a procedure in which convicts were stripped to the waist, tied behind a cart and whipped as it moved along the street. This was a common punishment for prostitutes or bawds as well as for theft, vagrancy, and begging.

20 **pillory** 'A device for punishment, usually consisting of a wooden framework mounted on a post, with holes or rings for trapping the head and hands' (*OED*, *n*. 1). Punishment at the pillory was often imposed for crimes such as sedition, perjury, fraud, or impersonation of a figure of authority.

21 **have...ears** i.e. have my ears nailed to the pillory and thus torn off.

21 **even reckoning** settling of grievances (see *OED*, Even *adj.* 13b; *OED*, Reckoning *n.* 6).

23 **concavities** cavities, i.e. earholes.

24–32, 69–72 Roberto repeatedly refers in this scene to subjecting Ursula to harsh physical punishment. He is never shown carrying out such actions, and they are treated with comic hyperbole, but the suggestion of domestic violence adds a disquieting edge to the representation of their marriage.

26 **till...again** until you soil yourself, until your offence is made evident.

27–32 **For...caterpillars** Roberto presents a carnivalesque reinterpretation of the punishments for treason: drawing, hanging, and quartering (a process that usually involved emasculation, disembowelling, beheading, and having the body cut into four parts) for men; drawing and burning at the stake for women; and simple beheading for some elite men and women.

27 **aught** anything.

28 **Look to't** Take heed, be careful.

28 **bring...quarters** get me through this with my body intact. The division of the body into four parts ('quartering') was part of the ritual punishment for traitors.

29 **cropped** i.e. have my limbs lopped off (see *OED*, Crop *v.* 4).

29 **flay thee** strip off your skin.

30–1 **hang...crows** i.e. use you as a scarecrow.

34 **headed** beheaded.

35 **But one** Roberto apparently means that there is only one of Thomazo, whereas he and Ursula are two.

36 **sha'not...grace** i.e. won't look half as attractive.

37 **goodly** splendid (said ironically).

384

THE GENTLEMAN OF VENICE   5·4

To see our faces grin upon two poles
To tell the gaping world how we came thither
To perch and stink in unity. Be wise   40
And leave Thomazo to the law.
URSULA Can you be so uncharitable? Oh, tyrant!

     Enter DUKE [*and*] MARINO.

May it please Your Excellence, my husband and
Myself –
ROBERTO [*Aside*] She has put me in already.
URSULA Humbly beseech a pardon for our son.   45
DUKE Your son Giovanni? Where is he?
URSULA   He waits
In the next chamber.
DUKE   Call him in. What is the fact?
It must be an offence next treason if we
Deny him pardon.
ROBERTO [*Aside*] I fear 'tis much about the matter.   50
DUKE What is the fact?

     Enter GIOVANNI.

URSULA We do beseech you grant a pardon first,
And then you shall know all.
DUKE   That were preposterous
Justice. Why dost thou kneel, Giovanni?
GIOVANNI To beg your mercy, sir, to him for whom   55
My mother kneels.
DUKE   She asks thy pardon.
GIOVANNI   Mine?
Let me offend first.
DUKE   He's innocent.
URSULA No matter what he says, my husband knows it –
ROBERTO [*Aside*] She'll make sure of me.

38–40 To...unity Roberto refers to the practice of setting the heads of traitors on poles on London Bridge as an example to others.

39 gaping staring in curiosity or wonder.

40 perch sit precariously.

48 next little short of.

50 I...matter i.e. I am worried that this might be true.

53 preposterous 1) back-to-front (*OED, adj.* 1a); 2) contrary to common sense, perverse (*OED, adj.* 2).

54–6 Giovanni apparently kneels when he enters, but it is not entirely clear when Ursula kneels, whether Roberto kneels too, and when each of them rise to their feet.

---

42 SD *and*] *Gifford; not in* Q/O   **44** Myself –] *Gifford;* My self. Q/O   **44 SD**] *Gifford subst.; not in* Q/O
46–7] *lineation this edn;* he? / He...Chamber. / Call Q/O   **50 SD**] *Gifford subst.; not in* Q/O
53–7] *lineation this edn;* all. / That...justice. / Why...*Giovanni?* / To...sir / To...kneeles / She...pardon. / Mine?...first. / Hee's Q/O
58 it –] *this edn;* it. Q/O   **59 SD**] *Gifford subst.; not in* Q/O

5·4   THE COMPLETE WORKS OF JAMES SHIRLEY, VOLUME 7

URSULA And if your highness will but grant the pardon,   60
    Your Grace shall not repent but thank me for
    The best discovery. I'll not bribe Your Excellence,
    But I will give you for it what you'll hold
    As precious as your dukedom.
DUKE   The old woman
    Raves. You had best send her to the house   65
    Of the *insani*.
ROBERTO [*Aside*] So she's to be whipped already.
DUKE What do you say, Roberto?
ROBERTO   I say nothing
    But that I think my wife will hardly mend upon't.
DUKE Upon what?
ROBERTO   On whipping, if it like your highness.
    She cannot feel those small corrections.   70
    I have tawed hunting-poles and hemp upon her,
    And yet could do no good.
URSULA Let not Your Grace mind him. [*Taking out a paper*] Give me a pardon,
    And if I do not make good all my promise
    You shall hang my husband and flay me alive.   75
DUKE What's that paper?
ROBERTO Gi't him; thou shouldst have done this afore.

               [*Ursula gives the Duke a document.*]

    [*Aside*] I am prepared. More bone and flesh upon me.
    If the business come to hanging were a courtesy.

---

62 **discovery** disclosure, revelation.
63 **for it** i.e. in exchange for the pardon.
63 **what** that which.
65–6 **house…*insani*** lunatic asylum (*insani* is the Italian for 'insane').
67 **What…say** The Duke does not hear what Roberto says, but he is aware that he is muttering to himself.
68 **mend upon't** be improved by it.
71 **tawed** whipped, thrashed (*OED*, *v.*¹ 3b).
71 **hunting-poles** sticks or staves used in hunting.
71 **hemp** rope.
73 **SD** O and Q do not indicate when Ursula rises, but this would be an appropriate moment.
73 **SD *paper*** This document, referred to as a 'paper' by the Duke (l. 76), provides the proof of Giovanni and Thomazo's true parentage. It may be a letter, or a signed affidavit, or another kind of document.
77 **Gi 't** Give it.
78 **More…me** This may mean something like 1) I wish I was more physically robust; or 2) I can see further physical punishment coming my way. The term 'bone and flesh' recalls Adam's words on the creation of Eve, 'This is now bone of my bones, and flesh of my flesh' (Genesis 2.23), which would cast Ursula as Eve and Roberto as Adam, suffering for her sake.
79 **were…courtesy** i.e. it would be a kindness/an act of generosity.

---

66 SD] *Gifford subst.; not in* Q/O   73 SD] *this edn; not in* Q/O
77 Gi't] *Gifford subst. (Give't);* Ge't Q/O   77 SD] *Gifford subst. (She gives a paper to the Duke.); not in*
Q/O   78 SD] *Gifford subst.; not in* Q/O

386

THE GENTLEMAN OF VENICE   5·4

URSULA Nay, 'tis there in black and white. You'll find it: 80
    Giovanni is your son that was the gardener,
    And he that is in prison poor Thomazo,
    My lawfully begotten.
DUKE   Changed in their infancy.
URSULA And since concealed out of ambition
    To see my own a great man.   85
ROBERTO [*Aside*] I feel the knot under my ear.
URSULA I durst not trust my husband.
ROBERTO [*Aside*] That was not much amiss.
URSULA He has not wit enough to keep my secrets.
ROBERTO [*Aside*] Oh, what a blessing has that man whose wife   90
    Knows when to hold her peace!
MARINO Sir, if we may compare their tracts of life,
    I shall believe your nobleness lived there
    In Giovanni, not suppressed in poverty,
    And their rude, coarse condition, notwithstanding   95
    The helps of education, which seldom
    Do correct nature, in Thomazo's low
    And abject spirit.
DUKE   I'm too full! I must
    Disperse my swelling joys or be dissolved.
    Summon our friends; invite Bellaura hither.   [*Exit Marino.*]   100
    Art thou my son?
GIOVANNI   I would I were so blessed.
    I owed you duty, sir, before, and now
    My knees incline with double force to humble
    The doubtful Giovanni.
                  [*He kneels.*]

---

83 **lawfully begotten** i.e. my legitimate child.
83 **Changed** Exchanged.
86 **I...ear** i.e. I feel the noose tightening around my neck.
88 **That...amiss** i.e. That's true enough, that wasn't so bad (i.e. not too incriminating).
92 **their...life** the ways in which they have passed their time (see *OED*, tract *n.*³ 1a–c), the courses of their
lives.
95 **their** i.e. that of Roberto and Ursula.
97 **low** 1) ignoble, base (*OED*, *adj.* 12a); 2) coarse, vulgar (*OED*, *adj.* 12c).
98 **abject** despicable, servile.
98 **too full** filled with emotion to the point of bursting.
99 **be dissolved** melt, dissolve into tears of joy.
104 **doubtful** uncertain, hesitating (*OED*, *adj.* 2).
104 **SD** Giovanni both humbles himself before the Duke and performs the son's act of doing his duty to his
father by kneeling before him to receive his blessing.

---

86 SD] *Gifford subst.; not in* Q/O   88 SD] *Gifford subst.; not in* Q/O   90 SD] *Gifford subst.; not in* Q/O
95 coarse] *Gifford;* course Q/O   100 SD] *Gifford subst.; not in* Q/O   104 SD] *this edn; not in* Q/O

387

5.4   THE COMPLETE WORKS OF JAMES SHIRLEY, VOLUME 7

DUKE   Let that name
  Be lost. Take all my blessings in Thomazo.   105
URSULA What think you of this, Roberto?
ROBERTO   Why, I think
  The duke is mad, and when he finds his wits
  He'll hang us both yet.
DUKE   Now I find the reason
  And secret of my nature. [*To Roberto and Ursula*] But tell me
  What, after so long silence, made you now   110
  Open the cloud that had concealed my son?
ROBERTO I know not, sir. – Now, Ursula.
URSULA The weakness of a woman, and a mother
  That would be loath to see her natural child
  Die like a bird upon a bough for treason.   115
  Nature will work, a mother is a mother,
  And your son, by the opening of this riddle
  Restored, I hope all shall be well again.
ROBERTO Would I were fair washed yet out of my pickle.
URSULA What think you now?
ROBERTO   I wish – I wish I could not think.   120

    Enter SENATORS [*and*] CORNARI.

CORNARI We hear of wonders, sir.
DUKE   This is my son.
CORNARI With our most glad embraces let us hold you.
GIOVANNI Ever a servant to your gravities.
ROBERTO   The sky clears up.

    Enter BELLAURA [*and*] MARINO.

---

  105 blessings A daily ritual in early modern households, a parental blessing involved parents laying their
hands on or just above the child's head and/or making a gesture to the heavens.
  105 in Thomazo i.e. in regaining your rightful name of Thomazo.
  107 finds...wits regains his sanity.
  108–9 Now...nature The Duke refers back to his confusion about his feelings for Giovanni in 4.2.98–104.
  111 cloud 1) state of obscurity; 2) deception.
  112 Now i.e. Now it is your turn
  115 like...bough A quasi-proverbial phrase. Ursula may mean that she does not want to see Thomazo die
helplessly or suddenly, or that he is a wronged innocent.
  116 work strive to achieve its own ends (*OED*, *v.* 11a).
  117–18 your...Restored i.e. now that this revelation has restored your son.
  119 washed...pickle i.e. taken out of my predicament (see *OED*, Wash *v.* 13e(a), *OED*, Pickle, *n.* 4a).
Compare the proverbial phrase 'to be in a sad pickle' (Tilley P276).
  120 SD SENATORS Candiano is not named, but he may appear among the other senators.
  123 gravities A form of address indicating respect.
  123 The...up i.e. Things are looking brighter.

---

  109 SD] *Gifford subst.; not in* Q/O   **120 wish – I wish**] *this edn;* wish, I wish Q/O; wish *Gifford*
  120 SD *and*] *Gifford; not in* Q/O   **123 SD** *and*] *this edn; not in* Q/O

388

THE GENTLEMAN OF VENICE   5.4

DUKE Bellaura, now receive not Giovanni
But Contarini's son, my dear Thomazo.   125
BELLAURA My heart hath wings to meet him.
GIOVANNI Oh, my happiness!
DUKE   Pause a little.
ROBERTO I melt again, Ursula: the duke points at us,
And carries fireworks in his eyes.
DUKE Though we did grant a pardon for your son,   130
You are subject to the censure of our laws
For this imposture.
ROBERTO I knew 'twould come. Now, telltale, will you beg
The favour we may hang till we be dead?
Sweet Giovanni-Thomazo, speak for us!   135
Not guilty, my lord, I am not guilty.
Spare me, and let my wife be burned, or hanged,
Or drowned, or anything you shall think fit.
You shall find me reasonable.
Who shall beg our pardon?
URSULA   Mercy! Oh, mercy!   140
GIOVANNI Let me beseech you for their pardon, sir.
They always used me civilly.
BELLAURA   Let me join.
SENATORS And all of us. This is a day of triumph.
DUKE It shall be so.
ROBERTO   A jubilee, a jubilee!
Here comes Thomazo. I shall speak treason   145
Presently.
URSULA   Now heaven preserve Your Sweet Graces.

    Enter THOMAZO [*and*] MALIPIERO.

---

125 **Contarini** This is the first time that the Duke's name is revealed.

126 **hath wings** is carrying me swiftly (see *OED*, Wing *n*. 2b), is flying out.

127 **SH1** The speech prefixes in O and Q at this point begin to refer to Giovanni as '*Tho.*' for 'Thomazo', and they later do the same in reverse for Thomazo, who is referred to as '*Gio.*' for 'Giovanni'. The characters' original speech prefixes are retained here to avoid confusion.

127 **Pause…little** Roberto's response indicates that the Duke's tone shifts and he appears to be angry.

128 **melt** 1) am overwhelmed with dismay (*OED*, *v.* 3a); 2) sweat excessively (*OED*, Melt *v.* 2e).

131 **censure** condemnatory judgement.

133 **telltale** someone who discloses secrets, often for malicious reasons.

134 **may…dead** i.e. be executed merely by hanging.

143 **a…triumph** i.e. not a day that should be marred by judicial violence.

144 **jubilee** 1) time of remission from the consequences of sin, especially in the Roman Catholic church (*OED*, *n.* 1b, 2); 2) occasion of celebration (*OED*, *n.* 4).

145 **speak treason** i.e. by calling his natural son Thomazo rather than Giovanni (and therefore failing to register his change of status).

---

127 **SH1**] *Gifford subst. and throughout;* Tho. Q/O   143 **SH**] Q/O *(Sen.)*

144–6] *lineation this edn;* so. / A…*Thomazo,* / I…presently. / Now Q/O

146 **SD** *and*] *Gifford; not in* Q/O

389

5.4 THE COMPLETE WORKS OF JAMES SHIRLEY, VOLUME 7

THOMAZO Mercy! Oh mercy, my indulgent father!

URSULA Art thou come, boy?

THOMAZO   Boy? Stand away, good woman.

URSULA I have procured thy pardon, marry have I, child.

THOMAZO I would 'twere true. Thou wert ever a loving crone.   150

ROBERTO You may believe her, son.

THOMAZO Son? The old fellow's mad!

URSULA   I say thou art pardoned.
    You must kneel to me now, and this good
    Old man, and ask us blessing.

MARINO Your name is proved Giovanni now. The duke   155
    Has found another son.

THOMAZO   What shall become of me?

DUKE You shall be only punished to return
    And dig as he hath done, and change your name
    To Giovanni. Nature was not willing
    You should forget your trade. Where's my Thomazo?   160

THOMAZO Are you my father?

ROBERTO   So my wife assures me.

THOMAZO Are you my mother?

URSULA   Aye, my dear child.

THOMAZO And you Signor Thomazo, that was I?

GIOVANNI And you Giovanni, with the inside outward.

THOMAZO And must I be a gardener? I am glad on't.   165
    Pray give me a couple of blessings, and a spade,
    And *fico* for this frippery. I'll thank
    My destiny that has yet kept my thread
    To a better use than hanging.

---

148 boy This would be a disrespectful way to refer to the Duke's son, but it is an appropriate way for a mother to address her son.

149 marry mild oath, derived from the name of the Virgin Mary, used here to give emphasis.

150 crone old woman.

153 kneel i.e. as a mark of filial respect.

164 with...outward i.e. now that your inner nature has been revealed.

167 *fico* a fig: a contemptuous gesture in which the thumb is thrust between two fingers of a closed fist, or inserted into the mouth (*OED*, Fig *n.*²; *fico* is the Italian for 'fig'). Thomazo probably makes this gesture as he speaks, an action that would underline his lack of refinement.

167 frippery fashionable dress.

168 thread life (referring to the representation of life in classical mythology as a thread that is spun out and cut off by the Fates).

---

147 SH] *Gifford subst. and throughout;* Gio. Q/O   **162** Aye] *Gifford subst. (*Ay*);* I Q/O

THE GENTLEMAN OF VENICE 5.4

CORNARI   Let nothing
  Of punishment profane this day. I must   170
  Implore your mercy upon this young man [*Gestures towards Malipiero*]
  Whose future life may recompense his past
  Impieties and make him serviceable
  To honour and good men.
DUKE   You show a charity,
  If I have heard a truth in some sad stories.   175
  He's yours and pardoned.
MALIPIERO [*To Cornari*]   You're a miracle
  Of goodness. 'Tis too much to look upon
  Whom I have with such impudence offended.
  Command me, sir, abroad until by some
  Years well-employed, a penance for my crimes,   180
  I may be thought one worthy to be owned
  Your kinsman.
DUKE   Again welcome, my Thomazo,
  My dearest pledge. Till now I was no father!
  In him the want of hope my thoughts oppressed,
  In thee my fortunes and my name are blessed.   *Exeunt.*   185

THE END

170 **profane** abuse, defile.
173 **serviceable** ready to do service.
174–5 **You…stories** i.e. You are displaying a remarkable degree of Christian love if all the bleak rumours (about Malipiero's behaviour) that I have heard are true.
181 **owned** acknowledged as.
183 **pledge** 1) hostage, especially a child-hostage; 2) child (*OED*, *n.* 4b). Children are sometimes described in early modern texts as 'a pledge of Gods goodnesse' (Boys 1610, R2v).
184 **him** i.e. the former Thomazo, now renamed Giovanni.
184 **want…hope** 1) lack of promise for the future (*OED*, Hope *n.*[1] 4b); 2) lack of confidence (*OED*, Hope *n.*[1] 2).

171 SD] *this edn; Pointing to Malipiero. Gifford; not in* Q/O
176 SD] *this edn; not in* Q/O   185 THE END] Q/O *subst. (*Finis.*)*

The Politician

EDITED BY

Duncan Fraser and Andrew Hadfield

THE
POLITITIAN,
A
TRAGEDY,

Prefented at *Salisbury* Court
BY HER
MAJESTIES SERVANTS;

WRITTEN
By JAMES SHIRLEY.

LONDON,
Printed for *H umphrey Moſeley* and are to be
ſold at his Shop at the *Princes Armes* in St.
Pauls Church-yard. 1655.

4. *The Politician*, quarto title-page (1655), Library of St Catharine's College, Cambridge, Z.49.

General Introduction

The Politician is an unusual play, hard to fit into perceived generic categories of drama. The play tells the story of Gotharus, a sly and ambitious Norwegian politician married to the virtuous Albina. He attempts to manipulate the weak (unnamed) king into making Haraldus, the son of his mistress, the formidable Marpisa, heir to the throne, by marrying her to the gullible ruler (Gotharus mistakenly believes that Haraldus is his son). Accordingly he persuades the king to send his only son, the popular prince Turgesius, and his disaffected, honest old uncle, Olaus, a man who cannot help speaking truth to power even when it is not called for, on a dangerous military expedition from which they are not expected to return. Like all of Gotharus's plans in this tragicomedy, Shirley's characteristic dramatic mode, it fails miserably.[1] Turgesius wins a notable victory and returns to Norway more popular than ever, so Gotharus tries to set father against son by forging letters that suggest the prince is plotting a palace coup to overthrow his father; he also arranges to have the prince assassinated. Haraldus proves too good-natured and lacking in ambition to be an adept conspirator, so Gotharus decides to get him drunk to make him easier to manipulate. Again, all these plans go badly awry. Poor Haraldus becomes seriously ill, partly a reaction to being plied with excessive drink, but also because he is convinced that Gotharus is his father. Marpisa persuades him that he is not, but nonetheless she has to admit that she is still Gotharus's mistress, at which point the distraught boy sadly expires. Gotharus's plan to assassinate Turgesius subsequently leaks out, and the people are furious to learn that their champion is under threat from within the court. Marpisa, blaming Gotharus for her son's death, turns against him and, with the furious army and the people at the gates, Gotharus decides that discretion is the better part of valour, and desperately hides in a coffin that has been prepared for Turgesius. The people carry it off for burial, believing it to contain the body of the prince, and immediately encounter the still living Turgesius along with Olaus. Breaking the coffin open, they discover the dead Gotharus. Marpisa reveals that she poisoned her former lover with a cordial, which she then takes herself. The king, realizing how wrong he has been about everything, offers to abdicate and let Turgesius rule, but he is persuaded not to by his son, who explains the need for an ordered monarchy and succession. Turgesius reveals that he is planning to marry Albina, the virtuous widow of Gotharus, demonstrating that, at last, order has returned to Norway.

---

[1] On Shirley and tragicomedy, see Clark 1992, ch. 4.

THE COMPLETE WORKS OF JAMES SHIRLEY, VOLUME 7

DATE AND PERFORMANCES

The Politician is probably the fifth of the six plays Shirley staged during his time as resident dramatist for the Werburgh Street Theatre in Dublin from 1636 to 1640. The first two to be performed are believed to have been *The Royal Master* and *The Constant Maid*, both most likely written in London before Shirley took up his post in Dublin, or immediately afterwards.[2] These were followed by four plays almost certainly all written in Ireland. Two were principally comic in nature, *The Doubtful Heir* (also known as *Rosania, or Love's Victory*, probably written in 1638 and published 1652) and *The Gentleman of Venice* (written 1639, published 1655). Then came the darker, more tragicomic, *The Politician* (also published in 1655), and finally Shirley's last Irish play, the notorious *St. Patrick for Ireland*, staged in Ireland and published in London in 1640, the year he returned to England.

There is no documentary evidence for *The Politician*'s date of composition or first performance, but Robert Fehrenbach argues convincingly that since Henry Burnell's play *Landgartha* (known to have been performed at Werburgh Street in March 1640) was clearly influenced by *The Politician* (notably with the inclusion of the character Marfisa, a response to Shirley's Marpisa), Shirley's play probably just pre-dated Burnell's (Fehrenbach 1980, liii–viii).[3] That would place its composition sometime early in 1638 or 1639 and its performance in late 1639 or possibly very early 1640.

The title page of the first edition tells us that it was also performed at the Salisbury Court theatre in London; if this is correct (the evidence of title pages cannot always be taken for granted), the performance would presumably have been between 1640 (when Shirley returned to England) and 1642 when the theatres were closed for the interregnum.[4] Since then there has been no known full performance of the play until the end of the twentieth century, though it is listed in most catalogues of plays published between Edward Archer's addendum to *The Old Law* (1656) and Halliwell's *Dictionary of Old English Plays* (1860) (Fehrenbach 1980, lviii–ix).[5]

The four public performances of *The Politician* since the 1640s that we are aware of have all been staged readings. The earliest of these was at the Globe Education Centre on 7 November 1999, and a recording of it is preserved in the Globe Theatre Archives. It was co-ordinated by James Wallace with programme notes by Maggy Williams, and the cast included Frances Barber (Marpisa), Terry McGinty (Gotharus),

---

[2] On the first performance of *The Royal Master* see Fehrenbach 1980, vii. Justine Williams wonders whether the play was specially written for the opening of the Werburgh Street Theatre (Williams 2010, 89–90). *The Constant Maid* was published in 1640 alongside *St. Patrick for Ireland*, but the original version may have an earlier date (Riemer 1966).

[3] Fehrenbach's *A Critical Edition of The Politician by James Shirley* (1980) is the most recent edition of the play, and the only one since William Gifford's, which appeared in volume 5 of his *The Dramatic Works and Poems of James Shirley*, 6 volumes (1833), and which in turn was the first edition since the original publication in 1655. The annotated text included in Edward Huberman's unpublished PhD thesis 'James Shirley's *The Politician*' (1934) is simply a photostat of the Wrenn copy in the University of Texas library (understood by Huberman, following the library's listing, to be an octavo but now correctly recognized to be a quarto); Huberman's notes record only emendations made by Gifford.

[4] As argued by Fehrenbach (1980, lviii–ix), the title page cannot be taken as definite evidence since seventeenth-century printers were casual about the accuracy of performance claims, and often used title pages as advertisements. But the associations between Shirley and the Queen's players who performed at Salisbury Court make it probable that *The Politician* was performed there.

[5] For further details of catalogue listings, see Fehrenbach 1980, ix–xiv.

398

THE POLITICIAN: GENERAL INTRODUCTION

Katy Odey (Albina), Colin Haigh (King of Norway), and Alec Linstead (Olaus). The reading was lively and theatrical, often inspiring the audience to laugh, especially when Sueno (Alan Cox) and Helga (Patrick Baladi) were on stage, their camp style of delivery striking a chord. Terry McGinty played Gotharus as a melodramatic villain to great effect, delivering his lines slowly and with great relish, and Alec Linstead was a suitably blunt and irritable Olaus. Frances Barber was also impressive as a manic Marpisa, much given to outbursts of evil laughter and able to spar with Gotharus once she became convinced of his responsibility for her son's death, a contrast to Katy Odey's measured and serene Albina. Tom Espiner was sympathetic as Haraldus, lost and out of his depth among scheming courtiers, and the banquet scene (3.2) was played as a contrast between the camp frolics of Helga and Sueno and the sad mixture of exhilaration and despair of Haraldus. Other scenes were also performed effectively, the rebels in Act 5 combining menace and pantomime humour, and the reading helped demonstrate how well-crafted and intelligently scripted Shirley's work invariably is.

The second performance took place at the Shakespeare Institute, Stratford-upon-Avon, on 27 June 2015, but unfortunately the recording, part of a marathon of Heywood and Shirley readings, has been lost.[6]

As part of the preparation for this edition there were two staged readings: one at the Attenborough Centre for the Creative Arts, University of Sussex, 13 March 2019, and the second at the Smock Alley Theatre, Dublin, 4 April 2019.[7] The Sussex performance was directed by Alex Brown with actors from the Department of Drama, University of Sussex, and the Dublin performance by Kellie Hughes, with actors from the Department of Drama, University College Dublin. Both performances successfully realized the tragicomic potential of the play, with Gotharus's plots becoming ever more exaggerated, absurd, and ineffective; Haraldus's death provoked a mixture of audience sympathy and laughter; and Helga and Sueno acted as a gossipy chorus for the first half of the play. The contrast between the malicious Marpisa and the virtuous Albina worked well on both occasions, and there were vigorously enjoyable rebels providing energy on stage in the second half. Both performances featured a strong lead from Gotharus.

SOURCES AND INFLUENCE

Norway, like other Scandinavian countries, was known to English readers and play-goers as a land of fierce, battle-hardened soldiers, with rough manners and heavy-drinking habits, lacking refined culture and religion. Olaus Magnus's definitive history, *Historia de Gentibus Septentrionalibus* was published in Latin in 1555, and a further edition of 1558 followed in Antwerp, which was widely disseminated throughout Europe. Although an English translation, *A Compendious History of the Goths, Swedes, & Vandals and Other Northern Nations*, did not appear until 1658, there were many accounts of the Norwegians that owed much to Olaus Magnus and it is possible that

---

[6] The editors are grateful to Martin Wiggins for this information.
[7] The performances were supported by the Sussex University Research Development Fund; the second in collaboration with the Department of English, Film and Drama at University College Dublin. The recording of the latter was funded by the Society for Renaissance Studies. For some details of the second performance see the *Irish Times* (Hadfield 2019).

Shirley's naming the blunt loyal general Olaus is an act of homage to the scholarly bishop of Uppsala. Descriptions of Norway and the Norwegians were easy to find and Shirley perhaps consulted Richard Hakluyt's *Principal Navigations, Voyages, Traffiques and Discoveries of the English Nation* (1599–1600), or the even more compendious *Hakluytus Posthumus, or Purchas his Pilgrimes* (1625), both of which contain detailed accounts of the Norwegians as a 'wild and savage' people (Hakluyt 1965, 1.245). *The Politician* does not contain definite allusions to Norwegian history, as Edward Huberman has noted, but the Norwegian setting is both informed and important (Huberman 1934, 23). Moreover, Shirley was an author who knew his dramatic tradition well and was drawing on the representation of the Norwegians as hardy warriors in *Hamlet*. His use of the Norwegian setting was noted by other dramatists and surely helps explain why Henry Burnell wrote *Landgartha*, another Norwegian play for the Irish stage (see 406–7).

The Politician is best read as an original play which makes knowledgeable use of earlier dramatic traditions, borrowing motifs from a large number of dramatists—Shakespeare, Jonson, Kyd, in particular. The play does have two obvious literary sources which are used to establish its plots, Sir Philip Sidney's *The Countess of Pembroke's Arcadia* (1590) and Lady Mary Wroth's *The Countess of Montgomery's Urania* (1621).[8] The similarities were first identified by Gerard Langbaine in his *An Account of the English Dramatick Poets* (1691), who noted, 'A Story resembling this, I have read in the first Book of the Countess of *Montgomery*'s *Urania*, concerning the King of *Romania*, the Prince *Antissius*, and his Mother-in-Law' (Langbaine 1691, 481).

The parallel is evident but not exact, because *Urania* is a complex web of different romance plots woven together in a polyphonic narrative, told by various characters over a lengthy period. In one of these the widowed king of Romania marries a 'young, politic and wicked' widow, who proceeds to wreck his happiness and government. Her 'damnable counsel' persuades him to banish his son, Antissius, because he is plotting against him, and the king is now isolated and surrounded by her favourites at court (Wroth 1621, 1.41). Banished to his uncle Seleucius's castle, Antissius becomes the focus for opposition to the regime now run by the queen. Like Olaus, Seleucius has no time for the scheming queen and frequently outlines her crimes.

The king calls Antissius back to court, a message he receives when Seleucius is absent, and he accepts the invitation, only to be ambushed while under escort and killed. His body is returned to Seleucius, Antissius's widow committing suicide and the rest of Seleucius's household determined to be revenged. Meanwhile the queen has grown tired of the weak king, and made her son heir to the throne. She eventually has a favourite murder the king so that she can act as her son's regent. She has all the courtiers who suspect her poisoned at a banquet, and, although she promises to marry the murderer, he discovers her attempting to seduce a foreign ambassador and reveals their crime. The queen and favourite are duly executed, but the revelations of court corruption trigger a popular revolt, the rebels calling for young Antissius, the son of the murdered prince, to replace the queen's son as ruler. Antissius arrives at court, defeats the son in single combat, and is proclaimed king to much celebrating.

---

[8] The most readily available analysis is Fehrenbach 1980, xxx–li. See also Huberman 1934, 2–15.

THE POLITICIAN: GENERAL INTRODUCTION

The similarities between this plot in *Urania* and Shirley's play suggest that he recalled Wroth's romance when planning *The Politician*. The feeble king of Norway resembles his counterpart in *Urania*, easily led astray by a determined amoral seductress, but Shirley has emphasized the monarch's inability to resist the sins of the flesh. Although Marpisa is also more licentious than her counterpart in the source, she is equally cunning and scheming, eager to advance her son for her own gain. Seleucius is a very similar character to Olaus: both are blunt, worldly, intemperate, and, in essence, loyal and good-hearted. Antissius and Antissius the younger bear a close resemblance to Turgesius. All three are virtuous and popular, standing outside the problematic values of the court, which are similar in both works, as are the rebels who are rough, easily swayed, loyal, and treacherous at the same time. Of course, Shirley extended the plot of *Urania* considerably, as Wroth's text contains no equivalent to the compelling character of Gotharus (developed from that of the queen's favourite, who serves as her minion), the drink–induced death of Haraldus, or Marpisa's suicide in the final act, to name only a few differences.

Shirley also appears to have consulted one of Wroth's principal sources, Sir Philip Sidney's *The Countess of Pembroke's Arcadia*, widely available after it was first published in 1590, especially as that romance contains a character named Marpesia.[9] A plot motif derived from *Arcadia* appears in *The Politician*. The King of Iberia's son, Plangus, falls in love with the wife of an ordinary citizen. Plangus, attempting to placate his father, carefully explains the lady's manifold qualities, which unfortunately inflames the king's desire and he sends his son off to battle. The lady refuses to become the king's mistress and demands that they marry and she become queen now that her citizen husband has died. When Plangus returns from the wars he finds his father, whose first wife had died soon after giving birth to Plangus, married with a son and a daughter. The queen, still desiring the son, makes advances to him and, when she is turned down, her lust turns to hate and she plots the downfall of both father and son. She convinces the king that the popular Plangus is planning to seize the throne, then lures Plangus to her chambers with the story that the king and his advisers are plotting to murder him. When Plangus appears brandishing his sword the king is waiting for him, having been told that he plans to assassinate his father and claim the throne. Plangus is exiled and stays with his cousin, Tiridates. Tiridates captures the treacherous servant who had been helping the queen hatch her plots and he tries to reveal her plans, but Tiridates's report is intercepted by the queen before it reaches the king. The king names the queen's son, Palladius, as heir and Plangus remains with Tiridates. The plot, like many in the *Arcadia*, remained unfinished at Sidney's death. Shirley undoubtedly knew both works, which were frequently used by dramatists as sources for plots: as is well known, *Arcadia* supplied the Gloucester sub-plot in *King Lear*, and the Plangus story was recycled in Beaumont and Fletcher's *Cupid's Revenge* (1615) (Huberman 1934, 19–20).

The Politician was also a source for other plays, such as Burnell's *Landgartha* (see 406–7), and Thomas Killigrew's tragedy *The Pilgrim* (1663), although that work may never have been performed in public.[10] Philip Major has recently commented that

---

[9] See Huberman 1934, 16–19. Huberman argues that *Urania* was a more important work for Shirley than *Arcadia* (16).

[10] On Shirley's influence on Killigrew see Fehrenbach 1980, lxiv–vii.

'there are sufficient parallels in structure, characterization and plot between the two plays for Shirley's to be considered Killigrew's prime source' (Major 2013, 189). The parallels are similar to those noted between *The Politician* and its sources. In *The Pilgrim* there is a weak ruler, Alphonso, Duke of Milan, who is deluded and manipulated by an ambitious woman, Julia, along with her lover, Martino. They have a son, Cosmo, who is virtuous and innocent, and whom they want to succeed as ruler, so they plan to murder the legitimate heir, Sforza. When he learns of their plans Cosmo disguises himself as a pilgrim in order to uncover the plot and bring the criminals to justice. In a bloody final act Cosmo kills his father, Martino, in a duel, and Julia stabs her son, thinking he is Sforza, before killing herself.

JAMES SHIRLEY IN IRELAND

Even though so much of Shirley's life is hidden from view, confusing, and invariably mysterious, his years in Ireland are often written about with a definitive confidence. Shirley went to Ireland in 1636, persuaded by his friend and collaborator, John Ogilby (1600–76), the Scots writer, theatre impresario, and dancing master (*ODNB* 2015). Ogilby was made the Irish Master of the Revels in 1633 by the autocratic Lord Deputy, Sir Thomas Wentworth (1593–1641, created earl of Strafford in 1640), who seems to have thought that a serious theatrical culture would help him establish rule in Ireland and would cement the often uneasy alliance of New English officials and Old English Dubliners.[11] Strafford was very keen on drama, planning numerous private performances in great houses.[12] Tasked with establishing a theatre in Werburgh Street in 1635, Ogilby chose James Shirley as the chief playwright. Shirley arrived in Dublin in November 1636, the actors following (probably later that month) in order to perform *The Royal Master* on 1 January 1637 (Williams 2010, 45, 332). Shirley was a good choice as by 1636, at the age of forty, he was the coming man of the Caroline stage; his rivals, John Ford, Philip Massinger, and Richard Brome, were all somewhat older.[13] The theatres in England were closed because of another bout of the plague, so a chance to find gainful employment for the next few years would surely have appealed to Shirley.

Shirley appears to have been a protégé of Strafford, who was executed on 12 May 1641. Shirley's first play performed in Ireland, *The Royal Master*, contained an epilogue addressed to the Lord Deputy, as well as to the earl of Kildare and to other major figures in Irish society.[14] The Werburgh Street Theatre was right in the heart of seventeenth-century Dublin, next to the castle and Christ Church Cathedral, a pointed contrast to the London theatres which had grown up a generation or so earlier in areas at the margins of the city jurisdiction.[15] Shirley was writing work to be produced next to the centres of power in English Ireland. Even so, as much criticism of the masque has pointed out in the last three decades or so, it does not automatically

---

[11] On Ogilby see also Fletcher 2000, 261–71. On Strafford see his *ODNB* entry; on his tenure as Lord Deputy see Kearney 1959.

[12] See Fletcher 2000, 201–4, 242–6, and *passim*.   [13] See Hadfield 2018.

[14] See Williams 2010, 94–132. For Strafford's political views see Kearney 1959.

[15] See Morash 2002, 6–10.

THE POLITICIAN: GENERAL INTRODUCTION

follow that courtly entertainments or plays staged for the authorities simply cele-brated the status quo and exalted the power of the monarch uncritically.[16] Intelligent writers who represent kingly or courtly power rarely do so in an unreflective manner and are invariably more subversive than many moderns imagine, even if they do support the regime.[17]

We should also acknowledge that, just as we are uncertain of the dates of compos-ition and revision of the plays, neither is it easy to pinpoint how the plays may be related to Irish issues. Shirley openly expressed his irritation with the Irish audience, who appear not to have been overly receptive to his brand of drama, as he famously pointed out in the prologue to *St. Patrick for Ireland*: 'We know not what will take; your pallets are / Various, and many of them sick I feare' (1640, A2r). Shirley is asserting, ostensibly at least, that his drama has been slighted, so he will give the audience what they want: a familiar tale of their patron saint, which will satisfy them.

The quotation seems straightforward enough and has usually been read as Shirley's irascible farewell to the Irish stage, taking his leave of an unappreciative audience.[18] However, things may not be quite what they seem. Throughout his time in Ireland Shirley had every reason to be a disappointed man. When Ben Jonson died in 1637 it looks as if Shirley—or his supporters—thought he would succeed the great man of English letters as poet laureate. In 'Upon Mr. James Shirley his Comedy, cal'd *The Royall Master*', one of its many prefatory verses, 'Dru. Cooper' assumes Shirley will be given the honour, making much of the fact that the play is called *The Royal Master*, whom he will now serve: 'Shirley stand forth, and put thy Lawrell on, / Phoebus next heire, now Ben is dead and gone' (1638, A3v).[19] Unfortunately for Shirley the post went to Sir William Davenant, and Shirley's failure was recorded for all to see in one of his own publications, which cannot but have been humiliating.

Shirley was a careful student of Jonson as well as a member of the self-styled 'Tribe of Ben', and his plays are littered with Jonsonian references.[20] The grotesque, child-switching Ursula in *The Gentleman of Venice*, for example, pays homage to Ursula the pig-woman in *Bartholomew Fair*, especially when she threatens to take revenge on her husband by letting a 'regiment of swine' in to destroy the garden that their son Giovanni has made (5.1.87). Jonson famously abused his audience in the prologue to *Poetaster* as 'base detractors and illiterate apes, / That fill up rooms in fair and formal shapes' (Jonson, *Poetaster*, Induction, 70–1). Shirley is not simply insulting his Irish audience for his English readers, but showing that he is the real heir of Ben, poet laureate, powerful, brilliant, and independent enough to have the right to shame those who are not worthy of his art. In other words, this insulting pas-sage in *St. Patrick for Ireland* is as much about Shirley's own status as a writer, back in England and looking for patronage and success, as it is simply an irritable, prejudiced complaint. We cannot be sure whether Shirley was venting his spleen or carefully tailoring his comments for English readers, perhaps deliberately misrepresenting his experience in Ireland. After all, the audience for plays at the

---

[16] On the critical and nuanced nature of court masques see Bevington and Holbrook 1998; Butler 2009; Knowles 2015.
[17] See Butler 1984.   [18] For analysis, see Lublin 2017.
[19] See also Williams 2010, 100–1, 131–2, on the laureateship, and Cooper's identity.
[20] See Scodel 1991, 142.

403

Werburgh Street Theatre, consisting of merchants, lawyers, and aristocrats, as well as commoners, was probably at least as sophisticated as those in many London theatres (Fletcher 2000, 272–3).[21] Nevertheless, as Justine Williams points out, the heterogeneous audience at the Werburgh 'more closely resembled that of the public theatres' in London than the exclusive private theatres with which Shirley is more frequently associated (Williams 2010, 190).

It is a fair assumption that Shirley's Irish plays had a distinct relevance to Ireland, but hard to know exactly what it was (especially as sections of the works may well have been altered for later publication). They must surely have been designed to engage an Irish audience; they may have failed if we believe published comments Shirley made for his English readers, but that does not mean that they do not contain themes, issues, and points related to the Irish situation. After all, Shirley's earlier plays had sought to engage his London audience with topical themes—notably, *The Young Admiral*, which explores issues of loyalty and treachery, and *Hyde Park*, which represents complicated love plots in a contemporary setting.[22] Furthermore, critics have found it almost impossible not to read one of his last plays, *The Cardinal* (1652), in terms of the rise of the other great absolutist figure of Charles' reign, William Laud, archbishop of Canterbury from 1633 until he was executed in 1645, who dominated the Church of England as Strafford dominated Anglo-Irish politics.[23] We should surely assume that the Irish plays have some topical relevance, however oblique, disguised, or even misconceived.

As this last example suggests, seeing Shirley as an apologist for aristocratic power, noble bloodlines, and court culture has probably led readers away from the topical significance of his writing, as well as made him seem such a second-rate and uninspiring figure.[24] Shirley wrote masques and poetry, but he also made his bread and butter through the competitive trial-by-audience of the stage, unlike, for example, Davenant, who had the queen's patronage.[25] We do not know how close Shirley was to Strafford: certainly he was far too humble to feature in Strafford's intimate social circle. But he may have played some role there and been on cordial terms with the good and the great in Anglo-Irish society, or been treated as a writer for hire. Certainly he managed to serve both the royalist and parliamentary regimes without any obvious issues. Shirley is often associated with the courtly culture of Henrietta Maria, but he is bold enough to mimic the ladies of the Catholic queen in *The Lady of Pleasure*.[26] Significantly, we do not know where his own religious sympathies lay. Eva Griffith (2010) has made a powerful recent case that Shirley was a practising Catholic. If so, her evidence may shed a new light on *St. Patrick for Ireland*, long read as a play which articulates the views of James Ussher (1581–1656), the Protestant Archbishop of Armagh, and the most powerful ecclesiastical figure in Ireland. Ussher argued that St. Patrick, coming to Ireland from Britain, founded the Church of Ireland to convert the heathen Irish which meant that the Irish Church was always subordinate to the natural descendant of the ancient British Church, the Church of England, but the play can also be read as

---

[21] We are grateful to Prof. Fletcher for illuminating conversations on the audience for Irish plays.
[22] See Bailey 2017, 72–85. On *The Grateful Servant* see Sharpe 1992, 706.
[23] See Yearling (ed.) 1986, 5–6 in Shirley, *Cardinal*. On Laud, see Carlton 1987.
[24] See Clark 1992, 153.   [25] See Edmond 1987, chs 4–5.
[26] See Huebert (ed.) 1986, 11–12 in Shirley, *The Lady of Pleasure*. Bailey argues that Shirley's plays draw 'attention to the shifting intricacy of religious realignment within the established Church', demonstrating the complicated patterns of allegiance that English recusants had to negotiate (2009, 119).

THE POLITICIAN: GENERAL INTRODUCTION

a plea for religious toleration.[27] It is possible that Shirley was at odds with his Irish political masters, his plays more subtle and pragmatic than has been realized.[28]

POLITICAL THEMES

Critics have not known what to do with *The Politician*. Commentators duly note its allusiveness, praise its skilful plotting but often also comment that its cleverness masks its lack of profundity.[29] The problem is that for too long political reading has meant allegorical reading, as though topical significance means a straightforward representation of a story that could be mapped onto reality without too much effort—a bit like the 'Murder of Gonzago' in *Hamlet*. One of the few essays on *The Politician* ingeniously, and sometimes persuasively, maps the plot of the play onto the story of the assassination of the duke of Buckingham (Keller 1997). Buckingham was the arrogant favourite of Charles' father, James I, who met his end on 23 August 1628, stabbed by the protestant John Felton, who was convinced, like many others, that the duke held undue sway over the king and promoted an elitist Catholicism which excluded the true religion of the majority of the population.[30]

There is something in this reading, but it is rather too literal and programmatic. People wrote and read pragmatically and analogically, a practice that should inform our attempts to reconstruct political readings of literary texts. Stories were tailored to the particular problems which an audience/readers might find most useful and relevant: they did not demand that an audience/readers map a play straightforwardly onto a particular series of characters, situations, or events. This more flexible approach to reconstructing the significance of literature will help us understand how Shirley's political plays work and how we might read such an obviously political work as *The Politician*.

It is most likely that *The Politician* is a reflection on the disastrous policies of Archbishop Laud and the Lord Deputy of Ireland, Strafford. Shirley may have been writing out of conviction from the outset, or he may have decided that it was safer to keep his head below the parapet and adapted his published play from the performance text to make this case after the outcome of the civil war became clear. What we witness in the play is a weak king who (until he realizes how wrong he is at the end) imagines that he is in control of his court and that his own plans work things out, but who has really ceded control to his chief politician, Gotharus, who, in turn, is not really the puppet-master he assumes he is.[31] The king has married the virtuous Albina (whom he himself desires) to Gotharus, imagining that he can then maintain her as his mistress, not realizing that his queen, Marpisa, is really united in her plans with Gotharus against him.

---

[27] See Cunningham 2007, 102; also Fletcher 2000, 274–5.

[28] It is also possible that Shirley's play was written to be in line with Strafford's policies, mingling Catholic and Protestant elements to suggest that a reconciliation between religious factions was possible and so undermining the more Calvinist position of the Church of Ireland bishops and bolstering the secular power of the Lord Deputy (see Lotz-Heumann 2005). We are grateful to John McCafferty for advice on Strafford's confessional politics.

[29] See, for example, Fehrenbach's comments in his otherwise excellent edition (1980, cxxiii–iv).

[30] See Treadwell 1998, 294–9.

[31] On weak kings in Caroline drama see Butler 1984, 76–83, and *passim*.

405

THE COMPLETE WORKS OF JAMES SHIRLEY, VOLUME 7

Despite her desire to do the right thing, and possessing the courage to warn the king that he needs to be faithful to his wife, Albina is caught between two awful men: the king, who threatens to tell her husband that she is having sexual relations with him if she refuses his advances, and Gotharus, who pretends to believe her unfaithful so that he can bully her into submission and control her.

This situation bears little obvious resemblance to what happened at the English court in the 1630s or in Ireland under Strafford's government. However, the audience witnesses a court spiralling out of control through cunning machinations and self-serving ambition, which could plausibly be mapped onto events in the British Isles in the late 1630s. Gotharus is in the tradition of stage Machiavels, his character and behaviour a nod to Richard III and Marlowe's Barabas. He boasts that he has no scruples and that destiny is in the hands of those who seize the day:

> Let weak statesmen think of conscience.
> I am armed against a thousand stings and laugh at
> The tales of hell and other worlds. We must
> Possess our joys in this, and know no other
> But what our fancy every minute shall
> Create to please us.

> (1.1.316–21)

Later, he advises the king to act swiftly against Turgesius, whom he is trying to frame, because 'He that aspires hath no religion, / He knows no kindred' (3.1.257–8), lines that purport to describe the prince but which really, as the audience knows, represent his own behaviour. Gotharus advises the king that a mighty oak can be 'cleft asunder' by 'a small wedge cut from the very heart / Of the same tree' (3.1.259–61). The king responds with typical hand-wringing despair: 'It frights me to apply [the analogy]. / Oh my misfortune – this is torment not / A cure' (3.1.261–3), showing that he has not the ability nor the will to deal with the gathering storm, a criticism that was frequently levelled at Charles.[32]

Certainly one reader, Henry Burnell, the first known Irish playwright for the public stage, read *The Politician* as a commentary on contemporary Irish politics. Burnell was inspired by Shirley's play—and probably also by his *St. Patrick for Ireland*—to counter Shirley's tale of perfidious treachery in Norway. Burnell was concerned to show the loyalty and honour of the Old English in Ireland, represented in *Landgartha* by Landgartha, the virtuous and noble doppelgänger of Shirley's Marpisa. Whereas Marpisa is scheming and self-interested, only realizing the errors of her ways when it is far too late, Landgartha is a faithful and honourable Amazonian queen. Landgartha is served by Marfisa, a 'humourous gentlewoman', distantly related to the queen, and whose presence in the play has been used to date *The Politician*, as Burnell, who may have collaborated with Shirley on some lost plays performed at the Werburgh Street Theatre, was surely alluding to his fellow dramatist's work and inviting comparisons between the two female characters by including a character with such an obviously significant name (Burnell, ed. Rankin 2014, 61). Marfisa might well be seen as a counterpart to Olaus in Shirley's play:

---

[32] See Carlton 1995, 108, 33–9, and *passim*.

406

THE POLITICIAN: GENERAL INTRODUCTION

she is witty, loyal, determined to defend her mistress and her cause at all costs, and a dangerous enemy.

Landgartha unites with Reyner, King of Denmark, to defeat the tyrannical Frollo, King of Sweden, but he betrays her. However, she is principled enough to come to his aid when he is threatened by Harald, his rival for the Danish throne, and the play ends with the possibility of reconciliation. It is not easy to map Burnell's play straightforwardly onto the existing political situation as a one-to-one allegory, but it is clear that its themes of treachery, betrayal, and reconciliation were included in a work in times of conflicting alliances and uncertainty, and it is hard not to read the weak and indecisive Reyner as a figure of Charles I, dithering and compromised in his Irish alliances.[33]

The same can be said of *The Politician*, which cannot be decoded simply nor does it provide an obvious political message. If figures like Gotharus are not to be trusted, then neither is a state in better hands when everyone is open and honest. Haraldus, as Gotharus the skilled politician recognizes, is not fit to rule, even if that is a role he may have to assume if he is shoe-horned in as heir apparent. Haraldus cannot either be groomed as the creature of Gotharus or function as a ruler of independent mind. Beginning to doubt at this point that Haraldus is his son, because 'At his years / I was prodigiously in love with greatness' (1.1.281–2), Gotharus complains that 'He is too tame and honest' (1.1.281).[34] This surely recalls the problem outlined in *2 Henry VI*, when the people of England had the uninspiring choice of either the virtuous but weak Henry VI or the arrogant brutal warlord, Richard, duke of York. While Gotharus advises Haraldus simply to bear the bad news he has received that his mother has been having an affair with Gotharus and carry on as normal, Haraldus falls into a debilitating melancholy from which he cannot recover.

The king of Norway feels free to indulge himself, imagining that the ruler is in control and can act without restraint. Doting on his manipulative queen, he passes ludicrous laws on a whim, demanding to the court that they 'Proclaim all pleasures free and while my fair / Queen smiles it shall be death for any man / I'the court to frown' (2.1.175–7). This is not welcome news for Olaus who, as he admits, cannot stand the queen and cannot disguise his feelings under any circumstances. When asked to be diplomatic he answers the king back with contempt:

> KING If Olaus be forgetful of good manners
> I shall forget his years and blood. Be temperate.
> OLAUS There's something in your blood that will undo
> Your state and fame eternally – purge that.
> You know I never flattered you. That woman
> Will prove thy evil genius.
>
> (3.1.3–8)

Shirley is interested in 'blood', as the carrier of genealogy, inheritance, social distinction, passion, weakness, and disease, but not in the uncritical manner that some commentators have argued.[35] We witness the classic dilemma of politics in a time before political institutions: how could a monarch be advised when they made obvious mis-

---

[33] See Gillespie 2006, 122–3.
[34] This turns out to be true as Haraldus's real father is Marpisa's dead husband.
[35] See, e.g., Clark 1992, 121–2, 125, and *passim*.

takes and nothing could bind them to respect sage advice or the will of the people? And when could they be resisted?[36] Shirley articulates the familiar dilemma of the Renaissance political play, an issue that was obviously relevant when the monarch had dismissed all assembled bodies, was thought to listen rather too much to his absolutist queen, and appointed unpopular advisers with similar tendencies who bolstered his position, isolating him from the people. Olaus speaks to the monarch as an equal trying to advise him to see sense: again, it is hard not to read his scornful address as the speech of an exasperated subject who could only take the monarchy seriously by dressing down the king. Olaus is right—the king, like Charles, is in danger of undoing his state and fame forever, and his offer to abdicate at the end acknowledges this, a solution that proved impossible in the real world.

Like Othello, Olaus claims that he has to 'speak truth in [his] unpolished words' (3.1.43) and he does so, refusing to recognize Marpisa as his queen, refusing to kneel to her, and by pledging his loyalty to Turgesius and instructing him never to think of Marpisa as his mother. When the king asks him to leave he tells his monarch how things really are:

> You have lost
> More honour in those minutes you were married
> Than we have gained in months abroad with all
> Our triumph purchased for you with our blood.
> Is this the payment, the reward for all
> Our faith?

> (3.1.51–6)

What the audience witnesses is a crisis in authority represented on stage, the monarch and his chief courtiers at irreconcilable odds. When the king threatens his opponents with execution—'Take heed / You do not talk your head off – we have scaffolds' (3.1.65–6)—Olaus dares him to do his worst:

> Let him take boldness but to move one hair
> That withers on my head out of his posture –
> He shall have more hope to o'ercome the devil
> In single duel than to 'scape my fury.

> (3.1.72–5)

Of course, in the real world it was the king's head which came off, as well as those of Strafford and Laud. If these lines were not revised for publication they were surely among the most prescient predictions of the seventeenth century.

And, hand in hand with the aristocratic opposition comes the mob fury of the soldiers and the people supporting Turgesius. The country does, inevitably, lurch into a bloody civil war. Turgesius, a decent military man, acknowledges the awful difference between military conquest and civil war. In their overseas conquest he recalls:

> We did there fight for honour and might use
> All the most horrid forms of death to fright
> Our enemies and cut our way to victory.

---

[36] See Sommerville 1986; Hadfield 2004.

THE POLITICIAN: GENERAL INTRODUCTION

> But give me leave to tell you, sir, at home
> Our conquest will be loss, and every wound
> We give our country is a crimson tear
> From our own heart. They are a viperous brood
> Gnaw through the bowels of their parent.
>
> (4.2.5–12)

On the battlements Gotharus speaks against the causes of civil war, claiming that the prince has been misled by poor advisers, 'Rash spirits' who have corrupted him 'with thought of hasty empire' (4.2.77–8).[37] The speech is a Machiavellian device which sounds as if it were true, but it is Gotharus himself who has turned king and prince against each other to serve his own ambitions. In doing so he has also let slip the dogs of war—almost literally—as the mob of soldiers and people imitate hunters in pursuit of their prey with the hunting cry of 'Follow, follow, follow' (4.4.96).[38] Their prey is, of course, the arch-traitor Gotharus, and they vow to catch and destroy him, whatever the consequences. His still-loyal wife, Albina, bravely confronts them with the threat of law and order, which they contemptuously dismiss:

> ALBINA How dare you run the hazard of your lives
> And fortunes thus, like outlaws without authority,
> To break into our houses? When you have done
> What fury leads you to't, you will buy too dear
> Repentance at the gallows.
> SECOND REBEL Hang the gallows and give us my lord, your husband!
>
> (4.4.86–91)

Authority has broken down completely and no one is in any position to carry out Albina's threat, as the rebel, imitating Olaus' defiance of the king, clearly realizes. The body politic is restored only with the restoration of the lawful king by the heir who accepts that he will wait his turn to rule.

---

[37] The words express the standard notion of civil war from Lucan onwards: see Armitage 2017.
[38] The cry was also produced on stage in Jonson's *Epicene* (3.7.41), first performed 1609 and a work Shirley would have known.

409

Textual Introduction

The Polititian, a Tragedy was published simultaneously in quarto and octavo in 1655, the two formats being printed from the same type settings. This creates a minor conundrum for bibliographers in that the two versions, though typographically identical, might be considered separate editions. Fehrenbach's solution, following Greg, is adopted here—that they are 'simultaneous issues' of the one edition, and for the purposes of establishing the text of a modern edition of the play can be treated as a single source (Fehrenbach 1980, xv, and Greg 1939–59, 2.861).

The title page reads as follows:

THE / POLITITIAN, / A / TRAGEDY, / Presented at *Salisbury* Court / BY HER / *MAJESTIES SERVANTS*; / [rule] / WRITTEN / By JAMES SHIRLEY. / [rule] / *LONDON*, / Printed for *Humphrey Moseley* and are to be / sold at his Shop at the *Princes Armes* in St. / *Pauls* Church-yard. 1655.

The quarto collates A–K4 L2 (A1 unsigned, A4 signed) and the octavo A–E8 F2 (A1 unsigned); each format has forty-two leaves paged 2–74, the page numeration 39, 40, 41, and 42 being repeated in error on G1r, G1v, G2r and G2v in both formats. A manuscript copy of the play came into the possession of the bookseller Humphrey Moseley, along with *The Gentleman of Venice*, presumably some time in the latter half of 1653 when he entered them both in the Stationers' Register.[1]

Given that the date of composition was the late 1630s, why Shirley delayed publication of this play for so long bears some examination. According to the *ODNB*, he published no fewer than sixteen of his plays during his four years in Dublin (*ODNB* 2005). Allan Stevenson notes that in 1637 the London bookseller Andrew Crooke entered into a partnership with the bookseller William Cooke, and between then and 1640 these two men produced ten Shirley plays, whilst Cooke also published *The Maid's Revenge* (1639) and *The Humorous Courtier* (1640) on his own. In 1638, Andrew Crooke along with his brother John teamed up with another London bookseller, Richard Sergier, and a Dublin bookseller, Thomas Allot, to publish *The Royal Master* simultaneously in London and Dublin, the play having two separate imprints: 'Printed by T. Cotes, and are to be sold by John Crooke, and Richard Serger [sic], at the Grayhound in Pauls Church-yard, 1638'; and, 'Printed by T. Cotes, and are to be sold by Thomas Allot and Edmond Crooke, neare the castle in Dublin, 1638' (Stevenson 1944, 142–3).

---

[1] *The Gentleman of Venice* was entered on 9 July 1653, and *The Politician* two months later on 9 September 1653 (Greg 1939–59, 2.856, 2.861).

THE COMPLETE WORKS OF JAMES SHIRLEY, VOLUME 7

Given this flurry of publishing activity, the number of publishers with whom Shirley was involved at this point in his career and, most intriguingly, the publication of *The Royal Master* in both England and Ireland at the same time, one might have expected him to have released *The Politician* to the press during his time in Dublin. One reason for not doing so could have been the political sensitivity of its content—content that might well have been less controversial when he did publish it, during the interregnum. However, as Moseley acquired seven other hitherto unpublished plays by Shirley in the early 1650s along with *The Politician*, perhaps there is no more to this delay than the simple fact that Shirley had quite enough to keep him occupied in the latter half of the 1630s publishing sixteen plays whilst at the same time writing for the Werburgh Street Theatre.

In the 1650s, however, with theatrical activity in London at an almost total standstill and no apparent end to that state of affairs in sight, his working life must have been very different. The comment in the Epistle Dedicatory to Walter Moyle that 'this is the last which is like to salute the public view in this kind' (Epistle Dedicatory, 14) has a decidedly valedictory tone, and this late flurry of publication may well have been Shirley dealing with such unfinished business as he had on his desk. It seems reasonable to assume, therefore, that *The Politician* was the very last play Shirley passed to Moseley. Though the playwright could not be certain that the publisher would necessarily have these last two plays printed in the order they were submitted, since *The Gentleman of Venice* did (just) precede *The Politician* through the press, Shirley's apparent confidence that this was to be the last play of his that would be published appears to have been justified.

We cannot be sure that Shirley himself passed the copy on to Moseley, but as publication was the only way he could have gained financially from his dramatic writings during this period, it would seem reasonable to assume that he did. Stevenson suggests that Shirley 'appears to have had the right of publication in his own hands, subject perhaps to release by his theatres' (Stevenson 1944, 143) and that last condition would not have applied at this date. The highly personal tone of his defence of the play in the Epistle Dedicatory also implies a close connection between the playwright and publication. Such an assumption is further supported by Moseley's publication in 1653 of Shirley's *Six New Plays*—*The Brothers*, *The Sisters*, *The Doubtful Heir*, *The Imposture*, *The Cardinal*, and *The Court Secret*—the last of which had, in fact, never been performed, so that work could not have provided him with any income other than through publication. Moreover, Paulina Kewes suggests that 'the information of the title-pages, which clearly state whether, when and where a given play was acted' was provided by Shirley, indicating that he 'actively participated in preparing them for the press' (Kewes 1995, 9).[2] We might finally note that the copy of *The Politician* used by the printer seems to have been particularly clear and clean, showing none of the signs of having been a working play-house copy: stage directions are concurrent with or very close to the action described, speech headings are consistently the names of the characters and never the actors, and there are a substantial number of unmarked exits

---

[2] The title page of *Six New Plays* states that 'The Five first were acted at the Private house in Black Fryers [...] The last was never Acted' and the title page of *The Court Secret* itself repeats that it was 'Never Acted, But prepared for the Scene at Black-friers'.

THE POLITICIAN: TEXTUAL INTRODUCTION

throughout the printed text. Moreover, as has been suggested, the play might have been revised between 1640 and 1653, which would also support the assumption that Shirley was the publisher's source for the manuscript.

Having registered them in mid-1653, Moseley published *The Gentleman of Venice* and *The Politician* in 1655, bringing out both in quarto and octavo formats simultaneously, an approach he also took that year with Lodowick Carlell's *The Passionate Lovers*. Kewes argues that a deliberate marketing strategy lay behind this, for its time an unusual procedure, that strategy being to fit the plays with Moseley's already established practice of publishing drama in octavo, a format that cost less to produce and hence could be sold more cheaply, and was therefore attractive to his main customer base, 'former Cavaliers and their families, by now seriously impoverished' (Kewes 1995, 11).

As the *Six New Plays* (1653) had been issued in octavo, making the two new plays available in that format would have enabled customers owning the earlier collection to purchase octavo copies of *The Politician* and *The Gentleman of Venice* to match, or even bind in the new plays with the earlier book, whilst 'owners of the previous quartos might keep their sets in uniform size' (Huberman 1934, 111).[3] Adopting this approach was therefore a neat way to maximize sales of dramatic texts in what would have been, during the interregnum, something of an uncertain market.

The Gentleman of Venice, Fehrenbach argues, went to press first. On the basis of type ornaments that appear in both plays Wilson F. Engel, in his edition of *The Gentleman of Venice*, suggests that Moseley chose William Wilson to print these plays (Engel 1976, vii).

The imprints at the bottom of the title pages, the heading 'The Epistle Dedicatory', and the signature 'James Shirley' at the end of this dedication all use the same setting of type for both plays, suggesting that the preliminaries went through the press one after the other, or at the very least hard upon one another (Fehrenbach 1980, xvii–xviii). In the imprints on the title pages, however, there are two variants: first, there is a gap between the 'H' and the 'u' of the publisher's name 'Humphrey' in the quarto copies of *The Gentleman* and in all copies of both sizes of *The Politician*; second, the 'e' of the word 'be' in 'are to be sold' is correctly placed in all copies of *The Gentleman*, but is significantly raised in all copies of *The Politician*. This leads Fehrenbach to conclude that were *The Politician* printed first 'we would have to believe that the compositor corrected one error in the imprint (in *be*) and ignored another even more obvious mistake (in *Humphrey*)' when he shifted the type from one galley to another (Fehrenbach 1980, xix).

For this edition, ten octavo and fifteen quarto copies of *The Politician* were collated separately. As was noted earlier, for the purpose of establishing the text the two formats can be treated as a single source, but their separate collation is necessary to establish the order in which the sheets for the two formats went through the press.

Fehrenbach argues that an examination of signature misprints in *The Gentleman of Venice* indicates that the octavo sheets for that play 'probably were printed before the

---

[3] The former was done with the British Library copy Cup.404.b.4(2); binding-in appears to have been done in some other cases, though the date of rebinding might have been later than 1655 (Fehrenbach 1980, xvii, n.).

413

THE COMPLETE WORKS OF JAMES SHIRLEY, VOLUME 7

quarto sheets' and that therefore 'there is no reason to believe that the process would have been changed for *The Politician*' (1980, xxiv). However, for *The Politician*, an examination of the press corrections and other textual variants across the two formats indicates that things were not so simple, and that in fact no consistent procedure of giving priority at the press to either the quarto or the octavo formes appears to have been followed.

For this play, the first forme to go to press was octavo A followed by quarto A and B; for octavo B and quarto C and D we have no help from press variants, but for the next two octavo (C and D) and four quarto (E, F, G, and H) formes the original order was clearly reversed, the quarto formes being imposed before the corresponding octavo formes; for the final formes, the earlier order of printing was then returned to, with octavo formes E and F preceding the quarto formes that match them (J and K, and L). An optical examination of the quarto and octavo copies in the British Library suggests that inner formes were imposed before outer formes.

The evidence for this order of imposition is set out in tabular form in the stop-press collation. We need, though, to consider that evidence in greater detail.

Concerning octavo A and quarto A and B, A4 is signed in the quarto sheets which, as Greg observes, 'is normal in octavo but not in quarto' and so 'suggests that when printing began, precedence was given to the octavo imposition' (Greg 1939–59, 2.861). There is also an error in line 4 of A8v in the octavo sheet in C.1 which is correct in all other octavo copies examined and in all the quarto copies, 't'the' being corrected to 'the', and this confirms Greg's conclusion that octavo sheet A preceded quarto sheets A and B through the press.

As has already been noted there are no press variants in octavo B and quarto C and D, so unfortunately we can say nothing about the order in which those sheets were printed.

The evidence for octavo C and quarto E and F is slender but persuasive. In the inner forme of the former quarto sheet, two letters—the 'e' of 'we' in line 35 of $4°E1v/8°C1v$, and the 'D' of 'Duke' in line 31 of $4°E2r/8°C2r$—are both clearly formed in some quarto copies but progressively fade during the printing of the quarto sheets with the degradation continuing through the octavo sheets until, in some octavo copies, they are almost invisible.[4]

There are, however, two other much more definite variants in the outer forme of quarto F. Both involve the insertion of a full stop after a stage direction, and in both cases in all quarto copies examined and in some but not all octavo copies the uncorrected version occurs. The first occurs in line 5 of $4°F1r/8°C5r$ after '*Enter Aquinus*' and the second in line 3 of $4°F4v/8°C8v$ after '*Drinks*'. The use of full stops after stage

---

[4] This variation cannot, strictly, be defined as a press variant as that involves a press stoppage, the removal of some type, and its replacement by one of the compositors; this would appear to be caused either by a slight, continuous displacement of the two pieces of type due to a loosening of the chase, or the progressive degeneration of their faces; it is possible, of course, that these faults were noticed towards the end of printing the octavo sheets and then, though corrected for the quarto, obstinately persisted in their course towards invisibility, but if that were the case one might expect to see at least one example of a reasonably clear formation of the letters in an octavo copy. As it is, the degradation from clarity in some quarto sheets to progressive faintness and finally almost entire absence in the octavo sheets is consistently graduated, suggesting that quarto E was printed before octavo C.

THE POLITICIAN: TEXTUAL INTRODUCTION

directions is remarkably consistent throughout *The Politician*, so it is far more likely that absent ones would have been noted and replaced rather than that existing ones be removed.[5] We can be confident, therefore, that quarto F preceded octavo C through the press, and can be reasonably certain that both the E and F quarto sheets were printed before the pages were re-imposed to make the octavo formes.

As to octavo D, quarto sheet G has two substantive errors which are corrected in some sheets for that format, but are corrected in all the octavo sheets, and another one which is not corrected until midway through the printing of the octavo D sheet. These errors are respectively: (1) 'egendring' in all quarto copies examined which is corrected to 'engendring' in all octavo copies (line 3 of 4°G1r/8°D1r); (2) 'Woh' in one quarto copy (line 36 of 4°G4r in L6.1), corrected to 'Who' in all other quarto and all octavo copies (8°D4r); (3) '*Go*' (the catch-word for 4°G2r/8°D2r, being the speech heading for Gotharus) in all quarto copies and three of the octavo copies (O.3, C.1, and C.2), which is corrected to '*Go.*' in all other octavo copies.

As two of those errors occur in the inner forme of G and the other in the outer forme, the whole of quarto sheet G must have been machined before either of the octavo formes was imposed. Whilst G was going through the press the pages for quarto H would have been set and it would seem logical at this point to have printed quarto sheet H, then reimpose both the G and H pages to make up the formes for octavo D. However, because there are no press corrections to quarto H in any of the copies examined for this edition we cannot be absolutely certain that it, too, was sent to press before being combined with G to make up octavo D, however likely this appears.[6]

Each of the octavo sheets E and F has one press variant that is wrong in octavo and correct in quarto copies, thereby indicating that the octavo formes were imposed first in both these cases. In line 37 of 4°K4r/8°E8r all of the octavo copies examined and most of the quartos have 'Lodie', which is corrected to 'Ladie' in the remaining quarto copies. In line 36 of 4°L1v/8°F1v 'annot' occurs in some octavo copies, this being corrected to 'cannot' in the remaining octavo and all quarto copies.

Why Wilson made these changes to the procedure for the press work we can only guess at. The conventional explanation would perhaps be a temporary shortage of type caused by other work being done alongside *The Politician* in the printing shop while 4°E–H /8°C–D were being set. But printing in octavo in itself, let alone simultaneously in quarto for the same book, would undoubtedly have put pressure on his type stock, and to build a definitive theory to account for the irregular pattern of printing on a type-shortage basis we would need to know, amongst other things, how many compositors were working on the specific days the changes were made, how long a day they worked and how efficiently, what other work was passing through the workshop

---

[5] There is, though, a stage direction without a full stop just two pages earlier, in the inner forme of sheet F: '*Har. drinkes*' (line 6 of 4°F3v/8°C7v).

[6] It is possible that once G inner was printed and H inner composed those eight pages were imposed to make the inner forme for octavo sheet D, then the outer forme of D imposed once G outer was clear of the press, before finally the two formes for quarto H were re-imposed and run off whilst the type used for quarto G was redistributed. Although the outer formes could, in theory, have been machined before the inner, an optical examination of several pages of the British Library copies of both *The Politician* and *The Gentleman of Venice*, as noted above, indicates that the inner formes were printed first.

415

THE COMPLETE WORKS OF JAMES SHIRLEY, VOLUME 7

at the same time as *The Politician*, what sort of size that work was, whether there were interruptions to press-work—the list is almost endless. In fact, to even attempt an explanation is, it has to be admitted, futile: the truth is that we cannot assume that composition on a given book kept pace with press-work in an orderly and regular manner, or that work in the shop was dedicated to only that book, and the work being done on it regular, consistent, and uninterrupted. Whatever the reason for these changes in the format order, though, we can be fairly sure that such decisions were not made on a whim: running a press was an expensive and financially complex business, and failure to maximize the efficient deployment of resources could have resulted in a considerable loss of income.

One final point worth noting about the press work is that though setting was almost certainly by forme rather than seriatim (because the latter would increase enormously the pressure on the type cases) there is no sign of that crowding of the later pages in a sheet which can be a consequence of setting by forme, the number of lines per page only varying between 35 and 37. Though this may simply be indicative of the skill of the workmen in Wilson's workshop, it could also be a consequence of the clarity of the copy they were working with, which would in turn be further reason to believe that the source of that copy was Shirley himself.

The information gained from such a detailed examination of the order of printing of the play has had, it should be acknowledged, no impact on editorial decisions about the text. What makes it worthy of discussion is that it reminds us how responsive to changing circumstances the mid-seventeenth-century printing workshop must have been, and that the successful management of such a complex business required considerable flexibility and a sharp mind.

That said, whilst there is always the possibility that this irregularity in the printing of *The Politician* was the result of mismanagement rather than a skilful response to some external factor, Wilson was also responsible for three of the plays printed in *Six New Plays*: *The Imposture*, *The Brothers*, and *The Court Secret*, so the fact that Moseley went back to him two or three years later to have *The Gentleman of Venice* and *The Politician* printed suggests that he trusted him to do a good job.[7] There is also the evidence of the text itself to suggest that Wilson ran an efficient business: the press-work presents an editor with very few problems, such press variants as there are leaving no room for doubt as to which is the corrected version. Because the predominant order of printing for the separate formats was octavo first, most of the press corrections had been done by the time the pages were re-imposed for the quarto printing, and in sheets E, F, G, and H, the correct state of such variants as there are is indisputable. We might also note here that because Shirley's only way of making money from his dramatic writing in the 1650s was by publication, this increases the likelihood that the copy provided to Wilson was a good, clear manuscript, possibly even in Shirley's own hand.[8] All these factors mean that the overall result of the work done in Wilson's workshop is a very clean quarto copy which has only one major substantive error (the correction for which is obvious), some minor substantive errors, and a few accidentals.

---

[7] See Engel 1978.
[8] *Cupid and Death* (1653) was, according to its title page, 'Printed according to the Authors own Copy'.

416

THE POLITICIAN: TEXTUAL INTRODUCTION

THE POLITICIAN: STOP-PRESS COLLATION OF 1655 OCTAVO AND QUARTO

Copies collated:

Quarto

BRISTOL	Bristol Central Library
C11.1	St Catharine's College Library, Cambridge, Z49
C11.2	St Catharine's College Library, Cambridge, Z59
D	Trinity College Library, Dublin, OLS B-2-990 no.2
E2	Edinburgh University Library, JA 169
HN	Huntington Library, 645647
L.1	British Library, 644.c.65
L.2	British Library, c.12.f.18.(5.)
L6.1	National Art Library (V&A), Dyce 25.C.99
O.1	Bodleian Library, Mal. 202 (3)
O.2	Bodleian Library, 4° S 3 Art.BS.
PARIS	Bibliothèque Nationale de France, YK–397
SHEF	Sheffield University Library, RBR 822.49 (S)
TEX	Harry Ransom Center, University of Texas, PR 3144 P6 1655
Y.1	Beinecke Library, Yale, Ih Sh66 655p

Octavo

C.1	Cambridge University Library, Brett-Smith.876
C.2	Cambridge University Library, Syn.7.63.383
C11.3	St Catharine's College Library, Cambridge, Z51
DUR (Bamb.)	Durham University Library, Bamburgh Q.7.29/2
HD	Harvard University Library, *EC65.Sh662.655gb
L.3	British Library, Cup.404.b.4.(2.)
L6.2	National Art Library (V&A), Dyce 25.E.38
LEEDS	Leeds University Library, Brotherton Collection Lt d SHI
O.3	Bodleian Library, Mal. 256 (8)
Y.2	Beinecke Library, Yale, Eliz21

Variants by forme:	*State 1*	*State 2*	
AB/A(o)			
4° B4v/8° A8v			
4	t'the	the	
	State 1	*State 2*	*State 3*
EF/C(o)			
4° F1r/8° C5r			
5	Aquinus	~	Aquinus.

417

4° F4v/8° C8v

	3	*Drinks*	*Drinks.*	A ~
		State 1	*State 2*	*State 3*

GH/D(i)
4° G2r/8° D2r

	cw	*Go*	~	*Go.*

4° G4r/8° D4r

	36	Woh	Who	~
		State 1	*State 2*	

GH/D(o)
4° G1r/8° D1r

	3	egendring	engendring
		State 1	*State 2*

IK/E(i)
4° K4r/8° E8r

	37	Lodie	Ladie
		State 1	*State 2*

L/F(i)
4° L1v/8° F1v

	36	annot	cannot

Distribution of variants:

AB/A(o)	*State 1*	*State 2*	
4°		BRISTOL, C11.1, C11.2, D, E2, HN, L.1, L.2, L6.1, O.1, O.2, PARIS, SHEF, TEX, Y.1	
8°	C.1	C.2, C11.3, DUR (Bamb.), HD, L.3, L6.2, LEEDS, O.3, Y.2	

EF/C(o)	*State 1*	*State 2*	*State 3*
4°	BRISTOL, C11.1, C11.2, D, E2, HN, L.1, L.2, L6.1, O.1, O.2, PARIS, SHEF, TEX, Y.1		
8°	C.1, C.2, O.3	C11.3, DUR (Bamb.)	HD, L.3, L6.2, Y.2

GH/D(i)	*State 1*	*State 2*	*State 3*
4°	L6.1	BRISTOL, C11.1, C11.2, D, E2, HN, L.1, L.2, L6.1, O.1, O.2, PARIS, SHEF, TEX, Y.1	
8°		C.1, C.2, O.3	C11.3, DUR (Bamb.), HD, L.3, L6.2, LEEDS, Y.2

THE POLITICIAN: TEXTUAL INTRODUCTION

GH/D(o)	*State 1*	*State 2*
	all quarto copies	all octavo copies
IK/E(i)	*State 1*	*State 2*
4°	C11.1, D, HN, L.1, L.2, O.2, PARIS, SHEF, TEX, Y.1	BRISTOL, C11.2, E2, L6.1, O.1
8°	C.1, C.2, C11.3, DUR (Bamb.), HD, L.3, L6.2, LEEDS, O.3, Y.2	
L/F(i)	*State 1*	*State 2*
4°		BRISTOL, C11.1, C11.2, D, E2, HN, L.1, L.2, L6.1, O.1, O.2, PARIS, SHEF, TEX, Y.1
8°	C.1, C.2, L.3, Y.2	C11.3, DUR (Bamb.), HD, L6.2, LEEDS, O.3

Uncorrected errors in both issues:

8° A3r/4° A3r, 12]	souldier [for souldiers]
8° A3r/4° A3r, 19]	aud [upturned 'n']
8° A3r/4° A3r, 22]	Aquinas [for Aquinus]
8° A4v/4° A4v, 19]	scatterrd [for scattered]
8° A7v/4° B3v, 16]	wives [for wife's]
8° B2r/4° C2r, 1]	*Ge.* [for *Go.* (SH Gotharus)]
8° B2v/4° C2v, 16]	and [for am]
8° B5v/4° D1v, 13]	*Go.* [for *Co.* (SH Cortes)]
8° C2v/4° E2v, 10]	To'ther [for T'other]
8° C7v/4° F3v, 23]	out [for on't]
8° C8v/4° F4v, 2]	to'ther [for t'other]
8° C8v/4° F4v, 6]	nos [for not]
8° D1r/4° G1r, 32]	*Entter* [for *Enter*]
8° D2r/4° G2r, 20]	'twell [for 'twill]
8° D5r/4° H1r, 21]	rewa [for reward]
8° D5v/4° H1v, 10]	Consin [upturned 'u']
8° D7r/4° H3r, 22]	thon [for thou]
8° D7r/4° H3r, 35]	Kign [for King]
8° D7v/4° H3v, 3]	you [for your]
8° E1r/4° I1r, 6]	see [for sees]
8° F2r/4° L2r, 35]	eare [for care]

419

The Politician

[THE EPISTLE DEDICATORY]
TO THE VERY MUCH HONOURED
WALTER MOYLE, ESQ.

Sir,

Though the severity of the times took away those dramatic recreations (whose language so much glorified the English scene) and perhaps looking at some abuses of the common theatres which were not so happily purged from scurrility and under-wit (the only entertainment of vulgar capacities), they have outed the more noble and ingenious 5

---

o WALTER MOYLE (1627–1701) Moyle was from a leading Cornish family and sat as Member of Parliament for Cornwall, Lostwithiel, and St. Germans between 1654 and 1660; nothing is known of his activity as a theatrical patron, but his son, Walter Moyle (1672–1721), also an MP, and a writer on politics and the classics, enjoyed the company of theatrical people such as Sheridan and Dryden at Will's coffee house in Covent Garden, a proclivity he may have inherited from his father. Fehrenbach (1980) provides a substantial biography of Moyle in Appendix II of his edition in which he suggests that Moyle and Shirley may have met through the Inns of Court (Moyle was admitted to the Inner Temple in 1653) and that they may have held similar political opinions.

2–6 Though...stages The theatres had long been seen by puritans as a source of moral corruption and they used their considerable influence in the parliamentary party (which then controlled London) to close them at the onset of the civil war (1642). They remained closed throughout the Commonwealth and Protectorate (1649–1660). Shirley appears to acknowledge that some theatrical entertainment was coarse and unedifying, but puts it down to the poor quality of the audiences rather than any innate failure of the dramatic form.

4 under-wit poor or inferior intelligence or understanding (*OED*, *n.* 1; this passage from *The Politician* is the only illustration given).

5 vulgar capacities the intellectual capabilities of ignorant, uneducated people.

5 outed driven out, expelled (*OED*, Out *v.* 1a).

Speech headings and names of characters have been silently regularized in this edition as follows:

In Q/O speech headings are consistently abbreviated but here are given in full throughout.

Prince Turgesius, who appears variously under that name, but also as 'Prince' in stage directions, with speech headings 'P.' or 'Pr.', is here 'PRINCE TURGESIUS' in entrances, but 'PRINCE' in speech headings and '*the prince*' in all other stage directions.

The rebels who appear in 4.4, 4.5, 4.6, and 5.2 are REBELS in stage entrances, and 'FIRST REBEL, SECOND REBEL, ALL REBELS' etc. in speech headings rather than '1, 2, Omnes' etc. as they appear in Q/O.

Soldiers are treated in the same way as rebels.

Variants in character names and speech headings are noted in the collation only where there is a substantive change, an error, or some other noteworthy irregularity.

This edition generally follows Q/O stage directions, with square brackets being used to indicate an editorial addition or change; stage directions are noted in the collation where there is a substantial departure from Q/O or another edition differs significantly from this one and offers a plausible alternative reading.

o THE EPISTLE DEDICATORY] *this edn; on second page only (A2v) in* Q/O

THE COMPLETE WORKS OF JAMES SHIRLEY, VOLUME 7

actions of the eminent stages. The rage yet hath not been epidemical; there are left many lovers of this exiled poesy who are great masters of reason and that dare conscientiously own this musical part of humane learning when it is presented without the stains of impudence and profanation.

Among these persons, sir, you deserve an honourable inscription. For my own part, this is the last which is like to salute the public view in this kind, and I have only to say that I congratulate my own happiness to conclude with so judicious a patron.

To make a doubt of your fair receiving this piece were to dishonour your character and make myself undeserving. Read at your leisure what is humbly presented to your eye and judgement, while I preserve my confidence in your virtue and good thoughts upon,

Sir,

the most humble honourer
of your worth,

JAMES SHIRLEY

---

6 rage mania, a vehement or passionate desire for something (*OED, n.* 4b, 5f).

6 epidemical universal (*OED, adj.* 2a). As 'rage' could have a quasi-medical implication there may be a glance also at the medical sense of 'epidemic'.

8 own acknowledge with approval (*OED, v.* 5, 6).

8 humane designating those texts or branches of study which concern humanity (*OED, adj.* 2).

9 impudence immodesty, indelicacy (*OED, n.* 1).

10 you...inscription Possibly in the sense 'you deserve to be written into this group', but 'inscription' may be used more simply in the sense of 'a dedication of a book to a person' (*OED, n.* 3b).

11 last...kind *The Politician* was the last play Shirley published; see Introduction, Textual History.

---

7 poesy] *Gifford; Posie* Q/O

THE POLITICIAN

THE NAMES AND SMALL
CHARACTERS OF THE PERSONS

KING OF NORWAY, *easy and credulous in his nature, and passionately doting upon*
  Queen Marpisa

GOTHARUS, *the politician, active to serve his pleasures and ambition, a great favourite*
  of the queen

TURGESIUS, *the prince, of a gallant disposition, and honoured by the soldier[s]*   5

DUKE OLAUS, *the king's uncle, old, choleric and distasted with the court*
  proceedings, disaffected to Gotharus and the queen but resolute and faithful to the
  prince

HARALDUS, *son to Marpisa, young, of a sweet and noble disposition, whom*
  Gotharus would form more bold and ambitious for the greatness he had designed   10

REGINALDUS } *captains*
AQUINUS

HORMENUS } *two honest courtiers*
CORTES

SUENO } *a couple of court parasites*   15
HELGA

[PETITIONERS]

[DOCTORS]

0 SMALL Brief (*OED, adj.* 7).

1 *easy* compliant, easily led (*OED, adj.* 12a).

3 GOTHARUS The first syllable (which is possibly the stressed one) could glance at both 'goth'—the type of an ignorant and destructive barbarian (*OED, n.* 2a)—and 'goat' (especially if the 'h' is not sounded or is suppressed)—an animal with a reputation for lechery. Fehrenbach notes Shirley's use of 'goth' in *The Lady of Pleasure*, *The Humorous Courtier*, and *Honoria and Mammon* in the sense of an uneducated, barbaric person, whilst the king refers to Gotharus as Marpisa's 'wanton goat' at 5.1.24.

3 *favourite* either in the specific sense of a person regarded with undue favour by a superior and chosen as an intimate (*OED, n.* 2), or just in the more general sense of someone preferred beyond others (*OED, n.* 1a).

5 *soldiers* Fehrenbach retains the singular of Q, suggesting it is equivalent to 'the military', but *OED* gives no such meaning.

6 *distasted* disgusted or offended (*OED, adj.* 2).

7 *disaffected* hostile (*OED, adj.*[1] 1).

7 *resolute* constant or steadfast; but it could also mean 'determined' or 'decided with regard to matters open to doubt', opinionated (*OED, adj.* 4b, 4a, and 3b).

15 *couple* mainly in the sense of two individuals who share common traits taken as a pair but the word was also strongly associated with pairing through emotional or amorous feelings (*OED, n.* 7a and 5a) and that meaning may be in play given the many suggestions of a homoerotic relationship between these two courtiers.

17 PETITIONERS i.e. People wishing to solicit Gotharus's interest in some personal matter; an unspecified number of them enter to him at 1.1.24 but leave immediately having said nothing.

18 DOCTORS Such characters are required in 4.3.1–23 and 5.2.215–20; they are named 'doctors' in the stage directions and speech prefixes in their earlier appearance but 'physicians' in the dialogue, stage directions, and speech prefixes of the later one.

THE . . . PERSONS] Q/O *subst.;* DRAMATIS PERSONÆ *Gifford*

5 *soldiers*] *this edn;* souldier Q/O

423

THE COMPLETE WORKS OF JAMES SHIRLEY, VOLUME 7

[OFFICERS]

SOLDIERS   20

REBELS

ATTENDANTS

MARPISA, *the queen, a proud, subtle and revengeful lady, from the widow of Count
    Altomarus advanced to royal condition by the practice of her creature and
    confidant, Gotharus*   25

ALBINA, *wife to Gotharus, a virtuous but suffering lady, under the tyranny of an
    imperious and disloyal husband*

[WAITING WOMAN *to Albina*]

---

22 ATTENDANTS i.e. Servants. Only one such character speaks in the play (4.4.63–72 and 92) and he is given
the speech prefix 'servant'; there would be many opportunities, however, for non-speaking extras to appear on
stage in such roles.

23 MARPISA Possibly a combination of 'mar'—to damage or harm (*OED*, *v.*1) and 'pis', French for 'worse',
and hence, 'someone who makes things or matters even worse than they already are'; Justine Williams (2010,
271) notes that according to George Crabb's *Universal Historical Dictionary* of 1825 there was a celebrated queen
of the Amazons named Marpesia, and such a source for the name would be entirely consistent with this character's
behaviour.

24 *advanced* promoted in rank (*OED*, Advance *v.* 2a).

24 *creature* instrument of a powerful patron, a puppet (*OED*, *n.* 4), with a strong suggestion of being a
despicable person (*OED*, *n.* 2c); compare 2.1.92, 100, and 198, and 4.1.37.

26 ALBINA From 'albus', the Latin for 'white' and hence a name indicative of purity, innocence, and virtue.
Justine Williams suggests that the name had a personal relevance for both Shirley and his Dublin audience
as Albanus the martyr gave his name to the English city of St Albans (where Shirley had been a clergyman
and schoolmaster in the 1620s), and Saint Albanus was an Irish bishop consecrated by St Patrick (Williams 2010,
278 n.).

28 WAITING WOMAN Non-speaking character who is on stage for only eight lines at 1.1.46–53.

---

28 WAITING . . . *Albina*] *Gifford subst.; not in* Q/O

424

THE SCENE: NORWAY.

1[.1]

Enter CORTES *and* HORMENUS.

CORTES It was a strange and sudden marriage.

HORMENUS Could he not love her for the game and so forth,
But he must thus exalt her? No less title
Than queen to satisfy her ambition?

CORTES 'Tis a brave rise!

HORMENUS   I did not prophesy   5
When the honest count her husband, Altomarus,
Lived, she would bring us on our knees.

CORTES   I hope
She'll love the king for't.

HORMENUS   And in his absence
Gotharus the king's minion, her old friend,
He has done this royal service beside what   10
Rests on accounts in her old husband's days.
I do suspect her son Haraldus was
Got with more heat and blood than Altomarus's
Age could assure her; but he's dead.

CORTES   ˙   God be with him.
Although I wo'not make oath for her chastity,   15

---

0 NORWAY See Introduction, Sources and Influence, for a discussion of the location.

1 Compare the conversation between Hamlet and Horatio about the proximity of the elder Hamlet's death and Gertrude's remarriage (*Hamlet*, 1.2.168–81).

2 **for…game** i.e. as a mistress.

5 **brave** impressive (sarcastic).

5 **prophesy** probably used loosely as in the sense 'anticipate', but possibly also establishing the antique setting of the play, as prophecy was invariably condemned in the sixteenth century, often as treason or seditious speech, following the 1542 revisions to the treason statutes (Bellany 2007, 45). Religious prophecies caused considerable disquiet.

7 **she…knees** Hormenus did not think that Marpisa would be so exalted that courtiers would have to kneel to her.

9 **minion** male favourite, with the clear implication that the minion is over-favoured, and, usually, rather close to the monarch. See Christopher Marlowe, *Edward II*: 'The king is love-sick for his minion' (1.4.87).

9 **friend** lover.

10 **service** sexual attention.

13 **got…blood** Illegitimate (natural) children were often thought to have been conceived with more lust and passion than legitimate ones: Shirley may have in mind Gloucester's boast about conceiving Edmund (*Lear*, 1.1.18–23). That Gotharus believes Haraldus to be his son is made clear later (see 1.1. 229-30). Haraldus's suspected illegitimacy would rule him out of the succession and further establishes Marpisa as a loose and lascivious fortune-hunter.

14 **but…dead** i.e. we cannot ask Altomarus if he really is Haraldus's father.

14 **God** Omitted from 1655 and replaced with a dash. Swearing in public was restricted by the 1623 Act against prophane Swearing and Cursing (21 Jac.), which led playwrights to remove oaths from their plays.

SCENE: NORWAY] Q/O *subst.*; *SCENE, the Capital of* Norway *Gifford*
1[.1]] *Gifford subst. (*ACT I. SCENE I.*)*; [I.i] *Fehrenbach;* Act. I. Q/O
11 accounts] *Fehrenbach;* accompts Q/O   14 God] *Gifford;* —— Q/O

I.I   THE COMPLETE WORKS OF JAMES SHIRLEY, VOLUME 7

That boy's good nature is an argument
To me Gotharus had no share in him.
He's honest, of a gentle disposition,
And on my conscience does pray sometimes.

> *Enter* GOTHARUS [*apart*] *reading a letter.*

HORMENUS   No more, we have a wolf by th'ear. What news   20
From hell? He cannot want intelligence, he has
So many friends there. [*Pause.*] He's displeased: there is
Some goodness in that letter, I will pawn
My head, that makes him angry.

> *Enter some with petitions*[.] *Gotharus frowns upon 'em*[. T]*hey return hastily.*

How his frown
Hath scattered 'em like leaves. They fly from him   25
As nimbly as their bodies had no more weight
Than their petitions. I would give an eye-tooth
To read but three lines.

GOTHARUS   [*Aside*]   Curse upon his victory!
I meant him not this safety when I wrought
The king to send him forth to war, but hoped   30
His active spirit would have met some engine
To have translated him to another world.
He's now upon return.   *Exit.*

HORMENUS   Would I had but
The harrowing of your skull. My genius gives me
That paper is some good news of the prince.   35
I would I knew it but concerned him.

CORTES   'Twas
My wonder the king would send his son abroad
To wars, the only pledge of his succession.

---

19 **SD** a common plot device in Shakespeare and other plays (see Dessen 1999, 131–2).
20 **we…th'ear** i.e. we are in a dangerous situation (Tilley W603).
21 **intelligence** information.
23–4 **goodness…angry** Hormenus jokes that only news of something evil could please Gotharus.
23–4 **I…head** i.e. I bet my life.
27 **give…eye-tooth** i.e. go to any lengths; *OED* cites this as the first usage of this now familiar phrase (*OED,* Eyetooth *n.* P1).
29 **wrought** manipulated (Fehrenbach).
31 **engine** instrument, especially of war. Again, the link to plot elements in *Hamlet* is clear—here, Claudius's attempted murder of Hamlet.
32 **translated** transported, sent.
33–4 **Would…skull** i.e. I wish I knew what you are thinking.
34 **genius gives me** instinct tells me.
36 **but** only.
38 **pledge** promise, hope.

---

19 **SD**   *apart*] *this edn; not in* Q/O   22 **SD**] *this edn;* —— Q/O   28 **SD**] *Fehrenbach subst.; not in* Q/O

426

THE POLITICIAN

HORMENUS He had a counsellor, this politician,
 That would prefer the prince to heaven, a place   40
 His lordship has no hope to be acquainted with.
 The prince and his great uncle, Duke Olaus,
 Would not allow these pranks of state, nor see
 The king betrayed to a concubine.
 Therefore it was thought fit they should be engaged   45
 To foreign dangers.

Enter ALBINA *and her* WAITING WOMAN.

 'Tis Madam Albina,
 Our great man's wife.
CORTES   The king did seem to affect her
 Before he married her to his favourite.
HORMENUS Dost think she's honest?
CORTES   I'll not stake my soul on't.
 But I believe she is too good for him,   50
 Although the king and she have private conference.
HORMENUS She looks as she were discontent.

Exeunt Albina [and her waiting woman].

CORTES   She has cause
 In being Gotharus's wife. Some say she loved him
 Most passionately.
HORMENUS   'Twas her destiny.
 She has him now and if she love him still   55
 'Tis not impossible she may be a martyr.
 His proud and rugged nature will advance
 Her patience to't.

---

 43 **pranks** a stronger sense than in modern English: evil deeds.
 47 **affect** favour, with a sense of sexual attraction.
 49 **honest** in a sexual and moral sense; compare Hamlet's words to Ophelia, 3.1.105–15.
 51 **private conference** again, implying a sexual liaison.
 53 **Some…him** Cortes and Hormenus are not sure what court gossip is true and whether Albina loves—or loved—the king or Gotharus.
 54 **destiny** meaning that whatever her feelings are, she is stuck with the undesirable Gotharus.
 55 **him…him** i.e. the king…Gotharus.
 56 **'Tis…martyr** Either because she loves Gotharus or because she does not.
 57 **His** i.e. Gotharus's.
 57 **rugged** rough.
 57–8 **advance…to't** i.e. test her patience until she reaches the level of martyrdom. Discussion among Catholics in the seventeenth century often concerned the issue of 'living martyrdom' and whether silent suffering deserved as much praise as bodily martyrdom.

---

 46 SD] Q/O *subst.;* ALBINA *and her Waiting-woman cross the stage. Gifford*
 52 SD] *Fehrenbach subst.; Exit Al.* Q/O

I.I   THE COMPLETE WORKS OF JAMES SHIRLEY, VOLUME 7

Enter HELGA *and* SUENO.

HELGA   Avoid the gallery!
SUENO The king is coming – oh, my lord, your pardon.
HORMENUS Nay, we must all obey.
CORTES [*Aside to Hormenus*]   I ne'er liked   60
    This fellow.
HORMENUS [*Aside to Cortes*] He is one of fortune's minions,
    The love of the choice ladies of the laundry.
    That's one that draws in the same team, but more
    Inclined to the knave. He is a kind of pendant
    To the king's ear, an everlasting parasite.   65
    The king! Albina returned with him.

        Enter KING *and* ALBINA.

KING   Leave us.

                Exeunt [*Hormenus, Cortes, Helga, and Sueno*].

    You're most unkind to yourself in my opinion.
    You know well who I am and what I have
    Advanced you to. Neither in virgin state
    Nor marriage to allow your king a favour?   70
ALBINA Sir, let the humble duty of a subject,
    Who shall with zealous prayers solicit heaven
    For you and your fair queen –
KING   Had you been wise
    That might have been your title, but the god
    Of love had with his arrow so engraven   75
    Gotharus in your heart you had no language
    But what concerned his praise, scarce any thought

---

58 **Avoid** Leave.
58 **gallery** 'covered space for walking in' (*OED, n.* 1).
61 **This fellow** It is not clear whether Cortes is referring to Helga or Sueno.
61 **one...minions** someone whose success depends upon good fortune rather than merit (Tilley F600).
62 **ladies...laundry** i.e. women of easy virtue; Williams (1994) glosses 'laundress' as 'whore'.
63 **one...team** i.e. like a team of horses, suggesting they are inseparable and, ideally, 'matched'—extremely similar.
64 **Inclined...knave** i.e. To act alone for base self-interest.
64–5 **pendant...ear** i.e. an earring. The image suggests that Sueno is a 'mere bauble' and a 'flatterer' (Fehrenbach).
65 **everlasting parasite** i.e. one that cannot be separated from the host.
70 **allow...favour** another sexual reference. It is now clear that the king has pursued Albina who has resisted his advances.

---

60 SD] *this edn; not in* Q/O   60 ne'er] *Fehrenbach;* never *Gifford;* near Q/O
61 SD] *this edn; not in* Q/O
66 SD2] *this edn;* [*Exeunt Cor. and Hor. before Enter* King *and* ALBINA., [*Exeunt Sue. and Hel. after* Leave us.– *Gifford; Exit. before Enter* King *and* Albina. Q/O

428

THE POLITICIAN   I.I

At liberty. I did imagine when
I had compassion of your sufferings
And gave thee a fair bride to my Gotharus   80
You would not lose the memory of my benefit
But, now in state and nature to reward it,
Consented to return my love.
ALBINA   Be pleased
To excuse the boldness of one question.
KING Be free, Albina.
ALBINA   Do not you love my husband?   85
KING There wants no testimony. Beside the rest,
My giving thee to him, dear to my thoughts,
Is argument I love him.
ALBINA   Would you take
Me back again? You but betrayed his faith
And your own gift to tempt me to forsake him.   90
KING You are more apprehensive. If you please
He shall possess you still. I but desire
Sometimes a near and loving conversation.
Though he should know't, considering how much
I may deserve, he would be wise enough   95
To love thee ne'er the worse. He's not the first
Lord that hath purchased offices by the free
Surrender of his wife to the king's use.
'Tis frequent in all commonwealths to lend
Their playfellows to a friend.
ALBINA   Oh, do not think   100
Gotharus can be worth your love, to be
So most degenerate and lost to honour.

78 **liberty** freedom, lack of restraint; the king implies that Albina cannot think of anyone other than Gotharus.
81 **benefit** gift, favour, with the clear meaning that he expects sexual benefits in return.
85 **Be free** Speak your mind, but with a hint of sexual suggestion.
86 **wants** lacks.
88 **argument** proof.
88–9 **Would…again** i.e. Would you take me back from Gotharus as your mistress?
91 **more** too.
92 **possess** with a sexual significance.
93 **near…conversation** i.e. intimacy
97 **free** willing, with sexual significance.
100 **playfellows** 'sharers in sexual pleasures' (Partridge 1955, 210). The king, in using the language of freedom and liberty, is degrading Albina to a sexual toy passed between men.
101–2 **to…honour** i.e. if Gotharus is what the king suggests he is then he cannot be worth taking seriously.

96 ne'er] *Gifford;* near Q/O

429

I.I   THE COMPLETE WORKS OF JAMES SHIRLEY, VOLUME 7

You have a queen to whom your vow is sacred.
Be just to her; the blessing is yet warm
Pronounced by holy priest. Stain not a passion   105
To wander from that beauty, richer far
Than mine. Let your souls meet and kiss each other
That while you live, the examples of chaste love,
Most glorious in a king and queen, we may
Grow up in virtue by the spring of yours   110
Till our top boughs reach heaven.
KING   You are resolvèd then
We must be strangers. Should my life depend
On the possession of your bosom, I
Should languish and expire, I see.
ALBINA   Good heaven
Will not permit the king want so much goodness   115
To think the enjoying of forbidden pleasure
Could benefit his life. Rather let mine
Ebb at some wound and wander with my blood
By your command ta'en from me. On my knee– [*She kneels.*]
KING Rise. [*Albina rises.*] I may kiss Albina –

    Enter GOTHARUS [*unseen by King and Albina*].

GOTHARUS   Ha!
KING   Th'ast shot   120
Another flame into me. Come you must –
ALBINA What?
KING   Be a woman. Do't, or I'll complain.

105 **Stain** Eclipse, obscure. 'Stain' could also be used to mean 'pollute' (especially of blood).

107 **Let...other** A neoplatonic image of the union of souls as more important than the union of bodies, particularly associated with the Carlomaria cult surrounding Charles and Henrietta Maria. Albina is trying to lead the king away from thoughts of sex.

111 **Till...heaven** A common image in the period: the virtue of the king and queen will inspire the rest of society and ensure that appropriate behaviour exists throughout all the social levels.

113 **bosom** seat of thoughts, emotions, and counsels, and hence suggesting the heart and, further, the intimacy between man and wife.

115 **want** lack.

117–19 **Rather...me** Like many virtuous women, such as Lucretia and Saint Ursula, celebrated in Medieval and Renaissance literary and art works, Albina prefers death to dishonour.

120–1 **Th'ast...me** Her virtue has only inflamed his lust for her.

122 **Be...woman** i.e. act sexually as women are supposed to do or, perhaps, show pity.

119 SD] *Gifford subst.; not in* Q/O
120 SD1] *Fehrenbach subst.;* [*Kisses her. after Albina– Gifford; neither in* Q/O
120 SD2] *this edn; Enter* Gotharus [*,unseen*]. *Fehrenbach; Enter behind* GOTHARUS *Gifford; Enter Gotharus. after* Ha! Q/O

430

THE POLITICIAN   I.I

ALBINA To whom?
KING   Thy husband.
GOTHARUS [*Aside*]   Horror!
KING   Think upon't.   *Exit.*
ALBINA What will become of miserable Albina?
    Like a poor deer, pursued to a steep precipice   125
    That overlooks the sea by some fierce hound,
    The lust of a wild king doth threaten here.
    Before me, the neglects of him I love,
    Gotharus my unkind lord, like the waves,
    And full as deaf, affright me.
GOTHARUS   How now madam?   130
    Come, can you kiss?
ALBINA   Kiss, sir?
GOTHARUS [*He kisses her.*]   What difference
    Between his touch and mine now? His perhaps
    Was with more heat but mine was soft enough.
    What has he promised thee? But that's no matter,
    Thou wo't be wise enough to make thy bargain.   135
    I father all, only the king shall give it
    A name: he'll make it master of a province.
ALBINA What means my lord?
GOTHARUS Thou think'st I am jealous now. Not I. I knew
    Before he doted on thee, and it is   140

123 **SH** GOTHARUS Fehrenbach gives 'Horror!' to Albina on the grounds that it expresses a reaction more likely to be hers than Gotharus's; however, the actor playing him could deliver the word in a number of ways that would make dramatic sense.
123 **Think upon't** The King's advances towards Albina now resemble those of Angelo towards Isabella in *Measure for Measure*, 2.4.
125–6 **Like…hound** A dramatic variation on the common poetic image of love being like hunting.
127 **wild** uncontrolled. In early modern political thought tyrants were imagined to be unable to control their desires which distorted their ability to rule themselves and the state they governed with temperance and reason.
130 **deaf** i.e. either the rough waves crashing on the shore seen from the cliff edge are loud enough to be deafening or both waves and Gotharus are deaf to her pleas.
130 **affright me** Albina is hunted by the lustful king so that she risks falling off a cliff into the crashing waves of her husband's anger.
133 **heat** lust, continuing references to heat and blood in the scene.
136–7 **I…name** i.e. I'll acknowledge it as my child but the king will provide for it.
137 **he'll…province** Refers to the practice of the monarch's illegitimate offspring being given land and titles. Gotharus suggests that Albina will allow him to bring up the king's child, who will be rewarded by his real father.
140 **Before** i.e. Before our marriage (with following 'that' implied).

123 **SH** GOTHARUS] Q/O *subst.;* [ALBINA]. *Fehrenbach*   123 **SD**1] *this edn; not in* Q/O
131 **SD**] *this edn;* [*Kisses her. after* can you kiss? *Gifford; not in* Q/O

I.I   THE COMPLETE WORKS OF JAMES SHIRLEY, VOLUME 7

To be presumed, having a veil to hide
Thy blushes – I do mean our marriage –
Thou mayst find out some time to meet and mingle
Stories and limbs. It may be necessary.
And 'cause I will be dutiful to the king   145
We will converse no more abed. I'll be
Thy husband still, Albina, and wear my buds
Under my hair close like a prudent statesman.
But 'twere not much amiss, as I advised
Before, and these new premises considered,   150
You appear abroad with a less train. Your wardrobe
Will make you more suspected if it be
Too rich, and some whole days to keep your chamber
Will make the king know where to find you certain.
ALBINA Will you have patience, my lord, to hear me?   155
GOTHARUS The world doth partly think thee honest, too.
That will help much if you observe good rules
And diet, without tedious progresses
And visiting of ladies expert in
Night revels, masques, and twenty other torments   160

142 **our marriage** Gotharus argues that their marriage is designed to hide the king's secret mistress and afford her respectability.

143–4 **meet...limbs** have sex and exchange stories, perhaps about court intrigue, in secret. Gotharus sees sexual intimacy in terms of court politics.

144 **necessary** i.e. to Gotharus's political advantage.

146 **We...abed** This continues the link between sex and conversation established in the scene. Gotharus is prepared to forgo his conjugal rights in the hope of political gain, but it is clear that he never wanted Albina anyway.

147–8 **wear...statesman** hide his cuckold's horns (buds) and keep quiet.

149–50 **as...Before** Gotharus argues that the current incident does not really change anything, letting the audience know that what they are now discussing has been considered before. It shows him to be a mean husband, intent on denying her both liberty and proper funds to support her role as his wife even before the new 'premises' arose.

150 **premises** facts, information.

151 **train** either 'an elongated back of a robe or skirt' (*OED*, *n.*² 2a), so related to the 'wardrobe' mentioned in the next sentence, or, more likely, the entourage that might be expected of a lady of her status.

153–4 **some...certain** Gotharus advises Albina how best to conduct her affair with the king, a moment that may be comic.

154 **certain** without fail.

156 **honest** chaste.

157–8 **good...diet** disciplined behaviour and careful expenditure (*OED*, Rule *n.*¹ 2a and Diet *n.*¹ 1 and 6).

158 **tedious** long, and so annoying to Gotharus who has to pay for them, not Albina.

158 **progresses** journeys.

159–61 **visiting...estate** Gotharus is also warning Albina, under the guise of advising her conduct to be moderate, that he will not maintain an expensive life-style, whilst also imagining her using panders—or pimps—to arrange sexual diversions in 'night revels'.

160 **masques** elaborate entertainments with music, dancing, and expensive costumes and disguises that might provide opportunities for covert sexual liaisons.

432

THE POLITICIAN   I.I

To an estate. Your doctors must be left too.
I wo'not pay a fee to have your pulse
Felt and your hand rolled up like wax by one
Whose footcloth must attend while he makes legs,
And every other morning comes to tell   165
Your ladyship a story out of Aretine
That can set you a-longing for diseases
That he may cure you; and your waiting-woman,
Whose curiosity would taste your clyster,
Commend the operation from her stomach.   170
Should you be sick, and sick to death, I would
Not counsel you to physic. Women are
Frail things and should a cordial miscarry
My conscience would be arraigned and I
Might be suspected for your poisoner.   175
No, no, I thank you. You're in a fine course
To ease me, wife. Or, if you must be loose
I'th'spring and fall, let the king bear the charges.
He will if you apply yourself.
ALBINA   I am wretched.
Why do you without hearing thus condemn me?   180

---

163 your...wax i.e. the doctor softly rolls his hand over Albina's hand, as if he were manipulating soft wax into a shape.

164 Whose...legs A complicated image as Gotharus's imagination races forward. A footcloth was an elaborate rug. Gotharus seems to be imagining a figure kneeling before Albina. 'Makes legs' suggests both kneeling in homage, so referring back to the image of the queen making her subjects kneel (1.1.7), but also with a bawdy connotation of intertwined legs. He combines doctor and lover as one composite cuckolding figure.

166 Aretine Pietro Aretino (1492–1556), Italian author of satirical and scandalous poetry, most famous as a pornographer.

167–8 That...you Gotharus imagines the doctor first inflaming Albina's lust and then profiting by treating her for the sexually transmitted diseases she would consequently contract, whilst she colludes in this as the doctor has become one of her lovers.

169 clyster enema injected, usually into the rectum, or the syringe used to effect this. 'Taste' has obvious sexual connotations to reinforce the sense of the 'clyster' as penis.

170 stomach thought to be the organ of all appetites, including sexual.

171 death meaning also orgasm, another common poetic image.

172 physic medical treatment.

173 cordial medicine, drug (possibly an aphrodisiac, or even sexual intercourse—see Williams 1994, entry for *cordial*).

174 My...arraigned My motives would be questioned (Fehrenbach); but the suggestion that he would feel guilt is hypocritical.

176 in...course going about things in the right way.

177 ease help, also satisfy (Rubinstein 1984, 85–6).

177 loose lascivious.

178 I'th'spring...fall Gotharus compares Albina to an animal on heat in the spring available for the stud, the king; 'spring and fall' mimics sexual activity; 'fall' refers both to autumn, and to Albina's fall from virtue.

178 charges weight, load (*OED*, Charge *n.* 1), with the suggestion of both sexual advances and the resulting illegitimate children, and a play on 'charges' as expenses.

---

167 a-longing] *this edn;* a longing Q/O

433

I.I   THE COMPLETE WORKS OF JAMES SHIRLEY, VOLUME 7

The lady lives not with a purer faith
To her loved lord than I have. Nor shall greatness,
Nor death itself, have power to break it.
GOTHARUS   Come,
These are but painted tears. Leave this. Have you
Prepared your last accounts?
ALBINA   They are ready sir.   185
Never was lady slaved thus like Albina.
A stipendiary – worse, a servile steward –
To give him an account of all my expenses.
GOTHARUS I'll have it so in spite of custom's heart
While you are mine. Accountless liberty   190
Is ruin of whole families. Now leave me;
We may talk more anon.   *Exit Albina.*
                    I have observed
This privacy before. Search here Gotharus:
'Tis here from whence mutinous thoughts conspiring
With witty melancholy shall beget   195
A strong-born mischief. I'll admit she be
Honest. I love her not, and if he tempt her
To sin that's paid him back in his wife's looseness
From whom I took my first ambition
And must go on till we can sway the kingdom,   200

184 **painted** false.
185 **accounts** account of her expenses. Gotharus's attempt to bully her financially helps to characterize him.
187 **stipendiary** hired employee.
187 **steward** Stewards were the chief servants in a household, in charge of all the accounts.
189 **custom's heart** convention (Shirley's coinage).
190 **Accountless** Unregulated, with a pun on the financial sense of 'accounts' (l. 185).
193 **privacy** secrecy.
194 **mutinous** rebellious, underhand.
195 **witty** feigned.
195 **melancholy** Caused by an excess of black bile in Renaissance humoral theory, it was often connected with the secrecy and conspiratorial plotting of the malcontent, a stock stage figure. Gotharus is a malcontent and is projecting his characteristics onto his wife.
196 **strong-born** substantial.
196–7 **I'll . . . honest** Just as Gotharus transferred his thoughts from the king to an imagined doctor and back again, so he now shifts from what he admits is imagined licentious behaviour by his wife to his own plans. Compare Iago's use of both his wife's and Desdemona's qualities for his own ends in *Othello*: 'And by how much she strives to do him good / She shall undo her credit with the Moor. / So will I turn her virtue into pitch, / And out of her own goodness make the net / That shall enmesh them all' (2.3.349–53).
197 **he** the king.
198 **looseness** promiscuity, lack of chastity, in contrast to Albina.
199 **ambition** quibbling on sexual satisfaction and plans to better himself.
200 **sway** influence, or, more strongly, become the rulers of (*OED*, *v*. 6b and 9a).

192 SD] *Gifford subst.; Exit Al. after* leave me, Q/O

434

THE POLITICIAN   I.I

Though we climb to't o'er many deaths. I first
Practise at home my unkindness to Albina;
If she do love me must needs break her heart.

     Enter HARALDUS.

HARALDUS My honoured lord.
GOTHARUS   Most dear Haraldus welcome,
  Preciously welcome to Gotharus's heart.   205
HARALDUS The queen my mother, sir, would speak with you.
GOTHARUS How excellently do those words become thee.
  'Tis fit Haraldus's mother be a queen:
  Th'art worth a princely fate. I will attend her.
HARALDUS I'll tell her so.
GOTHARUS   'Tis not an office for you.   210
HARALDUS It is my duty, sir, to wait upon my mother.
GOTHARUS Who i'th'court is not your servant?
  You do not exercise command enough.
  You are too gentle in your fortunes, sir,
  And wear your greatness as you were not born   215
  To be a prince.
HARALDUS   My birth sure gave me not
  That title. I was born with the condition
  To obey, not govern.
GOTHARUS   Do not wrong those stars
  Which early as you did salute the world
  Designed this glorious fate. I did consult   220

---

201 climb to't i.e. the monarchy.

201–2 I…Albina suggesting that his treatment of his wife is a part of his larger plot.

205 Preciously 'Very greatly; exceedingly, extremely' (*OED, adv.* 4).

207 excellently Gotharus is deliberately emphasizing his courtliness through the use of intensifiers, a contrast to his dark plotting.

209 princely fate fate that may not be wholly desirable and that prefigures Haraldus's miserable death. Gotharus's behaviour towards Haraldus here recalls that of Richard III towards the sons of Edward IV (*Richard III*, 3.1.61–94), which warns the audience that he will be the cause of their death.

210 office duty, function. Gotharus attempts to flatter Haraldus that he is of too high a status to act as a messenger.

214 gentle well-bred as well as mild, suggesting that Haraldus is not likely to function well in the rough world of the medieval Norwegian court.

215 as as if.

216 sure certainly.

217–18 I…govern A reference to the constantly discussed problem of whether those born in high positions were fit to govern.

218–20 Do…fate The common belief that the stars determine our character and destiny; compare *King Lear*, 1.2.101–15.

220 consult Gotharus appears to have cast Haraldus's horoscope.

211] *lineation this edn;* upon / My Q/O

435

I.I   THE COMPLETE WORKS OF JAMES SHIRLEY, VOLUME 7

And in the happy minute of thy birth
Collect what was decreed in heaven about thee.

HARALDUS Those books are 'bove my reading. But whate'er
My stars determine of me 'tis but late
I heard my mother say you are on earth   225
To whom I am most bound for what I am.

GOTHARUS [*Aside*] 'Tis a shrewd truth, if thou knew'st all.

HARALDUS   You have
Been more a father than a friend to us.

GOTHARUS (*Aside*) Friend to thy mother, I confess, in private –
The other follows by a consequence.   230
[*To Haraldus*] A father, my Haraldus? I confess
I was from thy nativity inclined
By a most strange and secret force of nature
Or sympathy to love thee like my own.
And let me tell thee, though thy mother had   235
Merit enough to engage my services,
Yet there was something more in thee considered
That raised my thoughts and study to advance
Thee to these pregnant hopes of state. Methinks
I see thee a king already.

HARALDUS   Good sir, do not   240
Prompt me to that ambition. I possess
Too much already, and I could, so pleased
My mother, travel where I should not hear
Of these great titles. And it comes now aptly:

---

222 **Collect** Gather the information, work out.

223 **Those books** i.e. Astrological texts; the stars.

223 **'bove...reading** too difficult for me.

224 **late** recently.

225–6 **I...am** In his simplicity Haraldus fails to realize that what his mother said could be taken to mean that Gotharus is his father, informing the audience that he lacks the wit to comprehend open allusions made in front of him. In this exchange Gotharus substantiates unconscious notions in Haraldus's words.

228 **us** i.e. mother and son.

230 **other** i.e. being a father.

233 **secret** mysterious.

236 **services** with clear sexual connotations.

237 **considered** respected, well-regarded.

239 **pregnant** The word carries a complex range of meanings here: weighty, compelling (*OED*, *adj.*²), promising, momentous, or receptive and ready (*adj.*¹ 1b, 2b, 3d).

242 **so** if it.

244 **aptly** appropriately.

223–4] *lineation Gifford;* what / E're my Q/O   227 SD] *Gifford subst.; not in* Q/O
229 SD] *Fehrenbach subst.; after* consequence, Q/O   231 SD] *Fehrenbach subst.; not in* Q/O

436

THE POLITICIAN   I.I

I should entreat your lordship to assist me   245
In a request to her. I know she loves you
And will deny you nothing. I would fain
Visit the university for study;
I do lose time methinks.
GOTHARUS   Fie, Haraldus,
And leave the court? How you forget yourself!   250
Study to be king! I shall half repent my care
If you permit these dull and phlegmatic
Thoughts to usurp – they'll stifle your whole reason.
Catch at the sun, divest him of his beams,
And in your eye wear his proud rays. Let day   255
Be when you smile, and when your anger points
Shoot death in every frown. Covet a shade?
Affect a solitude and books and forfeit
So brave an expectation?
HARALDUS   Of what?
GOTHARUS Of Norway's crown.
HARALDUS   Could there be any thought   260
Within me so ambitious? With what hope
Could it be cherished when I have no title?
GOTHARUS I that have thus far studied thy fortune
May find a way.

247–9 I…methinks Haraldus imagines that Gotharus has just declared a desire to help him, rather than
pursue his own goal of having a weak king that he can control. There is a comic irony in Haraldus's fears that
time is passing him by if he wishes to study at university, given his inability to read the underhand dealings at
court and in his immediate family. Students usually started university between the ages of fourteen and sixteen.
The echo of Hamlet's desire to return to university is obvious.
249–50 Fie…court Compare Claudius's desire that Hamlet stay in Denmark and not return to Wittenberg
(*Hamlet*, 1.2.112–17).
252 phlegmatic having excess phlegm, one of the four humours. A phlegmatic temperament was calm,
peaceful, and diffident, associated with water, passivity, and laziness.
253 usurp i.e. take possession (of your mind); here used in an absolute sense.
253 they'll…reason suggesting that Haraldus is allowing his nature to overcome his reason.
254 Catch at Reach for.
254 the sun the throne, punning on the king's son; compare *Hamlet*, 1.2.64–7: when Claudius calls Hamlet
'my son' and then asks, 'How is it that the clouds still hang on you?' the prince replies, 'Not so, my lord, I am too
much i'th'sun'.
256 points sharpens, an archery metaphor (*OED*, Point $v.^1$ 14a 'To give a point or points; to work or fashion
to a point or tapered end, to sharpen').
258 Affect Show an ostentatious desire for, assume (see *OED*, $v.^1$ 5).
259 brave fine, splendid. Compare Marlowe's Tamburlaine: 'Is it not brave to be a King, Techelles? … Is it
not passing brave to be a King?' (*Tamburlaine*, 2.5.51–3).
259 Of what? The question further exposes Haraldus's unsuitability as monarch.
262 cherished entertained, hoped for.
262 title claim to the throne, and being called 'Prince'.

251] *lineation Gifford;* King, / I Q/O

437

I.I   THE COMPLETE WORKS OF JAMES SHIRLEY, VOLUME 7

HARALDUS   The king —
GOTHARUS   Is not immortal
While he has physicians.
HARALDUS [*Aside*]   What's that he said?   265
[*To Gotharus*] The king is happy and the whole nation
Treasure up their hopes in prince Turgesius,
Who with his great uncle valiant Olaus —
GOTHARUS Are sent to th'wars where 'twill concern 'em
To think of fame and how to march to honour   270
Through death.
HARALDUS [*Aside*] I dare not hear him.
GOTHARUS   Or if they
Return —
HARALDUS   — They will be welcome to all good
Men's hearts and, next the king, none with more joy
Congratulate their safeties than yourself.
I am confident, my lord, you will remember   275
To see my mother and excuse me if,
To finish something else I had in charge,
I take my leave. All good dwell with your lordship.   *Exit.*
GOTHARUS But that I have Marpisa's faith, I could
Suspect him not the issue of my blood.   280
He is too tame and honest. At his years
I was prodigiously in love with greatness.
Or if not mine let him inherit but
His mother's soul. She has pride enough and spirit

   264–5 Is…physicians A thought that could be innocent enough, meaning that we are all mortal, but it also
suggests that Gotharus sees physicians as hired servants who will break the Hippocratic Oath for payment.
   267 Treasure up Put away or lay aside (anything of value) for preservation, security, or future use (*OED*,
Treasure *v.* 1).
   271 him i.e. Gotharus.
   274 yourself Haraldus tries to transform Gotharus to a loyal servant by speaking for him.
   277 had…charge i.e. important that I was entrusted to do. A slightly unusual construction.
   279–80 But…blood This comment, though it appears to confirm his faith in his mistress, also refers us back
to Gotharus's admission that Albina is honest but Marpisa 'loose' (see 1.1.196–9).
   279 faith word.
   281 tame and honest timid and virtuous.
   282 prodigiously immensely, particularly.
   284 pride also sexual desire (often associated with masculine desire).

   264–8] *lineation this edn;* Is…Physitians. / What's…happy, / And…hopes / In…uncle / Valiant Q/O
   265 SD] *Fehrenbach subst.; not in* Q/O   **266 SD]** *Fehrenbach subst.; not in* Q/O
   271 SD] *Gifford subst.; not in* Q/O

438

THE POLITICIAN   I.I

To catch at flames. His education   285
Has been too soft. I must new form the boy
Into more vice and daring. Strange, we must
Study at court how to corrupt our children.

    Enter MARPISA.

The queen!
MARPISA   My expectation to speak
With thee Gotharus was too painful to me –   290
I fear we are all undone. Dost hear the news?
The prince is coming back with victory.
Our day will be o'ercast.
GOTHARUS   These eyes will force
A brighter from those clouds. Are not you queen?
MARPISA But how Turgesius and his bold uncle   295
Will look upon me!
GOTHARUS   Let 'em stare out
Their eyeballs. Be you mistress still of the
King's heart and let their gall spout in their stomach.
We'll be secure.
MARPISA   Thou art my fate.
GOTHARUS   I must confess
I was troubled when I heard it first. Seem not   300
You pale at their return but put on smiles
To grace their triumph. Now you have most need
Of woman's art: dissemble cunningly.
MARPISA My best Gotharus.
GOTHARUS They shall find stratagems in peace more fatal   305
Than all the engines of the war. What mischief
Will not Gotharus fly to, to assure

---

  285 To...flames An image that suggests how fierce her ambition is, and (implicitly) that it may be doomed to failure. There is also a reference to Marpisa's natural heat and lust being so powerful that she might burst into flames.

  286 soft effeminate. Gotharus thinks that Haraldus needs to be more manly.

  287–8 Strange...children A particularly hard-hitting line, even within the tradition of anti-court drama, which saw the court as the root of all evil, corrupting the nation it was supposed to govern; see Tricomi 1989.

  289 expectation desire (pronounced here with five syllables).

  290 to me for me to contain myself.

  293 o'ercast spoiled by bad weather; overthrown.

  294 brighter i.e. brighter day (continuing the nature of his advice to Haraldus).

  298 gall bile, a bitter secretion of the liver, and hence bitterness of spirit.

  299 fate destiny, guiding spirit.

  302–3 you...cunningly This description provides an ironic context for Gotharus's desire for Haraldus to have a more manly education, when his own behaviour is based on deception.

  306 engines large military machinery, catapults, battering rams, siege engines, etc.

  307 fly to (immediately) practice.

I.I THE COMPLETE WORKS OF JAMES SHIRLEY, VOLUME 7

The fair Marpisa's greatness and his own
In being hers – an empire 'bove the world.
There is a heaven in either eye that calls   310
My adoration. Such Promethean fire
As, were I struck dead in my works, shouldst thou
But dart one look upon me it would quicken
My cold dust and inform it with a soul
More daring than the first.

MARPISA   Still my resolved   315
Gotharus.

GOTHARUS Let weak statesmen think of conscience.
I am armed against a thousand stings and laugh at
The tales of hell and other worlds. We must
Possess our joys in this, and know no other
But what our fancy every minute shall   320
Create to please us.

MARPISA   This is harmony.
How dull is the king's language. I could dwell
Upon thy lips. Why should not we engender
At every sense?

GOTHARUS   Now you put me in mind:
The pledge of both our hopes and blood, Haraldus,   325
Is not well bred – he talks too morally.
He must have other discipline and be fashioned
For our great aims upon him. A crown never

310–15 **There...first** A sacrilegious suggestion, as only Christ could be considered as able to raise the dead; compare 2.1.42–3 and note.

311 **Promethean fire** The Titan, Prometheus, stole fire from the Gods and gave it to man, planning to imitate the Gods by using it to bring images to life. Gotharus does not mention that the immortal was punished by being chained to a rock and having an eagle eat his liver for eternity.

313 **quicken** provide life to.

314 **dust** an allusion to Genesis 2:7: 'And the Lord God formed man of the dust of the ground, and breathed into his nostrils the breath of life; and man became a living soul.'

314 **inform** animate.

315 **More...first** Gotharus repays Marpisa's compliment, 'My best Gotharus' (1.1.304).

315 **Still...resolved** Always my determined.

316–18 **Let...worlds** Gotharus's cynicism identifies him as a stage Machiavel; compare Machevil in Marlowe's *The Jew of Malta*: 'I count Religion but a childish Toy' (Prologue, 14).

320 **fancy** imagination, desires.

323–4 **engender...sense** employ every sense to heighten and grow our pleasure in every way possible.

326 **bred** of the right character: more literally, properly aristocratic.

327 **discipline** teaching.

315–16] *lineation Gifford;* Still...Gotharus. Q/O

440

THE POLITICIAN   2.1

Became a stoic. Pray let me commend
Some conversation to his youth.
MARPISA   He is thine.   330
GOTHARUS He shall be every way my own.

     Enter HELGA.

HELGA The king desires your presence madam.
MARPISA I attend. You'll follow –   *Exeunt* [*Marpisa and Helga*].
GOTHARUS   Thee to death, and triumph in
My ruins for thy sake. A thousand forms
Throng in my brain. That is the best which speeds: 335
Who looks at crowns must have no thought who bleeds.

                                   Exit.

2[.1]

     Enter KING, HORMENUS, CORTES, [*and*] SUENO [*playing an instrument*].

KING This music doth but add to melancholy,
I'll hear no more. [*Sueno stops playing.*]
CORTES He's strangely moved.
HORMENUS   I cannot think a cause.
[*To Sueno*] You were wont to fool him into mirth. Where's Helga

---

329 Became…stoic i.e. Suited or befitted an ascetic philosopher; another possible reference to Hamlet, whose stoicism many critics see as an impediment to his effective action.

330 conversation i.e. education.

330 He…thine i.e. Take him in hand.

333–4 Thee…sake Gotharus realizes that he cannot control his passion for Marpisa and that it will have terrible consequences (as, indeed, it does); in this period all-consuming passion was invariably seen as destructive.

334–5 A thousand…brain Imagination was frequently represented as a chaotic and uncontrollable sequence of images and ideas that needed to be co-ordinated by the higher faculty, reason. Men were thought to be able to exercise their reason to control the imagination, women not; following his admission that he cannot control his passion for Marpisa, Gotharus is in danger of suggesting here that he is an effeminate man and so also prey to the dark feminine arts that overwhelm him.

335 speeds prospers; also with the sense of 'races'.

336 looks at aspires to.

1–17 The first seventeen lines of this scene suggest that it is Sueno who is providing the music, perhaps on a lute and perhaps also singing (see following notes) in an attempt to lift the king out of his melancholia. The belief that music relieves the dejected mind is an old one. The Book of Samuel relates how, when Saul was suffering from melancholic despair, 'David took an harp, and played with his hand: so Saul was refreshed, and was well, and the evil spirit departed from him' (I Samuel, 16:23); Shirley's contemporary, Robert Burton, suggested that 'besides that excellent power [music] hath to expell many other diseases, it is a soveraigne remedy against Despaire and Melancholy' (Burton 2.114). Sueno's musical efforts seem, unfortunately, to have no curative effect on the king, as was also the case for Shakespeare's melancholic Duke Orsino who cries out to his musicians: 'Enough, no more, / 'Tis not so sweet now as it was before' (*Twelfth Night*, 1.1.7–8).

---

331 SD] *this edn; after* thine. Q/O   **333 SD**] *Fehrenbach subst.; Exit.* Q/O

2[.1]] *Gifford subst. (*ACT II. SCENE I.*); [*II.i] *Fehrenbach;* Act. 2. Q/O

0 SD] *Fehrenbach subst.;* Enter *King, Hormenus, Cortes, Sueno.* Q/O   **2 SD**] *this edn; not in* Q/O

4 SD] *this edn; not in* Q/O

441

2.1   THE COMPLETE WORKS OF JAMES SHIRLEY, VOLUME 7

Your dear companion; no device between you   5
To raise his thoughts?
SUENO I am nothing without my fellow;
Music is best in consort.
HORMENUS Your buffoon'ry is musical belike.
CORTES Your jugglers cannot do some o'their tricks   10
Without confederacy.
SUENO   I'll try alone.
If please your majesty, there is –
KING That for your unseasonable and saucy fooling. (*Strikes him.*)
HORMENUS That was a musical box o'th'ear.
KING Leave us.   15
CORTES 'Tis nothing without a fellow; he knows
Music is best in consort.
SUENO   Would you had your parts!

                                        Exeunt [Sueno and Cortes].

KING Hormenus, you may stay.
HORMENUS   Your pleasure, sir.
KING Men do account thee honest –
HORMENUS 'Tis possible I may fare the worse.
KING   And wise.   20

---

5 **device** fanciful, witty, or ingenious expression (*OED, n.* 10).

6 **raise** animate, stimulate (*OED, v.*[1] 7a), with possibly a sexual innuendo suggesting male arousal (see next note).

7–8 **I...consort** This would support the idea that Sueno is playing an instrument (and possibly singing) in an attempt to amuse the king; however, both 'music' and 'consort' carry strong sexual connotations and the phrase thus hints at a homosexual relationship between the two court parasites (see Williams 1994, entry for *music*, where he notes the sexual innuendo in the phrase to 'play in consort' with others). Note that Cortes repeats the phrase sarcastically in l. 17. Another suggestion of homoerotic behaviour in a court context occurs in Shirley's *St Patrick For Ireland* when Ethne, one of the queen's daughters, asks Rodamant, the foolish servant of the magician, if his beloved is 'a man or a woman' (2.1).

9 **buffoon'ry** buffonry in Q, a common seventeenth-century spelling, as it was pronounced trisyllabically; the apostrophe allows for a modernized spelling which retains that pronunciation.

10 **jugglers** entertainers, but also tricksters (*OED*, Juggler *n.* 1 and 3); the word carried suggestions of sexual play; see Williams 1994, *juggling*: 'copulation—the figure is of play or legerdemain'.

11 **confederacy** union for joint action; in a bad sense, collusion (*OED, n.* 1 and 2) but again with a glance at conspiracy or collusion for sexual purposes and so completing the run of sexual innuendos.

13 **your...fooling** presumably the king is annoyed by Sueno's continuing to play and perhaps even singing this line in a foolishly comic manner.

17 **parts** melodies assigned to a particular voice or instrument in a piece of music (*OED*, Part *n.*[1] 13) and hence 'your share in this', but possibly also continuing the sexual innuendo by hinting at 'private parts' (*OED, n.*[1] 4) and hence a gratuitous jibe at Cortes's masculinity.

19 **Men...honest** See 1.1.196–7 and note.

20 **'Tis...worse** i.e. worse than Sueno; perhaps said aside.

---

9 buffoon'ry] *this edn;* buffoonery *Gifford;* buffonry Q/O

17 SD] *this edn; Ex[eunt* Cortes *and* Sueno]. *after* stay. *Fehrenbach;* [*Exit. after* consort., [*Exit. after* parts! *Gifford; Exit. after* Consort. Q/O

20–1] *lineation Fehrenbach;* 'Tis possible / I...worse. / And...sad? Q/O

442

THE POLITICIAN   2.1

Canst tell the cause why I am sad?
HORMENUS   Not I, sir.
KING Nor I myself. 'Tis strange I should be subject
  To a dull passion and no reason for it.
HORMENUS These things are frequent.
KING   Sometimes ominous,
  And do portend.
HORMENUS   If you enjoy a health   25
  What is in fate?
KING   I am king still, am I not?
HORMENUS We are all happy in't.
  And when time shall with the consent of nature
  Call you an old man from this world to heaven
  May he that shall succeed you, Prince Turgesius,   30
  The glory of our hope, be no less fortunate.
KING My son –
  I was too rash to part with him.
HORMENUS   We should
  Have thought his stay a blessing and did wish
  You would not have exposed such tender years   35
  To the rough war, but your commands met with
  His duty and our obedience.
KING   It is very
  Strange we of late hear no success. I hope
  This sadness is not for his loss. He has
  A kinsman with him loves him dearly – 'tis   40

---

  23 dull passion either an interesting oxymoron, as passion usually implies a state of intense or excited feeling, or passion in the sense of the condition of being acted upon by an external agency (see *OED, n.* 11).

  25 portend i.e. presage some unwelcome event (*OED, v.*[1] 1b).

  25–6 If…fate? i.e. 'If you are in a healthy state, what else can destiny have in store for you? Being healthy in itself portends good.' 'Health' would be soundness of both body and of mind, and could even be extended to spiritual well-being (*OED, n.* 1a and 4).

  29 Call Summon (*OED, v.* 13a), here with the specific additional sense of to the next world (*OED, v.* 15).

  32–4 My…wish This edition has followed the lineation of Q/O, as does Gifford, making 33 and 34 metrically regular, but leaving 32 highly irregular; Fehrenbach sets 'My son…with him' as one line and 'We should…did wish' as the next line, making the first line metrically regular and the second irregular, though no more so than many of Shirley's lines; however, two points can be made in justification of the Q/O lineation: first, the king is given another two-syllable line at l. 15 of this scene, so Shirley is clearly not worried by such extreme irregularity in his verse; second, the long hiatus after 'My son' is powerfully suggestive of a pregnant pause as the king dwells ruefully upon his decision to send his son and heir on a dangerous military mission.

  26] *lineation Gifford;* King / Still Q/O

443

2.1   THE COMPLETE WORKS OF JAMES SHIRLEY, VOLUME 7

The queen.

  Enter QUEEN [MARPISA] *and* HELGA.

    I feel my drooping thoughts fall off
And my clouds fly before the wind; her presence
Hath an infusion to restore dead nature.
My sweet, my dear Marpisa.
MARPISA   You sent for me.
KING I am but the shadow of myself without thee.   45

  Enter CORTES [*and*] SUENO.

No wonder I was sad. My soul had placed
All her delight in these fair eyes and could not
But think itself an exile in thy absence.
Why should we ever part, but chain ourselves
Together thus?
SUENO [*To Helga*] He's in a better humour I hope.   50
I do not think but His Majesty would cuff well,
His hand carries a princely weight.
HELGA [*To Sueno*]   A favour.
SUENO [*To Helga*] Would you might wear such another in your ear.
KING [*To Sueno*] Come hither, on this side.
SUENO [*To Helga*]   You were on that side before.
KING Wouldst not thou lose thy life to do a service   55
My queen would smile upon?
SUENO   Alas, my life

41–2 I...wind The king's meaning is perfectly clear—the presence of Marpisa revives his spirits—but 'fall off' and 'fly before' carry the meaning in a quite opposite direction, the former suggesting descent into a worse state, and the latter of trying to escape danger by flight; these under-currents of meaning point up Marpisa's presence as being malign and destructive to the king.

43 infusion A word used in theological discourse to describe the way the grace of God is imparted to human beings (*OED*, *n.* 2a) but which could also mean more negatively, 'insidious suggestion, insinuation' (*OED*, *n.* 2b); this underlying semantic ambivalence betrays the king's uncertainty as he strays into a theological minefield with his sacrilegious suggestion that Marpisa has the ability 'to restore dead nature'—i.e. bring the dead back to life.

52 weight strength, but possibly also 'impetus' (*OED*, *n.*[1] 3c) though this meaning is given as obsolete by the seventeenth century.

52 favour something given and worn as a mark of favour or allegiance (*OED*, *n.* 7a), in this instance, a bruise.

53 Would...ear Sueno sarcastically wishes Helga the same mark of 'favour' from the king as he has just received (see l. 13).

54 You...before Sueno suggests rather cattily that he has now replaced Helga in the royal favour by being invited into the king's confidence.

---

41 SD QUEEN MARPISA] *this edn;* MARPISA *Gifford;* Queen Q/O 50 SD] *this edn; not in* Q/O
52 SD] *this edn; not in* Q/O 53 SD] *this edn; not in* Q/O 54 SD1] *this edn; not in* Q/O
54 SD2] *this edn;* [*aside*]. *Fehrenbach; not in* Q/O

444

THE POLITICIAN   2.1

Is the least thing to be imagined. He
Is not a faithful subject would refuse
To kill his wife and children, after that
To hang himself, to do the queen a service.   60
KING Come hither Helga.
HELGA   Royal sir.
KING What would affright thy undertaking to deserve
The least grace from my queen?
HELGA   I cannot tell.
But I've an opinion the devil could not.
My life is nothing, sir, to obtain her favour,   65
I would hazard more: I have heard talk of hell –
So far she should command me.
HORMENUS [*To Cortes*]   Bless me, goodness!
What wretched parasites are these? How can
The king be patient at 'em? Here is flattery
So thick and gross it would endure a handsaw.   70
CORTES [*To Hormenus*] His judgement's, I fear, stupefied.
HORMENUS [*To Helga and Sueno*]   Come hither.
Which of you can resolve what serpent spawned you?
SUENO You are pleasant.
HELGA   My good lord, it hurts not you.

---

57 imagined thought about, taken into consideration—though a very late use of the word in that sense (*OED*, Imagine *v.* 3).

58 subject would elision of 'who' before 'would'.

62 What…undertaking i.e. 'What would you find so frightening that it would deter you from undertaking something'.

64 I've…not i.e. 'I believe not even the devil could frighten me from doing the queen a service'; the two courtiers vie with one another in obsequious hyperbole.

67 goodness substitution for 'God'; the avoidance of naming the deity in what is more an exclamation than an oath is an indication, perhaps, of how nervous dramatists were at this period of the profanity laws and their application to theatrical texts. Hugh Gazzard (2010, 520) notes an intensification during the Commonwealth period of the parliamentary battle to suppress profanity which culminated in 'a set of acts passed in 1650 which seemed to heighten the sense that the English criminal law was gaining the rigour of Mosaic code'; though these acts were not specific to the theatres (which were closed, anyway) they must have helped to define the atmosphere in which the publication of dramatic texts took place.

70 thick excessive in a disagreeable way (*OED*, *adj.* 3—though that sense is not given until 1884).

70 gross flagrant, monstrous (*OED*, *adj.* 4a).

70 endure either submit to or be impervious to (*OED*, *v.* 4a, 3b).

71 stupefied become stupid, deadened (*OED*, Stupefy *v.* 1).

72 resolve answer the question, explain, determine (*OED*, *v.* 17).

73 pleasant humorous, but with ironic suggestion; facetious (*OED*, *adj.* 4a).

---

67 SD] *Fehrenbach subst.; not in* Q/O   **71 SD1**] *this edn; not in* Q/O
71 SD2] *Fehrenbach subst.; not in* Q/O

2.1   THE COMPLETE WORKS OF JAMES SHIRLEY, VOLUME 7

There is necessity of some knaves, and so
Your lordship be exempted, why should you   75
Trouble yourself and murmur at our courses?

> *Enter* AQUINUS *hastily.*

AQUINUS The king?
HELGA   Peace.
SUENO   Your business?
AQUINUS   News from the field.
SUENO Good?
AQUINUS   Good.
HELGA   How?
SUENO   How, prithee?
AQUINUS The day, the field, the safety, oh, the glory
Of war is Norway's. Letters to the king –   80
HELGA Give 'em to me.
SUENO   Or me.
HELGA Trust not a fool with things of consequence.
He's the king's mirth – let me present the news.
SUENO Sir, I should know you, this is a knave
Would take to him all the glory of your report.   85
If please you, let me present the letters.
HELGA My liege!
SUENO   My sovereign!
HELGA   News!
SUENO   Good news!
HELGA   Excellent news!
SUENO The prince –
HELGA   The prince is –
SUENO   The enemy is – o'erthrown.
HELGA They have lost the day.
SUENO   Defeated utterly.
HELGA And all are slain.
SUENO [*To Marpisa*]   Madam, will you hear the news?   90

74–6 **There…yourself** i.e. 'There is a requirement that there are some knaves in the world and so—allowing that your lordship be excepted from that category—why should it bother you?'

76 **murmur at** complain or grumble about (*OED*, Murmur *v.* 1a); possibly, more intensively, criticize, accuse (*OED, v.* 1b), a Scotticism (probably brought over to Ireland by settlers from Scotland in the early years of the seventeenth century) that Shirley could have picked up in Dublin.

76 **courses** conduct, ways of acting, especially of a reprehensible nature (*OED*, Course *n.* 22b).

79 **safety** i.e. the deliverance from danger resulting from our victory (*OED, n.* 1d).

83 **mirth** something affording pleasure, an object of mirth, but possibly also of ridicule (*OED, n.* 2b and 4c).

84 **know you** make known to you, disclose to you (*OED*, Know *v.* 16).

---

90 SD] *Fehrenbach subst.; not in* Q/O

446

THE POLITICIAN   2.1

KING Say on. What is't you would relate?

HELGA One of my creatures, sir, hath brought you letters.

Aquinus delivers the letters.

My servant sir, one strengthened to your service
Out of my maintenance, an instrument of mine.
So please you to consider my duty in his service.   95

AQUINUS [*To Helga and Sueno*] Why hark you gentlemen, I have but mocked
Your greedy zeals. There's no such matter in
Those letters as you have told. We have lost all
And the prince taken prisoner. Will you not
Stay for the reward? You know I'm but your creature.   100
I look for nothing but your courtly faces
To pay my travel.

HELGA   We wo'not appear yet –   *Exeunt [Helga and Sueno].*

AQUINUS [*Aside*] How the rats vanish.

KING Read here, my best Marpisa, news that makes
A triumph in my heart great as the conquest   105
Upon our enemies. Hormenus, Cortes,
Our son will prove a soldier; was my sadness
Omen to this good fate, or nature feared

---

92 One…creatures i.e. One of my servants, but this is an insulting invention as Aquinus is a gentleman soldier and as such in the service of Prince Turgesius; Sueno is hoping that if he can claim to be responsible for Aquinus's actions he can also claim part of any reward due for them (see l. 95 and note). Aquinus gets his revenge for this affrontery—see ll. 96–102.

93 strengthened to i.e. increasingly committed to.

94 Out…maintenance As a result of my support (*OED*, Out of *prep*. 4a; Maintenance *n*. 2).

94 instrument agent or tool; the latter, derogatory sense, is probably closer (*OED*, *n*. 1).

95 consider…service i.e. take into account the dutiful part I have played in encouraging his loyal actions.

96 mocked deceived or fooled, possibly also disappointed (*OED*, Mock *v*. 1a and b).

97 zeals eagerness in pursuit of your aims (*OED*, Zeal *n*. 2a and 3), pluralized to apply to both of them; the word had negative connotations for those with an anti-puritanical outlook, as in Jonson's name for the character Zeal-of-the-Land-Busy in *Bartholomew Fair*.

98–9 We…prisoner Not true, as the king's next speech reveals; Aquinus says this to frighten the two parasites, and succeeds in doing so.

101–2 I…travel Pretending to play along with Sueno's appropriation of himself as a servant, Aquinus seems, rather cheekily, to be putting in a claim for his travel expenses, but 'travel' was homonymous with 'travail' so this is primarily a sarcastic 'admission' that he depends on them for reward for the trouble he has taken.

101 courtly befitting a court, but also implying servility (*OED*, *adj*. 2a, 4).

101 faces by metonymy, persons, but with a suggestion of both artificiality and effrontery (*OED*, Face *n*. 2e, 15).

102 appear yet be visible; remain in the presence, after all (*OED*, Yet *adv*. 5b).

105 great (as) great.

107–8 was…fate The king is referring back to his earlier conversation with Hormenus at ll. 18–25, specifically to the notion that extreme emotions that have no apparent cause can be a kind of omen.

108 nature (was it that) nature.

---

96 SD] *this edn*; [*aside to* Helga *and* Sueno]. *Fehrenbach; not in* Q/O   **102 SD**] *Gifford subst.; Exit.* Q/O
103 SD] *Fehrenbach subst.; not in* Q/O

447

2.1   THE COMPLETE WORKS OF JAMES SHIRLEY, VOLUME 7

The ecstasy of my joy would else o'ercome me?
They are returned victorious.

HORMENUS   Thanks to heaven!   110

KING [*To Aquinus*] And some reward is due to thee. Wear that
For the king's sake.

> [*He gives Aquinus a token.*]

AQUINUS   You too much honour me.

KING But something in Marpisa's face shows not
So clear a joy as we express. Forbear –
Wait till we call.   *Exeunt* [*Cortes, Hormenus, and Aquinus*].
                    Can this offend my queen,   115
To hear of happiness to my son? Oh, let
Thy eyes look bright: their shine hath force to make
The wreath of laurel grow upon his temples.
Why dost thou weep? This dew will kill the victory
And turn his bay to cypress.

MARPISA   Witness heaven,   120
There's not a tear that mourns for him. His safety
And conquest is most welcome and he shall
Have still my prayers he may grow up in fame
And all the glorious fortunes of a prince.
But while my wishes fly to heaven for blessings   125
Upon his head, at the same time I must
Remember in what miserable condition
My stars have placed me.

KING   What can make thy state

---

111 **Wear that** The king is clearly not giving Aquinus money but some sort of token that is merely symbolic of his gratitude; his lack of generosity contrasts with that of Olaus and Turgesius at 5.2.126 who distribute money to their loyal soldiers. Aquinus's response in l. 112 could be ironic rather than obsequious.

114 **Forbear** Leave us (*OED*, *v.* 4c).

117 **shine** radiance, but also, more literally, sunshine (*OED*, *n.*[1] 1a, 4a, 3a), that sense allowing the king to develop the subsequent metaphor in which Marpisa's eyes are a sun which has the life-giving power to make a laurel wreath (symbolizing victory) 'grow' on the prince's head.

119 **dew** i.e. her tears, a common assimilation, but continuing the 'sun' metaphor in that morning dew follows a hot, sunny day.

120 **bay** another name for the laurel.

120 **cypress** a coniferous tree associated with mourning, branches of it being used at funerals.

121–2 **His…is** Fehrenbach amends 'is' to 'are' but Shirley uses 'is' as a third person plural elsewhere (see 3.1.57, 3.3.25, and 3.3.42); *OED* notes that this is a Northern usage often employed by Shakespeare.

124 **fortunes** success, prosperity (*OED*, Fortune *n.* 4).

---

111 SD] *this edn; not in* Q/O
112 SD] *this edn;* [*Gives* Aquinus *a ring.*] *after* thee *Fehrenbach;* [*Gives him a ring. after* sake. *Gifford; not in* Q/O
115 SD] *Gifford subst.; Exeunt. after* forbear, Q/O

THE POLITICIAN   2.1

Guilty of such a name and so deject
Thy nobler thoughts? Am not I still the king   130
And is not fair Marpisa mine by marriage,
Crowned here my queen immortally?
MARPISA   Though I be
By royal bounty of your love possessed
Of that great title, sir, I have some fears.
KING You amaze me. Speak thy doubts at large.
MARPISA   The prince,   135
Dear to your love – and I still wish him so –
Dear to your people's hearts, I fear will think
Our marriage his dishonour. And Olaus
Your passionate uncle, no good friend of mine,
When he shall see to what a height your love   140
And holy vow hath raised me, most unworthy,
Will but salute Marpisa with his scorn
And by his counsel or some ways of force
Unchain our hearts and throw me from your bosom
To death or, worse, to shame. Oh, think upon me   145
And if you have one fear that's kin to mine
Prevent their tyranny and give me doom
Of exile ere their cruelty arrive.
I'll take my sentence kindly from your lips
Though it be killing.
KING   Let my son or uncle   150
Dare but affront thee in a look, I shall

129 **Guilty…name** i.e. deserve the punishment of being thus described (*OED*, Guilty *adj.* 4).

129 **deject** cast down, abase (*OED*, *v.* 3).

130 **Am…king** See l. 26 of this scene; the king's repetition of the phrase is indicative of his sense of insecurity.

132 **immortally** i.e. for ever, perpetually (*OED*, *adv.* 1).

133 **bounty** munificence, liberality (*OED*, *n.* 4).

135 **at large** freely and fully (*OED*, Large *adj.* P1a and c).

139 **passionate** hot-tempered and irascible, but also with a sense of being easily moved or susceptible to such passions (*OED*, *adj.* 2b, 1).

141 **holy vow** i.e. of marriage.

142 **salute** greet, conventionally in a polite or respectful manner so Marpisa's use of the word possibly has a tinge of irony.

143 **ways** courses of action, expedients (*OED*, Way *n.*[1] 18a).

144 **Unchain** Again, the semantic undertone is interesting as the word suggests that separation from Marpisa would be a liberation from captivity for the king.

147 **Prevent** With a sense of anticipating as well as stopping (*OED*, *v.* 1a).

147 **give…doom** pronounce judgement on me, sentence me (*OED*, Give *v.* 16, 18a; Doom *n.* 2).

150 **killing** fatal (*OED*, *adj.* 1a).

151 **in a look** with a look (*OED*, In *prep.*[1] 13b), the implication of the whole line being 'if one of them even so much as looks disrespectfully at you'.

2.1   THE COMPLETE WORKS OF JAMES SHIRLEY, VOLUME 7

Forget the ties of nature and discharge 'em
Like the corruption in my blood.

MARPISA   I can
Submit myself to them, and would you please
To allow my humbleness no stain to what   155
You have advanced me to, I can be their servant
And with as true a duty wait upon 'em.

KING   Thou art all goodness. Twenty kingdoms are
Too little for thy dowry. Who attends?

> *Enter* HORMENUS, [AQUINUS,] *and* CORTES.

Thus every minute I will marry thee   160
And wear thee in my heart. Vanish the thought
Of all thy sex beside and what can else
Attempt our separation. Th'art obscure
And liv'st in court but like a masquing star
Shut from us by the unkindness of a cloud   165
When Cynthia goes to revels. I will have

---

152 discharge primarily, dismiss from my service, but the next line brings the medical usage into play—to cause a body, wound, or organ to secrete corrupted matter (*OED, v.* 4b, 12b).

153 corruption...blood There may be a glance here at the legal phrase 'corruption of blood' whereby not only criminals but also their descendants were considered to be tainted by a crime and so lost rights of rank, title, and inheritance.

155 allow acknowledge (*OED, v.* 3a, 4); Marpisa is possibly suggesting a public acknowledgement—a clever amplification of her pretended humility.

155–6 stain...to i.e. a cause of disgrace to the position you have promoted me to (*OED*, Stain *n.* 3b; Advance *v.* 2a).

159 attends enters, presents themselves (*OED*, Attend *v.* 7).

161–2 Vanish...beside i.e. Let all thoughts of women other than you disappear from my mind. The king appears to have forgotten that only a short time ago he was trying to seduce Albina (see 1.1.66–123).

162 what...else i.e. whatever else can.

163 Attempt Try to effect (*OED, v.* 2) but possibly also, try with temptations (5a).

163 obscure both little known and concealed (*OED, adj.* 6, 1c), the latter meaning being played upon in the following image.

164–6 And...revels An oddly tautological and also ambivalent image: the primary sense is that Marpisa (the star) is like someone who goes to a masque (and hence is already disguised—*OED*, Mask *v.*⁴ 3), but who is further obscured by some other agency (the unkind cloud) when the goddess of the moon, Cynthia, has herself gone revelling (i.e. to a masque) and hence is not present in the sky to illuminate and reveal Marpisa (who is anyway hidden behind the cloud and also masked). To 'mask/masque' (the Q/O spelling is 'maskquing') had, however, connotations of hiding behind deceit, and we have just seen Marpisa behaving in exactly that way when she pretends to be humble and willing to submit herself to Olaus and Turgesius. Finally, 'mask' could also mean to ensnare in a net (*OED, v.*²), which describes well Marpisa's intentions towards the king. Once again, the tortuous and ambiguous phrasing reveals the king's true—though to him as yet unknown—position in relation to his new queen. For the idea that beautiful women at a festivity are like stars, cf. Capulet on his 'old accustom'd feast': 'At my poor house look to behold this night / Earth-treading stars that make dark heaven light' (*Romeo and Juliet*, 1.2.22–3). There is also surely a reference to Ben Jonson's play *The Fountain of Self-Love, or Cynthia's Revels* (1601).

---

159 SD] *Fehrenbach subst.; Re-enter* HORMENUS, CORTES, *and* AQUINUS. *Gifford; Enter* Horm. *and* Cortes. Q/O

450

THE POLITICIAN   2.1

A chariot for my queen richer than e'er
Was shown in Roman triumph, and thou shalt
Be drawn with horses white as Venus' doves
Till heaven itself, in envy of our bliss,   170
Snatch thee from earth, to place thee in his orb
The brightest constellation.
CORTES [*To Hormenus and Aquinus*] He dotes strangely.
KING Hormenus, Cortes, I would have you all
  Search your inventions to advance new joys.
  Proclaim all pleasures free and while my fair   175
  Queen smiles it shall be death for any man
  I'the court to frown.   *Exeunt [King and Marpisa].*
HORMENUS You ha'not so much love i'the court, Aquinus.
CORTES How do you like the queen?
AQUINUS   Why, she's not married?
  He does but call her so –
HORMENUS   And lies with her.   180
AQUINUS The prince yet knows it not.
HORMENUS   He'll meet it coming home.

      Enter GOTHARUS.

GOTHARUS Aquinus?

166–72 I…constellation The king now shifts to an image of Marpisa as being ostentatiously displayed
rather than hidden; he promises her a triumphal chariot (appropriate given her victorious seduction of the king)
which modulates into that of the goddess of love, conventionally seen as drawn by white doves (hence the white
horses of the king's extravagant picture); heaven, envious of the newly-weds' bliss, then translates Marpisa into
a 'constellation'—a group of stars—which, fixed to the celestial sphere (or 'orb') carrying the stars, makes her
ultimately an object of a universal gaze; this trope, entirely appropriate in the classical tradition from which the
king draws many of his references, is, however, couched equally in less appropriate Christian referents; he speaks
of 'heaven' rather than 'the gods', of 'bliss' which suggests the perfect joys of paradise, and even the doves are
awkwardly reminiscent of the holy spirit, frequently represented in Christian iconography by that bird; once
again, he edges dangerously close to profanity in an ironically self-reflective speech which Shirley takes care to
contextualize for the audience with Cortes's concluding comment, 'He dotes strangely'.
  169 Venus' Venus's would be the normal modern English form of the possessive, but the single 's' of Q/O is
kept to retain the metre.
  172 He…strangely An appropriate comment given the bizarre juxtaposition of images in the king's
speeches.
  174 Search…inventions i.e. Rack your brains (*OED*, Invention *n*. 4).
  174 advance promote, bring forward (*OED*, *v*. 1, 7a).
  174 joys occasions of gladness, mirth (*OED*, Joy *n*. 1b and c).
  178 You…Aquinus i.e. I'll bet nobody here dotes on you so ridiculously.
  179–80 Why…so i.e. Surely he can't have married this woman—he's just calling her his queen.
  180 lies…her i.e. has sex with her, but possibly with a pun on 'lies'—tells her these ridiculous things to fool
her into thinking he loves and will be faithful to her. The marriage, being consummated, is real.
  181 meet it encounter the news (*OED*, Meet *v*. 2).

169 Venus'] *Gifford;* Venus Q/O   172 SD] *this edn;* [*to* Hormenus]. *Fehrenbach; not in* Q/O
177 SD] *Gifford subst.; Exeunt.* Q/O   181 SD] *Gifford subst.; after* Aquinus? Q/O

451

2.1 THE COMPLETE WORKS OF JAMES SHIRLEY, VOLUME 7

AQUINUS   Sir.

GOTHARUS   You brought letters from the camp.

AQUINUS I did, my lord.

HORMENUS [*To Cortes*] What in the name of policy is now hatching?
  I do not like those fawning postures in him,   185
  How kind they are.

[CORTES] [*To Hormenus*] That soldier is thought honest.

HORMENUS [*To Cortes*] But if he cringe once more I shall suspect him;
  That leg confirms he is corrupt already.

GOTHARUS How does he like his father's marriage?

AQUINUS We had no fame on't there when I set forth.   190

GOTHARUS 'Twas strange and sudden, but we are all happy
  In the good prince's health and victory.
  The duke Olaus, too, I hope is well.

AQUINUS He was designed at my departure
  To be here before the army.

GOTHARUS   He will be welcome.   195
  You shall accept the price of a new armour,

---

184 hatching being plotted (*OED*, Hatch *v.*¹ 5c).

185 fawning servile (*OED*, *adj.* 2); as Hormenus appears to be observing the politician's behaviour the 'him' in this line might be thought to refer to Gotharus; it most probably, however, refers to Aquinus as it is unlikely Gotharus would fawn on a mere soldier, and the 'if he cringe once more' (l. 187) clearly applies to Aquinus.

186 kind pleasant (*OED*, *adj.* 8a), but used ironically: Hormenus is expressing his belief that pleasantness in them cannot be genuine, and so cannot bode well.

187 cringe bows sycophantically.

188 leg gesture of submission, bow (*OED*, *n.* 4).

188 already either indicating that he doesn't need Gotharus to corrupt him, or possibly in the sense 'straight away' (an intensification of *OED*, *adv.* 1).

190 fame on't report or rumour concerning the matter (*OED*, Fame *n.*¹ 1a).

191–2 'Twas...victory The import and structure of Gotharus's statement here provide a good example of his politic modus operandi as he tries to soften up Aquinus for his use. The opening half line suggests that Gotharus is on the side of those who regard the king's marriage with some suspicion, though we know that he is, in fact, the prime mover behind the match; the 'but' that links to the second half of the line, and the import of the phrase itself ('we are all happy') would appear to confirm that—'yes, it was an odd business, but everybody here is putting a brave face on it'; however, that 'but' and following phrase actually link to the next line, which, taken all together, suggest that the prince's victory is some compensation for these unfortunate developments at court; the actor playing Gotharus could get this across by seeming to change his mind at the line break about the direction his first line appears to be taking, making the comment about the prince's victory a kind of second thought; the overall effect therefore gives the impression that Gotharus is (a) disturbed by the marriage but (b) has 'inadvertently' given away his 'true thoughts' on the matter to Aquinus; he thereby prepares the ground for a relationship of trust between himself and Aquinus by seeming to accidentally take the soldier into his confidence.

194 designed intended or designated (*OED*, *adj.* 2 and 1).

196 price...armour i.e. sum of money sufficiently large to buy a new suit of armour (*OED*, Price *n.* 8), but the word 'price' could also mean a gift of money to secure a favour or support (*OED*, *n.* 9) so Gotharus may also be indicating to Aquinus that he expects something in return for this suit of armour.

---

184 SD] *Fehrenbach subst.; not in* Q/O   **186 SH**] *Gifford subst.; Go.* Q/O
186 SD] *this edn; not in* Q/O   **187 SD**] *this edn; not in* Q/O

452

THE POLITICIAN   2.1

And wherein any power of mine can serve you
I'th'court, command.
AQUINUS   I am your lordship's creature.

> *Exeunt [Aquinus and Gotharus].*

HORMENUS They are gone. I long to see the prince.
How do you think his Highness will   200
Behave himself to his new mother queen?
Will it be treason not to ask her blessing?
CORTES I am confident his uncle, brave Olaus,

> *Enter* HARALDUS [*unseen by Cortes and Hormenus*].

Wo'not run mad for joy of the king's marriage.
HORMENUS Let them look to't – there may be alterations.   205
HARALDUS [*Aside*] They talk sure of my mother and the king.
HORMENUS Secure as they account themselves, the prince
Must be received spite of Marpisa's greatness
And all the tricks of her incarnate fiend
Gotharus, who both plot, I fear, to raise   210
That composition of their blood
Haraldus –
HARALDUS [*Aside*] How was that?

198 **I…creature** Aquinus's use of the word 'creature' with obvious irony at l. 100 of this scene should alert us to consider whether he is using the word ironically here as well; if he is, that in turn would suggest that he has seen through Gotharus's ploy to affiliate him.

201 **mother queen** the term inevitably calls to mind Hamlet's 'mother queen', Gertrude, and the dilemma he is faced with in needing to be respectful towards his mother whilst also needing to respect the memory of the father whom she has dishonoured.

202 To ask Marpisa's blessing would be a mark of filial respect from Turgesius acknowledging her status as his parent; Hormenus deliberately exaggerates the 'crime' of not according her this respect.

205 **look to't** take heed, beware (*OED*, To look to, PV2 4c in Look *v*.).

205 **alterations** i.e. changes that they won't like, for example, who is raised in rank and favour, but possibly also suggesting a disordered state of the body politic (*OED*, Alteration *n*. 1a and 2b).

206 **sure** undoubtedly (*OED*, *adv*. 1a).

207 **they** i.e. Gotharus and Marpisa.

207 **account** consider, regard (*OED*, *v*. 6).

208 **received** primarily, welcomed and treated in a properly friendly way, but possibly also accepted as the king's son and hence by Marpisa as her step-son (*OED*, Receive *v*. 7, 2a).

208 **spite of** (in) spite of.

208 **greatness** grandeur (sarcastic).

209 **incarnate** embodied in human flesh (*OED*, *adj*. 1a).

210 **raise** promote, advance to higher status (*OED*, *v.*[1] 17), but also, following on the idea of Gotharus as a devil, conjure by magic (*OED*, *v*. 22a).

211 **composition** product, combination (*OED*, *n*. 19).

198 SD] *Gifford subst.; Exeunt.* Q/O
203 SD] *this edn; Enter behind,* HARALDUS. *Gifford; Enter* Haraldus. Q/O
206 SD] *this edn; not in* Q/O   212 SD] *this edn; not in* Q/O

453

2.1   THE COMPLETE WORKS OF JAMES SHIRLEY, VOLUME 7

HORMENUS   – the strange effect
Of their luxurious appetites. Though in him,
Poor innocence, suspecting not their sin,
We read no such ambition.

HARALDUS [*Aside*]   Oh, my shame!   215
What have my ears received? Am I a bastard?
'Tis malice that doth wound my mother's honour.
How many bleed at once? Yet now I call
To memory, Gotharus at our loving
Late conference did much insult upon   220
The name of a father and his care of me
By some strange force of nature. Ha! My fears
Shoot an ice through me. I must know the truth
Although it kill me.   *Exit.*

CORTES   Who was that – Haraldus?

HORMENUS I hope he did not hear us. Again Gotharus   225
And the two squirrels! More devices yet.

   Enter GOTHARUS, SUENO, *and* HELGA.

SUENO Let us alone, my lord – we'll quicken him.

GOTHARUS You must use all your art to win him to't.

HELGA Let us alone to make him drink, we are the credit
Of the court for that. He's but a child, alas: we'll take our time. 230

---

213 **luxurious** lecherous (*OED*, *adj.* 1).
214 **innocence** i.e. innocent person.
215 **read** perceive, discern (*OED*, *v.* 15).
216 **received** taken in, i.e. heard (*OED*, Receive *v.* 9c).
217 **malice** The word is perhaps used with the additional force of personification.
218 **How...once** i.e. How many suffer at this one stroke (at my mother's honour) (*OED*, At once *adv.* 10).
219–20 **loving...conference** recent affectionate conversation (*OED*, Loving *adj.* 2; Late *adj.*¹ 12; Conference *n.* 4). For the conversation Haraldus is referring to see 1.1.204–78.
220 **insult upon** exult in a proud or triumphant manner (*OED*, Insult *v.* 1); the term usually carried with it a sense of insolence or scorn prompting the exultation, and that sense may be absent from Haraldus's meaning here but present in Shirley's. Haraldus is referring to ll. 231–9 of his conversation with Gotharus in 1.1.
221–2 **his...nature** cf. Gotharus's lines at 1.1.232–4: 'I was from thy nativity inclined / By a most strange and secret force of nature / Or sympathy to love thee like my own.'
223 **Shoot...me** i.e. Chill me to the marrow.
226 **squirrels** The image is possibly based on Sueno and Helga's ability to adapt quickly to any situation in the court (see Tilley S797 for the proverbial nimbleness of the squirrel); there is also, perhaps, a hint at this animal's reputation for furtively hiding away what it has gathered. Compare *The Gentleman of Venice*, 3.4.17, where Malipiero refers to his drinking companions (though more companionably) as squirrels.
226 **devices** schemes, plots (*OED*, Device *n.* 6).
227 **Let...alone** i.e. Leave it to us.
227 **quicken** animate, invigorate (*OED*, *v.*¹ 1, 2).
228 **win...to't** prevail on him, overcome his reluctance (*OED*, Win *v.*¹ 9b).
229–30 **we...that** i.e. we have the best reputation in the court when it comes to drinking.

---

215 SD] *this edn; not in* Q/O

454

THE POLITICIAN   2.1

Enter OLAUS *attended with* CAPTAINS.

OLAUS Hormenus!
HORMENUS   My good lord Olaus, I
Joy in your safe return. How fares the prince?
OLAUS Well. Where's the king?
HORMENUS Kissing his new-made queen Marpisa.
OLAUS   Ha!
The king is married then.
GOTHARUS [*To Sueno and Helga*] Away!   *Exeunt Sueno and Helga.*
                        The Duke Olaus! Sir –   235
OLAUS I am too stiff for compliment,
My lord. I have rid hard –   *Exeunt [Olaus, Hormenus, Cortes, and captains].*
GOTHARUS   He has met the intelligence
And is displeased with the state of things at home.
This marriage stings him; let it. We must have
No trembling hearts, not fall into an ague   240
Like children at the sight of a portent,
But like a rock when wind and waves go highest
And the insulting billows dash against
Her ribs, be unmoved. The king must be saluted
With other letters which must counterfeit   245
The prince's character. I was his secretary
And know the art. Malice inspire my brain
To poison his opinion of his son.

---

236 stiff i.e. in the limbs from riding, but with also the underlying sense that Olaus is formal and lacks the
courtier's ease and any patience with Gotharus (*OED, adj.* 9).
236 compliment the observance of courteous ceremonies such as bowing (*OED, n.* 1a).
237 met found out, learnt.
237 intelligence news (*OED, n.* 6a).
238 home i.e. his native land (*OED, n.*¹ 5).
239 stings annoys or irritates intensely (*OED*, Sting *v.*¹ 5).
240 ague a bout of distress or fear (*OED, n.* 2).
241 portent an omen of a calamitous or terrifying event (*OED, n.* 1).
243 insulting as at l. 220, exulting in an insolent and scornful manner.
244 unmoved in both the physical and the emotional senses (the conclusion of a pathetic fallacy in which the
rock is 'insulted' by a raging sea which it confronts by baring its 'ribbed' chest).
244 saluted presented, possibly also with some sense of assailed (*OED*, Salute *v.* 2f and g).
246 character Gotharus primarily has in mind the prince's handwriting (*OED, n.* 4b) which he can imitate
having once been, as he says, the prince's secretary, but he also intends to falsely represent Turgesius's personality (*OED, n.* 9) to the king.
247 know...art i.e. have the ability to do that.
247 Malice...brain Either malice is personified, in which case that word is a vocative, or there is an ellipsis
of 'may' after 'Malice'.

---

235 SD1] *Fehrenbach subst.; not in* Q/O
235 SD2] *Gifford subst.; Exit Su. & Ho. after* married then. Q/O   **237 SD**] *Fehrenbach subst.; Exit.* Q/O

455

2.1   THE COMPLETE WORKS OF JAMES SHIRLEY, VOLUME 7

I'll form it cunningly. Ha! 'Tis Haraldus.

    Enter HARALDUS.

He looks sad.

HARALDUS [*Aside*] I dare not ask   250
My mother. 'Twere a crime but one degree
Beneath the sinful act that gave me life
To question her. And yet to have this fright
Dwell in my apprehension without
The knowledge of some truth must needs distract   255
My poor wits quite. [*He notices Gotharus.*] 'Tis he. I will take boldness
And know the worst of him. If I be what
I am already charactered, he can
Resolve my shame too well.

GOTHARUS   How is't my lord?

HARALDUS Never so ill, sir.

GOTHARUS   Art sick?

HARALDUS   Most dangerously.   260

GOTHARUS Where?

HARALDUS   Here, at heart, which bleeds with such a wound
As none but you can cure.

GOTHARUS   I'll drop my soul
Into it. Show me how I may
Be thy physician. To restore thy blood
I will lose all mine. Speak child.

---

249 it i.e. the letter, unless 'it' refers to the king's 'opinion of his son' which Gotharus intends to 'form [...] cunningly', i.e. manipulate to his own advantage.

250 sad serious, as well as in the usual modern sense.

251 crime...degree Haraldus is, as Hormenus did at l. 202, inflating the idea of filial disrespect. There was in law a concept of relative measures of criminality (*OED*, Degree *n*. 6d) but that was within specified offences rather than in the sense of ranking different crimes against one another, and the sense is illustrated in *OED* only from 1676.

252 sinful...life i.e. adultery rather than merely fornication, as the former involved the breaking of the seventh commandment.

254 Dwell Linger (*OED*, *v.* 5).

254 apprehension possibly simply the understanding (*OED*, *n.* 8) but it could also mean here fearful anticipation (*OED*, *n.* 11, 12).

255 knowledge...truth i.e. learning the truth of the matter.

256 boldness courage (*OED*, *n.* 1a).

258 charactered said or reputed to be (*OED*, Character *v.* 4).

259 Resolve Satisfy me regarding the question of (*OED*, *v.* 17a); convince me of (*OED*, *v.* 22a).

262 drop...soul Gotharus is offering his soul as medicine which he will drop like an ointment into Haraldus's heart (*OED*, Drop *v.* 13a).

264 restore reinvigorate, bring back to a state of health (*OED*, *v.*¹ 7a, b).

249] *lineation Fehrenbach;* cunningly. / Ha! Q/O

249 SD] Q/O *subst.; after* cunningly. *Fehrenbach; Re-enter* HARALDUS. *after* cunningly.– *Gifford*

250 SD] *Fehrenbach subst.; not in* Q/O   **256 SD]** *this edn;* [*Discovering* Gotharus.] *Fehrenbach; not in* Q/O

THE POLITICIAN   2.1

HARALDUS   This very love   265
  Is a fresh suffering and your readiness
  To cure my sorrow is another wound.
  You are too kind. Why are you so? What is
  Or can be thought in me fit to deserve it?

GOTHARUS Thou dost talk wildly to accuse me thus   270
  For loving thee. Could the world tempt me here
  And court me with her glories to forsake thee
  Thus I would dwell about thy neck and not
  Be bought from kissing thee for all her provinces.
  There is a charm upon my soul to love thee   275
  And I must do't.

HARALDUS   Then I must die.

GOTHARUS Forbid it gentler fates.

HARALDUS   If I could hear you wish
  Me dead I should have hope to live. Although
  I would not willingly deserve your anger
  By any impious deed, you do not know   280
  What comfort it would be to hear you curse me.

GOTHARUS [*Aside*] He's mad. [*To Haraldus*] Haraldus, prithee do not talk so.

HARALDUS Or if you think a curse too much to help me,
  Yet rail upon me, but do't heartily and call me –

GOTHARUS   What?

HARALDUS Villain, or bastard, sir – the worst is best from you.   285

265–7 This…wound Haraldus could be saying, 'it is precisely this love you express and your desire to help that hurts me more than ever'; but the word 'very' here could mean true, genuine (*OED*, *adj.* 1), or indicate the extremity of the degree of love shown by Gotharus (*OED*, *adj.* 8a).

271 here possibly indicating his heart.

272 court entice, allure (*OED*, *v.* 5), but the word is interesting coming from the mouth of such an adept resident of the court as Gotharus.

273–4 dwell…kissing such demonstrative physical affection between men would not have been unusual at this period.

274 bought from bribed (*OED*, Buy *v.* 5).

275 charm spell (*OED*, *n.*¹ 1a).

280 impious i.e. profane rather than criminal; entrapped by the belief that Gotharus is his father, Haraldus is possibly thinking again of the religious requirement that a child love and respect its parents.

284 rail upon abuse (*OED*, Rail *v.*⁵ 1a).

285 bastard strictly speaking a child born out of wedlock (*OED*, *n.* 1a) and since Gotharus and Marpisa were not married to one another Haraldus is taking 'out of wedlock' in the strictest sense. Contemporary law, however, was not so strict: since his mother was married at the time of his birth to Count Altomarus and they were neither judicially separated 'from bed and board' (as would appear from the information about their marriage) nor in two completely different countries at the time conception would have taken place, Haraldus, were he to have been Gotharus's child, could still have passed as legitimate. Richard Burn (1763, I.86) cites Edward Coke's *Institutes*: 'Lord Coke says, By the common law, if the husband be within the four seas, that is, within the jurisdiction of the king of England, if the wife hath issue, no proof is to be admitted to prove the child a bastard,

---

282 SD1] *Fehrenbach subst.; not in* Q/O   **282 SD2**] *this edn; not in* Q/O
285] *lineation this edn;* sir, / The Q/O

457

2.1 THE COMPLETE WORKS OF JAMES SHIRLEY, VOLUME 7

GOTHARUS Thou dost amaze me.

HARALDUS   Will you not for me?
  Then for my mother's sake, if you do love her
  Or ever did esteem her worth your friendship,
  Let me entreat you draw your sword and give me
  Something to wear in blood upon my bosom.   290
  Write but one letter of your name upon
  My breast I'll call you father by your love.
  Do something that may make me bleed a little.

GOTHARUS By that I dare not. Thou hast named, Haraldus,
  A father.

HARALDUS I but call you so. I know   295
  You are a stranger to my blood although
  Indeed to me your great affection
  Appears a wonder, nor can nature show
  More in a parent to a child. But if
  I be —

GOTHARUS What?

HARALDUS   I shall blush, sir, to pronounce it.   300
  There's something that concerns my mother will not
  Give it a name, yet I would be resolved
  That I might place my duty right. If I
  Must answer to your son you may imagine

unless the husband hath an apparent impossibility of procreation; as if the husband be [...] under the age of procreation, such issue is bastard, albeit he be born within marriage. But if the issue be born within a month or a day after marriage, between parties of full lawful age, the child is legitimate.' We are indebted to Martin Ingram for this note and the references. See also l. 309 of this scene.

290 Something...bosom The more usual ordering would be 'something in blood to wear upon my bosom'; Haraldus has in mind a kind of badge of dishonour such as the brand that criminals might have had inflicted upon them; a similar punishment was imposed on a woman taken in bed with a priest; she was paraded through the city bearing 'on her brest a letter of H. of yelowe wollen clothe in sygne and tokyn of a harlett and on her left shulder a picture of a woman in a preest goun' (Ingram 2017, 261); Haraldus, of course, chooses to ignore the fact that such punishments would have been more appropriate for his mother.

292 by because of, in consequence of (*OED, prep.* 36a), also in l. 294.

294 named either designated (me father) or uttered (the word 'father') (*OED*, Name *v.* 3a, 6b).

295 but merely (*OED, adv.* 2a).

296 stranger...blood person not kin to me (*OED*, Stranger *n.* 6).

298–9 nor...child i.e. there could be no better example of the natural bond of affection between parent and child. Bonds between parents and children were seen as determined by nature, and their breakdown, when it occurred, was seen as contrary to nature and hence 'unnatural'.

301 something...mother The 'concern' is that by naming himself a bastard Haraldus would automatically impugn his mother's honour.

303 place...right i.e. determine correctly where my duty (as a son) lies.

304 answer to i.e. answer to the name of, have the name of (*OED*, Answer *v.* 7).

---

292 father by your love.] *this edn;* father. By your love, *Gifford;* father, by your love; Q/O

458

THE POLITICIAN   2.1

I shall no more ask you a reason why   305
You have been so kind to me and to my mother.
GOTHARUS Thou hast said it: th'art mine own. 'Twas nature in me
That could not hide the actions of a father.
HARALDUS I am your base seed then.
GOTHARUS   Stain not thyself
With such a name, but look upon thy mother   310
Now made a queen.
HARALDUS   You made her first a strumpet,
And it would ask the piety of her son
To die upon that man that stole her honour.
Why did you so undo us? Why did you
Betray my mother to this shame? Or when   315
She had consented why should both your lusts
Curse my unsinning heart? Oh, I must be
For your vice scorned, though innocent.
GOTHARUS   None dare –
HARALDUS I should not by your virtue have been saved.
Where shall I hide my life? I must no more   320
Converse with men –
GOTHARUS   Thou art too passionate.
HARALDUS I will entreat my mother we may go
Into some wilderness where we may find
Some creatures that are spotted like ourselves
And live and die there, be companion   325
To the wild panther and the leopard. Yet

---

307 'Twas…me Again Gotharus appeals to the concept that nature determines relations between parent and child.

309 base seed illegitimate offspring (*OED*, Base *adj.* 6b; Seed *n.* 4); 'seed', however, has a more graphic application—semen (*OED*, *n.* 3)—which would be entirely in accord with Haraldus's horrified disgust at discovering what he now believes to be his true parentage.

312 ask be required from, be expected of (*OED*, *v.* 12b).

313 To…honour i.e. Take revenge on the man responsible for my mother's seduction; his self-image is so negative, though, that the person who dies in this imagined scenario is Haraldus rather than his enemy.

314 undo destroy, ruin, with a strong sense of the ruin being moral (*OED*, *v.* 8).

315 Betray (a) Expose, give up to by acting falsely; (b) lead astray, seduce (*OED*, *v.* 1b and 2; 4a).

319 I…saved i.e. Your ability and strength would not save me (from this disgrace). The tenses of the exchange, though, are odd: Gotharus's 'None dare' implies that he is thinking of any future effect on Haraldus, whose reply in the conditional 'I should not' seems to acknowledge that, but he then switches with 'have been saved' to the past, perhaps suggesting that it is now too late for Gotharus to protect him.

320 Where…life? i.e. Where shall I hide whilst I live?

324 spotted with regard to the animals, having a pattern of spots on their fur (though strictly speaking this applies only to the leopard), but with regard to himself and his mother, morally blemished (*OED*, *adj.* 1 and 3); Haraldus plays explicitly on the ambiguity in ll. 327–8.

---

316 lusts] *Gifford;* lust Q/O

3.1 THE COMPLETE WORKS OF JAMES SHIRLEY, VOLUME 7

They are too good for their converse; we are
By ours defiled – their spots do make them fair. *Exit.*

GOTHARUS 'Tis time that Sueno and his companion
Dispersed these clouds. Now to the king, with whom, 330
If the queen's beauty keep her magic, then
Our engines mount and day grows bright again. *Exit.*

3[.1]

Enter KING, QUEEN [MARPISA], OLAUS, REGINALDUS, AQUINUS,
HELGA [*and* SUENO].

KING Uncle, I am glad to see you.

OLAUS   I am not glad
To see you, sir.

KING   Not me?

OLAUS   Consorted thus.

KING If Olaus be forgetful of good manners
I shall forget his years and blood. Be temperate.

OLAUS There's something in your blood that will undo 5
Your state and fame eternally – purge that.

---

327 their converse that which is their opposite in the moral sense of 'spotted'—i.e. us (*OED*, Converse, *n.*³ 1b, though the earliest illustration for such a sense is 1786). Gifford and Fehrenbach's emendation of 'their' to 'our' to give the sense 'our conversation' is not necessary.

332 engines plots, machinations (*OED*, Engine *n.* 2).

332 mount prosper, rise in power, increase in strength (*OED*, *v.* 1b, 19a) with a glance at the idea of mounting a partner in order to have sexual intercourse (*OED*, *v.* 14), one of the aims of Gotharus's machinations.

332 day...again compare Richard of Gloucester's paean on the ascendancy of the House of York following their military success at Tewkesbury: 'Now is the winter of our discontent / Made glorious summer by this son of York' (*Richard III*, 1.1.1–2).

2 Consorted Married; given the sexual suggestion of 'consort' (see note to 2.1.7–8), Olaus is offering a fairly flagrant insult.

4 blood aristocratic birth (*OED*, *n.* 9a); possibly also his blood relationship to the king (*OED*, *n.* 8a).

4 temperate moderate, restrained (*OED*, *adj.* 1a).

5 your blood 'emotional disposition' shifting into 'passion, ardour' and also implying 'base or fleshly appetites' (*OED*, Blood *n.* 11, 12, 13).

6 state primarily the king's status as a ruler of a country, but also the country itself, and possibly the pomp and splendour associated with the position of a monarch (*OED*, *n.* 15, III, 16); the word also had specific medical applications and could refer to his personal health (including mental and emotional well-being) or to the point at which the symptoms of a disease were most severe (*OED*, *n.* 1b, 2a, and 9), meanings that could be linked with the following word 'purge'.

6 fame reputation, honour (*OED*, *n.*¹ 3a).

6 purge in the medical sense, expel harmful material from the body to restore health (*OED*, *v.*¹ 2d); also, to clear a person of moral defilement (3a, 4a); Shirley may additionally have had in mind a legal sense, to annul or atone for an offence (sense 6).

---

327 their converse;] Q/O *susbst.;* our converse. *Fehrenbach;* [our] converse. *Gifford*
332 SD] *Gifford subst.; Exeunt.* Q/O

3[.1]] *Gifford subst.* (ACT III. SCENE I.*); [III.i] *Fehrenbach*; Act. 3. Q/O
0 SD] *Fehrenbach subst.;* Enter K*ing, Queene, Olaus, Reginaldus, Aquinus, Helga.* Q/O

THE POLITICIAN   3.1

You know I never flattered you. That woman
Will prove thy evil genius.

KING   You're too saucy.

OLAUS Do not I know her? Was she not wife
To the Count Altomarus, a weak lord,   10
But too good for her, charmed by the flattery
And magic of her face and tongue to dote
And marry her. Born of a private family,
Advanced thus she grew insolent, and I fear
By pride and liberty and some trick she had   15
Broke her good husband's heart.

MARPISA   Sir, you much wrong me,
And now exceed the privilege of your birth
To injure mine.

OLAUS   We all know you can plead
Your own defence: you have a woman's wit.
Heaven send you equal modesty. I am plain.   20

MARPISA It would be held an insolence in others
And saucy boldness in the sacred presence
Thus of the king, to accuse whom he hath pleased
To take companion of his bed. And though

---

8 evil genius a malevolent spirit, one of a pair supposed to govern people's lives and influence them for good or ill (*OED*, Genius *n*. 2).

8 saucy impertinent, especially toward one's superiors (*OED*, *adj.*[1] 2a); the word had a much stronger force than it has now.

11–12 flattery…tongue The fact that the seductive capabilities of Marpisa's face and tongue are not respectively ordered possibly indicates Olaus's agitated state of mind.

12 dote The word could also mean to endow with riches and dignities (*OED*, *v.*[3]) but that sense was possibly obsolete by the time *The Politician* was written.

13 private family one without position in the world (*OED*, Private *adj.*[1] C2).

14 Advanced See note to 'The Names and Small Characters of the Persons', 24.

15 liberty sexually unrestrained behaviour (see *OED*, *n.*[1] 5).

15 trick ostensibly a particular and habitual way of behaving so as to deceive (*OED*, *n.* 1a, 7), but the word, as Williams (1994) notes, referred to the act of coition along with a range of other sexual activities, and Olaus, following on from his comment on Marpisa's 'liberty', clearly has that meaning in mind here.

18–19 you…wit i.e. you are sufficiently skilled in subtle argument not to need a lawyer to put your case. Marpisa's nineteen-line response (ll. 21–39) enthusiastically takes up Olaus's challenge.

20 modesty the ability to behave with sexual propriety as well as with reserve and humility (*OED*, *n.* 2 and 3).

22 boldness impudence (*OED*, *adj.* 2).

22–3 in…king The more usual order would be: 'thus in the sacred presence / Of the king'.

22 sacred frequently used as an epithet of royalty, possibly literally (as being ordained by God to rule) but possibly figuratively (as being entitled to the same reverence as is accorded to holy things) (*OED*, *adj.* 4).

24 take willingly accept as (*OED*, *v.* 23), possibly with a glance at the sense, possess sexually (*OED*, *v.* 43).

24–39 And…profession In this speech Marpisa constantly switches between referring to Olaus in the second and the third person, and between addressing both him and the king with the second person pronoun 'you'. The order is as follows: 'the author' (l. 27), 'his' (l. 29)—third person, Olaus; 'you're' (l. 31), 'you' (l. 32)—second person, Olaus; 'you' (l. 34)—second person, king; 'him' (l. 35)—third person, Olaus; 'you' (l. 36)—second person, Olaus; 'his' (l. 38)—third person, Olaus; 'your' (l. 39)—second person, Olaus. One might

461

3.1 THE COMPLETE WORKS OF JAMES SHIRLEY, VOLUME 7

It would become the justice of my cause   25
And honour to desire these black aspersions
May be examined further and the author
Called to make proof of such a passionate language
(Which will betray his accusation was
But envy of my fortunes) I remember   30
You're the king's uncle and 'tis possible
You may be abused by some malicious tale
Framed to dishonour me. And therefore I
Beseech you humbly, sir, to let this pass
But as an act in him of honest freedom –   35
Beside what else may give you privilege,
Being a soldier and not used to file
His language, blunt and rugged ways of speech
Becoming your profession.
OLAUS   Very good!
Although we ha'not the device of tongue   40
And soft phrase, madam, which you make an idol
At court and use it to disguise your heart,

wonder if this confusion is a consequence of—and hence indicative of—her agitation, but the elaborate and perfectly constructed ten-line sentence that runs from ll. 24 to 33 rather belies such an explanation. Certainly
Marpisa is excited, but not to the extent of her losing the ability to express herself; it may be, therefore, that this
excitement is indicated by her turning her attention alternately through this speech from Olaus to the king and
addressing them directly in turn, much as a prosecuting barrister might alternate between addressing the accused
in the dock and the judge on the bench for rhetorical effect during a trial, an idea that would be reinforced by the
weight of legal vocabulary in this speech (e.g. 'justice...aspersions...examined...make proof...accusation',
etc.). The editors of this edition do not consider Gifford's changes to the pronouns in ll. 36 and 39 to be necessary.
25 become befit, be proper for (*OED*, *v.* 8b). The word is attached to 'honour' (l. 26) as well as 'the justice of
my cause'.
26 aspersions false and unjust imputations that tarnish reputation (*OED*, Aspersion *n.* 6).
27 author inventor or instigator (*OED*, *n.* 4a, d).
29 betray reveal, against the person's will, the true nature of (*OED*, *v.* 6).
32 abused deceived (*OED*, Abuse *v.* 3b).
33 Framed Invented, fabricated (*OED*, Frame *v.* 6a).
35 honest done with good intentions even if misguided, not deserving of reproach (*OED*, *adj.* 4a, 1c).
35 freedom frankness, outspokenness, with the implication here of overstepping customary boundaries
(*OED*, *n.* 8a, b).
36 privilege i.e. the right to speak as you do; Marpisa may be including in this right that which comes with
the prerogative of rank (*OED*, *n.* 2b).
37 file polish, make smooth and elaborate (*OED*, *v.*¹ 1b).
38 rugged unsophisticated; perhaps also severe (*OED*, *adj.*¹ 5, 3).
39 Becoming See note to l. 25.
40 device...tongue i.e. ingenuity in using language.
41 soft phrase ingratiating or bland manner of expression (*OED*, Soft, *adj.* 19b; Phrase *n.* 1).
42 disguise...heart The heart was considered to be the seat not just of the emotions, but also of a person's
deepest feelings, will, temperament, and conscience (*OED*, Heart *n.* 9, 6, 7, 8, 13), all of which is comprehended
in Olaus's use of the word here. The fear that people should conceal this behind a show of false seeming is frequently expressed in the drama of the period: compare Iago's 'when my outward action doth demonstrate / The
native act and figure of my heart / ... 'tis not long after / But I will wear my heart upon my sleeve / For daws to
peck at' (*Othello*, 1.1.61–5).

462

THE POLITICIAN   3.1

We can speak truth in our unpolished words.
Thou art –
MARPISA   What am I?
OLAUS   Not the queen.
KING   She is
My wife, Olaus.
OLAUS   I must never kneel to her.   45
Nor the good prince, your son – the hope of war
And peace's darling, honour of our blood,
And worth a better kingdom than he's born to –
KING What of him?
OLAUS Must never call her mother.
KING   Dare you instruct him   50
Against his duty? Leave us.
OLAUS   You have lost
More honour in those minutes you were married
Than we have gained in months abroad with all
Our triumph purchased for you with our blood.
Is this the payment, the reward for all   55
Our faith? When thy young son, whose springing valour
And name already makes the confines tremble,
Returns like young Augustus crowned with victories,
Must a stepdame first salute him
And tread upon his laurel?

---

46 hope person on whom hopes are centred, who gives hope or promise for the future—in this case as a military leader (*OED, n.*[1] 4b).

47 darling favourite (*OED, n.*[1] 1b).

47 blood i.e. family.

51 Against…duty For the duty of children to their parents see notes to 2.1.201 and 202.

54 triumph victories (*OED, n.* 2a).

56 faith fidelity, loyalty (*OED, n.* 1a).

56 springing youthful, developing (*OED, adj.* 1c, d).

57 makes Gifford and Fehrenbach emend to 'make' but Shirley's grammar is perfectly reasonable: the adjective 'springing' attaches easily to both 'valour' and 'name' making the phrase 'springing valour / And name' a composite singular.

57 confines lands bordering our frontiers (*OED*, Confine *n.*[2] 1a).

57 tremble regard us with fear (*OED, v.* 1b).

58 Augustus Referenced here as the type of the great military commander. After the murder in 44 BCE of his adoptive father Julius Caesar and following a lengthy civil war, Gaius Octavianus (63 BCE–14 CE) took control of Rome and had himself declared Emperor; he was given the title Augustus ('venerable') by the senate and on his death he was deified. He was credited by many, including most of the great literary figures of the day, with reinstituting the ancient Roman virtues of hard work and the simple life, and presiding over a period of peace and cultural achievement at home whilst expanding the Roman Empire abroad—an activity which consolidated his reputation as a soldier. See also note to 3.1.156.

59 stepdame stepmother (*OED, n.* a); the term may have been chosen for what would appear to be its negative connotations, a marked feature of every illustration given by *OED*.

60 tread upon trample on so as to destroy (*OED*, Tread *v.* 5).

60 laurel i.e. laurel wreath of victory.

463

3.1   THE COMPLETE WORKS OF JAMES SHIRLEY, VOLUME 7

KING   Leave the court.   60

OLAUS May it not prove an hospital; 'tis i'th'way
   To change a title, lust and all the riots
   Of licence reeling in it by th'example
   Of one should least profane it. I am still
   Olaus and your father's brother.

AQUINUS [*To Olaus*]   My lord!

KING   Take heed   65
   You do not talk your head off – we have scaffolds.
   But the old man raves. Come my Marpisa.

OLAUS Then I will talk. Threaten my head,
   Command that parasite that dares do most
   In wickedness to show himself your servant;   70
   Give him his engine and his fee for hangman;
   Let him take boldness but to move one hair
   That withers on my head out of his posture –
   He shall have more hope to o'ercome the devil
   In single duel than to 'scape my fury.   75

61 **hospital** Originally signifying simply a lodging place for travellers such as pilgrims, the word became increasingly associated with charitable institutions for the care of the destitute, infirm, and, most famously perhaps, through the Bethlehem Hospital (Bedlam) in London, the insane. Though *OED* does not specify such a function in any of its definitions this is probably the kind of 'hospital' Olaus has in mind, since he goes on to elaborate in the following three lines the kind of inmate this 'court hospital' is likely to maintain—that is, those whose loss of a moral compass has led them into madness (immorality and madness being strongly linked in early modern psychological theory). *OED* does, however, give (*n.* 4): 'a house of entertainment; "open house"', the illustrations strongly suggesting that a brothel is the usual import of this usage, and Olaus may well be hinting at that meaning as well.

62 **title** possibly simply the name 'court', but it could also mean that which justifies a claim or right to something (in this case the court as the exemplary institution in the country) (*OED*, *n.* 12).

62 **riots** extravagant and dissipated displays (*OED*, Riot *n.* 3).

63 **licence** unrestrained liberty, disregard of propriety, especially with regard to sexual conduct (*OED*, *n.* 3b).

63 **reeling** whirling or rushing about in a wild and unruly manner with implications that this is under the influence of alcohol (*OED*, Reel *v.*[1] 2a, 3b, 8); perhaps also with a glance at the lively dance of that name (*OED*, Reel *n.*[3] 1), that being the kind of activity that moralists considered would lead to promiscuity, and possibly even at the sense of becoming unwound (*v.*[2] 1c) in a moral sense.

64 **should** (who) should.

64 **profane** desecrate by treating with disrespect or irreverence (*OED*, *v.* 1a).

66 **You...off** i.e. You don't say something treasonable and so be beheaded; there may also be a play on the idea of talking too much.

70 **show...servant** i.e. demonstrate to you that he is a loyal servant.

71 **engine** instrument of execution or torture—in this instance (as Olaus goes on to suggest that his executioner will be a hangman) a gibbet and, as hanging was a form of capital punishment restricted to the lower classes, Olaus thus chooses to interpret the king's threat of execution as especially offensive (*OED*, *n.* 4b).

72 **take boldness** take the liberty (*OED*, Boldness *n.* 1b).

73 **his posture** its position (*OED*, Posture *n.* 2a).

65 SD] *Fehrenbach subst.; not in* Q/O

464

THE POLITICIAN   3.1

AQUINUS [*To Olaus*] Sir –
KING   Our guard!
        [*Enter* SOLDIERS.]
OLAUS Look you, I'll bring no danger to your person;
    I love you too well. I did always use
    To speak; your father liked me ne'er the worse,
    And now I am cool again.   80
    You say you are married –
KING   We are.
OLAUS Then between you and I (and let none hear us)
    [*He whispers to the king.*] To make yourself, your son, and kingdom prosper,
    Be counselled to a divorce.
KING   Not, not
    To save thy soul. My son's life added   85
    To thine and lives of all the army shall
    Be divorced from this world first. You are my father's
    Brother and if you love my son, your pupil,
    So hopeful in your thoughts, teach him to come
    More humbly to us without thought to question   90
    Our marriage, or I'll find a chastisement
    For his rebellious heart. We will!   *Exeunt* [*King, Marpisa, and soldiers*].
OLAUS You must not. I wo'not leave him yet.   *Exit.*

---

78 did…use was always wont, in the habit of (*OED*, Use *v.* 22).
84 divorce As in the modern sense of the word, Olaus means a legal dissolution of the king's marriage to Marpisa, but at this date the word had a stricter sense and more serious implications for the separated couple. Such a dissolution could be only *divortium a mensa et thoro*—merely a separation from bed and board; it would not allow either partner to remarry as their union was initially legally valid and hence remarriage would constitute bigamy. If the union was within the prohibited degrees of kinship, or had not been physically consummated (as, respectively, was argued in the cases of Catherine of Aragon's marriage to Henry VIII and to his brother Arthur) it could then be *annulled*—that is, declared initially invalid—following which remarriage was lawful because effectively no marriage had originally taken place (see Rickman 2008, 17–18); the word thus reveals that part of Olaus's stratagem here is to remove an obstacle to Turgesius's succession to the throne.
84 Not, not the repetition is possibly emphatic, but it could be that the king is stuttering with rage; Fehrenbach emends to 'No, not'.
86 lives…army i.e. the life of every soldier in the army.
87 divorced here, forcibly separated from (*OED*, Divorce *v.* 4a).
89 hopeful promising (*OED*, *adj.* 2a).
93 I…yet The precise meaning of 'leave' in this phrase depends on who is meant by 'him'; if that is Turgesius, Olaus would be declaring his determination not to desert, or renounce his adherence to the prince (*OED*, Leave *v.*¹ 10); if it is the king, Olaus would be declaring his intention to pursue him and continue berating him on this matter (*OED*, *v.*¹ 13).

---

76 SD1] *Fehrenbach subst.; not in* Q/O   **76 SD2**] *Fehrenbach subst.; not in* Q/O
79 ne'er] *Gifford;* near Q/O   **83 SD**] *this edn; [aside to the king]. before* Then between *Fehrenbach; not in* Q/O
92 SD] *Fehrenbach subst.; Exit.* Q/O

3.1   THE COMPLETE WORKS OF JAMES SHIRLEY, VOLUME 7

REGINALDUS This freedom may engage his life to danger.

　　He is too passionate.

AQUINUS　　　　　　　He has said too much.　　　　　　　95

　　I'll venture speaking to him.　　　　　　　　　　　　*Exit.*

HELGA [*Aside to Sueno*] He's alone, now to him.

SUENO Noble sir, I have a suit to you.

REGINALDUS A courtier ask a suit of a soldier?

　　You'll wear no buff nor iron!　　　　　　　　　　　100

SUENO I come very impudently and I hope to thrive

　　The better for't. This gentleman, my friend,

　　A man of quality and in some grace with

　　The king, hath laid a wager with me of

　　Two hundred crowns I dare not pull a hair　　　　105

　　From your most reverend beard. Now if you please

　　To give me leave I'll win the crowns, laugh at him,

　　And drink your health at supper.

REGINALDUS　　　　　　　A hair from my beard?

SUENO But one hair, if shall please you.

REGINALDUS　　　　　　Come, take it.

　　　　　　[*Sueno plucks his beard.*]

SUENO I have pulled three, noble sir.　　　　　　　110

REGINALDUS 'Twas more than your commission. There's one, (*kicks him*)

---

94 freedom probably here undue openness in expressing an opinion, overstepping the bounds of decorum (*OED*, *n*. 8b), but it could include such ideas as enthusiasm (*OED*, *n*. 6) and nobility in behaviour (*OED*, *n*. 2).

94 engage expose (*OED*, *v*. 2), but perhaps with a glance at the military sense, to engage the enemy (*OED*, *v*. 18).

95 passionate see 2.1.139, where the word is also applied to Olaus.

97 to him i.e. approach him. Apparently Helga and Sueno talk privately to one another during this scene (they have played no direct part in the action so far) and in the course of their conversation make the wager referred to by Sueno in ll. 102–6; the episode that follows is presumably intended as a comic prefiguring of the quarrel between Olaus and Aquinus that occurs immediately afterwards, thereby dramatically highlighting the second, much more serious altercation; compare *Macbeth* 2.3, where the drunken porter, clearly incapable of carrying out his duty of overseeing access to the castle properly, comically parallels the state of the two chamberlains who, having been made drunk by Lady Macbeth, are rendered unable to control access to King Duncan.

98 suit Sueno means a request or entreaty (*OED*, *n*. 11a), but Reginaldus picks up and puns on the sense relating to clothing (see next note).

100 buff…iron military coat made of stout leather (*OED*, Buff *n*.² 2b), and a suit of armour.

103 in…grace in favour (*OED*, Grace *n*. 7).

105–6 pull…beard pulling a man's beard would normally be an extremely insulting gesture, especially to a soldier such as Reginaldus.

111 more…commission more than you were authorized to take (*OED*, Commission *n*.¹ 4a).

---

97 SD] *Fehrenbach subst.; not in* Q/O　　**109 SD**] *Fehrenbach; not in* Q/O

111–12 SD] *this edn;* 'Twas . . commission. [*Kicks him.*] There's one. *Kicks him* [*again.*] That's another. *Strikes him.* And…you / An…courtier. *Fehrenbach;* 'Twas more / Than…one, [*kicks him.*] – there's another, [*Again.* / And…courtier. [*Strikes him. Gifford;* 'Twas…one *Kicks him.* That's…Courtier. *Strikes him.* Q/O

THE POLITICIAN   3.1

That's another, *(strikes him)* and that will make you an upright courtier.
HELGA Ha, ha!
SUENO   Sir, I beseech you –
REGINALDUS Beg modestly hereafter; take within your bounds.
You have small beard to play upon. 'Tis fit   115
My fist should make an answer to your wit.
SUENO I have it to a hair. The choleric duke again?
I am gone!   *Exeunt [Sueno and Reginaldus].*

    Enter OLAUS [*and*] AQUINUS.

AQUINUS [*To Olaus*] Sir, you have been to blame.
OLAUS How dare you talk to me, sir?
AQUINUS 'Tis my duty, and I must tell you   120
Y'have built too much upon him as a kinsman
And have forgot the king.
OLAUS Take that for your impudence. *Strikes him with his cane [and] exit[s].*
AQUINUS I have it, and I thank you.   [*Exit.*]

    Enter KING, *reading of letters,* QUEEN [MARPISA, *and* SUENO].

---

112 **and that** there is possibly a missing stage direction here to strike Sueno again.
112 **that…courtier** i.e. that will teach you how to behave properly; having knocked Sueno to the floor, Reginaldus is probably using 'upright' with simple irony—i.e. Sueno is actually no longer standing up (*OED, adj.* 3), though it is possible that there is a play on the now obsolete sense, lying flat on the ground facing upwards (*OED, adj.* 2).
114 **modestly** with decorum or decency, unassumingly (*OED, adv.* 2 and 3), and possibly also playing ironically on Sueno's 'impudently' (l. 101), an antonym of this word.
115–16 **You…wit** i.e. Since you have so little beard that I cannot replace my lost hairs by taking some of yours it is only right that I repay your attempt at a joke with blows. Sueno's lack of beard would be seen as indicating a corresponding lack of masculinity.
117 **to…hair** exactly, precisely (*OED*, Hair *n.* P3).
118 **I…gone** Most likely 'I'm off', as in the modern 'I'm out of here', and a reaction to Reginaldus's moving towards him threateningly before leaving himself, rather than a response to the entrance of the choleric Olaus (who did not even speak to Sueno in the earlier part of this scene); the 'exeunt' in Q/O would therefore refer to the exits of both Reginaldus and Sueno. However, Sueno is given no direction in Q/O to re-enter with the king and Marpisa at l. 125, which is necessary as he speaks almost immediately; that could perhaps indicate that Sueno merely makes as if to leave when threated by Reginaldus and hides behind Helga meaning that he is still on stage when the king enters; directions for entrances and exits in Q/O are, though, not entirely complete so it is quite likely that Sueno should leave the stage after this line and re-enter with the king and Marpisa, as is indicated in this edition.
118 **to blame** Q/O have 'too blame' and *OED* (Blame *v.* 6) notes that when 'to blame' was used in the sixteenth and seventeenth centuries as the predicate after *be*, 'the *to* was misunderstood as *too*, and *blame* taken as adj. = blameworthy, culpable'.
121 **built…much** relied over-confidently (*OED*, Build *v.* 6b).
122 **forgot…king** i.e. forgotten that he is the king.
124 **have it** have received it (i.e. your blow), as in Mercutio's 'They have made worm's meat of me. / I have it, and soundly, too' (*Romeo and Juliet,* 3.1.107–8).

---

118 SD1] *this edn;* [Reginaldus *and* Sueno] *exeunt* [*separately*]. *Fehrenbach;* Exeunt. Q/O
118 SD2] *Fehrenbach subst.;* Re-enter OLAUS *and* AQUINUS. *Gifford; Ent. Ol. & Aqui.* Q/O
118 SD3] *Fehrenbach subst.; not in* Q/O   118 to] *Gifford;* too Q/O
123 SD] *Gifford subst.;* Exit. / Strikes him with his Cane. Q/O   124 SD1] *Gifford subst.; not in* Q/O
124 SD2] *Fehrenbach subst.;* Re-enter King *and* MARPISA, *followed by* SUENO. *Gifford;* Enter King, *reading of Letters,* Queen. Q/O

467

3.1   THE COMPLETE WORKS OF JAMES SHIRLEY, VOLUME 7

HELGA They are gone, sir, but have left prints of their fury.   125
  The angry duke has broke Aquinus's head
  For speaking dutifully on your behalf;
  T'other mute man of war struck Sueno, sir.
SUENO I hear his language humming in my head still.
KING Aquinus? Strike so near our presence?   130
SUENO Nay, these soldiers will strike a man if he do not
  Carry himself to a hair's breadth; I know that.
KING They shall repent this impudence. Look up
  My dear Marpisa: there's no tempest shall
  Approach to hurt thee. They have raised a storm   135
  To their own ruins.

      Enter a SOLDIER.

SOLDIER [*To Helga*] Sir, if you'll bring me
  To th'king you shall do an office worth your labour.
  I have letters will be welcome.
HELGA   You must give
  Me leave, sir, to present 'em from the prince.
          Soldier gives Helga the letters and exit[s].

  [*To the king*] Most excellent sir, my sovereign.   140
SUENO Letters? [*To Helga*] If you have a chain of gold –
HELGA [*To Sueno*] Go hang thyself!

---

    125 left...fury i.e. the traces of their violence (such as footprints) remain behind them (*OED*, Print *n.* 1b; Fury, *n.* 2a).
    126 broke...head cut, grazed, or bruised his head (*OED*, Break *v.* 5b); the word did not, in this phrase, mean anything as violent as fracturing the skull.
    128 mute taciturn, laconic (*OED*, *adj.* 2a, c).
    129 language his manner of expressing himself (*OED*, *n.* 1c) i.e. his blows; Sueno is picking up on Helga's 'mute'.
    129 humming i.e. the blows have made Sueno's head buzz, but he is also playing on the sense, to utter inarticulate vocal sounds (*OED*, *v.*¹ 2a).
    130 Strike...presence? It was considered an affront, and perhaps even treason, to draw a weapon or to engage in physical combat before a king (Fehrenbach); the disorder indicates how little control the king has over his court.
    132 Carry...breadth Conduct himself with exact propriety (*OED*, Carry *v.* 33a; Breadth *n.* 1b; and Tilley H28 and H29); there is also a rueful glance at the cause of the blows being Sueno's taking too many hairs from Reginaldus's beard.
    133 Look up Be cheerful, take courage (*OED*, Look up, PV3 in Look *v.*).
    137 office service or kindness (*OED*, *n.* 5).
    141 have are given, receive (*OED*, *v.* 10a).

---

136 SD2] *Fehrenbach subst.; not in* Q/O   **139 SD**] *position Fehrenbach; after* thy selfe. Q/O
140 SD] *Fehrenbach subst.; not in* Q/O   **141 SD**] *this edn;* [*To the king.*] *Fehrenbach; not in* Q/O
142 SD] *Fehrenbach subst.; not in* Q/O

468

THE POLITICIAN

3.1

SUENO — we will divide.

HELGA [*To the king*] I am most fortunate to present you, sir,
With letters from the prince, and if your majesty
Knew with what zeal I tender these —

[*He gives the letters to the king who reads them.*]

KING Ha! 145

HELGA He frowns. Where's the soldade? [*To Sueno*] You'll go my half?

KING Who brought these letters? Where's the messenger?

HELGA He was here but now. He's vanished!

KING Vanish thee too, and creep into the earth.

HELGA I shall sir. [*Exeunt Helga and Sueno.*] 150

KING The impudence of children. Read, Marpisa,
More letters from the proud ambitious boy.
He dares to give us precepts and writes here
We have too much forgot ourself and honour
In making thee our queen; puts on his grace 155
A discontent and says the triumph he
Expected, the reward of his young merit,
Will be ungloried in our sudden match
And weak election.

MARPISA This was my fear.

KING He threatens us, if we proceed, with his 160

---

146 soldade anglicized form of 'soldado', Spanish for 'soldier'.

146 You'll…half? Ostensibly Helga means—or intends Sueno to understand—half of the chain expected as reward, but seeing that the king is frowning and the soldier has disappeared he anticipates trouble and actually is inviting Sueno to share what he sees to be the imminent royal displeasure.

153 precepts instructions as to how to behave, especially with regard to moral conduct (*OED*, Precept *n.* 1a).

154 honour The king could be referring to his own honour or to the concept in general.

155 puts on adopts, assumes, possibly with additional sense of pretending or affecting (*OED*, Put on, PV2b, 5a in Put *v.*).

155 grace virtue, sense of duty and propriety (*OED*, *n.* 4b).

156 discontent strong displeasure, indignation (*OED*, *n.*¹ 1).

156 triumph the military display granted to a victorious general on his return to Rome (*OED*, *n.* 1a); both James VI and I and Charles I frequently represented themselves as triumphant Roman emperors bringing peace after the chaos of war (see Miller 2001, 107–27); Shirley may have in mind Mantegna's *Triumphs of Caesar* (1484–92), which were acquired by Charles I in 1629 and displayed in Hampton Court Palace.

158 ungloried deprived of its glory (*OED*, *v.*, where this line is one of the two illustrations of the word's usage).

159 weak election poor choice (*OED*, Election *n.* 2), specifically of the king, the 'our' in the previous line being the royal plural.

---

143 SD] *Fehrenbach subst.; not in* Q/O

145 SD] *this edn;* [Helga *gives the king the letters; the king reads.*] *after* prince. *Fehrenbach;* [*The king reads.* Gifford; *not in* Q/O

146 SD] *this edn;* [*aside to* Sueno]. *before* He frowns. *Fehrenbach; not in* Q/O

150 SD] *Fehrenbach subst.; not in* Q/O

3.1   THE COMPLETE WORKS OF JAMES SHIRLEY, VOLUME 7

Command and power i'th'army. Raise new forces
To oppose 'em and proclaim 'em rebels, traitors –
MARPISA Sir, I beseech you for the general good
Temper your rage. These are but words of passion.
The prince will soon be sorry for't. Suspect not   165
His duty. Rather than disgrace your son
Divide me from your heart – the people love him.
KING I'll hate him for't. Gotharus! Where's Gotharus?   *Exit.*
MARPISA This letter tastes of his invention.
He's active; it concerns us both.

    Enter ALBINA [*with some hesitation*].
                  Albina.   170

Nay, you may forward, madam.
ALBINA   I beseech
Your pardon – I did hope to have found my lord
Gotharus here.
MARPISA   The king asked for him
And is but new retired, who I presume,
If he had known of your approach, would not   175
Have gone so soon.
ALBINA   I have no business, madam,
With the king.
MARPISA   Come, do not disguise it thus.
I am covetous to know your suit.
But I am confident he will deny
You nothing, and your husband is of my   180
Opinion lately.
ALBINA   By your goodness, madam,

---

161 **Command** This could refer to Turgesius's position as a commander of the army, his power to order them to do his bidding, or the actual body of troops under his command (*OED, n.* 7, 3, and 8a).

164 **Temper** Restrain, control (*OED, v.* 7).

167 **Divide** Separate, sunder (*OED, v.* 5a).

169 **tastes** bears the mark (*OED*, Taste *v.* 9a).

170 **active** busy about or engaged in this matter—'on the case' would be a modern equivalent (*OED, adj.* 4a, 7).

171 **forward** advance (*OED, v.* 1).

174 **retired** withdrawn to a place of privacy (*OED, v.* 3a); the king remains the subject of the verb, and is also the antecedent of the following relative pronoun, 'who'.

177 **disguise...thus** put on this counterfeit show (*OED*, Disguise *v.* 6).

178 **covetous** eagerly desirous (*OED, adj.* 1a).

---

162 'em] *Fehrenbach;* 'm Q/O

168 Gotharus!...Gotharus?] *Gifford subst.; Gotharus,...Gotharus,* Q/O

170 SD] *this edn; Enter* Albina. *after both. Fehrenbach; Enter* Albina. *after* Albina. Q/O

470

THE POLITICIAN 3.1

Let me not suffer in your thoughts. I see
There is some poison thrown upon my innocence
And 'tis not well done of my lord Gotharus
To render me to your suspicion 185
So unhappy. 'Tis too much he has withdrawn
His own heart; he will show no seeds of charity
To make all others scorn me.
MARPISA If he do
You can return it, but take heed your ways
Be straight to your revenge. Let not my fame 190
And honour be concerned with the least wound.
ALBINA I understand not what you mean.
MARPISA I cannot
Be patient to hear the king commend
Your lip.
ALBINA I am betrayed.
MARPISA My phrase is modest.
Do not you love the king?
ALBINA Yes, with the duty – 195
MARPISA Of one that wants no cunning to dissemble
Her pride and loose desires.
ALBINA You are the queen.
MARPISA What then?
ALBINA I should else tell you 'tis ill done
To oppress one that groans beneath the weight
Of grief already, and I durst take boldness 200
To say you were unjust.

182 **suffer** endure shame or disgrace (*OED*, *v.* 1b).
185 **render me** most likely, portray or describe me in a particular way (*OED*, Render *v.* 3b, 4b), though possibly, surrender me (*OED*, *v.* 6c).
186 **unhappy** This adjective could qualify equally Albina, or Marpisa's suspicion of her.
186–8 **'Tis...me** Either, he has withdrawn too far his affection for me and shows not a glimmer of charity in making everybody else scorn me, or, it is too much to bear that he has withdrawn his affection for me and he will go to any lengths to make others scorn me as well.
188 **If...do** Were he to do so (subjunctive).
189 **return it** 'it' could refer to Gotharus's heart (i.e. you too could reject him), or to the word 'charity' used ironically, thus suggesting that Albina could respond to Gotharus as he has behaved towards her.
189 **ways** means of achieving that end (*OED*, Way *n.*¹ 19a).
191 **concerned with** i.e. troubled or adversely affected by (*OED*, Concern *v.* 4a, 6a; possibly earlier usages than those exemplified in *OED*).
196 **wants** lacks (*OED*, Want *v.* 1a).
197 **loose** wanton, immoral (*OED*, *adj.* 7).
200 **durst** would dare (conditional).

471

MARPISA	So, so.
ALBINA	I can

Contain no longer. Take from my sad heart
What hitherto I have concealed – in that
You may call me dissembler of my sorrows.
I am weary of my life and fear not what   205
Your power and rage can execute. Would you
Had no more guilt upon your blood than I
Have sin in my accounts; that way, my lord
Gotharus would not be so unkind to me.

MARPISA What's that you said so impudently, Albina?   210

ALBINA What I did think should have consumed me here
In silence. But your injuries are mighty
And, though I do expect to have my name
In your black register designed for death –
To which my husband will, I know, consent –   215
I cannot thus provoked but speak what wounds me.
Yet here again I shut the casket up,
Never to let this secret forth to spread
So wide a shame hereafter.

MARPISA	Thou hast waked

A lioness.

---

202 Contain Refrain from expressing my feelings (*OED*, *v.* 14b).

202 Take Hear and understand (*OED*, *v.* 21, 76a).

206 execute perform or carry into effect, with perhaps a glance at the sense 'put to death' (*OED*, *v.* 1, 6a).

206–9 Would...me A difficult passage in terms of both lexis and syntax. Albina's words might be paraphrased as, 'were you to have no more sins to account for than I will at the day of judgement, there would be nothing to cause my husband's cruel behaviour towards me (because he would not be being unfaithful to me)'. 'Blood' (*OED*, *n.* 12) is possibly the seat of passion, and hence implies Marpisa's lust, though it could equally be understood as meaning kindred (*OED*, Blood *n.* 8a), and hence be a reference to Haraldus, who is also the result of that lust; 'accounts' has the usual sense of 'a statement of financial transactions' (*OED*, Account *n.* 3) but could also suggest a statement of the discharge of moral responsibilities and hence the final reckoning at the day of judgement (*OED*, *n.* 6a and 7); finally, 'unkind' means not just hurtful but unnatural. These lexical and syntactical difficulties can be understood as resulting from the tension Albina is experiencing between her anger and sense of betrayal, and her awareness that she is exposing herself dangerously to the queen's ill-will and greater power.

211–12 What...silence i.e. What I would have expected to destroy me if I remained here in silence (*OED*, Shall *v.* 22d; Consume *v.*[1] 3a), which is to say, I had to speak or I would have died from the effort of restraining myself.

212 your injuries i.e. the sufferings you have wilfully and unjustly inflicted on me (*OED*, Injury *n.* 1).

214 black register more commonly 'black book', a record of those liable to censure or punishment (*OED*, Black book *n.* 2a), kept sometimes by an organization or, as here, by an individual.

214 designed destined, intended (*OED*, Design *v.* 7).

216 speak...me i.e. make clear what it is that causes my injuries.

217–19 Yet...hereafter i.e. Albina has now only the option of once more being silent, by which means she may hope to prevent her further shame. There may be an allusion in the passage to Pandora's Box which, on being opened, released all the ills which afflict human beings and, on being closed, retained only hope.

219–20 Thou...lioness proverbial: wake not a sleeping lion (Tilley L317).

THE POLITICIAN   3.1

ALBINA   Death cannot more undo me.   220
    And since I live an exile from my husband
    I will not doubt but you may soon prevail
    To give my weary soul a full discharge
    Some way or other; and i'th'minute when
    It takes her flight to an eternal dwelling   225
    I will forgive you both and pray for you.
    But let not your revenge be too long idle
    Lest the unmeasured pile of my affections
    Weigh me to death before your anger comes,
    And so you lose the triumph of your envies.   230
MARPISA You sha'not be forgotten, fear it not,
    And but that something nearer doth concern us
    You should soon find a punishment. The king!   *Exeunt [Marpisa and Albina].*
        Enter KING [*and*] GOTHARUS, *with a letter.*
KING He struck Aquinus! Helga saw him bleed.
GOTHARUS These are strange insolences. One go for Aquinus.   235
    Did Olaus bring these letters?
KING   No, some spirit,
    For he soon vanished. I have given my son

220 **undo** destroy (*OED*, *v.* 8a).
223 **discharge** relief from suffering (*OED*, *n.* 1).
228 **pile** this could mean simply a large heap of heavy objects (*OED*, *n.*⁵ 1a), but in view of the next line presumably refers to the weights employed in the method of torture and execution known as pressing to death or *peine forte et dure*. The procedure was enacted, usually in capital cases, when the accused refused to plead in order to protect their children's rights of inheritance.
228 **affections** powerful and intense emotions (*OED*, Affection *n.*¹ 1b).
229 **Weigh...death** See first note to l. 228.
229 **comes** occurs, is given effect (*OED*, Come *v.* 12).
230 **triumph...envies** i.e. your triumph over me brought about by your malice (*OED*, Envy *n.* 1a).
233 **find** meet with, receive (*OED*, *v.* 3).
233 **SDs** Since the announcement of the king's arrival by Marpisa, her exit with Albina, and the entrance of the king and Gotharus all form a sequence of related actions between ll. 233 and 234, and there is no change of location at this point, the present editors do not agree with Gifford that there should be a scene break after l. 233.
235 **insolences** acts of insolence (*OED*, Insolence *n.* 1c).
236–7 **some...vanished** When asked the whereabouts of the soldier who brought these letters Helga replies, 'He was here but now. He's vanished!' (3.1.148); the king referring to this person as a 'spirit' and his repetition of the word 'vanished' reinforce the idea that the bearer of these letters is demonic, and since it was Gotharus who forged them and sent the messenger, the idea of diabolic agency further attaches to him.
237 **given** consigned, entrusted (*OED*, Give *v.* 7).

227 too] *Gifford;* to Q/O
233 SD] *this edn;* [*Exit.*] *after* envies., *Enter King, Gotharus, with letter[s, and servants].* *after* punishment., *Ex[it].* *after* The king! *Fehrenbach;* [*Exit, followed by Albina.* / SCENE II. / ... / *Enter* King *and* GOTHARUS, *with letters. Gifford; Ex.* / *Enter* King, Gotharus, *with a Letter.* Q/O
237] *lineation Gifford;* vanish'd. / I Q/O

473

3.1   THE COMPLETE WORKS OF JAMES SHIRLEY, VOLUME 7

To the most violent men under the planets,
These soldiers.
GOTHARUS   And they'll cling to him like ivy,
Embrace him even to death.
KING   Like breeze to cattle   240
In summer, they'll not let him feed.
GOTHARUS   But make
Him fling unquiet.
KING   Most repineful, spleeny.
GOTHARUS Ready to break the twist of his allegiance.
KING Which they fret every day –
GOTHARUS These put upon his young blood discontents.   245
KING Dangerous –
GOTHARUS   Extremely dangerous.
KING   Swell him up
With the alluring shapes of rule and empire –
GOTHARUS And speak his strength with a proud emphasis,
Yours with a faint cold-hearted voice. Was ever

239–49 And...voice i.e. Turgesius's men will be so strongly attached to him that they will willingly die with him and, further, encourage his rebellious tendencies, leading him to see that his allegiance is to them rather than to his father. Throughout this passage 'they' and 'these' refer to the soldiers in Turgesius's army.
240 breeze type of fly (gadfly) which annoys cattle during the summer, sometimes to the point of distraction (*OED*, *n.*[1]).
242 fling of animals, to kick and plunge violently (*OED*, *v.* 3a).
242 unquiet i.e. unquietly, restlessly; *OED* gives no entry for the word used adverbially.
242 repineful discontented (*OED* notes 'rare' and gives only two illustrations, one of which is this line).
242 spleeny i.e. morose, spiteful; the spleen was believed to be the seat of melancholy.
243 twist...allegiance another revealingly contradictory verbalization from Gotharus: allegiance is figured as something intimately and strongly bound together in the way the various threads of a rope are (*OED*, Twist *n.*[1] 4a), but the word has also a strong sense of contortion or even distortion, ideas that could appropriately be applied to Gotharus's application of the concept.
244 fret gnaw at, wear away (*OED*, *v.*[1] 2a).
245 put upon impose upon in the sense of duping or fooling (*OED*, Put upon, PV2, 3 in Put *v.*).
245 blood primarily ardour, enthusiasm (see 3.1.5), but the sense 'sexual ardour, passion' (see 1.1.13) possibly prompts the following agitated and fantastical meditation by the king on Turgesius as an oedipal phallic rival.
247 shapes configurations, possibly visual, but with a sense of the supernatural, as though they are spectral or phantom beings tempting the prince (*OED*, Shape *n.*[1] 3a, 1d, 6c); however, the general tenor of this passage, the word 'swell', with its allusive suggestion of male sexual arousal, and the erotic connotations of 'alluring' all bring into question whether the sense 'sexual organs' (*OED*, *n.*[1] 16) is not also in play (see also note to ll. 239–49).
247 empire here in the general sense of supreme dominion or command over a territory—i.e. a synonym of 'rule' (*OED*, *n.* 5a, b).
248 speak make known, declare (*OED*, *v.* 15a).
248 emphasis force of expression (*OED*, *n.* 3).
249 Was Were; this was a common plural form of the past indicative of 'be' in the sixteenth to eighteenth centuries (see *OED*, Be *v.*). Gifford's emendation, followed by Fehrenbach, is unnecessary.

474

THE POLITICIAN   3.1

Such peremptory lines writ to a father?   250
KING Thy counsel – while the danger's yet aloof.
GOTHARUS Aloof? Take heed: hills in a piece of landscape
    May seem to stand a hundred leagues, yet measure,
    There's but an inch in distance. Oh, ambition
    Is a most cunning, infinite dissembler,   255
    But quick i'th'execution.
KING   Thy counsel.
GOTHARUS He that aspires hath no religion,
    He knows no kindred.
KING   I ask for thy advice.
GOTHARUS Have you not seen a great oak cleft asunder
    With a small wedge cut from the very heart   260
    Of the same tree?
KING   It frights me to apply it.
    Oh, my misfortune – this is torment not
    A cure.

        Enter AQUINUS.

GOTHARUS Aquinus! [*To the king*] Speak him gently, sir,
    And leave me to encourage him in a service
    Worth his attempt and needful to your safety.   265
    Noble Aquinus, our good king has sense
    Of the affront you suffered from his uncle
    And, as he is informed, for speaking but
    The duty of a subject.
AQUINUS   This is true, sir.
    I wear his bloody favour still; I never   270
    Took any blow so long on trust.

---

250 **peremptory** intolerant of contradiction, over-confident, imperious (*OED*, *adj.* 5).
251 **aloof** far off (*OED*, *adj.* 1).
252 **piece** painting (*OED*, *n.* 14a).
253 **stand** be situated at (*OED*, *v.* 19).
254 **There's…distance** i.e. if measured on the painting.
256 **i'th'execution** primarily, in being put into effect, but probably also with a hint at the sense of putting to death as a punishment (*OED*, Execution *n.* 8b).
257 **aspires** is ambitious.
258 **knows…kindred** does not acknowledge family ties or responsibilities (*OED*, Know *v.* 3).
263 **Speak** Address (*OED*, *v.* 20).
266 **sense** a full understanding (*OED*, *n.* 21a).
270 **I wear…still** i.e. the wound he gave me is still visible.
270–1 **I never…trust** i.e. I have never taken so long to pay back something I owed – in this case, a return blow (*OED*, Trust *n.* 7b).

263 SD2] *Fehrenbach subst.; not in* Q/O

3.1   THE COMPLETE WORKS OF JAMES SHIRLEY, VOLUME 7

KING I know thy spirit's daring and it shall become
  My justice to reward thy suffering.
  A storm now hovers o'er my kingdom;
  When the air is clear and our sky fair again   275
  Expect – nay challenge: we shall recompense
  What thou hast suffered for us with a bounty
  Worth all thy merits. I'th'mean time apply
  Thyself to my Gotharus and be counselled.   *Exit.*

AQUINUS My duty.

GOTHARUS   Th'ast no alliance to my blood,   280
  Yet, if thou think'st I do not flatter thee,
  I feel a friendly touch of thy dishonour.
  The blow – 'twas not well done of Duke Olaus.

AQUINUS You great men think you may do what you please,
  And if y'have a mind to pound us in a mortar   285
  We must obey.

GOTHARUS   That law is none of nature's,
  And this distinction of birth and royalty
  Is not so firm a proof but there are men
  Have swords to pierce it through, and make the hearts
  Of those that take this privilege from their blood   290
  Repent they were injurious.

AQUINUS   My sword
  Was quiet when he beat me.

GOTHARUS He did not, could not beat thee!

AQUINUS 'Twas worse – he cudgelled me. I feel it yet,
  Nor durst I strike again.

  272 become (a) befit or be in accord with; (b) set in a good light (*OED, v.* 7; 9).
  276 Expect...challenge The king starts by suggesting that Aquinus may confidently expect satisfaction for
  the indignity he has suffered, but then changes to the stronger assertion that he should demand his rights in this
  matter once the dispute with Turgesius has been settled (*OED*, Challenge *v.* 5); the king's following 'we shall
  recompense / What thou hast suffered' makes it clear that he will settle this affair, and that he is not suggesting
  Aquinus challenge Olaus to a duel (*OED, v.* 8), a course of action that would be inappropriate given the difference in status between them.
  278–9 apply Thyself direct yourself, give your attention (*OED*, Apply *v.* 13b).
  280–2 Th'ast...dishonour The word 'if' in this sentence should be understood as introducing a supposition
  which is considered to be true rather than a hypothesis which is assumed to be untrue (*OED,* If *conj.* 1, rather than
  3); hence Gotharus is saying, 'you have no kinship with me, but nonetheless, and working on the assumption that
  you do not believe I am flattering you by saying this, I am affected by your dishonour as a friend might be'.
  283 of by (*OED, prep.* 14).
  285 pound pulverize—i.e. as with a pestle in a mortar (*OED, v.*¹ 1a).
  288 so...proof such secure armour (*OED*, Firm *adj.* 2; Proof *n.* 9b).
  289 hearts see note to 3.1.42.
  290 take...blood i.e. presumptuously claim this privilege as a right of their birth (*OED*, Take *v.* 46a;
  Privilege *n.* 2; Blood *n.* 7, 9a).
  292 quiet inactive (*OED, adj.* 2b).
  295 again in return (*OED, adv.* 3a).

                                476

THE POLITICIAN   3.1

GOTHARUS   It could not be   295
A tameness in thy spirit but quick thought
That 'twas Olaus; not that in thy heart
There was no will to be revenged – for he
Is false to nature loves his injury –
But that there was no safety to return   300
Thy anger on his person.
AQUINUS   You're i'th'right;
That frighted me.
GOTHARUS   For he is not revenged
That kills his enemy and destroys himself
For doing his own justice. Therefore men
That are not slaves but free, these we receive –   305
Born and bred gentlemen in fair employments
That have and dare bid high again for honour
When they are wronged by men 'bove them in title,
As they are thought worthy a personal wound
In that, are raised and levelled with the injurer. 310
And he that shall provoke me with his weapon,
By making me his enemy makes me equal
And on those terms I kill him. But there is
Another caution to wise men, who ought
To cast and make themselves secure: that when   315
They have returned full payment for their sufferings
In fame, they may be safe without a guard.

298–9 for...injury i.e. because it is unnatural to love one's own injury.

300–1 there...person it was not safe to turn your anger back against him physically.

302–4 For...justice i.e. Because he who kills his enemy, but also causes his own death as a consequence of or with the object of enacting justice for himself, does not achieve revenge. As Gifford notes at l. 310, 'This long-drawn perplexed tissue of sophistry seems purposely calculated to bewilder the honest soldier. It may be read twice without being comprehended' (Gifford, 130). The sophistry continues to l. 362, but it will be noted that Aquinus is quite capable of matching Gotharus at this game; it will be seen later that he is playing Gotharus every bit as much as Gotharus thinks he is doing the same to Aquinus and this mutual strategy of deception goes a long way towards explaining the difficulty of the language in this passage.

305 receive admit into our favour or employment (*OED*, *v*. 4a).

306 fair honourable, reputable (*OED*, *adj*. 6).

307 That...honour i.e. That have in the past aimed to achieve honour, and dare do so again.

308 wronged injured (*OED*, Wrong *v*. 1).

309 personal directed at them personally, but also with some sense of bodily or physical injury (*OED*, *adj*. 4a, and 3b).

310 levelled placed on the same level.

315 cast the word has a wide range of meanings applicable to this context: calculate, anticipate, consider, contrive, scheme, determine, arrange, plan (*OED*, *v*. 38b, 41, 42, 43, 44, 45b).

315 secure certain to remain safe (*OED*, *adj*. 6a).

315–17 that...guard i.e. when they have repaid in full the injury done to their reputation, they will remain safe without the need for any further protection.

3.1   THE COMPLETE WORKS OF JAMES SHIRLEY, VOLUME 7

AQUINUS That, sir, is the prudence.

GOTHARUS   Yet I can direct thee
To be revenged with safety unto this.
What if I add, therein thou shall do service   320
That will oblige the commonwealth that groans
With fear of innovation, and make
The king thy friend by one expense of courage.
And having named the king thus, it must make
Thy thoughts secure from future loss and in   325
The present act no danger.

AQUINUS   Sir, be clear.
Make good what you have promised
And see if I be frighted; I have helped
Many give up the ghost.

GOTHARUS   Olaus used
Thee basely. How much would the kingdom suffer   330
If he were dead and laid into his tomb
Perhaps a year sooner than nature meant
To make his bones fit.

AQUINUS   I dare kill him, sir,
If I were sure the king would pardon me
That in my own revenge and any other   335

---

318 That…prudence cf. Fear (Suspicion) is one part of prudence (Tilley F135).

319 unto this concerning this (business) (*OED*, Unto *prep.* 19).

320 therein in doing so (*OED*, *adv.* 2).

321 oblige render indebted (to you) (*OED*, *v.* 9a).

321 commonwealth nation, state (*OED*, *n.* 2).

322 innovation revolution, rebellion (*OED*, *n.* 2b).

323 courage most likely used in its common current sense, but in the seventeenth century the word could also mean spirited energy, boldness, or even anger (*OED*, *n.* 3a, d, and b), and such senses may well be in play here.

324 thus i.e. as your friend.

325 secure from free from fear or anxiety with regard to.

325–6 in…danger i.e. (that) in the action I am now proposing you take (there will be) no danger.

327 Make good Fulfil.

329 give…ghost A common biblical phrase suggestive of a life cut short; see, e.g., King James Bible, Jeremiah 15.9: 'She hath given up the ghost; her sun is gone down while it was yet day'; and Job 14.10: 'But man dieth, and wasteth away; yea, man giveth up the ghost, and where is he?'

329 used treated (*OED*, Use *v.* 17a).

333 fit either verbal—fill or occupy perfectly (the shape of the tomb) (*OED*, *v.*¹ 8a); or adjectival—ready, prepared (for entombment) (*OED*, *adj.* 5a).

333–7 I…conscience There is nothing difficult about the language Aquinus is using here, but the syntax is tortured as Aquinus feels his way towards expressing himself with caution: 'I would dare to kill Olaus if I were sure the king would pardon me; I would do that to achieve my own revenge, and I would kill, with no exceptions, any other person the king regards as his enemy; I am required to do this by my belief that it is my moral duty to behave thus.' The dilemma recalls Pedringano's confidence in 3.6 of *The Spanish Tragedy* that he will be pardoned by the king for the murder he has committed.

478

THE POLITICIAN   3.1

Whom he calls enemy without exception.
To this I am bound in conscience. Sir, there needs
No conjuration for this nor art
To heighten me. Let me but hear the king
Will have it, and secure me.
GOTHARUS   Thou deserv'st him,   340
And mayst a statue for our great deliverer.
Yet, now I have thought better on't, we may
Save trouble in Olaus's tragedy
And kill him through another.
AQUINUS   Whom?
GOTHARUS   One that
Sits heavier on the king's heart and dwells in't   345
Such a disease as if no resolute hand
Cure him.
AQUINUS   I'll be his chirurgeon.
GOTHARUS   When I name him.
One that has had no will to advance thee
To thy deserts in wars – for all thy former

338 **conjuration** most likely, given the following 'art' (i.e. cunning or trickery, especially linguistic) the employment of magical charms or spells, the implication being that Aquinus sees Gotharus as a magician trying to raise an evil spirit to do his bidding; however, the word could also refer to conspiracies confirmed by an oath (*OED*, *n.* 4 and 1).

339 **heighten me** intensify my feelings (*OED*, Heighten *v.* 4).

340 **have it** cause or allow it (to be thus) (*OED*, Have *v.* 28a, 29).

340 **secure me** ensure my safety, protect me (*OED*, Secure *v.* 1a, b); possibly also, free me from worry or apprehensions (*OED*, *v.* 2a).

340 **him** i.e. as your protector or guardian.

341 **mayst** may (deserve). There is a possibility that Q/O's 'maist' is an old form of the verb 'make', still in seventeenth-century Northern use.

341 **for** as, as being (*OED*, *prep.* 19a).

343 **in** in the matter of, with regard to (*OED*, *prep.*¹ 17).

343 **tragedy** downfall (*OED*, *n.* 5).

344 **kill him** i.e. effectively put an end to his ambitions.

345–7 **dwells…him** The lines can be paraphrased as: '(this person) will remain a serious disease in the king's heart, so that (eventually) it will become impossible for even a determined or properly qualified person to cure it'. There is no clear or obvious connection, either semantic or grammatical, between the two phrases on either side of 'as if'; the first phrase is reasonably clear; in the second, there is probably (given Aquinus's reply to Gotharus in the next line, 'I'll be his chirurgeon') a play on 'resolute': (a) steadfast in achieving a fixed resolve (*OED*, *adj.* 4b), and (b) well qualified medically (*OED*, *adj.* 3b); the former meaning hints at the need of a man who will solve the king's problem through a decisive violent act and the latter sets up the disease metaphor that Aquinus pursues. 'Such' is merely an intensive.

347 **chirurgeon** surgeon (*OED*, *n.*).

347 **him** i.e. Turgesius.

348 **will** possibly intention (*OED*, *n.*¹ 5b) rather than merely desire or inclination (*OED*, *n.*¹ 1).

348–9 **advance…deserts** i.e. prefer you to those rewards that are due to you (*OED*, Advance *v.* 2a; Desert *n.*¹ 3).

349 **for** notwithstanding, in spite of (*OED*, *prep.* 23a).

3.1 THE COMPLETE WORKS OF JAMES SHIRLEY, VOLUME 7

And thy late services, rewarded with   350
A dull command of captain – but incensed
By Olaus now, who rules his heart, less hope
To be repaired in fortune.
AQUINUS Let him be the prince.
GOTHARUS   'Tis he.
AQUINUS   It honours my attempt.
And while his father holds him disobedient   355
I think him less than subject.
GOTHARUS Disobedient? Look there. (*Shows a letter.*)
AQUINUS This is the prince's hand.
GOTHARUS   But read his heart.
AQUINUS [*Takes the letter and reads.*] Impious! Above the reach of common faith!
I am satisfied he must not live. The way?   360
They would not trust me with his cup to poison it.
Show me the way. The king and queen!
GOTHARUS   Let's study.

    Enter KING *and* QUEEN [MARPISA *in conversation*].

MARPISA You have a faithful servant in Gotharus.
KING Upon his wisdom we depend.
GOTHARUS [*Aside to Aquinus*]   I have it.
He shall die like a soldier, thus – (*Whispers.*)
MARPISA   Their malice   365

---

350 late recent (*OED*, *adj.*¹ 12).
350 rewarded (which have been) rewarded.
351 incensed inflamed with anger, incited, stirred up (*OED*, Incense *v.*² 3b, 4).
352 less hope either understand an ellipsis: 'have less hope'; or, taking 'hope' as a verb rather than a noun, read, 'hope less (than you have hitherto)'; the syntax is complicated by Gotharus's failure to indicate his switching the grammatical subject from Turgesius to Aquinus.
353 repaired in fortune compensated (for your service) through great wealth (*OED*, Repair *v.*² 6; Fortune, *n.* 6).
354 Let...prince This declaration is exactly what Gotharus needs to lure Aquinus into carrying out his aims and as such might be seen as clumsy plotting on Shirley's part: the soldier, after all, has no quarrel with the prince so this is making things too easy for Gotharus. However, as noted at ll. 302–4, Aquinus's guarded response to Gotharus's tortured sophistry suggests that he is suspicious about where this conversation is leading, so this line could be read as his quickly picking up on the introduction of the prince into the discussion, and then following through on it to provoke Gotharus into finally revealing his hand.
354 honours confers dignity or credit on (*OED*, Honour *v.* 3a).
355 holds considers, regards (*OED*, Hold *v.* 12d).
356 less...subject i.e. below the consideration that should be given to any ordinary person in this kingdom.
359 Above...faith Beyond the comprehension of that ordinary loyalty that belongs to all human-kind (*OED*, Reach *n.*¹ 7a; Common *adj.* 1b; Faith *n.* 1a).
360 The way? i.e. By what means shall we achieve this?
365 Their i.e. Turgesius and Olaus.

---

359 SD] *this edn;* [*Aqu. reads. Gifford; not in* Q/O   **359**] *lineation Gifford;* reach / Of Q/O
362 SD] *this edn; Enter* King *and* Marpisa *after* the way., [Gotharus *and* Aquinus *walk aside and talk.*] *after* Let's study. *Fehrenbach; Enter* King *and* Queen. Q/O   **364 SD**] *Fehrenbach subst.; not in* Q/O

480

THE POLITICIAN   3.1

Doth only aim at me and if you please

To give me up a sacrifice to their fury –

KING Not for a thousand sons. My life and honours

Must sit with thine, Marpisa.

AQUINUS [*Aside to Gotharus*]   Sir, 'tis done.

GOTHARUS [*Aside to Aquinus*] This act shall make thee great. The king and queen!   370

Look cheerful royal sir, and think of honour

To crown the merit of this captain. Let

No trouble shake a thought. He will deserve

Your bosom, sir.

KING   He shall possess it.

[*Aside*] How, my Gotharus?

GOTHARUS [*Aside*]   Pray leave it to me.   375

It is not ripe yet for your knowledge, sir.

KING We'll trust thee. [*Aloud*] Come, Marpisa.

GOTHARUS Dearest madam! Come, Aquinus.

AQUINUS I attend your lordship.   *Exeunt.*

368 **honours** those qualities that confer on me dignity and exalted status.

369 **sit with** be consonant or in harmony with (*OED*, Sit with, PV2 2 in Sit *v.*).

369 **'tis done** i.e. consider it as good as done.

372–3 **Let...thought** i.e. Do not allow any trouble to disturb your thoughts.

373–4 **deserve...bosom** i.e. earn the right to be taken into your confidence, the bosom here being the location of a person's secret thoughts (*OED*, Bosom *n.* 6a); cf. 1.1.113 and note.

374 **possess** possibly in the looser, legal sense, 'occupy as a tenant might rather than as an owner' (*OED, v.* 1d), but the word also carried malign suggestions, such as to be dominated by another person, controlled by demonic power, or infected by a disease (6, 4, 2c).

375–7 **How...thee** Their conversation is aside and refers to the agreement they made earlier in the scene, in which Gotharus was to 'encourage [Aquinus] in a service / Worth his attempt and needful to [the king's] safety' (3.1.264–5). The king's parting instructions to Aquinus were 'apply / Thyself to my Gotharus and be counselled' (ll. 278–9), so here he is asking Gotharus what transpired.

369 SD] *Fehrenbach subst.; not in* Q/O

370 SD] *this edn;* [*to* Aquinus]. *before* This act, [*To the king.*] *after* great. — *Fehrenbach; not in* Q/O

374–6] *lineation this edn;* He...Gotharus? / Pray...sir. Q/O   375 SD1] *Fehrenbach subst.; not in* Q/O

375 SD2] *Fehrenbach subst.; not in* Q/O   377 SD] *this edn; –* Gifford; *not in* Q/O

THE COMPLETE WORKS OF JAMES SHIRLEY, VOLUME 7

[3.2]

Enter HARALDUS, SUENO, [*and*] HELGA, *at a banquet.*

SUENO My lord, you honour us.

HELGA   If we knew how
To express our duties –

HARALDUS   No more ceremony.
Your loves engage me, if some discontents
Make me not seem unpleasant. Yet I must
Confess I was more prompted to th'acceptance   5
In hope to cure a melancholy.

HELGA   With your pardon,
It does too much usurp on your sweet nature
But, if your lordship please, there is a way
To banish all those thoughts.

HARALDUS   I would call him doctor
That could assure me that.

SUENO   I am of his   10
Opinion, sir, and know the best receipt
I'th'world for sadness.

HARALDUS   Prithee what?

---

0 SD *banquet* probably the least elaborate form of this entertainment is meant—a wine drinking carousal (*OED*, *n.*[1] 4). Fruit and sweetmeats were often served with the wine, as would have been the case with Capulet's 'trifling foolish banquet' (*Romeo and Juliet*, 1.5.121; *OED*, *n.* 3a) but there is no indication in the dialogue that any food is available here. *The Gentleman of Venice* contains a similar drinking scene (3.4) in which Thomazo, the supposed son of the Duke, and his dissolute companions try to get the elderly courtier Marino drunk, but here without success; during this scene Thomazo explicitly asks if there is food and is told it is being prepared.

2 **duties** acts of respect due to a superior (*OED*, Duty *n.* 1); as Haraldus cuts him short with his 'No more ceremony', we can imagine that Helga's speech is accompanied by much obsequious bowing and scraping.

2 **ceremony** deferential courtesy (*OED*, *n.* 2).

3 **engage** The force of the word is obvious enough—Haraldus is acknowledging that Sueno and Helga have prevailed on him to come out of himself and accept their offer of sociability—but there is no precise meaning that fits easily with the phrase that follows (see next note); win over or charm by pleasing qualities, invite, persuade or induce cover, in the light of ll. 5–6, the most likely range of meanings (*OED*, *v.* 9a, 10, 8a); the word could also, however, take us in a quite different direction—'ensnare' (11a)—which would be perfectly appropriate given what is to follow.

3–4 **if...unpleasant** The double negative is odd and makes the phrase seem self-contradictory; however, the phrase could be read as a slightly detached qualification of the first part of the sentence: 'your loving behaviour wins me over—if the things that cause my unhappiness do not cause me to appear unfriendly'.

4–6 **Yet...melancholy** i.e. Nonetheless, I have to admit it was more my hope of finding a cure for my melancholy that prompted me to accept your invitation than a recognition of the kindness of your gesture.

7 **It** i.e. Melancholy.

7 **usurp on** assume predominance over, encroach upon (*OED*, Usurp *v.* 2c, 9).

10 **assure** guarantee (*OED*, *v.* 7a).

11 **receipt** prescription, or the medicine made up according to that prescription (*OED*, *n.* 12a).

[**3.2**]] *Gifford subst.* (SCENE II.) *(though actually Scene III); [*III.ii.*] Fehrenbach; no scene division in* Q/O
1–2] *lineation Gifford;* If...duties. Q/O

482

THE POLITICIAN   3.2

SUENO   Good wine.

HARALDUS I have heard 'em talk so. If I thought there were
    That operation –

HELGA   Try sir.

SUENO My humble duty – 'tis excellent wine!   15

HARALDUS Helga!

HELGA   Your lordship's servant.

HARALDUS (*Drinks*)   'Tis pleasant.

SUENO It has spirit. Will you please
    Another trial that prepares more sweetness?
    Health to the queen.

HARALDUS   I thank you. [*They drink.*]

HELGA With your pardon, fill to me.   20
    Your Grace should have it last.

HARALDUS   She is my mother. (*Haraldus drinks.*)

SUENO She is our royal mistress, heaven preserve her.
    Does not your lordship feel more inclination
    To mirth? There is no spell 'gainst sorrow like
    Two or three cups of wine.

HELGA   Nothing, believe't,   25
    Will make your soul so active. Take it liberally.

HARALDUS I dare not trust my brain.

SUENO   You never tried?

HELGA You'll never know the pleasure then of drinking;

---

14 **operation** power to effect (a cure) (*OED*, *n.* 3a).
16 **Helga!** Presumably Haraldus lifts his glass to toast Helga at this point.
17 **spirit** lively and inspiring quality (*OED*, *n.* 14a).
17 **Will…please** i.e. Will it please you (to undertake).
18 **trial** test (of the efficacy of this cure) and, possibly, experiment (*OED*, *n.*¹ 2a, 4).
18 **prepares** provides or produces (*OED*, Prepare *v.* 5a, 6a).
18 **sweetness** delightful feelings, pleasure (*OED*, *n.* 6), but also literally.
20–1 **With…mother** These lines probably indicate stage action more than anything else: Helga first excuses himself to Haraldus for turning away from him—'With your pardon'—in order to ask Sueno (or possibly a servant if production allows for non-speaking extras) to fill his glass—'fill to me'—and then, turning back to Haraldus, suggests that he might take a bit more time over getting drunk—'have it (i.e. make it) last'; Haraldus justifies his enthusiastic drinking by appealing to his filial affection for the queen.
24 **spell** charm or cure; the word also has sinister suggestions of malign forces at work.
26 **active** lively (*OED*, *adj.* 4a).
26 **liberally** plentifully, but also implying unrestrainedly, and in that sense having a suggestion of immoral behaviour (*OED*, *adv.* 1, 2).

---

16 SD] *this edn; drinks. Before* Helga. *Fehrenbach;* Drinkes. *after* pleasant. Q/O
19 SD] *this edn;* [Drinks. *after* queen! *Gifford; not in* Q/O
21 SD] *this edn;* Haraldus *drinks. after* preserve her. *Fehrenbach; Har. drinkes after* inclination Q/O
24 mirth?] *Gifford;* mirth, Q/O

3.2 THE COMPLETE WORKS OF JAMES SHIRLEY, VOLUME 7

I have drunk myself into an emperor.

SUENO In thy own thoughts.

HELGA   Why, is't not rare that wine,   30
Taken to the extent, should so delightfully
Possess the imagination? I have had my queens
And concubines –

HARALDUS   Fine fancies.

HELGA   The king's health!
Give me't in greater volume, these are acorns.
Sueno, to thee. I'm sprightly but to look on't.   35

SUENO What rare things will the flowing virtue raise
If but the sight exalt you? To your grace,
The king's health!

HARALDUS   Let it come. I'll trespass once. [*They drink.*]

HELGA That smile became you sir.

HARALDUS (*Drinks.*)   This cup doth warm me.
Methinks I could be merry.

SUENO   Will your grace   40
Have any music?

HARALDUS   Anything.

HELGA   Strike lustily! (*Music [plays].*)

HARALDUS I have begun no health yet, gentlemen.

SUENO Now you must honour us.

HARALDUS   Health to the prince!

---

29 into...emperor i.e. into thinking myself to be an emperor.

30 rare excellent (*OED, adj.* 5b).

31 to...extent i.e. to the fullest extent; such a definition is not recorded directly by *OED*, but Shirley might be using the term in the legal sense, which seems to imply such a meaning (see *OED*, Extent *n.* 2b, illustration for 1768).

32 had sexually enjoyed (*OED*, Have *v.* 13a)—but again, only in his dreams, as Haraldus is quick to point out.

34 Give...acorns addressed again to Sueno or a servant whom Helga criticizes for dispensing only quantities such as might fill an acorn cup.

35 I'm...on't i.e. Merely looking at it makes me feel cheerful and vivacious.

36 What...raise 'raise' can suggest stir up, make cheerful and, possibly, restore to a former status or revitalize; however, given the direction in which Helga has taken the conversation in ll. 30–3, the word could carry a suggestion of 'phallic tumescence' (Williams 1994, entry for *raise*).

36 flowing virtue i.e. wine, 'virtue' having the sense of supernatural, magical, or divine power (*OED, n.* 8a, 9a, 3a).

37 exalt elate with joy (*OED, v.* 2b), but also lift up or elevate (1a), possibly extending the sexual innuendo of 'raise'.

38 Let...come i.e. Come what may.

38 trespass commit sin, transgress (*OED, v.* 1a).

41 lustily with a will, cheerfully (*OED, adv.* 2).

---

33 health!] *Gifford;* health, Q/O   **35** on't] *Gifford;* out Q/O   **38** health!] *this edn;* health. Q/O
38 SD] *this edn; Drinks. Fehrenbach; not in* Q/O   **39 SD**] *this edn; after* me, Q/O
40–1] *lineation Gifford;* Will...musick? Q/O   **41** lustily!] *Fehrenbach;* lustily. Q/O
41 SD plays] *this edn; within Gifford; not in* Q/O   **43** prince!] *Gifford;* Prince. Q/O

484

THE POLITICIAN   3.2

HELGA That is your title, sir, as you are son to a queen.
HARALDUS My father was no king. Father? I'll drown   45
  The memory of that name. (*Drinks.*)
HELGA The Prince Turgesius's health.
SUENO   He's not far off
  By the court computation. Happiness now
  To Prince Haraldus's mistress!
HELGA   With devotion.
HARALDUS Alas, I am too young to have a mistress.   50
HELGA Sir, you must crown it.
HARALDUS   These are complements
  At court, where none must want a drinking mistress.
SUENO Methinks loud music should attend these healths –
HARALDUS So, shall we dance? (*Drinks.*)
HELGA   We want ladies.
HARALDUS I am as light. Thou shall go for a lady.   55
SUENO Shall I? ([*They*] *dance.*)
  Is not this better than to sigh away
  Our spirits now?
HARALDUS   I'm hot.
HELGA A cup of wine is the most natural cooler.
HARALDUS You are my physicians, gentlemen. (*Drinks.*)   60
SUENO Make it a health to my lord Gotharus –
  I'll pledge it as heartily as he were my father.
HARALDUS Whose father? ([*He*] *throws wine in Sueno's face.*)

48 **computation** estimation, reckoning (*OED, n.* 2).
49 **devotion** enthusiastic loyalty (*OED, n.* 5).
51 **crown it** i.e. bring this to a successful conclusion by obtaining a mistress (*OED*, Crown *v.*[1] 7b), or, possibly, complete the toast by responding to it.
51 **complements** forms or requirements of social behaviour which complete the proper gentleman (*OED*, Complement *n.* 8, 7).
55 **I...lady** Possibly punning on the idea of being light-headed through drink, Haraldus initially seems to be suggesting that he has those 'woman-like' qualities of lightness—i.e. is frivolous, fickle, wanton (*OED*, Light *adj.* 14a, 16, 14b)—and hence is liable to sin; he then, perhaps chastened by that thought, changes his mind and suggests Sueno should be the one to 'go for (i.e. pass for) a lady' (thereby reinforcing the suggestion of effeminacy attaching to that character).
58 **spirits** here, the vital energies of the mind that give rise to action and feeling, especially vivacity and cheerfulness (*OED*, Spirit *n.* 16, 17); they could also be, however, seminal fluids (Williams 1994, entry for *spirit*) and to 'sigh them away' might be seen as equivalent to Shakespeare's 'expense of spirit in a waste of shame' (Sonnet 129, l. 1).
58 **hot** a symptom of Haraldus's increasing inebriation (*OED, adj.* 8d) and a foreshadowing of the fever that will subsequently afflict him.
59 **cooler** cooling medicine; prostitute (*OED, n.* 2a, 5 and Williams 1994, entry for *cooler*).
63 **Whose father?** Haraldus presumably hears a stress on Sueno's 'my' which implies Haraldus's bastardy.

44] *lineation Fehrenbach;* sir, / As Q/O   49 mistress!] *Gifford;* mistress. Q/O
56 **SD**] *Fehrenbach subst.;* [*dances.*] *after* light; *Gifford; Dance.* Q/O   63 **SD** *He*] *this edn; not in* Q/O

485

3.2   THE COMPLETE WORKS OF JAMES SHIRLEY, VOLUME 7

SUENO   Mine I said.

HARALDUS   Cry mercy.

SUENO Nay 'tis but so much wine lost. Fill 't again.

HARALDUS I'll drink no more.

HELGA   What think you of a song?   65

SUENO A catch. To't boys.

                         ([*They sing a*] *song.*)

HARALDUS Shall we to bed, gentlemen?

I did not sleep last night.

HELGA   If your grace

Desire to sleep, there's nothing to prepare it

Like t'other cup.

HARALDUS   A health to both your mistresses! (*Drinks.*)   70

SUENO You do us grace.

HELGA [*Aside to Sueno*] There's hope of his conversion.

HARALDUS I am not well. What wheels are in my brains?

Philosophy affirms the earth moves not –

'Tis here methinks confuted. Gentlemen,

You must be fain to lead me to some couch   75

Where I may take a nap and then I'll thank you.

I'll come again tomorrow.

SUENO   Every day

For a twelve-month.

HELGA   That will make you a good fellow.   *Exeunt.*

---

66 **catch** song in which each singer progressively repeats the last line sung by the previous singer (*OED*, *n.*² 3).

70 **t'other** one more (*OED*, Tother *adj.* 5b).

72 **What…brains?** On the face of it Haraldus is simply saying that his head is spinning as the alcohol takes its effect, but the word 'wheels' appears to provoke a series of correlative ideas that lead to the next line: the term 'wheel' was used of the spheres on which planets were understood to revolve around the earth, and the philosopher's wheel was the alchemical process by which elements were converted into other elements (*OED*, Wheel *n.* 10, 15b).

73 **Philosophy…not** Despite the fact that Copernicus had challenged this idea more than a century earlier, the view that the earth was the centre of the universe persisted in both some scientific thinking and popular belief; this is another indication, perhaps, that the play is set in the past.

74 **confuted** proven to be false (*OED*, Confute *v.* 2).

75 **fain** willing, or possibly obliged, to act as suggested (*OED*, *adj.* 3a, 2b).

78 **fellow** besides the usual meanings *OED* gives 'a friend or companion in feasting, drinking' (*n.* 3) but has no illustration later than 1542.

---

66 SD] *this edn;* SONG. *Gifford; Song. after* asong? Q/O   70 mistresses!] *Gifford;* Mistresses. Q/O

71 **SD**] *Fehrenbach subst.; not in* Q/O

78 **SD**] *this edn; Ex*[*eunt,* Sueno *and* Helga *helping* Haraldus]. *Fehrenbach;* [*Exeunt, leading in Haraldus. Gifford; Exit.* Q/O

THE POLITICIAN   3.3

[3.3]

> *Enter* PRINCE TURGESIUS, REGINALDUS, [*and*] SOLDIERS *marching.*
> OLAUS [*enters and*] *meets* [*them*]. *They salute and whisper.*

PRINCE You tell me wonders.

OLAUS   'Tis all truth. We must
Stand on our guard. 'Tis well we are provided.

PRINCE Is it not some device to make us fear,
That at our entertainment we may find
Our joys more spacious?

OLAUS   There is some device in't.   5

PRINCE It is not possible a father should
Be so unkind to his own blood and honour.

OLAUS My life was threatened.

PRINCE   Who durst threaten it?

OLAUS The king your father.

PRINCE   Oh, say not so, good sir.

OLAUS And if you please him not with your behaviour   10
Your head may be soon humbled to the axe
And sent, a token of his love, to your stepdame,
The queen. I trifle not.

PRINCE   For what sins
Hath angry heaven decreed to punish Norway
And lay the scene of wrath in her own bowels?   15

---

2 **provided** prepared and in a state of readiness, well equipped (*OED*, *adj.* 2, 1).

3 **fear** apprehensive rather than frightened (*OED*, *v.* 7a).

4 **That** i.e. In order that, or with the objective that.

4 **entertainment** reception (by the king).

5 **more spacious** greater (*OED*, Spacious *adj.* 3a).

5 **There ... in't** Olaus's repetition of 'device' stresses the notion of trickery or deceit latent in the word. Olaus, of course, suspects a device of Gotharus's making.

7 **unkind** unnaturally cruel (*OED*, *adj.* 5); the word was stronger in this period (see note to 3.1.206–9).

7 **honour** the nobility of mind and upright behaviour that would be expected of him, and the dignity of his exalted position (*OED*, *n.* 2a, 3a).

8 **durst** dared.

11 **humbled** lowered in dignity, abased, but also, as one had to kneel to be beheaded, literally be forced to bow down in an act of humility (*OED*, Humble *v.*¹ 2, 3a).

15 **lay ... bowels** i.e. locate the manifestation of God's retribution in the heart of the state; the word 'scene', with its theatrical associations, points up the events as particularly dramatic.

[3.3]] *Gifford subst. (*SCENE III.*) (though actually Scene IV);* [III.iii.] *Fehrenbach; no scene division in* Q/O
0 SD] *this edn; Enter* [*at one side,*] Turgesius, *Reginaldus,* [*and*] *soldiers marching;* [*at the other,*] Olaus; *they salute and whisper. Fehrenbach; Enter at one side, prince* TURGESIUS, REGINALDUS, *and Soldiers marching; at the other,* OLAUS; *they salute, and whisper. Gifford; Enter Prince* Turgesius, Reginaldus, *Souldiers march-ing,* Olaus *meets, they salute and whisper.* Q/O

487

3.3 THE COMPLETE WORKS OF JAMES SHIRLEY, VOLUME 7

I did suspect, when none came forth to meet
Our victory, to have heard of some misfortune,
Some prodigies engend'ring. Down with all
Our pride of war – the garlands we bring home
Will but adorn us for the sacrifice,   20
And while our hairs are decked with flowers and ribbons
We shall but march more gloriously to death.
Are all good women dead within the kingdom
There could be found none worth my father's love
But one whose fame and honour is suspected?   25

OLAUS Wouldst they were but suspected.

PRINCE   Marpisa?

OLAUS Her preferment was no doubt
Gotharus's act, for which 'tis whispered
She pays him fair conditions, while they both
Case up the king's eyes or confine him to   30
Look through such cunning optics as they please.

PRINCE I'll have his heart.

OLAUS   But how will you come by't?
He's safe in the king's bosom, who keeps warm
A serpent till he find a time to gnaw
Out his preserver.

18 **prodigies engend'ring** abnormal and monstrous creatures being born as portents of an imminent calamity (*OED*, Prodigy *n.* 1, 2; Engender *v.* 3).

19 **pride...war** magnificent display of our warlike achievements, compare *Othello*, 3.3.355–9, 'O, farewell!...Pride, pomp, and circumstance of glorious war!'

19–20 **garlands...sacrifice** garlands of flowers and ribbons adorned both triumphant warriors and sacrificial beasts in classical times.

24 **There** (So that) there.

25 **fame** reputation for good character (*OED*, *n.*¹ 2a); the word, as used here, was synonymous with 'honour'; they were effectively one quality, and hence perhaps Shirley's choice of the singular 'is' here; however, he does use 'is' as a third person plural elsewhere. Gifford's emendation to 'are' is not necessary (see also 2.1.121–2, 3.1.57, and l. 42 of this scene).

26 **Marpisa?** Punctuated thus in Q/O; though it is also an exclamation, marking it as a question reinforces Turgesius's sense of utter disbelief that his father could have chosen such a wife.

29 **pays...conditions** gives him in return certain things that he demands—i.e. her sexual favours (*OED*, Condition *n.* 1a).

30 **Case up** Cover over (*OED*, Case *v.*¹ 1).

30 **confine** restrict (*OED*, *v.* 7a).

31 **cunning optics** skilfully constructed optical instruments, here most likely spectacles which had a reputation for allowing people to see more than was actually there, as in Lear's 'Get thee glass eyes, / And, like a scurvy politician, seem / To see the things thou dost not' (*King Lear*, 4.5.166–8).

32 **his** i.e. Gotharus's.

33–5 **keeps...preserver** To nourish a viper (or snake) in one's bosom was proverbial (Tilley V68) and derived from the story of a man who found a frozen snake and warmed it back to life in his bosom, only to be repaid with a bite from the treacherous snake when it woke up; Shirley adds to the horror by having the snake residing actually inside its preserver's body and then gnawing its way out through his flesh; see also 4.2.11–12 and note.

488

THE POLITICIAN   3·3

PRINCE   We had died with honour   35
By the enemy's sword. Something might have been read
In such a fall as might have left no shame
Upon our story, since 'tis chance of war,
Not want of valour, gives the victory.
This shipwrecks all and eats into the soul   40
Of all our fame; it withers all the deeds
Is owing to our name.

     Enter CORTES.

CORTES Health to the prince!
OLAUS   Cortes, welcome. What news?
CORTES These letters will inform his Highness.   [*Cortes gives letters to the prince.*]
OLAUS Sent from the king, Cortes? Has he thought upon't?   45
Are we considerable at last and shall
The Lady Gewgaw, that is perched upon
His throne, be counselled not to take too much
Upon her? Will Gotharus give us leave
To be acquainted with the king again? Ha!   50
CORTES These letters come, sir, from Aquinus.
OLAUS [*Aside*]   How?

---

35 We had i.e. We would have; Fehrenbach amends to 'Had we' and retains Q/O's comma after 'sword' in l. 36, but the elliptical phrasing here and the use of a comma where modern punctuation would have a full stop are both typical of Shirley.

36 read made out, understood, seen (*OED, v.* 7a).

37 fall being struck down in battle.

38–9 'tis ... victory cf. Ecclesiastes, 9:11: 'the race is not to the swift, nor the battle to the strong ... but time and chance happeneth to them all.'

40 soul i.e. the very existence (*OED, n.* 6a).

41 all ... fame i.e. the fame of each one of us.

41 withers blights, destroys the glory of (*OED*, Wither *v.*² 7), but the physical notion of withering remains strong and transfers to the immaterial 'deeds' to evoke a powerful image of decayed memorials of military victory such as wilted garlands, faded flags, and 'bruisèd arms hung up for monuments' (*Richard III*, 1.1.6).

42 Is Fehrenbach amends unnecessarily to 'Are'.

45 thought upon't thought better of it.

46 considerable thought to be worthy of consideration or regard (*OED, adj.* 4).

47 Gewgaw Gaudy trifle or toy, used disparagingly of people (*OED, n.* 1a, c).

47 perched seated in an elevated (and perhaps precarious) position (*OED, adj.*² 3); possibly also with a glance at the sense, presumptuous, self-assertive (*OED, adj.*¹).

48–9 take ... her assume authority without warrant, behave presumptuously.

---

44 SD] *this edn;* [*gives letters to* Turgesius]. *before Cortes's next speech Fehrenbach; not in* Q/O
51 SD] *Fehrenbach subst.; not in* Q/O

489

3.3   THE COMPLETE WORKS OF JAMES SHIRLEY, VOLUME 7

I hope he mentions not the broken pate
I gave him and complains on't to the prince.
I may be apt to make him an amends
With such another.

PRINCE [*To Olaus*]   Sir!

OLAUS   What's the matter?   55

PRINCE Read. I am planet-struck. Cursed Gotharus!
What would the traitor have? [*He gives letters to Olaus.*]

OLAUS 'Tis here, I take it. [*He reads.*] He would have you sent
Yonder and has took order with Aquinus
For your conveyance hence at both their charges.   60
But now you know the plot, you wo'not trust
Your life as he directs.

PRINCE   Not trust Aquinus?

OLAUS You are desperate – hark you, I do suspect him
And I ha' cause. I broke his head at court
For his impertinent counsel when I was   65
In passion with the king. You sha'not trust him:
This may be cunning to revenge himself.
I know he has a spirit. Come, you sha'not
Be cheated of your life while I have one
To counsel you.

PRINCE   Uncle, I am unmoved.   70
He is a soldier: to that name and honour
I'll trust a prince's life. He dares not be

---

52 pate head, specifically the crown (*OED, n.*[1] 1a).

54 apt inclined (*OED, adj.* 4d).

54 make...amends exact retribution (for his complaining); possibly, ironically, make an improvement (to his previous injury) (*OED*, Amends *n.* 2a, 4a).

56 planet-struck flabbergasted; the image evokes the idea of being rendered idiotic by an extremely unusual planetary conjunction.

59 Yonder Vague term indicating anywhere in the near or far distance, but Olaus presumably means the court.

59 took order made arrangements (*OED*, Order *n.* 18).

60 conveyance removal, possibly with the sense of getting rid of (*OED, n.* 3).

60 hence another vague indication of distance—away from here (*OED, adv.* 1).

61 wo'not will not.

63 desperate either, reckless, too ready to take unnecessary risks, or, in a situation where there is no room for hope (*OED, adj.* 4a, 2).

68 spirit courage, a readiness to assert and defend himself (*OED, n.* 13a); possibly also with reference to the spirit as the seat of angry feelings (*OED, n.* 12).

---

55 SD] *Fehrenbach subst.; not in* Q/O

57 SD] *this edn;* [*gives letters to* Olaus]. *before* Read. *Fehrenbach; not in* Q/O   **58 SD]** *this edn; not in* Q/O

THE POLITICIAN   4.1

A traitor.
OLAUS   I have read that one prince was
  So credulous and 'scaped. But Alexander,
  Though he were great, was not so wise a gentleman   75
  As heaven in that occasion might have made him:
  The valiant confidence in his doctor might
  Ha' gnawn his bowels up and where had been
  My gallant Macedonian? Come, you shall
  Consider on't.
PRINCE   I am resolved already: 80
  March to the city. Every thought doth more
  Confirm me. Passion will not let you see,
  Good uncle – with your pardon – the true worth
  And inside of Aquinus: he is faithful.
  Should I miscarry 'tis my single life,   85
  And 'tis obedience to give up our breath
  When fathers shall conspire their children's death.   *Exeunt.*

4[.1]

            Enter KING [*and*] GOTHARUS.

GOTHARUS You may surrender up your crown. 'Twill show
  Brave on Turgesius's temples, whose ambition
  Expects it.
KING   Nay, Gotharus –
GOTHARUS   Has my care
  Cast to prevent your shame – how to preserve

73–9 I...Macedonian According to Plutarch, in 333 BCE Alexander, king of Macedonia, was in Cilicia pursuing Darius III when he fell so ill that his doctors refused to treat him, fearing that he was going to die anyway and they would be blamed for his death. His friend, Philip, a physician, offered to cure him, but even as he was preparing the medicine Alexander received a letter warning him that Philip had been bribed by Darius to kill him. Alexander refused to believe the accusation and hid the letter under his pillow; when Philip came in with the medicine, he gave Philip the letter to read and looked cheerfully upon his friend while he drank the potion. To begin with it appeared to be killing him, so powerful was its effect on his body, but it quickly drove out the malady and restored him to complete health.
82 **Confirm** Convince (*OED, v.* 9).
84 **inside** inward nature (*OED, n.* 2c).
85 **miscarry** come to harm or be killed (*OED, v.* 1a).
85 **my...life** i.e. I am the only person who will be killed (*OED,* Single *adj.* 2a).
86–7 **And...death** Like Haraldus, Turgesius takes a strong line on the duty of obedience that a child owes its parent.
  1 **You may** 'may' here expresses merely possibility (*OED, v.*¹ 5)—i.e. you may as well; Gotharus is pursuing his strategy of making the king see Turgesius as a direct threat to his rule.
  1–2 **show Brave** look splendid.
  3–5 **Has...possess** 'cast' here is best taken in the sense 'contrived, calculated, planned', giving the whole phrase a meaning like 'has the care which I have contrived to prevent your being shamed, and to preserve the honour and exaltation in which you are held...'.

4[.1]] *Gifford subst.* (ACT IV. SCENE I.); [IV.i.] *Fehrenbach;* Act. 4. Q/O

                              491

4.1   THE COMPLETE WORKS OF JAMES SHIRLEY, VOLUME 7

The glories you possess by cutting off   5
A canker that would eat into your trunk
And hinder your fair growth – and do you make
A scruple to be cured?
KING   I did but mention –
And nature may excuse – he is my son.
GOTHARUS The more your danger when he dares be impious.   10
The forfeit of his duty in this bold
And hostile manner to affright your subjects
And threaten you with articles is already
The killing of your honour and a treason
Nature abhors, a guilt heaven trembles at,   15
And you are bound in care of your own province
To show your justice and not be partial
To your own blood. But let your kingdom suffer,
Her heart be torn by civil wars; 'tis none
Of mine. And let him in the blood of many   20
Fathers be made a king, your king, and you
That now command be taught obedience.
Creep to your child, exchange your palace for
A prison, and be humbled till you think
Death a preferment. I have but a life –   25
KING Which I will cherish. Be not passionate,
And I consent to all thou hast contained.

6 **canker** cancerous growth.
7–8 **make...scruple** hesitate, are unsure that you want to be.
9 **nature...excuse** nature may pardon me, i.e. it is natural that I should mention that he is my son.
10 **impious** 'wanting in natural reverence and dutifulness, esp. to parents. Rare' (*OED*, *adj.* 2).
11 **forfeit** 'breach or violation' (*OED*, *n.* 1).
12 **affright** frighten, terrorize.
13 **articles** 'Terms, conditions' (*OED*, Article *n.* 3b), with the sense of a legally binding agreement.
14–15 **treason...at** i.e. disloyalty in defying the Crown and the unnaturalness of a son in disobeying his father.
16 **province** country, and also 'duty, business' (*OED*, *n.* 1 and 9).
19 **civil wars** The destruction wrought by civil war was often thought to be worse than enduring tyranny. Gotharus is working on a king's worst fears to claim that lack of resolution risks both treason and civil war. See Thomas Lodge's play about the Roman civil wars between Sulla and Marius, *The Wounds of Civil War* (*c*. 1594).
19–20 **none...mine** i.e. it doesn't matter to me.
20–1 **in...Fathers** One of the staple horrors of civil war was the spectacle of sons killing fathers and fathers killing sons, as in 2.5 of *3 Henry VI* where Henry, during the battle of Towton, observes first a son discovering that he has killed his father, and then a father discovering he has killed his only son.
27 **contained** outlined.

492

THE POLITICIAN

4.1

Thou art my friend.

GOTHARUS I would be, sir, your honest chirurgeon
And when you have a gangrene in your limb   30
Not flatter you to death, but tell you plainly
If you would live, the part so poisoned must be
Cut from your body.

KING   And I wo'not shake
With horror of the wound but meet my safety
And thank my best preserver. But art sure   35
Aquinus will be resolute?

GOTHARUS   Suspect not.
He is my creature.

Enter HORMENUS.

HORMENUS The prince, your son –
KING   Is a bold traitor,
And they are rebels join with him.

GOTHARUS What of the prince, Hormenus?   40
HORMENUS He is very near the city with his army.
KING Are the walls fortified?
HORMENUS   They are.
KING We wo'not trust him nor the ruffian
Olaus, that incendiary.

Enter MARPISA.

GOTHARUS   The queen!
MARPISA   Oh, sir!
KING There are more wounds in those sad accents   45
Than their rebellion can give my kingdom.

MARPISA My boy, my child, Haraldus –
KING   What of him?

28 **friend** friendship signified a relationship between equals, and so was hard for monarchs to countenance. The king is again showing his gullibility and weakness in acceding to Gotharus's demands and cunning rhetoric.

29–31 **I…death** Gotharus continues the medical metaphor, common in the literature of *speculum principis* (mirrors for princes), advising monarchs how to govern and how to listen to advice. Flattery was invariably considered a particular danger which undermined effective government, the irony being that Gotharus is flattering the king in his speech in order to manipulate his government, emboldened by the king's declaration that Gotharus is his friend and so his equal.

32–3 **part…body** i.e. killed to preserve the security of the realm. The metaphor acknowledges that such a course of action is dangerous, as was amputation before modern hygiene and anaesthetics.

37 **creature** here implying that Gotharus has total control over his servant and can demand anything of him, including that he commit murder.

43 **ruffian** stronger than in modern English, a 'brutal or lawless villain; a violent criminal, a thug' (*OED*, *n*. 1).

44 **incendiary** someone who inflames a situation, especially a political one. A relatively new usage in the seventeenth century (see *OED*, *n*. 2a).

45 **accents** sounds, especially of music.

44 SD] *Fehrenbach subst.; after* Queen. Q/O

493

4.2 THE COMPLETE WORKS OF JAMES SHIRLEY, VOLUME 7

MARPISA Is sick, is dying, sir.

GOTHARUS   Forbid it, heavens!
　He was in health –

MARPISA   But if I mean to see him
　Alive, they say I must make haste.   50
　The comforts of my life expire with him.   *Exit.*

GOTHARUS The devil's up in arms and fates conspire against us.

KING Mischiefs tumble like waves upon us.

HORMENUS Sir, it will be necessary
　You lend your person to direct what shall   55
　Be further done i'th'city. Aquinus hath
　Charge of the gate and walls that offer
　The first view to the enemy.

KING   He is trusty and
　A daring soldier. What, at stand, Gotharus?

GOTHARUS I was thinking of the queen, sir, and Haraldus,   60
　And grieve for the sweet child.

KING   Some fever. Would my
　Son were in his state; but soon we shall
　Conclude his destiny if Aquinus prosper.
　But to the walls!

GOTHARUS   I attend. [*Aside*] My very soul
　Is in a sweat. [*Aloud*] Hormenus –

HORMENUS   I wait on you.   *Exeunt.*   65

[4.2]

Enter PRINCE TURGESIUS, OLAUS, CORTES, REGINALDUS, [*and*] SOLDIERS.

PRINCE The gates are shut against us soldiers.

OLAUS Let our engines
　Tear 'em and batter down the walls.

PRINCE   Good uncle,

---

53 Mischiefs Bad luck, often implying a malevolent cause (see *OED*, Mischief *n.* 2a and b); cf. Mischiefs, like waves, never come alone (Tilley M1004).

55 lend…person provide the assistance your presence will afford (*OED*, Lend *v.*² 2e).

59 at stand immobile, transfixed.

65 in…sweat i.e. troubled.

2 engines see note to 1.1.306.

48–9] *lineation Gifford;* Forbid…health—— Q/O

64 SD] *Fehrenbach subst.; not in* Q/O   **65 SD1**] *this edn;* – *Gifford; not in* Q/O

[4.2]] *Gifford subst.* (SCENE II.*); [IV.ii.] Fehrenbach; no scene division in* Q/O

THE POLITICIAN   4.2

Your counsel I obeyed i'th'wars abroad:
We did there fight for honour and might use   5
All the most horrid forms of death to fright
Our enemies and cut our way to victory.
But give me leave to tell you, sir, at home
Our conquest will be loss, and every wound
We give our country is a crimson tear   10
From our own heart. They are a viperous brood
Gnaw through the bowels of their parent. I
Will rather die without a monument
Than have it bear my name, to have defaced
One heap of stones.

   Enter GOTHARUS *on the walls* [*above, with*] HORMENUS [*and*] AQUINUS.

CORTES   Gotharus on the walls?   15
OLAUS Hormenus and Aquinus? Now a speech
 An 'twere at gallows would become him better.
GOTHARUS Thus from my master to the prince of Norway:
 We did expect and had prepared to meet
 Your victory with triumphs and, with garlands   20
 Due to your fate and valours, entertained you.
 Nor has your army sacrificed so many
 Warm drops of blood as we have shot up prayers
 That you might prosper and return the pledge
 Of all our hope and glory. But when pride   25
 Of your own fames and conquest in a war

---

6 horrid horrifying.

8–11 But...heart A further reminder of the devastating effects of civil war and that even the victors lose.

11–12 viperous...parent Vipers were thought to be such vicious creatures that babies ate their way out of their mother's body to be born, killing the parent. The image was commonly used to represent heresy or treason, the most serious crimes which were committed by those who should be the most loyal, and so a fitting image for the horrors of civil war (see Loewenstein 2013, 60).

13 monument grand funeral monuments were usually commissioned by the person themselves and often constructed before they died as an enduring symbol of the significance of their lives.

14–15 to...stones i.e. as one who has defaced even a small part of the city.

17 An 'twere As if; 'And' in Q/O (*OED*, And *conj.*[1] 13a).

17 gallows In speeches given from the gallows the condemned man or woman supposedly accepted their fate and praised the merciful monarch (see Sharpe 1985).

21 valours courage, but also intrinsic worth or merit, what a person has achieved through their own merit (*OED*, Valour *n.* 1c and Valor *n.* 2a.). By putting 'fate' first here, Gotharus slips in a sly insinuation that Turgesius's success should be attributed more to his good luck than his courage.

24 pledge promise, hope (of safety).

---

15 SD] *this edn; Enter* [*above,*] *on the walls, Gotharus, Hormenus* [*and*] *Aquinus. Fehrenbach; Enter* Gotharus *on the walls,* Ho. Aqui. Q/O

17 An] *Gifford;* And Q/O

495

THE COMPLETE WORKS OF JAMES SHIRLEY, VOLUME 7

Hath poisoned the obedience of a son
And tempted you to advance your sword new bathed
In enemies blood 'gainst your country's bosom,
Thus we receive you, and declare your piety   30
And faith lost to your country and your father.
PRINCE My lord, all this concerns not me. We have
But done our duties and return to lay
The trophies at his feet whose justice did
Make us victorious more than our own valour.   35
And now, without all titles but his son,
I dare hell's accusation to blast
My humble thoughts.
GOTHARUS   Sir, give us leave to fear
Not your own nature, calm as the soft air
When no rude wind conspires a mutiny –   40
OLAUS Leave rhetoric and to th'point: why do not
The gates spread to receive us and your joys
Shoot up in acclamations? I would have
Thy house give good example to the city
And make us the first-born fire.
GOTHARUS   Good heaven knows   45
How willingly I would sacrifice myself
To do a grateful service to the prince.
And I could wish, my lord, you were less passionate
And not inflame his highness' gentle spirit
To these attempts.

---

30 **Thus** i.e. In armed resistance.

30 **piety** true religion, pity. Piety or pity often carried the sense of proper devotion, indicating that the safety of the realm demanded pity for the people who needed to be protected from their enemies. True piety, Gotharus suggests, involves correct martial conduct.

36 **titles** Turgesius renounces his civic and military honours for rhetorical effect, just as he earlier claimed he had no interest in a funeral monument.

37 **blast** discredit.

38–40 **give...mutiny** Gotharus blames Olaus for the civil war, pretending that he only wishes to act as peacemaker.

45 **first-born fire** Olaus appears to be suggesting that Gotharus's house should be set on fire as the first part of their victory celebrations. In Numbers 18:17 the first-born of certain animals should be offered to God as a burnt offering, so an alternative reading could be that Olaus is demanding that they are given the right to sacrificial offerings in return for their service. Gifford amends to 'first bonfire', but 'first-born fire' gives a good sense of the destruction of a house being like the loss of a child, imagery that is continued by Gotharus in his subsequent speech as he offers to sacrifice himself.

47 **grateful** pleasing, agreeable.

48 **passionate** with the sense that the passions have overwhelmed Olaus's reason.

49 **inflame** continuing the image of the 'first-born fire', Gotharus cleverly deflects Olaus's speech demanding that he abandon rhetoric and sacrifice his house by suggesting that it is Olaus who is actually causing the fires of civil war through inciting Turgesius, the first-born son of the king.

49 **highness'** The final 's' is omitted to maintain the metre.

THE POLITICIAN   4.2

PRINCE   I am ignorant, Gotharus,   50
  Of what you mean. Where is the king, my father?
AQUINUS Where a sad father is, to know his son
  Bring arms against his life.
PRINCE   How now, Aquinus?
OLAUS Dare you be saucy? Oh, that gentleman
  Is angry. His head aches with the remembrance of   55
  My truncheon.
AQUINUS   'Twas a valiant act
  And did become the greatness of Olaus,
  Who by the privilege of his birth may do
  A wrong and boast it.
OLAUS   Shall these grooms affront us?
PRINCE [*To Aquinus*] Have you commission to be thus insolent?   60
  [*To Olaus*] They do not know us.
GOTHARUS   Yes, and in our hearts
  Bleed that our fears of your unjust demand
  Compel us to this separation.
PRINCE Demands? Is it injustice for a son
  To ask his father's blessing? By thy duty,   65
  Gotharus, I command thee: tell my father
  His son desires access. Let me but speak with him.
GOTHARUS I have not in your absence, sir, neglected
  What did become my service to your Highness,
  To take his anger off.
PRINCE   What riddle's this?   70
GOTHARUS But let me, with a pardon, tell your grace

54 **that gentleman** Aquinus.
56 **truncheon** club, staff.
56–9 **'Twas…it** Aquinus asserts that Olaus can only get away with his behaviour because he is of noble birth;
'valiant' is clearly sarcastic, implying that Olaus is simply a bully.
59 **grooms** servants (contemptuous); compare Lear's description of Oswald, Goneril's steward, when Regan
suggests that Lear return to Goneril's house: 'Persuade me rather to be slave and sumpter / To this detested
groom' (*King Lear*, 2.2.389–90).
60 **commission** i.e. authority from the king (continuing Aquinus's discussion of rank). There follows a series
of speeches which employ the language of authority and service: 'duty' (l. 65); 'access' (l. 67); 'neglected' (l. 68);
'service' (l. 69).
64 **Demands?** Gifford regularizes the 'demand' in l. 62 to demands, but there is no particular reason to do
so. Turgesius is horrified at the idea that he would makes demands on his father, not just the specific one of which
he is accused.
70 **take…off** calm his anger.
70 **riddle** Turgesius does not know that Gotharus has forged a letter which has made the king angry.

54] *lineation Gifford;* saucy? / O Q/O   60 SD] *Fehrenbach subst.; not in* Q/O
61 SD] *Fehrenbach subst.; not in* Q/O

497

4.2 THE COMPLETE WORKS OF JAMES SHIRLEY, VOLUME 7

The letters that you sent were not so dutiful.
You were to blame to chide and article
So with a king and father. Yet I said,
And pawned my conscience, 'twas no act of yours –   75
I mean entire – but wrought and formed by some
Rash spirits to corrupt you with ambition,
Feeding your youth with thought of hasty empire
To serve their ends, whose counsel all this while
Did starve that sweetness in you we all hoped for.   80
OLAUS Devices! More devices!
PRINCE   I am amazed,
And if the king will not vouchsafe me conference
I shall accuse thy cunning to have poisoned
My father's good opinion.

     Enter KING [*above*].

GOTHARUS   Innocence
May thus be stained. [*To King*] Pray let your justice clear me.   85
KING What would our son?
PRINCE   Thus pay his filial duty. [*He kneels.*]
KING 'Tis but counterfeit if you bring no thought
To force our blessing in this rude manner. How
Dare you approach? Dismiss your soldiers.
OLAUS Not the meanest knapsack.   90
That were a way to bring us to the mercy
Of wolves indeed; Gotharus grinds his teeth
Already at us.
KING [*To Olaus*] We shall talk with you, sir,

73–4 **article...with** bring charges against.

75 **pawn'd...conscience** pledged, risked my conscience (with the implication that Gotharus had to be insincere in defending Turgesius).

76 **entire** free from alien admixture (*OED*, Entire *adj*. 6a). It describes the 'act' of the previous line and implies that it was Olaus's idea—one of the 'Rash spirits' of l. 77.

78 **hasty empire** i.e. taking the crown too early.

81 **Devices** Tricks.

82 **vouchsafe...conference** promise me an interview.

84–5 **Innocence...stain'd** Ironically Gotharus feels that he is being falsely accused.

85 **clear** exonerate.

87 **bring no thought** i.e. come so thoughtlessly.

88 **in...manner** i.e. with an army. Shirley may be drawing a parallel with Rome where to prevent civil war, generals were not allowed to enter the city with their armies when they returned from campaigns.

90 **meanest knapsack** i.e. smallest, least well-supplied soldier.

---

84 SD] *Fehrenbach subst.; Enter* King *on the walls. Gifford; Enter* King. Q/O
85 SD] *Fehrenbach subst.; not in* Q/O   86 SD] *Gifford subst.; not in* Q/O
93 SD] *Fehrenbach subst.; not in* Q/O

THE POLITICIAN   4.2

Hereafter. [*To the prince*] I command thee by thy duty
Thou owe'st a father and a king: dismiss   95
Your troops.
PRINCE   I will.
OLAUS   You shall not. That were fine
So we may run our heads into their noose.
You give away your safety.
PRINCE   I will not
Dispute my power. Let my entreat prevail
For their dismission.
OLAUS   You may dismiss   100
Your head and mine, and be laughed at. These men
Are honest and dare fight for us.
PRINCE   I know
Their loves and will reward it, dear, dear uncle.
GOTHARUS [*Aside to Aquinus*] How he prepares his tragedy, Aquinus.
Let not thy hand shake.
AQUINUS   I am resolute.   105
GOTHARUS And I, for thy reward.

                    [*The prince speaks to some soldiers and they leave.*]
                    'Tis done, the soldiers
Disperse already.
OLAUS [*To the prince*] If any mischief follow this,
Thank your credulity.
PRINCE [*To King*]   May I now hope for access?
KING Descend Gotharus and Aquinus
To meet the prince. While he contains within   110
The piety of a son we shall embrace him.   [*Exeunt Gotharus and Aquinus above.*]

---

99 dispute discuss.
99 entreat request.
100–1 You…mine i.e. You might as well say goodbye to our heads as we will surely lose them if you take that course of action.
106 reward a grim pun as Gotharus plans to kill Aquinus. The quibble, coming immediately after Gotharus's reference to 'tragedy' recalls the *double entendres* of many Jacobean tragedies (see Brooke 1979).
110–11 contains…son restrains himself (*OED*, Contain *v.* 13a) and behaves as a proper son should.

---

94 SD] *Fehrenbach subst.; not in* Q/O
100 dismission] *Gifford;* dimission Q/O   **100** dismiss] *Gifford;* dimiss Q/O
103 reward] *Gifford;* rewa Q/O   **104 SD**] *Fehrenbach subst.; not in* Q/O
106 SD] *this edition;* [*Speaks with the soldiers.*] *after* uncle, [*Exeunt soldiers.*] *after* reward. *Fehrenbach;* [*exeunt Soldiers.*] *after* reward. *Gifford; not in* Q/O
107 SD] *Fehrenbach subst.; not in* Q/O   **108 SD**] *Fehrenbach subst.; not in* Q/O
111 SD] *this edn;* [*Exeunt* King, Gotharus, Hormenus, *and* Aquinus.] *Fehrenbach; not in* Q/O

499

4.2   THE COMPLETE WORKS OF JAMES SHIRLEY, VOLUME 7

PRINCE When I degenerate let me be accursed
   By heaven and you.
OLAUS [*To the prince*] Are you not pale to think on't.
PRINCE [*To Olaus*] It puzzles me to think my father guilty. [*He makes to leave.*]
OLAUS I do not like things yet.

   As the prince is going forth a pistol is discharged within. He falls.

PRINCE   Oh, I am shot! I am murdered!   115

   [*Enter* GOTHARUS *and* AQUINUS.]

OLAUS [*To Aquinus*] Inhuman traitor! Villain!   (*Olaus wounds Aquinus.*)
GOTHARUS [*Aside*] So so, his hand has saved my execution.
   'Tis not safe for me to stay. They are both sped rarely.   *Exit.*
OLAUS [*To King*] Oh, my dear cousin. Treason! Treason!
KING   Where?
OLAUS In thy own bosom. Thou hast killed thy son.   120
   [*To Reginaldus and Cortes*] Convey his body – guard it safe.

                  [*They take up the prince's body and exeunt.*]

                                        And this

   Perfidious trunk I'll have it punished
   Past death and scatter his torn flesh about
   The world to affright mankind. [*To King*] Thou art
   A murderer, no blood of mine.

            [*Exeunt Olaus and soldiers carrying the body of Aquinus.*]

      [*Enter* GOTHARUS *above.*]
GOTHARUS   'Tis done,   125

---

112 **degenerate** fall away from my proper allegiance and ancestral qualities, revolt (*OED v.* 1a, 4).
113 **pale** frightened.
117 **execution** i.e. Gotharus's plot to murder Aquinus.
118 **sped** dispatched, killed.
118 **rarely** unusually (implying with good fortune).
122 **Perfidious trunk** i.e. Aquinus's body.
123–4 **scatter...mankind** alluding to the practice that traitors' body parts were publicly displayed (usually on city walls) as a warning to others.
125 **no...mine** i.e. he will no longer acknowledge the king as his kin. There may also be a reference to the surviving family of traitors losing titles, status, and land because their blood was tainted by the crime, unless the monarch decided to pardon them.

---

113 SD] *Fehrenbach subst.; not in* Q/O   114 SD1] *Fehrenbach subst.; not in* Q/O
114 SD2] *this edn; not in* Q/O
115 SD2] *this edn;* [*Enter* Aquinus, *below.*] *after* murder'd!, [*Enter* Gotharus, *below.*] *after* Olaus *wounds* Aquinus., [*Enter the king, below.*] *after* Gotharus's exit *Fehrenbach; not in* Q/O
116 SD1] *Fehrenbach subst.; not in* Q/O   117 SD] *Fehrenbach subst.; not in* Q/O
119 SD] *this edn; not in* Q/O   121 SD1] *Fehrenbach subst.; not in* Q/O
121 SD2] *this edn; not in* Q/O   124 SD] *this edn;* [*To the King. after* Thou art *Gifford; not in* Q/O
125 SD1] *this edn;* [*Exeunt, all save the king, bearing the bodies. Enter* Gotharus, *above.*] *Fehrenbach;* [*Exeunt, bearing the bodies. Gifford; not in* Q/O
125 SD2] *this edn; Re-enter* GOTHARUS *above. Gifford; not in* Q/O

500

THE POLITICIAN   4.3

And all the guilt dies with Aquinus, fallen
By Olaus's sword most happily, who but
Prevented mine. This act concludes all fear.
KING He was my son – I must needs drop a tear.

> *Exeunt [King, Gotharus and Hormenus above].*

[4.3]

>   HARALDUS *discovered sick, [with]* QUEEN [MARPISA, OFFICERS, *and*] DOCTORS.
MARPISA It is not possible! He catch a fever
By excess of wine? He was all temperance.
DOCTOR He had a soft and tender constitution,
Apt to be inflamed. They that are most abstemious
Feel the disorder with more violence.   5
MARPISA Where? Who assisted him in this misfortune?
He had some company.
DOCTOR   He was invited,
He says, by Sueno and Helga to a banquet
Where in their mirth they, careless of his health,
Suffered him drink too much.
MARPISA   They poisoned him.   10
[*To officers*] Go apprehend the murderers of my child.   [*Exeunt officers.*]
If he recover not, their death shall wait

---

126 guilt…Aquinus Gotharus's assumptions are problematic as intention to kill was almost as serious a crime as actually committing murder, therefore it is not obvious that 'guilt dies with Aquinus'. The issue of intention and actions was discussed at length in Thomas Aquinas, *Summa Theologica*, 2.12–18. Aquinas is clear that evil intentions, like murder, are evil, whatever the outcome. Aquinus's name may perhaps involve a joke about the philosopher, especially if Shirley was, as many assume, inclined to Catholicism.

128 This…fear Gotharus concludes that Fortune has acted in his favour and he is now safe.

0 SD DOCTORS The number of doctors who enter is unspecified and, contrary to the practice regarding the rebels who speak in the following three scenes and in 5.2, Q/O makes no distinction between them in their speech headings. As the number of doctors who enter, and which one delivers which speech, is essentially a performance decision this edition follows Q/O. Q/O follows the same practice when doctors are required at 5.2.215–20.

1–2 It…wine The dangers of excessive drinking were recognized in the early modern period: Robert Greene was thought to have died in 1592 after a 'surfett of pickle herring and renish wine' (Harrison 1922, 13). Marpisa's incredulity is because Haraldus, young as he is, is not given to excessive consumption.

3–4 He…inflam'd Illness was usually imagined in terms of the functioning of an individual's constitution and the need for it to be correctly balanced, rather than caused by an invasive disease (see Porter 1997, 198). The doctor argues that Haraldus is especially vulnerable to disease because of his weak, untried constitution.

10 Suffered him Allowed him (to).

10 poisoned It was commonly feared that ruthless *politiques* would employ poison, often inspired by Italian practices (see Thomas 2012). Poison was frequently seen as a woman's weapon: see 4.4.44n.

12–13 wait Upon follow, accompany.

---

129 SD] *this edn; Exeunt* Q/O
[4.3]] *Gifford subst. (*SCENE III.*); [*IV.iii.*] Fehrenbach; no scene division in* Q/O
0 SD *with…*DOCTORS] *this edn; Marpisa, physicians[, and officers] Fehrenbach;* MARPISA, *and* Physicians *Gifford;* Queen, Doctors Q/O
11 SD1] *Fehrenbach subst.; not in* Q/O   **11 SD2**] *Fehrenbach; not in* Q/O

501

4.3   THE COMPLETE WORKS OF JAMES SHIRLEY, VOLUME 7

Upon Haraldus. But pray you tell me, gentlemen,
Is there no hope of life, have you not art
Enough to cure a fever?

DOCTOR   We find madam   15
His disease more malignant by some thought
Or apprehensions of grief.

MARPISA   What grief?
You're all imposters and are ignorant
But how to kill.

HARALDUS   Is not my mother come?

MARPISA Yes, my dear son, and here shall weep myself   20
Till I turn Niobe unless thou givest me
Some hope of thy own life.

HARALDUS   I would say something,
Were you alone.

MARPISA [*To Doctors*] Leave us.   [*Exeunt Doctors.*]
                          Now my Haraldus,
How is it with my child?

HARALDUS   I know you love me
Yet I must tell you truth: I cannot live.   25
And let this comfort you: death will not come
Unwelcome to your son. I do not die
Against my will and, having my desires,
You have less cause to mourn.

MARPISA   What is't has made
The thought of life unpleasant, which does court   30
Thy dwelling here with all delights that nature
And art can study for thee, rich in all things

---

17 **apprehensions** feelings.
18 **imposters** fakes (quacks).
19 **But** Except for.
19 **how ... kill** Doctors took the Hippocratic Oath and promised to preserve life; the line appears to suggest that even good doctors were as likely to kill as cure.
20–1 **weep ... Niobe** Niobe was turned to stone by the gods so that she could escape her grief after the death of her twelve children, but her tears still flowed; compare Hamlet's: 'she followed my poor father's body, / Like Niobe, all tears' (*Hamlet*, 1.2.148–9). This exchange between Haraldus and his mother closely follows that between Hamlet and Gertrude in the closet scene when Hamlet, like Haraldus, first berates his mother for being unfaithful to his father and then expresses disgust and horror as he is compelled to recognize the mother's sexuality.
23 **Were you** (If) you were.
24 **I ... me** Perhaps an echo of Iago's words to Othello: 'My lord, you know I love you' (3.3.121). Marpisa does love Haraldus, but not in a conventional manner—using him for her own gain, which helps to generate the anxiety that kills him.
30–1 **which ... here** which (i.e. life) tries to make your staying in the world seem attractive.

---

23 SD1] *this edn; not in* Q/O   23 SD2] *this edn; [exeunt Physicians.] Gifford; not in* Q/O

502

THE POLITICIAN

4.3

Thy wish can be ambitious of? Yet all
These treasures nothing to thy mother's love,
Which to enjoy thee would defer a while   35
Her thought of going to heaven.
HARALDUS   Oh, take heed, mother – heaven
Has a spacious ear and power to punish
Your too much love with my eternal absence.
I beg your prayers and blessing.
MARPISA   Th'art dejected;
Have but a will and live.
HARALDUS   'Tis in vain mother.   40
MARPISA Sink with a fever into earth?
Look up, thou shall not die.
HARALDUS   I have a wound within
You do not see, more killing than all fevers.
MARPISA A wound? Where? Who has murdered thee?
HARALDUS   Gotharus –
MARPISA Ha! Furies persecute him!
HARALDUS   Oh, pray for him!   45
'Tis my duty though he gave me death –
He is my father.
MARPISA   How? Thy father?
HARALDUS He told me so, and with that breath destroyed me.
I felt it strike upon my spirits. Mother,
Would I had ne'er been born!
MARPISA   Believe him not.   50
HARALDUS Oh do not add another sin to what
Is done already. Death is charitable
To quit me from the scorn of all the world.
MARPISA By all my hopes, Gotharus has abused thee.
Thou art the lawful burden of my womb,   55
Thy father, Altomarus.
HARALDUS   Ha?
MARPISA Before whose spirit, long since taken up
To meet with saints and troops angelical,
I dare again repeat, thou art his son.

---

39 dejected close to despair, a deadly sin because the despairing refused to believe that God's mercy could save them (see Baseotto 2008). Robert Burton has a long section on the cure of despair which concludes *The Anatomy of Melancholy*. Marpisa is encouraging Haraldus to try to live, which will increase his chances of life and avoiding eternal damnation.

45 Furies In Greek mythology, goddesses of justice and vengeance who drive their guilty victims mad.

49 spirits vital life functions.

53 quit release.

54 By...hopes A mild oath; see *Richard II*, 1.1.68: 'By all my hopes, most falsely doth he lie'.

54 abused wronged, deceived.

503

4.3 THE COMPLETE WORKS OF JAMES SHIRLEY, VOLUME 7

HARALDUS Ten thousand blessings now reward my mother! 60
    Speak it again and I may live. A stream
    Of pious joy runs through me. To my soul
    You've struck a harmony next that in heaven.
    Can you without a blush call me your child
    And son of Altomarus? All that's holy 65
    Dwell in your blood forever. Speak it once,
    But once again.
MARPISA   Were it my latest breath,
    Thou art his and mine.
HARALDUS   Enough, my tears do flow
    To give you thanks for't. I would you could resolve me
    But one truth more: why did my lord Gotharus 70
    Call me the issue of his blood?
MARPISA   Alas, he thinks thou art –
HARALDUS What are those words? I am undone again.
MARPISA Ha?
HARALDUS   'Tis too late to call 'em back. He thinks I am his son –
MARPISA I have confessed too much and tremble with
    The imagination. Forgive me child, 75
    And heaven, if there be mercy to a crime
    So black as I must now, to quit thy fears,
    Say I have been guilty of. We have been sinful
    And I was not unwilling to oblige
    His active brain for thy advancement by 80
    Abusing his belief thou wert his own.
    But thou hast no such stain; thy birth is innocent
    Or may I perish ever. 'Tis a strange
    Confession to a child but it may drop
    A balsam to thy wound. Live, my Haraldus, 85
    If not for this, to see my penitence
    And with what tears I'll wash away my sin.
HARALDUS I am no bastard then.

62 **pious** faithful to parents (as well as religion).

63 **harmony...heaven** Haraldus now feels he can remain on earth instead of needing to escape to heaven. He experiences heavenly harmony on earth.

67 **latest** last.

68 **tears...flow** continuing the Niobe references.

74–5 **I...imagination** i.e. 'I have confessed too much and tremble with the knowledge of having done so'.

78 **We** Gotharus and Marpisa.

79 **oblige** i.e. 'place a further obligation on'.

81 **Abusing** i.e. Encouraging.

82 **stain** dishonour of illegitimacy.

83 **perish ever** die for all time (continuing the earlier discussion of salvation/damnation).

85 **balsam** healing, soothing agent (*OED*, *n.* 2a, 3).

87 **tears...sin** Marpisa casts herself as Mary Magdalene, whose tears before Jesus were thought to have washed away her sins (Luke 7:37–8), a subject frequently represented in art and poetry, notably Richard Crashaw's poem, 'The Weeper' (1646).

68 SH] *Gifford subst.; not in* Q/O   72] *lineation Gifford;* undone / Agen. Q/O

504

THE POLITICIAN   4·3

MARPISA   Thou art not.
HARALDUS But I am not found while you are lost:
   No time can restore you. My spirits faint.   90
MARPISA Will nothing comfort thee?
HARALDUS   My duty to the king.
MARPISA He's here.

      Enter KING.

KING How is't Haraldus? Death sits in's face.
HARALDUS Give me your blessing and within my heart
   I'll pray you may have many. My soul flies   95
   'Bove this vain world. Good mother, close mine eyes. [*He dies.*]
MARPISA Never died so much sweetness in his years.
KING Be comforted, I have lost my son too –
   The prince is slain.

      Enter OFFICERS *with* HELGA.

                          How now?
MARPISA Justice upon the murderer of my son.   100
   This villain Helga and his companion,
   Sueno, have killed him. Where's the other?
OFFICER   Fled madam,
   But Helga does confess he made him drunk.
HELGA But not dead drunk – I do beseech you, madam.
KING Look here what your base surfeit has destroyed.   105
HELGA 'Twas Sueno as well as I. My lord Gotharus
   Gave us commission for what we did.
MARPISA [*Aside*] Again Gotharus! Sure he plotted this.
KING Hang him up straight.
HELGA   I left no drink behind me –
   If I must die let me have equal justice   110
   And let one of your guard drink me to death, sir.
   Or if you please to let me live till
   Sueno is taken, we will drink and reel

89 i.e. As long as you are (morally) lost I cannot think of myself as found.
104 **dead drunk** The first citation in the *OED* is 1599: Helga's pun, perhaps the result of his panicking, is nonetheless extremely insensitive, and reveals his lack of understanding of Haraldus's feeble constitution.
105 **base surfeit** i.e. vulgar or tasteless excess.
109–14 **I...together** Helga is perhaps still too intoxicated to deal with the gravity of the situation in which he finds himself and his lines are delivered with a mixture of bravado, confusion, and desperation.

90] *lineation Gifford; you, / My* Q/O   93] *lineation Gifford; Haraldus? / Death* Q/O
96 SD] *Gifford subst.; not in* Q/O
99 SD] *this edn; Enter officers with Helga*[, *drunk*]. *Fehrenbach; after* now. Q/O
108 SD] *Fehrenbach subst.; not in* Q/O

505

4.4   THE COMPLETE WORKS OF JAMES SHIRLEY, VOLUME 7

Out of the world together.

KING   Hence, and hang him.

Exeunt [Officers with Helga].

      Enter HORMENUS.

HORMENUS Sir, you must make provision against   115
  New danger. Discontent is broke into
  A wild rebellion and many of your subjects
  Gather in tumults and give out they will
  Revenge the prince's death.

KING   This I did fear.
  Where's Gotharus? [*Aside*] Oh, my fright, my conscience   120
  Has furies in't. [*Aloud*] Where's Gotharus?

HORMENUS Not in the court.

KING   I tremble with confusions.

Exeunt [King and Hormenus].

MARPISA I am resolved. My joys are all expired,
  Nor can ambition more concern me now.
  Gotharus has undone me in the death   125
  Of my loved son. His fate is next. While I
  Move resolute, I'll command his destiny.   *Exit.*

[4.4]

      Enter GOTHARUS.

GOTHARUS How are we lost. The prince Turgesius's death
  Is of no use since 'tis unprofitable
  To the great hope we stored up in Haraldus.
  It was a cursèd plot directed me
  To raise his spirit by those giddy engines   5

---

114 **Hence** (Take him) hence.
115–19 **Sir…death** Disorder in the country follows disorder at court; compare *Hamlet*, 4.3.1–11.
118 **tumults** disorderly crowds, mobs.
120–1 **Oh…in't** The king would be unlikely to admit his guilt out loud.
121 **furies** see l. 45. The king imagines he is being justly punished for allowing Haraldus to die.
124 **more** (any) more.
126–7 **While…resolute** i.e. So long as I continue to act with determination.
1 **How…lost** i.e. We are completely lost.
5 **giddy engines** foolish instruments (Sueno and Helga).

---

114 SD1] *Gifford subst.*; Exeunt. Q/O   120 SD] *this edn; not in* Q/O   121 SD] *this edn; not in* Q/O
122 SD] *Gifford subst.*; Exit. Q/O
[4.4]] *Gifford subst.* (SCENE IV.*); [IV.iv.] Fehrenbach; no scene division in* Q/O

506

THE POLITICIAN 4.4

That have undone him – their souls reel to hell for't.
How will Marpisa weep herself into
The obscure shades and leave me here to grow
A statue with the wonder of our fate.

    Enter ALBINA.

ALBINA Sir.
GOTHARUS Do not trouble me.
ALBINA   Although   10
  I am not partner of your joys or comfort
  Yet let your cruelty be so mindful of me
  I may divide your sorrows.
GOTHARUS   Would thy sufferings
  Could ease me of the weight, I would
  Empty my heart of all that's ill to sink thee   15
  And bury thee alive. Thy sight is hateful;
  Ask me not why but in obedience
  Fly hence into some wilderness. The queen!   *Exit Albina.*

    Enter QUEEN [MARPISA].
  Great queen, did any sorrow lade my bosom
  But what does almost melt it for Haraldus,   20
  Your presence would revive me. But it seems
  Our hopes and joys in him grew up so mighty
  Heaven became jealous we should undervalue
  The bliss of th'other world and build in him
  A richer paradise.
MARPISA   I have mourned already   25
  A mother's part and, fearing thy excess
  Of grief, present myself to comfort thee.
  Tears will not call him back and 'twill become us

---

6 reel hurtle, stagger drunkenly (*OED*, *v.*[1] 10b, 8b) but perhaps also, harking back to 3.2.54–9, dance (*OED*, *v.*[3]).

7–9 A variation on the Niobe myth. Gotharus imagines Marpisa weeping until she descends into the gloomy underworld of Hades ('The obscure shades') while he turns to stone out of astonishment at what has happened to them ('the wonder of our fate'); 'wonder' could also mean strangeness, specifically malign, as in 'great distress or grief' (*OED*, *n.* 5c).

12 let...me i.e. let me be aware of your suffering.

13 divide share.

13–16 Would...alive i.e. Were it possible that your suffering could relieve me of the pain of mine, I would empty my heart of everything unpleasant in it to overwhelm you and bury you alive.

19 lade load, burden.

20 But what Other than what.

21–5 But...paradise Their ambitions for Haraldus threatened to obscure their belief in the significance of the afterlife, and hence inspire divine wrath.

---

18 SD1 and 2] *Gifford subst.; Enter* Marpisa. *after* wilderness., *Exit* Albina. *after* queen. *Fehrenbach; Enter Queene. Exit* Alb. *after* The Queeen. [*sic*] Q/O

507

4.4   THE COMPLETE WORKS OF JAMES SHIRLEY, VOLUME 7

(Since we two are the world unto ourselves –
Nothing without the circle of our arms   30
Precious and welcome) to take heed our grief
Make us not oversoon like him that's dead
And our blood useless.
GOTHARUS   Were you present madam
When your son died?
MARPISA   I was.
GOTHARUS   And did you weep
And wish him live and would not heaven at   35
Your wish return his wandering ghost again?
Your voice should make another out of atoms.
I do adore the harmony and from
One pleasant look draw in more blessings
Than death knows how to kill.   40
MARPISA [*Aside*] He is recovered from his passion.
GOTHARUS What's this? Ha!
MARPISA   Where?
GOTHARUS   Here, like a sudden winter
Struck on my heart. I am not well o'th'sudden. Ha!
MARPISA My lord, make use of this – 'tis cordial. (*Gives him a box of poison.*)
I am often subject to these passions   45
And dare not walk without this ivory box
To prevent danger. They are pleasant.
'Tis a most happy opportunity.
GOTHARUS Let me present my thanks to my preserver

    Enter ALBINA.

And kiss your hand.
MARPISA   Our lips will meet more lovingly. [*They kiss.*]   50
ALBINA [*Aside*] My heart will break.

---

  30 without outside, beyond.

  31–3 to…useless i.e. their fate may too quickly follow that of Haraldus if they do not control their melancholy at his death.

  37 Your…atoms Gotharus poetically adapts Lucretius's theory that atoms were the basic, indestructible unit of matter to suggest that Marpisa can create another son to replace Haraldus using her voice (perhaps an acknowledgement that Haraldus will live on if they talk about him). Shirley was among the many writers and thinkers interested in Lucretius in the seventeenth century (see Barbour 1998, 46, 54–5).

  38 harmony i.e. of your voice.

  39 look either a glance at or a look from Marpisa.

  41 He has got over his anger; but the observation is ironic—Marpisa recognizes immediately the politic intention behind Gotharus's hyperbolic sympathy.

  44 cordial medicine for the heart (*OED, n.* a; also *adj.* 2a).

  44 SD *Gives…poison* On poison as a woman's weapon, see Martin 2005, xiv.

  45 passions afflictions, illness.

  48 happy opportunity fortunate coincidence (with heavy dramatic irony).

---

41 SD] *Gifford subst.; not in* Q/O   **50 SD**] *this edn; not in* Q/O   **51 SD**] *Fehrenbach subst.; not in* Q/O

508

THE POLITICIAN   4·4

MARPISA   Your lady. We are betrayed.
   She sees us kiss and I shall hate her for't.
GOTHARUS [*To Albina*] Does this offend your virtue?
ALBINA   You're merciless.
   You shall be a less tyrant, sir, to kill me.
   [*To Marpisa*] Injurious queen!
MARPISA   Shall I be here affronted?   55
   I shall not think Gotharus worth my love
   To let her breathe forth my dishonour, which
   Her passion hath already dared to publish,
   Nor wanted she before an impudence
   To throw this poison in my face.
GOTHARUS   I'll tame her.   *Exit.*   60
ALBINA I wo'not curse you, madam, but you are
   The cruellest of all womankind.
   I am prepared to meet your tyrannies.
          [*Re-*]*enter* GOTHARUS *with a pistol; at the other door, a* SERVANT.
SERVANT   My lord,
   We are undone. The common people are
   In arms and violently assault our house,   65
   Threat'ning your lordship with a thousand deaths
   For the good prince, whose murder they exclaim
   Contrived by you.
GOTHARUS The fiends of hell will show more mercy to me.
   Where shall I hide me?
                      [*He drops the pistol.*]
MARPISA   Alas, they'll kill me too.   [*Exit.*]   70
SERVANT There's no staying – they have broke the wall of
   The first court. Down at some window, sir.
                  Albina takes up the pistol.
GOTHARUS Help me! Oh, help me! I'm lost!   [*Exeunt Gotharus and Servant.*]

---

51 betrayed exposed.
54 a less tyrant i.e. less of a tyrant.
55 Injurious Damaging, harmful.
58 publish broadcast.
59 wanted lacked.
60 poison i.e. defamatory accusations (but referring also to Marpisa's actions).
63 tyrannies crimes, violent acts.
67 exclaim proclaim loudly (*OED*, *v*. 3).
72 Down at Get out through.

---

52 sees] *Fehrenbach;* [saw] *Gifford;* see Q/O   **53 SD**] *Fehrenbach subst.; not in* Q/O
55 SD] *this edn; not in* Q/O   **63 SD** *Re-enter*] *Gifford; Enter* Q/O   **70 SD1**] *this edn; not in* Q/O
70 SD2] *Gifford; not in* Q/O   **71–2**] *lineation this edn;* There...wall / Of...sir. *Gifford;* There's...Court, /
Down...sir. Q/O   **72 SD**] Q/O *subst.;* [Gotharus *drops*] *the pistol;* Albina *takes* [*it*] *up. Fehrenbach;* [Goth.
drops the pistol, which Albina takes up. Gifford   **73 SD1**] *Fehrenbach subst.;* [*Exit with Serv. Gifford; not in* Q/O

4.4   THE COMPLETE WORKS OF JAMES SHIRLEY, VOLUME 7

REBELS (*Within*)   Down with the doors!
    This way, this way!

      Enter REBELS.

ALBINA   He that first moves this way
    Comes on his death. I can despatch but one   75
    And take your choice.
FIRST REBEL   Alas, good madam,
    We do not come to trouble you,
    You have sorrow enough. We would talk
    With my lord, your pagan husband.
SECOND REBEL   Aye, aye, where is he?
THIRD REBEL   That traitor.   80
FOURTH REBEL   Murderer of our prince.
ALBINA   You're not well informed –
    Aquinus killed the prince.
SECOND REBEL   But by my lord's correction.
    We know his heart and do mean to eat it.
    Therefore let him appear. Knock down the lady,
    You with the long bill.   85
ALBINA   How dare you run the hazard of your lives
    And fortunes thus, like outlaws without authority,
    To break into our houses? When you have done
    What fury leads you to't, you will buy too dear
    Repentance at the gallows.   90
SECOND REBEL   Hang the gallows and give us my lord, your husband!

      Enter SERVANT.

SERVANT   [*Privately to Albina*] He's escaped madam. Now they may search.

      Enter more REBELS.

---

75 **I…one** Albina's pistol, typically for this period, is single-shot.

76 **And** Used to emphasize that the rebels have to choose who is to be shot (see Abbott 1869, 71).

79 **pagan** unchristian, ungodly.

82 **correction** i.e. responsibility ('control, governance' *OED*, *n*. 5), but as it is a lower class character speaking it is possible that the word is a malapropism for 'direction' (and that Gifford, who amends to 'direction', was thinking along the right lines).

83 **heart…it** recalling Turgesius's threat to have Gotharus's heart at 3.3.32, but also perhaps with reference to the spectacular scene in John Ford's *'Tis Pity She's A Whore* (first performance 1626), in which Giovanni enters with his sister's heart on his dagger (5.6).

85 **long bill** halberd, a combination of a pike and an axe.

91 Albina has given the rebels the idea of hanging Gotharus, a form of execution not usually undertaken for those of noble birth.

---

73 **SH2 SD2**] *Fehrenbach subst.; Within*—— Q/O

76 **SH**] *this edn;* 1 [REBEL]. *Fehrenbach;* 1 *Reb. Gifford;* 1. Q/O *(and thus throughout remainder of scene for Rebel SHs)*

76–7] *lineation Fehrenbach;* Alas…you, Q/O   88 houses?] *Gifford;* houses, Q/O

92 **SD1**] *this edn; not in* Q/O

THE POLITICIAN   4.5

ALBINA [*Privately to Servant*] But where's the queen? She must not be betrayed.
FIRST REBEL This way, this way – he got out of a window
  And leapt a wall. Follow, follow!   [*Exeunt Rebels.*]   95
REBELS (*Within*) Follow, follow, follow!
ALBINA   Oh, my poor Gotharus.

         [*Re-*]*enter* QUEEN [MARPISA].

  Madam you are secure. Though you pursued
  My death I wish you safety.
MARPISA   I have been
  Too cruel, but my fate compelled me to't.   *Exit.*
ALBINA I am become the extremest of all miseries.   100
  Oh, my unhappy lord!   *Exeunt* [*Albina and Servant*].

[4.5]

         Enter SUENO [*disguised*].

SUENO Helga is hanged. What will become of me?
  I think I were best turn rebel: there's no hope
  To walk without a guard, and that I shall not
  Want to the gallows. Heathen halberdiers
  Are used to have a care and do rejoice   5
  To see men have good ends.

         Enter GOTHARUS.

GOTHARUS   I am pursued.
SUENO [*Aside*] My lord Gotharus? Worse and worse. Oh, for a
  Mist before his eyes!

95 **Follow, follow** A hunting cry (see Ben Jonson, *Epicoene* (first performance 1609), 3.7.50).

100 **miseries** Albina appears to be imagining herself as a visual allegory of misery.

2–4 **there's…gallows** i.e. there's no chance of surviving unless one has a body-guard, which I will not lack if taken to the gallows.

4 **Heathen halberdiers** i.e. Soldiers with halberds, who guarded prisoners and escorted them to the gallows, a job which might be seen as conflicting with Christian belief.

5 **Are…care** Perform their work with customary care.

6 **good ends** here, ironic, but executions were supposed to save the soul of the criminal who repented, so the condemned were given time to do so before they died.

8 **Mist…eyes** to prevent him seeing Sueno; proverbial, to cast a mist before one's eyes (Tilley M1017).

93 SD] *this edn; not in* Q/O   93 queen?] *Gifford;* Queene, Q/O
95 SD] *Gifford subst.; not in* Q/O   96 SH1 SD1] *Fehrenbach subst.; Within*— Q/O
96 SD2] *Gifford subst.; Enter* Queen. Q/O   101 SD] *Fehrenbach subst.; Exit.* Q/O
[4.5]] *Gifford subst.* (SCENE V. *);* [IV.v.] *Fehrenbach; no scene division in* Q/O
0 SD] *Gifford subst.; Enter* Sueno. Q/O   7 SD] *Fehrenbach subst.; not in* Q/O
7–8] *lineation this edn;* My…worse. / Oh…eyes. *Fehrenbach;* My…for / A…eyes! *Gifford;* My…eyes. Q/O

511

4.5   THE COMPLETE WORKS OF JAMES SHIRLEY, VOLUME 7

GOTHARUS   You sha'not betray me sir.

> [*He attacks Sueno.*]

SUENO Hold, my lord. I am your servant, honest Sueno.
GOTHARUS Sueno, off with that case! It may secure me.   10
    Quickly or –
SUENO   Oh my lord, you shall command my skin.

> [*They exchange clothes.*]

    Alas, poor gentleman, I'm glad I have it
    To do your lordship service.
GOTHARUS   Nay, your beard too.
SUENO Yes, yes, anything. [*He gives Gotharus his false beard.*]
    Alas, my good lord, how comes this?   15
GOTHARUS Leave your untimely prating – help!
    You'll not betray me?
SUENO   I'll first be hanged.
REBELS (*Within*) Follow, follow!
GOTHARUS Hell stop their throats. So, so, now thy reward.
SUENO It was my duty. Troth sir, I will have nothing.   20
GOTHARUS Yes, take that, and that, for killing of Haraldus. (*Wounds him.*)
    Now I'm sure you will not prate.
SUENO   Oh, murder! [*Falls down.*]
REBELS (*Within*) Follow, follow!
GOTHARUS I cannot 'scape. O help, invention!

> *He bloodies himself with Sueno's blood, and falls down as dead.*

> *Enter* REBELS.

FIRST REBEL This way they say he went.

> [*He sees Gotharus.*]
>
>   What's he?   25

SECOND REBEL One of our company I think.
THIRD REBEL Who killed him?
FOURTH REBEL   I know not.

---

10 **case** clothes, disguise.
11 **command** demand to have (*OED*, *v.* 7).
16 **prating** prattling, idle talk.
21 **that, and that** These words mimic the thrust of the dagger.
24 **invention** inspiration, ingenuity.
25 **What's he** Who's he?

---

8 SD] *Fehrenbach subst.; [Draws a poniard.* Gifford; *not in* Q/O
11 SD] *this edn;* [They exchange clothes.] *after* anything. *Fehrenbach;* [They exchange dresses. *after* help! *Gifford; not in* Q/O
14 SD] *this edn; not in* Q/O   18 SH SD] *Fehrenbach subst.;* [Within.] *Gifford; Within--- Q/O
22 SD] *this edn; not in* Q/O   23 SH SD] *Fehrenbach subst.;* [Within.] *Gifford; Within--- Q/O
25 SH] *this edn;* 1 REBEL. *Fehrenbach;* 1 Reb. *Gifford;* 1. Q/O *(and thus throughout remainder of scene for Rebel SHs)*
25 SD] *this edn;* [Discovering Gotharus disguised.] *Fehrenbach; not in* Q/O

THE POLITICIAN   4.6

SECOND REBEL   Let's away.
 If we can find that traitor he shall pay for all.
FOURTH REBEL Oh, that I had him here, I'd teach him –
SECOND REBEL This way! This way!
SUENO   Oh!   30
THIRD REBEL Stay, there's one groans.
SUENO   Oh!
SECOND REBEL Nay, 'twas hereabouts. Another dead?
FOURTH REBEL He has good clothes. Gotharus? The very cur.
THIRD REBEL 'Tis Gotharus. I have seen the dog.
SECOND REBEL 'Tis he, 'tis he!
SUENO   Oh!   *Exit Gotharus [unnoticed]*.   35
SECOND REBEL Now 'tis not he. If thou canst speak my friend –
SUENO Gotharus murdered me and shifted clothes.
 He cannot be far off. Oh! [*He dies.*]
FIRST REBEL That's he that lies dead yonder. Oh, that he were
 Alive again that we might kill him one after another!   40
THIRD REBEL He's gone.
SECOND REBEL   The devil he is. Follow, follow!
THIRD REBEL This way – he cannot 'scape us. Farewell friend:
 I'll do thee a courtesy. Follow, follow!   *Exeunt [Rebels, with the body of Sueno]*.

[4.6]

> *Enter* OLAUS, PRINCE [TURGESIUS *disguised*, CORTES, *and*] AQUINUS.

OLAUS So, so, in this disguise you may to th'army,
 Who though they seem to scatter are to meet
 By my directions. Honest Aquinus, you –
 You wait on the prince – but sir – (*Whispers [to the prince]*.)
CORTES [*To Aquinus*] Were you not wounded?   5

---

33 good clothes sumptuary laws dictated that only certain ranks were permitted to wear particular clothes or use certain colours so aristocrats could be identified by their clothes (see Jones and Stallybrass 2000, 188–9).

36 Now An emphatic stressing the negative force of the statement (*OED*, *adv.* 7b); it could be an error for 'No' but there is insufficient evidence to warrant emendation.

43 courtesy The rebel probably means that he will do Sueno the 'courtesy' of burying him; it is also possible that he stabs Sueno thinking that he is still alive in order to put him out of his misery.

1 you Turgesius.

27–8] *lineation Fehrenbach;* Let's...find / That...all. *Gifford;* Lets...Traytor, / He...all. Q/O
35 SD] *this edn;* Goth. rises, and steals off. *Gifford;* Exit Gotha. Q/O   **38 SD**] *Fehrenbach subst.; not in* Q/O
40 another!] *Gifford;* ano-ther. Q/O   **42–3**] *lineation Fehrenbach;* This...courtecy. / Follow, Q/O
43 SD] *this edn;* [*Exeunt Rebels. Gifford; Exit.* Q/O

[4.6]] *Gifford subst.* (SCENE VI.); [IV.vi.] *Fehrenbach; no scene division in* Q/O
0 SD] *this edn; Enter* Olaus, Turgesius, [*disguised,*] Aquinus[, *and* Cortes]. *Fehrenbach; Enter* OLAUS, TURGESIUS, AQUINUS, *and* CORTES. *Gifford;* Enter *Olaus, Prince, Aquinus.* Q/O
4 SD] *this edn;* [*Whispers Tur. Gifford;* Whispers. Q/O   **5 SD**] *Fehrenbach subst.; not in* Q/O

513

4.6   THE COMPLETE WORKS OF JAMES SHIRLEY, VOLUME 7

AQUINUS   I prepared a privy coat, for that I knew Gotharus
  Would have been too busy with my flesh else.
  But he thinks I'm slain by the duke and hugs
  His fortune in't.
PRINCE   [*To Olaus*] You'll follow.
OLAUS   And bring you news. Perhaps the rabble are   10
  In hot pursuit after the politician.
  He cannot 'scape them: they'll tear him like
  So many hungry mastiffs.
PRINCE   I could wish they had him.
OLAUS   Lose no time.   *Exeunt [the Prince and Aquinus].*
                    Cortes, stay you with me,
  Not that I think my house will want your guard.   15
CORTES   Command me, sir.
OLAUS   Was ever such a practice by a father
  To take away his son's life?
CORTES   I would hope he may not be so guilty; yet I know not
  How his false terrors, multiplied by the art   20
  Of this Gotharus, may prevail upon him
  And win consent.
OLAUS   Aquinus has been faithful
  And deceived all their treasons, but the prince
  Is still thought dead. This empty coffin shall
  Confirm the people in his funeral   25
  To keep their thoughts revengeful –
REBELS   (*Within*) Follow, follow!
OLAUS   – Till we are possessed of him that plotted all.
CORTES   The cry draws this way.
  They are excellent bloodhounds.   30

6 **privy coat** 'Armoured coat (usually of chain mail) worn concealed under ordinary clothing' (*OED*, C1 Privy coat in Privy *n.*).
7 **too...else** i.e. eager to attack me.
8 **hugs** delights in, congratulates.
13 **mastiffs** hounds used in bear-baiting, a common image in drama: see *Macbeth*, 5.7.1–2; Höfele 2011, 42–8. The image can be linked to the hunting cries of the rebels.
15 **my house** Olaus's reference to his house here and at l. 50, along with Gotharus's later statement that he was forced into Olaus's house (l. 36), indicate that this scene takes place at Olaus's residence.
17 **practice** plan, plot.
22 **win consent** win (his) approval.
23 **deceived** thwarted.
25 **Confirm...funeral** Convince everyone that he is really dead.
26 **keep...revengeful** maintain their eagerness for revenge.

9 SD] *Fehrenbach subst.; not in* Q/O
14 SD] *Fehrenbach subst.;* [*Exeunt Tur. and Aqu. after* him. *Gifford; Exit. after* Mastives. Q/O
19 SH] *Gifford subst.; Pr.* Q/O   27 SH SD] *Fehrenbach subst.;* [*Within.*] *Gifford; Within—* Q/O
28 SH] *this edn; line given to Olaus, after* revengeful, *Gifford; no direct SH in* Q

514

THE POLITICIAN   4.6

Enter GOTHARUS.

GOTHARUS As you are men defend me from the rage
  Of the devouring multitude. I have
  Deserved your anger and a death but let not
  My limbs inhumanely be torn by them.
  Oh, save me!
REBELS (*Within*) Follow, foll–
OLAUS   Blest occasion.   35
GOTHARUS I am forced to take your house and now implore
  Your mercy but to rescue me from them
  And be your own revenger. Yet my life
  Is worth your preservation for a time.
  Do it and I'll reward you with a story   40
  You'll not repent to know.
OLAUS   You cannot be safe here.
  Their rage is high and every door
  Must be left open to their violence –
  Unless you will obscure you in this coffin
  Prepared for the sweet prince that's murdered   45
  And but expects his body which is now embalming.
GOTHARUS That? – Oh, you're charitable.
REBELS (*Within*)   Follow, foll–
GOTHARUS Their noise is thunder to my soul.

                He goes into the coffin.

                    So, so.

        Enter REBELS.

OLAUS How now, gentlemen, what means this tumult?
  Do you know that I possess this dwelling?
FIRST REBEL   Yes, my lord,   50

---

34 Perhaps an allusion to the fate of Actaeon, who, as a punishment for watching Diana bathing, was transformed by the goddess into a stag and torn to pieces by his own hounds.

35 and 47 **Follow, foll—** The first of these abbreviated cries could be intended to suggest that the rebels are getting further away and hence the sound of their voices is diminishing, but that does not effectively explain the second—since at that point they are clearly nearer their prey. Perhaps on hearing this second cry, Gotharus, in his anguish at the imminent approach of his pursuers, speaks over the last syllable.

35 **Blest occasion** Fortunate chance.

36 **take** occupy (*OED*, *v*. 64a); see also note to l. 15.

38 **be...revenger** take revenge yourself.

38–41 **Yet...know** We never discover what Gotharus's story might be. It may be an empty promise, a sign of his desperation as he runs out of options.

42–3 **every...violence** no doors will keep out such forceful enemies.

44 **obscure you** hide yourself.

46 **expects** awaits (*OED*, Expect *v*. 10).

---

35 SH1 SD] *Fehrenbach subst.; [Within.] Gifford; Within— Q/O*
47 SH2 SD] *Fehrenbach subst.; [Within.] Gifford; Within— Q/O*
50 SH] *this edn; [1] REBEL. Fehrenbach; Reb. Q/O*

4.6 THE COMPLETE WORKS OF JAMES SHIRLEY, VOLUME 7

But we were told my lord Gotharus entered
And we beseech you give him to our justice.
He is the common enemy and we know
He killed the prince.
OLAUS You may search if you please:
He can presume of small protection here. 55
But I much thank you for your loyalties
And service to the prince, whose bloodless ruins
Are there, and do but wait when it will please
His father to reverse a cruel sentence
That keeps him from a burial with his ancestors. 60
We are forbid to do him rights of funeral.
FIRST REBEL How, not bury him?
SECOND REBEL Forbid to bury
Our good prince? We'll bury him, and see
What priest dare not assist us.
THIRD REBEL Not bury him?
We'll do't and carry his body in triumph 65
Through the city and see him laid i'th'great tombs.
FIRST REBEL Not bury our prince? That were a jest indeed.
CORTES 'Tis their love and duty.
SECOND REBEL We'll pull the church down but we'll have our will.
THIRD REBEL Dear prince, how sweet he smells.
FIRST REBEL Come countrymen, march, 70
And see who dares take his body from us.

[*Exeunt Rebels with the coffin.*]

CORTES You cannot help.
OLAUS They'll bury him alive.
CORTES He's in a fright.
OLAUS So may all traitors thrive. *Exeunt.*

55 **presume of** expect.
57 **bloodless ruins** i.e. lifeless remains, though 'bloodless' might refer to the prince's having been embalmed.
67 **jest** (cruel) joke.
69 **but we'll** i.e. if we don't.
70 **sweet...smells** another possible indication of embalmment, the rebel imagining that it has been done expensively, but he might also be suggesting that the prince was a saint—as their bodies, being thought incorruptible, were supposed not to smell of decay. Shirley might also be engaging in some sly dramatic irony here by suggesting that Gotharus has befouled himself either through terror or because (as we learn later) he dies in the coffin.
73 **in...fright** terrified; Cortes may also be commenting on the reason for the smell coming from the coffin.

53–4] *lineation Gifford;* Give...common / Enemy...prince. *Fehrenbach;* He...Prince. Q/O
62 **SH1**] *this edn;* 1 [REBEL]. *Fehrenbach;* 1 Reb. *Gifford;* 1. Q/O *(and thus throughout remainder of scene for Rebel SHs)*
71 **SD**] *this edn; not in* Q/O
73 **SD**] Q/O; [*Exeunt Rebels with the coffin, followed by Cor. and Olaus. Gifford*

516

THE POLITICIAN   5.1

5[.1]

     Enter KING *and* QUEEN [MARPISA].

KING Oh, I am lost, and my soul bleeds to think
  By my own dotage upon thee.
MARPISA   I was cursed
  When I first saw thee, poor wind-shaken king!
  I have lost my son.
KING   Thy honour, impious woman,
  Of more price than a son or thy own life.   5
  I had a son too, whom my rashness sent
  To another world, my poor Turgesius.
  What sorcery of thy tongue and eyes betrayed me?
MARPISA I would I had been a basilisk to have shot
  A death to thy dissembling heart when I   10
  Gave myself up thy queen. I was secure
  Till thou with the temptation of greatness
  And flattery didst poison my sweet peace,
  And shall thy base fears leave me now a prey
  To rebels?
KING   I had been happy to have left   15
  Thee sooner. But be gone! Get to some wilderness
  Peopled with serpents and engender with
  Some dragon like thyself.
MARPISA   Ha, ha!
KING Dost laugh, thou prodigy, thou shame of woman?
MARPISA Yes, and despise thee, dotard. Vex till thy soul   20
  Break from thy rotten flesh; I will be merry
  At thy last groan.
KING   Oh, my poor boy! My son!
  His wound is printed here. That false Gotharus,

1–2 **to think…dotage** i.e. that it was as a consequence of my own foolishness.
3 **wind-shaken** agitated (suggesting cowardly).
4 **Thy honour** i.e. It is your honour you have lost.
8 **sorcery…me** the common misogynist complaint that men were led astray by women (often through witchcraft).
9 **basilisk** mythical beast that could kill by looking at a victim.
19 **prodigy** monster.
20 **dotard** imbecile; Marpisa sarcastically turns back on the king the word he applies derisively to his love for her in the first speech of this scene.
20 **Vex** Fret, grieve (*OED*, *v*. 4b).

5[.1]] *Gifford subst.* (ACT V. SCENE I.*);* [V.i.] *Fehrenbach;* Act. 5. Q/O
0 SD QUEEN MARPISA] *this edn;* MARPISA *Gifford;* Queene Q/O

517

5.1   THE COMPLETE WORKS OF JAMES SHIRLEY, VOLUME 7

Your wanton goat, I fear practised with thee
His death.

MARPISA   'Twas thy own act and timorous heart, in hope   25
To be secure. I glory in the mention,
Thou murderer of thy son.

    Enter HORMENUS.

HORMENUS Oh sir, if ever, stand upon your guard.
The army which you thought scattered and broke
Is grown into a great and threatening body –   30
Led by the Duke Olaus, your loved uncle,
Is marching hither. All your subjects fly to him.   *Exit.*

MARPISA Ha, ha!

KING   Curse on thy spleen. Is this a time for laughter
When horror should afflict thy guilty soul?
Hence, mischief.

MARPISA   Not to obey thee, shadow of a king,   35
Am I content to leave thee and, but I wo'not
Prevent thy greater sorrow and vexation,
Now I would kill thee, coward.

KING   Treason! Treason!

MARPISA Aye, aye – who comes to your rescue?

KING   Are all fled?

MARPISA Slaves do it naturally.

KING   Canst thou hope to 'scape?   40

MARPISA I am mistress of my fate and do not fear
Their inundation, their army coming.
It does prepare my triumph. They shall give
Me liberty and punish thee to live.

KING Undone, forsaken, miserable king!   *Exeunt severally.*   45

---

24 wanton goat goats were traditionally associated with lechery: see *Othello* 3.3.408 and 4.1.265.

24 practised carried out.

33 spleen organ thought to control the emotions. The King implies that Marpisa has no control over hers, as she laughs inappropriately.

35 mischief devil, wicked person.

35 shadow an ironic reflection on the king's earlier declaration to Marpisa that 'I am but the shadow of myself without thee' (2.1.45).

40 Slaves...naturally i.e. The lower classes are natural cowards (with the implication that the king is acting like one of them).

42 inundation flood, mass.

44 punish...live i.e. if you are allowed to live that would be worse than dying.

518

THE POLITICIAN   5.2

[5.2]

Enter PRINCE [TURGESIUS], OLAUS, CORTES, AQUINUS, [*and*] SOLDIERS.

PRINCE Worthy Aquinus, I must honour thee,
  Thou hast preserved us all. Thy service will
  Deserve a greater monument than thanks.
AQUINUS Thank the duke, for breaking o' my pate.
OLAUS I know 'twas well bestowed, but we have now   5
  Proof of thy honest heart.
AQUINUS But what, with your highness' favour, do you mean
  To do with your father?
PRINCE   Pay my duty to him.
  He may be sensible of his cruelty
  And not repent to see me live.   10
OLAUS But, with your favour, something else must be
  Considered. There's a thing he calls his queen,
  A limb of Lucifer; she must be roasted
  For the army's satisfaction.
AQUINUS   They'll ne'er digest her.
  The king's hounds may be kept hungry   15
  Enough perhaps and make a feast upon her.
PRINCE I wonder how the rabble will bestow
  The coffin.
OLAUS   Why, they'll bury him alive
  I hope.
PRINCE   Did they suppose my body there?
OLAUS I'm sorry he will fare so much the better.   20
  I would the queen were there to comfort him –
  Oh, they would smell and sweat together rarely.

---

4 breaking…pate beating me over the head.
5 well i.e. powerfully, with considerable strength.
7 highness' pronounced 'highness'.
7 favour permission.
9 sensible aware.
13 limb…Lucifer an accomplice or follower of Lucifer, in this case a witch; in *The Gentleman of Venice* Thomazo refers to a prostitute as a 'limb of wantonness' (3.4.54).
13–14 roasted…satisfaction i.e. burnt at the stake, the conventional punishment for witches, to satisfy the soldiers' desire for vengeance. There is also a play on the idea of roast meat as food and hence a suggestion of cannibalism. See note to l. 61.
14 digest suggesting that the soldiers will not be satisfied even by such a cruel death and that she might instead be devoured by hunting dogs: see 4.6.32.
17 bestow dispose of.
21 comfort him continuing the black humour of the scene.
22 smell…sweat referring to their mutual lust, and a macabre variation of Hamlet's imagining his mother and Claudius enacting the primal scene: 'Nay, but to live / In the rank sweat of an enseamèd bed' (*Hamlet*, 3.4.81–2).

[5.2]] *Gifford subst.* (SCENE II.*); [V.ii.] Fehrenbach; no scene division in* Q/O
0 SD PRINCE TURGESIUS] *this edn;* TURGESIUS *Gifford;* Prince Q/O

519

5.2   THE COMPLETE WORKS OF JAMES SHIRLEY, VOLUME 7

AQUINUS He dare as soon be damned as make a noise,
  Or stir or cough.
OLAUS   If he should sneeze!
CORTES 'Tis his best course to go into the ground   25
  With silence.
PRINCE   March on. [*A trumpet sounds within.*]
                 Stay, what trumpet's that?

     Enter REBELS, *with a trumpet before the coffin, marching.*

OLAUS They are no enemies – I know the coffin.
AQUINUS What rusty regiment ha' we here?
OLAUS They are going to bury him – he's not yet discovered.
  Oh, do not hinder 'em – 'tis a work of charity.   30
  [*To the prince*] Yet now I do consider better on't
  You may do well to show yourself; that may
  Be a means to waken the good gentleman
  And make some sport before the rascal smell.
  And yet he's in my nostril; he has perfumed   35
  His box already.

    [*The Rebels*] *see the prince, throw down the coffin, and run to kneel and embrace him.*

ALL REBELS 'Tis he, 'tis he, the prince alive! Hey!
AQUINUS What would he give but for a knife to cut
  His own throat now?
ALL REBELS   Our noble prince alive?
PRINCE That owes himself to all your loves.   40
AQUINUS What? What trinkets ha' you there?
FIRST REBEL The Duke Olaus told us 'twas the prince's body,
  Which we resolved to bury with magnificence.
AQUINUS So it appears.
OLAUS   'Tis better as it is.
SECOND REBEL There's something in't – my shoulder is still sensible.   45
  Let's search. Stand off –

---

25 course…ground a pun on 'corse' (i.e. corpse).
28 rusty this could refer to their clothes—shabby, worn out, the result of having been on campaign for some time—or their behaviour—undisciplined, raucous (*OED, adj.*[1] 8c, 4b and 5).
31 consider…on't think better of it.
34 rascal smell as a corpse. See *Hamlet* 4.3.35–6: 'if you find him not this month, you shall nose him as you go up the stairs into the lobby'.
35–6 perfumed…already impregnated his coffin with a smell (again with the suggestion that Gotharus has soiled himself in fear).
38 he i.e. Gotharus.
44 appears…is Olaus suggests that the reality they encounter (Turgesius alive and Gotharus captured) exceeds the magnificent appearance of the funeral procession.
45 still sensible still feels (the weight of the coffin).

---

26 SD1] *Fehrenbach subst.;* [*Trumpet sounded within. after* silence. *Gifford; not in* Q/O
31 SD] *this edn;* [*To Turgesius.*] *after* on't.– *Fehrenbach*   36 SD] Q/O *subst. (but after* hey. *line 37)*
37 SH] *this edn;* OMNES REBELS. *Fehrenbach; Omnes Reb. Gifford; Om. Reb.* Q/O
39 SH] *this edn;* OMNES REBELS. *Fehrenbach; Omnes Reb. Gifford; Om. Rebel.* Q/O
42 SH] *this edn;* [1] REBEL. *Fehrenbach; Reb.* Q/O   45 SH] *this edn;* 2 REBEL. *Fehrenbach; 2 Reb.* Q/O

THE POLITICIAN   5.2

OLAUS Now do you scent him gentlemen? He would forgive
    The hangman to despatch him out o'th'way.
    Now will these mastiffs use him like a cat,
    Most dreadful rogues at an execution.   50
    Now, now. [*They open the coffin.*]
FIRST REBEL 'Tis a man. Ha! Gotharus, the thing we whet our teeth for.
ALL REBELS Out with the traitor and with the murderer! Hey, drag him!
OLAUS I told you.
FIRST REBEL Hold! Know your duty, fellow renegades!   55
    We do beseech thee high and mighty prince,
    Let us dispose of what we brought – this traitor.
    He was given us by the duke. Fortune has
    Thrown him into our teeth.
OLAUS   And they'll devour him.
ALL REBELS We beseech your highness.
OLAUS   I do acknowledge it.   60
    Good sir, grant their boon and try the cannibals.
SECOND REBEL I'll have an arm.
THIRD REBEL   I'll have a leg.
    I am a shoemaker – his shinbone may be useful.
FOURTH REBEL I want a sign. Give me his head.
PRINCE Stay. Let's first see him. Is he not stifled?   65
THIRD REBEL I had rather my wife were speechless.
OLAUS The coffin, sir, was never close.
PRINCE   He does not stir.
FIRST REBEL We'll make him stir, hang him. He's but asleep.
SECOND REBEL He's dead! Hum –
OLAUS Dead? Then the devil is not so wise as I took him.   70
PRINCE He's dead and has prevented all their fury.

47–8 He...o'th'way i.e. He would rather the hangman dispatched him than experience the fate waiting for him.
61 try...cannibals test the man-eaters. An uncomfortable image continuing the suggestion of cannibalism
in 'roasting' and 'digest' above. Another suggestion of cannibalism occurs in *The Gentleman of Venice*, when
Thomazo, thinking that Florelli might have fallen in the river after escaping their attempt on his life, wonders
whether 'we may eat his nose / In the next haddock' (3.1.4–5).
63 shinbone Shoemakers used tools made of shinbones in the preparation of leather and to finish the welt of shoes.
64 sign The rebel may be a barber-surgeon who wants to display a sign which advertises his trade and the
severed head will either look like the red and white pole they used or represent one of the heads he shaves.
65 stifled suffocated, strangled.
67 close tightly shut.

51 SD] *Gifford; not in* Q/O   52 SH] *this edn;* 1 REBEL. *Fehrenbach;* 1 Reb. Q/O
53 SH] *this edn;* OMNES REBELS. *Fehrenbach; Omnes Reb. Gifford; Om. Reb.* Q/O
53 murderer!...him!] *this edn;* murderer....him! *Fehrenbach;* Murderer!...him. *Gifford;* murderer,...him. Q/O
55 SH] *this edn;* 1 REBEL. *Fehrenbach;* 1 Reb. Q/O
55 Hold!...renegades!] *this edn;* Hold!...renegades.- *Gifford;* Hold,...renegades, Q/O
60 SH1] *this edn;* OMNES [REBELS]. *Fehrenbach; Omnes Reb. Gifford; Om.* Q/O
60–1] *lineation Fehrenbach;* I...boone, / And...Caniballs. Q/O
62 SH1] *this edn;* 2 [REBEL]. *Fehrenbach;* 2 Reb. *Gifford;* 2. Q/O *(and thus for remainder of scene for Rebel SHs
until l. 129)*
62–3] *lineation this edn;* Ile...Shoomaker, / His...useful. Q/O

521

5.2   THE COMPLETE WORKS OF JAMES SHIRLEY, VOLUME 7

AQUINUS He was not smothered – the coffin had air enough.

OLAUS He might ha' lived to give these gentlemen
  Some content.

FIRST REBEL   Oh, let us tear his limbs.

PRINCE Let none use any violence to his body.   75
  I fear he has met reward above your punishment.

SECOND REBEL Let me have but his clothes.

THIRD REBEL   He is a tailor.

SECOND REBEL Only to cut out a suit for a traitor by 'em,
  Or any man my conscience would wish hanged.

FOURTH REBEL Let me have a button for a relic –   80

PRINCE No more.

OLAUS   There is some mystery in his death.

  Enter KING.

  The king! Obscure a little, nephew – [*The prince retires.*]

KING To whom now must I kneel? Where is the king?
  For I am nothing and deserve to be so.
  Unto you, uncle, must I bow and give   85
  My crown: pray, take it. With it give me leave
  To tell you what it brings the hapless wearer
  Beside the outside glory, for I am
  Read in the miserable fate of kings.
  You think it glorious to command but are   90
  More subject than the poorest pays you duty,
  And must obey your fears, your want of sleep,
  Rebellion from your vassals, wounds even from
  Their very tongues whose quietness you sweat for,
  For whose dear health you waste and fright your   95
  Strength to paleness and your blood into a frost.

---

76 he...punishment i.e. he has got his just deserts from an authority higher than you.

77 He The second rebel.

80 relic people who attended executions often took tokens from the bodies of criminals (handkerchiefs, scraps of clothing, removable body parts).

82 Obscure...little Hide yourself for the time being.

84 nothing compare *King Lear*, 2.2.184: 'Edgar I nothing am', and the numerous other quibbles on 'nothing' in that play.

88 outside external.

89 Read in Know about, have read about. The speech owes much to both Henry IV's soliloquy which concludes 'Uneasy lies the head that wears a crown' (*2 Henry IV*, 3.1.4–31) and Henry V's meditation the night before Agincourt (*Henry V*, 4.1.230–84).

91 poorest pays i.e. poorest who pays.

94 sweat work, suffer.

73–4] *lineation Fehrenbach;* He ... content. Q/O
82 SD] *this edn;* [Turgesius *retires.*] Fehrenbach; [*Tur. retires.* Gifford; *not in* Q/O

522

THE POLITICIAN   5.2

You are not certain of a friend or servant
To build your faith upon; your life is but
Your subjects' murmur and your death their sacrifice.
When looking past yourself to make them blest   100
In your succession, which a wife must bring you,
You may give up your liberty for a smile
As I ha' done and in your bosom cherish
More danger than a war or famine brings.
Or if you have a son – my spirits fail me   105
At naming of a son.
PRINCE [Coming forward] Oh, my dear father.
KING Ha! Do not fright me in my tears which should
    Be rather blood for yielding to thy death.
    I have let fall my penitence, though I was
    Counselled by him whose truth I now suspect   110
    In the amaze and puzzle of my state –
PRINCE Dear sir, let not one thought afflict you more.
    I am preserved to be your humble son still.
    Although Gotharus had contrived my ruin
    'Twas counterplotted by this honest captain.   115
KING I know not what to credit. Art Turgesius?
PRINCE And do account your blessing and forgiveness,
    If I have erred, above the whole world's empire.
    The army, sir, is yours –
OLAUS   Upon conditions –
PRINCE [To Olaus] Good sir – [To the king] and all safety meant your person.   120
OLAUS Right, but for your gypsy queen, that cockatrice.
KING She's lost.

---

99 murmur furtive expressions of discontent.

99 sacrifice the king will be the scapegoat for his subjects.

101 Monarchs have to worry about marriage and the succession, and sacrifice their personal happiness for the good of the state they govern. Marriage alliances were thought to be—and invariably were—among the most important factors in securing the stability of the realm and its happiness.

103–4 in … brings an allusion to his own recent marriage. There may be a political allusion because it was well-attested that Charles I and Henrietta Maria, whose marriage was later seen as ideal, had not taken to each other when first married, and the queen's Catholicism turned many against the monarchy (see Sharpe 1992, 306).

107 Ha! … me The King thinks that Turgesius is an apparition or ghost.

109 let fall failed to pursue, allowed to lapse (*OED*, Let *v*. 22c).

110 truth honesty, loyalty.

111 i.e. As a result of the confused and bewildering condition of my nation. The word 'state' could also refer to the king's mental condition or his status as a monarch (*OED*, *n*. 1b and 22a).

121 gypsy queen suggesting lasciviousness, sexual immorality. 'Gipsy' had connections to Egypt, and Shirley probably has *Antony and Cleopatra* in mind: 'a gipsy's lust' (1.1.10) and 'Like a right gipsy hath at fast and loose / Beguiled me' (4.12.28–9).

121 cockatrice synonym for basilisk (see 5.1.9), also implying a whore.

---

106 SD] *Gifford subst.; not in* Q/O   **120 SD1**] *Fehrenbach subst.; not in* Q/O
120 SD2] *Fehrenbach subst.; not in* Q/O

5.2   THE COMPLETE WORKS OF JAMES SHIRLEY, VOLUME 7

OLAUS   The devil find her.

KING   She's false.

OLAUS That gentleman Jack-in-a-box, if he could speak,
  Would clear that point.

KING   Forgive me, gentle boy.

PRINCE Dear sir, no more.

AQUINUS   Best dismiss these gentlemen.   125

OLAUS The prince's bounty. [*He gives them money.*]
                      Now you may go home
  And, d'ye hear, be drunk tonight – the cause requires it.

FIRST REBEL We'll show ourselves good subjects.

ALL REBELS Heaven bless the king and prince and the good duke!   *Exeunt.*

KING My comforts are too mighty; let me pour   130
  More blessings on my boy.

PRINCE   Sir, I am blest
  If I stand fair in your opinion.

KING And welcome, good Olaus.

OLAUS   You're deceived;
  I am a ruffian and my head must off,
  To please the monkey madam that bewitched you,   135
  For being too honest to you.

KING   We are friends.

OLAUS Upon condition that you will –

KING   What?

OLAUS Now have I forgot what I would have.
  Oh – that my Lady Circe that transformed you
  May be sent – whither? I ha' forgot again.   140
  To the devil, any whither, far enough.
  A curse upon her; she troubles me both when

---

123 Jack-in-a-box Sharper or cheat (*OED*, Jack-in-the-box *n.* 2a). A grim joke about Gotharus's situation.
125 these gentlemen i.e. the rebel soldiers.
127 drunk Scandinavian nations—especially Danes—were known for their love of heavy drinking: see
Othello, 2.3.71–3; *Hamlet*, 1.4.9–18.
128 good subjects loyal citizens, no longer rebels, with a joke that they will drink heavily as requested.
135 monkey madam monkeys, like goats were thought to be lecherous; see *Othello*, 3.3.408 and Partridge
1955, 193.
136 too...you too honest with you. Olaus is reminding the king of their earlier encounter where his (just)
criticisms of the king's behaviour nearly got him executed, 'Take heed / You do not talk your head off – we have
scaffolds' (3.1.65–6).
137 Upon...will Presumably Olaus is about to tell the king to reform his ways but thinks better of it.
138 forgot Olaus's hesitation indicates the uncomfortable nature of this dialogue for both men.
139 Circe Witch in *The Odyssey* who turned men into swine.
141 any whither anywhere.

123] *lineation Fehrenbach;* That Gentleman / Jack...speake, Q/O   **126 SD**] *Gifford subst.; not in* Q/O
129 SH] *this edn;* OMNES [REBELS]. *Fehrenbach;* Omnes Reb. *Gifford;* Om. Q/O

524

THE POLITICIAN   5.2

I think on her and when I forget her.

    Enter ALBINA.

KING Gotharus's wife, the sorrowful Albina.
ALBINA If pity dwell within your royal bosom   145
  Let me be heard: I come to find a husband.
  I'll not believe what the hard-hearted rebels
  Told me, that he is dead – they loved him not
  And wish it so – for you would not permit
  His murder here. You gave me, sir, to him   150
  In holy marriage. I'll not say what sorrow
  My poor heart since hath been acquainted with,
  But give him now to me and I'll account
  No blessing like that bounty. Where, oh where
  Is my poor lord? None tell me? Are you all   155
  Silent or deaf as rocks? Yet they sometimes
  Do with their hollow murmurs answer men.
  This does increase my fears; none speak to me?
  [*To the king*] I ask my lord from you, sir. You once loved him,
  He had your bosom; who hath torn him thence?   160
  Why do you shake your head and turn away?
  Can you resolve me, sir? [*She sees the prince.*] The prince alive,
  Whose death they would revenge upon Gotharus!
  Oh, let me kiss your hand. A joy to see
  You safe doth interrupt my grief; I may   165
  Hope now my lord is safe too. I like not
  That melancholy gesture. Why do you make
  So dark your face and hide your eyes as they
  Would show an interest in sorrow with me?
  Where is my lord? Can you or any tell me   170
  Where I may find the comfort of mine eyes,
  My husband? Or but tell me that he lives
  And I will pray for you. Then he is dead
  Indeed, I fear.
PRINCE   Poor lady.
AQUINUS   Madam, be comforted.
ALBINA Why, that's well said – I thank you gentle sir.   175

---

156 Silent…rocks Combining two proverbs, 'As still as stone' and 'as deaf as stone' (Tilley S877 and S879).
157 hollow murmurs echoes.
158 This The silence.
162 resolve answer.
169 an…sorrow sympathy.
173 you. Then There is presumably a lengthy pause between these two sentences while Albina waits for the answer that never comes.

159 SD] *this edn; not in* Q/O   **162 SD**] *this edn; not in* Q/O

525

5.2   THE COMPLETE WORKS OF JAMES SHIRLEY, VOLUME 7

You bid me be comforted; blessing on you.
Show me now reason for it. Tell me something
I may believe.
AQUINUS   Madam, your husband's dead.
ALBINA And did you bid me, sir, be comforted
  For that? Oh, you were cruel. Dead? Who murdered him?   180
  For though he loved not me in life I must
  Revenge his death.
PRINCE   Alas you cannot.
ALBINA   No?
  Will not heaven hear me, think you? For I'll pray
  That horror may pursue the guilty head
  Of his black murderer. You do not know   185
  How fierce and fatal is a widow's curse.
  Who killed him? Say!
AQUINUS   We know not.
ALBINA   You're unjust.
PRINCE Pursue not sorrow with such inquisition,
  Lady.
ALBINA Not I? Who hath more interest?
KING The knowledge of what circumstance deprived him   190
  Of life will not avail to his return.
  Or, if it would, none here know more than that
  He was brought hither dead in that enclosure.
ALBINA Where?
AQUINUS   In that coffin, lady.
ALBINA   Was it charity
  Made this provision for him? Oh my lord,   195
  Now may I kiss thy withered lip, discharge
  Upon thy bosom a poor widow's tears.
  There's something tempts my heart to show more duty
  And wait on thee to death, in whose pale dress
  Thou dost invite me to be reconciled.   200
KING Remove that coffin.
ALBINA   You're uncharitable.
  Is't not enough that he is robbed of life
  Among you but you'll rob me of his body?
  Poor remnant of my lord, I have not had
  Indeed so many kisses a great while.   205

186 widow's curse Widow's curses were proverbially dangerous. In Chaucer's *Friar's Tale* a demon hauls a Summoner (who summoned the accused to ecclesiastical courts) down to hell after he is cursed by a widow he swindles.
198–200 Albina considers (but rejects) the idea of suicide.
204 remnant remainder.

187 Say!] *Fehrenbach;* saie. Q/O

526

THE POLITICIAN   5.2

Pray do not envy me, for sure I sha'not
Die of this surfeit. He thought not I was
So near to attend him in his last and long
Progress that built this funeral tenement
Without a room for me. The sad Albina   210
Must sleep by her dead lord. I feel death coming
And, as it did suspect, I durst not look
On his grim visage; he has drawn a curtain
Of mist before my eyes. [*She faints.*]
KING   Look to the lady.
PRINCE Look to Albina. Our physicians!   215

    [*Enter* DOCTORS.]

There is not so much virtue more i'th'kingdom.
If she survive this passion she is worth
A prince and I will court her as my blessing.
Say, is there hope?
DOCTOR   There is.
PRINCE Above your lives preserve her.
DOCTOR   With our best art and care. 220

                         Exeunt [Doctors] with Albina.

OLAUS She has almost made me woman too. But
  Come, to other business.

    Enter QUEEN [MARPISA].

AQUINUS   Is not this the queen?
OLAUS The queen of hell. Give her no hearing but
  Shoot, shoot her presently without more repentance.
  There is a lecherous devil in her eye: 225
  Give him more fire. His hell's not hot enough.

---

207 surfeit i.e. of kisses, but it could also imply an excess of emotion which, in early modern medical theory, was thought to be potentially fatal.

209 Progress Journey, a common image of death.

209 funeral tenement i.e. the coffin, the last house that Gotharus will inhabit.

214 Look...lady cf. *Macbeth*, 2.3.98.

215 SD See note to 4.3.0 SD.

217 passion bodily crisis caused by excess of emotion. Gloucester dies when he is caught ''Twixt two extremes of passion' (*Lear*, 5.3.190).

221 made...too made me cry (adopt female characteristics).

223 queen...hell most probably the Whore of Babylon, the most frequently represented woman associated with the devil.

224 presently immediately.

224 repentance regret.

---

214 SD] *this edn;* [*Swoons. Gifford; not in* Q/O   **215 SD**] *this edn; Enter* Physicians. *Gifford; not in* Q/O
219 SH] *this edn; Phy.* Q/O   **220 SH** DOCTOR] *this edn; Phy.* Q/O
220 SD] *this edn;* [*Exeunt with Albina. Gifford; Exit with* Albina. Q/O
222 SD QUEEN MARPISA] *this edn;* MARPISA *Gifford; Queene* Q/O

5.2   THE COMPLETE WORKS OF JAMES SHIRLEY, VOLUME 7

Now shoot!
PRINCE   Be temperate, good sir.
MARPISA Nay, let his choleric highness be obeyed.
AQUINUS She is shot-free.
MARPISA The prince alive? Where is Gotharus?   230
OLAUS Your friend that was.
MARPISA   It is confessed.
OLAUS Your stallion.
MARPISA   He has more titles sure.
OLAUS Let but some strangle her in her own hair.
MARPISA The office will become a noble hangman.
OLAUS Whore!
MARPISA   I'll not spend my breath upon thee,   235
I have more use on't. Does Gotharus live?
AQUINUS You may conjecture, madam, if you turn
Your eyes upon that object. [*He points to the coffin.*]
MARPISA   It has wrought then.
KING What has wrought?
MARPISA   His physic, sir, for the state megrim.
A wholesome poison which in his poor fears   240
And fainting, when the rebels first pursued him,
It was my happiness to minister
In my poor boy's revenge, killed by his practice.
PRINCE Poisoned?
OLAUS   She is turned doctor.
MARPISA   He becomes
Death's pale complexion. And now I'm prepared.   245
PRINCE For what?

227 **temperate** Olaus's excessive anger balances Albina's grief.
229 **shot-free** i.e. bulletproof.
231 **friend** now used clearly to mean lover.
232 **stallion** stud, as in current usage.
232 **titles** referring to Olaus's eagerness to reach for insulting names.
233 Marpisa presumably is displaying her long hair, something traditionally associated with unmarried (available) or lascivious women and with madness.
236 **on't** for it.
237 **conjecture** here meaning 'see for yourself', as Aquinus directs her to the coffin.
238 **wrought** worked.
239 **physic** medicine.
239 **state megrim** The word 'megrim' could describe a fit of dizziness or vertigo (*OED*, Megrim *n.*[1] 1c) and this would fit well with Marpisa's following reference to Gotharus's 'poor fears / And fainting, when the rebels first pursued him'; 'state' could, in a medical context, refer to the crisis of an illness (*OED*, State *n.* 9), giving 'the height of his attack of dizziness', but it could also act in a quasi-adjectival way with reference to a person's exalted position or political power (*OED*, State *n.* 15b, and see illustrations to C2.a.(a)), and that may well be the way it is being used here—dizziness brought about by his exalted position.
244 **She...doctor** Another dig at the reputation of physicians for killing more often than curing.
244–5 **He...complexion** Death suits him.

238 SD] *this edn; not in* Q/O   239] *lineation Gifford;* His...sir, / For...Megrim. Q/O

528

THE POLITICIAN   5.2

MARPISA   To die.
OLAUS Prepared to be damned. A seven years killing
   Will be too little.
MARPISA   I pity your poor rage.
   I sha'not stay so long nor shall you have
   The honour, sir, to kill me.
OLAUS   No? Let me try.   250
MARPISA Ha, ha!
OLAUS   Dost thou laugh, hell-cat?
MARPISA Yes, and scorn all your furies. I was not
   So improvident to give Gotharus all
   My cordial; you may trust the operation.
   Here's some to spare, if any have a mind   255
   To taste and be assured. [*To Olaus*] Will you, my lord?
   'Twill purge your choler rarely.
OLAUS I'll not be your patient, I thank you.
MARPISA This box was ever my companion,
   Since I grew wicked with that politician,   260
   To prevent shameful death, nor am I coy
   To pleasure a friend in't. [*She takes the poison.*]
OLAUS   Devil's charity!
MARPISA It works with method and doth kill discreetly
   Without a noise. Your mercury is a rude
   And troublesome destroyer to this medicine.   265
   I feel it gently seize upon my vitals.
   'Tis now the time to steal into my heart.
KING Hast thou no thought of heaven?

---

250 Let . . . try Olaus may start to take hold of her here.
251 hell-cat common term for an evil woman, and yet another from Olaus's range of familiar insults.
253 improvident lacking in foresight.
257 purge expel from the body; it was common medical practice at the time to give emetics and laxatives in the belief that they could get rid of harmfully excessive humours such as, in Olaus's case, the yellow bile that caused choler; Marpisa's medical advice is, however, tinged with sarcasm.
259–60 i.e. Since becoming Gotharus's lover and accomplice I have always kept this box close to me.
261–2 nor . . . in't 'coy', 'pleasure', and 'friend' all have strong connotations of sexual activity, but it is not clear who exactly is meant by 'friend'. It could be ironic, and hence another taunt aimed at Olaus, or it could be the box of poison, which she now intends to embrace and so die (i.e. enjoy an orgasm with). Even when about to commit suicide, Marpisa resorts to sexual puns.
262 in't with it.
263 method systematically, methodically.
264 mercury Mercury was used as a cure for syphilis but was known to be acutely poisonous if carelessly administered. It was thought to have caused the death of Sir Thomas Overbury, who died in the Tower on 14 September 1613, leading to the murder trial of Sir Robert Carr and Frances Howard, one of the biggest scandals of James's reign (Bellany 2007, 52).
265 to i.e. compared to.

---

256 SD] *Fehrenbach subst.; not in* Q/O   **262 SD**] *this edn; not in* Q/O

5.2   THE COMPLETE WORKS OF JAMES SHIRLEY, VOLUME 7

MARPISA   Yes, I do think
Sometimes, but have not heart enough to pray.
Some vapour now rises 'twixt me and heaven;   270
I cannot see't – lust and ambition ruined me.
If greatness were a privilege i'th'other
World, it were a happiness to die a queen.
I find my conscience too late: 'tis bloody
And full of stains. Oh, I have been so wicked   275
'Twere almost impudence to ask a pardon,
Yet for your own sakes pity me. Survive
All happy and if you can, forgive, forgive. [*She dies.*]
KING Those accents yet may be repentance.
PRINCE   She's dead.
KING Some take their bodies hence.
PRINCE   Let them have burial.   280

[*Exeunt soldiers with the bodies of Gotharus and Marpisa.*]

KING 'Tis in thee, Turgesius,
To dispose all, to whom I give my crown. [*He offers the prince his crown.*]
Salute him king, by my example.

[*The king kneels and others follow suit.*]

PRINCE   Stay.
Upon your duty stay. Will you be traitors?
Consent your lawful king should be deposed?   285
Sir, do not wound your son and lay so great
A stain upon his hopeful, his green honour.

268–79 Yes…repentance It is not clear whether Marpisa repents in this speech or whether she is so focused on earthly matters that she simply seeks approval from those who witness her death and, as a suicide, her chance of salvation was not clear. However, final repentance was always possible. William Camden describes a gravestone of a man who fell off his horse with the epitaph: 'My friend judge not me, / Thou seest I judge not thee: / Betwixt the stirrup and the ground, / Mercy I askt, mercy I found' (Camden 1974, 420). The king's comment ensures that the audience is uncertain whether Marpisa genuinely repents for her sins before she dies, but is offered that possibility.
270 vapour a mist or fog rising from the ground, and hence of satanic origin; cf. the machiavellian Flamineo's 'Oh, I am in a mist' (Webster, *The White Devil*, 5.5.260), spoken as he dies at the hands of Isabella's revengers.
279 accents words, comments.
281–3 'Tis…example The King's attempt to abdicate suggests that he has no real understanding of the burdens and responsibilities of those who govern. Such sudden transformations of political authority at moments of crisis are unlikely to ensure secure rule, as Turgesius's following speech recognizes.
284 traitors Turgesius's use of the word invokes the problem, familiar in many history plays, of where obedience lay when monarchs did not fulfil their duties, or, as here, acted against the interests of the Crown. The doctrine of the king's two bodies, public and private, distinguished the office of the monarchy from its particular incumbent. Often this enabled subjects to claim that they were acting in the interests of the Crown in opposing the monarch, a position the now-dispersed rebels did not articulate, but which lay at the heart of their actions. Turgesius acts promptly to ensure that there can only be one ruler, saving the king and kingdom from the consequences of his actions. Abdication, as in Shakespeare's *Henry VI* plays and *Richard II*, led to protracted civil war. *The Politician* was written in the late 1630s as Charles I clashed ever more seriously with mounting opposition (see Introduction, 405–9).
287 green immature, youthful.

---

278 SD] *Gifford subst.; Moritur.* Q/O   **280 SD**] *Gifford subst.; not in* Q/O   **282 SD**] *this edn; not in* Q/O
283 SD] *this edn; not in* Q/O

530

THE POLITICIAN   5.2

I now enjoy good men's opinions;
This change will make 'em think I did conspire
And force your resignation. Wear it still.   290
By justice and yourself, it shall not touch
My brow till death translate you to a kingdom
More glorious and you leave me to succeed,
Bettered by your example in the practice
Of a king's power and duty.
KING   This obedience   295
Will with excess of comfort kill thy father
And hasten that command thou wouldst decline.
PRINCE Receive this captain and reward his faith
To you and me. [*He presents Aquinus to the King.*]
KING [*To Aquinus*] Be captain of our guard.
[*To Olaus*] And, my good uncle, to your care I leave   300
The soldiers; let the largesse speak our bounty
And your love.
OLAUS   Aye, this sounds well, fellow soldiers.
Trust me, beside your pay, for the king's bounty.
SOLDIERS (*Within*) Heaven preserve the king and prince!
OLAUS Not a short prayer for me?
ALL SOLDIERS [*Within*]   Heaven bless the duke!   305
Heaven bless the duke!
OLAUS   Why so, money will do much.
KING A bright day shines upon us. Come, my son –
Too long a stranger to the court. It now
Shall bid thee welcome. I do feel my years
Slide off and joy drown sorrow in my tears.   *Exeunt omnes.*   310

THE END

289–90 This…resignation The king has not thought through the implications of his proposed abdication and the monarchy is compromised as the play concludes. Either the incumbent remains, having shown himself to be a problematic ruler who does not want the role, or a new king takes over, not ready or prepared, under a cloud of suspicion.
292 translate transport.
296–7 excess…decline Imbalance of the passions again threatens to overwhelm one of the characters. Parallels are evident to the ending of the folio version of *Lear*, when the king dies imagining that Cordelia might live.
297 command rank, position, rule.
301 largesse gift of money.
301 bounty beneficence, gracious liberality in giving (*OED*, *n.* 4 and 5a, b).
306 Why…much Olaus retains his cynicism, albeit in a more jovial form.

---

290 Wear] *Gifford subst.;* were Q/O   **299 SD1]** *this edn;* [*Presents Aqu. Gifford; not in* Q/O
299 SD2] *this edn; not in* Q/O   **300 SD]** *this edn; not in* Q/O
304 SH SD] *this edn;* SOLDIERS. *Fehrenbach;* Sold. *Gifford; Within Sol.* Q/O
304] *lineation Fehrenbach;* Heaven preserve / The…Prince. Q/O
305 SH2] *this edn;* OMNES SOLDIERS. *Fehrenbach; Omnes Sold. Gifford; Om. Sol.* Q/O
305 SD] *this edn; not in* Q/O   **305–6]** *lineation this edn;* Heaven…Duke, heaven…Duke. Q/O
310 THE END] Q/O *subst. (FINIS.)*

531

BIBLIOGRAPHY

Abbott, E. A. *A Shakespearian Grammar*. London: Macmillan, 1869.

Anon. *The Northhampton-shire lover, or, A Pleasant dialogue between a Northampton-shire gentleman and a marchants daughter of London to the tune of Falero lero lo*. London: for H. Gosson, 1625. STC (2nd ed.) / 18662.5.

Anon. *The Resolution of the Women of London to the Parliament*. London: for William Watson, 1642. Wing / R1159.

Armitage, David. *Civil Wars: A History in Ideas*. New York: Alfred A. Knopf, 2017.

Astington, John H. 'Jolly, George (bap. 1613, d. in or before 1683), actor and theatre manager.' *Oxford Dictionary of National Biography*. Oxford: Oxford University Press, 2004.

Astington, John H. 'The *Messalina* Stage and Salisbury Court Plays', *Theatre Journal* 43 (1991), 141–56.

Bacon, Francis. *Historia vitae et mortis*. London: by John Haviland for Matthew Lownes, 1623. STC (2nd ed.) / 1156.

Bacon, Francis. 'Of the True Greatness of Kingdoms and Estates', in *Essays or Counsels, Civil and Moral*, ed. Brian Vickers. London: Folio Society, 2002.

Bailey, Rebecca A. '"A Conflict More Fierce Than Many Thousand Battles": Staging the Politics of Treason and Allegiance in James Shirley's Maritime Plays, *The Young Admiral* and *The Court Secret*', in *James Shirley and Early Modern Theatre: New Critical Perspectives*, ed. Barbara Ravelhofer. Abingdon, Oxon: Routledge, 2017, 72–85.

Bailey, Rebecca A. *Staging the Old Faith: Queen Henrietta Maria and the Theatre of Caroline England, 1625–1642*. Manchester: Manchester University Press, 2009.

Baker, Donald C. 'The "Angel" of English Renaissance Literature', *Studies in the Renaissance* 6 (1959), 85–93.

Barbour, Reid. *English Epicures and Stoics: Ancient Legacies in Early Stuart Culture*. Amherst: University of Massachusetts Press, 1998.

Baseotto, Paola. '*Disdeining Life, Desiring Leaue To Die*': *Spenser and the Psychology of Despair*. Stuttgart: Ibidem, 2008.

Bawcutt, N. W. (ed.). *The Control and Censorship of Caroline Drama: The Records of Sir Henry Herbert, Master of the Revels 1623–73*. Oxford: Oxford University Press, 1996; published online, 2013.

Beal, Peter (ed.). '*Catalogue of English Literary Manuscripts 1450–1700 (CELM)*.' *Institute of English Studies*, 7 June 2017, http://www.celm-ms.org.uk. Accessed 30 August 2020.

Beaumont, Agnes. 'The Narrative of the Persecution of Agnes Beaumont', in John Bunyan, *Grace Abounding with Other Spiritual Autobiographies*, ed. John Stachniewski with Anita Pacheco. Oxford: Oxford University Press, 1998, 191–224.

Beaumont, Francis and John Fletcher. *The Dramatic Works in the Beaumont and Fletcher Canon*, gen. ed. Fredson Bowers. 10 vols. Cambridge: Cambridge University Press, 1966–96.

Behn, Aphra. *The young king, or, The mistake*. London: Printed for D. Brown *et al.*, 1683. Wing / B1776.

Bellany, Alastair. *The Politics of Court Scandal in Early Modern England: News Culture and the Overbury Affair, 1603–1660*. Cambridge: Cambridge University Press, 2007.

Bentley, Gerald E. *The Jacobean and Caroline Stage: Dramatic Companies and Players*. 7 vols. Oxford: Clarendon Press, 1941–68.

Bergel, Giles and Ian Gadd (eds). *Stationers' Register Online*, http://stationersregister.online. Glasgow: University of Glasgow, CREATe, n.d. Accessed 23 September 2019.

BIBLIOGRAPHY

Betham, William. *The Baronetage of England*. 5 vols. Ipswich: Printed for William Miller, Old Bond-Street, London, 1801–5.

Bevington, David and Peter Holbrook (eds). *The Politics of the Stuart Court Masque*. Cambridge: Cambridge University Press, 1998.

Bevington, David *et al.* (eds). *English Renaissance Drama: A Norton Anthology*. New York and London: W. W. Norton, 2002.

Billing, Christian M. *Masculinity, Corporality and the English Stage 1580–1635*. Farnham: Ashgate, 2008.

Boys, John. *An Exposition of the Dominical Epistles and Gospels, Used in Our English Liturgie*. London: Printed by Felix Kyngston for William Aspley, 1610. STC (2nd ed.) / 3459.3.

Braddick, Michael J. *The Nerves of State: Taxation and the Financing of the English State, 1558–1714*. Manchester: Manchester University Press, 1996.

Brome, Richard. *Richard Brome Online*, gen. ed. Richard Cave. London and Sheffield, 2010. https://www.dhi.ac.uk/brome. Accessed 30 August 2020.

Brooke, Nicholas. *Horrid Laughter in Jacobean Tragedy*. New York: Rowman & Littlefield, 1979.

Burn, Richard. *Ecclesiastical Law*. 2 vols. London: Printed by H. Woodfall and W. Strahan; and sold by A. Millar, 1763.

Burnell, Henry. *Landgartha: A Tragie-Comedy*, ed. Deana Rankin. Dublin: Four Courts, 2014.

Burton, Robert. *The Anatomy of Melancholy*. Oxford: Printed by John Lichfield and James Short, for Henry Cripps, 1621. STC (2nd ed.) / 4159.

Burton, Robert. *The Anatomy of Melancholy*, ed. Thomas Faulkner, Nicolas Kiessling, and Rhonda Blair. 6 vols. Oxford: Oxford University Press, 1989–2000.

Butler, Martin. *The Stuart Court Masque and Political Culture*. Cambridge: Cambridge University Press, 2009.

Butler, Martin. *Theatre and Crisis 1632–1642*. Cambridge: Cambridge University Press, 1984.

Butler, Todd. 'Power in Smoke: The Language of Tobacco and Authority in Caroline England', *Studies in Philology* 106.1 (Winter 2009), 100–18.

Callon, Gordon. *William Lawes: Collected Vocal Music Part 1: Solo Songs*. Middleton, WI: A-R Editions, 2002.

Camden, William. *Britain, or A chorographicall description of the most flourishing kingdomes, England, Scotland, and Ireland etc.*, trans. Philemon Holland. London: Impensis Georgii Bishop & Ioannis Norton, 1610. STC (2nd ed.) / 4509.

Camden, William. *Remains Concerning Britain*. Wakefield: EP Publishing, 1974.

Carlell, Lodowick. *The Passionate Lovers*. London: Printed for Humphrey Moseley, 1655. Wing / C581.

Carlton, Charles. *Archbishop William Laud*. London: Routledge, 1987.

Carlton, Charles. *Charles I: The Personal Monarch*. 2nd ed., London: Routledge, 1995.

Casady, Edwin. *Henry Howard, Earl of Surrey*. New York: Modern Language Association, 1938.

Cavendish, William, Duke of Newcastle. *The country captaine and the Varietie, two comedies written by a person of honor*. London: Printed for Hum. Robinson and Hum. Moseley, 1649. Wing / N877.

Cavert, William M. *The Smoke of London: Energy and Environment in the Early Modern City*. Cambridge: Cambridge University Press, 2016.

Celovsky, Lisa. 'Ben Jonson and Sidneian Legacies of Hospitality', *Studies in Philology* 106.2 (2009), 178–206.

Cerasano, S. P. 'The Chamberlain's–King's Men' in *A Companion to Shakespeare*, ed. David Scott Kastan. Oxford: Blackwell, 1999, 328–45.

Chalfant, Fran C. *Ben Jonson's London: A Jacobean Placename Dictionary*. Athens, GA: University of Georgia Press, 1978.

534

BIBLIOGRAPHY

Chambers, E. K. *The Elizabethan Stage*. 4 vols. Oxford: Oxford University Press, 1923.

Chapman, George. *An Humorous Day's Mirth*, ed. Charles Edelman. Manchester: Manchester University Press, 2010.

Cheney, Liana De Girolami. 'The Oyster in Dutch Genre Paintings: Moral or Erotic Symbolism', *Artibus et Historiae* 8.15 (1987), 135–58.

Clark, Ira. *Professional Playwrights: Massinger, Ford, Shirley and Brome*. Lexington: University Press of Kentucky, 1992.

Clark, Sandra. 'Cervantes' "The Curious Impertinent" in Some Jacobean Plays', *Bulletin of Hispanic Studies* 79 (2002), 477–89.

Clark, William S. *The Early Irish Stage*. Oxford: Clarendon Press, 1955.

Clouston, R. W. M. 'The Church Bells of Renfrewshire and Dunbartonshire', *Proceedings of the Society of Antiquaries of Scotland* 82 (1947), 146–92.

Coke, Edward. *The Selected Writings and Speeches of Sir Edward Coke*, ed. Steve Sheppard. 3 vols. Indianapolis, IN: Liberty Fund, 2003.

Coope, Rosalys. 'The "Long Gallery": Its Origins, Development, Use and Decoration', *Architectural History* 29 (1986), 43–84.

Cotton, Charles. *The Compleat Gamester*. London: Printed by A. M. for R. Cutler and to be sold by Henry Brome, 1674. Wing / C6382.

Crowther, Stefania. 'James Shirley and the Restoration Stage'. Unpublished PhD thesis, University of Warwick, 2017.

Cruickshank, C. G. *Elizabeth's Army*. Oxford: Oxford University Press, 1946.

Cunningham, Jack. *James Ussher and John Bramhall: The Theology and Politics of Two Irish Ecclesiastics of the Seventeenth Century*. Farnham: Ashgate, 2007.

Cutts, John. 'Drexel Manuscript 4041', *Musica Disciplina* 18 (1964), 151–202.

Cutts, John. 'Original Music for Two Caroline Plays—Richard Brome's *The English Moore; or The Mock-Marriage* and James Shirley's *The Gentleman of Venice*', *Notes and Queries* 33.1 (1986), 21–5.

Davenant, William. *The Tragedy of Albovine, King of the Lombards*. London: Printed [by Felix Kingston] for R. M[oore], 1629. STC (2nd ed.) / 6307.

Davenport, Robert. *A pleasant and witty comedy: called, A new tricke to cheat the Divell*. London: Printed by John Okes, for Humphrey Blunden, 1639. STC (2nd ed.) / 6315.

Daye, Anne. '"Youthful Revels, Masks, and Courtly Sights": an introductory study of the revels within the Stuart masque', *Historical Dance* 3.4 (1996), 5–22.

Dekker, Thomas. *The Belman of London*. London: [By E. Allde] for Nathaniell Butter, 1608. STC (2nd ed.) / 6482.

Dekker, Thomas. *The Dramatic Works of Thomas Dekker*, ed. Fredson Bowers. 4 vols. Cambridge: Cambridge University Press, 1953–61.

Dekker, Thomas and Thomas Middleton. *The Roaring Girl*, in *English Renaissance Drama: A Norton Anthology*, ed. David Bevington *et al*. New York and London: W. W. Norton, 2002.

Dent, R. W. *Proverbial Language in English Drama Exclusive of Shakespeare, 1495–1616: An Index*. Berkeley, CA and London: University of California Press, 1984.

Dessen, Alan C. and Leslie Thomson. *A Dictionary of Stage Directions in English Drama, 1580–1642*. Cambridge: Cambridge University Press, 1999.

Dibdin, Charles. *A Complete History of the English Stage*. 5 vols. London: Printed for the author, 1800.

Drouillard, Tara. 'The Prison System', *The Map of Early Modern London*, ed. Janelle Jenstad. Victoria: University of Victoria, 2018. http://mapoflondon.uvic.ca/PRIS1.htm. Accessed 20 June 2019.

Duffin, Ross W. *Some Other Note: The Lost Songs of English Renaissance Comedy*. Oxford: Oxford University Press, 2018.

535

BIBLIOGRAPHY

Dugan, Holly. *The Ephemeral History of Perfume: Scent and Sense in Early Modern England.* Baltimore: Johns Hopkins University Press, 2011.

Dutton, Richard. 'The St. Werburgh Street Theater, Dublin', in *Localizing Caroline Drama: Politics and Economics of the Early Modern English Stage, 1625–1642.* New York and Basingstoke: Palgrave Macmillan, 2006, 129–55.

Dyson, Jessica. *Staging Authority in Caroline England: Prerogative, Law and Order in Drama, 1625–1642.* Farnham: Ashgate, 2013.

Edelman, Charles. 'George Chapman's *All Fools*', *The Explicator* 72.1 (2014), 49–52.

Edelman, Charles. *Shakespeare's Military Language: A Dictionary.* London and New Brunswick, NJ: Athlone Press, 2000.

Edmond, Mary. *Rare Sir William Davenant: Poet Laureate, Playwright, Civil War General, Restoration Theatre Manager.* Manchester: Manchester University Press, 1987.

Engel, Wilson F. (ed.). *The Gentleman of Venice.* Salzburg: Universität Salzburg, 1976.

Engel, Wilson F. 'William Wilson, printer of five plays by James Shirley', *Papers of the Bibliographical Society of America* 72.1 (1978), 88–9.

Esche, Edward J. 'Stages to Pages: The Four Quartos of Shirley's *The Constant Maid*', *TRANS. Internet-Zeitschrift für Kulturwissenschaften*, 16 (2006). http://www.inst.at/trans/16Nr/09_6/esche16.htm. Accessed 30 August 2020.

Evans, Geraint. 'The Minotaur of the Stage: Tragicomedy in Spain', in *Early Modern Tragicomedy*, ed. Subha Mukherji and Raphael Lyne. Woodbridge, Suffolk: D. S. Brewer, 2007, 59–75.

Evans, Jennifer. '"They are called Imperfect men": Male Infertility and Sexual Health in Early Modern England', *Social History of Medicine* 29 (2016), 311–32.

Eyre, G. E. Briscoe. *A Transcript of the Registers of the Worshipful Company of Stationers, from 1640–1708 A. D.* 3 vols. London: Roxburghe Club, 1913–14.

Fairholt, F. W. *Costume in England: A History of Dress to the End of the Eighteenth Century.* 4th ed., enl. and thoroughly rev. by H. A. Dillon. London: G. Bell, 1896.

Fairholt, F. W. and H. A. Dillon. *A Glossary of Costume in England.* Facsimile reprint of *Costume in England.* 2 vols. 3rd ed., London: G. Bell, 1885.

Falconer, Alexander F. *A Glossary of Shakespeare's Sea and Naval Terms.* London: Constable, 1965.

Fehrenbach, Robert J. (ed.). *A Critical Edition of The Politician by James Shirley.* New York: Garland, 1980.

Fehrenbach, Robert J. 'The Printing of James Shirley's *The Polititian* (1655)', *Studies in Bibliography* 24 (1971), 144–48.

Fletcher, Alan. *Drama, Performance, and Polity in Pre-Cromwellian Ireland.* Cork: Cork University Press, 2000.

Fletcher, John. *The Bloody Brother.* London: Printed by R. Bishop, for Thomas Allott, and Iohn Crook, 1639. STC (2nd ed.) / 11064.

Fletcher, John. *The Womans Prize: or, The Tamer Tamed*, in *Comedies and Tragedies written by Francis Beaumont and John Fletcher.* London: Printed for Humphrey Robinson and for Humphrey Moseley, 1647. Wing / B1581.

Florio, John. *Queen Anna's New World of Words.* London: Printed by Melch. Bradwood [and William Stansby], for Edw. Blount and William Barret, 1611. STC (2nd ed.) / 11099.

Foakes, R. A. (ed.). *Henslowe's Diary.* 2nd ed., Cambridge: Cambridge University Press, 2002.

Ford, John. *'Tis pitty shee's a whore.* London: Printed by Nicholas Okes for Richard Collins, 1633. STC (2nd ed.) / 11165.

Ford, John. *'Tis Pity She's a Whore*, ed. Brian Morris. London: Ernest Benn, 1968.

Forker, Charles R. '"A little more than kin, and less than kind": Incest, Intimacy, Narcissism, and Identity in Elizabethan and Stuart Drama', *Medieval and Renaissance Drama in England* 4 (1989), 13–51.

536

BIBLIOGRAPHY

Forker, Charles R. 'Review of *The Gentleman of Venice*, ed. Wilson F. Engel', *Yearbook of English Studies* 9 (1979), 332–3.

Forsythe, Robert Stanley. *The Relations of Shirley's Plays to the Elizabethan Drama*. New York: Columbia University Press, 1914.

García, Luciano Nicolás. 'Presencia Textual de España y de la Literatura Española en la Obra Dramática de James Shirley (1596-1666)'. Unpublished PhD thesis, Universidad de Jaén, 1998.

Gazzard, Hugh. 'An Act to Restrain Abuses of Players (1606)', *Review of English Studies* 61.251 (September 2010), 495–528.

Gifford, William (ed.). *The Dramatic Works and Poems of James Shirley now first collected; with notes by the late William Gifford; and additional notes, and some account of Shirley and his writings by the Rev. Alexander Dyce*. 6 vols. London: John Murray, 1833.

Gilbert, Allan H. (ed.). *Literary Criticism: Plato to Dryden*. New York: American Book Co., 1940.

Gillespie, Raymond. *Seventeenth-Century Ireland: Making Ireland Modern*. Dublin: Gill, 2006.

Graham-Dixon, Andrew. 'Unravelling the Riddle of Rembrandt's *The Night Watch*', *Christie's Online Magazine* (3 April 2019). https://www.christies.com/features/Andrew-Graham -Dixon-on-The-Night-Watch-by-Rembrandt-9786-1.aspx. Accessed 4 July 2019.

Greg, W. W. *A Bibliography of the English Printed Drama to the Restoration*. 4 vols. London: The Bibliographical Society, 1939–59.

Griffith, Eva. '"Till the state fangs catch you": James Shirley the Catholic: Why it does not matter (and why it really does)', *TLS* (2 April 2010), 14–15.

Guarini, Battista. *Compendio della poesia tragicomica*. Venice: Giovanni Battista Ciotti, 1601.

Gurr, Andrew. *The Shakespearean Stage 1574–1642*. Cambridge: Cambridge University Press, 1970.

Gurr, Andrew. *The Shakespearean Stage 1574–1642*. 4th ed., Cambridge: Cambridge University Press, 2009.

Haaker, Ann. 'The Plague, the Theater, and the Poet', *Renaissance Drama*, n.s. 1 (1968), 283–306.

Hadfield, Andrew. 'Culture and Anarchy in Mid-Seventeenth-Century Ireland: the strange case of James Shirley at Werburgh Street', *Literature Compass* 15 (2018), n.p.

Hadfield, Andrew. 'The Politician by James Shirley is back on the Dublin stage (after almost 400 years)', *The Irish Times* (3 April 2019). https://www.irishtimes.com/culture/books/ the-politician-by-james-shirley-is-back-on-the-dublin-stage-after-almost-400-years- 1.3846701. Accessed 24 April 2019.

Hadfield, Andrew. *Shakespeare and Renaissance Politics*. London: Methuen, 2004.

Hair, P. E. H. 'Bridal Pregnancy in Earlier Rural England Further Examined', *Population Studies* 24.1 (1970), 59–70.

Hair, P. E. H. 'Bridal Pregnancy in Rural England in Earlier Centuries', *Population Studies* 20.2 (1966), 233–43.

Hakluyt, Richard. *The Principal Navigations, Voyages, and Discoveries of the English Nation*, ed. D. B. Quinn and R. A. Skelton. 2 vols. Cambridge: Cambridge University Press, 1965.

Hall, J. L. 'A Critical Edition of Two Plays by James Shirley: "The Grateful Servant" and "The Constant Maid" '. Unpublished M.Litt. thesis, University of Oxford, 1958.

Hall, Joseph. *Resolutions and decisions of divers practicall cases of conscience in continuall use amongst men, very necessary for their information and direction in these evil times. In four decades.* London: Printed for N.B. And are to be sold by R. Royston, 1650. Wing / H407.

Happé, Peter. '"And you meane to rise at court, practise to caper": The Representation of the Court in James Shirley's Plays, 1631–36', in *James Shirley and Early Modern Theatre: New Critical Perspectives*, ed. Barbara Ravelhofer. Abingdon, Oxon: Routledge, 2017, 48–58.

BIBLIOGRAPHY

Harrison, G. B. (ed.). *Gabriel Harvey: Foure Letters*. London: Bodley Head, 1922.

Heavey, Katherine. 'A New Way to Please You: Helen of Troy in early modern comedy', *Renaissance Studies* 28.3 (2014), 426–42.

Heavey, Katherine. 'Performing "in the likeness of a petticoat": Playing Helen of Troy and Medea in the Drama of James Shirley', *Postgraduate English* 19 (March 2009), 2–22. http://www.dur.ac.uk/postgraduate.english. Accessed 30 August 2020.

Henning, Basil Duke. *The History of Parliament: The House of Commons, 1660–1690*. 3 vols. London: Secker & Warburg, for the History of Parliament Trust, 1983.

Heylyn, Peter. *Mikrokosmos: A Little Description of the Great World*. Oxford: Printed by John Lichfield and William Turner, and are to be sold by W. Turner and T. Huggins, 1625. STC (2nd ed.) / 13277.

Heywood, Thomas. *The Fair Maid of the West. Or, a Girle Worth Gold*. London: Printed [by Miles Flesher] for Richard Royston, 1631. STC (2nd ed.) / 13320.

Hilton, John. *Catch that catch can, or A choice collection of catches, rounds, & canons for 3 or 4 voyces*. London: Printed for John Benson & John Playford, 1652. Wing / H2036.

Hoenselaars, A. J. *Images of Englishmen and Foreigners in the Drama of Shakespeare and his Contemporaries*. Rutherford, NJ and London: Fairleigh Dickinson University Press and Associated University Presses, 1992.

Höfele, Andreas. *Stage, Stake, & Scaffold: Humans & Animals in Shakespeare's Theatre*. Oxford: Oxford University Press, 2011.

Hollar, Wenceslas. *Ornatus Muliebris Anglicanus*. [London, 1640]. STC (2nd ed.) / 13599.5.

Horbury, Ezra. *Prodigality in Early Modern Drama*. Woodbridge: Boydell & Brewer, 2019.

Hotson, J. Leslie. 'George Jolly, Actor-Manager: New Light on the Restoration Stage', *Studies in Philology* 20.4 (October 1923), 422–43.

Hotson, J. Leslie. *The Commonwealth and Restoration Stage*. Cambridge, MA: Harvard University Press, 1928.

Howard, Jean E. 'Crossdressing, The Theatre, and Gender Struggle in Early Modern England', *Shakespeare Quarterly* 39.4 (1988), 418–40.

Howard, Jean E. *Theater of a City: The Places of London Comedy, 1598–1642*. Philadelphia, PA: University of Pennsylvania Press, 2007.

Huberman, Edward. 'James Shirley's *The Politician*'. Unpublished PhD thesis, Duke University, 1934.

Huberman, Edward. 'Bibliographical Note on James Shirley's *The Polititian*', *The Library*, 4th series, 18 (1937), 104–8.

Hume, Robert D. 'Dr. Edward Browne's Playlists of "1662": A Reconsideration', *Philological Quarterly* 64.1 (Winter 1985), 69–81.

Ingram, Martin. *Carnal Knowledge: Regulating Sex in England, 1470–1600*. Cambridge: Cambridge University Press, 2017.

Johnson, Anthony W. 'Urban(e) Visualization and Early Modern Drama: Ben Jonson's "Spectral Cities"', *Nordic Journal of English Studies* 17.1 (2018), 26–73.

Johnson, James H. *Venice Incognito: Masks in the Serene Republic*. Berkeley: University of California Press, 2011.

Johnson, William Savage (ed.). *The Devil is An Ass by Ben Jonson*. New York: Henry Holt, 1905.

Jones, Ann Rosalind and Peter Stallybrass. *Renaissance Clothing and the Materials of Memory*. Cambridge: Cambridge University Press, 2000.

Jonson, Ben. *The Cambridge Edition of the Works of Ben Jonson Online*, ed. David M. Bevington, *et al.* 2014. http://universitypublishingonline.org/cambridge/benjonson/. Accessed 4 July 2019.

Jonson, Ben. *The Devil is An Ass*. New York: Henry Holt, 1905. See Johnson. *The Devil is An Ass by Ben Jonson* above.

BIBLIOGRAPHY

Jonson, Ben. *The Devil is an Ass*, ed. Peter Happé. Manchester and New York: Manchester University Press, 1994.

Jonson, Ben. *Volpone or The foxe*. [London]: Printed [by George Eld] for Thomas Thorpe, 1607. STC (2nd ed.) / 14783.

Jorgens, Elise Bickford. *English Song 1600–1675: Facsimiles of Twenty-Six Manuscripts and an Edition of the Texts*. 12 vols. New York: Garland, 1986–89.

Judges, A. V. (ed.). *The Elizabethan Underworld: A Collection of Tudor and Early Stuart Tracts and Ballads*. 1930; repr. Oxford: Routledge, 2002.

Kearney, Hugh F. *Strafford in Ireland, 1633–41: A Study in Absolutism*. Manchester: Manchester University Press, 1959.

Keller, James R. 'James Shirley's *The Politician* and the Demand for Responsible Government in the Court of Charles I', *Journal of the Rocky Mountain Medieval and Renaissance Association* 18 (1997), 179–99.

Kermode, Lloyd (ed.). *Three Renaissance Usury Plays*. Manchester: Manchester University Press, 2009.

Kewes, Paulina. ' "Give me the sociable Pocket-books": Humphrey Moseley's Serial Publication of Octavo Play Collections', *Publishing History*, 38 (1995), 5–21.

Killigrew, Thomas. *Comedies and Tragedies*. London: Printed for Henry Herringman, 1664. Wing / K450.

King, T. J. 'Shirley's *Coronation* and *Love Will Find out the Way*: Erroneous Title-Pages', *Studies in Bibliography* 18 (1965), 265–69.

King, T. J. 'Staging of Plays at the Phoenix in Drury Lane, 1617–42', *Theatre Notebook* 19.4 (Summer 1965), 146–66.

Kirsch, Arthur C. 'A Caroline Commentary on the Drama', *Modern Philology* 66.3 (February 1969), 256–61.

Knowles, James. *Politics and Political Culture in the Court Masque*. Basingstoke: Palgrave Macmillan, 2015.

Koslofsky, Craig. *Evening's Empire: A History of the Night in Early Modern Europe*. Cambridge: Cambridge University Press, 2011.

Kurz, Hilde. 'Italian Models of Hogarth's Picture Stories', *Journal of the Warburg and Courtauld Institutes* 15.3/4 (1952), 136–68.

Kyd, Thomas. *The Spanish tragedie, containing the lamentable end of Don Horatio, and Bel-imperia: with the pittifull death of olde Hieronimo*. London: Printed by Edward Allde, for Edward White, [1592]. STC (2nd ed.) / 15086.

[Kynaston, Francis]. *The Constitutions of the Musaeum Minervae*. London: Printed by T. P[urfoot] for Thomas Spencer, 1636. STC (2nd ed.) / 15099.

Langbaine, Gerard. *An Account of the English Dramatick Poets*. Oxford: Printed by Leon. Lichfield, for George West, and Henry Clements, 1691.

Leinwand, Theodore B. 'London's Triumphing: The Jacobean Lord Mayor's Show', *CLIO: A Journal of Literature, History, and the Philosophy of History* 11.2 (Winter 1982), 137–53.

Leonard, H. H. 'Distraint of Knighthood: The Last Phase, 1625–41', *History*, 63.207 (1978), 23–37.

Leslie, Michael. '*The New Academy; or, The New Exchange*: Critical Introduction', in *Richard Brome Online*, gen. ed. Richard Cave. London and Sheffield, 2010. https://www.dhi.ac.uk/brome. Accessed 30 August 2020.

Lodge, Thomas. *The Wounds of Civill War*. London: John Danter, 1594. STC (2nd ed.) / 16678.

Loewenstein, David. *Treacherous Faith: The Specter of Heresy in Early Modern English Literature and Culture*. Oxford: Oxford University Press, 2013.

Lope de Vega Carpio, *Arte nuevo de hacer comedias en este tiempo*, ed. Juana de José Prades. Madrid: C.S.I.C., 1971.

BIBLIOGRAPHY

Lope de Vega Carpio. *El hombre por su palabra. Comedia famosa*, in *Segunda Parte de la Parte Veinte de las Comedias de Lope de Vega Carpio*. Madrid: por la viuda de Alonso Martín, 1625.

Lopez, Jeremy. 'Time for James Shirley' in *James Shirley and Early Modern Theatre: New Critical Perspectives*, ed. Barbara Ravelhofer. Abingdon, Oxon: Routledge, 2017, 17–31.

'Lord Chamberlain's List (1641)', *Lost Plays Database*. https://lostplays.folger.edu/Index.php/Main_Page. Accessed 15 March 2019.

Lotz-Heumann, Ute. 'Confessionalisation in Ireland: Periodisation and Character, 1534–1649' in *The Origins of Sectarianism in Early Modern Ireland*, ed. Alan Ford and John McCafferty. Cambridge: Cambridge University Press, 2005, 24–53.

Lublin, Robert I. 'Shirley's Dublin Days: A Nervous Première of *St. Patrick for Ireland*' in *James Shirley and Early Modern Theatre: New Critical Perspectives*, ed. Barbara Ravelhofer. Abingdon, Oxon: Routledge, 2017, 108–23.

Magnus, Olaus. *A Description of the Northern Peoples, 1555*, ed. P. G. Foote. 3 vols. London: Hakluyt Society, 1996–98.

Major, Philip. ' "This Lemon in mine eye": Writing the Exile in Thomas Killigrew's *The Pilgrim*' in *Thomas Killigrew and the Seventeenth-Century English Stage: New Perspectives*, ed. Philip Major. Farnham & Burlington: Ashgate, 2013.

Malone, Edmond. 'An Historical Account of the Rise and Progress of the English Stage', in *The Plays and Poems of William Shakespeare*, ed. Edmond Malone. 10 vols. London: H. Baldwin, 1790, vol. 1, pt 2, 1–284.

Marlowe, Christopher. *The Complete Works of Christopher Marlowe*, ed. Roma Gill *et al.* 5 vols. Oxford: Oxford University Press, 1986–98.

Marlowe, Christopher. *The Jew of Malta*. Ed. James R. Siemon. 3rd ed., London: Methuen, 2009.

Marston, John. *The Malcontent. Augmented by Marston. With the additions played by the Kings Maiesties servants*. London: Printed by V[alentine] S[immes] for William Aspley, 1604. STC (2nd ed.) / 17481.

Martin, Randall (ed.). *Women and Murder in Early Modern News Pamphlets and Broadside Ballads, 1573–1697*. Farnham: Routledge, 2005.

Massinger, Philip. *The Plays and Poems of Philip Massinger*, ed. Philip Edwards and Colin Gibson. 5 vols. Oxford: Clarendon Press, 1976.

Mayerne, Louis Turquet de. *The Generall Historie of Spaine*, trans. Edward Grimeston. London: Printed by A. Islip, and G. Eld, 1612. STC (2nd ed.) / 17747.

McLaren, A. N. *Political Culture in the Reign of Elizabeth I: Queen and Commonwealth 1558–1585*. Cambridge: Cambridge University Press, 1999; repr. 2004.

McEvilla, Joshua J. 'The Original Salisbury Court Players of Richard Brome's *The Antipodes*', *Notes and Queries* 59 (2012), 168–71.

McEvilla, Joshua J. 'A Catalogue of Book Advertisements from English Serials: Printed Drama, 1646–1668', *Papers of the Bibliographical Society of America* 107 (2013), 10–48.

McGraw-Hill Dictionary of Scientific and Technical Terms. 6th ed., New York: McGraw-Hill, 2003.

McKerrow, R. B. *Printers' & Publishers' Devices In England & Scotland 1485–1640*. London: Bibliographical Society at the Chiswick Press, 1913.

Meli, Domenico Bertoloni. 'The Collaboration between Anatomists and Mathematicians in the mid-Seventeenth Century with a Study of Images as Experiments and Galileo's Role in Steno's *Myology*', *Early Science and Medicine* 13 (2008), 665–709.

Middleton, Thomas. *The Famelie of Love. Acted by the children of his Maiesties Reuells*. London: Printed [by Richard Bradock] for Iohn Helmes, 1608. STC (2nd ed.) / 17879.

Middleton, Thomas. *Thomas Middleton: The Collected Works*, gen. ed. Gary Taylor and John Lavagnino. 2 vols. Oxford: Oxford University Press, 2007–13.

Middleton, Thomas. *A Trick to Catch the Old One*, in *Thomas Middleton: Five Plays*, ed. Bryan Loughrey and Neil Taylor. Harmondsworth: Penguin, 1988.

BIBLIOGRAPHY

Miller, Anthony. *Roman Triumphs and Early Modern English Culture*. Basingstoke: Palgrave, 2001.

Miller, C. William. 'A London Ornament Stock: 1598–1683', *Studies in Bibliography* 7 (1955), 125–51.

Monahin, Nona. 'Decoding Dance in Shakespeare's *Much Ado About Nothing* and *Twelfth Night*', in *The Oxford Handbook of Shakespeare and Dance*, ed. Lynsey McCulloch and Brandon Shaw. Oxford: Oxford University Press, 2019, 49–82.

Morash, Christopher. *A History of Irish Theatre, 1601–2000*. Cambridge: Cambridge University Press, 2002.

More, Thomas. 'Supplication of Souls', in *The Complete Works of St. Thomas More*, ed. Frank Manley, Clarence H. Miller, and Richard C. Marius. 15 vols. New Haven: Yale University Press, 1990, vol. 7.

Moryson, Fynes. *An Itinerary Written by Fynes Moryson, Gent*. London: J. Beale, 1617. STC (2nd ed.) / 18205.

Moryson, Fynes. *Shakespeare's Europe: Unpublished Chapters of Fynes Moryson's Itinerary*, ed. Charles Hughes. London: Sherratt & Hughes, 1903.

Munro, Lucy. 'Dublin Tragicomedy and London Stages', in *Early Modern Tragicomedy*, ed. Subha Mukherji and Raphael Lyne. Woodbridge, Suffolk: D. S. Brewer, 2007, 175–92.

Munroe, Jennifer. *Gender and the Garden in Early Modern English Literature*. Aldershot: Ashgate, 2008.

Nason, Arthur Huntington. *James Shirley, Dramatist: A Biographical and Critical Study*. New York: Arthur H. Nason, 1915.

Nevile, Jennifer. *Footprints of the Dance: An Early Seventeenth-Century Dance Master's Notebook*. Leiden: Brill, 2018.

Ó Hannracháin, Tadhg. 'Plantation, 1580–1641', in *The Oxford Handbook of Modern Irish History*, ed. Alvin Jackson. Oxford: Oxford University Press, 2013, 291–314.

ODNB. Oxford Dictionary of National Biography. Oxford: Oxford University Press, 2004-.

OED. Oxford English Dictionary. Oxford: Oxford University Press, 2000-.

Partridge, Eric. *Shakespeare's Bawdy: a Literary & Psychological Essay and a Comprehensive Glossary*. London: Routledge & Kegan Paul, 1955.

Paster, Gail Kern. 'Unbearable Coldness of Female Being: Women's Imperfection and the Humoral Economy', *English Literary Renaissance* 28.3 (1998), 416–40.

Pecke, Samuel (ed.). *A Perfect Diurnall*, 269 (29 January–5 February 1655). London: Printed by Edw. Griffin, [1649–55].

Peele, George. *Merrie conceited Jests of George Peele Gentleman*. London: Printed by G[eorge] P[urslowe] for F. Faulkner, 1627. STC (2nd ed.) / 19543.

Pick, Samuel. *Festum Voluptatis, or The Banquet of Pleasure*. London: Printed by E[lizabeth] P[urslowe] for Bernard Langford, 1639. STC (2nd ed.) / 19897.

Playford, John. *The English Dancing Master: or, Plaine and easie rules for the dancing of country dances, with the tune to each dance*. London: Printed by Thomas Harper, and are to be sold by John Playford, 1651. Wing / P2477.

Porter, Henry. *The Pleasant History of the Two Angry Women of Abington*. London: [By Edward Allde] for William Ferhrand [i.e. Ferbrand], 1599. STC (2nd ed.) / 20122.

Porter, Roy. *Medicine: A History of Healing: Ancient Traditions to Modern Practices*. London: Michael O'Mara, 1997.

Ravelhofer, Barbara (ed.). *James Shirley and Early Modern Theatre: New Critical Perspectives*. Abingdon, Oxon: Routledge, 2017.

Ravenscroft, Thomas. *A briefe discourse of the true (but neglected) vse of charact'ring the degrees, by their perfection, imperfection, and diminution in measurable musicke, against the common practise and custome of these times*. London: Printed by Edw: Allde for Tho. Adams, 1614. STC (2nd ed.) / 20756.

BIBLIOGRAPHY

Richards, R. D. 'The Lottery in the History of English Government Finance', *The Economic Journal* 44.Supp. 1 (1 January 1934), 57–76.

Rickman, Johanna. *Love, Lust, and License in Early Modern England: Illicit Sex and the Nobility.* Aldershot: Ashgate, 2008.

Riemer, A. P. 'Shirley's Revisions And The Date Of *The Constant Maid*', *Review of English Studies* 17.66 (1966), 141–8.

Rivière, Janine. *Dreams in Early Modern England.* London: Routledge, 2017.

Rollins, Hyder E. 'Samuel Pick's Borrowings', *Review of English Studies* 7.26 (1931), 204.

Rowlands, Samuel. *The Famous Historie, of Guy, Earle of Warwick.* London: [E. Allde for William Ferbrand], 1609. STC (2nd ed.) / 21378.

Rowley, William. *All's Lost By Lust.* London: Printed by Thomas Harper, 1633. STC (2nd ed.) / 21425.

Rowley, William. *A Match at Mid-night. A pleasant comoedie: as it hath beene acted by the Children of the Revells.* London: Printed by Aug. Mathewes, for William Sheares, 1633. STC (2nd ed.) / 21421.

Rubinstein, Frankie. *A Dictionary of Shakespeare's Sexual Puns and their Significance.* London: Macmillan, 1984.

Salgado, Gamini (ed.). *Cony-Catchers and Bawdy Baskets: An Anthology of Elizabethan Low Life.* Harmondsworth: Penguin, 1972.

Sanders, Julie. *The Cultural Geography of Early Modern Drama, 1620–1650.* Cambridge: Cambridge University Press, 2011.

Sanders, Julie. ' "Powdered with Golden Rain": The Myth of Danae in Early Modern Drama', *Early Modern Literary Studies* 8.2 (September 2002), 1–23.

Schreyer, Kurt. ' "Here's a knocking indeed!": *Macbeth* and the Harrowing of Hell', *The Upstart Crow* 29 (2010), 26–43.

Schulten, Paul. 'Physicians, Humour and Therapeutic Laughter in the Ancient World', *Social Identities* 7.1 (2001), 67–73.

Scodel, Joshua. *The English Poetic Epitaph: Commemoration and Conflict from Jonson to Wordsworth.* Ithaca, NY: Cornell University Press, 1991.

Shakespeare, William. *The Complete Works*, ed. John Jowett, William Montgomery, Gary Taylor, and Stanley Wells. 2nd ed., Oxford: Oxford University Press, 2005.

Sharpe, J. A. ' "Last Dying Speeches": Religion, Ideology and Public Execution in Seventeenth-Century England', *Past & Present* 107 (1985), 144–67.

Sharpe, Kevin. *The Personal Rule of Charles I.* New Haven: Yale University Press, 1992.

Shirley, James. *Poems &c. By James Shirley.* London: Printed [by Ruth Raworth and Susan Islip] for Humphrey Moseley, 1646. Wing (2nd ed.) / S3480.

Shirley, James. *The Cardinal*, ed. E. M. Yearling. Manchester: Manchester University Press, 1986.

Shirley, James. *The Coronation a Comedy.* London: Printed by Tho. Cotes, for Andrew Crooke, and William Cooke, 1640. STC (2nd ed.) / 22440.

Shirley, James. *Cupid and Death. A Masque.* London: Printed by T[homas] W[arren], for J. Crook, & J. Baker, 1653. Wing (2nd ed.) / S3464.

Shirley, James. *The Gentleman of Venice.* London: Printed for Humphrey Moseley, 1655. Wing / S3468 and S3469.

Shirley, James. *The Gentleman of Venice.* Salzburg: Universität Salzburg, 1976. *See* Engel. *The Gentleman of Venice* above.

Shirley, James. *The Gentleman of Venice.* Unpublished PhD thesis, Rijksuniversiteit Gent, 1981. See Vermeulen. 'James Shirley's *The Gentleman of Venice*: A Textual Edition With Some Introductory Notes' below.

Shirley, James. *The Lady of Pleasure*, ed. Ronald Huebert. Manchester: Manchester University Press, 1986.

Shirley, James. *The Polititian, a Tragedy.* London: Printed for Humphrey Moseley, 1655. Wing / S3482 and S3483.

BIBLIOGRAPHY

Shirley, James. *The Politician*. New York: Garland, 1980. *See* Fehrenbach. *A Critical Edition of The Politician by James Shirley* above.

Shirley, James. *The Royall Master*. London: Printed by T. Cotes, 1638. STC (2nd ed.) / 22454.

Shirley, James. *Six New Playes*. London: Printed for Humphrey Robinson, and Humphrey Moseley, 1653. Wing / S3486.

Shirley, James. *St. Patrick for Ireland. The First Part*. London: Printed by I. Raworth, for R. Whitaker, 1640. STC (2nd ed.) / 22455.

Shirley, James. *St Patrick for Ireland*. New York: Garland, 1979. *See* Turner. *A Critical Edition of James Shirley's* St. Patrick for Ireland below.

Shirley, James. *The Wedding. As it was lately acted by her Majesties Servants, at the Phenix in Drury-Lane*. London: Printed [by Nicholas Okes] for John Grove, 1629. STC (2nd ed.) / 22460.

Sidney, Philip. *An Apologie for Poetrie*. London: Printed [by James Roberts] for Henry Olney, 1595. STC (2nd ed.) / 22534.

Smith, Thomas. *De Republica Anglorum*. London: Printed by Henrie Midleton for Gregorie Seton, 1583. STC (2nd ed.) / 22857.

Sommerville, J. P. *Politics and Ideology in England, 1603–1640*. Harlow: Longman, 1986.

Steggle, Matthew. *Richard Brome: Place and Politics on the Caroline Stage*. Manchester: Manchester University Press, 2004.

Steggle, Matthew. 'A Lost Jacobean Tragedy: *Henry the Una* (c. 1619)', *Early Theatre* 13.1 (2010), 65–81.

Stern, Tiffany. ' "I Have Both the Note, and Dittie About Me": Songs on the Early Modern Page and Stage', *Common Knowledge* 17.2 (2011), 306–20.

Stevens, David. 'The Stagecraft of James Shirley', *Educational Theatre Journal* 29.4 (December 1977), 493–516.

Stevens, David. 'The Staging of Plays at the Salisbury Court Theatre, 1630–1642', *Theatre Journal* 31 (1979), 511–25.

Stevenson, Allan H. 'Shirley's Dedications and the Date of his Return to England', *Modern Language Notes* 61 (1946), 79–83.

Stevenson, Allan H. 'James Shirley and the Actors at the First Irish Theater', *Modern Philology* 40.2 (November 1942), 147–60.

Stevenson, Allan H. 'Shirley's Publishers: The Partnership of Crooke and Cooke', *The Library* 4th ser., 25.3–4 (1944), 140–61.

Stevenson, Allan H. 'Shirley's Years in Ireland', *Review of English Studies*, 20.77 (1944), 19–28.

Stockwell, La Tourette. *Dublin Theatres and Theatre Customs (1637–1820)*. New York and London: B. Blom, 1968.

Štollová, Jitka, 'Plotting Paratexts in Shirley's *The Politician*', in *James Shirley and Early Modern Theatre: New Critical Perspectives*, ed. Barbara Ravelhofer. Abingdon, Oxon: Routledge, 2017, 139–52.

Stonex, Arthur Bivins. 'The Usurer in Elizabethan Drama', *PMLA* 31.2 (1916), 190–210.

Stow, John. *A Survay of London. Contayning the originall, antiquity, increase, moderne estate, and description of that citie*. London: Imprinted by John Wolfe, 1598. STC (2nd ed.) / 23341.

Stow, John. *A Survey of London. Reprinted from the Text of 1603*, ed. Charles Lethbridge Kingsford. 2 vols. Oxford: Clarendon, 1908.

Stróbl, Erzsébet. 'Queen Elizabeth and the "Judgement of Paris" ', *The AnaChronisT* 18.2 (2018), 207–28.

Taylor, John. *All the Workes of John Taylor the Water-poet. Beeing sixty and three in number. Collected into one volume by the author: with sundry new additions, corrected, revised, and newly imprinted*. London: Printed by J[ohn] B[eale], Elizabeth Allde, Bernard Alsop, and Thomas Fawcet] for James Boler, 1630. STC (2nd ed.) / 23725.

BIBLIOGRAPHY

Thomas, Catherine E. 'Toxic Encounters: Poisoning in Early Modern English Literature and Culture', *Literature Compass* 9 (2012), 48–55.

Thornbury, Walter. 'Clerkenwell: (part 2 of 2)', in *Old and New London: Volume 2*. London: Cassell, Petter & Galpin, 1878, 328–38. *British History Online*, http://www.british-history.ac.uk/old-new-london/vol2/pp328-338. Accessed 23 May 2019.

Tilley, Morris Palmer. *A Dictionary of the Proverbs in England in the Sixteenth and Seventeenth Centuries: a Collection of the Proverbs found in English Literature and the Dictionaries of the Period*. Ann Arbor, MI: University of Michigan Press, 1950.

Tomlins, Thomas Edlyne. *The Law-dictionary: Explaining the Rise, Progress, and Present State of the British Law*. 2 vols. London: Payne *et al.*, 1820.

Treadwell, Victor. *Buckingham and Ireland, 1616–1628: A Study in Anglo-Irish Politics*. Dublin: Four Courts, 1998.

Trevisan, Sara. 'The Impact of the Netherlandish Landscape Tradition on Poetry and Painting in Early Modern England', *Renaissance Quarterly* 66.3 (Fall 2013), 866–903.

Tricomi, Albert. *Anti-Court Drama in England, 1603–1642*. Charlottesville, VA: University Press of Virginia, 1989.

Trumbach, Randolph. *The Rise of the Egalitarian Family: Aristocratic Kinship and Domestic Relations in Eighteenth-Century England*. New York: Academic Press, 1978; repr. Elsevier, 2013.

Tucker Murray, John. *English Dramatic Companies 1558–1642*. 2 vols. Boston, MA: Houghton Mifflin, 1910.

Turner, John P., Jr. (ed.). *A Critical Edition of James Shirley's* St. Patrick for Ireland. New York: Garland, 1979.

Vaught, Jennifer C. 'Introduction: Men Who Weep and Wail: Masculinity and Emotion in Early Modern English Literature', in *Masculinity and Emotion in Early Modern English Literature*, ed. Jennifer C. Vaught. Aldershot: Ashgate, 2008, 1–23.

Verbeke, Demmy. 'Swag-Bellied Hollanders and Dead-Drunk Almaines: Reputation and Pseudo-Translation in Early Modern England', *Dutch Crossing* 34.2 (2010), 182–91.

Vermeulen, Lieven. 'James Shirley's *The Gentleman of Venice*: A Textual Edition With Some Introductory Notes', Unpublished PhD thesis, Rijksuniversiteit Gent, 1981.

Verstille, E. J. *Verstille's Southern Cookery*. New York: Owens and Agar, 1866; repr. Kansas City, MI: Andrews McMeel, 2014.

Vicary, Grace Q. 'Visual Art as Social Data: The Renaissance Codpiece', *Cultural Anthropology* 4.1 (February 1989), 3–25.

Wabuda, Susan. 'Bishops and the Provision of Homilies, 1520 to 1547', *The Sixteenth Century Journal* 25.3 (Autumn 1994), 551–66.

Walen, Denise A. *Constructions of Female Homoeroticism in Early Modern Drama*. New York and Basingstoke: Palgrave Macmillan, 2005.

Walsham, Alexandra. *Providence in Early Modern England*. Oxford: Oxford University Press, 1999.

Webster, John. *The White Devil*, ed. John Russell Brown. London: Methuen, 1966.

Webster, John. *The Works of John Webster*, ed. David Gunby *et al.* 4 vols. Cambridge: Cambridge University Press, 1995–2019.

Whitney, Geffrey. *A Choice of Emblemes, and other Deuises*. Leyden: In the house of Christopher Plantyn, by Francis Raphelengius, 1586. STC (2nd ed.) / 25438.

Wickham, Glynne, Herbert Berry, and William Ingram (eds). *English Professional Theatre, 1530–1660*. Cambridge: Cambridge University Press, 2000.

Williams, G. *A Dictionary of Sexual Language and Imagery in Shakespearean and Stuart Literature*. 3 vols. London: Athlone Press, 1994.

Williams, Justine. 'The Irish Plays of James Shirley, 1636–1640'. Unpublished PhD thesis, University of Warwick, 2010.

544

BIBLIOGRAPHY

Williams, Maggy. '*The Doubtful Heir* by James Shirley'. Programme note for the Shakespeare's Globe Read Not Dead production, 2008.

Wirsung, Christof. *The General Practise of Physicke*. London: [Printed by Richard Field for] Georg. Bishop, 1605. STC (2nd ed.) / 25864.

Wood, Julia K. 'William Lawes's Music for Plays', in *William Lawes (1602–1645): Essays on his Life, Times and Work*, ed. Andrew Ashbee. Aldershot: Ashgate, 1998, 11–67.

Wright, Celeste Turner. 'Some Conventions regarding the Usurer in Elizabethan Literature', *Studies in Philology* 31.2 (April 1934), 176–97.

Wroth, Mary. *The Countesse of Mountgomeries Urania*. London: Printed [by Augustine Mathewes?] for John Marriott and John Grismand, 1621. STC (2nd ed.) / 26051.

Wroth, Mary. *The Countess of Montgomery's Urania*, in *An Anthology of Seventeenth-Century Fiction*, ed. Paul Salzman. Oxford: Oxford University Press, 1991.

Wroth, Mary. *Loves Victorie*. Huntington Library, San Marino, CA. Manuscript shelfmark HM 600 (c. 1619).

Wurzbach, Wolfgang von. *Lope de Vega und Seine Komödien*. Leipzig: Dr. Seele, 1899.

Yarwood, Doreen. *Costume of the Western World*. Guildford: Lutterworth, 1980.

Zucker, Adam. *The Places of Wit in Early Modern English Comedy*. Cambridge: Cambridge University Press, 2011.